East Central and Southeast Europe

EAST CENTRAL AND SOUTHEAST EUROPE

**1976
Edition**

CLIO PRESS

SANTA BARBARA, CALIFORNIA
OXFORD, ENGLAND

A HANDBOOK OF LIBRARY AND ARCHIVAL RESOURCES IN NORTH AMERICA

Paul L. Horecky / Chief Editor
David H. Kraus / Associate Editor

The research reported herein was performed
pursuant to a contract with the
U. S. Department of Health, Education, and Welfare, Office of Education,
under PL 85—864, Title VI, Section 602,
as amended , and PL 480.

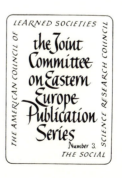

LEARNED SOCIETIES
THE AMERICAN COUNCIL OF
the Joint
Committee
on Eastern
Europe
Publication
Series
Number 3.
SCIENCE RESEARCH COUNCIL
THE SOCIAL

Library of Congress Cataloging in Publication Data
Main entry under title:

East Central and Southeast Europe
    (Joint Committee on Eastern Europe publication
series; no. 3)
    Includes Index
    1. Europe, Eastern—Library resources—United
States. I. Horecky, Paul Louis, 1913–
II. Kraus, David H. III. Series: Joint Committee
on Eastern Europe, Publication Series–Joint
Committee on Eastern Europe; no. 3.
Z2483.E2 [DJK9]   947'.007   76-28392
ISBN 0-87436-214-8

    Clio Books
American Bibliographical Center—Clio Press
2040 Alameda Padre Serra
Santa Barbara, California 93103

European Bibliographical Center—Clio Press
Woodside House, Hinksey Hill
Oxford OX1 5BE, England

Composed, printed and bound in the United States of America

Contents

Foreword

IN 1966 THE Subcommittee on East Central and Southeast European Studies (SECSES) of the American Council of Learned Societies (ACLS) and the Social Science Research Council (SSRC) initiated a survey of language and area studies and of the corresponding bibliographic resources in the field, which led in 1970 to the publication by the University of Chicago Press of the following three volumes: *Language and Area Studies, East Central and Southeastern Europe: A Survey* by Charles Jelavich, *East Central Europe: A Guide to Basic Publications,* and *Southeastern Europe: A Guide to Basic Publications,* the latter two under my direction and editorship. The important tasks of describing and evaluating the major research resources on these areas and of identifying what was available and where, remained outside the scope of these publications.

The present handbook can be traced to an ACLS-appointed Advisory Committee on Library Needs, which, in 1968, under the chairmanship of Professor Peter Sugar of the University of Washington, was directed to ascertain strengths and weaknesses of East Central and Southeast European library and archival resources in North America and to recommend measures for an effective dissemination and improved utilization of these materials on a nationwide scale. A questionnaire-based survey, launched to that end, strongly suggested that the preparation of an inventory of research collections on these areas was a desideratum deserving high-priority consideration. Many respondents felt that, even with the use of existing library and union catalogs and bibliographic lists, researchers often had to waste a good deal of time and effort in identifying key collections and materials for their work. There were substantial indications that libraries often lack detailed knowledge of the riches preserved within their own walls and sometimes grope in the dark when it comes to assessing the various components of their own area holdings. One tends to lose sight of the forest for the trees.

As a followup to these initiatives, a Research and Library Resources Advisory Committee, consisting of 10 scholars and librarians who represented major libraries in the field, was subsequently constituted under ACLS auspices and under my chairmanship, with the mandate to evolve project guidelines, structure, scope, methodology, and prospective participants for the handbook, with the organization, preparation, and publication of which I was charged by ACLS.

The present volume is intended to provide scholars, librarians, students, and researchers with a basic reference tool for the study of the essential collections available in major libraries, archives, and research institutions in the United States and Canada, by outlining the profiles of these collections and offering broad guidance to their subject and area contents. The focus is on the humanities and the socioeconomic and political sciences. The following countries are covered: Albania, Bulgaria, Czechoslovakia, East Germany, Greece, Hungary, Poland, Romania, and Yugoslavia. The term "East Germany" was used by the contributors in their surveys because the materials they described encompassed the postwar military government, the German Democratic Republic (1949-), and East Berlin. Moreover, by the time of the official recognition of the German Democratic Republic by the United States in September of 1974, the *Handbook* had reached a stage where major textual and terminological changes were no longer feasible, because they would have entailed considerable delay in publication.

In concept and execution, this volume is the result of a truly cooperative undertaking, with some 40 participating research libraries, archives, and special institutions and a far larger number of individual contributors. Area resources of institutions with leading strength are described and analyzed, country by country, in major surveys ranging from 2,000 to 5,000 words in length. In addition, shorter aggregate reports survey in lesser detail selected collections of substantial area strength or describe holdings in institutions of specialized subject concentration. An effort was made to include general information on conditions of access, organization, and location of area collections and reading rooms, photocopying facilities, special catalogs and files, and bibliographic data for printed materials which deal with the collections concerned. The arrangement is alphabetical by institution. Within an institution, where applicable, the extensive surveys appear first, alphabetically by country, with the summary surveys following.

In general, author, title, and other bibliographic citations, as well as transliteration, were left intact as reported by the contributors, on the ground that the best finding aid for the user of a particular library is the version in that library's catalog. Editorial changes were made, however, in regard to place names: the commonly accepted English version is given in lieu of the vernacular one (e.g., Rome instead of Roma); the Latin place name of early works is retained (e.g., Basilae instead of Basel); and, for cities the official name of which has changed over the years, the form used at the time of publication is preferred (e.g., Lemberg, Lwów, L'viv).

Most of the contributions to the *Handbook* were received in late 1972 and the first half of 1973 and reflect the state of the collections and services as of that period. Following the processing, editing, and synchronization of the mass of information assembled, and negotiations with prospective publishers, the final manuscript was submitted for publication in the first half of 1975. Only minor updating was feasible in the galley stage.

Author acknowledgments appear at the end of the individual report. As a rule, these collections surveys were authored by resident librarians or members of the faculty of the institution surveyed. Sometimes, it became necessary to invite outside experts to visit a given institution for the purpose of preparing descriptions of specific sectors of the collection, with the assistance of the resident library staff, to whom these outside specialists owe a debt of gratitude for their most valuable cooperation. In such cases, the author's professional affiliation in the credit line differs from the institution of which he surveyed the holdings. A subject and area guide with references to collections by areas, subjects, and institutions, should facilitate the use of this reference aid.

A truly cooperative enterprise such as this could not have come to fruition without the sympathetic understanding and full collaboration of a spate of individuals. It is with deep appreciation that I acknowledge the spirited response of the directors of the participating libraries and the chairmen of the various Slavic and East European university departments who readily pledged the cooperation of their institutions and staffs. My foremost thanks go to the team of contributors who, despite other ongoing assignments and commitments, assumed the exacting and challenging task of surveying multifaceted research collections and summarizing their findings within stringent limitations of length. Quite frequently, additional abridgement proved inevitable during the editorial stage, if the mass of data collected were to be compressed into a single volume of manageable size and accessible price. I am grateful to the contributors for their forbearance in this respect.

A vital role in the realization of this project was played by my two friends and editorial aides, David H. Kraus and Frederick B. Mohr, whose seasoned bibliographic skills and thorough area knowledge were instrumental in processing and organizing the assembled data. To Mrs. Marisa Vandenbosch, I am greatly indebted for the alacrity and intelligence which she dedicated to the preparation of the manuscript, making numerous useful suggestions in the process. Parts of the manuscript were readied competently by Miss Johanna T. Craig, who helped out when time was of the essence. Again this time, my wife, Emily I. Horecky, performed ''yeoperson's'' work on numerous occasions when there was a need for her administrative and reviewing talents.

This volume would not have seen the light of day without the unflagging support and wise counsel of Dr. Gordon B. Turner, Vice President, ACLS, who also arranged for joint financial support by ACLS and the U.S. Office of Education. Dr. Carl P. Epstein and Ms. Julia A. Petrov, specialists on the staff of the latter agency, were at all times most understanding and responsive to project problems and needs.

I was fortunate to enjoy the guidance and support of my colleagues of the Joint Committee on Eastern Europe, ACLS and SSRC, in whose publication series the present volume appears as Number 3.

Paul L. Horecky

The Alliance College Polish Library

The history of the Alliance College Polish Library is intimately connected with the history of the institution. When the Polish National Alliance opened its doors to the specific educational needs of Polish American youth in 1912, the Library was an integral part of the educational program. The fire of January, 1931 which destroyed the College, located in the former Rider Hotel, an internationally known landmark, destroyed the Library in its entirety, including precious, irreplaceable letters of noted Polish and American statesmen (Washington, Jefferson, Kościuszko, et al.). Thus, the present collection dates from after the fire.

The efforts of such persons as Alphonse S. Wolanin, Marion Moore Coleman, Walter Kondy, Danuta Obojska, and those who supported these individuals saw the collection through its formative years. In 1970, with the advent of the present librarian, Mrs. Rena A. Lamparska, a concerted effort was made to develop the collection into a scientifically designed library. The services of various consultants and evaluators were employed including Mr. Joseph Placek (University of Michigan), Mrs. Hanna Zasada (University of Warsaw), Mrs. Elżbieta Motyl (Polish Academy of Science), Dr. Leon Twarog and Dr. Jerzy Krzyżanowski (Ohio State University), The Pennsylvania State Department of Education, and most recently, Mrs. Wanda Kronman-Czajka (University of Warsaw).

Primarily the Library is concerned with Polish studies, including Polish literature, linguistics, history, government, foreign relations, sociology, economics, geography, art, music, folklore, civilization, intellectual life, and Poles in America in historical, sociological, and cultural aspects. Special attention is paid to reference publications, i.e.: bibliographies, biographies, biobibliographies, encyclopedias, dictionaries, directories, and the like. Materials in these subject areas support the curricular needs of Alliance College students and faculty as well as researchers and scholars in the community at large. It is the aim of the Library to have available in the collection every major work published within its various fields of specialization as well as exhaustive, comprehensive materials in certain designated areas.

The reference collection has been richly developed. In the realm of Polish national bibliographies, the Library has at its disposal a wide range of bibliographies: current—*Przewodnik Bibliograficzny, Bibliografia Zawartości Czasopism,* retrospective—*Bibliografia Polska* of Karol Józef Teofil Estreicher and its continuation edited by Karol Estreicher; as well as prospective—*Zapowiedzi Wydawnicze.* There is also a large reference collection of foreign Polonica (e.g., works by Zabielska, Danilewicz and Nowak, Kowalik, Wolanin, Waldo, and Trypućko); special literary bibliographies (among them, *Bibliografia Literatury Polskiej "Nowy Korbut," Polska Bibliografia Literacka, Rocznik Literacki*); monographic works covering translations of Polish literary works, (e.g., works by Guttry, Ryll and Wilgat, Maciuszko, Coleman, and Taborski); biobibliographical works including Starowolski, Korzeniewska, Bartelski, and others; bibliographical and biobibliographical monographic works pertaining to specific authors (e.g., K. Piekarski's *Bibliografia dzieł Jana Kochanowskiego* . . . , and a wide range of *kalendarze życia i tworczości* of the major writers); bibliographies of certain literary genres; bibliographies of Polish literary journals published in Poland and abroad; and many others.

In the special bibliographies section particular attention is devoted, next to literature, to historical references, including the fundamental works by Finkel and Płoski; as well as *Bibliografia*

Historii Polski, edited by Madurowicz-Urbańska, et al.; and the current *Bibliografia Historii Polskiej,* initiated by Baumgart. There are also monographic reference works pertaining to specific historical subjects (e.g., bibliographies of the January Uprising by J. Gąsiorowski and E. Kozłowski, Chojnacki's bibliography of books printed in Poland in conspiracy under the Nazi occupation, bibliographies pertaining to the defensive operations in September, 1939, and others). Added to this, the Library has gathered references on separate branches of historical writings, for example: E. Maliszewski's *Bibliografia pamiętników polskich . . . ,* Budzyk's bibliography of the Polish Parliament's constitutions of the 17th century, Daszkiewicz and Gąsiorowski's bibliography on militarism, Symonolewicz's bibliography on the subject of nationalism, plus many more. Mention should be made of the bibliographies of bibliographies found in the Library, of which the works of Hahn and Sawoniak, as well as the *Bibliografiia Bibliografii i Nauki o Książce,* merit special attention.

This is merely a general indication of some of the implements and tools utilized by the Polish Library staff to complete and develop an in-depth collection as well as to serve as a source of information for all other interested parties.

Two major areas of interest are history and literature. With respect to Polish philology (i.e., literature and linguistics), it is important to underline that the Library contains publications on the history of Polish literature; literary criticisms; Polish literary texts of various genres (novel, short story, poetry, drama); works on the theory of literature; works on comparative literature provided one of the literatures is Polish; works on linguistics and Polish textbooks; works on the method of teaching Polish literature and the Polish language; works on Polish dialects and folk literature.

In the general history section, the primary aim is to complete classical historical works of the Polish school and to complete this section systematically with new publications. Within the range of each particular subject group, the concern is to collect the most general and monographic works as well as contributory and smaller pieces. The most vivid subject groups are those associated with the Polish immigration movement, World War II, and Polish history after 1945.

The Library holds a wide range of periodicals, newspapers, and university proceedings (representing all areas of specialization of the collection) published in Poland, France, England, Canada, and the United States, with special emphasis on the Polish American press. For example, the Library currently receives *The Polish Review, Kultura* (Paris and Warsaw), *Wiadomości* (London), and, more specifically in the area of Polish literature, *Pamiętnik Literacki, Tworczość, Dialog, Poezja,* and *Oficyna Poetów,* to name but a few. A similar situation exists with historical periodicals, including *Kwartalnik Historyczny, Acta Poloniae Historica, Dzieje Najnowsze, Studia Historyczne, Przegląd Historyczny,* among others. Special attention is paid to Polish American questions. The Library receives *Polish American Studies, Ethnicity, Polish American Community Life,* etc. in this area of study.

In addition to current periodicals, the Library possesses various periodicals no longer published such as *Bellona, Tygodnik Powszechny, Kłosy, Goniec Krakowski,* as well as the magazine *Poland* (subsequently *Poland-America*), and *Trybuna Polska* (Erie, Pa.). Special arrangements have been made to secure complete files on microfilm of *Tygodnik Illustrowany* (Warsaw, 1859-1939), *Życie* (Kraków, 1897-1900), and *Życie* (Warsaw, 1887-91).

Access to the collection is available through standard interlibrary loan procedures as well as through individual letters of inquiry for specific information. Photocopying services are available.

Numerous bibliographies of the holdings of the Alliance College Polish Library on special subjects have been compiled. These bibliographies are available to all interested parties upon request and include such topics as Non-current Polish and Polish American periodicals, Polish Folklore, Polish Literature and Linguistics in the Current Periodicals Collection, as well as a detailed description of the Polish Library. Additionally, information concerning new acquisitions is printed. The Library contributes information concerning its holdings to the Library of Congress for inclusion in the *National Union Catalog*.

The collection is arranged according to the Library of Congress classification system. A special series catalog has been initiated.

Extensive exchange programs have been established with libraries, institutions, and publishing centers in the United States, Canada, Poland, France, and England along with direct purchase arrangements, to make certain that the Library can fulfill its stated aims, goals, and direction. This includes standing orders for series, specific title requests, and statements of the collection's profile (which is under constant revision). Since 1972, as a result of a federal grant from the United States Office of Education utilizing frozen funds in Poland, the acquisition program has been stepped up. The expectation of receiving such a grant in the coming years, as well as the continuation and expansion of the exchange program, point to an optimistic outlook for the future of the Library and will push the annual acquisition rate well beyond the current figure of 2,000 pieces.

At present, there are over 21,000 books available through this collection, over 200 titles of current and non-current Polish and Polish American periodicals and university proceedings, approximately 2,000 pamphlets dealing with various topics, including Polish Americana, a large collection of Polish postage stamps, original and reproduced works of art, posters, maps, films, and slides, as well as language and music records and an interesting collection of old Polish imprints.

A part of the Polish National Alliance Archives is found in the Library in the form of 176 volumes of newspaper clippings. These clippings, gathered by Paweł Widera from various Polonia publications in the United States, concentrate on Polonia itself, Polonia's organizations, and on Polish questions.

The Library has made a sincere effort to incorporate into its objectives the thousand-year-old heritage of Poland. The aims, objectives, and programs of the Library have been, and will continue to be, constantly re-evaluated in order to meet the evolving needs of students and faculty at Alliance College as well as scholars and researchers at large. The Library is committed to keeping abreast of national and international developments, such as the American Bicentennial and the Kopernik Anniversary celebration, and reflecting this in its constitution.

James R. Przepasniak and
Rena A. Lamparska

University of British Columbia

General Information

The East Central and Southeast European materials at the University of British Columbia are located in the Main Library building. The Library's policy is to maintain open access to the collection for all users, whether or not they are associated with the University.

During the academic session, the Library is open from 8 a.m. to 12 midnight Monday-Friday, from 9 a.m. to 5 p.m. on Saturday, and from 12 noon to 12 midnight on Sunday. Users interested in the East Central and Southeastern European publications should consult the Slavic Bibliographer, the Slavic Reference Librarian in the Humanities Division, or the Slavic Cataloguer.

The materials in the Library's collections may be located through the main card catalog, divided in this case into an author-title catalog and a separate subject catalog. The UBC Library uses the Library of Congress classifications and subject headings. New acquisitions which have not yet been cataloged are accessible through computer printouts which are frequently updated and cumulated.

Although UBC has a small Slavonic Studies Reading Room, its holdings have been disregarded in this survey since they are mainly duplicates of materials available in the Main Library.

The core of the East Central and Southeast European collection is located in the Main Library. Since it is considered an integral part of the main collection, it is scattered throughout the entire building and is interfiled with all the other library materials. The main exceptions to this arrangement are the reference works, which are located in the appropriate Reference Division (the Humanities Division, the Social Sciences Division, the Fine Arts Division, etc.).

Books may be borrowed for various lengths of time, depending on the status of the borrower. In addition, the UBC Library participates in the interlibrary loan program. Photocopying facilities are readily accessible, and the Library has numerous Xerox machines.

The Collections

The Library's Slavic and East European collection has been built systematically only since the 1940s. Its main growth and development took place during the 1950-68 period. Generous grants from the Canada Council, Mr. W. Koerner, and Mr. H. R. Macmillan have made possible the purchase of large, valuable sets of periodicals and continuation sets.

Although it is impossible to estimate accurately the size of this collection, since no special records have ever been kept and since the materials are scattered throughout the whole range of LC classifications, it is possible to hazard a guess that the East Central and Southeastern European collection ranges in size between 35,000 and 45,000 volumes. As a further aid to estimating the scope of the collection, the Library subscribes to 258 currently published periodicals in the fields of humanities and social sciences, emanating from the countries under discussion.

The Czechoslovak Collection

This is an exceedingly strong and wealthy collection. Of the 9,000 to 10,000 volumes pertaining to Czechoslovakia, over 6,000 volumes are concentrated in the fields of history, political science, and related social sciences. In fact, the Czech history collection is the best in Canada and probably one of the best on the North American continent. It is rich in rare sets of academic and learned societies' publications. It is particularly strong in its coverage of Czech history of the 15th-17th centuries (especially the Renaissance, Reformation, and Hussite periods), and of the 19th and 20th centuries. The language-literature section (about 2,000 volumes) is considerably weaker. The bulk of the literature collection is made up of sets of collected works of the major 19th-century and the early 20th-century authors. The Slovak literature section is particularly weak.

The Library subscribes to 57 Czech periodicals, 19 in the field of history and archeology, six in political science, nine in other social sciences, 10 in language, philology, Slavistics, etc., and only three devoted to literature.

The following larger sets are listed to indicate the nature of this collection: *Archiv český*, v. 1-37 (Prague, 1840-1944); *Čas* (Prague, 1888-91, 1893-98, 1901-07); *Časopis archivní školy*, v. 1-16 (Prague, 1923-33); Česká akademie věd a umění, Prague. Třída I. *Historický archiv*, v. 1- (Prague, 1893-; UBC has about half this set); *Česká revue*, v. 1-6 (Prague, 1897-1903) and ser. 2, v. 1-22 (Prague, 1907/08-1929/30; UBC set nearly complete); Česká společnost nauk, Prague. Třída filozofsko-historicko-jazykopytná. *Věstník* (nearly complete for 1885-1942); Československá akademie věd. *Věstník*, v. 1- (Prague, 1891-); *Československý časopis historický*, v. 1- (Prague, 1953-); *Český časopis historický*, v. 1-50 (Prague, 1895-1949); *Český lid*, v. 1-31 (Prague, 1892-1931; incomplete from 1949 to date); *Dav*, v. 1-9 (Prague, 1924-37); *Fontes rerum bohemicarum*, v. 1-6, -8 (Prague, 1871-1907, and 1932); *Kritický měsíčník*, v. 1-9 (Prague, 1938-48); *Kulturní tvorba*, v. 1-33 (Prague, 1963-68, nearly complete); *Květy*, v. 1-73 (Prague, 1879-1915); *Literární listy* (Prague, 1968, nearly complete); *Naše doba*, v. 1-55 (Prague, 1893-1949); *Osvěta*, v. 1-51 (Prague, 1871-1921); Prague. Národní museum. *Časopis*, v. 1-116 (Prague, 1827-1947); *Slovenský přehled*, v. 1- (Prague, 1899-; almost complete); Verein für Geschichte der Deutschen in der Sudetenländern. *Mitteilungen*, v. 8-75 (Prague); Czechoslovak Republic. Laws, statutes, etc. *Nové zákony a nařízení*, v. 1- (Prague, 1939-) Czechoslovak Republic. Nejvyšší soud. *Rozhodnutí ve věcech trestních*, v. 1-29 (Prague, 1919-48); Slovakia. Laws, statutes, etc. *Slovenský zákonník* (1939-45); *Slovenské pohľady*, v. 1- (Bratislava, 1884-; UBC has v. 1, 3-87, i.e., 1884, 1886-).

The Czech collection also includes all the major reference works, such as statistical yearbooks, bibliographies (e.g., Č. Zíbrt. *Bibliografie české historie*, v. 1-5), periodical indexes (e.g., *Články v českých časopisech* and *Články v slovenských časopisech*), biographies, dictionaries, and encyclopedias.

The Yugoslav Collection

This collection contains between 10,000 and 11,000 volumes, about 7,000 of which are concentrated in the fields of history, political science, and the related social sciences. Modern history and politics are particularly well represented. Other materials in the collection are distributed throughout all disciplines, with no exceptional strengths in other specific areas.

The collection includes vast and remarkably complete holdings of publications of the Yugoslav academies and the learned societies such as Matica srpska and Matica hrvatska. The language-literature section contains about 2,500 volumes, much of it in the form of large sets of collected works of the major 19th- and 20th-century Croatian, Serbian, and Slovenian authors.

The Library subscribes to 46 Yugoslav journals, 14 in the fields of history and archeology, seven in political sciences, 13 in the other social sciences, and only five dealing with linguistics, philology, and literature.

The following sets are listed to indicate the scope and the strengths of this collection: *Arhiv za pravne i društvene nauke*, v. 1-59 (Belgrade, 1906-41); *Čas*, v. 1-36 (Ljubljana, 1907-42); *Danica horvatska, slavonska i dalmatinska* [*Danica ilirska*], v. 1-20 (Zagreb, 1835-66; UBC has v. 1-15); *Hrvatsko kolo* (Zagreb, 1905-55); Jugoslavenska akademija znanosti i umjetnosti. *Rad,* v. 1- (Zagreb, 1867-; UBC has nearly complete set from 1873 to date); Jugoslavenska akademija znanosti i umjetnosti. *Starine na svijet,* v. 2-53 (Zagreb, 1870-1966); *Ljubljanski zvon,* v. 1-45 (Ljubljana, 1881-1925); Matica srpska, Novi Sad. *Letopis,* v. 116-408 (1874 to date) *Nova Evropa,* v. 1-33 (Zagreb, 1920-40); Slovenska matica v Ljubljani. *Letopis* (Ljubljana, 1876-1912); Slovenska matica v Ljubljani. *Narodni kolendar* (1886, 1871-1907); the following publications of the Srpska akademija nauka i umetnosti, Belgrade: *Glas,* v. 1- (1887-); *Godišnjak,* v. 1-10, 18- (1887-97, 1904-); *Posebna izdanja,* v. 1- (1888-, first 4 issues lacking); *Zbornik radova,* v. 1- (1949-, almost complete); *Spomenik,* v. 1-111 (1888-1961); *Zbornik za istoriju, jezik i književnost.* 1. Odelj: *Spomenici na srpskom jeziku,* v. 1- (1902-); *Zbornik za istoriju, jezik i književnost.* 2. Odelj. *Spomenici na tutim jezicima,* v. 1-19 (1904-21); *Zbornik za istoriju, jezik i književnost srpskog naroda.* 3. Odelj., v. 1-13; Serbia. Laws, statutes, etc. *Zbornik zakona i uredaba,* v. 1-63 (1840-1910).

The collection contains a large number of important reference works, including statistical yearbooks, periodical indexes (e.g., *Bibliografija Jugoslavije; članci i književni prilozi u časopisma,* sections A-C), bibliographies (e.g., Cankar, I. *Slovenski biografski leksikon*), encyclopedias (e.g., *Enciklopedija Jugoslavije*), numerous sets of Croatian, Serbian, and Slovenian etymological dictionaries, and national, subject, and general bibliographies.

The Polish Collection

This collection of between 13,000 and 14,000 volumes is divided between the field of history and the allied social sciences and the field of language and literature. A few rare and important sets are included, but there is no particular focus on any one subject. The main strength of the history section is in the period from the 16th to the 20th century, for which materials in related fields such as political science, sociology, and economics are also available. Most of the publications, however, are post-1945. The main focus of the language and literature section, which comprises about 6,000 volumes, is on 19th- and 20th-century writers. Sets of collected works of many of the major literary figures are lacking, however, and the collection is uneven.

The Library subscribes to 92 Polish journals, 58 of which are in the humanities, 15 in history, and six in archeology. In addition, 28 journals cover the various social sciences.

The collection includes a considerable number of publications of the Polish Academy of Sciences and the numerous learned societies, most of which are from the post-1945 period. Among the large sets in the collection are: *Acta historica res gestas Poloniae,* v. 1-13 (Kraków, 1878-1910; UBC has v. 1-3, 5-7, 10); *Archiwum Literackie,* v. 1- (1956-); *Chimera,* v. 1-10 (Warsaw, 1901-07); *Krytyka,* v. 1-16 (Kraków, 1899-1914; UBC has partly on microfilm); *Kultura,* v. 2- (Paris, 1947-); *Kwartalnik Historyczny,* v. 1- (1887-; almost complete); *Nowe Drogi,* v. 1- (Warsaw, 1947-; UBC has 1965 to date); *Pamiętnik Literacki,* v. 42- (1951-); *Pamiętnik Słowiański,* v. 1- (1949-); *Państwo i Prawo,* v. 4- (1949-); Poland. Laws, statutes, etc. *Dziennik Ustaw Rzeczypospolitej Polskiej* (1918-39, some post-1945 years); *Pomniki Dziejowe Polski,* ser. 1, v. 1-6; ser. 2, v. 1- (second series incomplete); *Prace Filologiczne,* v. 1-17 (Warsaw, 1885-1937, microfilm); *Prace Polonistyczne,* v. 11- (1953-); *Przegląd Historyczny,* v. 1- (Warsaw, 1905-; UBC has partly on microfilm); *Przegląd Zachodni,* v. 1- (1945-); *Rocznik Sławistyczny,* v. 1- (Kraków, 1908-, almost complete, partly on microfilm); *Sobótka,* v. 1- (1946-); *Sprawy Międzynarodowe,* v. 14- (Warsaw, 1961-); *Twórczość,* v. 18- (1963-); *Wiadomości,* v. 1- (London, 1945?-; a few early issues missing); *Wiadomości Literackie,* (Warsaw, 1924-39; microfilm); *Z Pola Walki,* v. 1- (1958-); *Źródła Dziejowe,* v. 1-24 (1876-1915; UBC has v. 1-9, 11); *Monumenta medii aevi historica res gestas Poloniae,* v. 1-19 (1874-1927).

8   University of British Columbia

Among the many important reference works in the collection are statistical yearbooks, periodical indexes (e.g., *Bibliografia Zawartości Czasopism*), biographies (e.g., *Polski Słownik Biograficzny*), encyclopedias (e.g., Gloger, Z., *Encyklopedja staropolska* and *Wielka encyklopedia powszechna PWN*), numerous large sets of etymological, specialized, and general dictionaries (e.g., Linde, M.S.B. *Słownik języka polskiego*), national and special bibliographies (e.g., *Bibliografia historii polskiej;* Finkey, L., *Bibliografia historii polskiej, Polska bibliografia literacka*) and general bibliographies (e.g., *Korbut;* Estreicher, K., *Bibliografia polska*).

The Hungarian Collection

The Hungarian collection comprises about 1,500 volumes, mostly in the field of history and the allied social sciences. Much of the material is in Western European languages, although published in Hungary. The language and literature sections are quite small.

The Library subscribes to 13 Hungarian journals, primarily in the fields of history, political science, and archeology. A large part of these are in languages other than Hungarian. Some of the larger Hungarian sets are: *Acta historica,* v. 1- (Budapest, 1951-); *Hungarian Quarterly,* v. 1-6 (Budapest, 1936-41); Magyar Szocialista Munkáspárt. Központi Bizottság. Párttörténeti Intézet. *Párttörténeti Közlemények,* v. 1- (Budapest, 1955-; two volumes missing); *Századok,* v. 1- (Budapest, 1867-); *Történelmi Szemle,* v. 1- (Budapest, 1958-); *Ural-altaische Jahrbücher,* v. 1- (1921-).

Among the Hungarian reference works available are the statistical yearbooks, a periodical index *(Magyar folyóiratok repertóriuma),* encyclopedias (e.g., *Révai nagy lexikona, Új magyar lexikon*), dictionaries (e. g., *A magyar nyelv történeti-etimológiai szótára, A magyar nyelv értelmező szótára*), bibliographies (e.g., Sajó, G. & Soltész, E., *Catalogus incunabulorum;* Kosáry, D., *Bevezetés a magyar történelem forrásaiba és irodalmába;* Apponyi, A., *Hungarica, Régi magyarországi nyomtatványok,* etc.), and various atlases.

Other Collections

The Bulgarian collection contains some 600 volumes, which are evenly distributed between the social sciences and the humanities. The Romanian collection comprises about 400 volumes, most of which relate to the social sciences; many are in languages other than Romanian. The Library subscribes to 14 Romanian journals, six of which are in the field of history and six in the social sciences. Some Romanian reference works are also available. Fewer than 100 volumes dealing with Albania are in the collections, and only about 400 volumes relating to modern Greece are available. The Library's East German collection, however, has experienced considerable growth, and the Library receives a broad selection of East German journals.

I. Fiszhaut-Laponce
University of British Columbia

University of California at Berkeley

The East Central and Southeast European collections of the University of California Library, Berkeley, are excellent in agriculture, economics, folklore, earth sciences, biology, forestry, mathematics, history, international relations, linguistics, and literature. They are strong in the political sciences, sociology, ethnography, anthropology, and are adequate in music and philosophy. All of the area's academies and practically all the universities and principal scholarly institutions are very well represented in the Library's holdings. The Library has fine holdings exclusive of materials which do not fall within the range of the general library collection, e.g., law and medicine.

Slavic studies may be said to have begun at Berkeley in 1901 with the offering of courses in Slavic languages and history by Professors G. Noyes and Thomas Bacon. Since then faculty members, too numerous to mention individually, have contributed and are contributing significantly to the growth of the Library. Historical events, faculty and student needs, course requirements, the establishment of the Institute of Slavic Studies in 1948, now defunct, all contributed to and accelerated the development of the Library collection. The Library currently maintains 514 active exchange ties with East Central and Southeast European countries to complement its other acquisitions. In all, the collections surveyed contain approximately 83,000 volumes.

Questions on the individual country collections may be referred to the Bibliographical Division, Acquisition Department of the General Library.

The Library's materials, except for the Masaryk-Benes Library, are integrated and dispersed throughout the entire Library collection. Access to the holdings is furnished by the Public Catalog, by author, title, and added entries, by a Subject Catalog and a Shelf List, and a printed catalog published in 1963.

Albania

Although Berkeley has a research collection of great resources, it is limited by funds and channeled in its development by teaching requirements. There is scarcely any demand for Albanian materials, consequently the Library has only a minimal collection in the area. It does possess the important bibliographies, some statistical material, dictionaries, descriptive works, a few titles on Scanderbeg, works by S. Skendi, F. Noli, N. Jokl, E. Hozha (Hoxha), some histories of Albanian literature and works on folklore. The series, *Albanische Forschungen,* and periodicals, *Arhiv za arbansku starinu, jezik i etnologiju* (1923-26), *Studia albanica, Studime historike, Novaía Albaniia,* and the *Anuari statistikor i R. R. SHI* are a small part of the collection. The Library has about 400 volumes on Albania.

Bulgaria

Bulgaria is represented by a useful collection. Although the number of volumes can conservatively be estimated at about 4,500 there are unfortunate gaps. About 50 percent of the items listed in Pundeff's *Bulgaria; a Bibliographic Guide* are in the collection.

Materials are present in all subjects but somewhat thinly spread. The Library does possess the basic reference aids, bibliographies, surveys, but does not cover the fields as thoroughly as needed. Nonetheless, the collection is adequate for good and even some intensive work.

Although the documents from Bulgaria are not minuscule the collection lacks the *Dŭrzhaven vestnik*, but it has fairly good representation in statistics. The collection is short on literary anthologies and individual authors though it does have the outstanding writers. Currently the Library receives approximately 175 periodicals as well as the entire periodical output of the Academy excluding nongeneral library materials such as animal husbandry and veterinary medicine. The collection includes the *Bibliografiski iztochnitsi za istoriiata na Turtsiia i Bŭlgariia* and a selected number of the publications of the National Library and the University at Sofiia.

Czechoslovakia

The Czechoslovak collection at Berkeley is a substantial working collection with most of the necessary bibliographic apparatus including the national bibliographies, the *Bibliografický katalog*, continued by *České knihy* and *Slovenské knihy*. Retrospective works include Doucha's *Knihopisný slovník československý . . . 1774-1864, Soupis československé literatury za leta 1901-1925*, Rizner's *Bibliografia slovenského písomníctva . . . od najstarśich čias do konca r. 1900*, supplemented by Miśianik's *Bibliografia slovenského písomníctva do konca xix. stor. . . .* The principal encyclopedias are present from *Ottův slovník naučný, Slovenska vlastiveda*, to the ongoing *Československá vlastivěda*.

Although the collection does not contain as much as it ought in the field of literature it is sufficient to support graduate studies. There is an adequate collection in linguistics, grammars, and dictionaries. History is more thoroughly represented, including such works as Palacký, *Geschichte von Böhmen, Balbín, Miscellanea historica regni Bohemiae* and *Epitome rerum Bohemicarum*, Dobner's *Monumenta historica Boemiae nusquam antehas edita*, Hajek's *Böhmische Chronik. Bibliografie české historie*, an essential aid, is also present.

Of particular interest, however, and a unique collection is the Masaryk-Beneš Library purchased from Dr. Arne Laurin, editor of the former Prager Presse. The collection contains 1,904 volumes and is maintained as a unit in the Library's holdings. It contains 200 works written by Masaryk, including translations of some of his titles. Most of them are first editions. It also includes 1,297 works about Masaryk as well as titles by his wife, Mrs. Charlotte Masaryk, and his son and daughter. Besides these separate works there are 36 scrapbooks with clippings about Masaryk's life and death, altogether several thousand pages with clippings from many countries written in as many different languages. Additionally, there are several hundred loose sheets with pasted clippings and some hundred complete copies of newspapers with various articles on Masaryk and a number of photographs. Masaryk's archivist and literary secretary stated that Laurin's collection is second only to the materials contained in the Library of the Masaryk Institute in Prague. Prof. Kerner noted that it is a unique collection, one of the rare sources for the history of a period in European history in general, especially 1918-38, and in the remarkable history of Czechoslovak democracy in particular.

The Beneš portion of the collection contains his works and lectures, including the parliamentary speeches which had not been published, in all 139 book units. Further works about Beneš and his politics number 109 items, a total of 248 titles by and about Beneš. There are also two scrapbooks with newspaper clippings mainly concerning Beneš' resignation and a large number of photographs and newspaper copies with articles about him. Titles complementing this collection are added whenever possible. The Masaryk-Beneš Library is not represented in the Public Catalog; it has a typewritten index which is listed as volume 1 of the collection.

A gift of 1,700 volumes from the collection of Dr. Livingstone Porter, priest, historian, and lecturer, was presented to the Library by his widow in 1955. It included 1,280 volumes in Czech, a valuable research collection, and a full run of the periodical *Bratislava; Časopis pro výzkum Slovenska a Podkarpatské Rusi.* There were also volumes in German, English, and French dealing with the political, economic, and religious history of Central and Eastern Europe including, as well, the nucleus of a collection on the Lusatians. That nucleus has been expanded so that at present it is a rich body of research material.

At present, the Library subscribes to more than 175 periodicals and series from Czechoslovakia. Additionally, except for a few titles which do not fall within the scope of the Library collection, the Library receives the entire output of periodicals of the Czechoslovak Academy of Sciences, the Slovak Academy of Sciences, and periodicals from the universities in Prague, Brno, Bratislava, and other institutions in the country. Titles such as *Slovenské pohl'ady, Naše doba, Česká revue, Český lid, Slovenské divadlo, Archiv orientální, Eirene, Ars, Historický časopis,* and Národní museum. *Časopis* are part of the holdings.

East Germany

The collection, about 2,000 volumes, is well equipped with the necessary general bibliographic and essential reference aids. General works are available in most disciplines.

History is adequately covered. However, there are only about 100 document titles in the collection. Literature, theater, music, and art are treated in varying degrees of thoroughness.

Periodical and series publications of the Deutsche Akademie der Wissenschaften zu Berlin, the Humboldt-Universität zu Berlin, the Leipzig University, and the Sächsische Akademie der Wissenschaften are received in substantial numbers. In addition to the above mentioned, the Library receives *Deutsche Fragen,* 1958-, *Geographische Berichte,* the *Wissenschaftliche Veröffentlichungen* of the Leipzig Deutsches Institut für Länderkunde, *Petermanns geographische Mitteilungen, Leipziger Stadtgeschichtliche Forschungen, Schriften zur Theaterwissenschaft,* etc. Fifty-seven exchanges assist in the growth of the collection.

Greece

Greek and Latin were prominent in the University's curriculum of 1869-70. A separate department of Greek was formed in 1896 and it remained so until 1937, when it was combined into the Department of Classics. Consequently, it is not surprising to find that the Greek collection exceeds 20,000 volumes. Ancient, medieval, and modern Greek history account for 3,458 volumes; Greek language, history of literature, 4,064 volumes; classical Greek literature, 8,745 volumes; Byzantine and modern Greek, 592 volumes; classical Greek philosophy, 2,721 volumes; a total of 16,228 for those major classifications.

For a brief period in the recent past no attempt was made at complete coverage of publications from Greece until a few years ago when publications of research value in the social sciences were selected from the *Bulletin analytique de bibliographie hellénique.* Currently the Library is securing Greek materials on a blanket program which began with 1970 imprints. The Greek document collection is very strong in statistics and census material but has no parliamentary reports and very few administrative reports.

Basic bibliographic titles including Legrand's works are well represented. The Library has just received the important Greek encyclopedia, *Eleutheroudakē synchronos enkyklopaideia,* 12 v. (1965-67). Very few of the fundamental works in history, language, or literature are lacking. A small number of Greek titles in the Rare Book Collection is also of interest.

Periodicals and series include titles such as *Berliner Byzantinische Arbeiten, Byzantion; Revue internationale . . . , Dumbarton Oaks Papers, Studi bizanti e neoellenici, Vizantiiskii vremennik, Parnassos, Nea hestia, Byzantinisch-neugriechische Jahrbücher, Athena, Syngramma periodikon,* to list a few.

Hungary

The recent introduction of Hungarian into the language and literature program has spurred interest in Hungarian materials. Berkeley has a good research collection of basic Hungarian works indispensable to the study of Hungarian history, language, literature, and culture. The Library contains works of such famous Hungarian historians as Hóman, Lukinich, Szekfű, and Katona's *Historia Critica Rerum Hungariae . . . ,* 42 v. (1779-1817). The complete works of I. Széchényi and L. Kossuth are part of the collection. Hungarian literature is represented by Balassi, Vörösmarty, Arany, Madách, Jókai, Petőfi, Babits, Ady, Attila József, Kassák and contemporary writers as Déry, Illyés, Juhász, Passuth, and Németh to cite some names.

Among the many bibliographic tools in its holdings the Library has Petrik, *Magyar könyvészet;* Szabó, *Régi magyar könyvtár;* Apponyi, *Hungarica;* Kont, *Bibliographie française de la Hongrie 1521-1910; Magyar folyóiratok repertóriuma;* Szinnyei, *Magyar írók élete és munkái; Pallas nagy lexikon; Révai nagy lexikon;* and *Új magyar lexikon.*

Periodicals in the collection range from *Magyar Tudomány, Budapesti Szemle, Magyar Földrajzi Értesítő,* v. 15- (1887-), *Archaeológiai Értesítő,* v. 2- (1869-), *Századok, Statisztikai Szemle, Magyar Nyelv, Nyelvtudományi Közlemények,* 36- (1901-), *Egyetemes Philológiai Közlöny, Irodalomtörténeti Közlemények,* to *Nyugat.* The Library has about 10,000 volumes devoted to Hungarian linguistics, literature, and history.

Poland

The Polish collection, with approximately 12,000 volumes, is an excellent research facility, strong in linguistics, literature (major authors are represented very well), and history. Other subjects, also with fundamental works as a base, are no mean adjuncts to the total collection, whether in political science, art, biology, agriculture, mathematics, economics, or archeology.

Bibliographic and reference works are in good supply. Major encyclopedias, dictionaries, and biographies are at hand, from the *Wielka encyklopedia powszechna,* to the *Słownik języka polskiego,* and *Polski słownik biograficzny.* The catalog lists 108 document entries under Poland, most far from complete.

Listed under the Academy, Kraków, are more than 50 periodical entries, half of them complete runs; there are almost as many under the Academy in Warsaw; 70 periodical runs of varying length are under societies; and the universities in Poznań, Lublin, Kraków, Warsaw, and Lwów do not lag far behind in titles relevant to the collection of the general library. Other titles among the 450 currently received include *Acta Poloniae Historica, Antemurale,* 9- (1965-), *Archaeologica Polona, Biblioteka Warszawska, Dialog,* 6- (1961-), *Ekonomista, Materiały i Prace Antropologiczne, Pamiętnik Literacki, Polish Review, Rocznik Slawistyczny,* and *Twórczość.* All in all the Polish materials are a solid contribution to the Library research resources.

Romania

Containing about 2,300 volumes, the Romanian collection covers a surprisingly broad range of fields. It has a fairly large number of bibliographic tools, the *Bibliografia Republicii Populare Romîne,* 8- (1959-), *Bibliografia românească veche, 1508-1830, Bibliografia periodicelor din*

RPR, 7- (1959-), *Publicaţiunile periodice româneşti,* v. 1 for 1820-1906, and various other titles, among them a good number of Academy bibliographies.

Although the language is not taught, the Library has a good selection of dictionaries and some grammars. Literature, except for a few prominent writers, is poorly represented. The history titles do permit more than mere browsing.

A very good proportion of the periodical publications of the Academy under its various names is in the Library, many of them in their entirety. Among periodicals in the collection there are *Revue des études roumaines, Revista d' histoire littéraire, Revista de etnografi şi folclor, Biblioteca istorică, Fontes rerum Transylvanicarum, Cronicile medievale ale Romîniei,* 2- (1959-), *Fauna Republicii Populare Romîne,* as well as *Flora Republicii Populare Române.*

There are about 150 titles in the Documents Department, some of them periodicals in various stages of completeness. The Library maintains an active exchange with 46 institutions; thus the collection will continue to grow.

Yugoslavia

Since participating in the Farmington Plan in 1953 the Library has been receiving all monographs of research value published in Yugoslavia. It was a recipient of Yugoslav materials under the PL 480 Program, which ran from 1967 to 1973. It also subscribes to a selection of scholarly periodicals in all subjects. Its holdings include a good collection of government documents for the period since 1945, materials about Yugoslavia from Western Europe and America. Standard bibliographic tools such as *Bibliografija Jugoslavije* are basic portions of the collection. Humanities, social sciences, architecture, art, engineering, and natural sciences are well represented. The collection is particularly strong in economics, history, international relations, and literature.

The Library has good holdings of Yugoslav 19th-century periodicals, e.g., *Hrvatska vila, Leptir, Otadžbina, Kolo* (some issues missing), *Delo, List za nauke, književnost i društveni život, Letopis Matice srpske* (some gaps but quite complete) and *Godišnjica Nikole Čupića.* Additionally, the Library contains among other titles, *Južnoslovenski filolog, Ljubljanski zvon, Historijski zbornik, Jugoslovenski istoriski časopis.*

Holdings of the Matica hrvatska, Srpska akademija nauka i umetnosti, Jugoslovenska akademija znanosti i umjetnosti, the University at Belgrade, and other institution publications are present in varying degrees of completeness.

The Library is fortunate in possessing the major bibliographies, encyclopedias, reference tools, biographies, historical works, and statistical publications necessary for intensive research on Yugoslavia. Currently, the Library is receiving more than 400 periodicals and series from Yugoslavia and adding about 750 monographs annually to its holdings of approximately 31,000 volumes.

Rudolf Lednicky
University of California at Berkeley

University of California at Los Angeles

General Information

The University Research Library is located on the North Campus and is open to all users, with free access to all stacks and service from 7:45 a.m. to 11 p.m. from Monday through Thursday and from 7:45 a.m. to 5 p.m. on Friday, 9 a.m. to 5 p.m. on Saturday, and 1 to 11 p.m. on Sunday. The Slavic Bibliographer is responsible for the collection. The holdings are reflected in the general alphabetical catalog (under author, title, and subject) and, for acquisitions up to 1963, in the printed *Dictionary Catalog of the University Library, 1919-1962*, 129 v. (Boston: G. K. Hall, 1963). A helpful aid is the mimeographed "Slavic Studies: A Checklist of Periodicals and Serials in the University Research Library at UCLA," compiled by E. Alex Baer in 1965. The Library uses the Library of Congress classification and shelving system, with the exception of a backlog of books from various subject fields temporarily classified and shelved as PG 9900. The loan regulations vary depending on the borrower's status, but in most cases monographs are loaned for two weeks; periodicals are not loaned to off-campus borrowers. The same regulations apply for interlibrary loans. There are numerous photocopying machines available at a rate of five cents per copy. Outside orders placed through interlibrary loan services are charged 15 cents per copy, with a minimum of $5.00.

The UCLA Research Library initiated a large-scale collecting policy in the Central and East European area only in the early 1960s. Before that time, Slavic acquisitions efforts had been focused on prerevolutionary Russia, with Soviet and East European titles acquired largely through exchange agreements with libraries, institutes, and universities. The energetic buying program pursued since 1962 has resulted in the formation of excellent research collections for most of the Slavic countries, particularly Czechoslovakia and Poland. Among the non-Slavic countries, Hungary and East Germany are well represented in literature, linguistics, and history, while modern Greece has a small but balanced collection which supports an active teaching program in postclassical and modern Greek studies. Albanian materials have not been systematically collected, but modern Albanian writers from both Tirana and Priština (Yugoslavia) are present in significant numbers.

Bulgaria

THE UNIVERSITY OF California has the distinction of being the first American institution approached by the Bulgarian Literary Society (the present Bulgarian Academy of Sciences) in 1908 for exchange of publications, a fact which produced fruitful arrangements maintained to the present (Radka Peicheva-Gospodinova, "Nauchnata periodika ot SASht i Velikobritaniia v knizhnite fondove na BAN," Izvestiia na Tsentralnata biblioteka pri Bŭlgarskata akademiia na naukite, v. 5, 1969: 143-157). UCLA also has exchange agreements with Bulgaria's two other leading institutions, the University of Sofia and the Cyril and Methodius National Library, and receives serials in the medical and technical sciences from three other sources. Through exchange and purchase a collection of some 3,000 volumes has been accumulated, reflecting in its makeup the two traditionally strongest fields of scholarship in Bulgaria, philology and history. There are also significant acquisitions outside these two main fields.

The most important feature of the collection is the extensive set of publications of the Academy, which go back to 1869, and *Periodichesko spisanie na Bŭlgarskoto knizhovno druzhestvo v Braila.* The Academy's publications to 1953 are listed (with contents for the periodicals and serials) in its *Opis na izdaniiata na Bŭlgarskata akademiia na naukite, 1869-1953* (Sofia, 1956), which UCLA has along with its 1926 *Opis* (important for authors omitted in the 1956 edition) and *Katalog na izdaniiata na BAN* for 1870-1958. See also M. Pundeff, "The Bulgarian Academy of Sciences (On the occasion of its centennial)," *East European Quarterly,* September, 1969: 371-86. UCLA has the 12 issues of *Periodichesko spisane* published in Brăila, Romania (1870-76) and the 71 issues published in Sofia (1882-1911). It also has the Academy's old *Spisanie* (1911-50, with gaps); the new *Spisanie* (1953-, with gaps); the *Sbornik,* 41 v. (1911-49; except v. 40); the *Letopis* for 1899-1942 (1901-47); *Izvestiia na Bŭlgarskoto arkheologichesko druzhestvo* (1910-20) and its continuation *Izvestiia na Bŭlgarskiia arkeologicheski institut* (1921-52), as well as *Bibliografiia na bŭlgarskata arkheologiia, 1879-1955* published by the institute in 1957; the series "Bŭlgarska Biblioteka" (1884-85 and 1902-36), "Bŭlgarski Starini" (1906-45), "Materiali za istoriiata na Sofiia" (1910-43), and others, some with gaps. The library has complete sets of the massive *Sbornik za narodni umotvoreniia i narodopis,* initiated in 1889 for folklore and ethnographic, linguistic, and historical studies and currently in its 53d volume, and *Dokumenti za bŭlgarskata istoriia* (1931-51).

Among the older (and now rare) monographic publications of the Academy at UCLA are A. Teodorov-Balan, *Bŭlgarski knigopis za sto godini, 1806-1905* (1909) [Here and hereafter Sofia is the place of publication, unless otherwise indicated], which laid the foundation of Bulgarian bibliography; the three-volume edition of *Sŭchineniia* of Marin S. Drinov (1909-15), the Academy's first president; the *editio princeps* of Paisii's *Istoriia slavenobolgarskaia,* edited by Iordan Ivanov (1914); Ivanov's *Bŭlgarski starini iz Makedoniia* (1908); G. A. Il'inskii, *Opyt sistematicheskoi Kirillo-Mefod'evskoi bibliografii* (1934) and its continuation by M. Popruzhenko and S. Romanski, *Kirilometodievska bibliografiia za 1934-1940 god.* (1942); and Nikola V. Mikhov's basic compilations *Bibliografski iztochnitsi za istoriiata na Turtsiia i Bŭlgariia* (1914-34), *Naselenieto na Turtsiia i Bŭlgariia prez XVIII i XIX v.; bibliografsko-statistichni izsledvaniia* (1915-35), and *Bibliographie des articles de périodiques allemands, anglais, français et italiens sur la Turquie et la Bulgarie* (1938).

Among the more recent publications received from the Academy are the anniversary volumes for Balan (1955), Drinov (1960), Paisii (1962), Cyril and Methodius (1963), Cyril (1969), Romanski (1960), and Mikhov (1959), all valuable additions. UCLA has also received the major series in progress: *Izvori za bŭlgarskata istoriia* (1954-), V. Nikolaev, *Vodnite znatsi v khartiite na srednovekovnite dokumenti ot bŭlgarskite knigokhranilishta* (1954), "Epigrafska poreditsa" (1955-), "Trudove po bŭlgarska dialektologiia" (1965-), "Bŭlgarska dialektologiia; prouchvaniia i materiali" (1962-), *Bŭlgarski dialekten atlas* (1964-), the three-volume *Rechnik na sŭvremenniia bŭlgarski knizhoven ezik* (1955-59), and "Biobibliografii na bŭlgarski ucheni" (1953-; with gaps). The Library currently receives the occasional (for the most part annual) *Izvestiia* of the majority of the Academy's institutes, including those for literature (1952-), linguistics (1952-), history (1951-), archeology (continuing the earlier *Izvestiia* cited above), ethnography (1953-), music (1952-), law (1956-), philosophy (1954-), as well as *Izvestiia* of the Academy's library (1959-) and of its scholarly archives (1957-), in some cases with gaps.

Finally, the recently compiled guides to the biobibliographies of the Academy's members and scholarly staff, its organization and officers, scientific institutions in Bulgaria, etc., are for the most part available at UCLA: *Sto godini Bŭlgarska akademiia na naukite, 1869-1969, I,*

Akademitsi i chlenove-korespondenti (1969); *Bulgarian Academy of Sciences Reference Book 1969* (1969); *Bŭlgarskata akademiia na naukite sled 9 septemvri 1944; spravochna kniga* (1958); *Nauchni uchrezhdeniia v Bŭlgariia, 1966; spravochnik* (1967); and *Les études balkaniques et sud-est européennes en Bulgarie; guide de documentation* (1966).

In contrast to the Academy publications, those of the University of Sofia, also very numerous (see M. Pundeff's "The University of Sofia at Eighty," *Slavic Review,* September 1968: 438-46), are inadequately represented in the UCLA collection. The Library has four of its bibliographies, *Bibliografiia na Sofiiskiia universitet "Sv. Kliment Okhridski," 1904-1942* (1943); *Bibliografiia na izdaniiata na Sofiiskiia universitet "Kliment Okhridski," 1956-1965* (1969); *Bibliografiia na disertatsiite zashtiteni v Bŭlgariia, 1929-1964* (1969), which reflects dissertations defended not only at the University, but at Academy institutes and other scholarly institutions in the country; and *Biografsko-bibliografski sbornik* (1968), reflecting the biobibliographies of the teaching staff of the Faculty of Slavic Philologies. The Library also has *Almanakh na Sofiiskiia universitet Sv. Kliment Okhridski* (1940), presenting biobibliographic data on the teaching staff, and *Istoriia na Sofiiskiia universitet Sv. Kliment Okhridski prez pŭrvoto mu polustoletie, 1888-1938* (1939), both compiled by Mikhail Arnaudov. The main body of the University publications is in its *Godishnik,* which is divided into subseries for each of the faculties. The subseries represented by considerable numbers of volumes at UCLA are those of the Faculties of Philosophy and History, Slavic Philologies, Law, and Western Philologies. UCLA also has volumes 1 and 3-5 of the nine volumes of *Izvestiia na seminara po slavianska filologiia* and all five volumes of "Trudove na statisticheskiia institut za stopanski prouchvaniia."

From the National Library in Sofia UCLA receives the biweekly national bibliography for books *Bŭlgarski knigopis* (1897-), which is available in print for 1900 to the present and on microfilm for 1897-1945. The gaps in *Bŭlgarski knigopis* and other aspects of Bulgarian bibliography are discussed by Tsenko Tsvetanov in *Bŭlgarska bibliografiia; istoricheski pregled i dneshno sŭstoianie* (1957), which UCLA has. It does not, however, currently receive the selective list of articles and reviews, *Letopis na periodichniia pechat* (1952-), which it has only to 1960. The Library has *Opis na rŭkopisite i staropechatnite knigi na Narodnata biblioteka v Sofiia,* 4 v. (1910-); *Bŭlgarska vŭzrozhdenska knizhnina; analitichen repertoar na bŭlgarskite knigi i periodichni izdaniia, 1806-1878,* 2 v. (1957-59); *Bŭlgarski periodichen pechat, 1844-1944; anotiran bibliografski ukazatel,* 3 v. (1962-69); *Obzor na arkhivnite fondove, kolektsii i edinichni postŭpleniia sŭkhraniavani v Bŭlgarski istoricheski arkhiv,* 3 v. (1963-); and various bibliographies and publications of the former Bulgarian Bibliographic Institute, now absorbed into the National Library, including its *Godishnik,* 9 v. (1945-62).

A particularly noteworthy feature of the collection is a set of the stenographic records of the National Assembly, *Stenografski dnevnitsi,* which UCLA has for 1879-1971. It includes the minutes of the constituent assembly of 1879 and the special (grand) national assemblies and has only minor gaps. Another special feature is the state gazette for promulgation of laws, *Dŭrzhaven Vestnik,* available for 1920-68, also with minor gaps. Of the numerous indexes to Bulgarian legislation, however, UCLA has only *Spravochnik po zakonodatelstvoto na Narodna Republika Bŭlgariia* (1957), which covers the period from September 9, 1944, to June 30, 1957. It should be noted, however, that in the area the Los Angeles County Law Library has substantial holdings, including indexes, for the identification and study of Bulgarian law. In the area of statistics, UCLA has a complete set of *Statisticheski godishnik na Tsarstvo Bŭlgariia* (1909-42) and the volumes for 1960, 1961, and 1965-70 of its successor, *Statisticheski godishnik na Narodna Republika Bŭlgariia.*

In the well-represented field of modern literature, UCLA has the works of most of the major writers and some of the minor and younger ones listed in *Bŭlgarski pisateli; biografii, biblio-*

grafiia, by Georgi Konstantinov and others (1961) and *Bibliographische Einführung in das Studium der neueren bulgarischen Literatur (1850-1950),* by Peter Gerlinghoff (Meisenheim am Glan, 1969). Both these items are available in the Library. In the case of prewar writers, however, postwar editions of collected and edited works have been acquired, as a rule, rather than original or early editions. The same characteristic of acquisition of postwar works is evident in history of literature and criticism; for example, while the library has Boian Penev's *Bŭlgarska literatura; kratŭk istoricheski ocherk* in its 1946 edition, it does not have his indispensable *Istoriia na novata bŭlgarska literatura* published in 1930-36. The acquired translations are few compared to what the available guide *Bŭlgarska khudozhestvena literatura na chuzhdi ezitsi; bibliografski ukazatel, 1823-1962,* by Veselin Traikov (1964) lists, but the library can boast a copy of the first translation in any language of Ivan Vazov's classic novel *Under the Yoke* (London, 1894).

In the related field of oral literature and folklore, UCLA can also boast copies of the first editions of *Bugarske narodne pesme,* compiled by Stefan Verković (Belgrade, 1860), and *Bŭlgarski narodni pesni,* collected by Dimitŭr and Konstantin Miladinov (Zagreb, 1861), as well as *Chansons populaires bulgares inédites,* translated by Auguste Dozon (Paris, 1875). It has the relatively rare *Trem na bŭlgarskata narodna istoricheska epika ot Momchila i Krali Marka do Karadzhata i Khadzhi Dimitra* (1939) and *Senki iz nevidelitsa; kniga na bŭlgarskata narodna balada* (1936), both compiled by Bozhan Angelov and Khristo Vakarelski, as well as the new 13-volume collection *Bŭlgarsko narodno tvorchestvo,* edited by M. Arnaudov and others (1961-65).

Taking at random noteworthy acquisitions, primarily of prewar vintage, UCLA has the following:

In linguistics, Stefan Mladenov's *Geschichte der bulgarischen Sprache* (Berlin, 1929) and *Etimologicheski i pravopisen rechnik na bŭlgarskiia knizhoven ezik* (1941); Liubomir Miletich's *Die Rhodopemundarten der bulgarischen Sprache* (Vienna, 1912); Balan's *Bŭlgarska gramatika* (1930) and *Nova bŭlgarska gramatika* (1940); Beniu Tsonev's *Istoriia na bŭlgarskii ezik* (1940); and P. S. Kalkandzhiev, *Bŭlgarska gramatika* (Plovdiv, 1936).

In history, Vasil Zlatarski's *Istoriia na bŭlgarskata dŭrzhava prez srednite vekove,* 3 v. in 4 (1918-40); Konstantin Jireček's *Geschichte der Bulgaren* (Prague, 1876) and his emendations *Istoriia na Bŭlgarite; popravki i dobavki ot samiia avtor* (1939); his *Das Fürstentum Bulgarien* (Vienna, 1891); Felix Kanitz's *Donau-Bulgarien und der Balkan,* 3 v. (Vienna, 1879-80), and its French edition *La Bulgarie danubienne et le Balkan* (Paris, 1882); R. Leonow, ed., *Geheime dokumente der russischen Orient-politik, 1881-1890* (Berlin, 1893); Ofeikov (pseud. of Atanas Shopov), *La Macédoine au point de vue ethnographique, historique, et philologique* (Plovdiv, 1887); Simeon Radev's *La Macédoine et la renaissance bulgare au XIX-e siècle* (1918); Zhecho Chankov, *Geografski rechnik na Bŭlgariia, Makedoniia, Dobrudzha i Pomoraviia* (1918); Miletich's *Razorenieto na trakiiskite bŭlgari prez 1913 godina* (1918); Iordan Ivanov's *Les Bulgares devant le Congrès de la paix; documents historiques, ethnographiques et diplomatiques,* 2d ed. (Berne, 1919); Dimitŭr Mishev's *Bŭlgariia v minaloto; stranitsi iz bŭlgarskata kulturna istoriia* (1916) and its English translation *The Bulgarians in the Past* (Lausanne, 1919); Alois Hajek's *Bulgariens Befreiung und staatliche Entwicklung unter seinem ersten Fürsten* (Munich, 1939).

In church history, Todor Burmov's *Bŭlgaro-grŭtskata tsŭrkovna raspria* (1902); Drinov's *Istoricheski pregled na Bŭlgarskata tsŭrkva ot samoto i nachalo i do dnes* (Vienna, 1869); Khr. Vŭrgov, *Konstitutsiiata na Bŭlgarskata pravoslavna tsŭrkva i razvoi na Ekzarkhiiskiia ustav* (1920); Stefan Tsankov and others, eds., *Pravilata na sv. Pravoslavna tsŭrkva s tŭlkovaniiata im,* v. 1 (1912); Metropolitan Kliment of Turnovo, *Sŭchineniia,* 2 v. (1968), his biography under his lay name Vasil Drumev, by Iurdan Trifonov (1926); *Tsŭrkoven arkhiv,* 5 v. in 2 (1925); *Deset godini Bŭlgarska patriarshiia 10 mai 1953–10 mai 1963* (1963); three of the late Patriarch Kiril's works: *Sŭprotivata sreshtu Berlinskiia dogovor* (1955), *Graf N. P. Ignatiev i bŭlgarskiia tsŭrko-*

ven vŭpros (1958), and *Prinos kŭm bŭlgarskiia tsŭrkoven vŭpros* (1961); *Godishnik na Dukhovnata akademiia "Sv. Kliment Okhridski"* and the *Godishnik* of its predecessor, the Faculty of Theology of the University of Sofia, with gaps.

In economics, Ivan Sakazov's *Bulgarische Wirtschaftsgeschichte* (Berlin, 1929); Georgi Danailov's *Les effets de la guerre en Bulgarie* (Paris, 1932); Leo Pasvolsky's *Bulgaria's Economic Position* (Washington, 1930); Zhak Natan's *Istoriia ekonomicheskogo razvitiia Bolgarii* (Moscow, 1961); Kiril Lazarov's *Ekonomicheskoe razvitie Narodnoi Respubliki Bolgarii* (Moscow, 1963).

In politics, Dimitŭr Blagoev's *Sŭchineniia*, 20 v. (1957-64); L. Trotskii and Kh. Kabakchiev, *Ocherki politicheskoi Bolgarii* (Moscow, 1923); *Bŭlgarskata komunisticheska partiia v rezoliutsii i resheniia na kongresite, konferentsiite i plenumite na TsK, Tom I, 1891-1918*, 2d ed. (1957); *Istoriia na BKP, 1885-1944; bibliografiia; materiali publikuvani sled 9 septemvri 1944 g.* (1965); *Istoriia Bolgarskoi kommunisticheskoi partii* (Moscow, 1960); biobibliographies of Kabakchiev (1958), Vasil Kolarov (1947), and Vŭlko Chervenkov (1950). Additional UCLA holdings in these and other fields are identified in M. Pundeff's *Bulgaria: A Bibliographic Guide* (Washington, 1965; reprint, New York, 1968).

In newspapers and periodicals, the collection is also limited, but a number of valuable and rare periodicals published before 1944 are in it. UCLA receives only two current newspapers, *Rabotnichesko Delo* and *Literaturen Front*, and has *La Parole Bulgare* for 1937-40. The rarest acquisition is *Bŭlgarski knizhitsi* (Constantinople, 1858-60). The complete or nearly complete periodicals of that vintage are: *Bŭlgarska sbirka* (1894-1915); *Uchilishten pregled* (1896-1949) and *Arkhiv na Ministerstvoto na narodnoto prosveshtenie*, which replaced it in 1909-11; *Spisanie na Bŭlgarskoto ikonomichesko druzhestvo* (1896-1949); *Izvestiia na Bŭlgarskoto istorichesko druzhestvo* (1905-); *Bŭlgarska istoricheska biblioteka* (1928-33); *Bŭlgarska misŭl* (1925-44); *Makedonski pregled* (1924-43); *Izvestiia na Bŭlgarskoto geografsko druzhestvo* (1933-42); *Prosveta* (1935-43); and *Izkustvo i kritika* (1938-43).

Finally, among the periodicals and serials published since 1944 of which UCLA has complete or nearly complete sets are: *Istoricheski pregled* (1945-); *Bŭlgarski ezik* (1951-); *Literaturna misŭl* (1957-); *Bŭlgarski ezik i literatura* (1953-); *Bŭlgarska muzika* (1948-); *Études historiques* (1960-); *Études balkaniques* (1964-); *Balkansko ezikoznanie* (1959-); *Izvestiia na Dŭrzhavnite arkhivi* (1957-); *Izvestiia na Narodnata biblioteka "Kiril i Metodi"* (1952-); and *Bibliotekar* (1954-).

Marin Pundeff
California State University, Northridge

Romania

THE UCLA ROMANIAN collection is composed of about 5,000 volumes; the annual intake is about 200. Approximately 75 percent are in Romanian, 20 percent in Western languages, and 5 percent in Russian. Most of the collection has been acquired through exchanges. During the past 15 years the Library has maintained regular exchange relations with some 30 partners, including the Library of the Romanian Academy in Bucharest and its branches in Cluj, Iaşi, and Timişoara, the Central State Library, the universities of Bucharest, Cluj, Iaşi, and Timişoara, and national and local museums. Since the growth of its Romanian holdings has depended heavily upon these exchanges, and since there has been little retrospective buying, the collection consists largely of works published since the mid-1950's. Runs of periodicals and serials form the most significant part of the collection, while the monographic literature is, on the whole, modest. By disciplines, the collection is strongest in history and language, but even here its usefulness for research is limited.

Bibliographic and Reference Aids

The Library possesses a number of standard bibliographies and reference works. Of general interest are *Anuarul cărţii din Republica Populară Română* (1953-54), *Bibliografia Republicii Socialiste România, cărţi, albume, hărţi, note muzicale* (since 1958), and *Bibliografia periodicelor din RSR* (since 1959), all published by the Bibliotecă Centrală de Stat in Bucharest. There are also several indispensable bibliographies of periodicals, including Nerva Hodoş and Al. Sadi Ionescu, *Publicaţiunile periodice româneşti (ziare, gazete, reviste),* v. 1, 1820-1906, (Bucharest, 1913) and its continuation for the period 1907-18 (Bucharest, 1969), and *Bibliografia analitică a periodicelor româneşti* (Bucharest, 1966-); such basic bibliographies in the humanities and social sciences as Ioan Bianu, Nerva Hodoş, and Dan Simonescu; *Bibliografia românească veche,* 4 v., (Bucharest, 1903-44), and Andrei Veress, *Bibliografia română-ungară,* 3 v. (Bucharest 1931-35); and inventories of manuscripts in the Library of the Romanian Academy in Bucharest, among them Ioan Bianu, *Catalogul manuscriptelor româneşti,* 2 v. (Bucharest, 1907-13), and Constantin Litzica, *Catalogul manuscriptelor greceşti* (Bucharest, 1909). Holdings of general statistical materials are largely confined to *Anuarul statistic al României* (Bucharest) for the years 1915-16, 1926, 1929, 1937-40, and *Anuarul statistic al RSR* (Bucharest) for the years since 1958.

History

The strength of the Library's holdings in history lies in its periodical and serial collections. On ancient history, for example, it has *Acta Musei Napocensis,* v. 1- (Cluj, 1964-); *Arheologia Moldovei,* v. 1- (Bucharest, 1961-); *Dacia,* first series, v. 1-2, 5-6 (Bucharest, 1924-36), and second series, v. 1- (Bucharest, 1957-); Gheorghe Popa-Lisseanu, *Izvoarele istoriei Românilor,* v. 1, 4-6, 8-10 (Bucharest, 1934-36); *Materiale şi cercetări arheologice,* v. 2-8 (Bucharest, 1956-61); *Studii şi cercetări de istorie veche,* v. 3-13, 15- (Bucharest, 1952-62, 1964-); and on history generally, Academia Română, *Bulletin de la section historique,* v. 1-9 (Bucharest, 1912-21); *Cercetări istorice,* edited by Ion Minea, v. 1-16 (Iaşi, 1925-43); Comisiunea Monumentelor Istorice. *Buletinul,* v. 1-32 (Bucharest, 1908-39); *Ephemeris dacoromana,* v. 1-10 (Rome, 1923-45); *Revista istorică,* edited by Nicolae Iorga, v. 5-20 (Bucharest, 1919-34); *Anuarul Institutului de Istorie din Cluj,* v. 1- (Cluj, 1958-); *Revue Roumaine d'histoire,* v. 1- (Bucharest, 1962-); *Studii. Revistă de Istorie,* v. 10-11, 13-14, 17- (Bucharest, 1957-58, 1960-61, 1964-); and *Studii şi materiale de istorie medie,* v. 1-5 (Bucharest, 1956-63).

There are only a few collections of sources; those that are complete or rare are T. Codrescu, *Uricariul cuprinzător de hrisoave, anafarale, tratate şi alte acte ale Moldo-Valahiei,* v. 3, 5, 7-10, 15, 18-23 (Iaşi, 1892-95); a number of volumes of *Documente privind istoria României,* series A. *Moldova,* 11 v. (Bucharest, 1951-57) and series B. *Ţara Românească,* 13 v. (Bucharest, 1951-60), and *Războiul pentru independenţă,* v. 1-9 (Bucharest, 1952-55); Mihai Costăchescu, *Documentele moldoveneşti înainte de Ştefan cel Mare,* 2 v. (Iaşi, 1931-32); Ioan Bogdan, *Documentele lui Ştefan cel Mare,* 2 v. (Bucharest, 1913); and Nicolae Iorga, *Acte şi fragmente cu privire la istoria Românilor adunate din depozitele de manuscrise ale Apusului,* 3 v. (Bucharest, 1895-97).

Of the general multivolume histories of the Romanians, besides the older *Chronica Românilor* by Gheorghe Şincai, 2d ed., 3 v. (Bucharest, 1886), the Library has complete only Alexandru D. Xenopol, *Istoria Românilor din Dacia Traiana,* 6 v. (Iaşi, 1888-93) and Nicolae Iorga, *Geschichte des rumänischen Volkes,* 2 v. (Gotha, 1905). The holdings of specialized studies and supporting collections of documents on any given period or subject are too incomplete to allow more than basic research. There are, nonetheless, a few monographs by Iorga, P. P. Panaitescu, Constantin C. Giurescu, and Andrei Oţetea and selected writings by Ioan Bogdan and Dimitrie Onciul. The holdings of Romania's foreign relations mainly concern those with Russia from the middle of the 19th century to the present.

There are only a few works on Romanians outside the Old Kingdom. Transylvania is covered best. There are studies of the Romanian national movement up to 1918 and minority problems (mainly Magyar) afterwards; several collections of sources, including Ioan Lupaş, *Documentele istorice transilvane*, v. 1 (Cluj, 1940-), and *Documente privind istoria României*, series C. *Transilvania*, 6 v. (Bucharest, 1951-55); and a few serial and periodical collections (incomplete), such as *Apulum*, v. 1-2, 4-9 (Alba Iulia, 1939-71), *Revue de Transylvanie*, v. 1-5 (Cluj, 1934-39), and *Korrespondenzblatt des Vereines für Siebenbürgische Landeskunde*, v. 19-41 (Hermannstadt, 1896-1918).

Language and Literature

The collection includes a small number of descriptive works and grammars, mostly in Western languages, by Ovid Densuşianu, Alf Lombard, Sever Pop, Sextil Puşcariu, Alexandru Rosetti, and Kristian Sandfeld and Hedvig Olsen. Most of the recent standard dictionaries and linguistic atlases are also available. The main strength of the holdings lies in periodicals and serials. There are, for example, numerous recent publications of the Romanian Academy, e.g., *Studii şi cercetări lingvistice*, v. 5- (Bucharest, 1954-   ); *Revue de linguistique*, v. 1-8 (Bucharest, 1956-63) and its continuation, *Revue roumaine de linguistique*, v. 9- (Bucharest, 1964-   ); *Fonetică şi dialectologie*, v. 1-7 (Bucharest, 1958-71); *Limba română*, v. 9- (Bucharest, 1960-   ); *Limbă şi literatură*, v. 2-26 (Bucharest, 1956-70); *Romanoslavica*, v. 1-17 (Bucharest, 1958-70), *Cercetări de lingvistică*, v. 2- (Cluj, 1957-   ), and *Studii şi cercetări ştiinţifice. Filologie*, v. 7-15 (Iasi, 1956-64) and its continuation, *Anuar de lingvistică şi istorie literară*, v. 16- (Iaşi, 1965-   ). There are also a few university publications, including *Bulletin linguistique*, v. 8, 11, 13, 15-16 (1940-48) and *Analele . . . Filologie*, v. 8- (1959-   ) of the University of Bucharest, and *Studia Universitatis Babeş-Bolyai*, series philologia, v. 7- (1962-   ) of the University of Cluj.

The holdings on literature are small and fragmentary. There are only a few of the standard histories, for example, Nicolae Cartojan, *Istoria literaturii române vechi*, v. 1 (Bucharest, 1940), and the rarity, George Călinescu, *Istoria literaturii române dela origini până în prezent* (Bucharest, 1941). Literary criticism is represented by recent editions of the works of Titu Maiorescu, Pompiliu Constantinescu, Tudor Vianu, and Şerban Cioculescu, among others. There are few works by the chief poets and prose writers; Vasile Alecsandri, Ion Creangă, and Ioan Slavici are probably the best represented. The holdings on folk literature consist mainly of a few recent anthologies from Oltenia, Maramureş, and Transylvania and *Revista de folclor*, v. 1-8 (Bucharest, 1956-63) and its continuation, *Revista de etnografie şi folclor*, v. 9- (Bucharest, 1964-   ).

Other Disciplines

The Library possesses some useful items on economic development and commerce. There are several valuable periodicals covering the interwar period: *Buletinul institutului economic românesc*, v. 1-17 (Bucharest, 1922-38); *Raport statistic de mişcarea porturilor României*, 5 v. (Bucharest, 1934-39); and *Correspondance économique roumaine*, v. 16-22 (Bucharest, 1934-40), and the current *Viaţa economică*, v. 4- (Bucharest, 1966-   ). Monographic literature deals primarily with the history of agricultural development and the peasant question in the 19th and 20th centuries.

On social conditions and demography there are *The Rumanian Journal of Sociology*, v. 2 (Bucharest, 1964-   ), *Recensămîntul populaţiei din 21 februarie 1956*, 4 v. (Bucharest, 1959-61),

Buletinul demografic al României, v. 1-9 (Bucharest, 1932-40), and several works by Sabin Manuila on the rural population.

The significant holdings dealing with intellectual and cultural life also consist mainly of periodicals. On law, there is little material except *Revue roumaine des sciences sociales. Série des sciences juridiques,* v. 8- (Bucharest, 1964-   ) and *Studii și cercetări juridice,* v. 9- (Bucharest, 1964-   ). Philosophy is represented by *Revista de filozofie,* v. 12- (Bucharest, 1965-   ) and *Analele . . . Filozofie,* v. 8 (1959-   ) of the University of Bucharest. In addition to a few important monographs by George Oprescu, Ioan D. Ştefănescu, and Virgil Vătăşianu, the holdings on art and music include *Studii și materiale de istoria artei,* v. 1, 5-8, 10 (Bucharest, 1958-63); *Studii și cercetări de istoria artei. Seria teatru, muzică, cinematografie* and *Seria arta plastică,* both v. 11- (Bucharest, 1964-   ); and *Studii de muzicologie,* v. 2- (Bucharest, 1966-   ).

Keith Hitchins
University of Illinois at Urbana-Champaign

Yugoslavia

UCLA'S YUGOSLAV COLLECTIONS were greatly expanded in the 1960s in connection with the University area studies program. In the spring of 1961 Joel M. Halpern, then a member of the Department of Anthropology at UCLA, received a grant from the National Science Foundation for 18 months of research in Yugoslavia. University authorities made approximately $30,000 available to Mr. Halpern for library purchases in Yugoslavia. At that time the Yugoslav holdings of the UCLA Library were modest; a 1961 survey listed most of the nonserial titles in about a dozen pages. The serial holdings received through exchange and subscription totaled over 130, including titles in the natural sciences. By 1972 the Yugoslav holdings were estimated at about 40,500 titles. Approximately 18,500 titles had been acquired by purchases made in Yugoslavia in 1961-62 under Mr. Halpern's supervision, 8,000 titles were obtained on blanket order between 1963 and 1967, and approximately 14,000 titles were received under the PL-480 program between 1967 and 1971, with an annual intake of Yugoslav materials under that program of approximately 3,000 items.

Under the present UCLA Library policies, the following subject categories of Yugoslav materials are collected: literature, literary history and criticism, and linguistics; in the humanities—history, folklore, music, dance, art (sculpture and painting); in the social sciences—anthropology (in the Yugoslav context—ethnology, archeology, and folklore); economics—industry, agriculture, trade, and commerce; and politics, including domestic affairs and foreign relations; natural science—geology, physical, political, and economic geography. General reference works such as dictionaries and encyclopedias are also acquired. Among the categories not systematically collected, but for which the Library has residual or specialized holdings, are medicine, law, agriculture, physical sciences and technology, art exhibit catalogs, vanity press literature, poetry, and materials published in Yugoslav languages outside Yugoslavia. Almost all the more than 18,000 book titles purchased in 1961-62 were brief-listed. Most of the acquisitions are brief-listed in the multivolume complete UCLA card catalog produced in folio book format in 1962, subsequent to the acquisitions of 1961-62. The purchases of 1961-62 included about 1,000 titles of newspapers, periodicals, serials, and almanacs totaling some 10,000 items; thus 28,000 pieces were acquired overall. Approximately 70% of the books collected were in Serbian or Croatian, with Slovene forming perhaps 20% of the total. The remaining 10% was made up of publications in Macedonian, Albanian, Romanian, Bulgarian, Hungarian, Italian, German, and French, with some Russian titles.

Serbo-Croatian linguistics and literature form the main strength of the collections and are substantially supplemented by historical materials. These strengths are exemplified by the holdings of the publications of three major learned societies, the Serbian Academy of Sciences and Arts in Belgrade, the Yugoslav Academy of Sciences and Arts in Zagreb, and the Serbian Society in Novi Sad. For example, the Library has complete runs of most of the various serials published by the Srpska akademija nauka i umetnosti, such as the *Glasnik, Godišnjak, Posebna izdanja, Spomenik,* and in specialized fields as *Srpski dijalektološki zbornik, Srpski etnografski zbornik, Zbornik za istoriju, jezik i književnost srpskog naroda, Naš jezik,* and *Južnoslovenski filolog,* among others. For the Jugoslavenska akademija znanosti i umjetnosti there are *Djela, Grada, Monumenta,* and *Radovi,* as well as specific items such as *Codex diplomaticus regni Croatiae, Dalmatiae et Slavoniae, Zbornik za narodni život i obicaje južnih slovena;* and for the Matica srpska in Novi Sad there are the *Letopis, Zbornik za književnost i jezik,* and *Zbornik za filologiju i lingvistiku.* The runs of all these serials are extensive. As an example, the *Letopis* of the Matica srpska is one of the earliest South Slavic scholarly periodicals, beginning publication in 1824; the Library has virtually a complete run, all but three of the more than 410 volumes that had been issued by 1971. Similarly the Library has nearly all of the *Posebna izdanja* of the Serbian Academy, which had reached 445 volumes by 1971.

The Department of Special Collections has some 18th-century works. Illustrative of these are: Stefan Novaković, *Dissertatio brevis ac sincera Hungari auctoris de gente Serbica perperam Rasciana dicta ejusque meritis ac factis in Hungaria. Cum appendice privilogiorum eidem genti elargitorum* (1790); and Jovan Rajić, *Istoriia raznyh slavenskih narodov, naipache bolgar, horvatov i serbov,* I-IV and supplement (Vienna, 1794-95) (the Library also holds an 1823 edition of this item).

A comprehensive view of the language and literature holdings of UCLA may be achieved by making an item-by-item comparison with a comprehensive survey such as that of Jerkovich (George C. Jerkovich), "The Library's South Slavic Collection," *Books and Libraries at the University of Kansas,* v. 4, no. 3, (December 1966). The strength and diversity of the UCLA collections in these fields may be illustrated by references to a number of major and minor authors in the various South Slav literatures selected somewhat randomly from the Jerkovich survey. The earliest Croatian writers, from Dalmatia and more specifically Dubrovnik (Ragusa), include Sisko Menčetić (1457-1527) and Džore Držić (1461-1501) whose works are represented in two editions, 1870 and 1937. The famous playwright Marin Držić (1510-67), whose works continue to be performed, is well represented (five anthologies, including an 1875 edition of his *Djela,* plus three editions of his *Dundo Maroje* including an English translation by Sonia Bicanić and works about him by Frano Čale, Živko Jeličić, Miroslav Pantić, and Franjo Švelec).

Following the Renaissance period there was the era of Protestantism in Slovenia and Croatia represented in the work of Primož Trubar, 1508-86 (4 editions of his works, including collections of psalms and epistles and two surveys of his work by France Kidrić and Mirko Rupel). Among the most famous 17th-century writers was the Dubrovnik poet Ivan Gundulić, 1588-1638 (five anthologies and more than a dozen editions of his poems, many from the early 19th century). The 18th century is documented by authors such as Filip Grabovac, Matija Antun Reljković, Andrija Kačić-Miošić, and Tito Brezovački, who have been discussed by Croatian critics such as Ljubomir Maraković and Antun Barac (there are 13 works for the latter, while the others are represented in several anthologies dealing with each author individually).

The 19th-century Illyrian movement, so important in forming a South Slav national consciousness at the literary level, is exemplified in the writings of Ljudovit Gaj, Stanko Vraz (five anthologies), Ivan Mažuranić (three anthologies and eight editions plus one English translation of his *Smrt Smail-age Čengijića*).

The romantic period in 19th-century Croatian literature has many representatives: Luka Botić (two works) and Vjenceslav Novak (14 works, several in a number of editions, plus eight anthologies) are typical of the coverage, while August Šenoa has perhaps the most extensive representation (13 of his separate works, plus nine anthologies and a 20-volume set of his collected works).

Modern Croatian authors are very well accounted for both in their diversity and in collected works of the most prominent: August Cesarec (1893-1941) is represented by 11 volumes, Miroslav Krleža (1893-   ) by 25 volumes. Contemporary poets and novelists of the postwar period are also represented, such as Josip Pupačić, Milivoj Slaviček, Nikola Šop, Zlatko Tomičić, Ivan Raos, Mirko Božić, and Krsto Špoljar, to name a few.

Serbian literature, as befitting the multinational nature of Yugoslavia, needs to be taken as a separate entity. A crucial early figure is Dositej Obradović (1742-1818), an enlightened monk and extensive traveler, who knew Western literatures (he is represented in five anthologies plus three editions of his work from the first half of the 19th century and five monographs about his work). Perhaps the most famous Serbian writer of the early 19th century was Vuk Stefanović Karadžić (1784-1864) who, in his long life, produced substantial works in the diverse fields of history, ethnography, folklore, and linguistics; he is famous primarily as the reformer of the Serbian literary language (over 90 volumes in the collection, including several early 19th-century editions and nine monographs written about his career).

Equally well-known is Petar Petrović Njegoš, also known as Petar II, Prince Bishop of Montenegro (1813-51), whose most famous work is *Gorski vijenac* (Mountain Wreath), a poem of the fight for freedom (eight editions of the poem, seven anthologies of his work, 10 monographs on his writings, and 17 volumes of his collected works).

Like the Croatian literature of the same period, the Serbian literature of the 19th century is manifested in the UCLA collections in the works of many authors. Among the more important are Svetozar Marković, best known for his role in the formation of Serbian socialism and as a strong influence on Serbian realism (seven anthologies and two monographs on his writings) and the playwright and satirist Branislav Nušić (64 volumes, including various editions, and three monographs about him).

The most famous contemporary Yugoslav author is perhaps the Nobel Prize winner Ivo Andrić (30 anthologies, 30 volumes of collected works, and nine volumes of analysis of his writings in several languages), whose works on his native Bosnia have attracted worldwide attention.

Even in a very brief survey of Serbian literature it is necessary to mention the names of Oskar Davičo, Dobrica Ćosić, and Branko Ćopić (collectively represented by over 100 volumes).

Macedonian literature has established itself in the postwar period, and is most abundantly represented in the works of the critic Blaže Koneski (33 volumes) and the works of the novelist Slavko Janevski (22 volumes), as well as by some dozen other authors.

Slovenia has a long literary tradition dating from the 16th century and the writings of Primož Trubar. In the 19th century perhaps most significant is the work of the romantic poet France Prešeren who was influential in articulating a national consciousness (33 works, including 26 anthologies and four studies on the poet). Another important Slovene poet who represented the "Liberals" of the late 19th century was Ivan Cankar (over 100 volumes); 20th-century Slovene writers are abundantly represented. Important to an understanding of Slovene literary life are the journal *Ljubljanski zvon,* 56 v. (1881-1941), and the *Letopis,* 36 v. (1869-1912) of the Slovenska matica v Ljubljani.

There is a large collection of dictionaries of Serbo-Croatian (30) of which the most important are the *Rječnik hrvatskogo ili srpskog jezika* (Zagreb academy, JAZU, 18 volumes at present) and *Rečnik srpskohrvatskog književnog i narodnog jezika* (Belgrade academy, SAN, 7 volumes at present). There are also multivolume dictionaries produced by Matica srpska and Matica hrvatska in 1967. Among the more interesting bilingual dictionaries is a Serbo-Croatian-Romani dictionary edited by Rade Uhlik (1947). The Library also has a half-dozen Macedonian dictionaries and some dozen Slovene ones. There are extensive collections on Serbo-Croatian dialects, as well as grammars, etymologies, and general language histories.

The Yugoslav holdings in the field of literature can be most precisely documented, because of the author designation. Owing to incomplete cataloging of the collections, the extent of specific holdings is more difficult to establish in other fields, where the author is not the primary identifying feature (e.g., periodicals and serials).

Most of the monographs cited in the survey of source materials on Yugoslav history at the University of Kansas are in the UCLA Library (George C. Jerkovich and Galina Kuzmanovich. "A survey of source materials on Yugoslav history," *Books and Libraries at the University of Kansas,* v. 9, no. 1, September 1971). An idea of the diversity of the UCLA collection can be gained by citing some well-known historians of Yugoslavia and the number of titles listed in the card catalog for each: Ferdinand Šišić (15), Vladimir Ćorović (17), Josip Horvat (12), Hermann Wendel (13). This approach can be applied in other fields as well. Thus the late Milenko Filipović, a distinguished Serbian ethnologist who worked in Bosnia, Macedonia, the Vojvodina, and Slovenia, as well as Serbia proper, is represented by 10 titles; Rudolf Bičanić, the late Croatian economist, who was also interested in social history, is represented by an equal number; 24 volumes are listed for Jovan Cvijić, the founder of the Serbian school of human geography and investigations of population migrations before World War I. Fourteen titles are listed for Stjepan Radić, the founder of the interwar Croatian Peasant Party, 14 for Slobodan Jovanović, the prewar Serbian historian, while 60 titles are cataloged for the former Vice President of Yugoslavia Edvard Kardelj. Other figures, for example, Filipović and Bičanić are well represented by both prewar and postwar items.

A partial listing of some 19th- and early 20th-century periodicals of literary and social significance may help indicate an additional dimension of the collection: *Bosanska vila,* v. 1-21 (1885-1913); *Brankovo kolo za zabavu, pouku i književnost,* v. 1-19 (Sremski Karlovac, 1895-1913); *Bratstvo,* (Belgrade, 1887-, incomplete); *Danica, list za zabavu i književnost* (Novi Sad, 1860-, incomplete); *Godišnjica Nikola Čupica* (Belgrade, 1877-, incomplete); *Hrvatska misao* (Zagreb, 1902-05); *Hrvatska mladost* (Zagreb, 1916-17); *Književnik; časopis za jezik i poviest Hrvatsku i Srbsku, i prirodne znanosti,* v. 1-3 (Zagreb, 1864-66); *Otadžbina; književnost, nauka, društveni život,* v. 1-32 (Belgrade, 1875-92); *Srpske novine; službeni dnevnik Kraljevine Serbije u Krfu* (1916-18) (the newspaper of the Serbian government in exile on Corfu); *Serbska pčela* (Budapest, 1830-41, incomplete); *Srpski Sion* (1895-1907); *Srpsko-dalmatinski magazin* (Zadar, 1836-, incomplete); *Straža* (Novi Sad, 1878-79); *Vienac, zabavi i pouči,* v. 1-35 (Zagreb, 1869-1903).

The collection includes some 19th-century law codes, statistical series, and parliamentary records for Serbia, Croatia, Bosnia, and Montenegro. The series are generally incomplete. The following holdings are intended to be illustrative rather than exhaustive: Serbia. *Zbornik zakona,* 15 v. (1840-63); Serbia. *Narodna skupština. Protokoli* (1859-); Serbia. *Uprava državna statistike. Statistički godišnjak,* (1893-1905); Montenegro, *Code général des beins pour le principauté* de Montenegro de 1888 (1892); Croatia-Slavonia, *Dnevik Sabora* (1861-); Croatia-Slavonia. *Zemaljsko-vladni list* (1850-); Croatia-Slavonia. *Zemaljski statisticki ured* (1895-); *Manuale del regno di Dalmazia* (Zara, 1871-); *Glasnik Zakona i Naredba za Bosnu i Hercegovinu* (1887-).

Also of importance are the various museum journals, especially those from the interwar period and earlier which are difficult to obtain in many major libraries in the United States. These include: Belgrade. Etnografski muzej, *Posebna izadanja. Editions spéciales* (1930-); Skopje. *Glasnik Skopskog naučnog Društva,* v. 1-10 (1925-39); Sarajevo. Zemaljski muzej, *Glasnik,* v. 1-55 (1889-1943).

On another level there are certain World War II newspapers, official gazettes, and various government documents from the independent Croatian fascist state. For Belgrade this collection includes the occupation newspapers issued under German auspices, *Novo vreme* (May 16, 1941-August 30, 1944) and *Opštinske novine* (April 1941-June 1941). For Zagreb illustrative items are: *Hrvatski Narod, glasilo hrvatskog ustaškog pokreta* (1941-44), *Narodne novine, službeni list* (1941-44), *Brzopisni zapisnici* (NDH, 1942), *Hrvatsko državno pravo* (1944), *Časopis za hrvatsku poviest* (1943).

The potential user of the UCLA Yugoslav collections may find it profitable to consult the printed catalog of the UCLA Library card file as well as the card catalog itself. The printed catalog includes subject and sometimes added entries, as well as author and title entries, and yields such materials as local calendars and almanacs issued both before and since the Second World War by such diverse groups as Moslem and Catholic clergies in Bosnia, the Croatian Peasant Party, Serbian cooperative unions, local political and administrative organizations.

The Library has some specialized collections of Yugoslav materials, for example, elementary school textbooks for the various republics as well as the minorities—Albanian, Bulgarian, Hungarian, Romanian, Turkish; private collections of documents relating to materials presented at the peace conference at Versailles after the First World War when the Yugoslav state was being established (much of this material was produced in limited editions in French and English); materials on ethnic and boundary questions concerned with the Trieste dispute of the 1950s; literature on the Partisan movement in all its aspects and on the workers' movement in Yugoslavia prior to World War II as interpreted by contemporary Yugoslav historians.

The acquisition programs begun in the 1960s added provincial periodicals, scholarly series, statistical, and economic publications. These provincial publications are particularly important in Yugoslavia where the spirit of localism is strong.

Joel M. Halpern
University of Massachusetts at Amherst

Other Countries

Albania

The relatively small but qualitatively excellent Albanian collection reflects a language and culture which are at present outside the university's teaching program, except within the general framework of Balkan studies. Consequently, no concerted attempt has been made in the past to collect Albanian materials in depth. However, since 1962 there has been a slow but steady influx of books and periodicals from Tirana and from Priština, capital of the Yugoslav autonomous region of Kossovo-Metohija and the center of a substantial Albanian population. As of 1974, UCLA had holdings of close to 2,500 volumes in Albanian or relating directly to Albania. The latter publications are largely in French, German, and English. The national book and periodical bibliographies, and government publications such as the official *Anuari statistikor* are present, as are such earlier scholarly works as Franz Manek's *Albanesische Bibliographie* (Vienna, 1909) and Émile Legrand's *Bibliographie albanaise* (Paris, 1912).

UCLA is surprisingly strong in scholarly periodicals relating to Albanology, particularly in folklore, ethnology, and literature. Eight serial titles, primarily in these areas, are received from Tirana University and the National Library at Tirana. In addition, UCLA holds the *Studia albanica* (Tirana, 1964-   ), the *Studi albanese* (Rome, 1965-   ), *Albanische Forschungen* (Wiesbaden), *Gjurmime albanologjike* (v. 1-, 1962-   ), an important ethnological journal from Priština; and complete files of both the *Studime historike* and *Studime filologjike* (both 1964-   ), published at the University of Tirana.

In linguistics and literary history, UCLA holds an almost complete selection of the classic works in this field, including Maximilian Lambertz' *Lehrgang des Albanischen: Grammatik* (1959), his *Albanisch-deutsch Wörterbuch* (1954), Stuart Mann's *Historical Albanian-English Dictionary* (1948) and his *Albanian Literature* (1955), Nelo Drizare's *Albanian-English Dictionary* (1957) and his *Spoken and Written Albanian* (1947), and Dhimiter S. Shuteriqi's definitive work, *Historia e letërisë shiqipe* (Tirana, 1959-   ), of which two volumes have appeared to date. There is also a fairly wide selection of current works in the fields of description and travel, economic conditions, foreign relations (especially with Turkey and Greece), and both contemporary and Byzantine history. In addition, there are some older works on the 15th-century national hero Georgios Kastriōtēs, or Scanderbeg, including a rare 18th-century English tragedy on this theme by William Havard (1733).

The great folk epic by Gjergj Fishta, *Lahuta e Malcis,* is represented in Maximilian Lambertz' German translation, *Die Laute des Hochlandes* (1958), and is analyzed in Lambertz' critical work, *Gjergj Fishta und das albanische Heldenepos* (1949). Current literary and political works are being added to the collection, although there are only four titles by Communist Party leader Enver Hoxha, including *Vepra,* v. 4 (1970) and *Zwanzig Jahre des neuen sozialistischen Albaniens* (1964). Writers Giuseppe Schirò (1865-1927), Ismail Kadare, and Azem Shkreli (1938-   ) are represented by examples of their poetry and prose, as are a number of other contemporary poets and novelists, many of them from Priština.

Czechoslovakia

In support of the Slavic teaching and research program at UCLA, the Czech and Polish areas rank second only to Russian, with strong Czech holdings in 19th-century literature, contemporary linguistics, and folklore. Before 1963, Czech and Slovak holdings were minimal, but more recent acquisitions in the two languages have increased the collection to approximately 10,000 titles, with subject concentration well balanced between literature/linguistics and the social sciences. Prague and Brno tend to surpass Bratislava and Martin as sources of current acquisitions, but Slovak holdings are exceptionally good, as the result of a nearly 2,000-volume purchase made in 1966. Collection scope in both Czech and Slovak is broad, embracing bibliographies (both current and retrospective); lexicographic aids; history, literature, and philosophy from Hus and Comenius through Hašek, Nezval, and Čapek to the present; folklore; theoretical and applied linguistics; politics, economics, and official government publications.

Reference and bibliographic tools are well represented in the UCLA collection, with complete files of both *České knihy* and *Slovenské knihy,* as well as holdings from 1922 of their pre-1951 predecessor, the *Bibliografický katalog.* Periodicals are indexed in the *Články v českých časopisech* (1953-) and the earlier *České časopisy.* Notable in literary bibliography are L'udovít Rizner's *Bibliografia slovenského písomníctva,* 6 v. (1929-34), which lists publications up to 1900, and Josef Jungmann's *Historie literatury české* (1825). For historians, there is Čeněk Zíbrt's *Bibliografie české historie,* 5 v. (1900-12) covering the period from the beginnings to the 17th century. In bibliophilia, there are two unusual and complete journal sets: *Bibliofil* (1923-40) and *Český bibliofil* (1910-38).

Pertinent encyclopedic works include the essential *Československá vlastivěda,* 10 v. (1929-36), its Slovak counterpart *Slovenská vlastiveda,* 5 v. (1943-49), and the present unified work-in-progress, *Československá vlastivěda* (1963-   ), which embraces both cultures. The basic general encyclopedia, *Ottův slovník naučný,* 34 v. (1888-1940), is available, as is the more recent

Československá akademie věd (hereafter abbreviated as ČAV) publication, *Příruční slovník naučný,* 4 v. (1962-67). For Slovakia, UCLA has the *Slovenský náučný slovník* (3 v., 1932).

In lexicography, UCLA has excellent coverage. Important dictionaries include Jan Gebauer's *Slovník staročeský* (a 1970 reprint of the 1903 edition); the ČAV work which supplements it, *Staročeský slovník* (1968-   ); the definitive *Slovník jazyka staroslověnského* (1958-   ); the standard contemporary dictionary *Slovník spisovného jazyka českého* (1966-71); its Slovak counterpart, the *Slovník slovenského jazyka,* 6 v. (1959-68), and the comprehensive reference dictionary *Příruční slovník jazyka českého,* 9 v. (1935-55). In addition, there are eight bibliographies of Slovak publications by the contemporary scholar Jozef Kuzmik, and important bibliographies of incunabula in the scholarly libraries of Prague, Bratislava, Martin, and Olomouc.

Government publications, an important source of political and economic statistics, include the *Statistická ročenka ČSSR, Statistické přehledy, Statistický obzor,* and *Československá statistika.* An index to such publications is furnished by Jaroslav Podzimek's *Bibliografie československé statistiky a demografie, 1945-1968.*

In general periodicals and monographic serials, UCLA is especially well-endowed. In history, linguistics, and ethnology, there are many complete or nearly full runs of important journals, including the *Časopis pro moderní filologii* (1911-   ), *Listy filologické* (1874-1951), the *Historický archiv* of the ČAV (1893-1949), the *Český časopis historický* (1895-1949), and its successor, the *Československý časopis historický* (1953-   ). The collection also boasts a 1907-45 file of the *Zprávy* of the Economics Section of the ČAV. Another unusually complete journal set is the *Rozpravy* of Sections 1-3 of the ČAV, including articles on literature, history, linguistics, and philosophy, from 1891 to 1972. The *Časopis* of the Matice moravská in Brno, an important cultural-historical journal, is represented from 1869 to date. One of the more unusual holdings is a complete run of the literary journal *Lumír* (1873-1939). UCLA also has a full set of the historical-ethnological journal *Český lid* (1892 to date). Two additional journals of note are the *Archiv český,* 37 v. (1840-1941), of which UCLA has nearly complete holdings, and the *Spisy* of Brno University's Faculty of Philosophy (1923-), which now numbers over 165 monographic titles in literature, linguistics, and the social sciences. Aside from subscriptions, UCLA receives 122 titles in the humanities and social sciences alone from 31 Czech universities and scholarly institutes.

Holdings for Czech prose and poetry, from the beginnings to the contemporary period, are outstanding for a collection of this size. Particularly impressive are the Comeniana; writings by and about František Palacký; and the large selection of works by Karel Čapek, often in first editions. Special mention must be made of the unusually rich Comenius holdings. This collection, if books in the William Andrews Clark adjunct are included, numbers over 200 titles by or relating to the 17th-century educator, philologist, and philosopher. Among the most noteworthy are many contemporary editions of the *Janua linguarum reserata,* dating from 1649 to 1670, and of the *Orbis sensualium pictus* from 1659 into the 19th century, with translations of the latter work into most of the major European languages. In the 19th and 20th centuries, such notable authors as Kollár, Krofta, Mácha, Jan Neruda, Arne Novák, Hašek, Jirásek, Němcová, Nezval, and Vrchlický are represented in depth. Among Slovak writers there are considerable holdings of Bernolák, Botto, Šafárik, Štúr, Palárik, and Hurban Vajanský. Czech folklore holdings are very strong, and include variant editions of the works of Karel Erben, among them an 1862 edition of *Nápěvy prostonárodních písní českých.* Contemporary writing has excellent coverage, including an almost complete representation of the works of Holub, Hrabal, Kundera, and many others.

Augmenting the impressive Czech collection is the Geyer purchase of Slovak materials, acquired in 1966 and numbering close to 2,000 volumes. Among authors strongly represented are Jan Kollár and Ľudovít Štúr and his circle. In the postwar period, UCLA has representative works of Bodenek, Karvaš, Král, Mináč, and many others. Over 150 volumes deal with Slovak literary criticism and theory, and over 100 titles with Slovak history, ethnography, and topography. Archeology, folk art, and music account for over 200 titles, among them Béla Bartók's Slovak folk songs (Bratislava, 1959). In periodicals, the Geyer purchase includes a complete file of the *Časopis* of the Šafárik Scientific Society and 1912-35 holdings of *Prúdy; Revue mladého Slovenska.* In its entirety, this wide-ranging collection, covering almost every aspect of Slovak life and culture in the 19th and 20th centuries, is an outstanding research resource for Slovak studies.

East Germany

It is difficult to gauge the size of the East German collection in terms of volumes, for separate accession statistics have not been kept since the 1945 partition and the establishment of the German People's Republic in 1949. However, the German collection has traditionally been, along with the French and Spanish collections, the largest foreign-language bloc in the UCLA Research Library's holdings. Over the past 20 years, receipts from East Germany have not diminished, and they now number around 15,000 volumes. Exchange agreements with the Akademie der Wissenschaften in Berlin have been in force for many years, and the Library has extensive retrospective holdings of both their monographic and serial publications. Other current materials have been acquired largely on blanket order (Harrassowitz), with the Zentralantiquariat der DDR in Leipzig serving as a prime source of reprints and antiquarian imprints.

The collection is above average in statistical materials and government publications, and holds a good percentage of titles in this category as listed in Fritz Epstein's *East Germany; a Selected Bibliography* (Library of Congress, 1959). Among them are publications of the Staatliche Zentralverwaltung für Statistik, including the *Statistisches Jahrbuch der DDR* (UCLA has 1955-), the *Jahrbuch der DDR* (1956-), and the *Bevolkerungstatistisches Jahrbuch der DDR* (1967-). Legislative and legal publications are also adequately represented. Reference materials on the GDR are strong, among them *GDR: 300 Questions, 300 Answers* (Berlin, 1968) and *Current Documents from the GDR* (Berlin, 1962-). There are complete holdings of the Federal Republic of Germany publication on East Germany, *A bis Z* (formerly *SBZ von A bis Z,* 1953-), a valuable reference tool.

Publications relating to more literary areas are also well covered, including the leading East German encyclopedia, *Meyers neues Lexikon,* 8 v. (Leipzig, 1961-64) and the literary encyclopedia, *Lexikon sozialistischer deutscher Literatur* (Leipzig, 1964). Periodicals and monographs concerning bibliography, libraries, and the book trade are quite strong and include a number of publications of the Deutsche Staatsbibliothek (Berlin). There is a full run of *Der Bibliothekar,* the East German public library journal, from 1947 through 1972. Book-trade journals and the publications of the Deutsches Zentralarchiv are also represented. Considerable resources for the study of Sorbian (Wendish) are available, largely emanating from the Institut za Serbski Ludospyt in Bautzen.

East German politics and economics are well covered, both in German and in translation, and number about 500 titles. Among significant periodical publications are the major East German historical journal *Zeitschrift für Geschichtswissenschaft* (1953-) and the various publications of Berlin's Institut für Marxismus-Leninismus.

In the field of belles lettres the coverage is erratic—good in some areas, weak in others. The major journals, *Neue deutsche Literatur* and *Sinn und Form,* are present, and there are surprisingly good holdings of important postwar East German writers. Berthold Brecht is represented in depth, and Johannes R. Becher by his *Gesammelte Werke,* along with 31 works by and about him, including a 1959 tribute to him by Walter Ulbricht. Other writers with substantial representation include Stefan Heym, Stephan Hermlin, Franz Fühmann, Peter Huchel, Christa Wolf, Volker Braun, and Wolf Biermann. The student literature of protest is also here, in a 1968-70 collection of underground newspapers and pamphlets from Berlin University. Although there are some conspicuous gaps (e.g., Johannes Bobrowski, Peter Hacks, Günter Kuhnert), this is in general a strong, diversified collection with emphasis on linguistics and the contributions of major contemporary literary figures.

Greece

As with most of the non-Slavic Balkan areas, the UCLA modern Greek collection has been built, and quite recently, in response largely to teaching needs. While there is no bibliographer for classical, Byzantine, or contemporary Greek, pertinent materials have been steadily acquired through a blanket order for current books (with Lagoudakis in Athens), exchanges, and direct faculty requests. The present holdings of 19th- and 20th-century titles in the humanities and social sciences are estimated at about 6,000 volumes, with considerable strength in important contemporary authors and general reference works, as well as excellent resources in Byzantine literature and art history. The serials exchanges, most of them dating back to the early 1950s, include 15 titles from four institutions and deal chiefly with the current Greek economic and political situation and with historical and archeological studies.

The area of governmental and statistical publications is well covered, with approximately 100 titles ranging from the 1968 Constitution, the latest census, and the foreign trade yearbook to various official publications in agricultural statistics, public finance, and demography. The central statistical bureau (Ethnikē Statistikē Hyperēsia), aside from its economic and demographic output, has published a politico-geographical atlas of Greece (1965) and an industrial atlas, with figures based on the 1963 census. UCLA has both.

The range of current periodicals received is fairly wide, focusing on literature and history. Major titles of note include a complete run of the preeminent Greek literary journal *Nea Hestia* (1927 to date), *Balkan Studies* (1960 to date), *Byzantinisch-neugriechische Jahrbücher* (1920 to date), *Neos Hellenomnemon* (1904-27), *Parnassos* (1877-95, 1959-62), and *Charioteer* (1960 to date). In addition, the Library holds many specialized titles, such as the émigré journal *Demokratia, Kritika chronika,* and *Architectonikē*.

Reference holdings are adequate for all but the specialist researcher. The collection includes most of the major tools cited in Horecky's *Southeastern Europe; a Guide to Basic Publications* (Chicago, 1969). In bibliography, there are the *Bulletin analytique de bibliographie hellénique* (Horecky #950), which lists both monographs and periodicals, and the *Deltion hellēnikēs vivliographias* [*Bulletin of Greek Bibliography*, Horecky #951], a variant edition of the preceding title. The *Hellēnikē vivliographia* (1800-63) of Demetrios Ghinēs (1957) records Greek books published anywhere in the world during this period. Encyclopedias are represented by the definitive Greek work, the *Megalē Hellēnikē Enkylopaidea,* 24 v. (1926-34) and biographical works by the standard *Mega Hellēnikon biographikon lexikon* (1958-), which provides current data on approximately 2,700 Greek personalities. Dictionaries are adequately covered, with the nine-volume *Dēmētrakou mega lexikon tēs Hellēnikēs glōssēs* (1936-50), Julian Pring's *Oxford Dictionary of Modern Greek* (1968), and such standard compilations as those of Liddell and Scott, Charalampēs, and Divry (1969).

In modern literature, the UCLA collection is excellent, with almost complete holdings of the works of such major figures as Gēorgios Valetas, the 19th-century poet Dionysius Solomos, the great modern poets Constantin Cavafy and George Seferis, and the prose writers Stratēs Myrivēlēs and Nikos Kazantzakis. There is a very good representation of bibliographic, historical, and critical works in Greek and English devoted to these and other contemporary literary figures, including an impressive group of holdings of the literary historian Kōnstantinos Dēmaras. His works include four Greek and French editions of the classic *Historia tēs neoellēnikēs logotechnias* [History of Modern Greek Literature], as well as the *Neoëllenikē epistolografia* and a translation of Cavafy's poems into French.

The collection, as a whole, can be characterized as well-balanced, with good to excellent representation of the major literary figures in both the Byzantine period and the modern era, and possessing solid resources for linguistic, literary, and historical research.

Hungary

The UCLA Hungarian holdings are remarkably strong, reflecting the intrinsic scholarly value of a language and culture often slighted in academic programs. The collection covers a broad spectrum, includes approximately 5,000 volumes, and emphasizes literature and linguistics, with history, folklore, and cultural anthropology also well represented.

Serials holdings are broadly based and include such important government periodicals as the *Statistical Yearbook* issued by the Központi Statisztikai Hivatal (UCLA has 1949-), the *Statisztikai Szemle* (1923-), and the most recent national census (1970). Nearly 50 exchange partners (libraries, universities, museums, and institutes) contribute a sizable number of general and scholarly periodicals to the collection. The exchanges of greatest magnitude are with the Hungarian National Library (Országos Széchényi Könyvtár), which sends seven titles in literature and bibliography, the Magyar Nemzeti Múzeum in Budapest (11 titles), the Hungarian Academy of Sciences (Magyar Tudományos Akadémia) (39 titles), the University at Debrecen (25 titles), and the University at Szeged (10 titles). The subject matter varies, focusing largely, however, on literature and the social sciences, with more specialized topics (e.g., geography, music, art, ethnology, archeology) being received from other of the remaining 40-odd exchanges. Important newspapers such as *Szabad Nép* and many scholarly journals of broad interest (e.g., *Nyugat, Századok*) are available in the periodicals section of the Library.

The literature and linguistics component of the Hungarian collection numbers some 3,000 titles, of which approximately 300 are lexicographical and linguistic works. Basic sources such as the *Nova Grammatica Hungarica* of Albert Molnár (1574-1653) and the *Ungarische Grammatik* of József Tompa (1905-) are here, as are the three-volume Hungarian-Latin-German dictionary of Gábor Szarvas and the 1953 and all later editions of the Hungarian-English, English-Hungarian dictionaries of the contemporary lexicographer László Országh. The eclectic bilingual dictionary collection also includes recent compilations in Hungarian-Bulgarian, Hungarian-Czech, Hungarian-French, Hungarian-German, Hungarian-Romanian, Hungarian-Russian, Hungarian-Serbocroatian, and Hungarian-Swedish. As supplementary material, there is a substantial number of dialectological and phonological works.

One of the most striking features of the collection is the in-depth coverage of many 18th-20th century writers. There are sizable, and often complete, holdings for such major figures as the prose writer and translator Kelemen Míkes (1690-1762); the poet János Arany (1817-82); the "Hungarian Pushkin," Sándor Petőfi (1823-49); the dramatic poet Imre Madách (1823-64), whose epic poem *Az ember tragédiája* is present in 10 versions and translations; the novelist Mór Jókai (1825-1904); the novelist and short-story writer Kálmán Mikszáth (1847-1910); the poet Endre Ady (1877-1919); the novelist Zsigmond Móricz (1879-1942); the poet-translator Mihály Babits (1883-1941); the prolific fiction writer Frigyes Karinthy (1887-1938); the prose writer and dramatist Tibor Déry (1894-); the contemporary poet-translators Lőrinc Szabó (1910-57) and Attila József (1905-37); the novelist Lajos Zilahy (1891-); and the philosopher-critic György Lukács (1885-1971). Most of their works are represented both in Hungarian and in all available English translations and constitute a valuable research resource for Hungarian studies.

Poland

The Polish collection, now numbering close to 11,000 titles, is noteworthy on many levels but chiefly for its excellent coverage of modern literature and linguistics and for the extensive holdings of journals and monographic series from the great Polish universities and learned societies, among them the Polska Akademia Nauk in Warsaw, Kraków, and Gdańsk, and the universities of Warsaw, Poznán, Łódź, Toruń, Wrocław, Kraków, and Wilno. In building the collection, an endeavor has been made to assemble a representative cross section of contemporary Polish culture. As a reflection of the teaching program, emphasis has been placed on the humanities, particularly history, literature, linguistics, and folklore. The collection is in a process of constant development, with an annual increment of approximately 1,000 volumes from purchase and exchange sources.

The major Polish reference, lexicographic, and bibliographic research tools are all available at UCLA, including the national bibliography, *Przewodnik Bibliograficzny* (1928-) and the national periodical index, *Bibliografia Zawartości Czasopism* (1966 to date). In all, over 150 titles deal with Polish bibliography, catalogs of library collections, encyclopedic works, and dictionaries. Among the more significant are the *Polski Słownik Biograficzny* (1935-), now in its 17th volume; the *Wielka Encyclopedia Powszechna PWN* (1962-); the monumental *Bibliografia Literatury Polskiej "Nowy Korbut"* (1963-), which continues the earlier four-volume work of Gabrjel Korbut; Ludwik Finkel's definitive historical bibliography, *Bibliografia historyi polskiej* (covering the period from the beginnings to 1815), and its continuation to 1914; Wiktor Hahn's standard *Bibliografia bibliografij polskich* (1956); and v.1-33 of Karol Estreicher's *Bibliografia Polska,* compiled over a period of a century, and listing all Polish publications from 1455 to 1900. Incunabula in Polish libraries are described in *Inkunabuły w bibliotekach polskich* (1970), and there are several individual catalogs for such rich collections as those at the libraries of Wrocław and Kraków.

UCLA's holdings in Polish periodicals and scholarly journals are particularly strong. Receipts from exchange agreements alone now total 190 titles from 30 institutions, including the Polska Akademia Nauk and its branches and the university libraries of Warsaw, Poznań, Łódź, Lublin, and Gdańsk. Many of these exchanges have been operative since the 1930s and 1940s, ensuring nearly unbroken runs of major monographic serials. Among important general periodicals represented in the collection are the distinguished literary monthly *Twórczość;* the important emigre literary journal *Kultura* (published in Paris); and the scholarly quarterly *Pamiętnik Literacki,* which UCLA holds from 1952. Newspapers have somewhat limited coverage, and include the daily *Trybuna Ludu* (Warsaw), the weekly *Polityka* (Warsaw), and the fortnightly literary review *Współczesność.* Kraków is represented by the weekly *Tygodnik Powszechny.* There is a good sampling of government publications, with holdings of the official statistical yearbook, *Rocznik Statystyczny,* since 1950 and of the *Biuletyn Statystyczny* (1957-66, 1971-).

Polish historical sources in the collection date from the 15th century and include the works of the eminent historian and Archbishop óf Lwów, Jan Długosz (1415-80), whose *Historica polonica* is present in the original Latin and in a modern Polish translation. Later works of note include the 10-volume *Historya narodu polskiego* by the 18th-century historian Adam Naruszewicz and 25 titles by the contemporary historian Oskar Halecki. Other important titles held by UCLA are the great dictionary of Slavic antiquities from the earliest times to A.D. 1200, *Słownik Starożytności Słowiańskich* (1961-); *Polska Ludowa; Materiały i Studia* (1965-), and the comprehensive Polska Akademia Nauk publication *Historia Polski* (1958-), projected as the first Marxist synthesis of Polish history.

Also noteworthy in the UCLA Slavic collections are the extensive holdings in folklore and ethnomusicology, with Poland no exception. Oskar Kolberg, the celebrated 19th-century folklorist, is represented by 24 titles, including a 35-volume set of his monumental *Lud; jego zwyczaje, sposób życia, mowa . . .* (1857-1907), which surveys the customs, folk arts, and folk music of the various cultural and linguistic regions of Poland and the adjacent territories. These holdings complement UCLA's excellent collection of Kolberg's Czech contemporary Karel Erben.

Although the UCLA collection is perhaps strongest in 19th- and 20th-century literature, there are substantial secondary holdings in lexicography and linguistics. Among titles of considerable interest are the *Słownik jezyka polskiego* (1958-69), the major dictionary of contemporary Polish, now complete in 11 volumes; the excellent two-volume Kościuszko Foundation *English-Polish, Polish-English Dictionary* (The Hague, 1964); and such specialized tools as the *Słownik języka Jan Chryzostoma Paska,* 2 v. (1965-), a glossary of the language of the 17th-century memoirist; the *Słownik języka Adama Mickiewicza* (1962-), which performs the same service for the great 19th-century poet; the *Słownik polszczyzny XVI wieku* (1965-), a comprehensive dictionary of 16th-century Polish; the *Słownik staropolskich nazw osobowych* (1965-); the *Słownik staropolski* (1953-); and Sławski's definitive etymological dictionary, *Słownik etymologiczny języka polskiego* (1952-), now in its fourth volume. The collection is also rich in philological journals and includes the Polish contributions made to the literature and linguistic sessions of the Fourth, Fifth, and Sixth International Congresses of Slavists held in Moscow, Sofia, and Prague (1958, 1963, 1968).

Polish literary holdings, from the beginnings to the contemporary period, are distinguished both for quality and breadth of coverage. Almost no author of significance, from Kochanowski (1530-84) to Stachura (1934-), is unrepresented. Beginning with the works of Kochanowski, Mikołaj Rej, and Frycz Modrzewski in the 16th century, the collection has representative to complete holdings of such writers as the prolific 17th-century poet Wacław Potocki, along with his contemporary Jan Morsztyn. For the 18th-century period, writers strongly represented include the historian Naruszewicz (his letters and poems), Ignacy Krasicki, Julian Niemcewicz, the poet and adventurer Jan Potocki, the satirist Stanisław Potocki, Wojciech Bogusławski, and Stanisław Trembecki.

The 19th-century collection is widely inclusive, with excellent holdings for such major figures as the great Romantic poets Mickiewicz, Słowacki, and Krasiński. Słowacki is represented not only by the 24-volume *Dzieła* (1930-31), and the 14-volume edition of 1959, but also by many works of Słowacki criticism from Polish and English-language sources. Further strong holdings in this period include the works of the poet Cyprian Norwid, the novels of Henryk Sienkiewicz and of the prolific Ignacy Józef Kraszewski, the novels of Bolesław Prus, the plays of Stanisław Wyspiański, and the novels of Stefan Żeromski. Turn-of-the-century writers are represented by the philosopher-critic Stanisław Brzozowski, the poet Bolesław Leśmian, and the surrealist novelist-playwright Stanisław Ignacy Witkiewicz.

In the contemporary period, when philosophy, literature, and social protest are as often commingled as in the France of Camus and Sartre, there is an extremely wide sampling. The range varies from the concentration camp novels of Tadeusz Borowski (d. 1951) to the drama of the absurd of Sławomir Mrożek. Almost all of the published works of the following important contemporary poets, dramatists, and novelists can be found at UCLA: Jerzy Andrzejewski, Kazimierz Brandys, Andrzej Brycht, Witold Gombrowicz (in both Polish and English translations), the brilliant poet Zbigniew Herbert, the novelist Marek Hłasko, Jarosław Iwaszkiewicz, the philosopher Leszek Kołakowski, the critic and Shakespearian scholar Jan Kott, Maria Kuncewiczowa, the satirist Stanisław Lec, the poet-critics Artur Międzyrzecki and Czesław Miłosz, the dramatist Mrożek, the philosopher-critic Zdzisław Nadjer, the novelist and short-story writer Marek Nowakowski, Jerzy Pieterkiewicz, Teodor Parnicki, the poet Tadeusz Różewicz, the noted prose writer Adolf Rudnicki, and the poet Kazimierz Wierzyński. Important literary critics and historians of whom the library has strong holdings include Antoni Potocki (his *Polska litera-tura współczesna*, 1911-12), Wacław Lednicki, Manfred Kridl, Czesław Miłosz, and Juliusz Kleiner. In sum, the collection is a well-balanced one, particularly rich in belles lettres, and is being maintained at a consistently high level.

Rosemary Neiswender
University of California at Los Angeles

University of California at Santa Barbara

General Information

The Nikić Collection for the Study of Balkan Peoples is in the Library of the University of California at Santa Barbara, in a room on the fourth floor designated for special collections and purchases. The collection is accessible during the week from 8 a.m. to 11 p.m. and on holidays from 9 a.m. to 5 p.m. For information about specific items in the collection, the Slavic Librarian should be consulted. The collection was purchased during 1971-72, and general catalogs of the collection, including a listing of books by author, will be completed in 1973.

The Collection

The Balkan Collection was purchased from Dr. Fedor Nikić, a retired university professor now living in Belgrade, Yugoslavia. Before World War II Professor Nikić taught international law, constitutional law, and diplomatic history at the University of Belgrade and at the Law Faculty in Subotica. He is the author of several books and articles published in prewar Yugoslavia and was for a time Undersecretary of State in the Ministry of Education in Belgrade. His private library was created over several decades and is the work of a connoisseur who had in mind not only the fulfillment of the requirements of his own studies but also the formation of the nucleus of a library for a future Balkan Institute.

The Nikić Collection was created to foster general studies of Balkan peoples. It is estimated that the collection contains approximately 13,000-15,000 volumes dealing with the Balkan peoples and their history, politics, social development, economy, law, religion, education, and cultural development in general. The materials cover primarily the 19th and 20th centuries. The largest part of the collection is in the Serbo-Croatian language, followed by Bulgarian, Russian, German, French, and English. The largest part relates to the Yugoslav peoples and, to a lesser degree, to the Bulgarians, Greeks, Albanians, Romanians, and Turks.

For Yugoslavia, the section dealing with the Serbs is the most extensive. Its most valuable volumes are the 19th- and 20th-century periodicals, political pamphlets, books referring to the history of the Orthodox Church, almanacs, and festschifts, as well as writings by Serbian historians and statesmen.

Periodicals and journals constitute the heart of the collection. Among them are nearly complete series of *Letopis Matice srpske* (Novi Sad, 1826-1905); *Glasnik srpskog učenog društva* (Belgrade, 1847-92); *Otadžbina* (Belgrade, 1875-83, 1887-92); *Delo* (Belgrade, 1894-99, 1902-15); *Srpski književni glasnik* (Belgrade, 1901-14, 1920-41); *Prilozi za književnost, jezik, istoriju i folklor* (Belgrade, 1921-30, 1954-69); *Matica* (Novi Sad, 1866-70); *Glasnik istorijskog društva* (Novi Sad, 1928-40); *Javor* (Novi Sad, 1874-93); *Brankovo kolo* (Sremski Karlovci, 1895-1900, 1902-07, 1909-11); *Srpsko-Dalmatinski magazin* (1852-59, 1861-62, 1864-71); and *Arhiv za pravne i društvene nauke* (Belgrade, 1906-14, 1920-41). Journals published during the interwar period in Skoplje are also available, e.g., *Glasnik skopskog naučnog društva* (1925-39) and *Godišnjak Skopskog filozofskog fakulteta* (1930-40), as well as other journals published in Zemun, Novi Sad, and Belgrade (including publications of the Professor's Association, 1894-96).

The Serbian Academy of Sciences and Arts is represented through its *Godišnjak* (1921-41); the publications of the Serbian Scientific Society, which preceded the Academy, are also in the collection. Among the Academy's publications are a practically complete series of the *Naselja* (1902-60) of Professor Cvijić.

Pamphlets dealing with the political, constitutional, judicial, and cultural history of Serbia form the next most important part of the collection. Typical examples are the Protocols of the 1868 Topčider Skupština, which elected Prince Milan; pamphlets concerning the rule of Prince Michael; texts of the 1869 and 1901 Serbian Constitutions; electoral laws for the elections in 1870, 1889, 1890, and 1903; and various items concerning the political parties from the 1880s and their programs, political disputes, etc.

An extensive part of the collection relates to the history of the Serbian Church, especially its development in Vojvodina. Representative Church and religious journals are: *Pravoslavlje* (Belgrade, 1871-73); *Hrišćanski Vesnik* (Belgrade, 1879-90, 1892-95, 1901-05, 1910-14); *Srpski Sion* (1891-1906), published in Novi Sad and Karlovci; and the collection *Bogoslovski Glasnik* (Karlovci, 1902-14). A very important source for the history of the Church is the *Šematizam* for the dioceses in Dalmatia and Istria, Boka, Dubrovnik, and Spič, as well as for Dabro-Bosnia, Zahum-Hercegovina, and Banja Luka-Bihać (incomplete). Other books refer to the development of monasteries in Serbia, Macedonia, and Vojvodina. There are also religious textbooks such as *Srednji katihizis pravoslavna narodna učilišta* (Vienna, 1876), service books, and Church Canons.

The almanacs or calendars are a special part of the collection, which includes, among others, *Orao* (Novi Sad, 1885, 1890-94, 1896), *Srbobran* (Zagreb, 1893-1914), and *Pančevac* (1874). Among the festschifts are those dedicated to various Serbian scholars and politicians (Bogdan Popović, Sima Lozanić, Jovan Sundečić, Vasilj Grdjić, Danilo Ilić, Petar Kočić, and others) and those of various political or cultural institutions and associations (Soko, Njegoš). The history of Serbian education may be traced in a variety of school textbooks, for example, the lectures which A. Mallet delivered to the young King Alexander Obrenović, *Histoire diplomatique de l'Europe . . .* , (Paris, 1893); various European and Serbian histories (M. Zečević, 1880; A. Majkov, 1876; V. Karić, 1887); and the translation of B. Kallay's *Istorija srpskog naroda* (Belgrade, 1882). Some books deal with the history of Serbian cities (Šabac, Jagodina, Topola, Kruševac, Smederevo, Niš, et al.), with the Eastern question (M. Jankovich and J. Grouitch, *Slaves du sud ou le peuple Serbe avec les Croates et les Bulgares,* Paris, 1853); and with Serbian activities in Macedonia at the turn of the century. Of special interest are books referring to the role of women, such as the journal *Žena* (Novi Sad, 1911-13, 1918, 1919), and the almanac *Srpkinja* (Sarajevo, 1913). A large part of the collection comprises works by such prominent Serbian scholars and politicians as Dositej Obradović, Milan Milićević, Stojan Novanković, Jaša Tomić, Polit Desančić, Tihomir Djordjević, Jovan Ristić, Vladimir Ćorović, and Stanoje Stanojević. The following Serbian socialists are also represented: Svetozar Marković, Vasa Pelagić, Dragiša Lapčević, Dušan Popović, Dimitrije Tucović, Sima Marković, and Filip Filipović.

Among the materials which emphasize Croatia are the publications of the Yugoslav Academy of Sciences and Arts in Zagreb, including *Rad* (1868-1948) and *Starine,* as well as some of the *Stari hrvatski pisci.* Other Croatian periodicals are *Hrvatsko kolo* (1905-11, 1927-43), *Hrvatska revija* (incomplete, 1928-45) and *Hrvatska straža* (1903-04), and *Nastavni vjesnik* (incomplete). Other works deal with Croatian social, political, and cultural development. Geography is covered in *Zemljopis zemalja u kojima obitavaju Hrvati,* 2 v. (Zagreb, 1880-81), the history of the military border in Vanichek's *Specialgeschichte der Militärgrenze* (Vienna, 1875), the Urbanian laws in Croatia in Deželić: *Urbar Hrvatsko-Slavonski* (Zagreb, 1882), the Catholic Church in Croatia in D. F. Belaj's *Katoličko crkveno pravo* (Zagreb, 1901), and festschifts of associations and gymnasiums. Other volumes in the collection cover the political history of Croatia, relations with Vienna and Budapest, and Croatian political activity designed to achieve the recognition of national rights, for example, B. Šulek, *Hrvatski ustav i konstitucija 1882* (Zagreb, 1883) or *Narodna Misao* (Zagreb, 1897), as well as the pamphlet *Zur Sanierung der Verletzungen Croatisch-Ungarischen Ausgleiches* (Vienna, 1886) and F. Folnegović's pamphlet *Otvorite oči!* (Zagreb, 1896). General Croatian histories can also be found in the collection, including those by S. Balenović (1870), and O. Knežević. Other books deal with the history of Croatian cities (Karlovac, Klis, Zagreb, Split, etc.). Of importance for Croatian political and cultural history are the writings of such eminent Croatians as Antun Radić, Gjuro Szabo, Tade Smičiklas, Rudolf Horvat, J. Bösendorfer, Frano Supilo, and others. A special part of the collection contains books related to the development of Dalmatia and Dubrovnik.

The Montenegrin part of the collection contains such important histories of Montenegro as *Istoria o Černoj Gori*, written by the Bishop Vasilije Petrović and published in Moscow in 1754 (photocopy), Dj. Popović's *Istorija Crne Gore*, published in Belgrade in 1896, and M. Dragović's *Crnogorski mitropolit Vasilije Petrović Njegoš ili Istorija Crne Gore od 1750 do 1766 godine*, (Cetinje, 1884). Other valuable books in the Montenegrin segment are the biographies of Bishops V. M. G. Medaković, *Vladika Danil Petrović Njegoš* (Belgrade, 1896), and L. Popović, *Černogorjskih vladika Petar I*, (Kiev, 1897). Other works cover the Montenegrin wars with the Ottomans and Montenegrin development in the 19th century.

The highlights of the collection concerning Bosnia and Hercegovina are the stenographic records of the 1910-11 Bosnian Diet and pamphlets covering the Serbo-Croatian disputes over Bosnia, as well as the pamphlets published during the 1908 annexation crisis (by J. Cvijić, St. Stanojević, D. Vasiljević, G. Geršić, Z. Perić, et al.). Also of importance are the festschifts referring to the 1875 Bosnian uprising and the Eastern crisis, including studies, memoirs, and pamphlets. A part of the collection deals with the Austro-Hungarian rule over Bosnia, legislation, the ''Mlada Bosna'' movement, and the 1914 Sarajevo assassination. A few works are available on the Orthodox Church in Bosnia. General Bosnian histories include those of M. Prelog, V. Ćorović, St. Stanojević, Lj. Jovanović, and Vl. Skarić.

The Macedonian literature consists of pamphlets claiming Serbian rights over Macedonia (Sp. Gopčević, V. Marković, G. Jakšić, G. Petković, M. Dj. Milojević, V. Djerić, P. Cemović, Dj. Jelinić, St. Protić, and K. Stojanović). A smaller segment contains studies in post-World War II Macedonian historiography.

The Slovenian part of the collection is not extensive. There are some general Slovenian histories which are of interest, such as I. Gruden, *Zgodovina slovenskoga naroda* (Ljubljana, 1912); I. Mal, *Zgodovina slovenskega naroda* (Ljubljana, 1928, 1939); V. Bučar, *Politička istorija Slovenačke* (Belgrade, 1939); M. Krek, *Les Slovènes* (Paris, 1917); and Gestrin-Malik, *Slovenska zgodovina* (Ljubljana, 1950).

One part of the collection refers primarily to Yugoslavia after 1918 and covers the 1915-18 Yugoslav Committee in London, the development of the Yugoslav movement, the 1918 unification of the Yugoslavs, and postwar Yugoslav judicial, social, political, and economic development. Highlights include the pamphlets published by the Montenegrin Committee during World War I, as well as materials presented by the Yugoslav delegation at the Paris Peace Conference in 1919. Other books deal with Yugoslav finances, the cooperative and agrarian movement, sociology, and law.

The larger Balkan area is represented by books and studies of specific Balkan countries and works on Balkan ties with Europe and the Eastern question, e.g., J. Ilić, *Pokretači Istočnog Pitanja i Panslavizam* (Belgrade, 1898), A. De Saint Clair, *Le Danube* (Paris, 1899), and L. Sentupery, *L'Europe politique - la Russie, la Serbie, la Turquie* (Paris, 1895).

Among the rare Bulgarian items in the collection are Milan Savić's *Istorija bugarskog naroda do propasti države mu* (Novi Sad, 1878), as well as *Organicheskyi ustav na Istochna Rumeliia* (Plovdiv, 1879), Simeon Radev's *Stroitelite na sŭvremenna Bŭlgaria,* 2 v. (Sofia, 1911), Charles Serkis, *La Roumelie Orientale et la Bulgarie actuelle* (Paris, 1898), and Jurdan Jurdanov, *Istoriia na bŭlgarskata tŭrgoviia do osvoboždenieto* (Sofia, 1938). Works of Aleksandar Girginov, I. Sakazov, A. Hajek, B. M. Andreev, A. Benderev, A. G. Drandar, and L. Lamouche are also included.

The Greek part of the collection contains some early publications dealing with Greek politics, such as C. N. Levidis' book *Quelques mots sur la Grèce et 1e ex roi Othon* (Brussels, 1863), Ch. Tricoupi's pamphlet *Discours* (Belgrade, 1891), A. Softazade's study *La Crète sous la domination et la suzeraineté ottomanne* (Paris, 1902), and E. About's *La Grèce contemporaine* (Paris, 1883), as well as I. Psihari's *Autour de la Grèce* (Paris, 1897).

The Albanian segment is represented by P. Chiara's *L'Albania,* published in Palermo in 1869, and various pamphlets on Albania published in Belgrade, e.g., D. K. Jovanović, *O Arbanasima, istorijska studija* (Belgrade, 1880).

The Romanian part contains P. Battaillard's *Les Principautés de la Moldavie et de Valachie devant le Congès* (Paris, 1856), *La vérité sur la question des couvents dédiés en Moldo-Valachie* (Paris, 1863), and I. T. Ghica, *Les droits de péage aux Portes de Fers* (Paris, 1899). For the study of the Romanians in Transylvania, the pamphlet *Die Rumänische Frage in Siebenbürgen und Ungarn* (Vienna-Budapest, 1892) is of interest. T. Jonescu's *La politique étrangère de la Roumanie* (Bucarest, 1891) is also available, as is *Istorija Rumuna,* a 1934 translation of N. Iorga's work.

Dimitrije Djordjevic
University of California at Santa Barbara

University of Chicago

The University of Chicago developed a strong and wide-ranging program of studies on Balkan and Eastern Europe only in the early sixties. Although some fields, such as Slavic linguistics, Albanian, Modern Greek philology and literature, and Germanic studies have been in the realm of the University's interest for many years, the Library tended to collect only the basic publications dealing with Eastern Europe, especially works written in English, French, or German.

The intensive acquisition of materials in the languages of Eastern Europe started late in 1960, when Dr. Josef Anderle became the Social Sciences Bibliographer with additional responsibility for the Slavic area. In 1962 the Library established the position of Slavic Bibliographer and greatly expanded the allocation of funds for the Russian and East Europe acquisitions.

As of summer 1972, close to 90,000 volumes of the East European collection were housed in the University Library system. Most of these books are in the new Joseph Regenstein Library [JRL], but large blocs are to be found in the Law and Art Libraries. The stacks are open to the University's faculty, students, and staff. Access to the Library for persons not connected with the university is strictly controlled and it is advisable to contact the Library administration for details. The usual Library hours are: Monday-Thursday, 8:30 a.m.-1 a.m.; Friday, 8:30 a.m.-10 p.m.; Saturday, 9 a.m.-10 p.m.; Sunday, 12 noon-1 a.m.

The East European reference staff consists of the Bibliographer for Slavic and Balkan Studies and the Assistant Slavic Librarian, both in the Joseph Regenstein Library. East European books and serials are cataloged according to the Library of Congress classification system and are shelved by subject throughout the University Library.

The University Library system operates with a single dictionary card catalog, where the cards, regardless of language, are filed by author, title, and subject. This Public Catalog is on the first floor of Regenstein Library. The Law Library materials are listed in the Regenstein Public Catalog only by the main entry card.

A specialized Soviet and East European reference collection, comprising over 3,000 volumes, is located on the second floor of Regenstein Library.

The loan regulations are very liberal, but persons not connected with the University are restricted to building use of materials. Each floor of the Regenstein Library is equipped with one or more Xerox machines for public use. The Library's Photoduplication Department is located on floor B.

Since 1962, the average annual intake of materials dealing with the East European area has been close to 6,000 volumes. Recent pressures on the Library's book budgets have been offset by the many benefits which the University of Chicago has drawn from participation in the PL-480 Yugoslav and Polish programs.

The University's East European collection has strengths and weaknesses. The collections which would rank as both good and adequate for the University's needs are: Albania, Bulgaria, Czechoslovakia, East Germany, Greece, Hungary, and Yugoslavia. The Polish collection has many strong points, but the lack of 19th- and early 20th-century general and subject-oriented periodicals makes it uneven. The Romanian collection is clearly weak, especially for the interwar period. There are almost no retrospective newspaper files for any of the countries of the area. The present holdings are:

General Balkan and East European	4,340 volumes
Albania	530
Bulgaria	5,440
Czechoslovakia	22,400
East Germany	data not available
Greece	4,100
Hungary	5,320
Poland	17,160
Romania	2,720
Yugoslavia	13,600

Albania

This collection is by far the smallest. It has been developed to supplement the Newberry collection of the late Prince Louis-Lucien Bonaparte.

The prevailing part is made up of monographs in the following subjects: language, history, folklore, ethnography, and literature. The holdings are strong in grammars and dictionaries: F. Blanchus' *Dictionarium latino epiroticum* (1635); G. Meyer's *Etymologisches Wörterbuch der albanesischen Sprache* (1891); H. Pedersen's *Albanesische Texte mit Glossar* (1895).

The history section contains editions such as: *Fonti per la storia d'Albania; Acta et diplomata res Albaniae mediae aetatis illustrantia;* and *Acta Albaniae Veneta saeculorum XIV et XV* (1967-).

The serial holdings include: *Albania* (1897-1909); *Arhiv za arbanasku starinu* (1923-26); *Diturija* (1926-29); *Revista d'Albaniae* (1940-43); Tirana, Universitetit Shtetëror. *Buletin* (1948-63); *Nëndori* (1954-); *Shêjzat* (1957-); *Ylli* (1960-); *Gjurmime albanologjike* (1962-); *Etnografia Shqiptare* (1962-); *Jehona* (1963-); *Studia Albanica* (1964-); *Studime historike* (1964-); *Studime filologjike* (1964-).

The Law Library has the recent and contemporary legal materials, such as *Kodifikimi i përgjithëshëm i legjislacionit në fuqi të RPSh* (1945-57, 1958-). Albanian Communist Party publications are collected.

With regard to Albanian literature the Library, since 1962, has been collecting novels and poetry published in both Tirana and Priština.

Bulgaria

The University of Chicago Bulgarian collection covers language, literature, folklore, ethnography, history, geography, political science, and bibliography. To be noted are official publications, including sets such as: Bulgaria. *Dŭrzhaven vestnik* (1870-); Bulgaria. Narodno sŭbranie. *Stenografski dnevnitsi* (1879-); *Statisticheski godishnik* (1909-42, 1943/46-).

Bulgarian academic publications include: Bŭlgarskoto knizhevno druzhestvo. *Periodichesko spisanie* (1882-1910); *Lietopis* (1899-1910); Bŭlgarska akademiia na naukite. *Spisanie* (1911-50); *Lietopis* (1911-40); *Sbornik* (1913-49); Sofia. Universitet. *Godishnik* (1904-).

The larger collections in history, literature, and ethnography are: *Sbornik za narodni umotvoreniia i narodopis* (1889-); *Bŭlgarska istoricheska biblioteka* (1928-33); Bŭlgarsko istorichesko druzhestvo. *Izvestiia* (1905-); *Rodina* (1938-40); *Istoricheski pregled* (1945-); *Izvori za bŭlgarskata istoriia* (1954-); *Balkanski pregled* (1946-49); *Bŭlgarska misŭl* (1926-43); *Zlatorog* (1920-43); *Bŭlgarska rech* (1926-43).

The Bulgarian literature section consists of some 2,500 volumes. It contains two, possibly unique collections: 63 titles of Bulgarian anthologies and literary almanacs and 1,368 titles of Chitov's collection of Bulgarian poetry published between 1845-1945. This collection has been hand-bound and is treated as follows: 890 titles were cataloged as the *Collection of Bulgarian Poetry, 1845-1945,* in 121 volumes. The remaining titles of Chitov's collection were cataloged as monographs. The entire collection has a typewritten catalog list in Cyrillic.

Czechoslovakia

The University's major interests in Czechoslovak studies cover the following subjects: language, literature, folklore, ethnography, history, economics, geography, sociology, political sciences, and bibliography. The Library also has major Czechoslovak publications in art, law, and music.

The language section contains the old grammars and lexicons such as: J. Konstanc, *Lima linguae Bohemicae* (1667), V. Rosa, *Grammatica linguae Bohemicae* (1672), V. Jandyt, *Grammatica linguae Boëmicae* (1715); Grammars of J. W. Pohl, F. M. Pelcl, J. Dobrovský, J. Nejedlý, V. Hanka; dictionaries of K. I. Thám, J. Jungmann, and A. Bernolák's *Slowár slowenskí,* 6 v. (1825-27).

The Czech and Slovak literature section consists of some 6,000 entries and contains works of all major writers, annotated and variorum editions, literary periodicals, and critical studies. The holdings extend even to lesser known writers, such as J. Deml who is represented by 53 titles.

The history collection contains over 5,000 volumes and compares well with the recently published detailed surveys by Josef Anderle (in P. L. Horecky [ed.] *East Central Europe: A Guide to Basic Publications,* Chicago, 1969) and in the *Austrian History Yearbook* (1970-71). T. G. Masaryk is represented by 154 entries and E. Beneš by 100 entries. The Library has a large collection of Hussitica and Comeniana. The local histories of Czechoslovakia cover many Czech, Moravian, and Slovak cities.

The official publications are represented by collections of laws, stenographic transcripts of parliamentary debates, and statistical publications.

The holdings of institutional publications extend to academies, universities, pedagogical institutes, museums, archives, and local historical societies.

The periodical collection is extensive and contains such little-known titles as: *Hlasatel český* (1806-19); *Krok* (1821-27); *Archa* (1912-40); and *Fronta* (1927/8-39). The retrospective holdings of Czech and Slovak newspapers are inadequate. The Library has only: *Prager Tagblatt* (1915-45); *Lidová demokracie* (1945-64, 1968-), and *Literární noviny* (1952-68). The following three newspapers are currently received: *Rudé právo, Pravda,* and *Lidová demokracie.*

The Special Collections of the University of Chicago Library contain some 50 Czech rare books including works of Daniel Adam z Veleslavína, Comenius, Balbín, T. Pešina z Čechorodu, and the first edition of Bible Kralická, the famous ''Šestidílka.'' Located here are two interesting collections: The Bezruč collection, covering the years 1899-1961, and consisting of 280 pieces. It contains all editions of Bezruč's poetry and their translations published in Czechoslovakia and elsewhere. All pieces are autographed and some contain the author's corrections and notes. Included, also, are a few of Bezruč's letters.

The second collection, The Czech and Slovak Emigration Archives, consists of more than 6,000 pieces which are not included in the total count of volumes. The foundation of these archives was laid by the gift of Dr. Zdeněk Hruban, who donated his collection of books and other printed and source material produced by Czech and Slovak communities in the United States since 1848. The Czech and Slovak Emigration Archives now include personal papers, manuscript material and publications of Czech and Slovak groups from the entire Western world. The collection has a provisory card index.

East Germany

Due to the classification used for the publications originating in the German Democratic Republic, it is impossible to provide an approximate count of volumes. The University of Chicago holdings of East German publications are considered strong both in humanities and social sciences. The University's Germanic Department as well as subject scholars in history, political science, law, economics, geography, music, and art have had continuing interests in this area for many years. Particularly noticeable are the holdings of serial publications of East German academies and universities.

Greece

In general, the Modern Greek collection is good in language, especially dialects, folklore, history, and literature. Again, as with the Albanian collection, The University of Chicago Library consciously relies on the Newberry holdings of the Bonaparte Collection which has all the major early grammars and lexicons.

The classical and Byzantine periods of Greece are covered more evenly and to a greater depth than the modern period. Perhaps the following example will illustrate this point. The Library catalog shows 33 entries for Adamantios Koraēs, the great scholar of modern Greece; 19 entries represent his editions of Greek and Latin classics. Though the Library has his *Atakta,* 5 v. (1825-35) it lacks many important works published during his lifetime. Occasionally the Greek holdings will reveal a rare title such as the English version of the 1844 *Constitution* (Athens, 1844).

It should be pointed out that after 1964 the Library made a great effort to fill the gaps, especially in holdings of Modern Greek periodicals. Since 1970 the Library has been participating in the Modern Greek Studies Association Cooperative Library Project which provides an adequate selection of current publications.

Hungary

Although the University of Chicago does not have any specific program in Hungarian studies, at present, there always was enough interest within the Humanities and Social Sciences Divisions to allow for the development of a basic core Hungarian collection which now consists of some 5,320 volumes. The collection includes bibliographies, encyclopedias, official statistical publications, and monographic and serial publications of the universities and the Academy.

The language section contains old grammars such as A. Gubernáth's *Institutionum linguae et litteraturae Hungaricae,* 2 v. (1802-03), and S. Gyarmathi's *Affinitas linguae Hungaricae cum linguis Fennicae originis* (1799); the dictionaries of D. Márkus, *Magyar jogi lexikon,* 6 v. (1898-1907), and Z. Gombocz, *Magyar etymológiai szótár* (1914-44). Among the larger sets in linguistics the Library has: *Nyelvtudományi Közlemények* (1862-); *Magyar Nyelvőr* (1872-); *Magyar Nyelv* (1905-); *Magyar Népnyelv* (1939-49); *Magyar Nyelvjárások* (1951-).

The history collection with more than 2,000 volumes contains, among others, some large sets such as S. Katona, *Historia critica regum Hungariae,* 42 v. (1779-1817); a complete run of *Monumenta Hungariae historica* (1857-); *Történelmi Tár* (1855-1934); *Századok* (1867-); *Archivum Rákóczianum,* 12 v. (1873-1935); *Ungarische Jahrbücher* (1921-43); *The Hungarian Quarterly* (1936-42).

The Library has an extensive collection of Béla Bartók's works, as well as the recent publications in musicology.

The Law Library has the basic collection of Hungarian laws: Hungary. Laws, statutes, etc. *Corpus juris Hungarici* (1899-1949). Among the Hungarian rare books the Library has: Hungary. Laws, statutes, etc. *Corpus juris Hungarici, seu Decretum generale,* 3 v. (1696) and *Rubricae sive Synopses titulorum,* 3 v. (1734).

Hungarian geographical monographs and serials are well represented.

Poland

The Library's Polish collection covers the following subjects: bibliography, language, literature, folklore, history, geography, political science, economics, sociology, and anthropology. The greater part of the collection was acquired during the past decade and this fact, together with a general scarcity of Polish pre-World War II books, explains a certain unevenness in coverage and some substantial gaps, as in the holdings of Polish periodicals and newspapers.

The 16th- and 17th-century Polish works, especially those written in Latin, are represented by such titles as Marcin Kromer's *Polonia, sive de situ, populis, moribus . . .* (1577); Jan Herburt's *Chronica* (1588) and *Statuta Regni Poloniae* (1756); Stanisław Cardinal Hozjusz, *Opera* (Paris, 1562) and *Opera omnia,* edited by M. Dziergowski, 2 v. (1584); N. Copernicus, *De revolutionibus* (1543, 1566), *Astronomia instaurata* (1617); S. Starowski's *Polonia* (1656); M. K. Sarbiewski's *Lyricorum libri IV* (1634, 1684).

The section on Polish language comprises many 19th century grammars and dictionaries such as S. Müller's *Słownik polsko-rossyyski,* 2 v. (1829-30); Ch. C. Mrongowius' *Dokładny słownik polsko-niemiecki* (1835); S. B. Linde's *Słownik języka polskiego,* 6 v. (1851-60). The larger sets in the field of Polish linguistics include: *Język polski* (1913-); *Poradnik językowy* (1901-); *Slavia occidentalis* (1921-); *Studia z filologii polskiej i słowiańskiej* (1955-). Among the works on dialectology, the Library has J. Karłowicz's *Słownik gwar polskich,* 6 v. (1900-11) and F. Lorentz's works on Slovincian.

The collection on Polish history, which consists of some 3,000 volumes, offers a solid representation of the writings of Naruszewicz's historical school. The Library has his *Historya narodu polskiego* (10 v.) and the major works of his successors: J. Lelewel, W. Kalinka, Ks. Liske, A. Małecki, L. Finkel, St. Wojciechowski, St. Smolka, M. Bobrzyński, O. Balzer, who is represented by 15 titles, and others. Among the larger sets the Library's holdings include: *Pomniki dziejowe Polski* (1864-93, 1946-); an incomplete run of *Kwartalnik Historyczny* (1887-); *Akta Grodzkie i Ziemskie* (1873-1931); *Acta historica res gesta Poloniae illustrantia,* 13 v. (1878-1910); *Monumenta medii aevi historica* (1824-1927); *Biblioteka Krakowska* (1897-); *Rocznik Krakowski* (1898-); *Sobótka* (1946-); *Słownik geograficzny Królestwa Polskiego,* 16 v. (1880-1914).

The Polish literature collection consists of more than 7,000 volumes. All the major writers are represented by collected works, annotated and variorum editions, and critical studies. Literary periodicals such as *Ruch Literacki* (1960-), *Prace Polonistyczne* (1937-), *Archiwum Literackie* (1956-), *Rocznik Literacki* (1932-35, 1955-) are complete, but *Pamiętnik Literacki* (1902-) and *Twórczość* (1945-) are still incomplete.

The holdings of institutional publications extend to academies, universities, and local scientific societies, though they mostly cover only the post-World War II period.

With regard to official publications, the Library has the basic collection of laws *Volumina legum* (1733-1952, 1952-); Poland. Laws, statutes, etc. *Dziennik praw Królewstwa Polskiego,* 71 v. (1815-61); statistical publications, such as *Statystyka Polski* (1919-39) and Poland. Główny urząd statystyczny. *Rocznik statystyki* (1920/21-30) and *Rocznik statystyczny* (1930-).

The Library has an extensive collection of the works of Chopin. The works on Polish popular and folk music, as well as the works of Polish composers, are well represented.

Romania

This is the least developed collection of the East European area, showing pockets of strength but also omissions and gaps. Before 1960 the Library had virtually no holdings of publications in Romanian, and the few titles pertaining to Romania were concentrated in language and history.

The history section contains a few sets which should be pointed out: E. de Hurmuzachi *Documente privitóre la istoria Românilor;* G. Petrescu *Acte și documente relative la istoria renascerei României,* 11 v.; *Dacia* (1924-40, 1957-); *Revista istorică română* (1931-34); *Documente privind istoria României* (1951-); *Acta historica* (1959-); *Bibliotheca historica Romaniae* (1963-).

The publications of the Romanian academy and universities in the Library date only from the mid-sixties.

Yugoslavia

The Library's materials covering Yugoslavia were assembled during the sixties. Although the history of the Yugoslav collection at the University of Chicago is short indeed, it is better balanced than the Polish collection, especially in holdings of retrospective periodicals and serials.

The section on the three major languages of Yugoslavia, Serbo-Croatian, Slovenian, and Macedonian, is strong and has its required depth. The Library has all important 19th-century grammars and lexicons, such as J. Stulic's *Lexicon latino-italico-illyricum,* 2 v. (1801); his *Rjecsoslòxje,* 2 v. (1806); J. Voltic's *Ricsoslovnik* (1803); J. Kopitar's *Grammatik der slavischen Sprache in Krain . . .* (1808); U. Jarnik's *Versuch eines etymologikons des Slowenischen Mundart* (1832); V. S. Karadžić's *Srpski rječnik* (1852); works of Đ. Daničić, I. A. Berlich, and F. G. Metelko. The linguistic periodicals include: *Južnoslovenski filolog* (1913-); *Naš jezik* (1932-37, 1950-); *Jezik* (1952-); *Srpski dijalektološki zbornik* (1905-); *Slavistična revija* (1948-); *Časopis za slovenski jezik, književnost in zgodovino* (1918-31); *Slovenski jezik* (1938-41); *Jezik in slovstvo* (1955/56-); *Makedonski jazik* (1950-).

The Yugoslav literatures section, about 4,800 volumes strong, contains works of all major writers, annotated and variorum editions, critical studies, literary periodicals, and collections such as *Stari pisci hrvatski, Pet stoljeća hrvatske književnosti, Srpska književnost u sto knjiga,* and *Zbrana dela slovenskih pesnikov in pisateljev.* Among the major literary periodicals the Library has a complete run of *Ljubljanski zvon* (1881-1941); *Dom in svet* (1888-1944); *Srpski književni glasnik* (1891-1941); *Građa za povijest književnosti hrvatske* (1897-); *Hrvatsko kolo* (1905-43); *Savremenik* (1906-40); *Hrvatska revija* (1928-45).

Yugoslav poetry published since 1966 is collected comprehensively and treated by the Library as a special collection.

The collection on folklore and ethnography is well represented and includes major serials such as *Srpski etnografski zbornik* (1894-); *Zbornik za narodni život i običaje južnih Slavena* (1896-); *Prilozi za književnost, jezik, istoriju i folklor* (1921-).

The history collection, consisting of some 3,400 volumes, includes sets such as *Monumenta spectantia historian Slavorum meridionalium* (1868-), 49 v. published so far; *Codex diplomaticus regni Dalmatiae, Croatiae et Slavoniae,* 15 v. (1874-1934); *Monumenta historica liberae regiae civitatis Zagrebiae,* 19 v. (1889-1952); *Zbornik za istoriju, jezik i književnost srpskog naroda,* all three series (1902-); *Narodna starina* (1922-39); *Kronika slovenskih mest* (1934-40).

The Library holdings of Yugoslav institutional materials are extensive and include *Ljetopis* and *Rad* of the JAZU; *Letopis* (1934-) of the Slovenska akademija znanosti in umetnosti; *Letopis* (only 1865-) of the Matica srpska, Novi Sad; and publications of the universities in Ljubljana, Belgrade, and Novi Sad.

The University of Chicago Library's participation in the PL 480 Yugoslav program provided comprehensive coverage of current publications from 1967 to 1973.

Václav Laška
University of Chicago

University of Cincinnati

Greece

Introduction

The Modern Greek collection at the University of Cincinnati owes both its existence and its excellence to the late Carl W. Blegen, for many years Professor of Classical Archeology at the University. In 1930 he proposed to William T. Semple, Chairman of the Classics Department, the acquisition of works by Greek scholars in the fields of ancient Greek literature, history, and archeology. Professor Semple approved the idea, and from 1930 to 1961 he and Mrs. Semple provided generous funds for the purchase of Modern Greek books. Since 1961 the Classics Fund endowed by Mrs. Semple provides for the collection.

From the first purchases made in 1930-31 until his death in 1971, Blegen continued to buy Greek books, chiefly in Athens but also in Istanbul, London, Paris, and New York.

Soon after the initial purchases, the project expanded, first into related fields, such as linguistics, Byzantine and Modern Greek history, geography and topography, and then into all aspects of Modern Greece.

By 1940 the collection had grown to some 3,500 volumes. Almost no books were bought during 1940-46. Then over the next seven years the collection doubled in size. About 7,000 volumes are listed in the alphabetical catalog, edited by Niove Kyparissiotis, *The Modern Greek Collection in the Library of The University of Cincinnati. A Catalogue* (Athens, 1960), representing monographic holdings to 1952 and periodicals as of January 1954. When the Farmington Plan was inaugurated (1948), the University of Cincinnati assumed responsibility for buying scholarly books currently published in Greece on all subjects except law, medicine, and agriculture. (These exclusions have not been followed closely in the case of law and agriculture.) In 1974 the collection numbered around 20,000 volumes, a valuable asset and stimulus to Neohellenic studies in the United States.

Current purchases are being made at the rate of several hundred volumes a year. The Cincinnati collection has the advantage of being shelved apart in a room in the library of the Department of Classics, which occupies a floor of the University Library; thus the entire collection is immediately accessible. It is under the supervision of the Departmental Librarian. Since 1970 a full-time cataloger for the collection has been employed by the Cataloging Department of the Library. The cards for the Modern Greek books are interfiled with the cards of the classics collection proper. The entire department catalog (which follows the Library of Congress system) is adjacent to the main classics collection and the Modern Greek room.

Reference Works

Besides the indispensable bibliographies by Ghinis and Mexas, Legrand, Politis, and the Institut Français d'Athènes listed in Winchell's *Guide* (8th ed.), AA 516-524, the Cincinnati collection has the following: *Catalogue of the Gennadius Library,* American School of Classical Studies at Athens, 7 v. (Boston, G. K. Hall & Co., 1968); *Mega hellēnikon biographikon lexikon,* 5 v. to date (1958?-   ); the two older encyclopedias—*Megalē hellēnike engyklopaideia*, 24 v. with 4 suppl. v., and *Eleutheroudakē engyklopaidikon lexikon*, 12 v.; and two postwar encyclopedias—*Neōteron engyklopaidikon lexikon*, published by "Helios," 18 v., and *Domē*, lavishly illustrated and written in the *dēmotikē*, in progress. [The place of publication of Greek titles, when not stated, is understood to be Athens.] The other reference titles indexed under "Greece" in Winchell's *Guide* are also to be found in Cincinnati.

Periodicals and Serials

The chief strength of the Cincinnati collection lies in its extensive holdings of serial and periodical publications, which now include some 575 titles, representing almost all fields of knowledge. The collection also includes a number of periodicals published outside Greece proper. Not all sets—especially the older and the short-lived periodicals—are complete, but many scholarly journals in a variety of fields are found in complete runs. An up-to-date typewritten list in Greek, giving bibliographic data for each title and showing volumes that are lacking, is available in the Classics Department Library.

A number of the journals and series will be mentioned below in connection with specific subjects. A few titles, however, will serve now to indicate the variety and wealth of the periodical holdings. There is an almost complete set of *Hermēs ho logios* (Vienna, 1811-21), the rare first Greek periodical, an indispensable source for the intellectual background of the Greek Revolution. *Euterpē* (1847-55) was the first illustrated Greek magazine, *Pandōra* (1850-72) an early important publication in the humanities. *To neon kratos* (1937-41) recorded the cultural policies of the Metaxas dictatorship. *Sōtēr* (1877-92; lacks last four volumes) had the imprimatur of the Holy Synod of the Church of Greece. Indeed, the periodicals unfold with rich detail the intellectual history of Greece since 1821.

Especially important are the complete runs of the various series of the Academy of Athens, which encompass all disciplines: the *Praktika* [Proceedings] (1926-   ); the *Pragmateiai* [Treatises] (1935-   ); the *Hellēnikē bibliothēkē* [Library of Ancient Greek Classics], 4 v. (1935-40); the *Mnēmeia* [Monuments of Medieval and Modern Greek History], 6 v. (1933-70); *Diaphora dēmosieumata* [Various Publications], 3 v. (1943-64); and the publications of the six research centers supported by the Academy—the Historical Lexicon of Modern Greek, Greek Folklore, Medieval and Modern Greek History, History of Greek Law, Astronomy and Applied Mathematics, and Greek Philosophy.

Comparable to the Academy's publications in range and quality are the *epetērides* [yearbooks] of the several faculties of the Universities of Athens and Thessaloniki: the sets at Cincinnati are very nearly complete.

Also to be found are the series and publications of the Hetaireia Makedonikōn Spoudōn [Society for Macedonian Studies]. Besides the important historical journals *Hellēnika* and *Makedonika*, they include monographic series covering history, law, economics, philology, and theology. There are complete sets, too, of both the periodical *Balkan Studies* (1960-   ) and the monographs (138 v. to 1974) of the Institute for Balkan Studies, which is under the aegis of the Society.

Language and Literature

LINGUISTICS AND DIGLOSSY.   The linguistic materials of the collection are extensive, covering many aspects of Modern Greek. Special studies treat its history, etymology, syntax, grammar, vocabulary, dialects, and orthography. Besides the works of celebrated older philologists, such as Koraïs, Chatzidakis, and Psichari, the collection includes the complete writings of the late Manolis Triantaphyllidis, the chief advocate of the *dēmotikē* in his day, recently republished by the University of Thessaloniki. There is a good sampling of older grammars of ancient and modern Greek published before 1821 by presses abroad. Important older dictionaries include the unfinished *Kibōtos tes hellēnikēs glōssēs* by N. Logadis, covering A-Δ (Constantinople, at the Patriarchal Press, 1821). The *Historikon lexikon tēs neas hellēnikēs glōssēs* of the Academy of Athens, on a vast scale, has only reached gamma. Important special dictionaries include the *Etymologiko lexiko tēs koinēs neoellēnikēs,* 2d ed. (1967) by N. Andriotis; the *Antistrophon lexikon tēs neas hellēnikēs* (1967) by G. Kourmoulis; and the *Antilexikon,* 2d ed. (1962) by I. Vostantzoglou, modeled on Roget's *Thesaurus.*

Involved with the history of Modern Greek is the thorny, still unsolved "language question." The Cincinnati collection contains extensive materials on the bitter quarrel between "purists" and "demoticists." The earlier stages of the quarrel are recorded in the writings of I. Rizos Neroulos, P. Kodrikas, Koraïs, D. Vyzantios, D. Katartzis, G. Konstantas, and D. Philippidis; in more recent times it may be traced in the works of Chatzidakis, Psichari, A. Tzartzanos, A. Delmouzos, D. Glynos, and Triantaphyllidis. One of the treasures of the collection is the virtually complete set of *Ho Noumas* (1903-31), the chief organ of the "demoticists." The volumes of the *Deltio tou ekpaideutikou homilou* (1911-24) record the effort of the "demoticists" to reform Greek education.

LITERATURE.   The collection covers thoroughly the development of Modern Greek literature from its beginnings in the 11th century to the present. Virtually all of the titles cited in the valuable bibliography in L. Politis' *Historia tēs neas hellēnikēs logotechnias* (Thessaloniki, 1968) are to be found at Cincinnati.

Modern Greek literature written before 1453 is to be found in several collections, the most important of which are those of Sp. Lampros and the great French Neohellenist, Émile Legrand. Virtually all the writings of Legrand and of his successor, Hubert Pernot, exist at Cincinnati. For the study of Cretan literature in the 16th and 17th centuries Cincinnati has editions and studies by C. Sathas, S. Xanthoudidis, E. Kriaras, L. Politis, G. Megas, M. Manousakas, and others.

All of the major literary figures of the 18th, 19th, and 20th centuries, as well as many minor figures, are well represented: Kalvos, Solomos, Christopoulos, the Soutsos brothers, Zalokostas, Laskaratos, Polylas, Valaoritis, Palamas, Drosinis, Polemis, Roïdis, Papadiamantis, Cavafy, Sikelianos, Kazantzakis, Varnalis, Ritsos, Seferis, Venezis, Myrivilis, and many others.

In addition to the complete works of the major authors, there are translations and biographic and critical studies. There are also bibliographies of individual writers compiled by G. Katsimbalis. The numerous histories of Modern Greek literature, in several languages, include the standard work of C. Dimaras, *Historia tēs neohellēnikēs logotechnias,* 4th ed. (1968). Very numerous, too, are the anthologies of prose and poetry. The 48 volumes of the *Basikē bibliothēkē* constitute an anthology of Greek literature, in the broadest sense, since Medieval times. The introductions, biographic notes, and bibliographies in some of the volumes add to the value of this series.

The particular strength of the Cincinnati collection in literary and philological journals adds to the comprehensiveness of the literature section. These include *Athēna* (1889-   ), *Hestia* (1876-95), *Nea hestia* (1927-   ), *Nea grammata* (1935-39), *Parnassos* (1877-94, 1959-   ), *Hellēnikē dēmiourgia* (1948-54), and *Kainourgia epochē* (1956-64).

Religion

The large collection of materials pertaining to religion corresponds to the important role of the church in Greek history since 1453. Again, the collection contains many periodicals, ranging from the short-lived *Euangelikē salpingx* (Nauplion, 1834-35) to *Nea Siōn* (Jerusalem, 1904-   ), and including the official publications of the Church of Greece, *Ekklēsia* (1923-   ) and *Theologia* (1923-   ), as well as popular religious journals like *Zōē* (1911-   ) and *Aktines* (1938-   ). *Grēgorios ho Palamas* (Thessaloniki, 1917-   ) and the yearbooks of the theological faculties at Athens and Thessaloniki contain original sources and studies. Canon law is the special concern of the *Archeion ekklēsiastikou kai kanonikou dikaiou* (1946-   ).

Religious books, a large part of the production of the prerevolutionary Greek presses outside Greek lands, are well represented. A signal rarity in this field is the *Historia hiera, ētoi ta Ioudaïka* (Bucharest, 1716). There is a good sampling of the various service-books of the Greek Church. The popular *synaxaria* [saints' lives] include the first edition of K. Doukakis, *Megalē syllogē biōn hagiōn,* 14 v. (1889-97), and Nikodimos, *Neon martyrologion,* 3d ed. (1961).

Ecclesiastical history is represented by the general works of G. A. Mavrokordatos, A. Kyriakos, P. Vaphidis, G. Konidaris, Ch. Papadopoulos, and V. Stephanidis. In addition there are special studies of the Church in a particular place or period, e.g., Th. Papadopoullos, *The History of the Greek Church and People under Turkish Domination* (Brussels, 1952). Mt. Athos is the subject of many studies dealing with its art, history, and monastic life. There is an incomplete set of the *Hagioreitikē bibliothēkē,* which publishes new materials from Athos. Contemporary scholars and theologians like H. Alivizatos, Ieronimos Kotsonis (primate of Greece 1967-74), K. Bonis, I. Karmiris, P. Bratsiotis, and K. Mertzios have written on various topics, including canon law, the patriarchate, and leading church figures.

Philosophy

There is a respectable collection on the development of Modern Greek philosophy, which begins appropriately with the Athenian, Theophilos Korydalevs (1560-1646). Long ignored, this subject is now receiving the attention it merits. Cincinnati has the writings of major figures of four centuries: Korydalevs, Voulgaris, Koraïs, N. Doukas, P. Vraïlas-Armenis, Benjamin of Lesbos, Ph. Ioannou, Th. Voreas, E. Papanoutsos, and I. Theodorakopoulos. Their philosophical interests include esthetics, logic, law, religion, and epistemology. Indispensable for the study of Modern Greek philosophy is G. E. Voumvlinopoulos, *Bibliographie critique de la philosophie grecque depuis la chute de Constantinople à nos jours, 1453-1953* (1966). Many of the articles and books he lists are found at Cincinnati. Worthy of special mention are the critical editions, articles, and monographs by the members of the *Homilos meletēs hellēnikou diaphōtismou* [Circle for the Study of the Greek Enlightenment], published both in its journal *Eranistēs* (1963-   ) and separately. Much of the Circle's work naturally relates to Koraïs, the preeminent figure of the Enlightenment. Cincinnati's collection of his writings and of works about him is all but complete.

Folklore

The Cincinnati collection is very rich in folklore materials, embracing all facets of popular Greek culture—poetry, music, language, architecture, religion, medicine, and law. The collection includes the pioneer works of N. Politis (1852-1919), who established *laographia* as a major discipline; the studies of his successors S. Kyriakidis and G. Megas; and the important contributions of G. Spyridakis, D. Loukatos, and D. Petropoulos. Original materials as well as studies are to be found in the periodical *Laographia* (1909-   ), in the *epetēris* of the Academy of Athens' Center of Research in Greek Folklore (1939-   ), and in the many journals specializing in the history and culture of provinces and localities. Since the expulsion of the Greeks from Asia Minor, the popular culture of the refugees is being preserved and recorded in journals like the *Archeion Pontou* (1928-   ) and *Mikrasiatika chronika* (1938-   ).

History

The abundant materials at Cincinnati in Greek history since 1453 are best described under several chronological periods. Our survey will not extend beyond the decade of war, occupation, and civil conflict (1940-49).

TOURKOKRATIA (ca. 1453-1821; to 1912 in northern Greece and certain islands). Original sources on the Turkish period are to be found in a variety of publications, e.g., in the journal *Mesaiōnikon archeion* of the Academy of Athens; the *Archeion koinotētos Hydras, 1778-1832,* 15 v. (Piraeus, 1921-31); the several collections edited by C. Sathas; and in journals dealing with localities and provinces, especially those recently freed from Turkish rule, a good example of which is *Epeirōtika chronika,* 16 v. (1926-41). Secondary sources include older and newer treatises, e.g., Sathas, *Tourkokratoumenē Hellas* (1869), and D. A. Zakythinos, *He tourkokratia* (1957), and especially the large synthesis in progress, of which four volumes have appeared, by A. Vacalopoulos, *Historia tou neou hellēnismou* (1961-73). Special investigations are numerous. We can only provide here a sampling by topic and authors' names: on the church by M. Gedeon, Mertzios, Manousakas, and Papadopoullos; on law by D. S. Ghinis, I. Lykouris, P. Zepos, I. Visvizis, and N. Pantazopoulos; on the craft guilds by M. Kalinderis, Eleni Vourazeli-Marinakou, K. Koukkidis, and E. Georgiou; and on education by K. Amantos, T. E. Evangelidis, Manousakas, and G. Kournoutos. There are valuable studies of cities and provinces under Turkish rule by M. Sakellariou, Ph. Argenti, Vacalopoulos, N. Svoronos, and many others. On the major figure of Rigas Velestinlis there is abundant material, ranging from the short biography by Perraivos (1860) to the recent studies by L. Vranousis.

VENETIAN RULE (VARYING PERIODS AND PLACES—IONIAN ISLANDS, CRETE, AEGEAN ISLANDS, PELOPONNESUS, ETC.). On this subject, only less important than the *Tourkokratia* in Greek history after 1453, Cincinnati has the older publications of documents by Sathas, *Mnēmeia hellēnikēs historias,* 9 v. (Paris, 1880-90); by Lampros in several volumes of the *Deltion tēs historikēs kai ethnologikēs hetaireias tēs Hellados,* 9 v. (lst ser., 1883-1926); and by Sp. M. Theotokis in the *Mnēmeia* of the Academy. It also has the monographs and publications of sources which have appeared since the 1950s, many of them by the students of Professors Vacalopoulos and Manousakas at Thessaloniki, and Zakythinos and Tomadakis at Athens. Similar material is appearing in *Thēsaurismata* (1962-   ), the yearbook of the Istituto Ellenico di Studi Bizantini e Post-Bizantini in Venice.

GREEK REVOLUTION (1821-29). This, the epic subject of Modern Greek history, has stimulated the greatest amount of study and writing by Greek historians, professional and amateur. Much of this production can be found on the shelves of the Cincinnati collection. It includes the histories by contemporaries—A. Phrantzis, I. Philimon, M. Oikonomou, G. Theophilos, and Sp. Trikoupis—and the more recent works of G. Vlachogiannis, N. Moschopoulos, and D. Kokkinos. There are special studies on the army by Ch. Vyzantios and Vacalopoulos; on the navy by K. Alexandris and G. Lazaropoulos; on philhellenism by S. Lascaris, P. Karolidis, and Th. Vagenas; and on law by Visvizis. On the *Philikē Hetaireia,* besides the pioneer account of Philimon, there are memoirs of E. Xanthos and A. Xodilos, and the studies by S. Sakellariou, T. Kandiloros, V. Mexas, and E. Protopsaltis. Many studies relate to regions and to special events. The collection also possesses a wealth of biographies of revolutionary figures, including the *Bioi peloponnēsiōn andrōn kai tōn exōthen* (1888) by Photakos and the *Bioi paralēloi,* 8 v. (1869-76) by A. Goudas.

Sources and documents available in the collection include A. Mamoukas, *Ta kata tēn anagennēsin tēs Hellados,* 11 v. in 3 (1839-52); *Archeia Lazarou kai Geōrgiou Kountouriotou 1821-32,* 7 v. (1920-69); *Historikon archeion Dionysiou Rōma,* 2 v. (1901-06); *Archeion tou stratēgou Mpotsarē* (1934); *Athēnaïkon archeion* (1901) and the *Archeion tou stratēgou Makrygiannē,* 2 v.

(1907), both published by Vlachogiannis; and the vast *Historikon archeion Alexandrou Mauro-
kordatou,* 3 v. (1963-68; in progress), edited by Protopsaltis in the *Mnēmeia* series of the Academy.
The memoirists include Ch. Perraivos, A. Rangavis, N. Spiliadis, Th. Kolokotronis, N. Kasomoulis,
N. Ypsilantis, and Photakos. Mention should be made also of the series *Apomnēmoneumata
agōnistōn tou 21,* 20 v. (1955-57) edited by Protopsaltis. There are, besides, the diaries of Admirals
Sachtouris and Tsamados; and the rare work by A. Miaoulis, *Synoptikē historia tōn hyper tēs eleu-
therias tēs anagennētheisēs Hellados genomenōn naumachiōn,* 2 v. (Nauplion, 1883-36). Other
documents on the Revolution have been published by Sathas, P. Kontogiannis, G. Laïos, and
A. Daskalakis.

  PRESIDENCY OF KAPODISTRIAS (1827-31).   The Cincinnati collection offers considerable resources for the study of this critical period of Greek history. Published documents include:
Archeia tēs hellēnikēs palingenēsias, 2 v. (1857-62); the Mamoukas set already cited; *Constitutions, loix, ordonnances des assemblées . . . et du président de la Grèce* (1835); P. Kontogiannis,
ed., *Historika engrapha* (1927); A. Soutsos, ed., *Syllogē tōn eis to exōterikon dēmosion dikaion
tēs Hellados anagomenōn episēmōn engraphōn* (1858). Letters and memoirs include Kapodistrias' autobiography, edited and translated by M. Lascaris (1940); *Epistolai I. A. Kapodistria,* 4
v. in 2 (1841-43), edited by E.-A. Bétant; *Allēlographia I. A. Kapodistria–I. G. Eÿnardou 1826-
31* (1929), edited by Theotokis; *Anekdotē allēlographia* (1958), edited by D. Konomos; Th.
Kolokotronis, *Diēgēsis symbantōn tēs hellēnikēs phylēs apo ta 1770 heōs ta 1836* (1846).

  Biographies of Kapodistrias and monographs on the various phases of his career before 1827
and on his presidency include: Evangelidis, *Historia tou Iōannou Kapadistriou* (1894); A.
Idromenos, *Ioannēs Kapodistrias* (1900); Eleni Koukkou, *Ho Kapodistrias kai hē paideia 1803-
1823* (1958); S. Lascaris, *Capodistrias avant la révolution grecque* (Lausanne, 1918); S. Loukatos, *Ho Ioannēs Kapodistrias kai hē heptanēsos politeia* (1959); Th. Makris, *Ho Ioannēs Kapodistrias kai hē prokybernētikē tou drasis* (1964); D. Seremetis, *Hē dikaiosynē epi Kapodistria* (1959);
A. Despotopoulos, *Ho kybernētēs Kapodistrias kai hē apeleutherōsis tēs Hellados* (1959); and
A. Daskalakis, *Koraēs kai Kapodistrias* (1958).

  REIGN OF OTHO (1832-62).   The birth pains of the new Greek kingdom under the first
king are richly documented in the Cincinnati collection. One will find biographies of Otho and
Amalia by A. Kleomenis and Evangelidis; histories by P. Karolidis, T. Pipinelis, E. Kyriakidis,
and N. T. Voulgaris; and special studies of social, political, and diplomatic problems by S.
Maximos, T. Vournas, K. Grapsas, A. Skandamis, Z. Papantoniou, and E. Prevelakis. Among
important primary sources must be mentioned the *Ephēmeris tēs Kybernēseōs* (1833-63); the
Praktika of the National Assembly of Sept. 3, 1843 (1843); the *Praktika tēs Boulēs 1845-46,* 4 v.
(1846) and *1848-49,* 3 v. in 2 (1849); also the memoirs of Ch. Neezer, Makrygiannis, S. Pelikas,
N. Dragoumis, Gennaios Kolokotronis, and A. Rangavis; and other contemporary accounts, such
as Th. I. Kolokotronis, *Hai teleutaiai hēmerai tēs basileias tou Othōnos* (1881), L. Palaskas, *Ta
symbanta tou oktōbriou 1862* (1882), and E. Deligeorgis, *Politika hēmerologia, 1859-1862*
(1896).

  REIGN OF GEORGE I (1862-1913).   For the long, eventful reign of George I Cincinnati
has considerable holdings, including primary sources in the form of memoirs of leading civilian
and military figures; also the *Episēmos ephēmeris tēs syneleuseōs 1862-64,* 6 v. (1863-64); the
Praktika tōn synedriaseōn tēs en Athēnais B' ton hellēnon syneleuseōs 1862-64, 6 v. (1862-65);
Peri Charilaou Trikoupē ek dēmosieumatōn, 16 v. (1907-17); Deligeorgis, *Logoi politikoi, 1863-
1877* (1880); and L. Voulgaris, *Apokalyphthētō alētheia* (1878).

  There are many contemporary accounts of the disastrous war of 1897, in addition to the official account by Prince Constantine, *Ekthesis tēs A. B. Hypsēlotētos tou diadochou epi tōn peprag-
menōn tou stratou Thessalias kata tēn ekstrateian tou 1897* (1898). On the Cretan question and the

revolts of 1866 and 1897 the collection possesses much original material: codices of Cretan law (1858, 1868) and the *Kōdikes krētikēs politeias,* 2 v. (Chania, 1902); memoirs and personal accounts by I. Skaltsounis, P. Peridis, Prince George, and others. Recent studies include P. Mamalakis, *Ho agōnas tou 1866-69 gia tēn henosē tēs Krētēs,* 2 v. (Thessaloniki, 1942, 1947); N. Tsirintanis, *Hē politikē kai diplōmatikē historia tēs en Krētē ethnikēs epanastaseōs, 1866-68,* 3 v. (1950-51); Domna Dontas, *Greece and the Great Powers, 1863-1875* (Thessalonica, 1966). An important source is *Hē krētikē epanastasis 1866-1869,* consisting of the reports of the Greek consuls in Crete, edited by E. Prevelakis and V. Plagiannakou-Bekiari, 2 v. (1967, 1970, in progress; in *Mnēmeia* of the Academy).

On the Military League and the revolt of August 15, 1909, which brought Eleftherios Venizelos to center stage in Greek politics, the available materials include N. Zorbas, *Apomnēmoneumata* (1925); the history by A. Kyriakos, *Hē nea Hellas, 1897-1909* (1910); A. Theodoridis, *Hē epanastasis kai to ergon autēs* (1914); and the newer study by P. Tsitsilias, *Hē epanastasis tou 1909* (1964).

Cincinnati has much of the abundant literature on the struggle for Macedonia. Original sources, documents, memoirs, and special studies have been published by the Institute for Balkan Studies of the Society for Macedonian Studies. There are also the studies of N. Kazazis, *To makedonikon problēma* (1907); V. Colocotronis, *La Macédoine et l'hellénisme* (Paris 1919); and N. Vlachos, *To makedonikon hōs phasis tou anatolikou zētēmatos, 1878-1908* (1935).

For the Balkan Wars (1912-13) the collection contains primary materials in the form of memoirs, contemporary accounts, and the official record published by the Greek General Staff, *Ho hellēnikos stratos kata tous balkanikous polemous tou 1912-1913,* 3 v. and 3 supp. (1932).

REIGNS OF CONSTANTINE AND ALEXANDER (1913-23). Numerous biographies, memoirs, and accounts, many of them written in partisan passion, record this turbulent decade. Much of the literature focuses on Constantine and Venizelos, particularly the latter. I. Metaxas, *Hē historia tou ethnikou dichasmou* (1935), Ch. Stratigos, *Hē Hellas en Mikra Asia* (1925), and V. Dousmanis, *Hē esōterikē opsis tēs mikrasiatikēs emplokēs* (1928) defend the King's policy. Defense of Venizelos' policy is best seen in his statements to Parliament, *To programma tēs exōterikēs autou politikēs* (1915), in *Hoi historikoi logoi tou Eleutheriou Benizelou,* 2 v. in 1 (1936), and in the memoirs of some of his collaborators, e.g., P. Danglis, *Anamnēseis,* 2 v. (1965). P. Panagakos, *Symbolē eis tēn historian tēs dekaetias, 1912-1922* (1960) surveys the whole period. Georgios Ventiris, *Hē Hellas tou 1910-1920* (1931) writes as a Venizelist. S. P. Cosmin (Phocas-Cosmetatos) dealt with diplomatic history in *L'Entente et la Grèce pendant la grande guerre,* 2 v. (Paris, 1926), and published the relevant documents in *Dossiers secrets de la Triple Entente; Grèce 1914-1922* (Paris, 1969). Two volumes published (1958-61) by the Greek General Staff describe Greek military action in 1914-18.

On the Asia Minor campaign there is ample material, e.g., the memoirs of Prince Andrew and others, and studies by N. Kazazis, *Ethnika dramata kai problēmata* (1924); Ch. Angelomatis, *Chronikon megalēs tragōdias* (n.d.); E. Voutieridis, *Hē ekstrateia peran tou Sangariou* (1922); D. Ambelas, *Hē kathodos tōn neōterōn myriōn* (1937); and K. Boulalas, *Hē mikrasiatikē ekstrateia 1919-1922* (1959). A. A. Pallis, in *Greece's Anatolian Venture and After* (London, 1937), surveys its diplomatic and political aspects. The official history of the disaster is recorded in the multiple volumes and maps of *Hē ekstrateia eis tēn Mikran Asian* published by the Greek General Staff.

BETWEEN THE WARS (1923-40). The two-volume work of G. Daphnis, *Hē Hellas metaxy dyo polemōn* (1955), surveys these years. Also valuable is P. Pipinelis, *Historia tēs exōterikes politikēs tēs Hellados 1923-1941* (1948). There are numerous biographies and memoirs of the leading figures, Venizelos, George II, Kondylis, Plastiras, Gonatas, Metaxas, and others.

For the Republic (1924-35) there is *To ergon tēs kybernēseōs Benizelou kata tēn tetraetian 1928-1932* (1932), published by the Premier's Office. For Metaxas and his regime (1936-41) the collection has his *Logoi kai skepseis,* 1936-41, 2 v. (1969) and *Hēmerologion,* 4 v. (1951-64), and the official record, *Tessara chronia diakybernēseos Metaxa,* 4 v. (1940). The Central Committee of the Greek Communist Party in *Deka chronia agōnes, 1935-1945* (1945) and *Pente chronia agōnes, 1931-36* (1946) gives an account of its aims and activities.

WORLD WAR II, OCCUPATION, CIVIL WAR (1940-49).   Ample materials exist at Cincinnati for the study of all phases of these momentous events, at least insofar as sources and secondary accounts thus far published will allow. Most of the titles cited in the informed surveys of L. S. Stavrianos and E. P. Panagopoulos, "Present-Day Greece," *The Journal of Modern History,* v. 20, 1948: 149-158, and F. A. Spencer, *War and Postwar Greece: An Analysis Based on Greek Writings* (The Library of Congress, European Affairs Division, 1952), are to be found here. We give here only the briefest sampling of the Cincinnati titles. G. Goudis, in *Hē Hellas kata ton deuteron pangosmion polemon* (Alexandria, 1947), provides historical background; Kokkinos published important sources in *Hoi dyo polemoi 1940-1941,* 2 v. (1945-46); V. Papadakis, in *Diplōmatikē historia tou hellēnikou polemou* (1957), discusses diplomatic aspects. For military history the Greek General Staff published three volumes (1956, 1959, 1960). Personal accounts of the war are many. D. Koutsoumis, *Tessara chronia agnōstē hellēnikē historia* (Alexandria, 1946) writes the history of the Greek Government-in-exile. Materials on E. Tsouderos, Premier of the Government-in-exile, include a biography by Venezis, and several of his own works: *Logoi henos chronou* (Alexandria, 1942), *Gnōmes kai logoi* (1945), *Hellēnikes anōmalies stē mesē anatolē* (1945), and *Diplōmatika paraskēnia* (1949).

On the occupation (1941-44) there is the comprehensive compilation of D. Gatopoulos, *Historia tēs katochēs,* 4 v. (1946-47). The viewpoint of the Right is expressed by L. Piniatoglou, *Hellēnika problēmata* (1945) and that of the Left in the *Archeion ethnikēs antistasēs* (1946), published by the National Liberation Front (E.A.M.).

The resistance produced much writing, ranging from the study of resistance in a particular city or province to the large work of K. Antonopoulos, *Ethnikē antistasis,* 3 v. (1964). P. Enepekidis' work, *Hē hellēnikē antistasis 1941-1944* (1964), is based on the secret archives of the Wehrmacht in Greece. K. Pyromaglou, *Hē ethnikē antistasis* (1947), and Stephanos Saraphis, *Ho ELAS* (1946) are important accounts from the point of view of the E.D.E.S. and the E.A.M., respectively.

Our aim has been to describe the Cincinnati Modern Greek collection as a working library. It is large enough to enable scholars to investigate in detail many topics in the fields of history, literature, and institutions. In this survey we have emphasized the traditional humanities, in which the main strength of the collection lies; but there are also many books and periodicals relevant to the social sciences and technical subjects. Thus the monographs and periodicals on legal history since 1453 and on the law and constitutions of Greece since 1821 form a sizable collection. We have made only incidental mention of rarities. A careful search of the collection would no doubt reveal a number of items of great scarcity, some of which, like *Hoi athloi tēs en Blachia hellēnikēs epanastaseōs to 1821 etos* by Ilias Photeinos (Leipzig [=Braïla], 1846), are valuable as historical sources. Lastly, we note that the value of the Modern Greek collection is enhanced by Cincinnati's splendid library on classical antiquity and by a growing collection on Byzantine history and civilization.

Eva C. Topping and Peter Topping
University of Cincinnati

Cleveland Public Library

General Information

THE CLEVELAND PUBLIC Library is among the largest public libraries in the United States, with a total of 3.3 million volumes in its collections. The Main Library alone houses over 1.6 million volumes, of which 910,000 are in the reference collection and 710,000 circulate. With its extensive Main Library subject and reference collections, the Library meets the research and specialized needs of the reading public of greater Cleveland, as well as those of students and scholars nationwide.

Ordinarily the serious scholar would engage in in-depth research at the Main Library, which is located in the heart of downtown Cleveland and is easily accessible by local transportation from the Cleveland Hopkins Airport as well as from other parts of the metropolitan area. Parking facilities are available at nearby locations. The Library is open Monday through Thursday from 9 a.m. to 8:30 p.m. and Friday and Saturday from 9 a.m. to 6 p.m.

It is suggested that the out-of-town scholar outline his research plans to the Head of Main Library, 325 Superior Avenue, Cleveland, Ohio 44114 (telephone 216/241-1020), before coming to Cleveland. This will permit the Library to answer specific questions in advance and to arrange an introduction to the facilities and collections.

The Main Library is basically departmentalized by subject specialties, and the individual subject departments administer and develop their collections under the supervision of a department head. The public catalog (author, title, and subject interfiled) contains information on most titles in the Library (exceptions are indicated below under Foreign Literature Department). Those using the Library for the first time should consult the public catalog before advancing further. The Cleveland Public Library uses a modified Dewey classification system (the Brett classification), and call numbers obtained at other libraries may hence be of little value. In addition to the public catalog, each department has its own card catalog in its respective reading room. Materials on Russia and Eastern Europe—including those on Hungary and Poland—are an integral part of the departmental collections and do not constitute separate collections. Printed catalogs or bibliographies are not available on the Russian and East European materials of the Library.

As a research center the Main Library is responsible for building and maintaining distinctive, specialized scholarly collections characterized by both breadth and depth in the main subject fields. While these collections were assembled primarily with the specialist in mind, the materials are also accessible to the public. Owing to their rarity and exceptional value, some of these materials carry certain restrictions and must ordinarily be used in the Library.

The Cleveland Public Library actively participates in the interlibrary loan program and makes provisions for the release of certain reference books upon request. Modern photocopying facilities are available and materials may be duplicated upon permission.

Materials on Hungary and Poland are significant—in terms of both quality and quantity. Since its founding in 1869 the Library has been aware of the important contribution books make in the life of those who have arrived in the Cleveland area from East Central Europe. In many instances the first friendly contacts of immigrants have been with libraries, which have helped them find the key to life in a new land through books, information, and services. The Library has arranged for language classes, study, and other cultural opportunities for such newcomers and has provided reading materials about the United States and from their country of origin, both in English and in their native languages.

In general, materials about Hungary and Poland are part of the subject department collections. There are notable exceptions, however. The Foreign Literature Department, established in 1924, is custodian of a significant collection which in 1972 numbered 160,000 volumes in 38 languages, all in the circulating classification. Each language has its own card catalog and is shelved separately. Works in Polish number 8,500 volumes.

The location of the Hungarian language material is also an exception. The principal depository of this is one of the regional branches of the Cleveland Public Library, the Carnegie West Branch Library, located on the near west side of Cleveland in an area heavily populated by Hungarians. The collection, which has its own card catalog and is shelved separately, numbers 9,500 circulating volumes.

The materials selection policy of the Cleveland Public Library offers general guidelines concerning the acquisition of materials in foreign languages. The aim is to buy reasonably popular books on a great variety of subjects, as well as the standard works for adults and young people. Translations of those literary works that are regarded as classics are added in many languages.

Among the specific factors considered in acquiring foreign language materials are the requirements of the city's many nationality groups, teachers and students of foreign languages and literature, the needs of the scholarly community and local business and industry, the updating of subject areas of special interest, the comparative scarcity of published material on the subject, and the availability of materials in other libraries in the Greater Cleveland area.

Encyclopedias, dictionaries, bibliographies, maps, and similar basic reference and source materials are acquired on a continuous basis. The publications of foreign governments are not necessarily added. Scholarly journals and the publications of learned societies abroad are subscribed to regardless of whether they are in English or in another language, provided they complement and strengthen the existing collection.

Hungary

THE ACQUISITION OF titles relating to Hungary began at the Cleveland Public Library during the last decades of the 19th century. Many of the earliest Hungarian volumes received were gifts. Regular purchasing of titles in Hungarian began at the turn of the century, and the first volumes on Hungarian history and literature in English were acquired at about the same time. The Hungarian collection, located at the Carnegie West Branch of the Cleveland Public Library, has since grown to 9,500 volumes. Some 200-250 volumes are added annually. The Main Library subject departments house an additional 3,000 volumes, almost all of which are in the reference classification. No previous attempt has been made to compile a bibliography of these materials.

The truly unique and valuable research materials about Hungary are in the reference collections of the Main Library subject departments. This discussion will focus on the more significant holdings in these collections.

Bibliographies

Among the basic bibliographies available in the collections are: *Magyar Könyvészet,* 6 v. in 12 (Budapest, 1882-1942); Szabó Károly, *Régi magyar könyvtár,* v. 2-3 (Budapest, 1879-98); Sztripszky, Hiador, *Adalékok Szabó Károly Régi magyar könyvtár cimű munkájának I., II. kötetéhez; pótlások és igazítások, 1472-1711* (Budapest); Apponyi, Sándor, *Hungarica; Ungarn betref-*

fende im Auslande gedruckte Bücher and Flugschriften, 4 v. in 3 (Budapest, 1903-27); Kertbeny, Károly, *Bibliografie der ungarischen nationalen und internationalen Literatur* (Budapest, 1880); Kertbeny, Károly and Géza Petrik, *Ungarns deutsche Bibliographie, 1801-1860* . . . (Budapest, 1886); Magyar, Márta and Béla Kemény (comp.), *Ungarn, Hungary, La Hongrie; a Selection of Works About Hungary in Twenty Different Languages* (Budapest, 1931); and the alphabetical lists of books and periodicals published by the Hungarian Academy of Sciences in 1890, covering the years 1830-89 and in 1911, covering the years 1889-1910.

Also available is a catalog of serials published on Hungarian history entitled *Les éditions des sources de l'histoire Hongroise, 1854-1930* (Budapest, 1931), edited by Imre Lukinich. On the subject of geography, the Library has the work of Rezső Havass, *Magyar földrajzi könyvtár* . . . (Budapest, 1893). Agriculture is covered in a work published by Mezőgazdasági Múzeum Könyvtára, Budapest, *A magyar gazdasági irodalom első századainak könyvészete,* 1505-1805 (Budapest, 1934). Biographic information on prominent Hungarian agriculturalists is included. Kálmán Eperjessy'sī *A bécsi hadilevéltár magyar vonatkozású térképeinek jegyzéke* (Szeged, 1929), is an inventory of political, physical, and special maps, city plans, and military maps. In *Hazai és külföldi folyóiratok magyar tudományos repertóriuma; történelem és annak segédtudományai* (Budapest, 1874-85), József Szinnyei offers a comprehensive bibliography of Hungarian periodicals.

Encyclopedias

The most useful encyclopedia for research on Hungary before 1900 is *A Pallas nagy lexikona,* 18 v. (Budapest, 1893-1904). More up-to-date, but not without its weak points, is *Révai nagy lexikona,* 21 v. (Budapest, 1911-35). A recent multivolume general encyclopedia is *Új magyar lexikon,* 6 v. (Budapest, 1959-62). *Magyar zsidó lexikon* (Budapest, 1929), edited by Péter Ujvári, contains a wealth of information on the history, development, and life of Jews in Hungary, as well as vignettes of local Jewish congregations in the country and biographic data on outstanding Jewish leaders.

A biobibliographic set covering some 30,000 authors and their literary production is József Szinnyei's *Magyar írók élete és munkái,* 14 v. (Budapest, 1891-1914). *Honpolgárok könyve* (Pest, 1866), edited by Soma Vereby, comprises biographies of 21 Hungarian statesmen. Officers and members of the Magyar Tudományos Akadémia, together with their scientific activities and publications, are listed for 1926-40 in *Magyar Tudományos Akadémiai almanach* (Budapest). *Magyar életrajzi lexikon,* 2 v. (Budapest, 1967-68), edited by Ágnes Kenyeres, contains nearly 11,000 biographies of Hungarians who died before 1966. Constant Würzbach's *Biographisches Lexikon des Kaiserthums Oesterreich, enthaltend die Lebensskizzen der denkwürdigen Personen, welche seit 1750 in den oesterreichischen Kronländern geboren wurden oder darin gelebt und gewirkt haben,* 60 v. (Vienna, 1856-90), includes many Hungarians about whom it is difficult to locate reliable data elsewhere.

Travel Narratives and Geographical Descriptions

The Library's collections include an impressive number of rare and informative travel narratives and geographical descriptions of Hungary. Among these are the oldest published work on Hungary in the Library, Marcin Broniowski's *Martini Broniovii de Biezdzfeldea, bis in Tartariam nomine, Stephani Primi Poloniae regis legati, Tartariae descriptio, Transylvaniae ac Moldaviae descriptio Georgii a Reichesdorff, Georgii werneri de admirandis Hungariae hypomnemation* (A. Mylij, 1595). The *Neue Beschreibung des Königreichs Ungarn und darzu gehöriger Länder, Städte und vornehmster Oerter* (Leipzig, 1664), by Martin Zeiller (1581-1661), gives a short political history of Hungary and a description of the country. In *Totius regni Hungariae superioris e inferioris accurata descriptio* . . . (Frankfurt und Nurnberg, 1685), Georj Krekwitz gives extensive information on the geography, regions, towns, and fortifications of Hungary. The first part of Edward Brown's *A brief account of some travels in divers parts of Europe* (London, 1685), devoted to Hungary, includes a beautiful illustration of the famous bridge at Eszék. Robert Townson, who went to Hungary on behalf of the British East India Company to explore the country's mineralogy and physical geography, claimed that his *Travels in Hungary, with a short account of Vienna in the year 1793* (London, 1797) was the first geography book in English which dealt exclusively with Hungary. In *Travels from Vienna through Lower Hungary; with some remarks on the state of Vienna during the Congress, in the year 1814* (Edinburgh, 1818), Richard Bright depicts both the country and its residents.

The following titles appeared during the great Reform Period of Hungary; Marmont, Auguste F. L. V., *Voyage du marechal duc de Raguse en Hongrie, en Transylvanie*, 5 v. (Paris, 1837-38); Gleig, George R. *Germany, Bohemia, and Hungary, visited in 1837*, 3 v. (London, 1839); Paget, John, *Hungary and Transylvania; with remarks on their condition, social, political and economical*, 2 v. (London, 1839); Pardoe, Julia, *The city of the Magyar, or, Hungary and her institutions in 1839-1840*, 3 v. (London, 1840). These works report on politics, the reform Diet, cultural developments, navigation, taxation, and the nobility, as well as on the authors' travels.

Of particular interest is *The Goth and the Hun; or, Transylvania, Debreczin, Pesth, and Vienna, in 1850* (London, 1851) by Andrew A. Paton. This collection of articles sent to the *Times* between October 1849 and January 1850 covers the political milieu, physical destruction during the War for Independence, the inhabitants' attitudes toward the Austrian army of occupation, and the problems faced by the country.

Travel by foreigners to Hungary increased substantially after 1867, and the Library's collections include nearly 40 travel journals and descriptions covering the period from 1867 to 1914. An example is *Magyarland; Being the Narrative of Our Travels Through the Highlands and Lowlands of Hungary*, 2 v. (London, 1881).

Three titles offer information on the history, geography, politics, religious life, villages, and folklore of Transylvania: Gerando, Auguste, *La Transylvanie et ses habitants*, 2 v. (Paris, 1845); Boner, Charles, *Transylvania, its Products and its People* (London, 1865); and Gerard, Emily, *The Land Beyond the Forest; Facts, Figures and Fancies from Transylvania*, 2 v. (New York, 1888).

There are over 30 titles in the Library containing travel journals and descriptive narratives on 20th-century Hungary, most of them written during the interwar period.

Ethnography

The Library's ethnography collection, maintained in the John G. White Department of Folklore, Orientalia and Chess, includes many rare and unusual research materials on Hungarian folklore, linguistics, and medieval history. Among the titles available are the periodical *Ethnographia*, v. 10-54 (Budapest, 1899-1943) and *A magyarság néprajza*, 4 v. (Budapest, 1933-37), an extensive survey edited by Elemér Czakó. Village life, hunting, wedding customs, secular and religious holidays, and inaugural ceremonies for local officials are discussed by Sándor Réső Ensel in his *Magyarországi népszokások* (Pest, 1867). Other titles of special interest on folk life, superstitions, and religious concepts are Heinrich Wlislocki's *Aus dem Volksleben der Magyaren, ethnologische Mitteilungen* (Munich, 1893) and *Volksglaube und religioser Brauch Magyaren* (Münster, 1893).

Among more than 12 collections of fairy tales available is Nándor Pogány's *Magyar Fairy Tales from Old Hungarian Legends* (New York, 1930). The Library's fine collection of proverbs includes two books by János Erdélyi, *Magyar közmondások könyve* (Pest, 1851) and *A nép költé-*

szete; népdalok, népmesék és közmondások (Pest, 1869) as well as *Magyar közmondások könyve,* by Andor Sirisaka and *Magyar közmondások és közmondásszerű szólások* (Budapest, 1897) by Ede Margalits.

History

The Library's resources on the history of Hungary are significant indeed. In the collections of the John G. White Department and the History Department an unusually large number of rare books on Hungarian history in several languages are available. In a sampling of some 300 titles in this field, about half were found to be in Hungarian.

SOURCES.   Three of the most important works on early Hungarian history are: Deseriz, József I., *Josephii Innocentii Desericii de initiis ac majoribus Hungarirum commentaria . . .* , 5 v. in 4 (Buda, 1748-60); Pray, George, *Annales veteras Hunnorum, Avarum, et Hungarorum . . .* (Vindobonae, 1761); and Thierry, Amadee M., *Histoire d' Attila et de ses successeurs jusqu'à l'établissement des Hongrois en Europe; suivie des legendes et traditions,* 2 v. (Paris, 1865). The three works cited discuss the origin, migration, and organization of the Huns, the Avars, and the Magyars, with stress on their stay in the Danubian Basin before A.D. 1000.

The original home of the Magyars, their wanderings through Levedia and Etelköz, and their first contact with other East European peoples are considered by Géza Kuun in his *Relationum Hungarorum cum Oriente gentibusque Orientalis originis historia antiquissima* 2 v. in 1 (Claudiopoli, 1892-95). In *Rerum Hungaricarum scriptores varii; historici, geographici* (Francofurti, 1600), the origin and history of the Magyars up to the sieges of Szigetvár and Eger in the 16th century are described on the basis of chronicles and the earliest available written sources. The establishment of the Kingdom of Hungary, the election of the king, the administration of the state, ecclesiastical offices, and the military are discussed in *Respublica et status regni Hungariae* (Lugduni, 1634).

A critical examination of the chronicle of Simon Kézai is *M. Simonis de Keza presbyteri hungari scriptoris saeculi xiii . . .* (Budae, 1782). The Kézai chronicle, written in 1282-83 and dedicated to King Ladislas IV (1272-90), is a history of the Hungarians from earliest times to the year in which it was written. The facsimile edition of *Chronica Hungarorum impressa Budae 1473, typis similibus reimpressa* (Budapest, 1900) was prepared by Vilmos Fraknói. The original chronicle of Buda (1473), the first book printed on Hungarian history at Buda, covered the period from the origin of the Magyars to the coronation of King Matthias (1458-90). On the basis of medieval chronicles, Paulus S. Cassel's *Magyarische Alterthümer* (Berlin, 1848) narrates the Magyar's entry into their permanent homeland.

The Library has two scholarly works which analyze the most important medieval writings about Hungary. *Scriptores rerum hungaricarum tempore ducum regumque stirpis arpadianae gestarum,* 2 v. (Budapest, 1937-38) includes critical discussions by Hungarian historians on the earliest sources of Hungarian history. The Library possesses volumes 1, 3, 6, and 7 of C. A. Macartney's *Studies on the Earliest Hungarian Historical Sources* (Oxford, 1938-51), one of the most detailed scholarly studies available on Hungarian historical sources.

PERIODICALS.   Significant items in the Library's small collection of Hungarian periodicals include *Ungarische Jahrbücher,* v. 1-23 (Berlin, 1921-43), and its sequel *Ural-altaische Jahrbücher,* v. 1- (Wiesbaden, 1952-), a complete set of *Századok,* v. 1- (Budapest, 1867-), and *South Eastern Affairs,* 10 v. in 2 (Budapest, 1931-40).

GENERAL WORKS.   The oldest general works on Hungarian history in the collections are from the 1850s: *Geschichte der Ungarn,* 2 v. (Pest, 1851-55) by Mihály Horváth, János Mailáth's work *Geschichte der Magyaren,* 5 v. (Regensburg, 1852-53), and *Literarische Berichte aus Ungarn,* 4 v. (Budapest, 1877-80). Two titles of broad scope and rich in illustrations are Sándor

Szilágyi's *A magyar nemzet története,* 10 v. (Budapest, 1895-98) and *Magyar történet,* 2d. ed., 5 v. (Budapest, 1935-36), by Bálint Hóman and Gyula Szekfű. The latter includes extensive bibliographies on each period. A highly influential work on the philosophical viewpoint of Hungarian historians is Bálint Hóman's *A magyar történetírás új útjai* (Budapest, 1931).

HISTORY OF HUNGARY BEFORE 1526. The Library has two monographs on the House of Árpád. In *Ungarns Geschichtsquellen im Zeitalter der Arpaden* (Berlin, 1882), Henrik Marczali contributes a critical essay on the writings and legends found in contemporary chronicles in various languages regarding the period of the Arpads. Bálint Hóman offers a reassessment of the first King of Hungary in *King Stephen the Saint* (Budapest, 1938).

Péter Horváth, in his *Commentario de initiis ac maioribus Jazygum et Cumanorum eorumque constitutionibus* (Pest, 1801), discusses the origin, westward migration, and history of the Cumans, who entered Hungary in the 13th century.

The invasion of Hungary by the Mongol nomads in 1241 is discussed in Edouard M. Sayous' short but thoroughly documented essay *L'invasion des Mongols en Hongrie dans les années 1241 et 1242* (Paris, 1875) and in Iosif Schiopul's *Contribuţiuni la istoria Transilvaniei în secola XII şi XIII* (Cluj, 1932).

The Library has two works on Matthias Corvinus by Vilmos Fraknói, *Bibliotheca Corvina; la biblioteca di Mattia Corvino re d'Ungheria* (Budapest, 1927), and *Mathias Corvinus, König von Ungarn, 1458-1490* (Freiburg, 1891). Ornaments from these beautifully illustrated codices of the Corvina library are reproduced in Johann Csontosi's *Bildnisse des Königs Mathias Corvinus und der Königin Beatrix in den Corvincodexen* (Budapest, 1890). Dedicated to the Cleveland Public Library by the Mayor of Kolozsvár is the Matthias anniversary volume *Mátyás király emlékkönyv* (Budapest, 1902), edited by Sándor Márki. The life and influence of Princess Beatrix of Naples, the wife of Matthias, is appraised in Albert Berzeviczy's biography *Beatrice d'Aragona* (Milan, 1931).

THE 16TH CENTURY. The battle of Mohács (1526) is treated in Kemal Pasha Zadeh's narrative about this event, *Histoire de la campagna de Mohacz par Kemal Pacha Zadeh* (Paris, 1859), which also has a critical evaluation of the Pasha's account. Further, there is *Mohácsi emlékkönyv, 1526* (Budapest, 1926), edited by Imre Lukinics, a collection of essays by 12 modern Hungarian historians.

Antoine Bechet's *Histoire du ministère du Cardinal Martinusius, archeveque de Strigonie, primat et regent de Hongrie, avec l'origine des guerres de ce royaume, et de celles de la Transylvanie* (Paris, 1715) summarizes the period of Hungarian history following the battle of Mohács.

THE 17TH CENTURY. The Thirty Years' War is the subject of Sándor Szilágyi's *Actes et documents pour servir a l'histoire de l'alliance de George Rakoczy, prince de Transylvanie avec le Français et les Suedois dans la guerre de trente ans* (Budapest, 1874), which include 228 letters and documents in the original Hungarian and Latin concerning issues common to the two countries.

Hieronymus Ortelius' *Ortelius dedivivus et continuatus, oder Der ungarischen Kriegs-Empörungen historische Beschreibung in Ober- und Nieder-Ungarn wie auch Siebenbürgen von dem 1395. bisz in das 1607. Jahr,* 2 v. (Frankfurt, 1665), includes illustrations of 16th-century fortifications, military personnel, and political figures.

The second half of the 17th century—one of the most complex, tragic, and devastating periods in Hungarian history—is discussed in Jean Le Clerc's *Memoirs of Emeric Count Teckely . . .* (London, 1693), two different 1693 editions of which are also available in the original French as *Histoire d'Emeric, comte de Teleki, ou mémoires pur servir à sa vie* (Cologne, 1693). During the late 1680s, one of the major objectives of Austrian imperial policy was the recapture of Buda from the Turks. The Library has two slim volumes on the military operations at Buda. The first, an anonymous work, is *A true and exact relation of the Imperial expedition in Hungaria, in the year 1684; wherein is contained an impartial and full account of the siege and defence of the city of Buda; as also, the most remarkable actions from day to day of the Elector of Bavaria* (London, 1685). A beautiful map of the Buda region is inserted in the volume. The second title on Buda, by an army engineer Jacob Richards, *A journal of the siege and taking of Buda, by the Imperial army (under the conduct of the Duke of Lorrain, and his Electoral Highness the Duke of Bavaria) anno Dom. 1686* (London, 1687) is an eye-witness account.

An anonymous work, *Present state of Hungary; or, A geographical and historical description of that Kingdom together with the memorable battles and sieges that have happened there since the Turkish invasions; to which is added, a short account of Transilvania* (London, 1687), published shortly after the capture of Buda, may be the first extensive summary in English of the period of Turkish occupation in Hungary. The Turkish occupation of Hungary is thoroughly reassessed by Albert Lefaivre in his *Les Magyars pendant la domination ottomane en Hongrie, 1526-1722*, 2 v. (Paris, 1902). In *The seat of the war in Hungary, between the Emperor and the Turks; being an historical and geographical account of the ancient Kingdom of Hungary, and provinces adjoining to it* (London, 1717), the anonymous author offers a long and detailed report on the last serious Turkish military challenge to regain territories in southern Hungary. The history of the 1716 military campaign in Hungary against the Turks is the subject of *Hungarisch- und Venetianisches Kriegstheatrum auss welchem die höchst glücklichen Feld Züge . . .* (Leipzig, 1717), a richly illustrated volume describing the military preparations and the siege of Temesvár.

Of interest to the economic historian is Zsolt Pákay's *Veszprém vármegye története a török hódoltság korában a rovásadó összeirás alapján, 1531-1696* (Veszprém, 1942), which includes detailed tax figures based on census records for each locality and village in Veszprém County during the Turkish era.

THE 18TH CENTURY.   After the expulsion of the Turks from Hungary, many attempts were made to reestablish Hungarian independence. The popular rebellion under the leadership of Francis (Ferenc) Rákóczi II, Prince of Transylvania, was the most serious challenge to Habsburg rule in Hungary. The Library has two titles on the Rákóczi rebellion: *Hungary's Fight for National Existence, or the History of the Great Uprising Led by Francis Rákóczi II. 1703-1711* (London, 1913) by Ladislaus Hengelmüller, which includes a short biography of Rákóczi, and *II. Rákóczy Ferencz emlékirata a magyar hadjáratról, 1703-1711* (Győr, 1861), originally published in French in 1739, which treats Rákóczi's aims in reasserting the constitutional rights and independent growth of Hungary.

The constitutional significance, political development, and religious life of Transylvania as part of the history of Hungary are stressed by Lavrentio Toppeltinus in *Origines et occasus Transsylvanorum; sev erutae nationes Transsylvaniae, earumque ultimi temporis revolutiones, historica narratione breviter comprehensae* (Lugduni, 1667).

The reaction of the Transylvanian Diet to the extension of Josephine reforms to Transylvania and the Diet's petitions and delegations to the Habsburg court are discussed by Ferdinand Zieglauer in *Die politische Reformbewegung in Siebenbürgen in der Zeit Joseph's II. und Leopold's II.* (Vienna, 1881). Henrik Marczali's *Hungary in the Eighteenth Century* (Cambridge, 1910) is the best available overall survey on the period.

THE 19TH CENTURY.   Materials on the political history of Hungary for the pre-1848 period offer a wealth of information on the War of Independence, including nearly 80 titles on the 1848-49 period. Selected items will be mentioned here.

Two key military men offer an appraisal of their roles in the War of Independence in *My Life and Acts in Hungary in the Years of 1848 and 1849* (N. Y., 1852), by Arthur Görgei, and *Memoirs of the War of Independence in Hungary*, 2 v. (London, 1850), by György Klapka. Comparative analyses of leading personages associated with the War of Independence are presented by Lajos Steier in his *Görgey és Kossuth* (Budapest, 1924), and *Haynau és Paskievics* (Budapest, n.d.).

Personal reflections on the period of conflict are contained in *The Letters and Journal (1848-1849) of Count Charles Leiningen-Westerburg, General in the Hungarian Army* (London, 1911). Leiningen-Westerburg was one of 13 Hungarian officers executed at Arad on October 6, 1849.

Memoirs and writings about the events of 1848-49 are contained in: *Beniczky Lajos visszaemlékezései és jelentései az 1848-49-iki szabadságharcról és a tót mozgalomról* (Budapest, 1924) by Lajos Beniczky; Terézia Pulszky's *Memoirs of a Hungarian lady* (Philadelphia, 1850); and Rudolph Bárdy's *Adventures of Rudolph Bardy de Kovatsi, a Hungarian exile in Italy, Hungary and Turkey* (Rochester, 1855).

The Russian military intervention in Hungary and its consequences are discussed by an anonymous author in *Der Feldzug in Ungarn und Siebenbürgen im Sommer des Jahres 1849* (Pest, 1850) and in *Ein Oesterreichischer Commentar zu der Russischen Darstellung des ungarischen Revolutionskrieges* (Pest, 1851).

Foreign evaluations of the events of 1848-49 in Hungary are presented in: *Scenes of the civil war in Hungary, in 1848 and 1849; with the personal adventures of an Austrian officer* (Philadelphia, 1850); *Hungary and its revolutions from the earliest period to the nineteenth century. With a memoir of Louis Kossuth* (London, 1854); Blaze de Bury, Marie P. R., *Voyage en Autriche, en Hongrie, et en Allemagne, pendant les événements de 1848 et 1849* (Paris, 1851); and Pimodan, Beorges, Marquis de, *Souvenirs du général marquis de Pimodan, 1847-1849, avec une introduction et des notes par un ancien officier,* 2 v. in 1 (Paris, 1891).

The Library has a very large number of works by and about Louis (Lajos) Kossuth, the dominant political figure of his time. The collections include the following works by Kossuth: *Kossuth in New England; a full account of the Hungarian Governor's visit to Massachusetts* (Boston, 1852); *Select speeches of Kossuth* (New York, 1854); *La question des nationalities. L'Europe, l'Autriche et la Hongrie* (Brussels, 1859); *Souvenirs et écrits de mon exil; periode de la guerre d'Italie* (Paris, 1880); *Memoirs of my exile* (New York, 1880); and *Irataim az emigráczióból,* 13 v. (Budapest, 1880-1911). Kossuth's relationship to Napoleon III, Mazzini, and Cavour during the late 1850s is discussed in Luigi Chiala's *Politica segrete di Napoleone III. e di Cavour in Italia e in Ungheria 1858-1861* (Turin, 1895), and Eugenio Kastner's *Mazzini e Kossuth, lettre e documenti inediti* (Florence, 1929).

The response to Kossuth and the impression he made during his visits to England and the United States were described by numerous contemporary authors. The following include short biographies of Kossuth and reports on his activities on behalf of Hungary during the first years of his exile: *Authentic life of His Excellency Louis Kossuth, Governor of Hungary* (London, 1851); De Puy, Henry W., *Kossuth and his generals; with a brief history of Hungary* (Buffalo, 1852); Headley, Phineas C., *The life of Louis Kossuth, Governor of Hungary* (Auburn, N.Y., 1852); and Tefft, B. F., *Hungary and Kossuth; or, an American exposition of the late Hungarian revolution* (Philadelphia, 1852).

The British diplomatic position during 1848-49 is summarized by Charles Sproxton in his *Palmerston and the Hungarian Revolution* (Cambridge, 1919).

Following the War of Independence, the constitutional relationship between the Hungarian crown and the Habsburg dynasty remained the outstanding issue through the years of Absolutism. The evolution of the Hungarian Constitution is discussed in *The Political Evolution of the Hungarian Nation,* 2 v. (London, 1908), by Cecil M. Brabourne, a historical survey of the development of the Hungarian Constitution from 1222 on. The statesman Albert Apponyi, in *A Brief Sketch of the Hungarian Constitution and of the Relations Between Austria and Hungary* (Budapest, 1908), offers a summary of the milestones of constitutional developments, the idea of representative government on the national and county level, and the constitutional relationship between Hungary and the Habsburgs and, through them, between Hungary and Austria.

The constitutional crises were resolved in the articles of the Compromise of 1867. The most extensive single work concerning this historic document and its background is Louis Eisenmann's *Le compromis austro-hongrois de 1867. Étude sur le dualisme* (Paris, 1904). The so-called sub-Compromise of 1868 between Hungary and Croatia is discussed by G. Horn in his *Le compromis de 1868 entre la Hongrie et la Croatie et celui de 1867 entre l'Autriche et la Hongrie* (Paris, 1907).

The life and political career of Francis Deák, the Hungarian jurist who was primarily responsible for framing the Compromise of 1867, are discussed by Zoltán Ferenczi in *Deák élete,* 3 v. (Budapest, 1904). Deák's speeches are available in *Deák Ferencz beszédei; 1829-1873,* 6 v. (Budapest, 1903), edited by Manó Kónyi. The first Prime Minister of the Hungarian half of the Dual Monarchy, Julius Andrássy, is the subject of Eduard Wertheimer's *Graf Julius Andrassy, sein Leben und seine Zeit nach eingedruckten Quellen,* 3 v. (Stuttgart, 1910-13).

THE 20TH CENTURY. World War I brought monumental changes in the history and development of Hungary. The Treaty of Trianon virtually created a new Hungarian state. During the 1920s Hungarian diplomats, aristocrats, social scientists, and historians wrote an unusually large body of historical-political literature in the major West European languages. By and large the majority of these writers focused on the inadequacies which Trianon imposed on Hungary. The Library has over 30 titles in English and French on the diplomacy of World War I and the Treaty itself.

The fate of Transylvania was perhaps the outstanding issue for Hungary during the interwar period. The Library has some 25 titles on a variety of topics relating to Transylvania, including the history of the three "nations" of Transylvania, the Protestant churches and sectarian groups, the ethnic minorities in Romanian Transylvania, and the consequences of Hungary's loss of Transylvania.

The question of nationalities of the former Austro-Hungarian Monarchy is considered in about 30 works available in the Library; the Slovak and Ruthenian question and the Banat and Burgenland are considered in several of these.

In addition to the works mentioned above, the Library has almost 100 titles on a variety of topics relevant to the pre-1945 period. These include international relations, economics, sociology and statistics, industry, church history, culture and the arts, as well as memoirs and collected speeches of well-known figures in Hungary today.

The Library has a wealth of materials on the post-World War II period in Hungary. Numerous titles are available in the humanities and social sciences, particularly in history, political science, folklore, the arts, and travel.

Language

The Library has two periodicals on the Hungarian language: *Magyar Nyelv,* v. 20-34, 37-38 (Budapest, 1924-42) and *Magyarosan,* v. 1-13 (Budapest, 1932-43).

The collections contain several Hungarian dictionaries published over the last 70 years, including the scholarly volumes of László Országh, *Angol-magyar szótár* (Budapest, 1960) and *Magyar-angol szótár* (Budapest, 1953). In addition the Library has the excellent *A magyar nyelv értelmező szótára,* 7 v. (Budapest, 1959-62), chief editors Géza Barczi and László Országh. Of interest to the linguist is the unique dictionary by Ferenc Sztojka, *Magyar és czigány nyelv gyök-szótára; román alava* (Kalocsa, 1886).

The only reliable history of literary Hungarian is Manó Kertész's *Szállok az úrnak; az udvarias magyar beszéd története* (Budapest, n.d.).

Almost 40 Hungarian grammars are on the Library's shelves, including the oldest edition by J. Csink, *A Complete Practical Grammar of the Hungarian Language* (London, 1853). These grammars were published over the last 120 years, primarily with the English- or German-speaking student in mind, and contain very useful data for the linguist.

Literature

The Library's Literature Department houses many fine representative titles of Hungarian literature in English, German, and French. The Department has nearly 20 titles on the history of Hungarian literature and about 30 anthologies and collections of Hungarian poetry in translation. Among these are: Bowring, J. (tr.), *Poetry of the Magyars, preceded by a sketch of the language and literature of Hungary and Transylvania* (London, 1830); Stier, G. (tr.), *Sechsunddreissig ungarische Lieder und Gedichte aus Berzsenyi, Kölcsey und Vörösmarty übers* (Halle, 1850); Loew, W. N. (tr.), *Magyar Poetry* (n.p., 1899); Vállyi, Nóra, *Magyar Poems* (London, 1911); Petőfi, Sándor, *Sixty Poems by Alexander Petőfi* (Budapest, 1948); and Kunz, Egon F., *Hungarian Poetry* (Sydney, 1955). Several other eminent Hungarian writers are represented in the Department's collections, among them János Arany, Imre Madách, and László Németh. The collection includes 23 novels by Mór Jókai and 15 of Ferenc Molnár's works.

The Hungarian Language Collection at the Carnegie West Branch of the Cleveland Public Library

The Carnegie West Branch of the Library houses a 9,500-volume collection of works in Hungarian. The collection has its own card catalog and shelflist and is located in a separate reading room. No consistent guidelines were employed in developing the collection. A substantial portion of the Hungarian books was received from individuals and Hungarian cultural organizations in various parts of the United States and abroad. The collection was established to satisfy the literary, intellectual, and day-to-day needs of first-generation Hungarian immigrants residing in the Greater Cleveland area. For several decades Cleveland has had the largest Hungarian population in the United States, and the Hungarian resources of the Carnegie West Branch represent a valuable resource for this group. The collection includes works of general interest as well as specialized and scholarly materials.

The Library has made a conscientious effort over the years to acquire grammars and readers for Hungarians to use in learning English. Numerous grammars are available, including many published 40-50 years ago and thus of interest to the linguist. Hungarians who settled in the Cleveland area during the first decades of the 20th century were primarily from agricultural backgrounds, and to help them adjust to a technological society, the Library purchased materials in Hungarian on such subjects as motor repair, machinery used in shops, factories, and agriculture, aviation, winemaking, and distillation of spirits.

Also in the collection are such diverse items as Hungarian translations of the Bible, prayer books, religious literature, histories of the United States and other countries, illustrated guidebooks on Hungary, cookbooks, and works on political science, philosophy, mathematics, and geography. As much as 25 percent of the Hungarian material consists of translations from other languages. These include works by major world authors. The reference collection at the Carnegie West Library contains some 250 encyclopedias, atlases, dictionaries, collections of biographies, multi-volume sets of Hungarian histories, works on political science, sermons and essays, and collected works.

The largest category in the Carnegie West collection comprises some 6,200 volumes in the field of Hungarian literature. Many of the titles in this category have been acquired in several editions and in multiple copies to meet reader demand. Some 220 Hungarian authors are represented, and 3,700 different titles are available. The collection includes most if not all of the works of the leading 19th- and 20th-century Hungarian novelists, short-story writers, poets, and dramatists. The collection also contains works by less well-known writers, literary criticism, anthologies and collected works, and more than 40 volumes of anecdotes and fairy tales.

Poland

THE LIBRARY BEGAN collecting titles in the Polish language early in the 20th century, the first identifiable accession date being January 1906. From that period on the Library added titles in Polish on a regular basis. By 1912, the Library's catalog of Polish books comprised 77 pages.

At present the Foreign Literature Department holds 8,500 volumes of Polish books, with an annual increment of 240-300 volumes. The Main Library subject departments house an additional 2,000 volumes, almost all being in the reference classification. It is estimated that there are about 11,000 volumes of Polish-language books in the Cleveland Public Library system.

The truly valuable research materials on Poland are in the reference collections of the Main Library subject departments. The forthcoming discussion, therefore, will focus on the more important features of those collections, on the unusual and significant titles which may be of particular interest to the scholarly community.

Reference

The most significant Polish bibliography in the collection is that of Karol J. T. Estreicher, *Bibliografia Polska,* v. 1- (Kraków, 1872-), which covers the period 1455 to 1900, and lists publications about Poland published either in or outside the country. *Bibliografia historyi polskiej,* 3 v. (Kraków, 1906) by Ludwik Finkel records titles in the field of history to 1815. Leon N. M. Kryczyński's *Bibliografia do historji tatarów polskich* (Zamość, 1935) is comprehensive, with emphasis on Polish-Tartar relations from the 14th through the 19th century, but includes selected 20th-century publications.

The Library's Polish materials have representative coverage in Robert J. Kerner's *Slavic Europe; a Selected Bibliography in the Western European Languages, Comprising History, Languages and Literatures* (Cambridge, Mass., 1918) and Paul L. Horecky (ed.), *East Central Europe; a Guide to Basic Publications* (Chicago, 1969).

Periodicals

The Library has only a few periodicals in Polish: of special interest are *Przegląd Historyczny,* 15 v. (Warsaw, 1917-39) and *Rocznik Tatarski; Czasopismo naukowe, literackie i społeczne, poświęcone historij, kulturze i życiu tatarów w Polsce,* 3 v. (Wilno, 1932-38).

Sources

Source materials are found in three titles. The Library has in reprint form *Monumenta medii aevi historica res gestas poloniae illustrantia,* 18 v. in 15, facsimile (Kraków, 1874-1908). *Polska w kronikach tureckich xv i xvi w.,* by Eugeniusz Zawaliński, treats Tartar-Polish relations from the earliest mention of Poland in Turkish sources. Karol Lutostanski's *Les partages de la Pologne et la lutte pour l'independance* (Lusanne-Paris, 1918) contains 369 documents, treaties, and diplomatic acts relating to Polish history from 1756 to 1864.

Encyclopedias and Dictionaries

Recently the Library acquired the *Wielka encycklopedia powszechna PWN,* 13 v. (Warsaw, 1962-70). The large dictionary collection of the Library includes two up-to-date and comprehensive ones, *The Kosciuszko Foundation Dictionary; English-Polish, Polish-English,* 2 v. (New York, 1960-62) and the two-volume set edited by Jan Stanisławski, *The Great English-Polish Dictionary* (Warsaw, 1968) and *The Great Polish-English Dictionary* (Warsaw, 1969).

Description and Travel, Journals, and Handbooks

The Library's collections contain a number of very valuable travel journals on East Central Europe, including Poland. In *Änderte Beschreibung desz königreichs Polen und groszhertzogthums Litauen,* bound together and published with *Anzeigungen der vornehmsten Kriegs-handel* (Ulm, 1657), Martin Zeiller (1589-1661), who traveled extensively as a tutor of wealthy families, narrates the history of the Polish and Lithuanian lands in the first half of the 16th century. Zeiller's essay is particularly interesting for its emphasis on the alternative geographic place-names resulting from the different ethnic and linguistic influences in these areas. Seventeenth-century Polish life is described by Edward Brown in *A discourse of the original, countrey, manners, government and religion of Cossaks, with another of the Precopian Tartars. And the history of the wars of the Cossaks against Poland* (London, 1672). Another late 17th-century title of value is Gaspard Tende's *An account of Poland. Containing a geographical description of the country, the manners of the inhabitants, and the wars they have been engaged in; the constitution of that government; particularly the manner of electing and crowning their king; his power and prerogatives; with a brief history of the Tartars* (London, 1698). The Library possesses two editions of the travel journals of William Coxe, his *Travels into Poland, Russia, Sweden, and Denmark,* 3 v. (Dublin, 1784) and the five-volume 1802 edition. Conrad Malte-Brun's *Tableau de la Pologne, ancienne et moderne* (Paris, 1807) is a well-balanced overall introduction to early 19th-century Poland, its geography, frontiers, population, and culture. The social life and customs of Poles are treated by Robert Johnston in *Travels through part of the Russian empire and the country of Poland along the southern shores of the Baltic* (London, 1815). Volume two of the travel journal of J. Stephens, *Incidents of travel in Greece, Turkey, Russia and Poland,* 2 v. (N. Y., 1838) reports on the author's tour through Poland.

The Library has two editions of one of the earliest travel guidebooks published in English for the traveler and tourist in Eastern Europe, the *Handbook for Travellers in Russia, Poland, and Finland* (London, 1868). The same title went through several editions, the 1893 edition being the fifth, with the added subtitle: *Handbook for Travellers in Russia, Poland and Finland; including the Crimea, Caucasus, Siberia and Central Asia,* and with the text expanded and updated, including a section on Polish history.

Anthropology and Ethnography

Among the source materials the Library has one title on anthropology: Akademija Umiejętności, *Zbiór wiadomości do antropologii krajowej,* 18 v. (Kraków, 1877-95). The subject coverage includes anthropology, archeology, and ethnography.

The collection includes one periodical on ethnography, *Wisła, Miesięcznik Geograficzno-Etnograficzny* (Warsaw, 1887-94; the Library has v. 1-8). The monograph, *Lud nadrabski od*

Gdowa po Bochnie (Kraków, 1893) by Jan Świętek, a native of the region, contains a description of the customs, legends, and songs of the Raba river region. The festival customs, songs, and other characteristics of the local people are recorded in the work of Adolf Pleszczyński, *Bojarzy międzyrzeccy* (Warsaw, 1892).

The Polish composer and ethnographer Oskar Kolberg (1815-90) collected and published the findings of his numerous field trips to the Polish countryside. Of these publications the Library has six titles:

Chełmskie; obraz etnograficzny, 2 v. in 1 (Kraków, 1890);

Lud, jego zwyczaje, sposób życia, mowa, podania, przysłowia, obrzędy, gusła, zabawy, pieśni, muzyka i tance, 23 v. in 12 (Warsaw, 1857-90);

Mazowsze; obraz etnograficzny, 5 v. in 2 (Kraków, 1885-90);

Pokucie; obraz etnograficzny, 4 v. in 2 (Kraków, 1882-89);

Przemyskie; zarys etnograficzny (Kraków, 1891);

Wołyn; obrzędy, melodye, pieśni (Kraków, 1907).

These volumes contain descriptions of villages, the region, festivals, social life, and customs of the common people and include proverbs and folk songs.

History

The Library's collections contain a significant body of research material on Polish history: a few representative but choice titles are cited here. R. Roepell's *Geschichte Polens;* 850-1506, 5 v. (Hamburg, 1840-88); Stanisław Kutrzeba's *Historja ustroju Polski w zarysie,* 4 v. (Kraków, 1931), which presents a general outline of the history of the Polish crown from the earliest times to the 20th century, and to which a history of Lithuania is appended. Luther Saxton's *Fall of Poland,* 2 v. (New York, 1851), written immediately after the First Partition of Poland by a contemporary author, treats Polish history from the earliest times to 1772. The works of James Fletcher, *The History of Poland; from the Earliest Period to the Present Time* (New York, 1842) and Charles M. Forster, *Pologne* (Paris, 1840) are less detailed. The second half of volume two of John William's *The rise, progress, and present state of the Northern Government; viz., the United Provinces, Denmark, Sweden, Russia, and Poland,* 2 v. (London, 1777) focuses on Polish political developments. The author made keen observations about contemporary Poland, politics, and the life of the nobility. Polish culture and civilization are discussed by William R. Morfill in *Poland* (N. Y., 1900) and by Nevin Winter in *Poland of Today and Yesterday* (Boston, 1913).

MIDDLE AGES.   The earliest publication on Poland in the Cleveland Public Library is *Respublica, sine status regni Poloniae, Litvaniae, Prussiae, Livoniae,* Lugd: batavorum, ex officina Elzeviriana (1642), which includes a description of the Kingdom of Poland, Wallachia, the region and early history of Lithuania, the invasion of the Teutonic Knights, and the development of Livonia. Two other notable titles on the Middle Ages are Max Perlbach's *Preussisch-polnische Studien zur Geschichte des Mittelalters,* 2 v. in 1 (Halle, 1886), which includes the critique of a 13th-century Polish text, and Heinrich Zeissberg's *Die polonische Geschichtschriebung des Mittelalters* (Leipzig, 1873).

THE 16TH CENTURY.   In *Geschichte der Reformation in Polen* (Leipzig, 1911), Theodor Wotschke concentrates on the influence of the Protestant Reformation in Poland during the second half of the 16th century, examining the Lutheran and Calvinist wings of the Reformation and, briefly, sectarian movements in Poland. The life, work, and influence of Protestant Pastor Piotr Skarga (1536-1612) are evaluated by A. Berga in *Un Predicator de la cour de Pologne sous Sigismond III; Pierre Skarga (1536-1612)* (Paris, 1916), a scholarly study of political life and religious developments in Poland during the reign of Sigismund III. A short but interpretative essay on Sigismund III and his confrontation with the Polish nobility in 1592 is presented by Felix Wężyk in his *Der Conflict des Königs Sigismund III. Wasa mit den Polnischen Standen und der Inquisitionsreichstag vom 7. September 1592* (Leipzig, 1869).

THE 17TH CENTURY.   The wealth and depth of the collections of the Cleveland Public Library are reflected in the number of rare books on 17th- and 18th-century Poland. Polish history during the 17th century is surveyed by Ludwik P. Leliwa, *Jan Sobieski i jego wiek,* 4 v. (Kraków, 1882-83; the Library has v. 1-2). Emile Haumant in his *La guerre du Nord et la paix d'Oliva, 1655-1660* (Paris, 1893) considers the period of Polish history from the invasion of Poland by Charles X of Sweden in 1655 until his death in 1660; the Treaty of Oliva and the Austrian-Polish alliance is dealt with. The relations of Poland and France are surveyed by Kazimierz Waliszewski, *Polsko-francuzkie stosunki w xvii. wieku, 1644-1667* (Kraków, 1889). The only work in Spanish on Polish history in the Library is a collection of letters written by Pedro D. Ronquillo, *Mision secreta del embajador D. Pedro Ronquillo en Polonia 1674* (Madrid, Recreo, n.d.). The letters in this volume were written in 1674 by a Spanish ambassador to Poland to his colleague Pablo Spinola Doria, ambassador at the Austrian court, discussing his secret and unsuccessful mission to promote the candidacy of Charles of Lorraine as king of Poland.

John III Sobieski, king of Poland, and his reign is the subject of a number of the Library's important books. The policies and role of Sobieski in European diplomatic history, and more closely the relation of Poland to France, Turkey, Austria, and Hungary prior to 1683, are considered by J. Du Hamel de Breuil, *Sobieski et sa politique de 1674 à 1683* (Paris, 1894). With marked emphasis on French-Polish relations, S. Rubinstein in his *Les relations entre la France et la Pologne de 1680 à 1683* (Paris, 1913) concentrates on the question how and why hostilities grew between Sobieski and Louis XIV, ultimately leading to a complete break with the French and the conclusion of the Polish-Austrian alliance.

In addition to a long treatise on the life and political role of Sobieski, emphasizing the period from 1683 to 1696, a unique alphabetical listing of contemporary *dramatis personae* is added in the third volume (pp. 321-391) of Gabriel Coyer, *Histoire de Jean Sobieski Varsovie, roi de Pologne,* 3 v. (Warsaw, 1761). The life of Sobieski is described in another long account, N. A. Salvandy's *Histoire de roi Jean Sobieski et du royaume de Pologne,* 2 v. (Paris, 1855). Michel D. La Bizardiere in his *Histoire de la scission ou division arrivée en Pologne le XXVII.* (Paris, 1700) concentrates on the political and constitutional developments of Poland in 1696-97. The reign of the next elected king, Augustus II of Saxony, is treated by Jean Baptiste Desroches de Parthenay in *The history of Poland under Augustus II* (London, 1734).

THE 18TH CENTURY.   Nicholas Baudeau, in his *Lettres historiques sur l'état actuel de la Pologne et sur l'origine de ses malheurs* (Amsterdam, 1772), analyzes the relationship between Poland and Russia from 1500-1768. Nisbet R. Bain also concentrates on the history of Poland and Russia in his compendium *Slavonic Europe; a Political History of Poland and Russia from 1447 to 1796* (Cambridge, 1908). This analytical survey of the two countries covers a crucial period of history from the middle of the 15th to the end of the 18th century. A highly informative and readable history of Poland, published in the year of the Third Partition of Poland, is that of Stephen Jones, *The history of Poland from its origin as a nation to the commencement of the year 1795; to which is prefixed an accurate account of the geography and government of that country and the customs and manners of its inhabitants* (London, 1795). The reader will find a detailed discussion of international and domestic, but mostly constitutional developments in Valerjan Kalinka's *Der vierjährige polnische Reichstag, 1788 bis 1791* 2 v. (Berlin, 1896-98). Pierre Boye's monograph *Un roi de Pologne et la couronne ducale de Lorraine. Stanislas Leszczynski, et le troisième traité de Vienne* (Nancy, 1898) is a diplomatic history within the framework of a biography. Through the life of Stanisław I Leszczyński, who was twice the king of Poland, Boye exposes the rivalry and the international negotiations concerning the future of the Polish throne. The life of Stanisław I Leszczyński and his daughter is narrated in Charlotte Reaulx's work *Le roi Stanislas et Marie Leczinska* (Paris, 1895). The hegemony of candidates and the involvement of foreign powers concerning the Polish throne during 1733 is presented by a contemporary author P. Massuet in his *Histoire de la guerre présente,* (Amsterdam, 1735).

In his extensive work *Histoire de l'anarchie de Pologne, et du démembrement de cette république,* 4 v. (Paris, 1807), Claude C. Rulhière, man of letters and member of the French Academy, narrates the history of Poland during the early 18th century, focusing on the First Partition of the country. A compilation of valuable essays, letters, and documents on the First Partition is to be found in John Lind's *Letters concerning the present state of Poland. Together with the manifesto of the courts of Vienna, Petersburgh, and Berlin, and letters patent of the King of Prussia* (London, 1773). The internal struggle in Poland, the Russian intervention, and other contributing factors to the 1772 Partition are considered in Simon Askenazy's *Die letzte polonische Königswahl* (Göttingen, 1894).

Johannes Janssen in *Zur Genesis der ersten Theilung Polens* (Freiburg im Breisgau, 1865) treats Polish political developments from 1656 to 1775, with an emphasis on the events surrounding 1772. British historian George Eversley in *The Partitions of Poland* (New York, 1915) compares the four partitions of Poland from 1772-1815. Polish diplomat Michel K. Ogiński in his *Mémoires de Michel Oginski sur la Pologne et les polonais depuis 1788 jusqu'à la fin de 1815,* 4 v. (Paris, 1826-27), writes of his part in Polish foreign relations from 1790 and of the Napoleonic campaign in Russia during 1812. In her *Mémoires d'une polonaise pour servir a l'histoire de la Pologne, depuis 1764 jusqu' à 1830,* 2 v (Paris, 1841) Françoise Trębicka recalls the manners, social behavior, and life in Poland interwoven with stories and anecdotes about outstanding contemporaries whom she had known.

THE 19TH CENTURY.   The Austrian invasion of Poland in 1809 and the life of Poniatowski is considered by Roman Sołtyk in *Relations des operations de l'armée aux orders du Prince Joseph Poniatowski pendant la campagne de 1809 en Pologne contre les autrichiens* (Paris, 1841). The Polish support given to Napoleon during the Italian campaign is interpreted by Leonard Chodźko in *Histoire des légions polonaises en Italie, sous le commandement du général Dombrowski,* 2 v. (Paris, 1829). The role of Jerome Napoleon in the formation of the Duchy of Warsaw and Polish participation in Napoleon's Russian campaign during 1812 are examined in Abel Mansuy's *Jerome Napoléon et la Pologne en 1812* (Paris, 1930).

G. Sommerlatt's *Beschreibung des polnisch-russischen Krieges, 1830-1831* (Freiburg, 1823) gives a political and military account of the 1830-31 Polish Revolution and its aftermath, with reference to the posture of European powers during the conflict. Hunter Gordon offers an evaluation of 50 years of Polish constitutional developments and the different phases in the relationship of partitioned Poland to Russia in his *Considerations on the war in Poland, and on the neutrality of the European powers of the present crisis* (London, 1831). Two hundred thirty-seven letters and documents written by Lafayette on behalf of Poland between 1829 and 1834 were published by Marie Joseph Lafayette in *Le Général La Fayette et la cause polonaise* (Warsaw, 1934). Joseph Hordyński in *History of the late Polish revolution and the events of the campaign* (Boston, 1833) offers a political and military history on the Polish Revolution of 1830.

Two of the Library's holdings on the Polish Revolution of 1863 should be singled out: Stanisław Koźmian's *Das Jahr 1863; Polen und die europäische Diplomatie* (Vienna, 1896), which reviews the European scene in 1863, the international and revolutionary developments with a long discourse on the 1863 events in Poland, and Arthur P. Coleman's *The Polish Insurrection of 1863 in the Light of New York Editorial Opinion* (Williamsport, Pa., 1934).

THE 20TH CENTURY. Two of the most important problems facing the new Polish state established by the Treaty of Versailles were the drastic alteration of the borders of historic Poland, including the loss of direct access to the sea, and the high percentage of non-Polish minorities within the new state. Of the large number of monographs in the Library's collection which deal with these two important issues, we cite several representative titles.

Carl Budding in *Der polnische Korridor als europäisches Problem* (Danzig, 1932) examines the creation of the Polish Corridor and the complications and problems it created during the first decade of its existence. Henryk Bagiński, in *Poland and the Baltic; the Problem of Poland's Access to the Sea* (Edinburgh, 1942) writes in the geopolitical tradition, emphasizing Poland's vital need of direct access to the Baltic Sea.

Arthur Goodhart, appointed by President Wilson as counsel to the American Commission to Poland, which was charged with investigating the conditions of Jews, relates the Commission's findings in *Poland and the Minority Races* (N. Y., 1920). The rights, life, and economic conditions of the minorities in Poland after 1919 are discussed in a work edited by S. J. Paprocki, *Minority Affairs and Poland* (Warsaw, 1935). The civil rights, political life, economic condition, cultural and social organizations of another minority, the Ukrainians, are considered by M. Feliński in his *Ukraincy w Polsce odrodzonej* (Warsaw, 1931).

A well-rounded survey of the first decade of post-World War I Poland is presented by Marjan Dąbrowski in *Dziesięciolecie Polski odrodzonej 1918-1928* (Kraków, 1928).

Robert Machrey offers a historical analysis of western Poland and examines the condition of Poles after the German occupation of the area during 1939 in his *The Polish-German Problem* (London, 1941). Written from the German point of view is Hans Schadewaldt's *The Polish Atrocities Against the German Minority in Poland* (Berlin, 1940). The suffering of Jews in Poland and their armed resistance against the Germans during World War II is presented in a slim but serious work by Jacob Apenszlak and Moshe Polakiewicz, *Armed Resistance of the Jews in Poland* (N. Y., 1944).

Miscellaneous Works

In the research collections of the Library there are over 300 titles about Poland on a variety of subjects. A few sample titles will indicate the diversity of the subjects and the languages in which these miscellaneous works are published. Among these works is a Polish translation of the Koran by Władysław Kościuszko, 2 v. (Warsaw, 1858), including a biography of the prophet Mohammed, an introduction to Moslem religious holidays and customs, and a chronology of Polish-Turkish contacts from 1397 to 1790. George L. Watson's *A Polish Exile with Napoleon* (Boston, 1912) is a biography of Polish Captain Frederick J. Piontkowski (1786-1849), who accompanied Napoleon to his exile on St. Helena.

The recollections of Józef Piłsudski are contained in his *Joseph Pilsudski; the Memories of a Polish Revolutionary and Soldier* (London, 1931), which includes nearly everything Piłsudski had written about his personal experiences prior to 1923. A selection from the 10-volume set of Piłsudski's work is *Du Revolutionnaire au chef d'état 1893-1935* (Paris, 1935). The collection includes *Letters of Joseph Conrad to M. Poradowska, 1890-1920* (New Haven, 1940), edited by John A. Gee and Paul J. Sturm, and *The Paderewski Memoirs* (New York, 1938), by Ignace J. Paderewski and Mary Lawton.

The Library has over 100 titles in English and about 40 in other languages on Polish literature. Among these are translations of Polish poetry, drama, short stories, the history of Polish literature, and general surveys on Polish civilization and culture. The earliest publication is by Daniel Defoe, *The dyet of Poland, a satyr* (Danzig, 1705). Another item is John Bowring (ed.),

Specimens of the Polish poets; with notes and observations on the literature of Poland (London, 1827). The following three works on the art of Poland are worth noting: Aronson, Chil. *Art polonais moderne* (Paris, 1929); Holewinski, Jan. *Sketch of the History of Polish Art* (1916), and Kuhn, Alfred R. *Die polonische Kunst von 1800 bis zur Gegenwart* (Berlin, 1930).

POLISH LANGUAGE COLLECTION IN THE FOREIGN LITERATURE DEPARTMENT. The entire 8,500 volume collection housed in the Foreign Literature Department is written in Polish; the collection has its own card catalog and is shelved separately in the Department. The collection has been built over the past 50 years, primarily with the recently arrived and the established first generation Polish immigrant in mind. The reading interest of second and third generation Poles has influenced acquisitions only in recent years; thus the collection is aimed first and foremost at the general reader.

The material may be divided into five distinct categories:

(1) English grammars and textbooks have been acquired by the Library through the years to meet the Polish immigrant's need to learn English well in order to function and get ahead in his new country. Polish grammars for the English-speaking student have been purchased regularly since World War II.

(2) To aid the recently arrived Polish immigrant in adjusting to a more advanced and technological society a number of "instructional books" have also been acquired in Polish: These inform the reader how to repair his own appliances, his car, or other everyday items in the household. Other books teach him basic mathematics, including conversion tables, and offer practical aid with respect to employment or daily living.

(3) This category, "mixed subjects," includes Polish translations of the Bible, books on religious literature, philosophy, economics, popular history, short introductions to United States history and government, popular science, illustrated travel guidebooks on Poland, and cookbooks.

(4) About 15 to 20 percent of the Polish language collections consists of translations from other languages, being on the whole the world's best literature—Mann, Twain, Pushkin, Steinberg, Tolstoy, Voltaire, and many others.

(5) The last and by far the largest number of books in the collection (about 6,000 volumes or 70 percent of the total) comprises Polish literature, representing about 200 authors and 3,500 titles (some in several copies and different editions).

From the 16th century on, every period and literary school is represented by the works of several authors and titles written about them. From the period of Humanism and Reformation, the Library has nine titles by or about Jan Kochanowski, 10 titles by or about Mikołaj Rej, and six titles by or about Piotr Skarga.

The Baroque era is represented by works by or about Jan A. Morsztyn and the works of Jan C. Pasek. Selected works, poems, and satires by Ignacy Krasicki, Adam Naruszewicz, Jan Potocki, and others from the period of the Enlightenment are also available.

The collection is rich in works of the school of Romanticism: among others there are eight titles by Alexander Fredro, almost 50 by Józef I. Kraszewski, a representative number by Adam Mickiewicz, and some of the literary and political writings of Cyprian Norwid.

The writers of Positivism from the second half of the 19th century are represented by a large number of volumes (hereafter the number of volumes available for an author is given in parentheses after the author's name). Among them one can find the names of Adolf Dygasiński (10), Maria Konopnicka (18), Eliza Orzeszkowa (30), Bolesław Prus (20), and Henryk Sienkiewicz (11).

The following "Young Poland" authors are represented in the collection: Władysław Reymont (13), Leopold Staff (9), Kazimierz P. Tetmajer (13), Stanisław Wyspiański (11), Gabriela Zapolska (20), and Stefan Żeromski (26).

The writings of more than 15 authors from the interwar or Independent Poland period are part of the collection, among them: Maria Dąbrowska (9), Konstanty I. Galczyński (8); Jarosław Iwaszkiewicz (30), Maria Rodziewiczówna (33), and Julian Tuwim (8).

The post-World War II era is very scantily represented, with 12 titles each of Kazimierz Brandys and Stanisław Lem.

The authors and titles listed above constitute but a small portion of the Polish literature collection.

PAMPHLETS AND PAPERS.   The Cleveland Public Library does not maintain an archival collection in the East European field, rather it is primarily concerned with published works. However, it does have certain files which contain valuable materials.

The History Department maintains two well-organized files of rare political pamphlets pertaining to 20th-century Europe. The files are divided into two basic categories: (a) World War I, and (b) World War II, and within each the pamphlets are arranged by country. The subjects of these political pamphlets range from foreign relations, boundary disputes, the question of national minorities, to the problem of Galicia and the Ukraine. The papers were published in the United States or in Europe. Most of the pamphlets are highly opinionated, polemical, and offer practically no documentation.

(a) In the World War I file there are 30 pamphlets relating to Polish affairs. Most of the pamphlets were published during the interwar period.

(b) The Polish collection on World War II is very rich indeed, with 164 pamphlets arranged under 21 main topics. These pamphlets were published during the 1940s and 1950s.

The History Department offers yet another important source on Poland, namely 33 underground newspapers from the 1940-46 period. The number of available issues, the places of publication, origins, and subject matter of these papers vary, but all are in Polish.

Laszlo L. Kovacs
Purdue University,
formerly of
Cleveland Public Library

Columbia University

General Information

COLUMBIA UNIVERSITY LIBRARIES consist of 35 units, the focal point of which is Butler Library (hours: Monday through Thursday, 8:30 a.m. to 11 p.m.; Friday, 8:30 a.m. to 10 p.m.; Saturday, 10 a.m. to 6 p.m.; Sunday 2 p.m. to 10 p.m.). The materials dispersed in the various libraries can be located centrally through Butler Library's General Catalog, which is divided into an author and title catalog, a topical subject catalog, and a serials catalog.

The Reference Department on the same premises provides various services: assistance in locating material, consultation service for graduate students, and interlibrary loan.

The service hours of other libraries which have East Central and Southeastern European holdings are:

Avery Library: Monday through Thursday, 9 a.m. to 9 p.m.; Friday, 9 a.m. to 5 p.m.; Saturday, 1 p.m. to 6 p.m.;

Fine Arts Library, Schermerhorn Building: Monday through Thursday, 9 a.m. to 11 p.m.; Friday, 9 a.m. to 10 p.m.; Saturday, 10 a.m. to 6 p.m.; Sunday 2 p.m. to 10 p.m.;

Lehman Library, School of International Affairs Building: Monday through Friday, 9 a.m. to 9 p.m.; Saturday, 10 a.m. to 6 p.m.;

Law School Library: Monday through Friday, 8:30 a.m. to 12 midnight; Saturday, 9 a.m. to 7 p.m.; Sunday, 12 noon to 12 midnight;

Library of Business and Economics, Uris Building: Monday through Friday, 8:30 a.m. to 11 p.m.; Saturday, 10 a.m. to 6 p.m.; Sunday, 2 p.m. to 10 p.m.;

Microform Reading Room: Monday through Thursday, 9 a.m. to 9 p.m.; Friday, 9 a.m. to 5 p.m.; Saturday, 10 a.m. to 6 p.m.;

Music Library, Dodge Building: Monday through Thursday, 9 a.m. to 9 p.m.; Friday, 9 a.m. to 5 p.m.; Saturday, 10 a.m. to 6 p.m.;

Oral History Collection, Rare Book and Manuscript Library: Monday through Friday, 9 a.m. to 5 p.m.;

Special Collections Division: Monday through Friday, 9 a.m. to 5 p.m.; Saturday, 10 a.m. to 6 p.m.

Copying services of various types are available: quick copies, including coin-operated copying machines, and reader-printers for making copies of microforms. The Photographic Services Department in Butler Library (Room 110) can be contacted for more extensive copying orders.

Butler Library collects all materials in the humanities and the social sciences to the end of World War II. The Lehman Library collects materials on general international relations, international organizations; diplomacy; war, peace, and disarmament; foreign relations; and political, economic, social, historical, military, anthropological, and geographic events and developments within the post-World War II period. The Lehman Library also collects materials on the communist movement, beginning with 1917. Butler Library collects theoretical works on communism.

There is no special reading room for Slavic materials, but each library in the Columbia system provides reading facilities for the user. All current issues of newspapers from Eastern Europe are arranged alphabetically on shelves outside the Slavic and East European Acquisitions Section in the Lehman Library. Older issues are in nearby stacks. Major reference works are located in the main reference collection in Butler Library. The Lehman Library also has selected reference works.

The microform library on the fifth floor of Butler Library (Room 501) includes an uncataloged Slavic and East Central European microfilm collection (including 18th-century material). Inquiries about this collection should be made at the circulation desk of the International Affairs Library.

Persons not connected with Columbia University who wish to consult the Library collections must apply at the Library Information Office, Butler Library (Room 234), for a temporary reading permit.

Staff
Columbia University Libraries

Columbia University Publications Pertaining to Collections Described

Annual report: Hungarian-Finnish Acquisitions, 1968-1969 and 1969-1970.
Annual report on Russian, East Central European and Finno-Ugrian Acquisitions for the fiscal years 1958-1959 and 1959-1960.
Columbia University. Libraries. *Handbook.* 1969.
Columbia University. Institute on East Central Europe. *Newsletter,* no. 3, Fall, 1971.
Columbia University. Oral History Research Office. *Report.* 1969/70-1970/71.
Lotz, John. *Report on Uralic and Altaic Studies. 1958.* 34 p.
Papp, Alouis. *A Survey of the Growth of the Hungarian Collection at Columbia University Libraries.* 1969. 15 p.
Rare Books and Manuscripts at Columbia: Their Facilities and Use. New York: Columbia Library Columns, 1968.
Tezla, Albert. Memorandum to John Lotz, Director of the Uralic Center. 1966.

Albania

EVEN BEFORE WORLD WAR I, Columbia Library had acquired certain scholarly publications in Western European languages concerning Albania. Holdings in the Albanian language were added in the interwar period, particularly in the 1930s (a course in Albanian was introduced in 1932). In the postwar era, Albanian acquisitions at Columbia have increased significantly, but works from Albania proper have been rare.

Humanities

As an ancient land and a crossroad of civilizations, Albania has been of particular interest to European archeologists. C. Patsch's *Das Sandschak von Berat in Albanien* (Vienna, 1904) and C. Praschniker's *Archäologische Forschungen in Albanien und Montenegro* (Vienna, 1919) are among the early holdings of Columbia. Between the two wars, Italian and French missions carried out excavations in southern Albania, the first in Butrinto (Lat. Butrintum), opposite Corfu, and the second in Pojan (ancient Apollonia), not far from Berat. Columbia possesses L. M. Ugolini's *Albania Antica* (Rome, 1927) and *L'antica Albania nelle ricerche archeologiche italiane* (Rome, 1928), but the French archeological mission is represented only by one issue of *Albania* (Paris, 1939), containing studies of archeology, history, and art in Albania and the Balkans. The Albanian archeologists of today, in order to assert more emphatically the antiquity and Illyrianism of their people, have devoted their studies and excavations principally to Illyrian civilization. Their works, in Albanian but generally with a summary in French, are lacking in the Columbia Library.

The studies on the Albanian language are often dispersed in various scholarly works, yet Columbia is rather strong in individual linguistic studies. There is the work by the father of Albanology, J. G. Hahn, *Albanesische Studien* (Vienna, 1853), and the short studies on loan words by F. Miklošič. Various studies by reputed philologists of Romanian who later analyzed Albanian because of similarities between the two languages are represented: G. Weigand's Albanian grammar and dictionary; M. Roques' researches on ancient Albanian texts; and C. Tagliavini's study of the dialect of Borgo Erizzo, near Zadar in Yugoslavia. In the postwar period, two significant contributions to Albanian dialectology have been added: W. Cimochowski, *Le dialecte de Dushmani, description de l'un des parlers de l'Albanie du Nord* (Poznań, 1951); and *Albanski jazyk i ego dialekty* (Leningrad, 1968), by A. V. Desnitskaia, a linguist at Leningrad University. Of the works of the foremost Albanologist, N. Jokl of Vienna, Columbia possesses only one work, *Studien zur Albanischen Etymologie und Wortbildung* (Vienna, 1911). This study was recently supplemented through the acquisition of M. Camaj's *Albanische Wortbildung* (Wiesbaden, 1966).

Albanian written literature, of which the beginnings were ecclesiastic, is not rich. The majority of the Albanians being Moslems, the Turks had banned written Albanian. Although the earliest records date from the 15th century, the first work in Albanian is the *Missal* (1555) by Gjon Buzuku, of which Columbia has a reproduction and a transcription (Città di Vaticano, 1958) made by N. Resuli. This should be accompanied by the recent two-part critical study by E. Çabej, published under the auspices of the University of Tirana (Tirana, 1968). Secular literature, on the other hand, emerged at the time of the national revival following the Congress of Berlin (1878). There is a disparity in the holdings of Columbia. First, there are no complete works of any author. N. Frashëri, the great lyric poet, is represented by minor works and not by the beautiful collection of poems *Lulet e verësë* [Summer Flowers] (1958), and Gj. Fishta's masterpiece and national epic *Lahuta e Malcis* [The Lute of the Mountains], 2d ed. (Rome, 1958) is available only in a German translation, *Die Laute des Hochlandes*. Übersetzt, eingeleitet und mit Anmerkungen versehen von M. Lambertz (Munich, 1958). The same could be said about the other few writers of the revival. It seems no sound criterion was used for the selection, for significant authors are not represented. Whereas the works of the revival and after are mainly poetry, those of the postwar period are, for the most part, novels and short stories. Of the latter, those housed at Columbia have not come directly from Albania but rather by way of the University of Priština, in Yugoslavia. Founded as a branch of Belgrade University, Priština University has become since 1970 a full-fledged Albanian university, reprinting literary and linguistic works published in Tirana. As a sample of the literary prose of today's Albania, Columbia possesses a collection of *Albanian Contemporary Prose* (Tirana, 1963), translated into English, in which "social realism" predominates, and an interesting novel by I. Kadare translated into French as *Le général de l'armée morte* (Paris, 1970; preface de Robert Escarpit).

The written literature of the Italo-Albanians, the Albanians who settled in Southern Italy and Sicily after the fall of their country to the Turks, is also meager at Columbia. Stronger are the acquisitions of their oral literature. One can find M. Marchianò, *Canti popolari Albanesi delle colonie d'Italia* (Foggia, 1908), based on a 1737 manuscript, and D. Camarda, *Appendice al saggio di grammatologia comparata della lingua Albanese* (Prato, 1866), a collection of various folksongs from Albania proper and, primarily, from the Albanian settlements in Italy. However, A. Scura, *Gli Albanesi in Italia e i loro canti tradizionali* (New York, 1912) is missing. M. Lambertz's *Albanesische Märchen (und andere Texte zur albanischen Volkskunde)* (Vienna, 1922) serves as a link between the Italo-Albanian and Albanian folk literatures. From the collections of Albania proper, Columbia houses the three volumes published by the Folklore Institute of Tirana under the title *Mbledhës të hershëm të folklorit shqiptar, 1633-1912* [Old Collectors of Albanian Folklore, 1633-1912] (Tirana, 1961), but lacks two fundamental collections: V. Prennushi, *Kângë popullore gegënishte* [Popular Gheg Songs] (Sarajevo, 1911), and the four volumes of *Visaret e Kombit* [The Treasures of the Nation] (Tirana, 1937/1939).

Among the histories of literature, one can find at Columbia A. Straticò, *Manuale di lettera-tura Albanese* (Milano, 1896) and the two volumes *Histori e leterisë shqipe* [History of Albanian literature] (Priština, 1971), published by the University of Tirana. In the field of the history of language, there is H. Barić, *Istorija Arbanaškog jezika* (Sarajevo, 1959) and, especially, E. Çabej, *Hyrje në historinë e gjuhës shqipe; fonetika historike e shqipes* [Introduction to the History of the Albanian Language; the Historical Phonetics of Albanian] (Priština, 1970).

The holdings of dictionaries are quite strong. There are the three fundamental dictionaries: G. Meyer, *Etymologisches Wörterbuch der albanischen Sprache* (Strassburg, 1891); *Lexikon tēs albanikēs glōsses* [Dictionary of the Albanian Language] (Athens, 1904), by K. Christophorides, the foremost expert of the Albanian language, written in Greek characters but recently transliterated into Albanian by Tirana; and A. Leotti, *Dizionario Albanese-italiano* (Rome, 1937). Several bilingual dictionaries are available, among them Russian-Albanian and Serbocroatian-Albanian works.

Social Sciences

As a rule, Western historical works treat—rather superficially—specific periods of Albanian history as it relates to Western Europe. For the medieval period, including the significant times of Skenderbeg, Columbia is weak in publications but strong in source material. *Acta et diplomata res Albaniae mediae aetatis illustrantia*, 2 v., (Vienna, 1913-18), collected and edited by three well-known Balkan scholars—Thallóczy, Jireček, and Šufflay—is among its holdings for this period. Other pertinent works include the multivolume *Acta Vēneta Saeculorum XIV et XV*, still in process, collected and edited by G. Valentini, S. J., and the record-book *(Defter)* of the province of Albania, discovered in the archives of Istanbul and edited by H. Inalčik (Ankara, 1954), which throws light on the Albanian Christian timariots under the Ottomans around 1430-40. The collection of documents of the Medieval period would be complete if Columbia possessed some of the source material published by Tirana after World War II, particularly the volume of Ottoman sources referring to the Albanian-Turkish war of the 15th century (Tirana, 1968), and J. Radonić, *Djuradj Kastriot Skenderbeg i Albanija u XV veku (istoriska gradja)* (Belgrade, 1942).

For the period of the Napoleonic wars and the independent Albanian rulers, Ali Pasha of Janina and the Bushatis of Shkodër, Columbia's holdings are weak, particularly those on the Bushatis. On Ali Pasha, in addition to some separate publications, there are also travel books written by Englishmen and Frenchmen. Another important period is that of the Congress of Berlin (1878), but for this era the material on Albania is dispersed in general works dealing with that Congress and in official documents of the great powers. The same may be said about the period of the Young Turks and the Albanian resistance to them. Columbia possesses E.b.V. [Iora], *Die Wahrheit über das Vorgehen der Jungtürken in Albanien* (Vienna and Leipzig, 1911), and the more recent Russian contributions by I. G. Senkevich, *Osvoboditel' noe dvizhenie albanskogo naroda 1905-1912* (Moscow, 1959) and *Albania v period vostochnogo krizisa, 1875-1881* (Moscow, 1965). S. Skendi, *The Albanian National Awakening, 1878-1912* (Princeton, N.J., 1967) covers in detail the period from the Congress of Berlin to the independence of Albania.

For diplomatic history and foreign relations, Columbia holds several dissertations from French universities on political developments concerning Albania in relation to other powers. Greek and Yugoslav studies in diplomacy are primarily concerned with defending their countries' points of view with regard to boundaries. Most of the Greek studies Columbia has acquired deal with the Northern Epirus question. The classic work on that problem remains E. P. Stickney's *Southern Albania or Northern Epirus in European International Affairs, 1912-1923* (Stanford, Calif., 1926). After World War II, Professor G. Stadtmüller of the University of Munich initiated a series of publications entitled *Albanische Forschungen*. Ten volumes have appeared thus far, and Columbia holds all of them. They are mostly dissertations, of uneven value, treating the life and works of Austro-Hungarian consular officers active in Albanian affairs. Even after the end of the Italo-Austrian rivalry on the Adriatic, Italian writers continued to be actively interested in Albanian political developments, and Columbia possesses some of their works.

Columbia's collection of materials—principally in Western languages—relating to political developments in and around Albania in the postwar era is also strong. Only the speeches of Hoxha delivered at the various congresses of the Albanian Communist Party are in Albanian or Russian. There are also several publications in Russian discussing the political changes in the country as it pursued "the road to Socialism." These studies, however, stopped in 1961, when Albania established close ties with China. Previously studied by Western political scientists in relation to Russia, Albania is now studied in light of the connections with China. Columbia is in the process of increasing its acquisitions of publications on this phase of Albanian-Chinese relations.

Columbia's holdings on Albanian economics are not strong. Albanian source materials in this field, e.g., those on statistics, are not complete. The five-year plans may be found in the proceedings of the congresses of the Communist Party. Some economic studies of prewar Albania are available, as are a few made by the Russians before 1961.

As far as social life and customs are concerned, the acquisitions refer mostly to northern Albania, where a tribal society had existed. They date from before World War II and are in Western languages. In English there are some works by E. M. Durham, e.g., *High Albania* (London, 1909) and M. M. Hasluck, *The Unwritten Law in Albania* (Cambridge, Eng. 1954). This unwritten law, codified by Sh. K. Gjeçov and published in Albanian under the title *Kanuni i Lekë Dukagjinit* [The Code of Lekë Dukagjini] (Shkodër, 1933), is available in an Italian translation, *Codice di Lek Dukagjini ossia Diritto consuetudinario delle Montagne d'Albania,* tradotto dal P. Paolo Dodaj, a cura di P. G. Fishta e Giuseppe Schiro, introduzione Federico Patetta (Rome, 1941).

Periodicals

A valuable holding is *Arhiv za arbanasku starinu, jezik i etnologiju,* published in Belgrade during the period 1923-26 by H. Barić (3 v.). Holdings of the *Buletin per Shkencat Shoqerore* [Bulletin for Social Sciences] of the Institute of Sciences, Tirana, are complemented with *Buletin i Universitetit Shtetëror të Tiranës* [Bulletin of the State University of Tirana], Social Sciences series, which replaced it in Autumn 1957. For *Studia Albanica,* published by the Institute of Language and History of the University of Tirana, only a single issue is available. This journal is useful because many of its articles are in West European languages.

Rruga e Partisë [The Road of the Party], the theoretical organ of the Albanian Communist Party published at Tirana, is a valuable addition to Columbia's holdings. The same may be said about *Letërsia Jonë* [Our Literature] (Tirana), the monthly organ of the Writers' Union of Albania from 1946 to 1953, which was replaced by *Nëntori* [November] (Tirana).

Columbia also holds several years of *Shêjzat (Le Pleiadi),* a cultural, social, and artistic review published in Rome and devoted primarily to the Italo-Albanians and Northern Albania.

The Albanians of Kosovo (formerly Kosmet) are well represented at Columbia. One can find *Gjurmime albanologjike* [Albanian Researches], published by the University of Priština;

Përparimi (Priština), a cultural and scientific review; and *Jeta e Re* [The New Life] (Priština), a cultural and literary bimonthly founded in 1945.

Stavro Skendi
Columbia University

Hungary

THE HUNGARICA HOLDINGS (works by Hungarian authors or pertaining to subjects relevant to Hungary in any language) at the Columbia University Libraries have increased substantially in scope and importance over the last decade. The geographic area for collecting Hungarica is defined as the territory of the Carpathian Basin and the Danube Valley, i.e., Hungary's territory preceding the Treaty of Trianon (1920).

History of the Hungarica Collection

The earliest Hungarica acquisitions consisted mainly of source materials in history, statistics, geography, and philology, many of them in English, German, or Latin, and the works of great Hungarian classical authors.

An important milestone in the acquisition of Hungarica occurred in 1954 when the Department of Uralic and Altaic Languages was established at Columbia University and at about the same time East European studies were started by the Russian Institute. Although no separate budget was available for Hungarica acquisitions it increased constantly through gifts and purchases. Professor John Lotz, Head of the Department of Uralic and Altaic Languages, was instrumental in building the Hungarica collection, and personally donated ca. 750 volumes plus many valuable microfilms; an additional 300 volumes were received as gifts from various sources, and several hundred volumes accrued through purchase.

In connection with the National Defense Education Act (NDEA, Title VI.) of 1958, the Uralic and Altaic program at Columbia was expanded such that Hungarian studies could be pursued from elementary languages courses to a complete doctoral program. An annual library budget of $10,000 was established for the systematic purchase of current and retrospective material in Uralic and Altaic studies, the greatest part of which has been used for the acquisition of Hungarica. Columbia's Hungarica collection is now one of the largest and most important such collections in the United States. For details of the evolution of the collections, see Alouis Papp, *A Survey of the Growth of the Hungarian Collection at Columbia University Libraries* (1969). The acquisition program includes primarily language teaching materials and connected background coverage (in bibliography, handbooks, literature, geography, history and ethnology) to put the study of language and literature in the proper perspective. Works in the social sciences are acquired including history from protohistory to the latest period, economics, statistics, law, ethnology, and folklore. Selective material in the theater arts, music, fine arts, archeology, architecture, library science, as well as general and special bibliographies to cover these subjects have been acquired.

Systematic acquisitions began in 1958 when a full-time staff member was entrusted with the selection of Hungarica. The program includes purchase through dealers in the U.S. and abroad and exchange arrangements with scholarly institutions and learned societies in Hungary. This development is illustrated below by annual acquisition statistics, for some banner years:

	Year	Volumes
	1960/1961	2,050
	1961/1962	2,450
	1962/1963	2,110
or		
	1969/1970	3,500

Some special highlights in acquisitions were: the purchase of ca. 300 volumes from the Révay Collection containing a great deal of material about minority problems, in 1963; ca. 160 titles of German and Latin Hungarica monographs published between 1750-1850; a microfilm copy of the newspaper *Pesti napló* for 1850-1904; about 420 volumes of the diaries, minutes, and papers of the Hungarian and Transylvanian Diets and of parliamentary sessions from 1790/91 up to recent issues.

Hungarica have been acquired at a more cautious pace in recent years, owing to budgetary limitations, but a sizable number of publications from various countries has been acquired through the Public Law 480 program and through exchange programs.

Columbia University's Hungarica holdings as of April, 1972, were:

	Titles	Volumes
Monographs		ca. 32,000-35,000
Numbered series, annuals, etc.	137	4,532
Periodicals (incl. 26 current titles)	183	3,400
		Reels
Newspapers	103	179
Newspapers uncataloged	60	Pieces
Microforms (incl. 179 reels of newspapers)		200

In addition there are holdings in the Oral History Collection, in the Rare Book and Manuscript Library, and in the Music Library.

Bibliographic Sources

Some of the most important Hungarian bibliographies in the Library are *Magyar Könyvészet* (Bibliographia Hungariae) in all published volumes, and *Magyar nemzeti bibliográfia* (Bibliographia Hungarica) (1946-) with its supplements, as *Magyar folyóiratok repertóriuma* (Repertorium bibliographicum periodicorum Hungaricorum) (1953-). A partial bibliographical coverage of periodicals is possible through Dezsényi, Béla. *A magyar hírlapirodalom első százada, 1705-1805* [The First Century of Hungarian Periodical Literature, 1705-1805] (Budapest, 1941), or Kemény, György. *Magyarország időszaki sajtója 1911-től 1920-ig* [Periodical Press of Hungary, 1911-1920] (Budapest, 1942).

A guide to early printed books can be found in Sándor Apponyi's *Hungarica; Ungarn betreffend im Ausland gedruckte Bücher und Flugschriften* (Munich-Budapest, 1903-27).; in several bibliographies by Károly Szabó, or in the recent joint publication of the Hungarian Academy of Sciences and the National Széchényi Library: *Régi magyarországi nyomtatványok, 1473-1600* (Res litteraria Hungariae vetus operum impressorum, 1473-1600) (Budapest, 1971).

Hungarian Language

A general interest in linguistics accounts for the acquisition of early standard works in philology, dictionaries, etc., long before the teaching of Hungarian was made part of the curriculum at Columbia. Examples of such linguistic tools are dictionaries as József Budenz's *Magyar-ugor összehasonlító szótár* [Hungarian-Ugrian Comparative Dictionary] (Budapest, 1873-81), or Gábor Szarvas's *Magyar nyelvtörténeti szótár* (Lexicon linguae Hungaricae aevi antiquioris) (Budapest, 1890-93). The collection now contains about 100 volumes of early and modern dictionaries in various languages.

The works and also several festschrifts in honor of outstanding philologists of the older generation as Gábor Szarvas, Zsigmond Simonyi, Zoltán Gombocz, as well as works of contemporaries as Loránd Benkő, Béla Kálmán, Péter Hajdu, Lajos Lőrincze, and others are available. Reports on linguistic conferences, the *Uralic and Altaic Series* of Indiana University, *Nyelvtudományi közlemények* [Philological Publications] (1862-), *Magyar Nyelvőr* [Guardian of the Hungarian language] (1872-) are some examples of the holdings in this field.

The various Hungarian dialects are discussed in ca. 40 titles summed up in Benkő, Loránd. *Magyar nyelvjárási bibliográfia* [Bibliography of Hungarian Dialects] (Budapest, 1951).

Hungarian Literature

The Library has ca. 40 titles of bibliographies in this field, including three bibliographies for earlier works, several biobibliographies, and some periodicals. Early authors who wrote in Latin, as the humanist poet Janus Pannonius, contemporary of Matthias Corvinus, or the Cardinal Péter Pázmány are represented in the original as well as in Hungarian or other translations; the latter with 14 titles by and 10 about him; the poet count Miklós Zrívnyi with 16 titles by and 14 about him. The authors of the late 18th and of the first part of the 19th century who inaugurated the renaissance of the literary language, the great poets of the 19th century, as János Arany, Mihály Vörösmarty, Sándor Petőfi, and many others may be read in various early and recent critical editions as well as in translations. The extensiveness of the collection is indicated, e.g., by the 14 editions (incl. translations) of Imre Madách's *Az ember tragédiája* [The Tragedy of Man] and 10 titles about this work, as well as other dramas, and collected works of this author. The novelists of the 19th century, as Mór Jókai or Baron József Eötvös, are to be found in several editions and translations.

Among the 20th century's most important poets Endre Ady's works are abundantly represented. A manuscript of the English translations of his poems is in the Rare Books and Manuscript Library to which we shall refer later. The poets and authors of the younger age group, Attila József, Miklós Radnóti, Gyula Illyés, along with virtually all important authors publishing in and outside of Hungary are available in a variety of works.

Literary history and criticism of various periods and viewpoints are available, from the conservative Jenő Pintér to the literary aesthetics of György Lukács; the latter can be studied in 84 titles of his own and 11 works about him. Collections and anthologies present a wide panorama in this field, the holdings being the most complete in 19th and 20th century literature, poetry, and literary history and criticism. Over 150 titles on the Hungarian theater, film industry, as well as biographies and memoirs of actors are part of this collection.

Periodical publications in Hungarian literature and in various aspects of intellectual life are abundant: 121 titles in 1,563 volumes, e.g., the early literary periodical *Felsőmagyarországi Minerva* [Minerva of Upper Hungary] (1825-39); or *Nyugat* [The West] (1908-41); and its continuation *Magyar Csillag* [Hungarian Star] (1941-44). The Library holds several current literary periodicals published in and outside Hungary, e.g., *Magyar Műhely* [Hungarian Workshop], (Montrouge 1963-), which also treats contemporary Hungarian painting and sculpture. The figures cited above indicate the thoroughness of coverage, but include literary mediocrities in various editions as well as the above sampling of outstanding authors.

Folklore, Folk Songs, Folk Tales

Several volumes contain lore of the pre-Christian period and of their later versions in ballads and tales of Hungary and Transylvania. Collections in Hungarian folklore comprising ca. 50 volumes, as those compiled by János Berze-Nagy, Gyula Ortutay, Linda Dégh, and others are there to enjoy, some also in translation. Some earlier compilations of folk songs and ballads are available, e.g., János Kriza's *Vadrózsák: székely népköltési gyütemény* [Wild Roses; Collection of Szekler Folk Poetry] (Budapest, 1911), or Béla Vikár's *A magyar népköltés remekei* [Masterpieces of Hungarian Folk Poetry] (Budapest, 1911). Collections by Elek Benedek, Arnold Ipolyi, and János Kodolányi contain tales of Transylvania, Burgenland, of counties such as Baranya, Somogy, stories about betyárs (outlaws), et al. which add further variety; five periodicals are also available on the subject, as well as several bibliographies.

Ethnology

Works of Pál Hunfalvy about Hungarian ethnology provide a general picture of the last century's folkways. Otto Herman, István Győrffy, and others treat special aspects, still others write about kindred tribes of the Hungarians as the Jazyks, Kipczaks (Cumani), or of the people in the regions of Kiskunság and Ormánság. An example of studies of customs dating back to protohistory is Vilmos Diószegi's. *A sámánhit emlékei a magyar népi műveltségben* [Memories of the Shaman Cult in Hungarian Folkways] (Budapest, 1958).

History, Geography

The greatest strength of the Hungarica collection is its coverage of history through source material of early and recent periods. The Roman provinces of Pannonia, Dacia, and Moesia are within its collecting field and several bibliographies, e.g., János Banner's *Bibliographia archaeologica Hungarica, 1793-1943.* (Szeged, 1944), can be consulted on the subject. The Library's seven series of *Monumenta Hungariae historica* (published since 1857 by the Hungarian Academy of Sciences), although not complete, include an impressive 133 volumes; ca. 60 volumes of sources about Transylvania, 12 volumes about Croatia, 12 volumes about Slovakia, as well as Turkish, Austrian, and other sources are here for the researcher. Medieval Hungary, its kings, and other historical figures are discussed in a number of treatises. The king of greatest popular appeal, Matthias Corvinus, can be studied in 56 titles from fiction to scholarly examination of his historical role and of his impact on the humanists surrounding him. His Corvina Library of illuminated manuscripts at the royal castle in Buda is the subject of many works.

The numerous Hungarian uprisings can be followed in considerable depth: Ferenc Rákóczi's revolt against the Habsburgs is covered by the *Archivum Rákóczianum* and many other works including poetry and fiction; the uprising of 1848/1849 is documented and discussed in 84 titles and the events of 1956 in 83 titles (including several bibliographies). A moderate coverage of genealogy and military history is also available.

The fairly extensive holdings, comprising about 300 volumes, in religious history, including biographies, works about dioceses, monasteries, collections of sermons, etc., as well as some fine examples of Bible translations also deserve to be mentioned.

Geographic treatises as documented by early works of Hungarians and of foreign travelers are abundant. Certain regions such as Lake Balaton and the Danube Valley are well covered as are some counties, or cities, e.g., Sopron and Eger. The richest coverage is reserved for the capital with more than a hundred titles, including several bibliographies.

Historical periodicals and other serial publications provide a great variety of material in 26 titles and 1,396 volumes. Some samples on special subjects are: *Hadtörténelmi Közlemények* [Publications on Military History] (1888-1943; n.s. 1954-), or *Turul* (1883-1943), a genealogical journal. Historical material has adequate coverage in historiography including works of many persuasions from a conservative to a Marxist interpretation of history.

Agriculture and Labor

Hungary, the breadbasket of the Austro-Hungarian Empire, remained a country of large estates up to 1945. Land tenure therefore was the decisive factor in agricultural development and in the social and economic conditions of the peasantry. Several treatises are available on the history of feudal estates through the centuries, others present points of view in favor of or against large agricultural units. Bibliographies serve as guides to this material, which is covered somewhat marginally with ca. 30 volumes. The economic and social conditions of the peasantry are described from various angles: from scientific studies to those based on personal experiences of authors as Péter Veres, Pál Szabó, and Gyula Illyés.

Most of the Library's holdings in the field of labor pertain to the agricultural laborer, who constituted the greater part of the working class in pre-World War II Hungary. At present the Library has relatively few works on the problems of the industrial worker.

Oral History Collection

Interviews with selected prominent Hungarians are in the files of this Department, e.g., interviews with the politician Béla Fábián, the psychoanalyst Sándor Radó, and the Nobel laureates Albert Szent-Györgyi and Eugene P. Wigner.

The *School of Library Service* also has research resources in history, literature, et al., including extensive holdings on the history of printing, facsimile editions, and many serial publications of Hungarian libraries on a variety of subjects.

The *Rare Book and Manuscript Library* holds some treasures well worth reporting: a relatively early edition in contemporary binding of Bonfini, Antonio. *Rervm Vngaricarvm decades qvatvor, cvm dimidia* . . . (Basileae, ex officina Oporiniana, 1568), and Dilich, Wilhelm Schäffer. *Vngarische chronica* . . . (Cassel/ gedruckt durch Wilhelm Wessel/ 1600). A collection of selected poems of Endre Ady in English translation (Gen. MS. 70) has been donated to the Library by the translator Joseph Grosz. The collection also contains a letter of Lajos Kossuth, of 1852. Béla Bartók presented a valuable gift containing manuscripts of his music, including Rumanian and Turkish Folk-Music, plus the Serbo-Croatian Table of Materials, totaling approximately 2170 pages.

Microform Reading Room

The microforms considerably increase the historical and literary coverage of Hungarica. Many titles of periodical publications and newspapers have been added to the holdings recently. Although most newspapers have only a sampling of issues, those of the periods of 1848-49, 1918-19 and 1956 will be of special value; the latter are in the microform collection of the Lehman Library.

*   *   *

All the foregoing description pertains to the Butler Library. The following refers to the more important specialized, branch libraries of Columbia University.

Music Library (Dodge Building)

The photocopies of the aforementioned Bartók manuscripts, numerous publications about his work, and five first editions of his compositions are in this library. Zoltán Kodály's *Dix pièces pour le piano*. op. 3 with the composer's autograph, and several bibliographies and treatises on Hungarian music and composers represent this important branch of Hungarian art.

The Avery Library

This architectural library has a sizable collection, several hundred volumes, of Hungarian archeology, architecture, and related fields. Several retrospective and current periodicals are available; some point to the essential role of Hungarians in the Bauhaus, as the names of László Moholy-

Nagy, Marcel Breuer, and Farkas Molnár will testify. Publications of museums, mostly with foreign-language summaries, present other aspects. These holdings are also growing through exchange, as are the holdings of the *Fine Arts Library* in the Schermerhorn Building, which has several hundred works by and about Hungarian painters and sculptors, as well as works representing collections of Hungarian museums.

Library of Business and Economics (Uris Building)

The economic and industrial development of Hungary can be followed through its different stages in several libraries: the early phases in the Butler holdings, the late 19th and middle 20th centuries at the Business Library, and the period from 1945 in the Lehman Library. This also holds true for the various official statistical publications comprising many hundred volumes.

The Law School Library

Legal and parliamentary language in Hungary was mostly Latin up to the 1840s which accounts for the great number of Latin documents. The *Corpus juris Hungarici* can be studied from the earliest times to the latest publications; different collections of laws and statutes, as civil, commercial, criminal, et al. are available. Eight bibliographies serve as guides to Hungarian legal literature, as, e.g., a recent publication: Charles Szladits. *Hungary* [Bruxelles] 1963, which constitutes Section D/11 of *Bibliographical Introduction to Legal History and Ethnology,* edited by John Gilissen. Several legal dictionaries, treatises on financial law, labor law, military law, and public law offer a picture of the legal development of Hungary. This collection of ca. 500 titles of monographs in 570 volumes, 17 numbered monographic series in 260 volumes, and 15 periodicals in 134 volumes contains the basic material on Hungarian law and constitutional history. The International Law Collection of this library provides another aspect of Hungarica: e.g., 13 works by Francis Deák about international legal problems, Hungary's Peace Treaties, 10 titles about the Danubian states, and 80 titles about the Danube River and navigation problems.

Lehman Library (School of International Affairs Building)

The volume of materials on contemporary Hungarian history in this collection is steadily increasing. The documentation on Communism is in this library, as are recent statistics, economic and demographic studies, political treatises, periodicals, et al. Newspapers on microfilm present some interesting titles: issues of *Vörös Zászló* [Red Banner] published in Budapest, Moscow, Vienna, or others published in Paris, as *Szabad Szó* [Free Word] and *Párisi Munkás* [Paris Worker] are among them. This library has an additional 60 titles of uncataloged newspapers.

Rose Stein
Columbia University

Romania

THE ROMANIAN HOLDINGS of Columbia University, located mainly in the Butler General Research Library, with important segments in the Law, Lehman, Business School, and Avery (archeology and architecture) Libraries, and fragmentary collections in the Fine Arts, Music, Theological Seminary, and Teachers College Libraries, include approximately 3,800 volumes (exclusive of periodicals) in the humanities and in the political and socioeconomic sciences. The main University Card Catalog does not include entries for all of the subsidiary libraries' holdings.

In nearly every field the collections reflect a haphazard development, except for those specialized areas where the University has maintained some special research program for a long period (e.g., foreign and comparative law) or where the interests of faculty members have required the regular, methodical procurement of materials (e.g., folklore, linguistics, and literature).

Between 1948 and 1962 acquisitions in all areas aside from those just mentioned totaled fewer than 300 volumes, and it was not until 1968-69, when the Slavic Acquisitions Division of the Library system was reorganized and a separate East Central European bibliographer appointed, that an effort for the systematic and balanced collection of Romanian materials began.

Although Columbia's acquisitions of Romanian materials have increased markedly since 1968 through exchange and the establishment of the Nicolae Iorga Chair of Romanian and South East European Studies (1971), serious gaps remain, which limit the research value of the collections to the humanities, law, and demography.

General Bibliography

The serious deficiencies which have resulted from long neglect hamper the researcher on Romanian affairs at Columbia from his preliminary investigation of general bibliographies. Since no comprehensive bibliographic survey on Romania exists, one must rely on studies of limited scope. Columbia possesses Léon Savadjian's *Bibliographie balkanique, 1920-1939,* 8 v. (Paris, 1931-39), the Romanian Academy's *Bibliografia românească veche 1508-1830,* 3 v. (Bucharest, 1903-12), compiled by Ion Bianu and Nerva Hodoş, and the excellent Romanian bibliographies published since 1956 in *Südosteuropa-Bibliographie* (Munich), but lacks such key items as Gh. Cardaş, *Tratat de bibliografie* (Bucharest, 1931), the Romanian Academy's *Creşterea Colecţiunilor,* a semiannual catalog of the Academy Library's accessions from 1905-44, and the Academy's *Catalogul publicaţiunilor Academiei Române, 1867-1923* (Bucharest, 1924), with supplements (1924-30).

Columbia's bibliographic holdings are somewhat more satisfactory for post-World War II publications. They include the semimonthly catalog of new monographs Biblioteca Centrală de Stat. *Bibliografia Republicii Socialiste România: cărţi, albume, hărţi, note muzicale* [The Central State Library. Bibliography of the Socialist Republic of Romania: Books, Albums, Maps, Musical Scores] since 1956, though not the parallel index for periodicals, Biblioteca Centrală de Stat. *Bibliografia periodicelor din Republica Socialistă Română.* Both the State Library's *Anuarul cărţii din Republica Populară Română, 1952-1954* [The Book Annual of the R.P.R., 1952-54] (Bucharest, 1957) and the Academy's *Indexul lucrărilor ştiinţific publicate în periodicele şi culegerile editate de Academia R.P. Române, 1948-1954* [Index of Scientific Works Published in Periodicals and Collections Edited by the Academy of the R.P.R., 1948-54] (Bucharest, 1957) are reliable guides to early postwar materials. For the most recent period Columbia has received the monthly *Romanian Scientific Abstracts* series since 1964, and *Romanian Books: a Quarterly Bulletin* since 1968.

Of the most valuable bibliographies of more limited compass, Alexandre and Getta H. Rally's *Bibliografie franco-roumaine,* 2 v. (Paris, 1930), Endre Veress's *Bibliografia româno-ungară,* 2 v. (Bucharest, 1930), and Ioachim Crăciun's *Bibliographie de la Transylvanie Roumaine, 1916-1936* (Cluj, 1937) are in Columbia's holdings, however, Octav Păduraru's two invaluable works, *Anglo-Roumanian and Roumanian-English Bibliography* (Bucharest, 1946) and *Bibliografia românească: ştiinţă, technică, economie* (Bucharest, 1947) are not. Significant bibliographic information is also included in the comprehensive prewar *Encyclopedia României* [The

Encyclopedia of Romania], 4 v. (Bucharest, 1936-41), which is available in the main reference room of Butler Library.

Political and Socioeconomic Sciences

HISTORY AND POLITICAL SCIENCE.   Columbia's holdings on Romanian history, politics, and government are weak and reflect the lack of systematic acquisition. Columbia lacks the two best general histories, Constantin C. Giurescu's four-volume *Istoria Românilor* (Bucharest, 1940-44) and Nicolae Iorga's massive, nine-volume *Histoire des Roumains et de la romanité orientale* (Bucharest, 1937-44); thus one must rely on either the earliest "modern" history, A. D. Xenopol's *Istoria Romînilor din Dacia Traiană* [History of the Romanians from Trajan's Dacia], 12 v. in 3 (Iaşi, 1896) which is outdated or the equally problematic early work by Iorga, *Geschichte des rumänischen Volkes im Rahmen seiner Staatsbildungen,* 2 v. (Gotha, 1905). Neither Constantin C. and Dinu C. Giurescu's most recent compendium *Istoria Românilor din cele mai vechi timpuri şi pînă astăzi* [History of the Romanians from the Most Ancient Times to the Present] (Bucharest, 1971), nor the numerous lesser "general" works by Iorga in the Columbia collection (e.g., *La Place des Roumains dans l'histoire universelle* (1935) or *Istoria poporului românesc* [History of the Romanian People], 2 v. in 1 (1922)) represent as high a level of historiographic development as the missing works. The fundamental Marxist history, *Istoria României* [History of Romania], 4 v. (Bucharest, 1960-64) is already being sharply criticized in Romania on both historical and ideological counts, but taken together with the sizable number of new publications, acquired by Columbia since 1968 (see below) and works such as Michael Rura's *Reinterpretation of History as a Method of Furthering Communism in Rumania: A Study in Comparative Historiography* (Washington: Georgetown University Press, 1961) and Dionisie Ghermani's *Die Kommunistische Umdeutung der rumänischen Geschichte unter besonderer Berücksichtigung des Mittelalters* (Munich, 1967), it can serve as a basis for studies of historiography under the communists.

Columbia lacks most of the basic document collections and historical journals published between the union of Moldavia and Wallachia in 1859 and the conclusion of World War II, having only four of the 31 volumes of documents published in Euxodiu de Hurmuzachi (ed.), *Documente privitore la istoria Românilor* [Documents Concerning the History of the Romanians], 19 v. in 31 (Bucharest, 1887-1938), still the basic collection of documents on pre-19th century Romania. Of the relevant journals Columbia has the first eight volumes (1931-38) of *Revista istorica română*, an excellent journal published between 1931 and 1947, but this represents virtually the entire prewar periodical holdings of Columbia in Romanian history.

The situation in regard to source materials and periodicals remained much the same for nearly two decades after World War II. Columbia's holdings of the voluminous collections of documents covering individual provinces, events, and centuries published in the 1950s and early 1960s are spotty or nonexistent. And runs of major historical journals like *Studii: revista de istorie, Analele institutului de istorie a Partidului de pe lîngă C.C. al P.C.R.,* and *Studii şi articole de istorie* begin only in 1958 (v. 9), 1965 (v. 11), and 1969 (v. 3) respectively. Only the main foreign language journal, *Revue Roumaine d'histoire,* has been received since its founding (in 1962). Thus the Library does not have the documents and journals required for historical research on most topics. Columbia's secondary materials on Romanian history and politics merit special comment in a few areas. An excellent collection of early archeological and historical studies on ancient Dacia, including the pathfinding works of Vasile Pârvan, Vasile Christescu, and Nicolae Densuşianu of the 1920s, and extending back even to Grigore D. Tocilescu's *Dacia înainte de Romani* [Dacia before the Romans] (Bucharest, 1880), has been strengthened in recent years by the addition of considerable periodical material, e.g., *Studii şi materiale de istorie veche* and *Materiale şi cercetări arheologice* (published 1955-62 only), and numerous excellent monographs. Works by contemporary scholars like Hadrian Daicoviciu (*Dacii*, 1965), D. Tudor (*Oltenia Română*, 1968), and Mihail Macrea (*Viaţa în Dacia română* [Life in Roman Dacia], 1969) continue to update an already impressive collection in this area.

Worthy of note also is the large number of monographs by leading scholars and statesmen (e.g., Grigorie Antipa, Mircea Djuvara, Take Ionescu) dealing with Romania's diplomatic and military situation from 1914 to 1918. They provide excellent background for a proper evaluation of Columbia's wide range of materials on Romania at the Paris Peace Conference and in the League of Nations, on her nationality problems between the wars, especially in Transylvania (see below under Law). However, Columbia's holdings on the nationality problem in other regions and for other times are poor.

Although Columbia has added many recent works to her collection, she possesses virtually none of the pre-1965 Romanian materials (monographic studies, ideological journals such as *Lupta de Clasă*, documents, speeches, etc.) on the Communist regime. Newspaper holdings constitute the exception to this rule, and are an important research tool for the pre-Ceauşescu era. They include *Scînteia* (1950-64, 1966, 1969), *România Liberă* (1956-66), *Munca* (1956-64), and *Scînteia Tineretului* (1951, 1958-64), as well as more sporadic holdings of literary journals (e.g., *Gazeta Literară, Contemporanul*) and journals in languages other than Romanian.

LAW.   In sharp contrast to the situation in history, Columbia possesses an excellent collection of more than 500 volumes (microfilmed, mimeographed, or printed) in Romanian law and legal history. It is especially strong for the period between 1900 and 1945, and covers the whole spectrum of legal concerns, from the most fundamental, constitutional law, through administrative, civil, and criminal law, to laws on education, labor, property and inheritance, and commerce.

Of particular importance are the approximately 100 doctoral theses by young Romanian scholars of the immediate pre-World War I and interwar periods which form part of the working collection of the Law School's Parker School of Foreign and Comparative Law. Prepared at West European universities, most notably in France, but also in Germany and Austria, these theses constitute excellent supplementary studies for the researcher. Thus in the constitutional field, for example, as well as the constitutional documents themselves and "classic" studies such as F. E. Weinreich's *Die Verfassung von Rumänien von 1923* (Leipzig, 1933) and Sébastian Popesco's *La Constitution roumaine de 27 février 1938 et ses principes* (Paris, 1939), one can consult theses ranging from M. Orleanu's historical study *Esquisse sur l'évolution constitutionnelle de la Roumanie de 1821 à 1859* (Paris, 1935) to Alexandre R. F. Radulescu's more procedural work *Le contrôle de la constitutionnalité des lois en Roumanie* (Paris, 1935). Similar possibilities extend even to the fields of judicial organization, e.g., Grig. Munteano, *L'organisation judiciaire en Roumanie* (Paris, 1909) and comparative law in specialized areas, e.g., Georges Taşcă, *Considérations sur les lois relatives à la propriété rurale en Roumanie, Angleterre, et Irlande—étude de droit comparé* (Paris, 1907). Women's rights as well fall within the purview of the thesis collection, e.g., Marguerite Barzanescu, *La capacité juridique de la femme mariée en Roumanie* (Paris, 1936).

The collection is well balanced in regard to international law, disputes, and treaties. It reveals exceptional strength, however, only on the complex problem of Romania's position at the Paris Peace Conference and in the League of Nations. In both arenas the country's main concern was with the Hungarian nationality problem and the status of Transylvania, and the Columbia holdings on these problems are immense. In addition to the more important monographic works, they range from basic documents of the peace conference, e.g., *La Roumanie devant le Congrès de la paix, 1919* (8 v. in 1) to studies of major disputes before the League and League bodies, e.g., *La réforme agraire en Roumanie et les optants hongrois de Transylvanie devant la Société des nations,* 2 v. (Paris, 1927-28) and Walter Jahr, *Der ungarisch-rumänische Optantenstreit vor dem ungarisch-rumänischen Gemischten Schiedsgericht und vor dem Völkerbundsrat in den Jahren 1927-29* (Jena, 1930); and from collections and analyses of nationality legislation, as Constantin T. Petrescu and Th. Teişanu, *Codul naţionalităţii române, adnotat* (Bucharest, 1940), to dissertations representing a wide range of political and propagandistic as well as legal convictions, e.g., M. A. Laurian, *Le principe des nationalités et l'unité nationale roumaine* (Paris, 1923).

Although the legal collection does not include the actual codes, decrees, and regulations of the interwar period, published either independently or in the government's *Monitorul Oficial,* it does include Constantin Hamangiu's excellent treatise *Tratat de drept civil român,* 3 v. (Bucharest, 1928-29) and long runs of such major legal and judicial series as *Revista de drept public* [Journal of Public Law], v. 1-14 (1926-39), *Jurisprudenţa generală* [General Jurisprudence], v. 1-21 (1923-43), and the High Court of Cassation and Justice's *Buletinul Deciziunilor* [Bulletin of Decisions], v. 59-77 (1922-40). No legal sources for the first two decades of Communist rule are available.

ECONOMICS AND STATISTICS.   Columbia's library resources for economic history and statistics include some of the general histories, like N. Razmiriţa's *Essai d'économie roumaine moderne, 1831-1931* (Paris, 1932) and John M. Montias's excellent *Economic Development in Communist Rumania* (Cambridge, Mass., 1967), but not a majority of them. Crucial works such as Gheorghe Dobrovici's *Istoricul desvoltării economice şi financiare a României şi împrumuturile contractate, 1823-1933* (Bucharest, 1934) and Virgil Madgearu's *Evoluţia economiei româneşti după Razboiul Mondial* (Bucharest, 1940) are not to be found.

For economic history prior to 1914, there is a considerable body of compendia and monographs dealing with specialized topics which are invaluable supplements to the more general materials provided in the surveys of V. N. Madgearu, M. G. Obedenaru, and the Ministry of Agriculture, Industry, Commerce, and Domains, e.g., *La Roumanie, 1866-1906* (Bucharest, 1907). Works such as Academia R.P.R., Filiala Cluj. Institutul de Istorie şi Arheologie. *Dezvoltarea economiei Moldovei între anii 1848 şi 1864—contribuţii* [The Economic Development of Moldavia from 1848 to 1864] (Bucharest, 1963), Nicholas Moga's dissertation *Über die ländliche Hausindustrie in Rumänien* (Halle, 1901), and Leonida Colescu's fine study *Geschichte des Rumänischen Steuerwesens in der Epoche der Fanarioten, 1711-1821* (Munich, 1897) are especially important, given the paucity of documentary and statistical materials for this period. Columbia's holdings are limited to the Statistical Office's *Buletinul statistic al României* (1892-95, 1899-1905, 1905-14 only) and some Austro-Hungarian consular reports (Wien. Österreichisches Handels-Museum. *Rumänien: Wirtschaftliche Verhältnisse nach dem Berichten der . . . Konsularämter in Bukarest, Jassy, etc.*) for 1909-13.

The situation is very different for the interwar period. The Library has complete or very substantial holdings of statistical compilations for 1920-45, of which *Buletinul statistic al României* (1920-31, 1933, 1938-40), *Statistica societăţilor anonime* [Limited Companies] *din România* (1919-39), *Banque nationale de Roumanie. Bulletin d'information et de documentation* (1929-47), and the Ministry of Industry and Commerce's *Correspondance économique roumaine, bulletin officiel* (1927-41) are the most notable examples. They provide an excellent basis for the productive use of approximately 50 monographs by government agencies and individual economists which deal with virtually every facet of the Romanian interwar economy. State monopolies, the banking and credit system, raw material and energy production, industrial history and potential, and agricultural taxation and reform are some of the more significant topics covered by these monographs.

In economics, as in other disciplines, Columbia has very little of the monographic material published during the 1945-64 period. Complete holdings of the main statistical compilations,

Anuarul statistic al R.P.R. and *Buletinul statistic trimestrial,* are useful but not sufficient for research. Neither of the most important periodicals, *Probleme economice* or *Viaţa economică,* were received regularly until 1965.

If examined by subject categories rather than chronologically, by far the most outstanding feature of Columbia's holdings in economics is its extensive coverage of the history of Romanian foreign trade and tariff policies from the Middle Ages, e.g., Iancu I. Nistor, *Die auswärtigen Handelsbeziehungen der Moldau im XIV, XV, und XVI Jahrhundert, nach Quellen dargestellt* (Gotha, 1911) through the interwar period. An exceptional section on 19th-century trade and tariffs is highlighted by works of Dimitru Z. Furnica (1908), Valdimir Diculescu (1970), C. I. Baicoianu (1904), C. G. Antonescu (1915), and A. J. Stamatin (1914). For industry, agriculture, and finance the collection is much less satisfactory.

DEMOGRAPHY AND SOCIOLOGY.   The University has very strong holdings of demographic monographs, including all of the works of Romania's most outstanding demographer and interwar director of the *Institutul Central de Statistică,* Sabin Manuila. The censuses of 1930, 1941, and 1956, as well as detailed official studies based on them and on the census of December 19, 1912 (or January 1, 1913 new style) are kept together in Butler Library. The Library's holdings of the two principal periodicals in this field, *Buletinul demografic al României* (1938-40, 1942-48 only) and *Anuarul demografic* (1890-1900, 1931-38, 1945-46 only), are sporadic, but the major works on specific ethnic groups and regions are available, for example, Joseph Berkowitz's *La question des Israélites en Roumanie* (Paris, 1923), Friedrich Teutsch's *Die Siebenbürger Sachsen in Vergangenheit und Gegenwart* (Hermannstadt, 1924), and C. Constante and Anton Galopenţia's *Românii din Timoc* [The Romanians of Timoc], 2 v. (Bucharest, 1943-44) are available. The most important ethnographic maps are also in the collection.

Columbia's resources in sociology are good but less inclusive than in demography. Because of the association of Professor Philip E. Mosely with Dimitrie Gusti and his *Institutul Social Român* (Romanian Social [i.e. Sociological] Institute), most of that Institute's publications on rural sociology are in Columbia's Library. These publications, by Henri Stahl, Ion Conea, Anton Galopenţia, and Gusti himself, among others, constitute the basis of Romanian rural sociology down to the present day. The bibliography of the Institute's (by 1944 renamed the Romanian Institute of Social Sciences) publications, *Institutul de Ştiinţe Sociale al României, 25 ani de publicaţii, 1919-1944* (Bucharest, 1944) is included. The avalanche of material on rural sociology which began to appear in the mid-1960s is also in the collection. The new works include both historical studies such as Dan Prodan's exceptional *Iobăgia în Transilvania în secolul al XVI-lea* [Serfdom in Transylvania in the 16th Century], 3 v. (Bucharest, 1967-68) and more theoretical works like Z. Ornea's *Ţărănismul: studiu sociologic* (Peasantism: a Sociological Study) (Bucharest, 1969). However, this strong collection of materials does not extend beyond rural sociology into general sociological thought, industrialization, labor problems, and overall socioeconomic structure.

Humanities

In the humanities a good selection of general cultural history and outstanding resources in several subject categories give rise to overall strength.

CULTURAL HISTORY.   P. P. Panaitescu's two excellent volumes, *Introducere la istoria culturii româneşti* [Introduction to Romanian Cultural History] (Bucharest, 1969) and *Contribuţii la istoria culturii româneşti* [Contributions to Romanian Cultural History] (Bucharest, 1971, Silvan Panaitescu and Dan Zamfirescu, eds.) are the most recent additions to a collection of general cultural histories which includes Iorga's *Études roumaines,* 2 v. (Paris, 1923-24), Garabet Ibrăileanu's (d. 1936) *Spiritul critic în cultura românească,* new ed. (Iaşi, 1970) and many others, but few of Eugen Lovinescu's works. More specialized studies include Pompiliu Eliade's *De l'influence française sur l'esprit public en Roumanie* (Paris, 1898), and for comparison Alexandru Duţu's *Coordonate ale culturii româneşti în secolul XVIII, 1700-1821* [The Coordinates of Romanian Culture in the 18th Century, 1700-1821] (Bucharest, 1968), both of which concentrate on the Phanariot period, as well as materials on other critical matters of Romanian cultural history, e.g., Moldavian culture under Stephen the Great, Romanian intellectual history in the mid-19th century, and the Romanian cultural movement in Austria-Hungary. This variety of general cultural monographs provides ample background information for research in most major subject areas of the humanities.

LANGUAGE AND LITERATURE.   Language and literature are areas in which Columbia's holdings are exceptionally strong, due in part to the continual presence at Columbia since the 1930s of faculty with special interests in Romanian linguistics (E. Cristo-Loveanu, R. Austerlitz, T. Ferguson), and to the automatic receipt of many studies published as separate volumes in continuing series of monographs (e.g., *Materiale şi cercetări lingvistice*). The University's collection in this field comprises nearly 300 volumes. In addition to the basic studies of Alexandru Rosetti, Sextil I. Puşcariu, and Ovid Densuşianu, and extensive holdings in the major linguistic journals (e.g., *Limba română, Studii şi cercetări lingvistice, Fonetica şi dialectologie, Cercetări de lingvistică*, and *Romanoslavica*), specialized works, ranging in publication date from the mid-19th century to the present, abound on nearly every major topic—consonants, dialects, diminutives, etymology, foreign elements, phonetics and phonology, syntax, etc. Especially noteworthy is the selection in etymology, which includes the 19th-century grammars and etymological dictionaries of Ioan Alexi, Andreas Clemens, A. T. Laurian, J. C. Massimu, B. P. Hasdea, and Samuel Klein. Columbia's holdings of numerous late 19th-century studies on the dialects of the Aromuni—by Gustav Weigand, Tache Papahagi, Theodor Capidan, and a few others—represent the results of research which would be impossible to reproduce today.

In literature the collection is not as complete. It includes both of the major interwar bibliographies—that of Nicolae Georgescu-Tistu (1932) and the three-volume work by Gheorghe Adamescu (1921-28)—as well as the more recent *Bibliografia literaturii române, 1948-60* (Bucharest, 1965) edited by Tudor Vianu for the Romanian Academy, and recent general historical works such as Gheorghe Ivaşcu's *Istoria literaturii române* (Bucharest, 1969-71), but it is very deficient in periodicals (except for a nearly complete collection of the *Rumanian Review*) and it lacks the great histories of G. Călinescu and E. Lovinescu. A wide selection of the works of Romanian writers, numerous critical anthologies, and an excellent group of studies on specific topics in literary history and criticism, e.g., W. Bahner, *Das Sprach- und Geschichtsbewusstsein in der rumänischen Literatur von 1770-1880* (Berlin, 1967) or N. I. Apostolescu, *L'influence des romantiques français sur la poésie roumaine* (Paris, 1901), make the collection as a whole worth consultation.

FOLKLORE AND FOLK CULTURE.   After language, folklore is Columbia's strongest humanities subject category. Its strength derives from many sources: from anthologies of folktales ranging from E. C. G. Murray's *The National Songs and Legends of Roumania* (London, 1859) to the collections of Petre Ispirescu at the turn of the century, to the extensive collections published by the Romanian government since World War II; from special studies such as Marcu Beza's *Paganism in Roumanian Folklore* (Toronto, 1928) or Liviu Rusu's *Essai d'interpretation psychologique de la poésie populaire roumaine* (Paris, 1935); and from a complete set of the major folklore periodical *Revista de etnografie şi folclor*. The single most important item in the collection, however, is the 40-volume series published by the Romanian Academy between 1908 and 1931 under the rubric *Din vieaţa poporului român* [From the Life of the Romanian People]. Its monographs cover folklore, village customs, superstitions, games and dances, holidays, diseases and cures, and numerous other aspects of folklore and life in Romania, and provide extensive bibliographical material as well. The Library is currently receiving *Bibliografia generală a etnografiei și folclorului românesc* [A General Bibliography of Romanian Ethnography and Folklore] (Bucharest, 1968-), edited by A. Fochi and published under the supervision of M. Pop of the Institute of Ethnography and Folklore in Bucharest.

MUSIC.   Closely related to the field of folklore and custom is Columbia's substantial collection in Romanian folk music. Developed mainly under the impetus of Béla Bartók's stay at Columbia during his later years and of the ongoing Laura Boulton Collection and Research Project on World Music, the collection includes the works of Bartók (e.g., *Rumanian Folk Music,* ed. by Benjamin Suchoff, 3 v. (The Hague, 1967); or *Melodien der Rumänischen Colinde* (Vienna, 1935) and many of those of the leading Romanian musicologist Constantin Brăiloiu, e.g., *Vie musicale d'un village: recherches sur le répertoire de Drăguș, 1929-32* (Paris, 1960). Collections and analyses from both the 19th and 20th centuries, e.g., by F. W. Schuster (1862), Elena Văcărescu (1891), Artur Gorovei (1931), and Josef Kuckertz (1963), offer worthwhile research possibilities. The folk music of Maramureș, which was of particular interest to Bartók, is especially well represented.

Except for the folk area, however, Columbia holds only two significant works in Romanian musicology: Mihail G. Poslușnicu's *Istoria musicei la Români, de la Renaștere până' n epoca de consolidare a culturii artistice* [History of Romanian Music from the Renaissance to the Consolidation of Artistic Culture] (Bucharest, 1928) and the excellent annual publication *Studii de muzicologie* [Studies of Musicology] founded in 1965.

FINE ARTS AND ART HISTORY.   Columbia's library holdings in fine arts and art history display exceptional strength. The various pre- and postwar works of George Oprescu, N. Iorga, I. D. Ștefănescu, Grigore Ionescu, and Gheorghe Balș form the heart of a wide range of materials on Romanian painting, architecture, archeology, and religious and folk art included in the approximately 150-volume collection. In ancient art and archeology, Nicolae Densușianu's *Dacia preistorică* [Prehistoric Dacia] (Bucharest, 1913), the postwar monographic series *Arheologia Moldovei* [Moldavian Archeology] (begun in 1961), and *Biblioteca de Arheologie* [Archeology Library] (begun in 1957), as well as an ever increasing number of substantial studies by contemporary researchers, e.g., Dumitru Berciu, Hadrian Daicoviciu, D. Tudor, and Emil Condurachi, offer particularly impressive opportunities for research preparatory to field work in Romania.

Religion. Education. Philosophy.

The holdings in these three fields are weaker. In religion, the strongest of these three areas, Columbia has about 20 monographs, several of little value, to supplement N. Iorga's survey *Istoria Bisericii românești și a vieții religioase a Românilor* [History of the Romanian Church and the Religious Life of the Romanians], 2 v. (Valenii-de-Munte, 1908-09). The major works by Ștefan Mates, Ion Mateiu, or Ilarion Pușcariu are not included. Religion in Transylvania is treated in Johannes Crisan, *Beitrag zur Geschichte der kirchlichen Union der Romänen in Siebenbürgen unter Leopold I* (Leipzig, 1882); Andreas Schaguna, *Geschichte des griechisch-orientalischen Kirche in Oestereich* (Hermannstadt, 1862); and Erich Roth, *Die Geschichte des Gottesdienstes der Siebenbürger Sachsen* (Göttingen, 1954). The only religious periodical held by the University is *Biserica ortodoxă română* starting with volume 81 (1963).

The Columbia collection includes some monographic materials in the field of education, but by no means a complete or unusual collection. Interwar studies by N. Iorga, Grigore Tabacaru, and C. Angelescu, and recent historical efforts like Ariadna Camariano-Cioran's *Academiile Domnești din București și Iași* [The Princely Academies of Bucharest and Iași] (Bucharest, 1971) and Mircea

Tomescu's *Istoria cărţii româneşti de la începutul pînă la 1918* [The History of the Romanian Book from the Beginning to 1918] (Bucharest, 1968) constitute the holdings of value for the precommunist period, with few holdings for the post-1945 era.

Columbia's holdings in Romanian philosophy are limited primarily to C. I. Gulian's Marxist *Istoria gîndirii sociale şi filozofice în România* [The History of Social and Philosophical Thought in Romania] (Bucharest, 1964) and the Philosophy Institute's *Revista de filozofie*, which has been received regularly since 1965.

Paul A. Shapiro
Columbia University

Yugoslavia

THE YUGOSLAV COLLECTION of the Columbia University Library is located in the various departmental libraries. The two main collections are in Butler Library and the Herbert Lehman Library of the School of International Affairs. Specialized collections are located in other libraries, such as Law, Architecture, Fine Arts, Music, Journalism, the science libraries, and the Business Library. The Slavic and East European Acquisitions Section in the International Affairs Library maintains a catalog of Yugoslav backlog materials as well as a serials acquisition file of all Yugoslav periodicals received under PL 480 program and from other sources. Both of these records are available for consultation.

Prior to 1956 only occasional purchases of South Slavic materials were made by Columbia University. In 1956 the purchase of material from the South Slavic area increased in support of the new East Central European program. Collection emphasis was on broad subject categories, such as history, economics, government, Communism, philosophy, literature, linguistics, and general reference works.

A systematic approach to the acquisition of Yugoslav materials was initiated in 1965; the Columbia University Library joined the PL 480 Program in 1967.

In 1971-72 the total cataloged monograph holdings of Yugoslav material in the original languages in the Columbia Library were reported as 28,972 volumes. The areas most strongly represented in this collection are linguistics, literature, and history. Linguistics is the strongest of the three.

Bibliography and Reference

The Yugoslav collection is supported by a good base of reference and bibliographic works, including the latest encyclopedia published in Yugoslavia, *Enciklopedija Jugoslavije,* 8 v. (Zagreb, 1955-72), the earlier *Hrvatska enciklopedija,* 5 v. (Zagreb, 1941-45), Stanojević's *Narodna enciklopedija srpsko-hrvatsko-slovenačka,* 4 v. (Zagreb, 1925-29), and the new *Krajevni leksikon Slovenije* (Ljubljana, 1968-).

Dictionaries vary from the *Rječnik hrvatskoga ili srpskoga jezika* (Zagreb, 1880-) to *Rečnik srpsko-hrvatskoga književnog jezika* (Novi Sad-Zagreb, 1967-) and *Rečnik na makedonskiot jazik* (Skopje, 1961-66). Other important works are the one-volume *Srpski rječnik, istumačen njemačkijem i latinskijem riječima* (Vienna, 1852, and reprints) by Vuk A. Karadžić and the *Rječnik iz književnih starina srpskih,* 3 v. (Belgrade, 1863-64, and reprint) by Dj. Daničić. For the Slovene language there are J. Glonar's *Slovar Slovenskega jezika* (Ljubljana, 1935-36), M. Pleteršnik, *Slovensko-nemški slovar* (Ljubljana, 1894-95), A. Murko, *Slovensko-nemški in nemško-slovenski slovar* (Graz, 1832-33), and reprints of two old and valuable works by H. Megiser, *Thesaurus polyglottus* (originally published in Frankfurt, 1603-13) and his *Dictionarium quatuor linguarum* (originally published in Graz, 1592). The library has *Slovar slovenskega knjižnega jezika* (Ljubljana, 1970-) and numerous editions of multilingual and bilingual dictionaries.

The Library has all the major national bibliographic tools, including *Bibliografija Jugoslavije; knjige, brošure i muzikalije* (Belgrade, 1950-), *Bibliografija Jugoslavije; članci i književni prilozi u časopisima* (Belgrade, 1950-), *Bibliografija rasprava, članaka i književnih radova* (Zagreb, 1956-), *Bibliografija jugoslovenske periodike* (Belgrade, 1956-), and *Jugoslovenska retrospektivna bibliografska gradja; knjige, brošure i muzikalije, 1945-1967* (Belgrade), 24 v. to date. Earlier bibliographies include *Bibliografija srpske i hrvatske književnosti* for 1868-78 and 1883-84, published in the *Glasnik Srpskog učenog društva*, Kukuljević-Sakcinski, *Bibliografija hrvatska; Dio I. Tiskane knjige* (Zagreb, 1860), and *Hrvatska bibliografija, 1941-44, god 1-2* (1941-42). Earlier Croatian bibliographies at Columbia are G. Valentinelli's *Specimen bibliographicum de Dalmatia et agro labaetium* (Venice, 1842) as well as his *Bibliografia della Dalmazia e del Montenegro; Saggio* (Zagreb, 1855) and *Supplementi al Saggio . . .* (Zagreb, 1862), and C. Combi's *Saggio di bibliografia istriana* (Capodistria, 1864).

Among Slovene bibliographies the Library has J. Šlebinger's *Slovenska bibliografija za leta 1907-1912* (Ljubljana, 1913), *Slovenski časniki in časopisi; bibliografski pregled od 1797-1936* (Ljubljana, 1937), Simončič's *Slovenska bibliografija, I. del: Knjige (1550-1900)* (Ljubljana, 1903-05), and the current *Slovenska bibliografija* (Ljubljana, 1945-). Bosnia and Hercegovina is covered by Dj. Pejanović's *Štampa Bosne i Hercegovine 1850-1941* (Sarajevo, 1949) and *Bosansko-hercegovačka bibliografija knjiga i brošura, 1945-1951* (Sarajevo, 1953), D. Vuksan, *Pregled štampe u Crnoj Gori 1834-1934* (Cetinje, 1934), and M. Dragović, *Pokušaj za bibliografiju o Crnoj Gori* (Cetinje, 1892). For Macedonia the Library has the current *Makedonska bibliografija* (Skopje,1960-).

Columbia University Library has several editions of *Ko je ko u Jugoslaviji* (Belgrade, 1928, 1957, and 1970), as well as J. Radonić's *Slike iz istorije i književnosti* (Belgrade, 1938), *Znameniti i zaslužni Hrvati te pomena vrijedna lica u hrvatskoj povijesti od 925-1925* (Zagreb, 1925), Šime Ljubić's *Dizionario biografico degli uomini illustri della Dalmazia* (Vienna, 1856), Andra Gavrilović's *Znameniti Srbi XIX veka*, 3 v. (1901-04), and the *Slovenski biografski leksikon* (Ljubljana, 1925-). Columbia also has important bibliographies published by the Serbian and Croatian academies (SAN and JAZU): *Popis izdanja Jugoslavenske akademije 1867-1950* (Zagreb, 1951), *Popis izdanja Jugoslavenske akademije znanosti i umjetnosti u Zagrebu, 1945-1965* (Zagreb, 1966), and the *Pregled izdanja Srpske akademije nauka i umetnosti, 1847-1959* (Belgrade, 1961).

Linguistics

The Library has excellent resources for research in the Slovene, Serbo-Croatian, Macedonian, and Old Church Slavonic languages and their literatures. Besides complete runs of all major Slavic and general linguistics journals dealing with the South Slavic languages and such series as *Izvestiia otdeleniia russkogo jazyka i slovesnosti Akademii nauk* (St. Petersburg-Leningrad, 1896-1927), *Sitzungsberichte der philosophisch-historischen Classe der Kaiserlichen Akademie der Wissenschaften* (Vienna, 1848-), and *Denkschriften der Akademie der Wissenschaften philosophisch-historischen Classe* (Vienna, 1850-), Columbia has complete collections of all significant South Slavic linguistics journals and serials. The most representative of them are, for Serbo-Croatian: *Kovčežić za istoriju, jezik i običaje Srba sva tri zakona* (Vienna, 1849), *Južnoslovenski filolog* (Belgrade, 1913-). *Prilozi za književnost, jezik, istoriju i folklor* (Belgrade, 1921-), *Glasnik Jugoslovenskog profesorskog društva* (Belgrade, 1922-38; Columbia lacks individual volumes), *Anali* of the Filološki fakultet of Belgrade University (Belgrade, 1962-), the *Godišnjak* of the Filozofski fakultet in Novi Sad (Novi Sad, 1956-), serial publications of Matica Srpska: *Letopis* (Buda, Novi Sad, 1825-; individual volumes lacking), *Zbornik za književnost i jezik* (Novi Sad, 1953-), *Zbornik za filologiju i lingvistiku* (Novi Sad, 1957-), the following serial publications of the Serbian Academy of Sciences and Arts: *Glasnik*, v. 1-75 (1847-92), *Glas: filološko-istoriske i filosofske nauke* (1887-; individual numbers lacking), *Godišnjak* (1887-; individual numbers lacking), *Spomenik: filološko-istoriske i filosofske nauke* (1890-; individual volumes lacking), and its later subseries *Spomenik: Odeljenje društvenih nauka* (1948-), *Zbornik za istoriju, jezik i književnost srpskoga naroda:* Prvo odeljenje, *Spomenici na srpskom jeziku* (1902-; individual volumes lacking), Drugo odeljenje, *Spomenici na tudjim jezicima* (1904-; individual volumes lacking), Treče odeljenje, *Fontes Rerum Slavorum Meridionalium* (1932-; individual volumes lacking), *Posebna izdanja* in several classes: Filosofski i filološki spisi (1893-), Odeljenje literature i jezika (1950-), Institut za srpski jezik (1954-), and the journal *Naš jezik* (1949-), also published by the Serbian Academy of Sciences and Arts (SAN). For the Yugoslav Academy of Sciences and Arts (JAZU) in Zagreb, there are *Rad* (1867-), *Ljetopis* (1877-), *Djela* (1882-; individual volumes lacking), and *Zbornik za narodni život i običaje južnih Slavena* (1896-). Columbia has *Slovo* (1952-) and *Radovi* (1952-) of the Staroslavenski institut in Zagreb and three serial publications of the Filozofski fakultet of Zagreb University: its *Zbornik Radova* (1951-); *Radovi Slavenskog instituta* (1956-), and *Radovi Zavoda za slavensku filologiju* (1958-), as well as *Radovi Filozofskog fakulteta* (Zadar, 1959/60-) and *Jezik, časopis za kulturu hrvatskog književnog jezika* (Zagreb, 1952-). For Bosnia and Hercegovina there are the *Glasnik* of the Zemaljski muzej (Sarajevo, 1889-1916), *Wissenschaftliche Mitteillungen aus Bosnien und Herzegovina* (Vienna, 1893-1916), *Pitanja savremenog književnog jezika* (Sarajevo, 1949-52), and *Pitanja književnosti i jezika* (Sarajevo, 1954-).

For Slovenia, Columbia has the *Letopis* (Ljubljana, 1867-1912) of Slovenska Matica, *Zbornik znanstvenih in poučnih spisov* (Ljubljana, 1899-1912), *Izvestja* of the Muzejsko društvo za Kranjsko (Ljubljana, 1891-1909), *Carniola; Zeitschrift für Heimatkunde*, v. 1-2 (Ljubljana, 1908-09; new series, 1910-18), *Glasnik* of the Muzejsko društvo za Slovenijo (Ljubljana, 1919-45), *Časopis za zgodovino in narodopisje*, v. 1-35 (Maribor, 1904-40; new series, v. 1-, 1965-), *Časopis za slovenski jezik, književnost in zgodovino*. v. 1-8 (Ljubljana, 1918-31), *Razprave* of the Znanstveno in humanistično društvo v Ljubljani, Filološko-lingvistični odsek (Ljubljana, 1923-), *Slovenski jezik* (Ljubljana, 1938-41), *Slavistična revija* (Ljubljana, 1948-), and two publications of the Slovene Academy of Science and Art: *Dela* of the Razred za filološke in literarne vede (Ljubljana, 1950-) and *Razprave* of the Filozofsko-filološko-historični razred (Ljubljana, 1950-).

For Macedonia, Columbia has the *Glasnik* of the Skopsko naučno društvo (Skopje, 1925-30; individual volumes lacking), *Makedonski pregled* (Skopje, 1924-34, 1940-43), two serial publications of the Filozofski fakultet in Skopje: the *Godišen zbornik* of the Istorisko-filološki oddel (Skopje, 1948-) and the *Godišnjak* (Skopje, 1948-), as well as the *Diplomski raboti* (Skopje, 1950-). Macedonian material from Bulgaria includes *Sbornik za narodni umotvorenija, nauka i knižnina* (Sofia, 1889-), *Bŭlgarski Starini* (Sofia, 1906-45), *Spisanie na Bŭlgarskata Akademija na Naukite* (Sofia, 1911-50, 1953-), *Izvestija na Seminara po slavjanskata filologija pri Universiteta v Sofija* (Sofia, 1911-48), and *Sbornik na Bŭlgarskata Akademija na Naukite* (Sofia, 1913-49).

Columbia University Library has practically all significant studies contributing to Serbo-Croatian, Slovene, and Macedonian synchronic and diachronic linguistics in surveys, monographs, or journal articles by leading scholars past and present.

It should be noted that before 1945 Columbia's acquisition policy in Slavic linguistics emphasized older periodicals, but after the war a more balanced approach was taken. During the earlier period, a core collection of literature on Old Church Slavonic was acquired, which includes every major work in that language or an edition of its monuments. Many of these items have been placed in the Rare Book Collection, for example, the P. Nenadović edition of M. Smotrickij's *Slavonic Grammar* of 1755.

In the earlier period various basic dictionaries of the South Slavic languages were acquired, including, in addition to those already mentioned, Vuk S. Karadžić's *Srpski rječnik* (1818, 1852, 1898), I. Belostenec's *Gazophylacium seu Latino-Illyricorum onomatum aerarium* (Zagreb, 1740), J. Stulli's *Lexicon Latino-Italico-Illyricum,* 2 v. (Buda, 1801), J. Voltiggi's *Riczoslovnik illiricskoga, italianskoga i nimacskoga jezika* (Vienna, 1803), *Rječnik hrvatskog jezika,* 2 v. (Zagreb, 1901) by I. Iveković and I. Broz, M. Pohlin's *Tu malu besedishe treh jezikov* (Ljubljana, 1782), and M. Cigale's *Deutsch-slowenisches Wörterbuch,* 2 v. (Ljubljana, 1860).

Columbia possesses a number of valuable older and modern grammars of the Yugoslav languages. For Serbo-Croatian: Vuk S. Karadžić's *Pismenica* (Vienna, 1814, and later editions), his grammar of 1818 in J. Grimm's *Kleine Serbische Grammatik* (Leipzig-Berlin, 1824), a number of Dj. Daničić's works, such as *Oblici* (1863) and *Istorija oblika* (Belgrade, 1874), *Srbska sintaksa* (Belgrade, 1858), *Osnove srpskog ili hrvatskog jezika* (Belgrade, 1876), and *Razlike izmedju jezika srpskoga i hrvatskog* (Belgrade, 1857), and grammars by S. Novaković, Lj. Stojanović, M. Lalević, A. Belić, R. Aleksić, and M. Stevanović. There are also such works as *Institutionum linguae illyricae libri duo* by B. Kašić (Rome, 1604), *Grammatica della lingua illyrica* by F. M. Appendini (Dubrovnik, 1808), *Grammatik der illyrischen Sprache* by I. A. Brlić (Ofen, 1833), T. Maretić's *Gramatika i stilistika hrvatskoga ili srpskoga književnog jezika* (Zagreb, 1899), and M. Rešetar's *Elementar-Grammatik der Kroatischen (serbischen) Sprache* (Zagreb, 1916).

For Slovene, Columbia has A. Bohorič's *Arcticae horulae* (Wittenberg, 1584), B. Kopitar's *Grammatik der slavischen Sprache in Krain, Kärnten und Steyermark* (Ljubljana, 1808), V. Vodnik's *Pismenost* (Ljubljana, 1811), F. Levstik's *Slovenische Sprache nach ihre Redetheilen* (Ljubljana, 1866), and a series of editions of grammars by A. Janežić, A. Breznik, and J. Toporišić, including G. Svane's descriptive *Die Grammatik der slowenischen schriftsprache* (Copenhagen, 1958). For Macedonian there are, in addition to K. Kepeski's first grammar of modern Macedonian, the *Makedonski pravopis so pravopisen rečnik* (Skopje, 1950) by B. Koneski and K. Tošev, B. Koneski's *Gramatika na makedonskiot literaturen jazik,* v. 1-2 (Skopje, 1952-54, and later editions), and H. G. Lunt's *Grammar of the Macedonian Literary Language* (Skopje, 1952).

Columbia has rich collections of printed texts for linguistic and philological investigation of early languages and literatures of the Yugoslav peoples. For Slovene, there are the Freisingen monuments in various editions by P. J. Köppen (1827), B. Kopitar (1837), V. Vondrák (1896), S. Pirchegger (1931), F. Ramovš and M. Kos (1937), et al.; Jurij Dalmatin, *Biblia* (1584) (Munich, 1968, Facs.), and others. For Macedonian there are, in particular, Old Church Slavonic texts of Macedonian recension, for instance Dobromir's Gospel (V. Jagić, 1898), and the collection of *Stari tekstovi* of the Institut za makedonski jazik (Skopje, 1954-). For Serbo-Croatian (Medieval Serbian in particular) there are F. Miklosich's *Monumenta Serbica* (Vienna, 1858), M. Pucić's *Spomenici srpski od 1395 do 1423 . . . ,* 2 v. (Belgrade, 1858-62), Lj. Stojanović's *Stare srpske povelje i pisma,* 2 v. (Sremski Karlovci, 1929-34), and *Stari srpski rodoslovi i letopisi* (Sremski Karlovci, 1927). For the older Croatian Glagolitic tradition there are, among others, the series *Glagolitica: Publicationes Academiae Paleoslavicae Veglensis* (Veglae, 1903-16) by J. Vajs; older Croatian literature is available in the Yugoslav Academy (JAZU) publications *Starine,* v. 1- (Zagreb, 1869-), *Monumenta historico-juridica slavorum meridionalium* (Zagreb, 1877-1915), *Rad,* and *Djela.*

The dialectology of the Yugoslav languages is represented in Columbia by and large by the studies published in the serials and journals such as those mentioned above. For Serbo-Croatian there are monographs such as P. Ivić's *Dijalektologija srpsko-hrvatskoga jezika* (Novi Sad, 1956, with annotated bibliography), and special journals such as *Srpski dijalektološki zbornik* (Belgrade, 1905-) and *Hrvatski dijalektološki zbornik* (Zagreb, 1956-; v. 1 includes a complete bibliography of Kajkavian-Čakavian-Štokavian dialectology by M. Hraste). For the Slovene dialects, the Library has works by F. Ramovš, T. Logar, J. Baudouin de Courtenay, and J. Rigler, as well as a model treatment of one single feature of the Slovene dialects, *Les formes du duel en slovène*, by L. Tesnière, with *Atlas linguistique pour servir à l'étude du duel en slovène* (Paris, 1925). For Macedonian dialectology, Columbia has monographs by authorities such as V. Oblak, A. M. Seliščev, and A. Mazon, as well as A. Vaillant's *L'évangélaire de Kulakia* (Paris, 1938).

Folklore

The Library has most of the 19th-century editions of Yugoslav oral literature, in particular that of the Serbian and Croatian oral traditions. The most significant among them are various editions of V. S. Karadžić's *Srpske narodne pjesme* and the collections of folksongs by P. P. Njegoš, Dj. Rajković, M. Vasiljević, L. Marjanović, F. Kuhać, S. Mažuranić, B. Raić, V. Žganec, M. Parry, and A. B. Lord. The Bosnian-Hercegovian tradition is also well represented. Although Macedonian folklore appears mostly in the *Sbornik za narodni umotvorenja nauka i knjižnina*, Columbia also has the collections by the Brat'ja Miladinovci, S. Verković, and K. Šapkarev, *Slovenske narodne pesmi*, v. 1-4 (Ljubljana, 1895-1923) by K. Štrekelj, and the new *Slovenske ljudske pesmi* (Ljubljana, 1971), edited by Z. Kumer, cover the Slovene oral tradition.

In addition, there are numerous critical works on folklore by noted scholars such as F. Miklosich, V. Jagić, S. Novaković, R. Jakobson, L. Zima, T. Maretić, J. Polivka, F. Krauss, A. Schmaus, A. Soerensen, M. Braun, M. Kravcov, G. Geseman, M. Murko, and I. Grafenauer.

Literature

The Library's holdings of Slovene, Croatian, Serbian, and Macedonian pre-19th century literary works appear mostly in collections, series, and journals, rather than in the original publications. Thus, Medieval Serbian, Croatian, Dalmatian (Čakavian and Štokavian), Dubrovnik, and Kajkavian cultural traditions and the old Serbian and Croatian texts and monuments are available in Columbia's holdings of the serial publications of the Serbian (SAN) and Yugoslav (JAZU) academies, in *Slovo* and *Radovi* of the Staroslavenski Institut, and in other periodicals.

Croatian humanists and Latinists are represented in the JAZU series *Hrvatski latinisti* (Zagreb, 1951-) and in the two-volume *Hrvatski latinisti* published in the Matica Hrvatska series, Pet stoljeća hrvatske književnosti. The Dubrovnik Renaissance and Dalmatian Čajkavian and Štokavian literature is covered in the JAZU series *Stari hrvatski pisci* (Zagreb, 1869-), while several works of the Kajkavian literary tradition are found in the *Zbornik za istoriju, jezik i književnost srpskog naroda*, in *Posebna izdanja* of SAN, in *Monumenta spectantia historiam Slavorum Meridionalium* of JAZU, and in other serial publications of the two academies.

Older Slovene literary productions are represented at Columbia in such editions as *Slovenski protestantski pisci,* 2d ed. (Ljubljana, 1966) and in the *Zbrana dela slovenskih pesnikov in pisateljev,* as well as the recent facsimile editions of Trubar, Bohorić, and Dalmatin.

Monuments of the older Macedonian literature are dispersed in journals and serials, such as *Makedonski jazik, Sbornik na Bulgarska Akademiia na Naukite,* and *Spomenik* SAN; some are held as separate works of V. Jagić, A. Gianelli, and A. Vailland; some appear in anthologies by J. Ivanov, A. M. Seliščev; and some are being printed in the series *Stari tekstovi* of the Institut za makedonski jazik (Skopje, 1954-).

The Library has an extremely rich collection of comprehensive histories and literature surveys of individual traditions, such as P. J. Šafárik's *Geschichte der südslawischen Literatur,* edited by J. Jireček, 3 v. (Prague, 1864-65), M. Murko's *Geschichte der älteren südslawischen Litteraturen* (Leipzig, 1908), and his *Die Bedeutung der Reformation und Gegenreformation für das geistige Leben der Südslaven* (Prague, 1927), V. Jagić's *Historija književnosti naroda hrvatskoga i srpskoga, Staro doba* (Zagreb, 1867), B. Vodnik's *Povijest hrvatske književnosti, Knjiga I: Od humanizma do potkraj XVIII. stoljeća* . . . (Zagreb, 1913), and V. Lozovina's *Dalmacija u hrvatskoj književnosti; povijesni pregled regionalne književnosti u Dalmaciji, Hrvatskom primorju i Istri, 800-1890* (Zagreb, 1936), as well as works by Dj. Šurmin, M. Kombol, M. Medini, I. Torbarina's *Italian Influence on the Poets of the Ragusan Republic* (London, 1931), A. Pavičić, D. Prohaska, M. Hadžijahić's *Hrvatska muslimanska književnost prije 1878 godine* (Sarajevo, 1938), B. Drechsler, F. Bučar, A. Gavrilović, P. Popović, J. Skerlić's *Srpska književnost u XVIII. veku* (Belgrade, 1909 and other editions), T. Ostojić, J. Marn, I. Grafenauer, K. Glazer's *Zgodovina slovenskega slovstva,* v. 1-4 (Ljubljana, 1894-1900), F. Kidrič's *Zgodovina slovenskega slovstva, od začetkov do Zoisove smrti* (Ljubljana, 1938), L. Legiša's *Zgodovina slovenskega slovstva* (Ljubljana, 1956-71), and *Stranici od makedonskata kniževnost* (Skopje, 1952) by B. Koneski and H. Polenaković.

Beginning with the 19th century, the Serbian, Croatian, Macedonian, and Slovene literatures are exceptionally well represented at Columbia, often in original printings, but more frequently in the newer series of collected works in various editions.

Of note are Columbia's holdings of Serbian literary journals, beginning with such contemporary titles as *Književne novine* (Belgrade, 1948-), *Naša stvarnost* (Belgrade, 1953-), *Savremenik* (Belgrade, 1956-), *Književnost* (Belgrade, 1950-), *Književnost i jezik* (Belgrade, 1954-), *Delo; mesečni književni časopis* (Belgrade, 1969-), and *Književna kritika* (Belgrade, 1970-), and going back to earlier publications such as *Godišnjak N. Ćupića* (Belgrade, 1879-1941), *Prilozi za književnost, jezik i folklor* (Belgrade, 1894-1915), *Nova iskra* (Belgrade, 1899-1907), and such basic literary journals as Vuk S. Karadžić's *Danica* (Vienna, 1826-29, 1834), *Slavenno-serbskia viedomosti* (Novi Sad, 1792/93-99), *Slaveno-serbskij magazin Zaharije Orfelina* (Venice, 1768), and *Serbska pčela ili Novyi cvietnik* (Buda, 1836-41); of particular value are the complete holdings of the leading Serbian literary journal *Srpski književni glasnik* (Belgrade, 1901-14, 1920-40).

The Library has the collected works of a number of Serbian authors, published in the 19th century in the Serbian Državna izdanja, as well as collected works published in the monograph series "Biblioteka srpskih pisaca" (Belgrade, 1925-38); the Matica Srpska series, Srpska književnost u sto knjiga, and the annotated collections of Serbian classics published by Prosveta, for instance, the *Sabrana dela Vuka S. Karadžića,* an anniversary edition, planned in 30 volumes (Belgrade, 1965-). There are also collected works of contemporary Serbian authors as I. Andrić, M. Crnjanski, D. Ćosić, O. Davičo, P. P. Njegoš, B. Radičević, Laza Lazarević, Steven Sremac, and S. Matavulj, among others.

Columbia also has numerous critical anthologies, for example, B. Popović, *Antologija novije srpske lirike* (Zagreb, 1911; Belgrade, 12th ed., 1968), M. Pavlović, *Antologija srpskog pesnistva (XIII-XX vek)* (Belgrade, 1964), two anthologies in the monograph series, Srpska književnost u sto knjiga, *Srpski pesnici,* v. 1-2 (Novi Sad, 1971), and *Antologija srpske proze,* 2 v. (Belgrade, 1955), edited by V. Gligorić, et al., as well as works by A. G. Matoš and others.

Serbian literary history and criticism is represented by the works of B. Popović, *Ogledi iz književnosti i umetnosti* (Belgrade, 1914 and 1968) and *Ogledi, članci iz književnosti* (Belgrade, 1970), Dj. Šurmin, *Poviest književnosti hrvatske i srpske* (Belgrade, 1898), D. Bogdanović, *Pregled književnosti hrvatske i srpske* (Belgrade, 1915-16), J. Skerlić, *Istorija nove srpske književnosti* (Belgrade, 1912 and 1967), V. Gligorić, *Srpski realisti,* 6th rev. ed. (Belgrade, 1970), and

M. Kolarić, *Klasicizam kod Srba, 1790-1848* (Belgrade, 1965), as well as the most significant articles and books of literary scholars and critics published in the monograph series, Srpska književnost u književnoj kritici.

Croatian literary journalism is represented in the Columbia University Library in such old literary journals as *Danica horvatska, slavonska i dalmatinska* (Zagreb, 1835-49), *Kolo; članci za literaturu, umetnost i narodni život* (Zagreb, 1842-54), *Dragoljub* (Zagreb, 1868), *Hrvatsko kolo* (Zagreb, 1905-43), *Hrvatska revija* (Zagreb, 1928-44), *Književna republika* (Zagreb, 1923-24); and *Književnik* (Belgrade, 1928-39), as well as contemporary titles such as *Republika* (Zagreb, 1945-), *Forum; časopis odjelenja za suvremenu književnost* (Zagreb, 1964-), *Dubrovnik; književnost i umjetnost* (Dubrovnik 1967-), *Književna smotra* (Zagreb, 1969-), *Marulić; hrvatska književna revija (Zagreb, 1969-), Croatica; prinosi proučavanju hrvatske književnosti* (Zagreb, 1970-) and many others.

Columbia has a broad representation of critical and annotated editions of all the major Croatian authors of all periods, as well as various editions of selected and individual works ranging from A. Šenoa, A. G. Matoš, S. S. Kranjčević, Tin Ujević, to V. Nazor, Miroslav Krleža, and the youngest generation of Croatian writers and poets. A number of critical anthologies further complement the Library's excellent coverage of Croatian literature.

The Macedonian 19th-century writers are represented by the brothers Miladinov and Krste P. Misirkov. There is good coverage of contemporary Macedonian belles lettres in collected and individual works of all the major Macedonian writers and poets. *Antologija savremene makedonske poezije i proze* (Belgrade, 1961) and *Savremena makedonska poezija* (Belgrade, 1967) provide a general survey of Macedonian contemporary literature.

Macedonian literary history and criticism is covered by H. Polenaković, *Stranici od makedonskata književnost* (Skopje, 1952 and 1969), H. G. Lunt, "A Survey of Macedonian Literature," in: *Harvard Slavic Studies,* v. 1 (1953), B. Koneski, *Kon Makedonskata prerodba* (Skopje, 1959), and *Makedonska književnost: Ohridska škola* (Belgrade, 1968), as well as in scholarly journals containing the best studies in the field of literary history and criticism.

Slovene writers and poets are extensively covered in various of individual works and in annotated critical editions of collected works in the series *Zbrana dela slovenskih pesnikov in pisateljev* (Ljubljana, 1946-) and *Cvetje iz domačih in tujih logov* (Celje, 1933), *Monumenta Literarum Slovenicarum* (Ljubljana, 1954-). The Library has the complete works of Ivan Cankar, F. Levstik, I. Pregelj, F. Bevk, France Prešeren, to name some of the major authors.

Columbia's resources in the field of Slovene literary history and criticism are excellent, including all the major works from K. Glaser's *Zgodovina slovenskega slovstva* (Ljubljana, 1894-98), F. Kidrič, *Zgodovina slovenskega slovstva od začetkov do Zoizove smrti* (Ljubljana, 1929-38), I. Prijatelj, *Slovenska kulturno-politična in slovstvena zgodovina 1848-1895* (Ljubljana, 1955), A. Slodnjak, *Slovensko slovstvo* (Ljubljana, 1968), as well as his *Geschichte der slowenischen Literatur* (Berlin, 1958), *Zgodovina slovenskega slovstva* (Ljubljana, 1956-71) edited by L. Legiša, to *Zgodovina slovenskega slovstva* (Maribor, 1969-72) edited by J. Pogačnik, and a number of works by M. Boršnik, F. Vodnik, A. Ocvirk, B. Paternu, and others. The Library also has the monographic series *Razpotja; razprave, eseji, članki, kritike,* published in Maribor, and *Razprave in eseji,* published by Slovenska Matica in Ljubljana, and comprising studies on specific topics of literary history and criticism.

Ethnography is represented in the Library by a rich collection of primary and secondary sources. The journals include *Zbornik za narodni život i običaje južnih Slavena* (Zagreb, 1899-), published by JAZU, *Srpski etnografski zbornik,* v. 1- (Belgrade, 1902-), published by SAN, *Etnolog* (Ljubljana, 1923-44), *Slovenski etnograf* (Ljubljana, 1948-), both published by the Etnografski muzej, *Makedonski folklor* (Skopje, 1968-), among others. Monographs include

M. Milićević, *Kneževina Srbija* (Belgrade, 1876), most of the monographs of Jovan Cvijić, the works of Vuk S. Karadžić, J. Erdeljanović, T. Djordjević, V. Čajkanović, A. Radić, L. Kuba, J. Polívka, F. S. Krauss, E. Schneeweis, M. Gavazzi, J. Z. V. Popović's *Untersuchungen vom Meere* (Frankfurt and Leipzig, 1750), and the works of J. Pajek, K. Štrekelj, M. Murko, V. Möderndorfer, F. Marolt, V. Novak, N. Kuret, and others. There are ethnographic surveys, such as *Narodopisje Slovencev,* 2 v. (Ljubljana, 1944-52), edited by R. Ložar.

History

Columbia's extensive holdings in Yugoslav history begin with the 19th century. Almost every period and movement is represented, and extensive related materials in law, economics, politics, and government, as well as the principal general histories, are also available. Many of the early writings produced among the western South Slavs are being reproduced and printed with commentaries by the various Yugoslav academies. For example, Columbia has the *Monumenta tantia historiam slavorum meridionalium* (Zagreb, 1868-), a series published by the Jugoslavenska akademija znanosti i umjetnosti (JAZU), and others already named. Publications of the Srpska akademija nauka i umetnosti (SAN) are also well represented in the Library and include *Glasnik,* v. 1-75 (Belgrade, 1847-92), *Glas filološko-istoriske i filosofske nauke* (Belgrade, 1887-) and its later series, *Glas: Odeljenje društvenih nauka* (Belgrade, 1951-), *Spomenik filološko-istoriske i filosofske nauke* (Belgrade, 1890-), and its later series of the *Odeljenje društvenih nauka* (Belgrade, 1941-), *Zbornik za istoriju, jezik i književnost srpskoga naroda* (Belgrade, 1902-), and *Posebna izdanja,* with all its subseries. Publications of the Slovenska akademija znanosti in umetnosti (SAZU) in Ljubljana include *Letopis* (Ljubljana, 1943-), *Dela* of the Razred za zgodovino in družbene vede (Ljubljana, 1950-), *Razprave* (Ljubljana, 1950-). The Library's holdings of the publications of the Akademija nauka i umjetnosti Bosne i Hercegovine include *Djela* (Sarajevo, 1954-), *Godišnjak* (Sarajevo, 1956-), *Gradja* (Sarajevo, 1956-), *Ljetopis* (Sarajevo, 1970-), *Posebna izdanja,* and *Radovi* (Sarajevo, 1953-). Also present are the *Glasnik* of the Zemaljski muzej and the *Wissenschaftliche Mitteillungen aus Bosnien und Herzegovina* (Sarajevo-Vienna, 1889-1916). In Macedonia the Academy of Sciences was only recently formed from the Skopsko naučno društveno. Columbia has its *Glasnik* (Skopje, 1925-38) and the *Glasnik* of the Institut za nacionalna istorija, v. 1- (Sarajevo, 1957-).

The Library has a good range of older and current history journals such as *Bratsvo Društva Sv. Save* (Belgrade, 1887-1941), *Prilozi za književnost, jezik, istoriju i folklor* (1921-), *Godišnjica Nikole Ćupića* (Belgrade, 1877-1914; 1921-41), *Jugoslovenski istoriski časopis* (Belgrade, 1963-), *Letopis* of Matica Srpska (Novi Sad, 1825-), and its *Zbornik za društvene nauke* (Novi Sad, 1950-). For Croatia there are the *Arhiv za povjestnicu jugoslavensku* (Zagreb, 1851-75), published by I. Kukuljević-Sakcinski, the *Vjesnik Hrvatskoga arheološkog društva* (Zagreb, 1881-), *Starohrvatska prosvjeta* (Zagreb, 1895-1903; new series, 1927-28; and series 3, 1949-63), *Vjesnik za arheologiju i historiju dalmatinsku* (Split, 1885-), *Narodna starina* (Zagreb, 1922-35), *Historijski zbornik* (Zagreb, 1948-); and the *Vjesnik za etnografiju, etnologiju, antropologiju i prehistoriju* (Zagreb, 1935-38) of the Etnografski muzej of Zagreb. For Slovenia, Columbia has the *Glasnik* (Ljubljana, 1919-45) of the Muzejsko društvo za Slovenijo, and its earlier series *Carniola; Zeitschrift für Heimatkunde* (Ljubljana, 1908-09; new series, 1910-18), *Archiv für Heimatkunde* (Ljubljana, 1882-87), two publications of the Historischer Verein für Steiermark in Graz: *Mittheilungen* (1850-1903) and *Zeitschrift* (1903-), *Slovenska zemlja* (Ljubljana, 1892-1926), *Ljubljanski zvon* (Ljubljana, 1881-1941), *Zgodovinski časopis* (Ljubljana, 1947-), *Časopis za zgodovino in narodopisje,* v. 1-35 (Maribor, 1904-40), and its new series (1965-), *Časopis za slovenski jezik, književnost in zgodovino* (Ljubljana, 1918-31), *Kronika,* v. 15- (Ljubljana, 1967-).

Slovenska Matica in Ljubljana is represented by its *Letopis* (1866-1912) and *Zbornik,* v. 1-14 (1899-1912). For Montenegro, Columbia has *Istorijski zapisi,* v. 1- (Titograd, 1948-) and *Zapisi; Glasnik cetinjskog istorijskog društva* (Cetinje, 1935-41), *Južna Srbija,* v. 1-49 (Skopje, 1922-25), *Istorija* (Skopje, 1965-), and *Materiali za istoriiata na makedonskoto osvoboditelno dviženie* of the Makedonski naučen institut (Sofia, 1925-). The Library also holds various serial publications of the Yugoslav universities.

Individual monographs of the collection range from full histories of Yugoslavia to regional and local histories. Some of the earlier classical histories are also present, e.g., a number of scholarly editions of Presbyter Diocleas' Chronicle (by F. Šišić, V. Mošin, and S. Mijušković), of the *Zakonik cara Stefana Dušana, Istorija raznyh slavenskih narodov, najpače Bolgar, Horvatov i Serbov* (Vienna, 1795; Buda, 4 v., 1823). Three early works on Croatia and Dalmatia are reprinted in J. G. Schwandtner, *Scriptores rerum Hungaricum,* 3 v. (Vienna, 1746-48), Marko Marulić, *Regum Dalmatiae et Croatiae Gesta,* Paulus de Paulo, *Memoriale,* and Johannes Lucius, *De Regno Dalmatiae et Croatiae Libri sex.* Later contributors to the history of the Yugoslav area represented in the collection are Anton T. Linhart, *Versuch einer Geschichte von Krain und der übrigen Ländern der südlichen Slaven Österreichs,* 2 v. (Ljubljana, 1788-91), Johan Christian von Engel, *Geschichte des ungarischen Reichs,* 5 v. (Vienna, 1813-14), Leopold Rank, *History of Servia* (London, 1853), A. Dimitz, *Geschichte Krains von der ältesten Zeit auf des Jahr 1813,* 4 v. (Ljubljana, 1874-76), and J. W. Valvasor, *Die Ehre des Herzogthums Krain,* 2d ed., 4 v. (Rudolfswerth, 1877-79). Among the major histories, Columbia has K. Jireček, *Istorija Srba,* 2d ed., 2 v. (Belgrade, 1952), Stanoje Stanojević, *Istorija srbskoga naroda,* 2d ed. (Belgrade, 1910), Lajos Thallóczy, *Studien zur Geschichte Bosniens und Serbiens in Mittelalter . . .* (Munich, 1914), T. Smičiklas, *Povijest Hrvatske,* 2 v. (Zagreb, 1879-82), V. Klaić, *Povijest Hrvata od najstarijih vremena do svršetka XIX stoljeća* (Zagreb, 1899-1911), F. Šišić, *Pregled povijesti hrvatskoga naroda,* 3d ed. (Zagreb, 1962), J. Šidak, *Povijest hrvatskoga naroda g. 1860-1914* (Zagreb, 1968), B. Grafenauer, *Zgodovina slovenskega naroda,* 2d ed., 2 v. (Ljubljana, 1964-65), J. Gruden, *Zgodovina slovenskega naroda* (Celje, 1910), M. Kos, *Zgodovina Slovencev od naselitve do petnajstega stoletja* (Ljubljana, 1955), Ivan Prijatelj, *Kulturna i politična zgodovina Slovencev 1848-1895,* 3 v. (Ljubljana, 1938), as well as the 1955-61 edition published in Ljubljana in four volumes under the title *Slovenska kulturno-politična in slovstvena zgodovina 1848-1895,* V. Klaić, *Geschichte Bosniens vom dem ältesten Zeiten bis zum Verfalle des Königreiches* (Leipzig, 1885), Sima-Sarajlija Milutinović, *Istoriia Černe-Gore od iskona do noviega vremena* (Belgrade, 1835), Jaguš Jovanović, *Stvaranje crnogorske države i razvoj crnogorske nacionalosti . . .* (Cetinje, 1947), Ilarion Ruvarac, *Montenegrina; prilošci istoriji Crne Gore,* 2d ed. (Zemun, 1899), Dimitar Vlahov, *Iz istorije makedonskog naroda* (Belgrade, 1950), and *Istorija na makedonskiot narod,* 3 v. (Skopje, 1963) published by the Institut za nacionalna istorija. Individual regions and problems within Yugoslavia are also well covered.

A comprehensive, collective survey of the history of the nations of Yugoslavia is *Historija naroda Jugoslavije,* 2 v. (Zagreb, 1953-59), edited by A. Babić, et al.

In the postwar period, Yugoslavia has made special efforts to cover the partisan activities of World War II. This material is represented in Columbia, for example, by the major series, *Zbornik dokumenta i podataka o narodnooslobodilačkom ratu jugoslovenskih naroda* (Belgrade, 1949-), published by the Vojnoistorijski institut. There are also works on the early workers' movement.

Other holdings of value are microfilm copies of issues of the newspaper *Radničke novine* (Belgrade, 1902-07, 1908-10, 1918-21). The Library has long runs of *Politika* and *Borba* (earlier issues on microfilm) and *Slobodna riječ* (Zagreb, 1902-09, microfilm).

Finally, it should be noted that Columbia University Library has many archival publications, example, the *Gradja* (Belgrade, 1951-54) of the Državni Arhiv in Serbia, *Arhivski pregled* (Belgrade, 1965-), *Arhiv za pravne i društvene nauke* (Belgrade, 1968-), *Vjesnik* (Zagreb, 1899-1945) of the Državni Arhiv in Croatia, and the *Istorijska gradja* (Cetinje, 1959-) of the archives of the Montenegrin Republic.

Nina A. Lenček and Robert A. Karlowich
Columbia University

Other Countries

THE DEVELOPMENT OF Polish, Czechoslovak, and Bulgarian collections at Columbia parallels the general development of Slavic studies in the United States. Details may be found in Clarence A. Manning's *A History of Slavic Studies in the United States* (Milwaukee, 1957, pp. 32, 51-52, 73). With the establishment of the East Central European Institute in 1954 and the introduction of area studies, a precise policy on acquisition of Slavic material was adopted, by which the material acquired had to be directly related to course work and research. Emphasis was laid on the following broad subject divisions: history, economics, government, communism, philosophy, literature, linguistics, the social sciences, and reference works. The following is a very broad overview of what is available at Columbia in major subject areas as defined by the acquisition policy.

Poland

This collection owes much of its early growth to the professors who taught the Polish language and Polish literature at Columbia. The first Polish language course was taught in 1914; graduate instruction in Polish literature was begun in 1916, but the collections at that time were negligible. Professor Arthur Prudden Coleman, who taught Polish courses for 20 years until 1947, and Professor Manfred Kridl, who held the Adam Mickiewicz Chair for Polish literature (1948-55) contributed to the development of the Polish collection in language and literature and each donated a sizable personal collection to the Library. Professor Peter Brock was responsible for the acquisition of a number of rare 17th- and 18th-century items in Polish history.

Until recently, Polish material was not regularly selected for purchase and this partly accounts for gaps in holdings. Only in the last few years, through the cooperative effort of faculty members and the East Central European Bibliographer, national and trade bibliographies have been checked systematically. During 1972, Columbia began to receive current works, numerous journals, and newspapers under the Public Law 480 program. The major and provincial periodicals and newspapers currently received cover every aspect of Polish life, including pure and applied sciences. A recently established exchange program with Polish institutions of learning is an important source for obtaining their publications, and the publications and films necessary to complete Columbia's holdings in periodical and newspapers collections. Participating in the exchange program are: the Polish Academy of Sciences with its regional branches, seven universities, and numerous scientific societies and institutes located in Warsaw, Kraków, Gdańsk, Białystok, Kórnik, Łódź, Lublin, Poznań, Toruń, and Wrocław.

There is no separate catalog in the Library for Slavic holdings. Polish items are interfiled in alphabetical order in the General Card Catalogue which covers items in various languages. This makes an evaluation of the collection rather difficult. The General Card Catalogue is located on the third floor of Butler Library in the Reference Room. Here are also located the subject and periodical catalogs which do not differentiate between materials in Slavic and other languages. Polish materials are recorded in both of them. The Reference Librarian should be consulted on the peculiarities of the entries in subject and periodical catalogs. Since the materials are housed in various libraries of Columbia, the location is indicated on cards of the three catalogs. The Reference Room houses the national bibliographies and other general and specialized reference aids in Slavic and Western languages. The Slavic Bibliographer, located in the Lehman Library, can be consulted for specialized reference assistance.

The Polish collection presently comprises approximately 31,000 volumes, with an annual growth rate of about 600 volumes in the 1960s and 700 in the 1970s. The strength of the Polish collections lies in monographs. They mainly cover literature, linguistics, history, social sciences, and reference material.

The collection contains nearly 80 percent of the titles listed for Poland in Paul L. Horecky (ed.), *East Central Europe: A Guide to Basic Publications* (Chicago, 1969). The best coverage is found in the areas of general reference aids and bibliography, history, the state, the economy, literature and language, and includes many additional titles of recent imprint date. Most of the items missing pertain to the section on intellectual and cultural life, particularly in religion, music, art, education, demography, theater and cinema, community structure, and culture.

The Library has a strong collection of Polish and Western language reference works, covering monographs, periodicals, and newspapers. Almost all works listed in Józef Grycz i Emilia Kurdybacha's *Bibliografia w teorii i praktyce, oraz wykaz ważniejszych bibliogafij i dzieł pomocniczych* (Warsaw, 1953) are in the Columbia Libraries. An important bibliographic guide to Polish bibliographies is Wiktor Hahn's *Bibliografia bibliografij polskich,* 1921 edition and enlarged 1966 edition covering the period to 1950, later extended to 1960 by Henryk Sawoniak.

Important for historical studies is Ludwik Finkel's *Bibliografia historii polskiej* covering the period from the earliest times to 1815; and for the history of literature, Gabriel Korbut's *Literatura polska od początków do wojny światowej* and its continuation the *Nowy Korbut.* The most important of retrospective bibliographies is Karol Estreicher's *Bibliografia Polska,* which lists, in 40 volumes, all Polish works for the period 1455-1900. For monographic series published after World War II there is a very valuable bibliography entitled *Serie wydawnicze Polskiej Akademii Nauk i towarzystw naukowych* (1967). The best scholarly publications in all subjects are listed in these series.

The Polish history collection deserves special attention. The libraries have a comprehensive collection of material in Polish and Western languages facilitating the study of important periods of Polish history from the earliest times to the present. Particularly strong are the holdings of printed source materials. Numerous original publications comprise the primary sources on early Polish history. The most valuable original works owned by Columbia Libraries belong to the 16th and 17th centuries. They describe not only Poland's past, but also wars, mode of life, and foreign relations. Among them are 16th-century books printed in Kraków representing not only rare historical sources, but also presenting examples of early printing in Poland. They are: *Chronica Polonorum* by Maciej z Miechowa (1521), *De vetustatibus Polonorum . . .* by Justus Ludwig Dietz (1521) and *Sarmatiae Europeae descriptio . . .* by Aleksander Gwagnin (1578). The item of importance is a 16-volume set of *Acta Tomiciana* started by Piotr Tomicki and continued by Stanisław Górski. It consists of Polish state papers for the period 1499-1572. Of the important writers of the 16th century, Marcin Kromer is represented by seven works.

Significant publications of the 17th century include a chronicle by Paweł Piasecki, the Bishop of Przemyśl: *Chronica gestorum in Europa singularium* (1648) in the original and an 1870 Polish translation, and a history of Poland by Joachim Pastorius of Hirtenberg: *Historiae Polonae plenioris pars priorposterior . . . Interserta Cosacorum a Tataricae simul gentis descriptio ac multa alia* (1685). Among the prominent writers of the 17th century, the Library has three works by Szymon Starowolski, including his biobibliography *Scriptorum Polaniae* (1625) containing biographical and bibliographical data on one hundred Polish writers, an 1858 edition of *Dwór cesarza tureckiego i rezydencja jego w Konstantynopolu,* and a Russian translation of this work from the original manuscript in 1678 for Tsar Fedor Alekseevich, in time of preparation for war with the Turks. In addition, there are many 16th- and 17th-century books about Poland, including the memoirs of Jan Chryzostom Pasek and annals of Jan Długosz in post-World War II editions.

The original works of Poland's major historians of the 18th and 19th century are represented in the collection; however, the holdings are weak, often consisting of one volume and not always the most important one. For example, of the 10-volume *Historia narodu polskiego* by a distinguished historian of the 18th century, Adam Naruszewicz, the Library has only three volumes. While Joachim Lelewel is represented by several volumes of his collected works, and Stanisław Smolka by three, Ksawery Liske, Walerian Kalinka, and Stanisław Kętrzycki are represented by one work each. The Library holds one of the important works of the 19th century, a history of Poland by Józef Szujski, *Dzieje Polski podług ostatnich badań,* covering the period 1572-1795.

The turn-of-the-century historians are better represented in the collection, although their works are not complete. Szymon Askenazy's several works are available as well as the works of Wilhelm Feldman and Tadeusz Korzon. Feldman's *Geschichte der politischen Ideen in Polen seit dessen Teilungen,* covering 1795-1914, is present in 1st and 2d editions.

The historical material for the period between the wars is rich in works pertaining to international relations, diplomacy, and archeological investigations. Of importance as source material are memoirs of distinguished Polish statesmen and soldiers such as Józef Piłsudski, Edward Rydz-Śmigły, and Wincenty Witos. The studies of Poland's prehistoric times are covered by serial publications of various archeological institutes, learned societies, and university publications. Especially plentiful are the archeological studies concerning the western part of Poland because of border disputes between Poles and Germans. Numerous documents in the collection relate to the dilemma of the free city of Danzig, Polish-German and Polish-Soviet relations of 1933-1939, and border disputes.

Holdings on the World War II and postwar period are most plentiful. Worth noting are the documents pertaining to the origin of the war, the partisan movement, the Nurnberg trials, and memoirs and eyewitness accounts of the war period. The historical works of present-day Poland held in the collection pertain to social history and economic conditions, and include new studies by modern Polish historians of historical periods, and reissued classics.

Columbia has a fine collection of Polish law publications. Beginning with the Statutes of the Diet of Wiślica of 1347 up to the end of Poland's independence with the first partition in 1772, it covers all of the most important laws enacted by the Parliament and the kings. Occupying the place of honor among the treasures is an original set of *Volumina Legum* (1732), containing a compilation of most important Polish laws from the beginning to 1732. The Library holds a comprehensive collection of the Polish Supreme Court Jurisprudence covering the period between the wars, as well as a collection of laws and statutes for that period and various editions of codes with comprehensive changes and revisions. There is also a collection of penal law dating to the present, including the decisions of the Polish courts for the years 1921-38. The holdings include most of the compilations of Polish treaties concluded after the First World War, and a collection of German laws governing Poland during the war years 1939-45, issued in Kraków, the seat of German Government in Poland. In addition, a complete set of the laws enacted by the Polish Parliament (1943-45) is also in the collection. One of the most important historians of Polish public law, Oswald Balzer, is represented in the collection by four books.

The Polish literature, language, and linguistics collection offers a comprehensive body of material, although there are areas of both strength and weakness. Representatives of important literary trends in poetry, prose, and drama are included in the collection. The writers of post-World War II Poland are selectively included in the collection; however, the holdings of literary material for the 1950s are rather weak.

Beginning with the great poets of the 16th century, Klemens Janicki and Maciej Kazimierz Sarbiewski (Latin poetry), Jan Kochanowski (considered the father of Polish poetry), and Mikołaj Rey (the first Polish writer to forsake Latin in favor of his native tongue), the collection includes all major poets and writers up to and including those of the 20th century. The works of several 19th-century novelists are also available in English translation, e.g., the early translation of Henryk Sienkiewicz's *Quo Vadis* by Jeremiah Curtin (1896). It is interesting to note that Adam Mickiewicz is a singular author for whom the card catalog contains over 300 entries in Polish, Russian, and Western languages. Among them are several treasures. The Library owns the first edition of *Konrad Wallenrod* (St. Petersburg, 1828), *Pan Tadeusz* (Paris, 1832), and *Księga narodu polskiego i pielgrzymstwa polskiego* (Paris, 1832), as well as *Pisma* (Paris, 1861) in six volumes. Another item of interest is a three-volume set of his lectures on Slavic literature published in 1840-43, which he delivered at the Sorbonne.

Other prominent items in the literature collection are *Poezye Juliusza Słowackiego* (Paris, 1832), *Poezye Aleksandra Chodźki* (Poznań, 1833), and *Poezye Juliana Korsaka* (Poznań, 1833). The collection also contains major works on literary criticism and literary history, beginning with the 19th-century writings of Ignacy Matuszewski, Józef Szujski, and Piotr Chmielowski, and continuing with basic studies by pillars of literary criticism and literary history as Stanisław Tarnowski, Wilhelm Feldman, and Juliusz Kleiner. The period between the wars is represented by such literary critics as Jan Kot, Kazimierz Wyka, Stanisław Pigoń, and the contemporary period by Roman Pollak, Stefan Durski, and Michał Głowiński.

The linguistics collection has spotty coverage of the material before the 19th century and of the first two decades of the 20th century. The history of the Polish language is represented by works of Jan Baudouin de Courtenay, Tadeusz Lehr-Spławiński, and Aleksander Brückner, while present-day linguists Jerzy Kuryłowicz, Zdzisław Stieber, and Władysław Kuraszkiewicz are also represented. The works on language studies are for the most part outdated, the grammar books old, and the primary sources for language studies are lacking.

In the field of sociological studies, the Library has material covering sociological investigations for early and recent periods. The best sociologists of the interwar period and after World War II are represented in the collection. Adam Krzyżanowski, Henryk Tannenbaum, Stefan Czarniecki, Julian Hochfeld are some of the leading sociologists of the early 20th century whose works are represented in the collection. The number of present-day sociologists is greater and their publications more plentiful. The leading figure is Michał Kalecki, whose basic work, *Theory of Economic Dynamics,* is available in four different editions in both Polish and English. In addition, 16 other publications, of which 10 are in English, are also included in the collection. Oskar Lange, another leading economist, is represented by 38 works. American sociologists whose works focused on Polish immigrants in America are also included in the collection. Wenceslaus Kruszka and Miecislaus Haiman are representatives of this group. Basic statistical sources published by the Main Statistical Office are complete or nearly complete. With the exception of 1950, the Library has a complete set of Poland's censuses of the population.

Although religion played an important role in Poland's cultural and political history and much has been published on this subject, Columbia's holdings are insignificant. There are, however, some important items worth mentioning. A notable bibliography by Joachim R. Bar and Wojciech Zmarz, *Polska bibliografia prawa kanonicznego od wynalezienia druku do 1940* covers the materials pertaining to the legal position of the Catholic Church in Poland from the invention of printing until 1940. The modern edition of the statutes of Mikołaj Trąba, *Statuty synodalne Wieluńsko-Kaliske Mikołaja Trąby z r. 1420,* pertaining to the status of the Catholic Church in medieval Poland, is also available. Other items of interest are: a microfilm of the 1561 and 1566 editions of the catechism by Jan Laski, the Bishop of Weszprim, the modern editions of the Bible of Queen Jadwiga, and *Biblia Szaroszpatacka,* one of the oldest Bibles.

The strength in Polish periodicals lies in the post-World War II titles, and the years between the two wars are also well represented. The real weaknesses are found in the 18th- and 19th-century holdings. Columbia has almost no holdings for the 18th century and only some titles for the later part of the 19th century, lacking most of the important 19th-century émigré periodicals. The Library has an incomplete but growing collection of the major literary journals, including *Dziennik Literacki* (Lwów), *Przewodnik Naukowy i Literacki, Przegląd Polski, Chimera, Lamus, Pamiętnik Literacki, Skamander, Wiadomości Literackie,* as well as the complete set of the principal historical journal *Kwartalnik Historyczny. Zeszyty Historyczne* (Paris), and *Teki Historyczne* (London) are also present.

The holdings of newspapers for the 19th century are weak, but an effort is being made to acquire the most important titles, e.g., *Gazeta Warszawska* (1871-75) and *Kurier Warszawski* (1871-75) have been purchased on microfilm. The strength of the newspaper collection lies in the post-1950 titles. Over 55 titles are recorded for this period, published in Warsaw, Kraków, Radom, Łódź, Poznań, Białystok, Koszalin, Rzeszów, and Wrocław.

The government publications are represented by items from the Ministry of Education, the Ministry of the Interior, the Main Statistical Office, the Ministry of Foreign Affairs, the Ministry of Information, and the Ministry of Culture and Art.

Czechoslovakia

The Czech and Slovak collections at Columbia University Libraries are substantial. Rated as the second in the country by the survey conducted by Ruggles and Mostecky, the holdings have grown at an average rate of 450 volumes a year, constituting a collection today of some 30,000 volumes.

The history of the collection's development follows the pattern of the Polish collection. The materials were bought when they became available. Courses for Czech language study were offered in 1920 and elementary literature in 1931. The collection at that time consisted mostly of textbooks, grammars, dictionaries, and some fiction. It was only after the Second World War, when Professor Roman Jakobson was appointed the Thomas G. Masaryk Professor of Slavic Philology, that interest in building the collection increased. With the establishment of the East Central European Institute the need for scholarly research material was recognized and the areas to be developed were stated in the acquisition policy already mentioned.

In monographs, the strongest holdings are in the area of bibliography, literature, history, and social sciences. The bulk of the publications are in the Czech and Slovak languages, but there is a considerable number of volumes in English, German, French, and Russian. The coverage of the historical periods is uneven in literature as well as in history.

In literature, the belles lettres collection includes complete, or nearly complete sets of most of the classics. There is a set of collected works of Božena Němcová, the first woman writer who contributed to Czech literature. Gaps in coverage occur in fiction and poetry after 1870, and the coverage of biographies of major writers is spotty. Important works in literary criticism and the history of literature for the interwar period are included in the collection. The most important monographs in linguistics are present and some of the important Czech linguists such as Miroslav Komárek, Jan Stanislav, and Vincent Blanar are represented.

Historical surveys are available for all periods. Basic works are present on the prehistory of the country in post-World War II editions. The historical source material is weak for the period between the two wars, and comprehensive for the period 1938-45, including the documents on the resistance movement and Czechoslovak politics under the German occupation. There is a good collection of works by and about T. G. Masaryk, Václav Novotný, and other political leaders.

Seventy percent of the basic publications in all areas represented in the chapter on Czechoslovakia in Horecky's *Guide* are in the collection. While in the areas of language, literature, history, and the state, almost all items are present, the other areas have gaps. Demography, culture, community structure, philosophy, education, music, theater, and cinema are poorly represented, accounting for nearly all of the missing items.

The collection is strong in periodicals and serial publications. They have important research value. Some of the literary periodicals are: *Lumír, Ruch, Květy, Zlatá Praha, Host* and in linguistics: *Naše řeč, Slovenská reč,* and Listy filologické. Several periodicals cover intellectual life: *Volná myšlenka, Život, Věda a umění.* Historical periodicals include *Český časopis historický, Archivní časopis, Čas, Sborník historický,* to name a few.

Recently Columbia concluded exchange agreements with several institutions of learning, including the Czech and Slovak academies of sciences, major universities in Bratislava, Brno, Olomouc, and Prague, and the State Library. Their publications are received in the area of the social sciences, literature, philology, linguistics, history, economics, anthropology, and pure sciences.

Publications are also received from government institutions such as The Ministry of Foreign Trade, the Ministry of Foreign Affairs, the Ministry of the Interior, and the State Statistical Office.

Bulgaria

Columbia's holdings of Bulgarian materials comprise approximately 6,600 volumes with an annual growth rate of about 325 volumes for the last decade. Ninety-eight percent of Bulgarian publications are obtained through exchange agreements with the Vazov National Library, the Bulgarian Academy of Sciences, the Cyril and Methodius National Library, the University of Sofia, and the Institute of Higher Studies in Economics and Finance. The strength of the collection lies in literature and history, but recently the stress has been put on acquiring more social science material. Most publications are of post-World War II imprint date, but the years between the wars are also represented. The source materials are provided by the Bulgarian Academy of Sciences.

Sixty-five percent of the works cited in the chapter on Bulgaria in Horecky's *Guide* are in the collection. The strongest subject areas are literature and history, with good representation in general reference aids and bibliographies; the weakest areas are physical landscapes, demography, economic planning, psychology, education, theater, music, art, and cinema. Other subject areas have representative coverage.

Bulgarian literature dates from the second half of the 19th century. Columbia has a comprehensive collection of works by leading authors of the 19th and 20th century. Khristo Botev, Ivan Vazov, Konstantin Velichkov, Lyuben Karavelov, Stoyan Mikhailovski represent the 19th century, while prose and poetry of the 20th century are represented by Georgi Raychev, Atanas Dalchev, Elisaveta Bagryna, and many others.

Among periodicals, there is a good selection in literary, historical, and social science titles. The important literary journal *Zlatorog* (1928-43) is included in the collection. Two important periodicals of the Bulgarian Academy of Sciences, *Spisanie na Bălgarskata akademija na naukite* (1911-50), and *Sbornik na Bălgarskata akademija na naukite* (1913-49) are also in the collection.

Columbia currently receives 24 publications from the Bulgarian Academy of Sciences, including abstracts of Bulgarian scientific literature in geology, geography, economics, and law. Thirty-six titles are received from the University Library in Sofia, including its bibliography of publications, prospectus of the academic year, and *Studia Balcanica;* twenty-three publications are received from the Cyril and Methodius National Library, including *Bălgarski knigopis, Finansi i kredit, Parten zhivot, Literaturen front, Nove vreme, Iskustvo, Ezik i literatura,* and *Bibliotekar.*

The newspaper collection is strong in post-World War II titles. Over 20 titles cover the years 1950-60, but the holdings are incomplete. An attempt is being made to complete the periodical and newspaper holdings on microfilm. To date the holdings of 15 Bulgarian journals have been completed.

Leonarda Wielawski
Columbia University

Cornell University

General Information

Material from and about East Central and Southeastern Europe in the humanities and the social sciences is located for the most part in John M. Olin Library, the central research library. Library hours during the academic year are Monday through Thursday: 8 a.m.-12 midnight; Friday: 8 a.m.-10 p.m.; Saturday: 9 a.m.-10 p.m.; Sunday: 1 p.m.-12 midnight. Additional material in the social sciences may also be found in the Industrial and Labor Relations Library. Separate libraries for fine arts, law, and music also collect publications from East Central and Southeastern Europe.

All members of the Cornell community may borrow books from any library on campus. However, access to the stacks in the central research library is usually restricted to graduate students and faculty. Other libraries on campus (with the exception of the Music Library and the Agricultural and Biological Sciences Library) have unrestricted access. Library resources are also available for use by persons outside the Cornell community in the following ways:

Use of material within the Library. Any responsible person may consult an item in the Library. All persons will be asked to present suitable evidence of identity.

Copy service. In general, one copy of any library item will be made for an individual. For copyrighted books published within the last 56 years, permission is required. Microfilm or Xerox copies of library material may also be obtained by mail for the cost of reproduction and handling. A price list is available from Interlibrary Lending and Cooperative Reference Services, Cornell University Libraries, Ithaca, N.Y. 14853.

Loan for use outside the Library. Persons wishing to borrow books may do so through interlibrary loan. Periodicals in the central research library and all other libraries on campus collecting in the humanities and social sciences do not circulate. Most other material is available for lending within the United States and Canada. A detailed statement of policy is available from Interlibrary Lending and Cooperative Reference Services, Cornell University Libraries, Ithaca, N.Y. 14853.

The reference and bibliography section of the central research library includes most major bibliographies and finding aids needed for preliminary investigation and verification. These range from such standard comprehensive tools as the *National Union Catalog,* the British Museum's *General Catalog of Printed Books,* and the *Catalogue général des livres imprimés de la Bibliothèque nationale* to works pertaining more specifically to East Central and Southeast Europe such as *Südosteuropa-bibliographie, Sovetskoe slavianovedenie,* the New York Public Library's *Dictionary Catalog of the Slavonic Collection,* the various bibliographic guides published by the Library of Congress, etc. National bibliographies are available for all countries in East Central and Southeastern Europe with the exception of Albania for which the national bibliography has just recently been ordered.

The East Central and Southeastern Europe area collection is totally integrated into the general humanities and social sciences collection. There is no special reading room. Carrels placed throughout the stacks are available to a limited number of graduate students. Faculty members are assigned private or semiprivate studies also located directly in the stacks.

Requests for further information should be addressed to the Slavic Studies Librarian, 110 Olin Library, Cornell University, Ithaca, N.Y. 14853. Telephone: (607) 256-4969.

The goal in developing the East Central and Southeastern European collection at Cornell has been limited, as a rule, to creating a balanced collection of titles basic to a large research library as well as representative of each country in the area under discussion.

Newspapers currently received from East Central and Southeastern Europe are as follows: Czechoslovakia: *Rudé právo;* East Germany: *Neues Deutschland;* Greece: *To vema;* Poland: *Trybuna Ludu;* Yugoslavia: *Borba.* No newspapers are currently received from Albania, Bulgaria, Hungary, and Romania.

Among the over 800 serial titles in the social sciences and the humanities currently received from and about East Central and Southeastern Europe, over 80 are devoted exclusively to linguistics; 50 concern language and/or literature; and 110 cover history and its auxiliary disciplines. The collection also numbers approximately 40 currently received serial titles in archeology, 50 in bibliography and library science, 80 in economics and political science, 30 in anthropology, sociology, and psychology, and 20 in philosophy and esthetics. The Music Library currently receives about 20 serial titles and the Fine Arts Library about 40. An additional 250 currently received serial titles range across several disciplines in the humanities and social sciences.

Heavy coverage in history and archeology is also reflected in series holdings, where 117 titles or 34 percent of a total of about 350 currently received series are in these two subjects. A further breakdown of currently received series shows approximately 30 series in linguistics, 30 in literature, 20 in economics and political science, nine in bibliography and library science, six in philosophy and esthetics, eight in anthropology, sociology, and psychology, 25 in music, and 84 of a general nature.

In developing serial and series holdings, both currently and retrospectively, emphasis has been placed on the publications of the various institutes and academies of science in East Central and Southeastern Europe. If one considers Poland, for example, one finds that the Library currently receives at least 26 series or serial titles published by the Polska Akademiia Nauk (PAN) in the humanities and social sciences. In addition, there are at least 32 serial or series titles for which either complete or scattered retrospective holdings are available. Among retrospective titles for which Cornell has complete holdings is the *Archiwum* (1917-37), published by the Komisja do badań historji filozofii w Polsce of the Polska Akademia Umiejętności, as well as the *Prace i Materiały Anthropologiczno-Archeologiczne i Etnograficzne* (1920-27), published by the same academy's Komisja antropologiczna. One important title for which Cornell has only incomplete holdings, however, is the *Rocznik* of the Polska Akademia Umiejętności.

Currently the collection includes virtually all titles in the series *Prace* published by the PAN's Komisja historyczno-literacka as well as the *Prace* published by its Komisja językoznawcza. Literature is not as well represented, however, with only scattered holdings, for example, in the various series published by the PAN's Instytut badań literackich. Available also are the complete holdings to date for *Conferenze* published by the PAN's Biblioteca e centro di studia a Roma, as well as the *Conférences* published by its Centre scientifique in Paris. Among non-Academy publications the library has virtually complete holdings for the *Acta universitatis wratislawiensis* and its predecessors, Wrocław University's *Zeszyty Naukowe*, Series A and B.

Series and serial holdings for the academies of science in Czechoslovakia, Hungary, and Yugoslavia are also substantial, but the number of titles is not as numerous. Among titles from these countries for which Cornell has virtually complete holdings is the *Věstník* (1891 to date) of the Československá Akademie Věd and the *Věstník* (1885-1952) of the Česká *společnost nauk.* From Yugoslavia the Library holds the *Ljetopis* (1866/67 to date) of the Jugoslavenska Akademija Znanosti i Umjetnosti, as well as its *Rad* (1867 to date), *Starine* (1869 to date), and *Monumenta spectantia historiam Slavorum meridionalium* (1868 to date).

An area approach has not been taken in the development of the East Central and Southeast European collection at Cornell, and strengths usually result from library or faculty interest in particular disciplines rather than countries. Such strengths are reflected throughout all of the Library's holdings, whatever the geographical area. Conversely, weaknesses in this area collection generally reflect weaknesses in Cornell's collection as a whole. In the field of history, for example, where coverage is generally strong at Cornell, one may find complete holdings for all of the following major Czech and Slovak historical periodicals: *Český časopis historický* (1895-1949); *Československý časopis historický* (1953 to date); *Historica* (1959 to date); the *Věstník* (1885-1952) of the Česká společnost nauk, Třída filosoficko-historicko-filologická; and the *Časopis* (1869 to date) of the Matice moravská. Virtually complete holdings are available for the *Časopis* (1827 to date) of the Národní Museum in Prague and the series *Acta universitatis carolinae, Philosophica et historica* (1962 to date).

In linguistics, another discipline in which there is great interest, the collection includes such classical works as Erich Berneker's *Slavisches etymologisches Wörterbuch* (1924), Vatroslav Jagič's *Istoriia slavianskoi filologii* (1910), Georg Pekmezi's *Grammatik der albanesischen Sprache* (1908), and Albert Thumb's *Handbuch der neugriechischen Volkssprache* (1895). The collection also includes most of the major linguistic journals. For example, virtually complete holdings are available for the following Hungarian periodicals: *Magyar Nyelv* (1905 to date); *Magyar Nyelvjárások* (1951 to date); *Magyar Nyelvőr* (1872 to date); *Magyarosan* (1932-48); and *Nyelvtudományi Közlemények* (1862 to date).

In Slavic language and literature one finds complete holdings for all major journals such as *Archiv für slavische Philologie* (1875-1929); *Revue des études slaves* (1921-68); *Ricerche slavistiche* (1952 to date); *Scando-Slavica* (1954 to date); *Slavia* (1922 to date); *Die Welt der Slaven* (1956 to date); and *Zeitschrift für slavische Philologie* (1924 to date), etc.

Law holdings, on the whole undistinguished for the area under consideration, show good coverage for East Germany. The Law Library has complete holdings for the major journals *Neue Justiz* (1947 to date), *Der Schöffe* (1954 to date), and *Vertragssystem* (1957 to date), as well as the *Gesetzblatt der Deutschen Demokratischen Republik* (1949 to date), the *Entscheidungen des Obersten Gerichts der Deutschen Demokratischen Republik in Strafsachen* (1951 to date), and the *Entscheidungen des Obersten Gerichts der Deutschen Demokratischen Republik in Zivilsachen* (1951 to date).

The East Central and Southeastern European collection is not well developed in the social sciences. Particularly weak are holdings in statistical material and other types of government publications.

Anna K. Stuliglowa
Cornell University

Dumbarton Oaks

General Information

The Dumbarton Oaks Research Library (Trustees for Harvard University) is located at 1703 Thirty-second Street, N.W., Washington, D.C. 20007. The telephone number is (202) 232-3101. Hours are from 9 a.m. to 5 p.m., Monday through Friday, throughout the year, except legal holidays. Dumbarton Oaks is a noncirculating library, except through interlibrary loan. Limited Xerox facilities are available.

The primary function of the Library is to support the research activities of the Dumbarton Oaks Center for Byzantine Studies. It is also open to persons engaged in advanced research in the Byzantine and allied fields. Because of limited space for users, it is appreciated if those wishing to use the Library for an extended period will notify the Librarian in advance of their arrival.

The history of Dumbarton Oaks Research Library begins in 1936, when Mr. and Mrs. Robert Woods Bliss, then the owners of Dumbarton Oaks, with the aid of a small professional staff, began to assemble a research library as a complement to their collection of Late Classical and Byzantine art objects. When Mr. and Mrs. Bliss gave Dumbarton Oaks, together with its contents and surrounding grounds, to Harvard University at the end of 1940, the Library already comprised more than 10,000 volumes. At the end of June 1972, there were in excess of 80,000 volumes, and the collection continues to grow by about 2,500 volumes per year.

From the beginning, the focus of the collection has been the history and culture of the Byzantine Empire, construed in the broadest sense. Thus, an attempt has been made to cover in detail the antecedent Hellenistic civilization, the contemporaneous cultures of Islam and of Western Europe and, not least of all, the culture and history of the Orthodox Slavs, who were so profoundly influenced by Byzantium. The collection is strong in archeology, the history of art and architecture, editions of texts of ancient and medieval writers, theology, and church history. A large portion of the holdings in these areas consists of the publications of national academies, of national and local learned societies, and of museums.

There is little to be found in the collection on the recent history of the countries which come within the purview of this survey. The emphasis is upon the Middle Ages and earlier, although the Library does have substantial amounts of material on the Greeks and the Orthodox Slavs until about 1700.

Dumbarton Oaks has little material published in Albania or in Albanian and relatively little on Albania. Only a limited amount of material is available on Czechoslovakia, East Germany, and Poland. Those countries, although outside the geographic area of our concern, do have important scholarly traditions in the field of Classical and Byzantine studies, however, hence the collections include a considerable amount of material published in those countries. The Library also has a number of periodicals and some monographic material published in Hungary, mostly in foreign languages but some in Hungarian as well.

It is from the Balkans proper, especially from Yugoslavia, that Dumbarton Oaks has the greatest concentration of holdings pertinent to the geographic areas covered by this survey. The Library has a nearly complete run of the Serbian periodical *Starinar* from 1884 and very extensive holdings of the publications of the Academies of Belgrade and Zagreb beginning in the latter part of the last century. These include periodicals, monographic material, and published collections of documents.

The Library also has rich holdings of publications from the Greek-speaking world. One of the rarities is a complete run (1863-1911) of the *Syngramma Periodikon* of the Greek Philological Society of Constantinople (Istanbul). The chief publications of Turkey, Cyprus, Crete, and Greece are also available, principally in Greek but some in other languages, dealing with the ancient and medieval history of the Greek world.

Apart from books, the Library has two very valuable tools for research on the medieval history of the Balkans. The first is a card catalog, arranged by author, of every entry in the annual bibliography of Byzantine studies, published since 1892 in the *Byzantinische Zeitschrift*. Since there has never been a published cumulation of this bibliography, the card catalog of it constitutes a unique resource.

In addition to this card file, Dumbarton Oaks also has a copy of the Princeton Index of Christian Art. In its coverage of publications on Christian art to about the year 1200, it includes much material dealing with the geographical area of this survey.

Merlin W. Packard
Dumbarton Oaks

Duquesne University
Tamburitzans Institute of Folk Art

The Duquesne University Tamburitzans Institute of Folk Arts, 1801 Boulevard of the Allies, Pittsburgh, Pa. 15219, houses a highly specialized library of over 10,000 volumes, more than 200 films of staged and field-collected dances, a record and audiotape collection of more than 24,000 recorded items, and a music collection of 50,000 pieces. The associated museum displays folk instruments and some 1,000 original costumes. The folk arts represented are primarily native songs and dances of Eastern Europe (including Hungary). Inquiries should be directed to Mrs. Patricia French, Promotion Director.

Harvard University

General Information

THE HARVARD UNIVERSITY Library system consists of the Harvard College Library, i.e. the library of the Faculty of Arts and Sciences, and a large network of other units: libraries of other faculties, departmental libraries, special research libraries, etc.

The Harvard College Library includes, in turn, the Widener, Lamont, and Hilles (undergraduate), Houghton (rare books), and Fine Arts libraries. Widener is the main research library, devoted predominantly to humanities and social sciences.

The bulk of the Slavic collections is located in the Widener Library. Smaller, but significant, clusters are to be found in other units, mainly in the Law Library, Fine Arts Library, Music Library, and Peabody Museum Library. There is a degree of overlapping between the areas covered by the various libraries; for example works on ethnography will be found both in Widener and in the Peabody Museum Library.

Rare books and manuscripts are kept in the Houghton Library. Because of limited space there, and because the University owns an extraordinarily large number of old and valuable books, many items considered "rare" by the usual standards will be found on regular shelves, subject to special circulation rules.

Most units of the Harvard University Library are located in Cambridge, Mass. 02138. The Baker Library of the Graduate School of Business Administration is on Soldiers Field Road, Boston, Mass. 02163, and the Francis A. Countway Library of Medicine is at 10 Shattuck Street, Boston, Mass. 02115.

Harvard libraries exist primarily for the faculty and students of the University but welcome use by other scholars to the largest extent consistent with this primary purpose. Short-term library privileges can usually be given free of charge to visiting scholars; fees are charged for those who wish to have library privileges for more than one to three months.

Hours of opening for Widener Library are 9 a.m. to 10 p.m. Monday through Friday and 9 a.m. to 5 p.m. on Saturday during term time; during other times the Library closes at 5 p.m. Monday through Friday and at 1 p.m. on Saturday. Persons wishing to use other Harvard libraries should ascertain hours of opening before coming.

For information on Slavic collections in Widener Library, the person to be consulted is the Assistant Librarian for the Slavic Collections in the Harvard College Library. General information regarding Harvard libraries and collections may be obtained at the Reference Desk, Widener Library (Telephone 495-2411).

In the classification system used by Widener Library, the history and literature sections of most countries are located next to each other. This is the general pattern of the Slavic collections. For example, Polish History and Polish Literature form a single block between numbers Slav 519 and Slav 7166. The Slavic history classes include general periodicals (except Russian), as well general and historical bibliographies and encyclopedias. Aside from history in the strict sense, t Slavic history classification covers many topics in the areas of government, church history, ethr ogy, and economic and social conditions.

Classification practices have not been completely consistent over the years. A user who has found some works in his field classified with Czech history should not be surprised if he has to go to the Sociology or Economics shelves in order to locate other items on the same subject.

Some of the areas other than Slavic History and Literature where the student of Eastern Europe will find his materials are: Language, Philosophy, Folklore, Education, Archeology, and History of the Second World War.

Slavic materials in the Law Library are located in the International Legal Studies Library and are grouped by country, so that, for example, all documents and works pertaining to Polish law will be found occupying one continuous block of shelves.

Catalogs

A union catalog located in Widener Library functions as the central record for the whole system. Another card catalog, the so-called "Public Catalog," covers, with some exceptions, only the Widener holdings, and includes subject cards. A file listing newspaper titles by country is kept near the Central Reference Desk. A card catalog of Slavic serial holdings is available in the Slavic Division. The cards in it are grouped by country.

Widener cataloging practices differ in some respects from those of other libraries. The user should bear this in mind when studying the structure and peculiarities of the Widener card catalogs.

Printed shelflists provide an extremely valuable guide to the Widener collections. Among the lists already published is one covering the history and literature of the Slavic countries. It consists of three parts, each ordered according to a different principle: in classified order, alphabetically by author and title, and chronologically.

Of the records of the other libraries one should mention the multivolume photostatic catalog of the Peabody Museum Library. It is divided into two parts: Authors and Subjects. The subject heading system makes the catalog particularly useful for scholars approaching the material from the regional viewpoint; they will find the subject headings grouped by country, for example: Poland—Archeology—Axes; Poland—Folk-lore—Songs; Poland—Ethnography—Museums and Collections.

Guides and Pamphlets about the Harvard Collections

General information about the library system and the Widener Library in particular is available in a pamphlet entitled *The Research Services of the Harvard College Library* (Cambridge: Harvard University Library, 1973). This guide includes an index of subjects covered by different libraries within the system. It also contains a listing of other guides published by some of the University libraries. Conditions of access for scholars from outside Harvard are outlined in a leaflet entitled: *Use of Harvard College Library by Visiting Readers* (Cambridge, 1970). A history and description of the Slavic collections is contained in an article by Charles R. Gredler, "The Slavic Collection at Harvard," *Harvard Library Bulletin*. v. 17, no. 4, October 1969: 425-33. (Available in offprint)

Interlibrary loan and photocopying services

With the exception of the Fine Arts Library and Houghton, Harvard libraries participate in the interlibrary loan system.

The Widener Photographic Division accepts orders for microfilming and Xeroxing, subject to copyright restrictions. The Division also does work for a number of other libraries within the system, including the Music Library and Fine Arts Library. The Law, Medical, and Business School Libraries have their own photocopying facilities. Large-format film negatives, color photography, slides, and infrared and ultraviolet photography are available in the Photographic

Department of the Fogg Art Museum. Persons wishing to have materials searched and delivered to the Photographic Division for reproduction may send an order to the Photographic Reference Assistant, Widener Reference Desk. There is a minimum charge of $2.50 on all mail orders.

Gabriel Grasberg
University of Massachusetts, Boston
and Edwin E. Williams
Harvard University

Publications Pertaining to Harvard College and University Libraries and the Collections Described

Berlin, Charles. *The Judaica Collection at Harvard.* Cambridge, Mass., Harvard University Library, 1971. 8 p. [Reprinted from the *Jewish Book Annual,* v. 26 (1968/69)].

Gredler, Charles R. "The Slavic Collection at Harvard," *Harvard Library Bulletin,* v. 17, no. 4 (Oct. 1969): 425-33.

Harvard University. Library. *Harvard University Library, 1638-1968.* [Cambridge, Mass., 1969] 53 p.

Harvard University. Library. Kress Library of Business and Economics. *Annual Report, 1970/-71.* 4 p.

Harvard University. Library. *The Research Services of the Harvard College Library.* [Tenth impression, with revisions]. Cambridge [Mass., September, 1968]. 51 p.

Harvard University. Library. *Slavic History and Literatures,* Widener Library Shelflists, v. 28-31. Cambridge, Mass., 1971.

Idem., v. 40: *Finnish and Baltic History and Literatures* (1972).

Harvard University. Library. *The Kilgour Collection of Russian Literature, 1750-1920, with Notes on Early Books and Manuscripts of the Sixteenth and Seventeenth Centuries, Cambridge, Mass., 1959.*

Layton, Evro. "The Modern Greek Collection in the Harvard College Library," *Harvard Library Bulletin,* v. 19, no. 3 (July, 1971): 1-23.

Minadakias, Nikolaos. "Neoellenika Grammata sto Panepistemion Harvard," *Aktines,* etos 30, no. 284 (Oct. 1967): 299-305.

"The Slovak Collection of Harvard College Library," *Harvard Library Bulletin,* v. 7, no. 3 (1959): 299-311.

The Tercentennial History of Harvard College and University, 1936-1939. Cambridge, Mass., 1935.

Bulgaria

THE MAIN RESOURCES of the Harvard University Library pertaining to Bulgaria and the Bulgars are in the fields of the humanities and social sciences. Those resources are housed for the most part in the Widener Library and in the International Legal Studies Wing of the Harvard Law School Library. Publications on the natural sciences from Bulgaria are only very selectively acquired by the Harvard University Library, and there is no general collection of such materials anywhere in its constituent libraries.

An important Harvard collection of materials on the Bulgars that is not in Cambridge is the Dumbarton Oaks Library in Washington, D.C. This library has extensive holdings pertaining to the Southern Slavs in the medieval period. However, many of these holdings are duplicated in the other libraries of the Harvard University Library in Cambridge.

The major part of Widener Library's holdings pertaining to Bulgaria and the Bulgars will be found listed in volumes 30 and 31 of the *Widener Library Shelflist, Slavic History and Literatures,* volumes III and IV (Author and Title Listing), Harvard University Library, Cambridge, 1971. Other volumes of the *Shelflist* (e.g., *Bibliography, Economics*) contain further listings under such subheadings as "Balkans," "Bulgaria," "Macedonia," etc.

The largest group of holdings relative to Bulgaria in Widener Library is on Bulgarian history and literature, classified under the rubric *Slav*. For the history of this collection and details of its size and intake, see Charles R. Gredler, "The Slavic Collection at Harvard," in: *Harvard Library Bulletin,* v. 17, no. 4, October 1969: 425-33.

The collection relating to Bulgaria under the rubric *Slav* is particularly rich in works and treatises of belles lettres and cultural history, and it will support a very broad range of advanced research on those subjects. It is one of the two best collections on these subjects in the Western Hemisphere. It is also an excellent library on Bulgarian political history, and contains some publications in this field which are not in any other major library in North America (e.g., the journal *Demokratičeski pregled,* Sofia, 1902-27). The most extraordinary feature of this collection is its rich provision of complete runs of cultural and political journals for the whole period of modern Bulgarian literature and statehood.

The section of Widener Library's Slavic History and Literature collection that is devoted to Bulgarian history, statistics, description, and biographies (under Widener call numbers Slav 9097-Slav 9195) also abounds in statistical and other descriptive periodicals, e.g., the *Mesečni statističeski izvestija* of the Direktsija na statistikata, 1908 and later years, the *Annuaire statistique* (1909-42), *Kriminalna statistika* (1935-), *Dviženija na tărgovijata na Bălgarija* (1895-1912), *Mouvement de la population* (1881-), and other periodicals of description and statistics on emigration, education, foreign trade, and so forth.

Numerous publications of the Ministerstvo na narodnata prosveta from its inception onward are in this collection. In regard to bibliography, the publications of the Bălgarski bibliografski institut, Sofia, are found here, and also the major bibliographical publications of the National Library in Sofia from 1906 onward. There is also a complete run of *Informatsionen bjuletin za bibliografski spravki i kartoteki* (Sofia, 1959-).

Widener Library's holdings embrace also the learned publications of the universities of Sofia and Varna, and their several faculties, institutes, and imprints. Other learned Bulgarian institutes and societies whose publications are collected include the Bălgarski arxeologičeski institut, Bălgarski geologičesko družestvo, Bălgarsko geografsko družestvo, Bălgarsko ikonomičesko družestvo, the Varnensko arxeologičesko družestvo, and others.

The collection of Bulgarian belles lettres, classified Slav 9195 and following, incorporates major editions of all the major writers in Bulgarian literary history. Although oriented strongly toward the "classics" of Bulgarian literature, this collection is so fully representative of its subject that the researcher using it may generally expect to find the works of any author or any particular literary periodical in it, though there will be some occasional exceptions.

Elsewhere in Widener Library there are important holdings relative to Bulgaria in fields of knowledge other than history and literature. The section of Widener Library under the rubric Linguistics contains a comprehensive collection of grammars and dictionaries of Bulgarian, including numerous bilingual dictionaries of Bulgarian and such other languages as English, French, Modern Greek, Hungarian, Russian, and Turkish. Here too are linguistic monographs and materials for the study of Bulgarian dialects, such as the Bulgarian Dialect Atlas published by the Bulgarian Academy of Sciences. All the major published books, monographs, lexica, and other compilations of data for linguistic research on Bulgarian and its dialects will be found in this good collection. Periodicals pertaining to this field of knowledge are held separately under the rubric Philol (Philological Periodicals).

Philological periodicals in Bulgarian and primarily about the Bulgarian language are located under the call number Philol 628. Among the journals held are complete series of *Bălgarski ezik, Bălgarski ezik i literatura, Izvestija na instituta za bălgarski ezik, Trudove po bălgarska dialektologija,* and *Ezik i literatura.* Other journals housed in the periodical collection that contain material bearing upon Bulgarian are *Slavjanska filologija* and *Ricerche slavistiche.*

Both the serial and the special publications of the major Bulgarian institutions and societies of learning in the humanities and social sciences are in Widener Library. The holdings of this library are especially complete for the Bulgarian Academy of Sciences and its several institutes and sections, and the University of Sofia, its library, and its various faculties.

Certain other fields of knowledge in the humanities and social sciences besides history, literature, and language are selectively represented not only in Widener Library's holdings of the publications of Bulgarian learned societies, but also in other types of publication and in other, neighboring libraries that are satellites of Widener for particular academic subjects.

ARCHEOLOGY.   The guides and descriptions issued by the Naroden arxeologičeski muzej in Sofia are in the Slavic collection in Widener, while the series *Razkopki i proučvanija* is in the separate Archeology collection (abbreviation: Arc), also in Widener Library. The *Izvestija na Bălgarskoto arxeologičesko družestvo* is under Arc 302.2.6, and there is a substantial collection of individually published monographs for the whole field of Balkan archeology including numerous works in Bulgarian and/or on Bulgarian topics under the call numbers from Arc 936.29 through Arc 936.252. Widener Library's holdings are complemented by those in another unit of the Harvard University Library, the Library of the Peabody Museum of Archaeology and Ethnology, which is located at 11 Divinity Avenue in Cambridge. The Peabody Museum's library holds sixty-odd volumes relating to Bulgarian archeology under its designation LSoc 22, including *Arxeologija,* vol. 1 and following, 1959 and subsequent years, and such bibliographical aids as *Katalog na izdanijata na BAN; 1870-1944* (Sofia, 1956), and *Zentralblatt der Bulgarischen wissenschaftlichen Literatur* (Geschichte und Archäologie), (Sofia, 1959-). This library also has a small and random collection of books and monographs (about 50 volumes) on the archeology and ethnography of the entire Balkan Peninsula. Although the Library of Peabody Museum thus has a considerable collection, especially of works in Western European languages, it is too incomplete to be more than a marginal base for effective research on Bulgarian archeology. Taken together with the resources in Widener, it is a good research library on its subject.

ECONOMICS.   Books, monographs, and a number of journals pertinent to the economics of Bulgaria and acquired by the Library since 1945, such as *Narodno stopanstvo* (Sofia, 1904-43), are in the Slavic History and Literature collection reviewed above. Publications on Bulgarian economics acquired before 1945 are distributed according to subjects in the Economics collection (abbreviation: Econ). There are some general works on the economics of the Balkans, including Bulgaria, classified between Econ 2183.1 and Econ 2183.199. Other, more specialized works elsewhere in the Economics collection include material on Bulgarian money, banking, and transportation (railroads) in particular. The Baker Library of the Harvard Business School on Soldiers Field Road in Boston also has a few titles on Bulgarian commerce and economic conditions; for these, see the *Subject Catalogue of the Baker Library,* 2 (Boston, G. K. Hall, 1971).

EDUCATION.   There are 30 volumes relating to Bulgarian education in Widener Library's Education collection (abbreviation: Educ).

A few other fields of knowledge are slightly represented in the Bulgarian collection in Widener Library; some of these fields, such as philosophy, psychology, and sociology, are not represented by strong traditions of learning in Bulgaria, and hence there has not been a large volume of publications to collect. Nevertheless, Widener Library does have the publications since 1970 of the newly formed Institut po sotsiologija of the Bulgarian Academy of Sciences, and there are Bulgarian works on such topics as atheism and esthetics in Widener's Philosophy collection.

BIBLIOGRAPHICAL AIDS. In addition to those in the collections mentioned above, other Bulgarian bibliographical, librarians', and bookmen's materials are in the Bibliography and Bibliographical Periodical collections (abbreviations: B and BP) in the Widener Library. Bulgarian book publishers' catalogs, such as *Almanax; Bălgarski pisatel 1948-1968* (Sofia, 1968), and histories of Bulgarian libraries are found here.

FINE ARTS. Another subsidiary of the Harvard University Library, the Fine Arts Library in the Fogg Art Museum at 32 Quincy Street in Cambridge, has an excellent collection of publications on the fine arts in Bulgaria. This collection embraces publications in all the languages of Europe, and is entirely capable of supporting the full range of research on the various forms of fine arts as they are practiced in Bulgaria, or as attested in Bulgarian art history. Subjects covered are Bulgarian architecture, (folk) costume and fashions, modern painting, iconography, sculpture, and some applied (industrial) art. The section on early Bulgarian art is especially rich. Among the periodicals held here are such resources as the *Godišnik na Narodni muzej v Sofija* (Sofia, 1922 and later years).

A number of titles on Bulgaria in the Library of the Graduate School of Design supplement the holdings of the Fine Arts Library; these two libraries are located only two city blocks apart in Cambridge. See the *Catalogue of the Graduate School of Design* (Boston, G. K. Hall and Co., 1968) for the holdings of that library relative to Bulgaria.

THE LAW OF BULGARIA. After the Slavic History and Literature collection in Harvard College Library, the collection in Bulgarian on Bulgarian law in the Harvard Law School Library is the finest group of holdings relative to Bulgaria in the entire Harvard University Library system. This collection embraces several hundred titles, and comprehends not only Bulgarian law codes and law reviews, but a wealth of material on related subjects, such as public administration, insurance, taxation, customs, land reform, governmental history, housing, and so forth. This collection is a superb base for research into any aspect of legal order in Bulgaria since its independence.

Administrative, civil, constitutional, and criminal law are all thoroughly covered. Law periodicals in complete or nearly complete sets are particularly well collected, for example: *Juridičeski arxiv,* v. I- (Sofia, 1929-); *Pravna misăl* (1935-41 and 1957-); *Godišnik na Sofijskija universitet, Juridičeski fakultet,* v. VI- (1911-); *Rešenija na Vărxovnija kasatsionen săd po obštoto mu săbranie za 1892* (and subsequent years to date). Other periodicals not strictly legal in content but cognate with legal studies are equally abundant in this collection, for example: *Dăržaven vestnik,* v. III- (1881-); *Bălgarski letopis na periodičnija pečat,* v. I- (Sofia, 1952-); *Abstracts of Bulgarian Scientific Literature; Economics and Law,* v. I- (Sofia, 1958-).

FOLKLORE. A superb collection of publications of and on Bulgarian folklore is located in Widener Library under the call numbers from 27235.61.6 to 27235.99.40. These holdings thoroughly represent the published resources for research on the topics of Bulgarian popular epic and other oral poetry, folktale, custom, and ethnography, as well as poetic dialectology. There is also a number of original sound recordings of oral poetic performances made in the field in Bulgaria deposited in the Milman Parry Collection of Oral Literature, also in the Widener Library building. Taken together, these joint resources of printed and sound-recorded materials on Bulgarian folklore are the best collection on that subject outside Bulgaria itself.

David E. Bynum
Harvard University

Czechoslovakia

THE CZECHOSLOVAK COLLECTION of the Harvard College Library can be traced back to the 17th century, when the reading list of Dr. Holdsworth for the Master's Degree included *Janua linguarum* by "that brave old man Johannes Amos Comenius." Interest in literary Bohemia slackened, however, reviving only some two centuries later. This development is mirrored in the present collection in which the first, 1825, edition of Josef Jungmann's history of Czech literature might be chosen as a hallmark of the Czech literary renaissance. Two years earlier, in 1823, the Gesellschaft des vaterländischen Museums in Böhmen had held its first session. In the learned societies section of the Library (Harvard designation LSoc), the *Verhandlungen* (1824) of the aforenamed society is adjacent to the publications of the Czech Academy, whose series *Rozpravy* has appeared for many decades.

The main body of Harvard's Czechoslovak collection is located on the third floor of Widener Library and is classified according to the Harvard College Library system. It is a part of the Slavic collections as a whole, which begin with works on general Slavic history, literature, and old Slavic literature. Here the Czechs hold their own not so much by numbers as by the importance of their contributions. P. Šafařík's *Slovanské starožitnosti* (Prague, 1837), J. Kollár's *Rozpravy o slovanské vzájemnosti* (Prague, 1929), and *Zpráwa o Sjezdu slowanském W Praze, 1848* (microfilm) are among the many works which deeply influenced the political and intellectual history of the Slavic world. Czech studies in Church-Slavonic also deserve attention, whether J. Dobrovský's pioneering *Kirill i Metodii* (Moscow, 1825), translated into Russian by M. Pogodin, or M. Weingart's *Československý typ církevnej slovančiny* (Prague, 1949).

The collection proper has two major divisions: Czechoslovak history and Czech-Slovak literatures. Czechoslovak history includes periodicals, bibliographies, general history, history by periods, geography, economic history, local history, et al. and in 1971 numbered 4,808 works.

The Library's periodical collections include many relevant items, among them *Atheneum* (1883-93), once the tribune from which Professor T. G. Masaryk spoke to the intellectuals of the last decades of the century. *Červen,* in its three years of existence (1918-21), preserved the literary and artistic climate of the first years of the Czechoslovak Republic. *Gindy a Nynj* (1827), the first Czech literary magazine, and *Květy české* (1834) are available, as is the new *Literární archiv* (1966-) and *Lumír* (1851-1939), the literary voice of the second half of the 19th century. *Moderní revue* (1895-1900), the unadulterated expression of Czech symbolism and decadence, as well as many other periodicals, document the development of modern Czech intellectual history in its original state. *Var* (1949-53), edited by Z. Nejedlý, and *Život strany* (1964-) reflect contemporary Czechoslovakia.

The collection includes the standard bibliographic periodicals: *Český bibliografický katalog* (Prague, 1889-97), *Bibliografický katalog ČSR* (Prague, 1922-50), *Slovenské knihy* (Martin, 1954-), and *Bibliografický katalog ČSSR* (Prague, 1956-). Numerous encyclopedic works are available.

The historiography section contains many remarkable volumes, among them *Monumenta historica Boemiae* (1764-85), by Gelasius Dobner, the founder of modern Czech history. General treatises include *Über den Geist der böhmischen Gesetze* (Dresden, 1788), written by Adaugt Voigt, the outstanding figure of the Czech Enlightenment. Works in religious history include *Bohaemia pia* (Frankfurt, 1608) by Pontanus z Braitenberka, J. A. Comenius' *Historia persecutionum ecclesiae Bohemicae* (n.p., 1648), and Rudolf Říčan's *Die böhmischen Brüder* (Berlin, 1561).

The history of special periods is well represented. For the early periods one may consult V. Hájek's chronicle of 1541, in the critical edition of 1918-33 by F. Flajšhans and in the translation

(Annales Bohemorum) (1761-65) by G. Dobner. Houghton Library holds the original *Kronyka Czecská,* published in Prague in 1541. J. Dubravius' *Historiae regni Boiemiae* (Prostanae, 1552) is also available. The Czech Reformation and the Hussite movement and its representatives (Chelčický, Hus, Jeronym of Prague, and others) have been favorite subjects of Czech historians and are covered in detail. The Counter-Reformation is not as well represented, although the Library has such rare works as Adam Tanner's *Apologia, oder Schutzschrift der Societet Jesu* (Vienna, 1619) and *De Statu bohemico* (Frankfurt, 1621), B. Balbín's *Epitome historica rerum Bohemicarum* (Prague, 1677/83) and *Miscellanea historica regni Bohemiae* (Prague, 1679/87).

The Czech Enlightenment of the 18th century and the national revival of the first decades of the 19th century are traditional themes of Czech intellectual history. They culminate in the revolutionary year 1848, particularly attractive to Czech scholars. The period 1848-1919 continues to document and interpret the politicocultural development of the Czech nation. At this point short periods of history were introduced: 1914-18 records the activities of Czechs at home (Maffia) and of Masaryk and Beneš abroad during World War I. The history of the First Czechoslovak Republic includes the authors F. Peroutka, J. P. Papánek, J. Ripka, and, of those Englishmen who were experts on Czechoslovak affairs, R. H. B. Lockhart and R. W. Seton-Watson. These years were also analyzed and described from the Marxist point of view (Alena Gajanová, *ČSR a středoevropská politika velmocí,* 1967). The period of World War II, the German occupation, and the controversial years 1945-48 stand out distinctly. In the most recent special period of Czechoslovak history, the focus is on the personalities of Fučik, Gottwald, and Zápotocký and on the changes inside Czechoslovakia.

The numerous works classified under geography complement those of history. They include *Das jetzige lebende Königreich Böhmen* (1712), by P. Mauritius Vogt, which has many beautiful engravings. Economic history, demography, and statistics are well represented and cover all aspects of the Czechoslovak economy.

The largest number of works on local history relate to Prague. Rare old publications (Hammerschmied, Jan Floryán, *Prodromus gloriae Pragensae,* Vetero-Pragae, 1723) alternate with modern books with beautiful photographic documentation. For other areas, a monograph on the Moravian *Mikulov* (Brno, 1971), for instance, represents a new and interesting type of topographic study. The collection also includes ethnological studies on minorities (Sudeten-German, Slovak, Magyar, Ruthenian) and provinces (Bohemia, Moravia, Silesia, Slovakia, Ruthenia).

In 1971, the Library's collection of Czech and Slovak literature numbered some 6,260 titles. Czech literary history and criticism are represented by works of the foremost Czech literary historians: Jungmann, Vlček, Jakubec, Novák, Pražák, Vodička, Wellek, and Jakobson. Czech poetry and drama are covered in detail. Individual authors are divided into the 19th and the 20th centuries. For the earlier period some unusual publications may be discovered, for example, F. L. Čelakovský's *Odglos pieśni czeskich* (Wroclaw, 1845) and *Wothlos pěsni ruskich* (Prague, 1846); the original *Ohlas pjsnj ruských* (Prague, 1820) is in Houghton Library. The first edition of K. H. Mácha's *Máj* is also available.

It is the policy of Harvard College Library to acquire new critical editions of authors. The 65 volumes (1878-1913) of Jaroslav Vrchlický—to give an illustration—are duplicated by the 20 volumes of the critical edition of 1948-63. The collection is complete with biographic documentation, critical studies, and letters, including the microfilmed letters of Vrchlický to Teza, the originals of which are in the Biblioteca Marciana. In addition to the works of Karel Čapek or Jaroslav Hašek, the Harvard College Library has Russian essays and articles published about them or by them, some of which are in the microfilmed journals of the Russian Research Center.

The Czech collection was checked against the bibliography of the first volume of *Dějiny české literatury* (1959), which was produced by a team of specialists in the field and is as complete as possible. The first volume is divided into five sections covering the first centuries of Czech literacy, the 14th century, the Hussite period, the Reformation and Humanism, and the Counter-Reformation-Baroque period. It was found that only 8.12 percent of the items listed were not covered by the Harvard collection.

Harvard's collection of Slovak literature is built along the same lines as the Czech collection. It was described in the bibliography by Dmitry Čiževsky, a former professor at Harvard University, who stated that, with the exception of Vienna, the collection was without peer outside Czechoslovakia. He quoted its most valuable holdings, among them A. Bernolák's *Grammatica slovaca* of 1790, the 19th-century first editions of the Štúr generation, and the periodicals *Orol tatránski* (1843-48) and *Slovenskje pohladi* (1846-52). In 1953, Professor Čiževsky noted the need to fill gaps in the collection. By 1972, it had met his requirements insofar as possible. Slovaks are building on a solid tradition like that of Matica slovenská and its publications, which started in the middle of the last century (for example, *Letopis* and its 12 issues published between 1864-75). Particularly impressive is current Slovak research in various fields of folklore, the new editions of their classics and interesting publications of Baroque literature. The Slovaks proudly stress their resistance and military uprisings during World War II, the anniversary of which was celebrated with extensive documentary and commemorative literature and which was also recorded in fiction.

Czech and Slovak folklore is shelved on Widener floor B with folklore materials and studies of other nations. In 1971, the Slavic holdings numbered 1,000. The collection includes the old medieval legends of St. Wenceslaus and St. Catherine, including important textual criticism on them. Also available are V. Hanka's falsifications of Czech medieval poetry and the controversial literature on them which extends over some 150 years; the latest item in this group is M. Ivanov's *Záhada rukopisu královédvorského* (Prague, 1970). From the Romantic period date various pioneer collections of Czech and Slovak songs and fairy tales: J. Sušil's *Národní pjsně* (1835), K. J. Erben's *Písně Národnj* (1842-46), J. Kollař's *Národnie zpievanky* (1834-35), P. Dobšinsky and J. Škultéty's *Slovenské povesti* (1858-61), and many other works. The major folklore periodical, *Český lid* (1898-) is available in the Slavic section.

Czech authors are also represented in other collections at Harvard. The letters from J. V. Purkyně to Goethe (1787-1869), for example, are in the Harvard Medical School Library, and biographic materials on Purkyně are in the Fogg Museum, by the wife of one of Purkyně's sons (a painter), who wrote a memoir about her famous father-in-law. Czechoslovak art books, however, often intended for export, are provided with résumés in foreign languages, and are integrated into the general collections relating to art.

The Music Library has scores of the major Czech composers—Antonín Dvořák, Bedřich Smetana, Leoš Janáček, Bohuslav Martinů, Vitězslav Novák—and documentation on them. It regularly acquires music of contemporary composers, including P. Bořkovec (1894-1972), P. Eben (1922-), J. Feld (1925-), J. Hanuš (1915-), I. Hurník (1922-), V. Kalabis (1923-), J. Kapr (1914-), I. Krejčí (1904-), J. Rychlík (1916-64), K. Slavický (1910-), V. Štědroň (1900-) and V. Trojan (1907-). The Library subscribes to *Musica Bohemica antiqua.*

The Czechoslovak collection of the Law School Library is considered to be one of the most complete of its kind in the United States. Its emphasis is on the last hundred years; the 20th century and, particularly, the post-World War II years are well represented.

The collection lacks back numbers of Czech newspapers, both from the second part of the last century and from the period of the First Czechoslovak Republic. The 19th-century *Národní listy* is represented for 1916-20 (incomplete); for *České slovo*, the paper of National Socialists, the Library has microfilm for the period 1938-40. The Russian Research Center has sections of *Právo lidu* for 1945-48. Although the Russian Research Center subscribes to *Rudé právo*, it lacks back numbers. No record exists of the conservative *Národní politika*, the agrarian *Venkov*, and the liberal

Lidové noviny. The Widener reading room shelves the daily *Mladá fronta* and more than two dozen other periodicals, a few of them published by Czechs in exile. Lamont Library has the Slovak *Smena.*

Acquisition of Bohemica and Slovaca at Harvard is based chiefly on the bibliographic series *České knihy, Nové knihy, Slovenské knihy, Co nového vyjde, Czech Books in Print* (Artia), and *Science and Books* (Academia). During fiscal year 1971-72, Slavic acquisitions at Harvard numbered 15,484, of which Czechoslovak works comprised some 1,000-2,000 titles.

Milada Součková
Harvard University

East Germany

PRESENT-DAY EAST GERMANY came into existence in 1945 when the Soviet Union in keeping with wartime Allied agreements occupied this area. This report addresses itself to developments in this region since 1945 and deals in particular with the German Democratic Republic, which was founded in 1949. A separate chapter concerns itself with the special problems of East Berlin.

Harvard University's long-standing and profound interest in those academic disciplines that relate to the German cultural heritage has served as the basis for its significant collection on postwar developments in East Germany and, in particular, on the German Democratic Republic since 1949. The major responsibility for developing these holdings, which encompass a wide range of subjects, has rested primarily with the Specialist in Book Selection for the Germanic Languages.

Harvard's efforts in the East German field are therefore largely a continuation of its traditional procurement policies in the German field, i.e., they are aimed at developing a comprehensive research collection for the disciplines concerned with the study of German scholarship that this area represents on campus. Harvard has not adopted a policy of collecting for the purpose of area studies, i.e., for research lying outside the purview of its academic pursuits. Specifically, it has not acquired its East German collection in order to round out its contemporary Eastern European holdings. It has therefore a well-rounded East German collection, built around academic disciplines and developed with the same care as its earlier German holdings.

SIZE OF THE COLLECTION.   Harvard University Library records permit no estimate of the size of its East German holdings. It is this reviewer's opinion that Harvard University Library has about 20,000 East German monographs and about 300 East German periodicals in the humanities (including art and music), social sciences, theology, and law. These figures should be understood as encompassing general publications as well as those dealing with the German Democratic Republic but issued elsewhere. This opinion is subject to a 25 percent margin of error.

In describing Harvard University Library's East German collections in terms of sufficiency, one has to take into account its basic acquisitions criteria, its general objectives, and the availability of the pertinent material. In these terms and for the purpose of a general overview, the following estimate is offered:

Category	None	Selective (1%-50%)	Representative (51%-75%)	Comprehensive (76%-100%)
Books in the book trade: General, History, Political Science, Law, External Affairs, Philosophy, Language, Literature, Religion, Arts				X
Geography, Demography, Economics, Sociology, Education, Mass Media, Military Science			X	
Books not in the book trade		X		
Serials			X	
Maps		X		
Graphics and films	X			
Music scores				X
Records			X	

ACCESSIBILITY. Neither the Union Catalog nor the Public Catalog in Widener Library distinguishes between West and East German holdings.

The Union Catalog, which serves as the author catalog of Harvard University Library, provides for corporate entries for agencies of both the Federal Republic of Germany and the German Democratic Republic. These are interfiled in alphabetical order under the heading "Germany," together with the publications issued by the German Reich until 1945. Material published by agencies on the zonal level after 1945 are listed under the heading "Germany (Territory under Allied Occupation)" in alphabetical order by title and not by agency.

The Public Catalog, which serves the holdings of the Harvard College Library, follows the practice of the Union Catalog for its author entries and has no separate geographic category for identifying its subject references to East Germany. These are listed under "Germany" together with titles referring to the Federal Republic and to all of Germany.

This system of entries is counterbalanced by the availability of printed subject catalogs of other libraries, including those of the Library of Congress and of the Weltwirtschaftliches Institut in Kiel. Keeping in mind that Harvard College Library is conceived as a research library (as distinguished from a ready reference library), one can consider the subject controls it affords more than adequate for its East German collections.

Moreover, about 14 shelves of books on East Germany dealing with a wide range of subjects are classed together under call number groups "Ger. 2561 to Ger. 2569," providing a convenient reference to many works on this area.

Other libraries of Harvard University Library—in particular the Law School Library, the Andover-Harvard Theological Library, the West European Studies Library, and the Baker Library—distinguish in cataloging their East German holdings from other German entries and/or shelve publications on the German Democratic Republic together in one place.

There are no guides unique to the East German collections.

Books, Periodicals, and Newspapers

GENERAL PUBLICATIONS. Harvard University Library has a comprehensive collection of reference works pertaining to the German Democratic Republic. Its holdings include not only those published in East Germany but also reference works published in the Federal Republic of Germany dealing either with the country as a whole or specifically with East Germany, as well as general works published elsewhere.

Harvard College Library has an impressive collection of general research publications, in particular East German academy reports and the scholarly journals *(Wissenschaftliche Zeitschriften)* published by the various universities and colleges.

The Library subscribes regularly to several East German newspapers, including *Neues Deutschland.*

LAND AND PEOPLE.   Harvard University has no geography department. Yet, the Harvard College Library has a good collection of geographic studies on East Germany, exceeding the requirements for comparative and interdisciplinary research. Its holdings of other material, such as guide books, gazetteers, and the like, are representative.

Harvard University Library has a solid collection of the few available general demographic studies on East Germany. Its holdings of official statistical publications are not strong; in particular, gaps in census reports were noted.

HISTORY.   The Harvard College Library's holdings of treatises dealing with the history of East Germany since 1945 are comprehensive. Research on this period can also rely on the pertinent published sources, the major East German historical journals, specialized West German publications, and—as would be the case for any evaluation of the recent past—on the large body of material reflecting the contemporary scene and pertaining to politics, government, law, economics, and the like.

Holdings of contributions made by East German historians to other historical fields are by their very nature substantially larger, but also comprehensive, permitting research on all aspects of East German historiography.

POLITICS AND GOVERNMENT (INCLUDING MILITARY AND NAVAL AFFAIRS). Harvard College Library has extensive holdings on East German politics and government. Thus, its catalog lists some 140 titles under the subject heading "Sozialistische Einheitspartei Deutschlands" alone. This material is supplemented to a large extent by the East German collection in the Law School Library. Altogether, Harvard University Library's holdings of studies on this subject are comprehensive, being enhanced by a representative collection of secondary sources, such as Party publications and other material not in the book trade.

The Library's holdings pertaining to the East German armed forces are limited to major treatises and general reference works; the pertinent subject headings of its catalog, for instance, refer to four West German publications and five East German publications.

SOCIETY AND ECONOMY.   Harvard University Library's holdings of publications on the East German economy are mostly in the Harvard College Library and, to a lesser degree, in the Baker Library. Altogether, the collection stresses critical and analytical treatises, and since Western research dominates this field, holdings of East German publications are relatively not as strong. East European works are also represented. The holdings are extensive: thus, the subject headings "Economy, 1945-" and "Economic policy 1945-" under the catalog entry "Germany" refer the reader to 60 and 40 titles, respectively, pertaining to East Germany. Yet some major East German works describing certain segments of the economy are lacking. Holdings concerning the economic aspects of agriculture, forestry, and fisheries are weak, while those pertaining to the social and political aspects of agriculture, e.g., rural cooperatives, are representative.

The patterns of holdings on East German society are similar to those on the economy: a comprehensive collection of major analytical treatises, mostly Western, contrasts with a relatively weaker showing of East German publications, which may not be as critical but which have the advantage of having been prepared in closer physical proximity to the actual conditions.

Holdings in Harvard College Library pertaining to the only remaining Slavic group in East Germany, that of the Sorbs, have been actively developed since 1955, in regard to both current and retrospective publications. Postwar holdings dealing with the various aspects of this minority, in particular its cultural life, are comprehensive. There are some 200 titles in literature alone, and a recent Ph.D. dissertation has been prepared in the field of Sorbian philology.

LAW.   The Law School Library, a component of Harvard University Library, has a comprehensive collection of gazettes, statutes, commentaries, decisions, journals, and treatises pertaining to East German legal developments since 1945. This collection of some 1,000 titles is shelved together, and is for this reason an outstanding research tool. The Law School Library catalog has separate author entries for the German Democratic Republic, as well as for the "Russian Zone" for the immediate postwar period.

EXTERNAL AFFAIRS.   Publications pertaining to this limited field are well represented in Harvard College Library and are supplemented by Law School Library holdings as legal aspects form a significant element in the discussion of East Germany's international position.

LANGUAGE, LITERATURE, AND FOLKLORE.   Harvard College Library's holdings in the field of East German philology are comprehensive; they include dictionaries, journals, studies on postwar East German usage, and major works analyzing the dialects of this area.

The collection of works by and on East German writers reflects Harvard's traditionally strong academic interest in the field of German literature. Its holdings of major East German authors are outstanding and those of lesser ones representative. In regard to other aspects, such as official efforts to induce workers to write, coverage is selective.

The Library has a solid body of publications on East German folktales, folkways, and place-names.

EDUCATION AND SCHOLARSHIP.   General studies on East German education and scholarship largely published in the Federal Republic of Germany are strongly represented in Harvard College Library. Holdings of GDR publications on education, which are more specialized and often didactic in nature, are selective. There is not sufficient material on which a major piece of in-depth research on the school system could be based. However, East German publications focusing on academic developments are more strongly represented.

RELIGION AND PHILOSOPHY.   The Andover-Harvard Theological Library, a component of the Harvard University Library, reflects the University's long-standing interest in Protestant theology and, particularly, in German developments in this field. Thus, a special effort has been made to collect on the postwar period, resulting in a comprehensive collection on the Protestant churches in East Germany.

General works on the less numerous Catholic element are available at the Harvard College Library, but holdings of East German studies on specialized aspects of Catholic developments in East Germany are underrepresented.

East German studies in the field of philosophy focus on Marxism and Leninism and are well represented in Harvard College Library.

ARTS.   The Fine Arts and Music Libraries, which are housed separately, neither catalog nor shelve their East German acquisitions separately, but both libraries have endeavored to procure all significant publications issued in the German Democratic Republic. Their holdings of materials in the book trade can therefore be considered to be comprehensive. The Fine Arts Library has many exhibit catalogs, while the Music Library also collects sheet music and records. The Fine Arts Library has an older collection of photographs, indexed by locality, but has neither films nor graphics.

MASS MEDIA.   The Library has a comprehensive collection of the small body of major works dealing with East German mass media.

Special Collections

The Winsom Memorial Map Collection, which is located in the Lamont Building, is a component of the Harvard College Library. It was reopened about six years ago and has selective holdings of maps in the book trade and of atlases on East Germany. Its holdings of pre-1945 official survey maps are comprehensive, but postwar publications of this type cannot be procured from East Germany.

The Library of the West European Studies Center is a component of Harvard University Library and has a reference collection of some 75 monographs and a few journals dealing with East Germany. The books on East Germany are shelved together.

The Documents Division of Harvard College Library has custody of the East German statistical yearbooks, the 1964 census, and the stenographic records of the Länderkammer and the Volkskammer.

East Berlin

Harvard has a comprehensive collection of major works dealing with East Berlin. The subject headings of the Public Catalog of Harvard College Library list 10 titles on its international status, 17 on the June 17, 1953, uprising, and 19 on the Berlin Wall. The Law School Library has the East Berlin legal gazette *(Verordnungsblatt)*. Statistical coverage is weak, e.g., the two postwar censuses are lacking.

Arnold H. Price
Library of Congress

Greece

Introduction

THE MODERN GREEK collection at the Harvard College Library is one of the outstanding research collections in the United States in the field of Modern Greek studies. It contains approximately 30,000 books, pamphlets, periodicals, and documents, covering Modern Greek history, language and literature, education, religion, social customs, intellectual life and the arts, industry, the economy, national archives, official documents, and laws.

The collection was begun more than 150 years ago, primarily through gifts from classical scholars and others who donated their personal libraries to the college. Among the early benefactors were Edward Everett, a Greek scholar, orator, and statesman; Cornelius Felton, Professor of Greek for many years and President of the College from 1860 to 1862; and Euangelinos Apostolides Sophocles, a young scholar of Greek origin.

Another significant factor in the early development of the Modern Greek collection was the effect of the Philhellenic sentiment in the United States prompted by the Greek struggle for independence in the 1820s. Scholars, students, public figures, and statesmen became interested in Greek independence and, through their intellectual endeavors, actively contributed to an increasing awareness of Modern Greece as an awakening nation and a cultural heritage. As a result, materials found their way to the Library and today constitute some of the rarest resources of the Modern Greek collection. Systematic development of the collection was ensured when the Library began to receive endowments for the acquisition of Modern Greek materials. Funds established exclusively to support the acquisition of research material for Modern Greek studies include the Raphael Demos Fund (1964), the Cornelius Conway Felton Fund (1966), and the Harry K. Messenger and Ada Messenger Fund (1968).

The collection is basically general in character, although several special sections are of interest to the research scholar, in particular those in history, literature, and language. The general collection contains most of the basic works in a wide range of fields and includes a wealth of early publications, important sets of monographs and serials, the publications of universities, academies, and learned societies, the files of the great literary journals, government documents and archival material, and the basic bibliographies and reference works. In addition, it includes many obscure publications in history, criticism, methodology, and other important research areas.

It should be noted that, as a rule, the Library's collections are classified by subject rather than by language, and thus a great deal of material on Modern Greece is scattered through the various classes. The present survey covers primarily the Modern Greek holdings of Widener Library, which constitute the core of the Modern Greek collection at Harvard. Materials cataloged under the "Modern Greek" class are shelved in the southwest wing of the fifth floor of the Widener stacks, covering about 50 stack sections and numbering approximately 15,000 volumes, with an annual increase of about 2,000 volumes.

Collection Catalogs and Finding Aids

No printed catalog of the Modern Greek collection is available at this time, but the Library does maintain a number of up-to-date catalog files and subject indexes which provide information on the collection. The major finding aids for Modern Greek material include the Union Catalog, which contains complete files of author cards for all Modern Greek materials in all the University libraries, and the Widener Public Catalog, which lists Modern Greek material in the Harvard College Library by author and subject and, in many cases, by title, series, and name of editor or translator. A useful supplement to these catalogs is the Widener Shelflist for the Modern Greek collection, which also furnishes the investigator with a subject bibliography of the Modern Greek literature available in Widener. A card file for current books in Modern Greek which have been accessioned and cataloged since 1968 is also available.

The Serial Record for Modern Greek periodicals, serials, and newspapers is located in Room 191 of Widener Library. A visual record is available in Room 191 for locating current issues of Greek serials and periodicals which are shelved in the Periodical Room. A number of printed catalogs of Modern Greek collections in other American libraries and in foreign countries, primarily Greece, are available, including the *Catalogue of the Gennadius Library,* 7 v. (Boston, 1968), *Katalogos ton biblion tes Ethnikes Bibliothekes,* 5 v. (Athens, 1883-91), *Katalogos tes Bibliothekes tes Boules* (Athens), *Katalogos tes Bibliothekes tes Archaiologikes Hetaireias* (Athens, 1897-1906), *The Modern Greek Collection in the Library of the University of Cincinnati; a Catalogue* (Athens, 1960), and others.

Bibliography

The bibliographical resources of the collection include practically all the general bibliographies of Modern Greek materials and of books and periodicals on Modern Greece. In addition to the large printed bibliographical works, the Library has a growing number of subject and regional bibliographies, as well as catalogs of special collections, manuscripts, documents, maps, periodicals and newspapers, and other special material.

Although there is no national bibliography for Greece, a series of general bibliographies covering special periods in effect constitutes a "national bibliography" since 1476. The collection includes a complete run of this particular series, which is probably the most comprehensive bibliographic tool in Modern Greek. It runs as follows: E. Legrand, *Bibliographie hellénique, 1476-1790,* 11 v. (Paris, 1885-1928); B. E. Raste, *Hellenike bibliographia, 1791-1799* (Athens, 1969); G. Ladas and A. Chatzedemos, *Hellenike bibliographia, 1791-1795* (Athens, 1970); D. S.

Gkines and B. G. Mexas, *Hellenike bibliographia, 1800-63,* 3 v. (Athens, 1939-57); a continuation of this bibliography covering the period 1864-1897, compiled by N. Maures under the auspices of the Academy of Athens (to be published); N. G. Polites, *Hellenike bibliographia, 1907-1920,* 3 v. (Athens, 1909-32); Genikon Symboulion Bibliothekon tes Hellados, *Hellenike Bibliographia,* no. 1-9, 1930-39 (Athens, 1934-40). *Bulletin analytique de bibliographie hellénique, 1945-* (Athens, 1947), Comprehensive bibliographies have yet to be published for the years 1898-1906, 1921-30, and 1940-44.

Other general bibliographic guides include G. Phousaras, *Bibliographia ton hellenikon bibliographion, 1791-1947* (Athens, 1961); P. Moullas, *Bibliographia hellenikon symmeikton A´, 1888-1961* (Athens, 1969); D. Gkines, *Katalogoi hellenikon kodikon en Helladi kai Anatole* (Athens, 1935); E. Moschonas, *Agnosta kai spania monophylla sylloges N. Karabia* (Athens, 1966); G. Boumblinopoulos, *Bibliographie critique de la philosophie grecque* (Athens, 1966); N. Kyriazes, *Kypriake bibliographia* (Athens, 1935); *Oikonomike bibliographia tes Hellados* (Athens, 1928-37); A. Meliarakes, *Neoellenike geographike philologia, etoi katalogos ton apo tou 1800-1889 geographethenton hypo Hellenon* (Athens, 1889); and P. Horecky, *Southeastern Europe: A Guide to Basic Publications* (Chicago, 1969).

In addition, all the important bibliographic periodicals such as *Bibliographika, Deltion Hellenikes bibliographias, Ho bibliophilos, Hellenike bibliographia; Genike hellenike bibliographia, Hellenike bibliographike kai bibliophilike epitheoresis,* and *Ephemeris ton bibliophilon* are available in fairly complete files.

Reference

The collection of general reference materials on Modern Greece contains approximately 200 titles and includes all the representative basic works such as encyclopedias, Greek and foreign dictionaries, *Who's Who* and other biographical dictionaries, directories, yearbooks, specialized handbooks, comprehensive subject-field histories, and miscellaneous guides.

General encyclopedia sets include the *Megale Hellenike Egkyklopaideia,* Eleutheroudake's *Egkyklopaidikon Lexikon,* Chares Patses' *Nea Hellenike Egkyklopaideia,* the popular *Neoteron Egkyklopaidikon Lexikon "Eliou,"* and many others, including four 19th-century titles. There are, besides, several smaller sets or abridged editions of the larger ones such as "Papyros," *Epitomon egkyklopaidikon kai glossikon lexikon,* and Eleutheroudake's *Neon epitomon egkyklopaidikon lexikon.*

Among the subject-field encyclopedias and dictionaries the collection offers A. Martinos' *Threskeutike kai Ethike Egkyklopaideia,* Chares Patses' *Megale Egkyklopaideia tes Neoellenikes logotechnias,* G. Konstantinides' *Lexikon Hagion Graphon,* A. Konstantinides' *Lexikon koinonikon epistemon* and *Lexikon mythologias kai historias,* and G. Konstas' *Neoteron lexikon nomikes.*

All the standard and many older titles in Modern Greek, foreign, and technical dictionaries are available. Foreign-language dictionaries are available for a variety of languages, including Latin, English, French, German, Italian, Russian, Dutch, and Turkish.

Periodicals

One of the strengths of the Modern Greek collection lies in its long files of Greek periodicals. There are about 500 current and noncurrent titles in the collection and the holdings run approximately to 3,000 volumes.

The following partial list offers only a general indication of the scope and strengths of the Greek periodical collection. The PGr class of the Modern Greek collection has the largest holdings in the general periodicals section. The principal specialized journals on such subjects as history, literature, language and philology, archeology, Byzantine studies, church history and theology, business and economics, and the arts are classed in the corresponding subject classes together with the related material.

The most important general catalogs and reference guides to periodicals and newspapers are represented by A. L. Martin-Papazoglou, *Union Catalog of Scientific Periodicals in Greek Libraries. Athens Area* (Athens, 1968); *Bulletin analytique de bibliographie hellénique* (1945-); D. Gkines, *Katalogos Hellenikon ephemeridon kai periodikon, 1811-1863* (Athens, 1963); D. Margares, *Ta palia periodika* (Athens, 1954); K. Mager, *Historia tou hellenikou typou*, 3 v. (Athens, 1957-60); G. Laios, *Ho Hellenikos typos tes Biennes* (Athens, 1961); A. Koumarianou, *Ho typos ston agona 1821-1827*, 3 v. (Athens, 1971); and A. Panagiotopoulou-Gabatha, *Ta Hellenika Proepanastatika Periodika* (Athens, 1971).

The group of current general periodicals in the collection includes such titles as *Aktines; Dialogos; Eos; Euthyne; Hellenika themata; Hellenikos politismos; Hellenisme contemporain; Ilisos; Kainouria epoche; Kouros; Lotos; Makedonike zoe; Nea synora; Nea skepse; Nautike epitheorese; Periegetike; Panathenaia; Sezetesis; Stoa; Stratiotike epitheorese; Zygos.*

The collection includes an unusual file of Greek periodicals established during the 19th century. Among the most notable titles are *Hermes ho Logios, Ionios anthologia, Ephemeris Konstantinoupoleos, Apotheke ton ophelimon gnoseon, Eranistes, Philologikos synekdemos, Pandora, Euterpe, Philistor, Chrysallis, Ethnike bibliotheke, Mentor, Attikon hemerologion, Athenaion, Hestia, Parnassos, Phoibos, Apollon, Poikile stoa, Hebdomas,* and *Hellenismos.*

Also available are numerous Greek periodicals which are no longer being issued. Some of the most prominent in this group are *Harmonia, Panathenaia, Noumas, Parthenon, Melete, Kallitechnes, Politike epitheorese, Pyrsos, Hemerologion tes Megales Hellados, Episteme kai zoe, Ionios anthologia, Hellenika grammata, Neoellenika grammata, Phragkelio, Idea, Neon kratos, Pneumatike zoe, Ho Kyklos, Hellenike demiourgia, Eleuthera grammata, Epistemologos, Neoi rythmoi, Poietike techne, Kochlias, Kibotos, Prometheus, Pali, Agglohellenike epitheorese, Eikones,* and *Ekloge.*

Of special interest to those concerned with the history and achievements of the Greeks of the diaspora are a number of Greek literary and general periodicals published outside Greece, mostly by Greeks and Greek communities established in different parts of the world. Holdings in this important category include such titles as *Myria hosa* (Paris), *Ethnikon hemerologion* (Paris [and Athens]), *Hesperos* (Leipzig), *Hellas* (Leiden), *Hellenic herald* (London), *Serapion* (Alexandria), *Grammata* (Alexandria), *Deltion Panelleniou Henoseos en Amerike* (New York), *Satyros* (New York), *Athene* (Chicago), American Council for a Democratic Greece. *Bulletin* (New York), *Hellenicana* (New York), *Krete* (New York), *Krikos* (London), *Hellenike zoe kai skepse* (Zurich), *Hellenic Review* (Forest Hills, N.Y.), *Hellenism* (Chicago), *Charioteer* (New York), *Argonautes* (New York), *Greek Heritage* (Chicago), *Hellenika* (Ingolstadt), and *Greek Report* (London).

The proceedings and serial publications of the important learned and scientific societies, academies, research institutions, and universities are available practically without exception. Represented are the publications of the Academy of Athens; the Universities of Athens and Salonika; Archaiologike Hetaireia; Historike kai Ethnologike Hetaireia tes Hellados; Hetaireia Byzantinon Spoudon; Hetaireia Historikon Spoudon; Hellenike Laographike Hetaireia; Christianike Archaiologike Hetaireia; Hellenike Anthropologike Hetaireia; Kentron Neoellenikon Ereunon; Kentron Byzantinon Ereunon; Ethnikon Kentron Koinonikon Ereunon; Hetaireia Kretikon Spoudon; Kentron Mikrasiatikon Spoudon; Hellenic Society for Humanistic Studies; Society for Macedonian Studies; Istituto ellenico di studi Bizantini e postbizantini, Venice; Centre de Recherche Scientifique de Chypre, Nicosia; Institute Français d'Athènes; Center of Planning and Economic Research.

Modern Greek History

The history section of the collection includes most of the resources which are essential to research and graduate instruction in Modern Greek history. The extensive holdings are well distributed over all related fields but are especially strong in historical bibliography, primary source material, and political history. There is also significant material in social, cultural, ecclesiastic, and economic history as well as in biography.

The collection has most of the historical writings of the outstanding representatives of each period, together with complete sets of texts, monographs, and treatises. Coverage is most extensive for the Greek Revolution (1821-29), but the period of Turkish Domination or *Tourkokratia* (1453-1821) is also quite well represented. The holdings are abundant for the 19th and 20th centuries.

All the standard general histories of Modern Greece are available, as well as the most recent popular ones. Included are the works of K. Paparregopoulos, E. Kyriakides, P. Karolides, K. Amantos, Sp. Lambros, D. Kokkinos, A. Bakalopoulos, A. Daskalakes, G. Kordatos as well as those of G. Finlay, G. Hertzberg, W. Miller, C. W. Woodhouse, S. Sboronos, Heurtley, Cambell and Sheppard, E. S. Foster.

The various special fields of history are also well represented. Coverage of political and diplomatic history, the history of foreign relations, constitutional and parliamentary history, the history of law and governmental institutions, and military history is virtually complete. In addition, the collection has all the specialized bibliographic and reference aids, catalogs of manuscript collections, and guides to the literature of Modern Greek history.

Major bibliographic contributions to Modern Greek history are also found in historical periodicals such as *Deltion Historikes kai Ethnologikes Hetaireias, Mnemosyne, Athena, Hellenika, Thesaurismata, Epeteris Kentrou Ereunes tou Mesaionikou kai Neou Hellenismou, Hellenomnemon, Neos Hellenomnemon, Epeteris Hetaireias Byzantinon Spoudon, Kypriakai Spoudai, Makedonika, Archeion Euboikon Meleton, Kretika chronika, Epeirotika chronika, Thrakika, Mikrasiatika chronika, Thessalika chronika, Kerkyraika chronika, Balkan Studies, Byzantinische Zeitschrift, Byzantinisch-Neugriechische Jahrbücher, Vizantiiskii vremennik* (Moscow), *The Journal of Hellenic Studies, Revue des études grecques,* and *Rivista di studi bizantini e neoellenici.*

The collection also possesses most of the important reference guides and printed catalogs of Greek manuscript collections contained in the Archives of Mount Athos, National Library of Greece, Academy of Athens, the Monasteries of Meteora, Byzantine Museum of Athens, Patriarchate of Constantinople, Patriarchate of Jerusalem, University of Athens. School of Theology, Monastery of Mega Spelaion, Monastery of Saint John Theologos in Patmos, the Koraes Library of Chios, and others.

The source material for the Tourkokratia period includes K. Sathas' *Documents inédits relatifs à l'histoire de la Grèce au Moyen âge* (Paris, 1880-90); the published archives of the Academy of Athens, which are found in the volumes of *Epeteris tou Mesaionikou Archeiou and Mnemeia tes hellenikes historias;* I. Basdrabelles' *Historika archeia Makedonias;* and the published documents of the Historike kai Ethnologike Hetaireia tes Hellados.

Of the significant historical treatises dealing generally with Tourkokratia, the collection includes, among others, the works of A. Bakalopoulos, D. Zakythenos, K. Sathas, P. Karolides, G. Finlay, I. Zinkeisen, J. Hammer, N. Iorga, L. Stavrianos, T. Euangelides.

The collection of source materials on the Greek Revolution is substantially complete. It includes most of the published archives and sets of historical documents; the memoirs, correspondence, diaries, and autobiographies of prominent participants and other contemporaries; and all the important series of national treaties, constitutional texts, government papers, and diplomatic documents. It also has facsimile reprints and complete texts in later editions of all the important newspapers of the period, such as *Salpigx Hellenike, Hellenika chronika, Philos tou Nomou, Ephemeris ton Athenon,* and *Genike Ephemeris tes Hellados.*

All the important treatises and standard histories of the Greek Revolution are available in the collection, including many scholarly monographs containing the latest research results and interpretations. The collection of major 19th- and 20th-century works in Greek, English, French, and German is complete. Represented are the works of Sp. Trikoupes, A. Phrantzes, I. Philemon, L. Koutzonikas, K. Paparregopoulos, P. Karolides, D. Kokkinos, A. Daskalakes, G. Kordatos, P. Pipineles, F. Pouqueville, J. Jourdain, Th. Gordon, G. Finlay, G. Gervinus, Prokesch-Osten, K. Mendelssohn-Bartholdy, G. Hertzberg, and G. Isambert.

The collection also includes most of the primary sources and special studies relating to the Philike Hetaireia, the biographies of the prominent figures of the Revolution, and the Philhellenic movement, both American and European.

For the period since 1832 the collection has most of the essential source material, together with all the historical writings of the major authors. In addition, there are many monographs and special studies providing background material.

Primary sources for the study of recent and contemporary Greek history include most of the essential material that has been published. The Library has the memoirs, correspondence, and other published papers of such prominent statesmen as Nikolaos Dragoumes, Charilaos Trikoupes, Eleutherios Benizelos, Alexandros Papanastasiou, Andreas Michalakopoulos, Theodoros Pankalos, Stylianos Gonatas, Ioannes Metaxas, E. Tsouderos, Sophokles Benizelos, G. Papandreou, and P. Kanellopoulos. The official publications available include the published diplomatic documents of the Greek Ministry of Foreign Affairs, collections of treaties, laws, legislative journals and parliamentary debates, texts of the constitutions, court reports, and other important documents of the executive branch of the government.

Literature

Modern Greek literature is a particularly strong area in the collections, containing a very substantial and representative portion of the important literary material. Included are the best available editions of each recognized author in the fields of poetry, drama, fiction, and nonfiction. The collection also provides comprehensive coverage of literary history and biography, treatises on Modern Greek literature, and critical interpretations.

In addition, the section of reference aids for Modern Greek literature contains all the basic material necessary to cover the subject in a general way. It includes bibliographies, guides, encyclopedias, dictionaries, handbooks, brief outline-subject histories, collections of standard works and anthologies, the publications of learned societies, and comprehensive files of literary journals.

The following list includes some of the standard bibliographic and reference works for the study of Modern Greek literature: K. Demaras, *Historia tes neoellenikes logotechnias;* Linos Polites, *Historia tes neas hellenikes logotechnias; Bibliographikon deltion neoellenikes philologias.* 1959-65; *Bibliographia neoellenikes philologias.* 1966-   ; K. Demaras and others, *La Grèce modern et sa littérature. Orientation bibliographique en allemand, anglais, français, italien;* M. Manousakas, *Kritike bibliographia tou Kretikou theatrou;* Chares Patses, *Megale egkyklopaideia tes neoellenikes logotechnias;* G. Baletas, *Lexiko neoelleniko philologiko;* E. Kriaras, *Lexiko tes mesaionikes hellenikes demodous grammateias, 1100-1669; Who's who tou hellenikou theatrou;* G. Sideres, *Theatriko glossario.*

The Library has all the important journals in Modern Greek literature and philology, including *Nea hestia, Parnassos, Aiolika grammata, Diagonios, Nea poreia, Kritika phylla, Epitheorese logou kai technes* (Nicosia), *Kypriakos logos, Philologike protochronia, Prototype philologike epitheorese, Themata kritikes* (Nicosia), *Epoches, Kainouria epoche, Epitheorese technes, Athena, Eranistes, Hellenika, Thesaurismata, Platon, Philologos, Symmeikta, Philologike Kypros, Stasinos, Theatron, Anoichto theatro,* and *Thespis.*

Practically all the primary sources on Modern Greek literary authors are available in one form or another. The most important general sets included are *Basike bibliotheke, Hapanta Neoellenon Klassikon, Neoellenike logotechnia* (Ekdoseis Kollaros), *Nea hellenike bibliotheke* (Ekdoseis Hermes), and Linos Polites' *Poietike anthologia.* In addition to the general sets and the works of individual authors, the collection is also rich in anthologies of literature. All the early standard titles and the leading recent collections are available.

Holdings are virtually complete in each of the major periods of Modern Greek Literature, e.g., Medieval Greek and Byzantine literature, Cretan literature, the prerevolutionary period, the 19th century, and the 20th century, including contemporary authors. Leading authors are represented not only by original works and standard editions but also, in a number of cases, by translations.

For the study of the Greek enlightenment of the late 17th and 18th centuries, the collection has all the available works of the major writers, among them Eugenios Boulgares, Nikephoros Theotokes, Demetrios Katartzes, Daniel Philippides and Gregorios Konstantas, Neophytos Doukas, Panagiotes Kodrikas, Konstantinos Koumas, Konstantinos Oikonomos, Athanasios Psalidas, Theophilos Kaires, Neophytos Bambas, and Regas Belestinles.

Modern Greek poetry is represented by a large number of standard editions of all the important poets. Included are the complete works of Solomos, Kalbos, Palamas, Kabaphes, Sikelianos, Kazantzakes, Sepheres, Christopoulos, Belaras, Martelaos, Koutouzes, Tertsetes, Laskaratos, Typaldos, Balaorites, Markoras, P. Soutsos, A. Soutsos, Rizos-Ragkabes, Zalokostas, Orphanides, Paraschos, Soures, Drosines, Mabiles, Probeleggios, Polemes, Krystalles, Palles, Ephtaliotes, Grypares, Chatzopoulos, Porphyras, Malakases, Karyotakes, Lapathiotes, Telos Agras, Polydoure, Papatsones, Barnales, Athanas, Ouranes, Empeirikos, Eggonopoulos, Elytes, Ritsos, Brettakos, G. Themeles, and N. Karouzos.

Among the many significant and stimulating writings in fiction there are the works of Papadiamantes, Xenopoulos, Kazantzakes, Myribeles, Benezes, Kalligas, Bernadakes, Roides, Bikelas, Bizyenos, Psychares, Karkabitsas, Ephtaliotes, Palles, Kondylakes, Blachogiannes, Christobasiles, Traulantones, Chatzopoulos, Theotokes, Boutyras, Kontoglou, Papantoniou, Theotokas, Karagatses, Kastanakes, and Terzakes.

For the study of the Modern Greek drama and the theater, the collection has the plays of all the important playwrights representative of the various periods of Modern Greek dramatic literature from its beginnings to the present time. The history and criticism of Modern Greek drama, together with biographic and related material, are represented by such authors as A. Terzakes, Ai. Chourmouzios, Ph. Mpoumpoulides, M. Manousakas, N. Laskares, G. Sideres, K. Paraschos, S. Melas, Alkes Thrylos, Th. Athanasiades-Nobas, S. Karantinos, Ph. Polites, M. Valsa, International Theatre Institute, *The Modern Greek Theater,* and A. Empeirikos. Also included are a number of works on the Greek shadow theatre (Karagkioses) by such authors as G. Ioannou, K. Mpires, Soterios Spathares, Louis Roussel, Hans Jensen, and Giulio Caimi.

The best of Modern Greek literary history and criticism is represented by such authors as K. Demaras, E. Boutierides, A. Glaukos, A. Kampanes, G. Kordatos, M. Manousakas, Linos Polites, Ph. Mpoumpoulides, G. Zabiras, K. Sathas, I. Rizos Neroulos, A. Rankabes, K. Krumbacher, K. Dieterich, D. Hesseling, B. Knoes, Ph. Lebesgue, A. Mirambel, B. Lavagnini, C. Gidel, R. Nicolai, G. Apostolakes, I. M. Panagiotopoulos, Ph. Polites, Alkes Thrylos, A. Karantones, K. Paraschos, Petros Chares, G. Chatzines, Ares Diktaios, I. Chatzephotes, T. Malamos, P. Spandonides, A. Chourmouzios, M. Klaras, and M. Augeres.

Modern Greek Language

In the field of Modern Greek language and linguistics the collection is exceptionally strong in both Greek and foreign material. All the important language treatises, dialect studies, histories of the language and the language question, and essential studies of grammar and syntax are represented together with the principal bibliographies and language handbooks, standard grammars and dictionaries, and language and philology periodicals. The collection contains the linguistic treatises of A. Koraes, G. Chatzidakis, K. Krumbacher, A. Thumb, A. Meillet, M. Triantaphyllides, A. Megas, Gustav Meyer, A. Mirambel, A. Tzartzanos, K. Sathas, G. Kordatos, and S. G. Kapsomenos.

In addition to general language dictionaries, there are available essential sets of dictionaries and lexicons of special importance to the scholar in the field of Modern Greek language and linguistics in general. Included are such titles as Akademia Athenon. *Lexikon tes hellenikes glosses. Historikon lexikon tes neas hellenikes,* v. 1-4 (Athens, 1933-); I. Stamatakos, *Lexikon tes neas hellenikes glosses;* A. Tamasokles, *Etymologiko lexilogio tes Kypriakes dialectou;* Th. Bostanzoglou, *Analytikon orthographikon lexikon tes neoellenikes glosses;* and G. Kourmoules, *Antistrophon lexikon tes neas hellenikes.* Among the older works in the collection are Gerasimos Blachos, *Thesauros tes egkyklopaidikes baseos tetraglossos;* Charles Du Cange, *Glossarium ad scriptores mediae et infimae graecitatis;* Alexis de Sommevoire, *Tesoro della lingua greca-volgare et italiana;* and E. A. Sophocles, *Greek Lexicon of the Roman and Byzantine Periods.*

Folklore

The Library possesses one of the richest sources of Modern Greek folklore material assembled in the United States. All the important primary sources of folklore material are available, and in addition, the collection contains hundreds of works in the peripheral fields as well as reference works, handbooks, and folklore periodicals. The holdings can be divided into several groups relating to such aspects of folklore as folksongs and ballads, folk music and musical instruments, folk dancing and dramatic art, folktales, proverbs, beliefs, customs, folkspeech vocabularies, etc. Most of the bibliographic material is found in the volumes of the *Laographia* of the Greek Folklore Society and the *Epeteris tou Laographikou Archeiou* of the Academy of Athens. The series of Greek and foreign editions of folklore texts and translations is virtually complete. Most of the important scholarly treatises and popular writings on various aspects of Greek folk life are also available. Represented are the works of N. Polites, St. Kyriakides, G. Megas, D. Kampouroglou, G. Apostolakes, K. Romaios, G. Spyridakes, D. Petropoulos, and D. Loukatos. Among the significant foreign works on Greek folklore are studies by such authors as Johann Hahn, Lucy Mary Garnett, Bertrand Schmidt, Richard Dawkins, James Rennell, Hubert Pernot, Edmund Geldart, Andre Mirambel, Dirk Hesseling, John Lawson, Georges Lambelet, Melpo Merlier, Samuel Baud-Bovy, Martin Nilsson, Hedwig Leudeke, Marianne Klaar, Philip Argenti, D. H. Sanders, Bertrand Bouvier, and J. W. Baggally.

Special Collections

In addition to the book and periodical holdings included in the Modern Greek collection, there are in the Library three notable special collections of Modern Greek materials which, because of their unique character and content, add considerably to the research resources in the field of Modern Greek studies. These are the materials on the Modern Greek stage included in the Library's Theatre Collection, which is housed in the Houghton Library; a special collection of sound recordings of Modern Greek poetry, which is in the Woodberry Poetry Room in the Lamont Library; and a collection of tape recordings of Greek shadow theater plays (Karagkioses), which is part of the Archives of Oral Composition housed in Widener C.

The collection of material on Modern Greek theater is made up of hundreds of theatrical items of interest such as playbills and programs, prints and posters, press clippings, articles and critical comment from newspapers and magazines, biographies, photographs and autographs of performers, stage and costume designs, and other special articles, all relating to the recent and current history of the theater and dramatic art in Greece, and affording an intimate view of what has been happening in the Modern Greek stage from season to season throughout this last decade. This collection was started by Mr. Nikolaos Minadakis, who donated his personal collection of theatrical items relating to the native Greek theater and stage to the Library's Theater Collection.

The Woodberry Poetry Room Collection includes original recordings of poetry readings by contemporary Greek poets reading from their own works. Represented in this collection are such leading poets as Giorgos Sepheres, Giannes Ritsos, Odysseas Elytes, Kostas Barnales, Nikephoros Brettakos, Takes Papatsones, Nikos Eggonopoulos, Giorgos Themeles, Nikos Karouzos, Andreas Empeirikos, Aris Diktaios, and many others. In addition, there are readings from the poetry of Palamas and Kabaphes, as well as other selections.

The collection of Greek shadow theater plays was given to the Library by Prof. Cedric H. Whitman of the Classics Department in 1969. It consists of 62 tapes of shadow plays recorded in Greece, most of them during the actual performances; a full-length black-and-white film; about 200 color slides; a few actual puppets; and tapes of a number of personal interviews with shadow puppeteers. These materials are supplemented by various books on Greek folk theater.

Rare Books, Documents, and Microfilms

Rare materials in Modern Greek are kept in the Houghton Library. Included are such Greek items as early state documents, constitutions, laws and proclamations; collections of manuscripts, rare pamphlets, diaries, and newspapers, survivals from the period of the Greek Revolution; books from early Greek presses; and many original editions of such authors as Koraes, Rizos-Neroulos, Samuel Howe, Solomos, Kalbos, Myribeles, Kabaphes, and Giorgos Sepheres.

The Library's Document-Microtext Division includes in its holdings such Greek document sources as the complete statistical publications of the National Statistical Service of Greece and other material of government and nongovernment research bureaus. In addition, the collection contains microfilms of certain materials in Modern Greek, mainly rare titles and out-of-print publications.

Constantine A. Vlantikas
Harvard University

Hungary

THE AVAILABLE RESEARCH material for Hungarica at the Harvard University Library includes not only Hungarian language materials, but publications in the Slavic languages, modern Western languages, Latin, Hebrew, Turkish, et al. One of the earliest donations, with the bookplate: Gift of Jonathan Jackson of Newbury, 1764-66, is *An historical and geographical account of the ancient Kingdom of Hungary* . . . (London, Printed for A. Bettesnorth in Pater Noster Row n.d., 4, 379 p.).

The importance of the Hungarica collection can be ascertained from the following: No. 44 of Harvard University Library's *Widener Shelflist; Hungarian History and Literature* (1974) contains about 5,500 entries on the Hungarian language, literature, and history; the *Shelflist* provides only partial information on Hungarica, since many pertinent works are under different classifications, e.g., Transylvania is classified with Romania. In all, the Harvard University collections contain about 15,000 volumes of Hungarica.

Development of the Hungarica Collection

A general interest in the geography and history of Hungary over the years has brought many works to Harvard, among them several first editions as Johann Ferdinand Behamb's *Jo, Ferdinandi Behamb . . . Notitiae Hungariae antiquomodernae . . . Argentorati, Sumptibus G. A. Dolhopfii,* 2 pt. in 1 v. (1676). Systematic purchase was begun in the first quarter of this century under the directorship of Archibald Cary Coolidge, who acquired works of great research value dealing with the history of the Austro-Hungarian Monarchy.

The curriculum of Harvard University does not include the Hungarian language and Hungarian literature; thus no special fund was allotted for the regular acquisition of Hungarica and no reports are available on the annual intake. In the early 1960s works on the Hungarian language, literature, and history in Widener Library totaled about 1,000-1,500 volumes. This collection developed rapidly between 1962 and 1967, when the largest number of historical and literary works was acquired, chiefly through purchase, but also through exchange with the National Széchényi Library, the Library of the Hungarian Academy of Sciences, and with several Hungarian universities. Owing to curtailment of funds, at present only the most important publications are purchased, but Hungarica are also obtained through the Public Law 480 program; further, Hungarica publications from Romania and Slovakia, as well as extensive purchase of works on religious subjects, rare books, etc., continue to broaden the coverage.

Imrie de Vegh, economist and onetime honorary curator of East European literature in the Harvard College Library, and his widow donated rare Hungarica to the Houghton Library. Their donations include works of famous humanists of the 15th and 16th centuries.

Hungarica in the Various Libraries of Harvard University

The main body of Hungarica—language, literature, and historical materials—is housed in Widener Library. The general bibliographic coverage is thorough, comprising 21 titles in 75 volumes in addition to 17 titles on Eastern Europe. The Hungarian bibliographies include the standard ones, e.g., most volumes of *Magyar könyvészet* (Bibliographia Hungariae) as well as the bibliographies edited by Károly Szabó, Hiador Sztripszky, Károly Kertbeny, et al., and the national bibliography published after World War II, *Magyar nemzeti bibliográfia* (Bibliographica Hungarica), 1946- with its supplements, e.g., *Magyar folyóiratok repertóriuma* (Repertorium bibliographicum periodicorum Hungaricorum), 1953-.

Hungarian Language and Literature

The preliminary printout of the Widener Library shelflist on periodicals in Hungarian philology lists 30 titles (550 v.), many of which are publications of Hungarian universities or academies and learned societies in Hungary and abroad, e.g., the publication of the Hungarian Academy of Sciences, *Magyar Nyelvőr* [Guardian of the Hungarian Language] (1872-) or those of the Hungarian Institute of Stockholm University.

Cited are examples of earlier and modern bibliographies: the first biobibliography of Hungarian authors which includes some historical personalities as well, compiled by David Czvittinger, *Davidis Czvittinger Specimen Hungariae literae . . .* (Francoforti et Lipsiae . . . Jod. Guil Kohlesii, 1711), or recent works for the English reading public, as Tezla, Albert. *An Introductory Bibliography to the Study of Hungarian Literature* (Cambridge, Mass., 1964), and his *Hungarian Authors; a Bibliographical Handbook* (Cambridge, Mass., 1970). A special aspect is the basis of Mérö, Ferenc. *Emigrációs magyar irodalom lexikona.* [Lexicon of Hungarian Emigrant Literature] (Köln-Detroit [1966]).

There is fair sampling of classical and modern authors, but relatively few editions. The holdings include many first editions, some in Widener Library, others in the Houghton Library's collection of rare books (the latter are distinguished by an asterisk in the call number of the catalog cards). Some first editions are György Bessenyei's *A Holmi* (Béts, 1799); *A Bélteky ház,* 2 v. (Pest, Füskuti Landerer, 1832) by András Fáy; Sándor Petőfi's *Petőfi Sándor összes költeményei* (Pest, Emich Gusztáv, 1847); and Dezső Kosztolányi's *Négy fal között* (Budapest, Pallas, 1907).

Baron József Eötvös is represented in several collections: as a literary author in Widener, as a political thinker in the Law Library, as the minister primarily responsible for the emancipation of the Jews in Hungary in Judaica, and in the Houghton Library as well.

Among the outstanding poets of the recent period Attila József can be studied in the original, in French and German translations, and in several evaluative works; Gyula Illyés in a variety of 37 titles of his own, including translations. The newest products of Hungarian literature are available in a limited variety; however, a great number of literary periodicals (24 titles in ca. 600 volumes) can bridge this gap. Some of these periodicals with substantial holdings are: *Acta litteraria Academiae Scientiarum Hungaricae* (1957-), *Minerva* (1922-39), *Napkelet* [The East] (1923-39), *Nyugat* [The West] (1908-41), and its continuation *Magyar Csillag* [Hungarian Star] (1941-44).

History and Geography

These subjects can be found under several classifications, the bulk of them under Austria; the Ottoman and Romanian sections also contain a great deal of relevant material. The Hungarica collection is strong in historical source material, especially covering the period from the 17th to the first quarter of the 20th century.

Several special bibliographies published by the National Széchényi Library, bibliographies of military history, of maps, etc., are among them. About 30 titles of historiographic works are available, from those by Bálint Hóman and Gyula Szekfű of the earlier school to the works of Francis S. Wagner of recent date. Historical periodicals (56 titles in 422 volumes) as *Ungarisches Magazin; Beiträge zur vaterländischen Geschichte* (1781-87) or more recent ones as 32 volumes of *Huszadik Század* and 14 volumes of its continuation *Századunk,* 47 volumes of *Magyar Szemle,* and others are available. A current quarterly, *Magyar Történelmi Szemle* [Hungarian Historical Review] published in Buenos Aires, has a broader range than its title implies; it contains articles and reprints in various languages in the fields of linguistics, art, and archeology as well.

Some of the valuable sources are several series of *Monumenta Hungariae historica, Fontes rerum Hungaricum, Fontes rerum Transylvanicarum, Archivum Rákóczianum,* and the correspondence of the Transylvanian statesman Mihály Teleki, edited by Samuel Gergely. Further, there are 60 volumes of works by and about Lajos Kossuth, including some contemporary pamphlets; ca. 50 volumes by and about Count István Széchényi, including the first edition, Széchényi, István, grof. *Kelet népe* (Pest, Trattner-Károlyi bet., 1841).

There are some 300 volumes relating to the Hungarian uprising of 1848-49 and about 100 volumes, many in English, French, or Russian, pertaining to the events of 1956.

Genealogy is relatively well represented with important works, like the periodical *Turul* (1883-1943). Descriptions and histories of counties and cities can be found in *Magyarország vármegyéi és városai; Magyarország monográfiája* [Counties and Cities of Hungary], edited by János Sziklay and Samu Borovszky (Budapest, 1896-1911).

The Romanian section has some hundred volumes of source material and also good descriptive works, e.g., Balázs Orbán, *A Székelyföld leírása* [Description of Transylvania] (Pest, 1863-76).

The Ottoman section contains works about the Turkish-Hungarian wars and a work on the siege of Buda published in the very year of its liberation by the Imperial troops: *Diario, e relaçam decima-quarta do sitio & tomada da cidada de Buda* (Lisbon, Na officina di Miguel Deslandes, 1686, 80 p.).

Judaica Related to Hungarica

Since 1962 a concerted effort has been made to collect Judaica in less familiar languages, one of them Hungarian. Acquisition is so extensive that titles can also be retrieved by place of printing, e.g., Budapest (100-200 titles), Pozsony (200-300 titles), Munkács (300-400 titles), and several small towns as well. Numerous pamphlets and several Haggadas round out the holdings—altogether 200-300 volumes.

The collection of Izidor Ullmann, head of the Jewish Community in Nagyvárad, is of special interest as it includes the original handwritten catalog of the collection. Works of noted authors such as David Kaufmann and Vilmos Bacher, many of them in German, are available. Periodicals as *Mult és Jövő* [Past and Future], *Egyenlőség* [Equality], *Magyar-Zsidó Szemle* [Hungarian-Jewish Review] form part of the holdings. The Public Law 480 program provided a steady flow of Hungarian language material published in Israel.

Rare Books and Manuscripts (Houghton Library)

The quality and quantity of Hungarica in the Houghton Library is impressive. It is fitting to cite first a work about the great bibliophile of Hungary, King Matthias Corvinus, the incunabulum Cortesius, Thomas Alexander. *Alexandri Cortesii: De lavdibvs Matthiae Corvin. regis Hvng. ac Bohem.* liber i. ([Rome] Eucharius Silber, after June, 1485. [50] p.). The collection contains several other works about his reign by the humanists who formed part of his scholarly circle as Bonfini, Antonio. *Antonio Bonfinii Rervm vngaricvm decades qvatvor, cvm dimidia* . . . (Francofvrti apud Andream Wechelum, 1631).

His contemporary, the humanist poet Janus Pannonius, Bishop of Pécs, is represented by 12 titles, including two first editions, the earliest dated 1555; Pelbárt Temesvári, the Franciscan preacher and critic of King Matthias' lavish expenditures, by 10 titles, the earliest dated 1501.

Special attention is devoted to the numerous works of the author and Imperial court historiographer Johannes Sambucus (Zsámboki János) with holdings of ca. 15 original titles in addition to many volumes edited by him such as the works of Antonio Bonfini, István Verbőczy, et al.

Some recent publications can serve as guides to early Hungarica: Sajó, Géza, ed. *Catalogus incunabulorum quae in bibliothecis publicis Hungariae asservantur* . . . (Budapest, 1970), or a joint publication of the Hungarian Academy of Sciences and the National Széchényi Library *Régi magyarországi nyomtatványok, 1473-1600* (Res litteraria Hungariae vetus operum impressorum, 1473-1600) (Budapest, 1971).

The Manuscript Collection holds a German translation of János Thuróczy's *Chronica Hungarorum* (in unidentified hand) (Austria, [ca. 1500], 204 f.) (fMS Ger43), and a Latin manuscript dated Oct. 17, 1522 of the Hungarian monastic order, the Hermits of Saint Paul, *Constitutiones ordinis Sancti Pauli Primi heremitae* (Colophon, Langnów, 1522) (MS Lat197).

Fine Arts Library (Fogg Art Museum)

This collection has several hundred books on art and architecture in Hungary. However, works on archeology are mostly in the Widener collection. As there is hardly any subject approach, the user can only look for authorities on fine arts, names of cities, publications of museums, etc. About 10 titles of periodicals are in these holdings.

The Law School Library (Langdell Hall)

The Law School Library holds a good working collection of bibliographical and reference works, constitutional documents, collections of laws and statutes, legislative documents, treatises, and some periodicals. It has rich holdings of pre-1825 publications (about 60 volumes), among them several editions of Verbőczy's *Tripartitum*.

Many treatises of historical, sociopolitical interest, e.g., pertinent works of Baron József Eötvös are in this library: among holdings by 20th-century authors are 11 titles by Károly Szladits. The strongest coverage in general is to the end of World War I, with holdings of over 2,000 volumes of monographs and 10 titles (ca. 170 v.) of periodicals.

Kress Library of Business and Economics at the Graduate School of Business Administration

Several early works of interest are in this collection in material published before 1850, as the first edition of an early statistical work: Schwartner, Martin. *Statistik des Königreichs Ungern. Ein Versuch . . .* (Pest, Gedruckt bey M. Trattner, 1798, 5 p.1., [iii] xvi, 606 p.). Another work deals with the waterways of the Kingdom of Hungary: Rauchmüller von Ehrenstein, Franz. *Uebersicht der dem ungarisch adriatischen Meereshandel diendenden Landund Wasserstrassen, und der dazu gehoerigen Seehaefen . . .* 5 pt. in 5 v. (n. p., 1831). A good bibliography for research is: Dóczy, Jenő (ed.) *A magyar gazdasági irodalom első századainak könyvészete . . .* (Bibliographia litterarum Hungariae oeconomicarum e prioribus saeculis . . .) (Budapest, 1934-38); an early book on agriculture is the description of the Habsburg archducal estate of Alcsuth by J. N. von Török. The number of works about Hungary proper is small but many others about Austria complement the picture and make an interesting collection of Hungarica.

Andover-Harvard Theological Library

In the tradition of the founder John Harvard, the coverage of religious and related cultural material had foremost importance, which accounts for the rich holdings of the Andover-Harvard Theological Library and of Widener Library in these subjects. The policy of the Theological Library is to acquire all available works, be they books, pamphlets or periodicals, about Protestantism with special emphasis on early imprints. Among the ca. 200 titles (250 v.) cataloged on Protestantism in Hungary and Transylvania, 20 works have 18th century imprints. There are 18 titles about the Unitarian Church (which originated in Transylvania), including five by and about its first bishop, Ferenc Dávid. The most recent acquisitions are 500 books plus 200 pamphlets of Hungarica. Among the 36 titles of periodicals (ca. 230 v.) which span the period from the 1880s to the present, three are Unitarian publications.

Catholicism in Hungary is classified in Hungarian history in the Widener Library collection, which contains numerous monographs on church history, history of dioceses, monasteries, etc., as well as several works of Cardinal Péter Pázmány, the principal figure of Counter Reformation in Hungary.

In summary it may be said that the Harvard collections of Hungarica are principally retrospective, and that current materials are acquired on a highly selective basis from the general fund. The Andover-Harvard Theological Library, the Judaica Collection, the Houghton Library, et al. have their own budgets and continue to acquire works in their collecting fields. The 15,000 volume Harvard collection is one of the finest Hungarica collections in the country and offers various research possibilities.

Rose Stein
Columbia University

Judaica

JUDAICA IN THE Harvard College Library are located chiefly in Widener Library. Certain rare materials are in the Library's Rare Book Department (Houghton Library) and may be consulted subject to the conditions governing the use of the Harvard University Library. With the exception of serials, some pamphlets, and certain rarities, this material is available on interlibrary loan. A well-equipped Photographic Services Department is located on the premises for microfilming and Xeroxing; mail requests should be addressed to the Photographic Reference Assistant, Widener Library.

Bibliographic access to materials in Western Languages is through the Library's card catalogs (Union Catalog, by main entry; Public Catalog, by main entry, added entries, subjects, and selected titles). Much of this Judaica is now accessible through the volumes of the *Widener Shelflist Series;* vol. 39 *(Judaica)* and vol. 28-31 *(Slavic History and Literatures)* are especially helpful. There are separate card catalogs and shelflists for Hebrew and Yiddish. In addition, the Hebrew card catalog has been published in book form: Harvard University Library. *Catalogue of Hebrew Books,* 6 v. (Cambridge, 1968); idem, *Supplement I.* 3 v. (Cambridge, 1972). Access to articles in Jewish Festschriften is provided by the Library's recently published *Index to Festschriften in Jewish Studies,* compiled and edited by Charles Berlin (Cambridge, 1971).

The Collections

Publications on the history and culture of the Jewish communities of East Central and Southeastern Europe are a prominent feature of Harvard's extensive collection of Judaica. Of the approximately 150,000 volumes of Judaica, some 20,000 are publications originating in or dealing with Jewish life in that area.

This collection is primarily a result of the intensive development of the Library's Judaica collection over the past 40 years. In 1929 Harvard acquired a large and multifaceted collection of Hebraica from the famous bookseller Ephraim Deinard; this included several thousand imprints which became the nucleus of the Library's extensive collection of Hebraica from East Central Europe. It was, however, the acquisition in 1951 of the Felix Friedmann Collection of Hebraica and Judaica that provided Harvard with a preeminent collection of East Central European Hebraica. The bulk of the Friedmann collection was the library of Izidor Ullman, a wealthy bibliophile and leader of the Jewish community of Nagyvárad in Hungary. With this acquisition Harvard acquired a comprehensive collection of some 3,000 volumes of Hungarian Hebraica, as well as hundreds of Hebrew books printed in Czechoslovakia, Poland, and Greece. In 1957 the Library received by bequest the Judaica collection of the noted bibliophile Lee M. Friedman. This collection, which was probably the finest collection of Judaica in Western languages in the United States, was especially rich in materials (especially pamphlets) on antisemitism, Jewish-Christian relations, and local history and included much material on the Jews of East Central and Southeastern Europe. In addition, throughout this period a substantial Yiddish collection had been developed through the intensive efforts of A. A. Roback, noted psychologist and historian of Yiddish literature; this included several thousand Yiddish books from Poland. Finally, in 1962 the Library's Hebrew Division was established, and since that time it has pursued a policy of systematic and comprehensive acquisition of Judaica in all languages, both current and retrospective. In the course of the past decade, many gaps in the holdings of earlier materials have been filled, especially Judaica in the Hungarian and Czech languages. In addition, these various special acquisitions, as well as the Library's intensive acquisitions activity in the past decade, have yielded much material on East Central and Southeastern Europe published elsewhere in Europe, in the United States, and, especially, in Israel. To the extent that materials and funds remain available, the Library will maintain its policy of acquiring all printed Judaica pertaining to this geographic area.

In addition to the brief description below of the collection of East Central and Southeastern European Judaica imprints, a few words are in order regarding the vast quantity of other materials dealing with that area. In addition to more than a thousand volumes published elsewhere and dealing specifically with this topic, it should be noted that the Library's general Judaica often contains much information on this area. General histories of the Jews and of Jewish literature, Jewish encyclopedias and biographic dictionaries, and other reference tools in Jewish studies frequently include material on the Jews of that area. Especially useful are Jewish newspapers and periodicals such as the English *Jewish Chronicle,* the Yiddish *Jewish Daily Forward,* and the Hebrew *Ha-arets* and *Davar,* all of which the Library has complete on microfilm, and the German *Allgemeine Zeitung des Judenthums,* the French *Univers Israélite,* and the Jewish Telegraphic Agency's *Daily News Bulletin,* which the Library has in the original. The publications of organizations like the World Zionist Organization are also useful in this regard, especially its newspaper *Ha-Olam* (on microfilm), and the proceedings and reports of the Zionist Congresses, most of which are in the collection. The Library also has many publications of various "Landsmanschaften" which contain much material on their former homeland; e.g., *MB (Mitteilungsblatt;* German bulletin of immigrants from Central Europe), *Bialystocker Vegn* (Yiddish). In the past quarter of a century, Israel has understandably emerged as the leading publisher of Judaica, and much has been published, primarily in Hebrew, on the Jews of East Central and Southeastern Europe, virtually all of which is in the Library's Judaica collection. This includes several hundred Yizkor ("remembrance") books published there in Hebrew and/or Yiddish as memorials to the Jewish communities destroyed during World War II. Finally, it should be noted that many books and periodicals in the Library's general collection of materials on East Central and Southeastern Europe contain material on the Jews of that area.

Hungary

Judaica in the Hungarian language (approximately 1,000 volumes) is divided into two main categories. The first consists of material on the history and culture of the Jews in Hungary; this includes a large number of substantial monographs dealing with general Hungarian Jewish history, local history, and communal organizations, of the 19th and early 20th centuries. Particularly noteworthy is the large number of pamphlets from this period, especially those concerned with the "Jewish Question," antisemitism, and Zionism.

The second category of Hungarian language materials represents contributions of Hungarian Jewish scholars to general Jewish scholarship. In addition to the works of well-known scholars and the series of scholarly monographs published by the Budapest Rabbinical Seminary, the collection also has many monographs, especially doctoral dissertations, by lesser-known figures. Topics in rabbinic literature are most numerous, although Bible, philosophy, and history are also represented. Also included are many collections of sermons by Hungarian rabbis and Hungarian belles lettres by Jewish authors or on Jewish themes. Selected translations into Hungarian include editions of the Old Testament prepared by Jewish scholars and translations of Jewish liturgical works. In addition, Hungarian translations of Judaica published elsewhere are acquired as illustrations of the process of cultural transmission; these include both scholarly as well as publicistic and literary works.

Hungarian periodicals of Jewish interest are well represented. These include complete or substantial runs of scholarly journals, e.g., *Magyar Zsidó Szemle, Izraelita Magyar Irodalmi Társulat Évkönyve, Ha-Tsofeh Me-Erets Hagar* (Hebrew), and *Ben Chananja* (German); cultural and political journals, e.g., *Egyenlőség, A Magyar Zsidók Lapja;* literary journals, e.g., *Libanon, Múlt és Jövő;* community publications, e.g., *Új Élet, Magyar Izrael;* almanacs, e.g., *Naptára, Magyar Zsidók Naptára, Izraelita Családi Naptár,* and *Cultur-almanach;* and Hebrew rabbinic journals, e.g., *Va-Yelaket Yosef, Otsar Ha-Hayyim, Tel-Talpiot,* and *Bet Vaad Le-Hakhamim.* In addition, the Library has an extensive collection of Jewish Festschriften published in Hungary. Both the periodicals and Festschriften contain much material on all aspects of Jewish life in Hungary as well as many contributions to other areas of Jewish scholarship.

The Library's collection of Hungarian Hebraica (approximately 3,000 v.) includes large numbers of books printed in Budapest, Paks, Szatmár, Szinérváralja, Ungvár, and Vác. More than 25 other locales are also represented, including Debrecen, Dés, Huszt, Kecskemét, Kisvárdán, Klausenburg, Nagyvárad, Nyírbátor, Temesvár, Újhely, and Vranov. These works are primarily in the area of rabbinic studies: Biblical commentaries, homiletics, Talmudic commentaries, religious law (halakhah), responsa, and religious ethics. The well-known rabbinic scholars are especially well represented, along with a multitude of lesser-known scholars scattered throughout the Jewish communities of Hungary. Many of the later American and Israeli reprints of these Hebrew texts are also in the collection.

Poland

During most of the century and a half preceding World War II, Poland was the chief center of Hebrew, and especially Yiddish, publishing. The tremendous quantity of that Judaica in Hebrew and Yiddish accounts for most of the Judaica published in Poland, and the Library's collection of Polish Judaica reflects this. Harvard's Polish Hebraica (ca. 5,000 items) ranges over the entire field of Jewish studies, including history and politics, philosophy and theology, Hebrew literature and philology, translations into Hebrew, and all areas of rabbinic literature. The collection includes a good representation of the earliest period of Hebrew printing in Poland as well, with approximately 100 Lublin and Kraków imprints of the 16th and 17th centuries. There are over 3,000 Warsaw and 1,000 Lemberg imprints, with over 60 other imprints also represented, including Białystok, Biłgoraj, Drohobycz, Grodno, Jozefów, Korzec, Krotoszyn, Łódź, Nowydwór, Ostrog, Piotrków, Podgórze, Słutzk, and Tarnopol. The collection of Yiddish books and pamphlets (ca. 4,000 items) reflects Poland's primacy in the development of Yiddish literature. A large part of the collection consists of Yiddish belles lettres, including popular novels, tales, and dramas. There is, in addition, much historical material dealing with Jewish life in Poland as well as materials in other areas of Jewish studies. The collection includes much periodical material in Polish, e.g., *Biuletyn* (Żydowski Instytut Historyczny); in Yiddish, e.g., *Bleter far Geshikhte, Literarishe Bleter, Oyfgang, Yidishe Shriftn,* and *Folksshtime;* and in Hebrew, e.g., *He-Asif,*

Ha-Dor, Ha-Kerem, Ha-Mevaser, Luah Ahiasaf, Sefer Ha-Shanah (Sokołów), as well as a number of other journals which were published for a time in Poland, e.g., *Ha-Tsefirah, Ha-Magid,* and *Ha-Shiloah.*

Special mention should be made of a collection of Polish Hebrew and Yiddish ephemera relating to the Yiddish theater, Jewish education, politics, Zionism, and the reaction to the 1929 Arab massacre of Jews in Hebron. There is also a large collection of "Jednodniówka," i.e., publications similar to periodicals in format but intended as "one-time" publications.

The Polish-language Judaica (ca. 300 items) include primarily books and pamphlets on Jewish life in Poland but also contain contributions to other areas of Jewish scholarship. The former include surveys of Jewish history in Poland, local histories, organizational reports, and pamphlets on the "Jewish question."

Czechoslovakia

The collection of Czechoslovak Judaica includes some 500 items in Czech and German dealing with the history of the Jewish communities in the medieval and modern periods. For the latter period, antisemitism and Zionism are well represented, as well as belles lettres by Jewish writers. Periodicals include substantial runs of *Židovská ročenka, Kalendář česko-židovský, Židovský Kalendář, Židovské zprávy, Pascheles' Israelitischer Volkskalender, Jahrbuch der Gesellschaft für Geschichte der Juden in der Tschechoslowakei, Judaica Bohemiae,* and *Věstník židovských náboženských obcí v Československu.* Special mention should be made of a collection of broadsides issued by the government regulating Jewish life in Moravia during the 18th and 19th centuries. The collection also includes approximately 1,000 Hebrew books (chiefly rabbinics) printed in Czechoslovakia, primarily in Prague (300 items, one-fourth of them 16th- and 17th-century imprints), Bratislava, Brno, and Mukačevo (the last with some 250 19th- and 20th-century imprints).

Romania, Yugoslavia, Bulgaria, and Greece

The collection includes some 500 items (books, pamphlets, and periodicals) from Romania, Yugoslavia, and Bulgaria, approximately 300 in the vernacular languages and 200 in Hebrew, Yiddish, and Ladino (Judeo-Spanish). Periodicals include *Revista Cultului Mozaic* (Bucharest), *Jevrejski Almanah* (Vršac), *Jevrejski Pregled* and *Jevrejski Almanah* (Beogard), and *Godishnik* (Obshtestvena kulturno-prosvetna organisatsiia na evreite v Narodna Republika Bulgariia). Hebrew material is primarily rabbinic, and the Yiddish and Ladino is chiefly popular literature; imprints include Belgrade, Sarajevo, Sofia, Rustchuk, Botoşani, Bucharest, Czernowitz, Déva, Jassy, and Sziget. There are also numerous ephemeral items (posters, broadsides, leaflets) in Romanian and Yiddish dealing with political and cultural affairs.

The Library's collection of 400 Hebrew and 200 Ladino books with Greek imprints (chiefly Salonika) reflects the long history of Hebrew printing in that area (with some 50 items from the 16th and 17th centuries) and the shorter but very active period of Ladino publishing in the 19th and 20th centuries. The Greek Hebraica is primarily rabbinic; the Ladino material consists of popular works, both literary and general.

Charles Berlin
Harvard University

Poland

ABOUT THE TURN of the century Harvard University Library began to acquire Polish books in a more or less systematic manner, with emphasis on serial publications of learned societies, collections of historical sources, editions of literary classics, and significant scholarly monographs. History was stressed more than literature, but the coverage seems to have been uneven. Thus the collection, although a very good one, had gaps. Much of the impetus during the early stage of development was provided by Professor Archibald Cary Coolidge, who was Director of the University Library from 1910 to 1928, but whose special interest in the Slavic collections antedated the period of his tenure.

A radical shift occurred during the 1950s when the University greatly expanded its programs concerned with the Slavic countries, their literatures and languages. Through increased funds available for the purchase of books and the concerted efforts of Mr. Charles R. Gredler, at present Archibald Cary Coolidge Bibliographer and Assistant Librarian for the Slavic Collection, and Dr. Wiktor Weintraub, now Alfred Jurzykowski Professor of Polish Language and Literature, the Library has acquired virtually every significant item relevant to Polish studies published during the last 15-20 years, as well as a wide range of Polish scholarly publications on subjects not related to Poland, and has filled most of the gaps remaining from the previous periods. These efforts are being continued, but in somewhat lesser volume, owing to budgetary restrictions.

The Polish history and literature sections form the most substantial part of the collection. Excellent resources are also available for the study of many other aspects of Polish civilization, chiefly: law, art, music, folklore, philosophy, and religion.

Exact statistics are not available on the number of Polish books or works about Poland owned by the Harvard University Library system, but a conservative estimate, based on shelflists and other sources, indicates a total of about 50,000 volumes or 30,000 titles.

The section of Widener Library comprising history and literature of the Slavic countries lists 7,678 titles under Polish history and 7,522 under Polish literature, i.e., 15,200 titles (about 20,000 volumes) on Polish subjects in various languages. The number of works published in the Polish language is 12,514 titles (an estimated 16,000 volumes). The annual increment of Polish holdings of the University is now about 2,000 titles.

Bibliography

The collection includes a complete set of standard general bibliographies: retrospective (Estreicher), as well as current *(Przewodnik Bibliograficzny)*. The gaps for the periods during which the publication of *Przewodnik Bibliograficzny* was suspended are filled by other titles *(Bibliografia Polska, Urzędowy Wykaz Druków,* and *Nowa Książka). Bibliografia Zawartości Czasopism* provides an index to contents of periodicals. Polish publications issued abroad are covered by the yearbook *Polonica Zagraniczne* and by J. Zabielska's *Bibliography of Books in Polish or Relating to Poland.* An indication of the depth of the bibliographic holdings can be had from the following.

The Library has 21 of the 25 separately published retrospective special bibliographies that appear in Korpała's *Dzieje Bibliografii w Polsce* for the period 1918-39, and 97 of the 111 items published since 1944. The missing items were in fields outside Polish history and literature.

Encyclopedias and Dictionaries

Of the general Polish encyclopedias, Harvard lacks only *Wielka Ilustrowana Encyklopedia Powszechna* (the so-called "Encyklopedia Gutenberga," Kraków, 1929-38) and *Encyklopedia*

Powszechna Ultima Thule (Warsaw, 1927-38). The period between the two world wars is represented by *Encyklopedia Trzaski, Everta i Michalskiego* (Warsaw, 1927-38). Among the particularly noteworthy works located at Harvard is *Wielka Encyklopedia Powszechna Ilustrowana* (Warsaw, 1890-1912). Although never completed, this seems the most thorough of all works of its kind published in Poland. The holdings of special encyclopedias and dictionaries include several significant titles such as the monumental *Słownik Geograficzny Królestwa Polskiego* (Warsaw, 1880-1902), *Podręczna Encyklopedia Kościelna* (Warsaw, 1904-16), and *Encyklopedia Prawa Obowiązującego w Polsce* (Poznań, 1923-29).

On the other hand, Widener does not have *Encyklopedia Wojskowa* (Warsaw, 1931-39), *Encyklopedia Nauk Politycznych* (Warsaw, 1936-39), *Encyklopedia Wychowania* (Warsaw, 1933-39), and a number of other works published prior to World War II and devoted to special subject areas. Harvard book selectors of that period apparently were reluctant to buy specialized reference tools published in Polish unless they were devoted to specifically Polish subjects. This policy has been reversed since then, and fortunately so, as such works often contain valuable and not easily accessible information on various aspects of Polish life and civilization.

The field of general biography is represented mainly by *Polski Słownik Biograficzny*, the preparation of which is still in progress.

A number of interesting and valuable works may be found among collections of special biographies, for example: B. Sadok. *Żywoty Sławnych Ormian w Polsce* (Lwów, 1856); S. Ciampi. *Notizie di Medici, Maestri di Musica e Cantori, Pittori . . . ed Altri Artisti Italiani in Polonia e Polacchi in Italia* (Lucca, 1830); E. Kotłubaj. *Galeria Nieświeżska Portretów Radziwiłłowskich* (Wilno, 1857); Z. Szulc. *Słownik Lutników Polskich* (Poznań, 1953). In addition to providing a sample of somewhat esoteric works available in the area of Polish special biography this listing may also serve to illustrate the range and quality of the whole collection.

Scholarly Serial Publications

From the beginning of the Polish collection, major emphasis was placed on acquiring scholarly journals and other serial publications issued by learned societies and academic institutions. To evaluate the results of these efforts, the author searched a number of bibliographies and found that the coverage is virtually complete in all aspects of Polish studies and nearly complete in other areas of humanities and social sciences. The files of each serial publications were not checked for completeness, but general use over an extended period indicates that there are relatively few gaps.

General and Literary Periodicals. Newspapers

A full range of currently published general and literary periodicals is available for the student of present-day Poland. The situation is less satisfactory for the earlier period.

Let us first consider the 19th and the beginning of the 20th centuries. The following titles will be found in Widener either complete or largely so: *Biblioteka Warszawska, Tygodnik Petersburski* (on film), *Przegląd Poznański, Tygodnik Ilustrowany, Przegląd Polski, Przegląd Powszechny, Krytyka,* and *Chimera.* A few short-lived, but valuable, periodicals published by 19th-century Polish émigrés should also be mentioned: *Kronika Emigracji Polskiej, Trzeci Maj, Pismo Towarzystwa Demokratycznego Polskiego, Przegląd Rzeczy Polskich,* and *Roczniki Polskie.* Mickiewicz's *Tribune des Peuples* is available in a modern reprint.

Among the missing titles are: *Przegląd Naukowy, Przegląd Tygodniowy, Prawda, Wędrowiec, Głos, Reforma* and its continuation *Nowa Reforma, Ogniwo* and, finally, the two sets of *Życie,* one published in Warsaw, the other in Kraków. Most of these periodicals were involved in the important ideological and esthetic debates of the half century preceding World War I. Their absence is bound to be felt by students of modern Polish intellectual history.

The situation is better for the period 1918-39. The two most important literary periodicals of this time, *Wiadomości Literackie* and *Skamander*, are available partly on film and partly in original. The set of Skamander is complete; that of *Wiadomości Literackie* nearly so. Other titles from that period held by Widener include: *Zdrój, Droga, Myśl Niepodległa*, a reedition of the communist *Nowy Przegląd, Przegląd Powszechny, Przegląd Współczesny, Przegląd Warszawski, Myśl Narodowa*, and *Tygodnik Ilustrowany*. Missing are *Kwadryga, Zwrotnica, Prosto z Mostu, Epoka, Sygnały*, and *Żagary*.

The difference noted between the quality of the current and retrospective holdings of Polish periodicals is also applied to newspapers, but the contrast is much sharper. Except for fragmentary microfilm of the socialist *Robotnik* there are no significant files of any Polish newspaper prior to 1944. The years of transition to airtight communism, 1944-48, are adequately covered by microfilms of *Głos Ludu, Robotnik*, and *Gazeta Ludowa*. For the Stalinist- and post-Stalinist era there are either complete or at least substantial files of *Trybuna Ludu, Głos Pracy, Życie Warszawy, Zielony Sztandar*, and *Żołnierz Wolności*.

The paucity of Polish newspapers reflects a conscious policy of long standing. Traditionally Widener Library had kept its newspapers holdings to a minimum level. The shift of research interests and the development of microfilm technique during recent decades have brought about a reversal of this policy, but the effects of the former limitations are still felt in many areas, and very keenly so in the field of Polish studies. The Slavic Division of Widener Library intends to fill the gaps in newspapers and periodicals by ordering microfilms.

History

The collection of source and documentary materials, some of them contained in multivolume sets, forms perhaps the most important element of the Polish History section. All the significant sources to the history of Poland prior to the partitions are found here, with the exception of the *Volumina Legum*, of which Harvard has only two parts. The following is a partial list of the important items: *Acta Historica Res Gestas Poloniae Illustrantia* (Kraków, 1878-1909); *Acta Tomiciana* (Poznań, 1852-   ); *Akta Grodzkie i Ziemskie z . . . Archiwum . . . Bernardyńskiego* (Lwów, 1868-1935); *Codex Diplomaticus Regni Poloniae et Magni Ducatus Lithuaniae* (Wilno, 1758-1764): *Monumenta Medii Aevi Historica Res Gestas Poloniae Illustrantia* (Kraków, 1874-1927); *Monumenta Poloniae Historica* (Lwów, 1864-1893); *Monumenta Polonia Vaticana* (Kraków, 1913-   ); *Scriptores Rerum Polonicarum* (Kraków, 1872-1917); Vilenskaia Kommissiia dlia Razbora Drevnikh Aktov. *Akty* (1865-1912); *Starodawne Prawa Polskiego Pomniki* (Warszawa, 1856-   ).

To the above materials the Library has been adding more recent publications containing sources both to older and to modern history. A gap in the latter category is the absence of stenographic reports of the Polish parliament during the period between the two wars. (The Library possesses on film the reports for the years 1919-22 only.)

The pattern of a strong collection of older publications serving as the basis for continuing expansion also is evident from the Library's holdings of secondary historical works. A student of Polish history is likely to find any contemporary monograph in his field of interest, and he will be able to read widely in the works of historians of previous generations: Bobrzyński, Szujski, Kalinka, Korzon, Askenazy, or Naruszewicz.

The collection offers abundant resources on local history. For example, in the section devoted to the city of Kraków there are more than one hundred titles besides the 16-volume *Rocznik Kra-*

kowski and the 111-volume *Biblioteka Krakowska.* About a much less important locality, the city of Kielce with the surrounding region, the reader will find about a dozen titles.

Genealogy and Heraldry, as well as Military, Church, and Economic History are other fields where the coverage seems excellent.

Most works on Polish history during World War II are not classified with the History of Poland. However the subject may be conveniently mentioned here. The Library's extensive holdings reflect the emphasis that this area has been given in Polish research and publishing. The émigré publications provide balance to the literature issued in Poland.

Literature

The Literature Collection has been built with the same care as the Polish History section and on similar principles. Consequently it has achieved an equal level of excellence. One of its most outstanding segments is the Mickiewicz collection, comprising eight editions of his complete works, numerous editions of selected works and individual titles, as well as over two hundred and fifty entries of criticism and biography. Although considerably larger than any other collection devoted to a single author, it is representative of the prevailing standards.

The Library has not limited its efforts to major authors. It has also extensively acquired works by and about secondary and lesser writers. For example, Michał Czajkowski is represented by an edition of his works in 12 volumes, eight separately published titles, and four items about him. There are ten titles by Stanisław Brzozowski and six critical works devoted to him.

These collections are supplemented by a full assortment of scholarly serial publications, general histories of literature, as well as works on special periods or subjects. Among the important multivolume collections one might mention the *Biblioteka Pisarzów Polskich,* published around the turn of the century, and both series of the more recent *Biblioteka Narodowa* (one devoted to Polish writers and the other to translations from foreign languages).

Groups of books related to Poland are scattered throughout classes other than Polish History and Literature. Following are some of the significant clusters.

Polish Language

The cards under the heading "Polish Language" occupy a full catalog drawer. Substantial segments of the collection are devoted to Old Polish and to various regional dialects. Practically every item of recent theoretical literature on the Polish language will be found on the shelves.

Folklore

The center of the collection consists of the editions of Kolberg's works: the original edition as well as the monumental edition (now nearing completion) in more than 65 volumes. Aside from these, and from current scholarly and popular publications, there are 19th-century studies on folklore, collections of tales, etc. Much relevant material may also be found in the Ethnography section of the Polish History class and in the files of *Wisła, Lud,* and other periodicals. The holdings of the Peabody Museum Library will likewise be of interest for the student of Polish folklore.

Education

The Library collects works on the history and current problems of education in Poland as well as writings by and about Polish educators. Soon most of these items will be transferred to the newly built Education Library. The part of this collection to remain in Widener probably will be that containing the history and official documents of academic institutions, including university catalogs, lists of faculty, and annual reports, some of them going back to the turn of the century.

Philosophy

The Polish philosophy section contains more than a hundred titles, including 19th-century editions of works by Hoene-Wroński, Libelt, and Jan Śniadecki, as well as a number of critical works devoted to these authors. Works by Polish philosophers on specific subjects are not kept here but are classified by those subjects.

Archeology

Two collections on the archeology of Poland, one in Widener and the other in Peabody Museum Library, provide intensive coverage of the subject. Much of the archeological literature published during recent decades is also of importance for Polish medieval history.

Scattered Holdings

Many works valuable for Polish studies are scattered in small clusters, or individually, throughout the whole library. To give just one example: in the Sociology section, among books dealing with the situation of women in different countries, there are several works devoted to the status and problems of women in Poland. The only practical approach to such scattered material is through the subject catalog, or through entries for the authors.

Students of Polish affairs will find much material in works in Polish which do not deal specifically with Poland and thus risk being overlooked. For example, *Mała Encyklopedia Ekonomiczna* is a reference work covering the whole range of the discipline, but is of particular interest to students of Polish economic conditions or Polish economic thought.

Houghton Library

Among the rare Polish books preserved in the Houghton Library are:
1. A number of early 16th-century Latin works published in Kraków; among them: *Opusculum de Arte Memoratiua* (1504), attributed to Jan of Dobczyce; Jan Głogowczyk's *Computus Chirometralis* (1511) and his *Tractatus Preclarissimus in Judicijs Astrorum* (1514).
2. First or very early editions of works by old Polish historians: Maciej z Miechowa, Gwagnin, Heidenstein, Decius, Pastorius, Piasecki, Solikowski, Kobierzycki.
3. First edition of Kochanowski's Latin elegies.
4. A group of early 17th-century Raków imprints, including many works by Smalcius.
5. A 1556 Polish translation of the New Testament (Kraków, Szarffenberger) and a 1561 illustrated folio edition of the Bible (the so-called Biblia Leopolity, published in Kraków by Szarffenberger). The latter is the first complete edition of the Bible printed in the Polish language.

A very tentative search of the Houghton Library manuscript catalog brought to light the following holdings related to Polish personalities or subjects:
1. A number of Mickiewicz items contained in the *Literary Papers of Zinaida Volkonskaia* (Accession no. *67-152). These are chiefly prose translations into French of Mickiewicz's poems, some of them done by the author himself, and some in his own hand.
2. Several of Mickiewicz's letters to Margaret Fuller d'Ossoli included in her family papers.

3. Letters, mostly in autograph, by or concerning: Kościuszko, Pułaski, Paderewski, Walerian Krasiński, Modjeska, Gurowski, and Wincenty Lutoslawski (including seven of his letters to William James).
4. Two documents from the royal chancery dated 1571 and 1687.

The Law Library

The Polish collection of the International Legal Studies Library is estimated at 2,000 to 3,000 volumes. The collection covers the periods of Polish independence as well as the 19th-century period of Russian rule. Materials specifically concerning the provinces incorporated into Austria and Prussia are kept with these countries.

The Library owns sets of *Dziennik Praw* and *Dziennik Ustaw* (publications containing authoritative texts of laws) extending from the time of the Duchy of Warsaw (1808) through the era of the Kingdom of Poland and subsequent forms of Russian administration until 1871, and then from 1918 to the present time. Besides the official codes, collections of laws in special fields, of judicial decisions, and of administrative regulations, the Library also collects extensively monographic literature on Polish law. The holdings of legal periodicals include: *Czasopismo Prawniczo-Ekonomiczne, Ławnik Ludowy, Nowe Prawo, Państwo i Prawo, Palestra, Ruch Prawniczy i Ekonomiczny, Rada Narodowa,* and *Przegląd Ustawodawstwa Gospodarczego*.

A number of 16th-, 17th- and 18-century compilations of old Polish laws are found both in the International Legal Studies Library and in the Polish History section of Widener.

Music Library, Fine Arts Library, and Peabody Museum Library

All three libraries have been acquiring a full range of recent Polish scholarly publications in their fields. The Music Library also buys scores by reputable Polish composers.

Except for the latter category, most of the acquisition for the Music and Fine Arts libraries is done by the Slavic Division of Widener. Holdings of older materials in these libraries are comparable to those of Widener.

The Peabody Museum Library specializes in Anthropology, Ethnology, and Prehistoric Archeology. In conjunction with the Ethnology and Folklore holdings of Widener and with the sections of the Fine Arts Library devoted to folk art, its collections provide comprehensive coverage of the whole field of Polish traditional folk culture.

The Andover-Harvard Theological Library

Most works on Polish church history will be found in Widener. However, Andover-Harvard Theological Library owns a valuable collection on the Polish antitrinitarian movement. It includes many early works published outside Poland (among them an edition of *Bibliotheca Fratrum Polonorum*). A group of Raków imprints of this religious movement is kept in Houghton Library.

Gabriel Grasberg
University of Massachusetts,
Boston

Yugoslavia

THE MAIN RESOURCES of the Harvard University Library pertaining to Yugoslavia and the Yugoslavs are in the fields of the humanities and social sciences. Those resources are housed for the most part in the Widener Library and in the International Legal Studies Wing of the Harvard Law School Library on Massachusetts Avenue in Cambridge.

A large part of Widener Library's holdings pertinent to Yugoslavia and the Yugoslavs will be found listed in sections 30 and 31 of the *Widener Library Shelflist; Slavic History and Literatures,* v. 3 and 4, Author and Title Listing (Cambridge, Harvard University Library, 1971). Other volumes of the *Shelflist* contain further listings under such subheadings as "Balkans," "Yugoslavia," "Croatia," "Serbia," "Slovenia," etc.

The largest group of holdings relative to Yugoslavia in Widener Library is on history and literature and classified under the rubric Slav. For the history of this collection and details of its size and intake see Charles R. Gredler, "The Slavic Collection at Harvard," in *Harvard Library Bulletin,* v. 17, no. 4, October 1969.

The collection relating to Yugoslavia under the rubric *Slav* is particularly rich in works and treatises of belles lettres and cultural history, and it will support a very broad range of advanced research on those subjects. It is also a good reference library on Yugoslav political history, with most of the basic historical works on Yugoslavia and Yugoslavs for the period before World War II. But it does not excel in this field, nor does it contain much special or unique material on that subject.

A special feature of the collection is its richness in 19th- and early 20th-century periodicals in Serbian and Croatian. Some of these are rarities, especially in the complete or nearly complete runs found here, e.g., *Leptir* and Živanović's *Venac* (Belgrade). The user of this library should note, moreover, that a number of these rare periodicals which are not in much demand and hence not in the stacks in Widener, such as *Bosanska vila,* are in the New England Deposit Library; several days' notice may be required to obtain them. But the more prominent journals are in the stacks, and most are in complete runs, for example: *Glasnik* (Belgrade), 1847-; *Srpski književni glasnik* (Belgrade), 1901-; *Delo* (Belgrade); *Prilozi za književnost, jezik, istoriju i folklor* (Belgrade); *Danica ilirska; Hrvatska revija* (Zagreb); *Forum* (Zagreb); *Južnoslovenski filolog.*

In this collection too are numerous basic contemporary economics periodicals, e.g., *Ekonomist, Ekonomika preduzeća* (Belgrade), *Ekonomski pregled* (Zagreb), *Finansije* (Belgrade).

Most of Harvard University Library's bibliographic resources pertaining to Yugoslavia are also in this collection, e.g., *Bibliografija Jugoslavije* (Belgrade, 1950-69) and *Jugoslovenska retrospektivna bibliografska građa,* 20 v. (Belgrade, 1945-62).

A few works on Yugoslav sociology are classified under Slav 8203. A larger group of books on economics follows under Slav 8204, and there is a good collection of Yugoslav statistics under Slav 8205. Numerous works, mostly recent, on the Yugoslav constitution are at Slav 8207, and there is a full collection on the Yugoslav Communist Party at Slav 8208. Works of description and history of Yugoslavia and its several provinces are at Slav 8210-Slav 8460.

The collection comprises, further, major editions of all the prominent belletrists throughout the history of Serbo-Croatian literature. It is particularly rich in poetry and theater, from the Dalmatian Renaissance to little editions and ephemera (including the so-called "primitives") of this century.

Sections of the collection devoted to Slovenian literature (Slav 9000-Slav 9046) and Macedonian literature (Slav 9056-Slav 9096) are equally comprehensive and diverse; there are more than 400 volumes of (Yugoslav) Macedonian belles lettres. In addition to major editions of all the prominent writers in Slovenian literary history, older Slovenian literary and cultural periodicals are also thoroughly represented, e.g., complete series of *Koledar družbe sv. Mohorja* (Celovec, 1881-) and *Časopis za zgodovino in narodopisje;* also *Čas: znanstvena revija* (Ljubljana, 1907-); *Ljubljanski zvon; Slovenski etnograf; Letopis Matice slovenske;* in regard to bibliography, the complete series of *Slovenska bibliografija,* 1947-.

In summary, a researcher studying the literatures of Yugoslavia (or its erstwhile provinces) may generally assume that the works of a particular author or a particular periodical are in this library, though there will of course be some exceptions.

Elsewhere in Widener Library there are considerable holdings relative to Yugoslavia in other fields of knowledge besides history and literature. The section of the Library under the rubric Linguistics incorporates a comprehensive collection of dictionaries and grammars for each of the Slavic languages of Yugoslavia. Here, too, are linguistic monographs and dialectical atlases and studies, e.g., *Srpski dialektološki zbornik* (3295.40.12). All the major published books, monographs, dictionaries, and compilations of data for linguistic research on Slovenian, Serbo-Croatian, and Macedonian will be found in this good collection. Periodicals pertaining to this field of knowledge are classified separately under the rubric Philol (Philological Periodicals).

Philological periodicals in and about primarily the South Slavic languages are located under the call numbers Philol 625-Philol 640. Here are found complete series of, e.g., *Slovenski jezik, Jezik in slovstvo, Naš jezik, Filologija, Makedonski jazik, Zbornik za filologiju i lingvistiku, Anali filološkog fakulteta,* and *Slovo; časopis staroslovenskog instituta u Zagrebu.*

Both the serial and the special publications of all the major institutions of learning in Yugoslavia are in Widener Library. Publications by the predecessors of present-day institutions should be sought under the modern institutional names; thus, see under the Union Catalogue heading "Srpska akademija nauka i umetnosti" for its publications and those of the earlier Društvo srpske slovesnosti, Srpsko učeno društvo, and Srpska kraljevska akademija. Publications by the various institutes, sections, galleries, and bureaux of academies are also listed under the current names of the parent institutions. Thus under Jugoslavenska akademija znanosti i umjetnosti will be found listed, for example, its published bibliographies and catalogues, the series *Stari pisci hrvatski, Codex diplomaticus regni Croatiae, Dalmatiae et Slavoniae,* most of *Posebna djela, Građa za povijest književnosti hrvatske, Hrvatski dijalektološki zbornik, Izveštaj o radu* (1960 and subsequent years), and substantially complete runs of: *Ljetopis; Djela; Rad; Prirodoslovna istraživanja; Starine; Zbornik za život i običaje hrvatskoga naroda, Izdanja Historijskog instituta, Zbornik Historijskog instituta,* etc.

Other Yugoslav institutions of learning whose publications are thus collected and cataloged are: the Zemaljski muzej u Sarajevu, both its *Anali* and *Glasnik,* and the earlier *Wissenschaftliche Mittheilungen aus Bosnien und der Hercegovina* (Vienna, 1893-1916); the Skopsko naučno društvo; the Akademija nauka i umjetnosti Bosne i Hercegovine, formerly the Naučno društvo N. R. Bosne i Hercegovine (especially its *Djela, Građa,* and *Radovi*); the universities of Belgrade, Novi Sad, Zagreb, Ljubljana, Sarajevo, and Skopje, and their several faculties, institutes, and sections for the humanities and social sciences; the ethnographic museums in Belgrade and Zagreb; the Leksikografski zavod in Zagreb; and so forth.

Among the scientific serials and periodicals of learned societies held in Widener Library are some series devoted to natural sciences, e.g., publications of the Mathematical Institute in Belgrade, the Department of Mathematics of Belgrade University, and the Belgrade Astronomical Observatory. But the Harvard University Library is very selective toward publications on the natural sciences in the South Slavic languages, and there is no general collection of such materials at Harvard.

Some other fields of knowledge in the humanities and social sciences besides history, literature, and language are represented in the Yugoslav collection in Widener Library, but only very selectively.

Archeology

There is a substantial collection of individually published monographs for the whole field of Balkan archeology classified under the rubric Archeology and under the call numbers Arc 936.29-Arc 936.252. The Widener Library holds numerous pertinent journals too: *Starinar* (Belgrade), *Arheološki vestnik* (Ljubljana), *Vjestnik* (old and new series) of the Hrvatsko arheološko društvo, the publications of the Zavod za zaštitu i naučno proučavanje spomenike kulture (Arc 302.27), and so forth. Widener's holdings are complemented by those in another unit of the Harvard University Library, the Library of the Peabody Museum of Archaeology and Ethnology, which is located at 11 Divinity Avenue in Cambridge. The Peabody Museum's library holds 60-odd volumes, mostly on Yugoslav archeology, under its designation LSoc 140, including a set of the *Glasnik Skopskog naučnog društva* (Skopje, 1925-35; but lacking volumes 4, 6, 9, and 10). This library also holds a small and random collection of books and monographs (fewer than 60 volumes) on the archeology and ethnography of the entire Balkan Peninsula. Even though the Library of Peabody Museum has a considerable collection of publications in English, French, German, and Russian, it cannot sustain any substantial research on Yugoslavia or its former provinces.

Economics

Numerous books and periodicals relative to Yugoslav economics and economic history are found in the Widener Library under its rubrics Economics and Economics Periodicals. Among the periodicals are such resources as *Ekonomski zbornik, Statistička revija* (Belgrade, 1951-) and *Statistički bilten* (Belgrade, 1952-). Books and monographs on Yugoslav economics published since 1945 are in the Slavic History and Literature collection, reviewed above. Those published before 1945 are distributed according to subjects in the Economics collection (rubric: Econ). There are numerous volumes in this collection on Yugoslav banking, finance, corporations, money, land and agrarian relations, railroads, postal service, etc. The Baker Library of the Harvard Business School on Soldiers Field Road in Cambridge receives some current publications on Yugoslav economics and business but discards most of them. It holds a dozen Yugoslav journals on these subjects, but many are incomplete. It also has 40-odd titles on Yugoslav commerce, economic conditions, and finance in its permanent collection; for these, see the *Subject Catalogue of the Baker Library,* v. 10 (Boston, G. K. Hall and Company, 1971). The Littauer Library in Littauer Center on Massachusetts Avenue in Cambridge has a modest collection on Yugoslav labor relations, unions, and workers' councils, classified Littauer 202W.

Education

There are about 100 volumes relating to Yugoslav education in Widener Library's collection on Education (rubric: Educ) under the call numbers Educ 1211-Educ 1220.

Other Subjects

A number of fields of knowledge are not represented or only slightly represented in the Yugoslav collection in Widener Library. In some cases (e.g., psychology, sociology) the tradition of such learning is relatively slight in Yugoslavia itself, hence there is scanty publication on those subjects to collect. Other subjects, such as divinity and war (military science), have not been acquired for Yugoslavia and its former provinces, although these subjects are well developed in Yugoslav learning.

There are a few Serbo-Croatian works on ethics and morality, esthetics, religion, and psychology in Widener Library's Philosophy collection (rubric: Phil), and isolated titles also in the

Sociology collection (rubric: Soc). But these materials are not remotely sufficient to sustain research on these subjects relative to Yugoslavia and the Yugoslavs.

Bibliographical Aids

In addition to those in the Slavic Collection mentioned above, other bibliographic, librarians', and bookmen's materials on Yugoslavia are in the Bibliography (rubric: B) and Bibliographical Periodical (rubric: BP) collections in the Widener Library. Yugoslav book publishers' bibliographies and catalogs, as well as catalogs of the Seventh and subsequent International Book Fairs at Belgrade (1962 and following years) are in the Bibliography collection, where there are also publications on Yugoslav printing and bookmaking (B 5732-B 5736) and an important group of holdings on the history of Yugoslav libraries (B 8835-B 8840).

Other cataloging and descriptive publications on various aspects of Yugoslav learning are dispersed by subject throughout the Harvard University Library system; note particularly Ivo Babić's *Scientific Institutions in Yugoslavia,* (Belgrade, 1958, LSoc 4051.2.4) and other material on Yugoslav institutions and societies of learning in the same location in Widener Library, as well as related publications such as *Finansiranje naučnoistraživačke delatnosti* (Belgrade, 1967) in the Littauer Library.

The Houghton Library of rare books and manuscripts, which is a satellite of the Harvard College Library located beside the Widener Library on Harvard Yard, holds some *rara* that are supplementary to the collection on Yugoslav history and literature in Widener, e.g., Marko Marulić's *Bene vivendi Instituta* and *Evangelistarium* (Parisiis, 1545), or the first edition of France Prešeren's *Poezije* (Ljubljana, 1847) and a folio sheet printed on four pages containing an acrostic thought to be Prešeren's first published work. But Houghton Library's possession of such individual pieces is only a sporadic outgrowth of the collecting for Widener Library's main stock on Yugoslavia and does not indicate any comprehensive richness in Yugoslav rare books and manuscripts. The entire Harvard University Library contains, for example, very few of the Croatian Latinistic works cataloged in the Jugoslav Academy's publication *Iugoslaviae Scriptores Latini Recentioris Aetatis* (Zagreb, 1971) although Widener Library does have a copy of this catalog itself.

Fine Arts

The Fine Arts Library, located in the Fogg Art Museum at 32 Quincy Street in Cambridge, has an excellent collection of publications and other materials on the fine arts in Yugoslavia and its former provinces. This collection is fully capable of supporting research on the various forms of Yugoslav fine arts, both as practiced by Yugoslavs, or on Yugoslav soil, and as embodied in the artistic possessions of Yugoslavia whether of Yugoslav provenience or not. The resources of this Library range from a fine collection of architectural photographs and slides through museum publications from Yugoslavia and books and monographs on a broad spectrum of art forms to art periodicals of both popular, or commercial, and scholarly appeal.

The collection is divided into four parts: books and monographs; periodicals; photographs; slides. Among the books and monographs are those of all the prominent art critics and art historians, both recent and earlier: e.g., Oto Bihalji-Merin and Gabriel Millet. In addition to the properties of the metropolitan museums of art in Yugoslavia, subjects well covered include Byzantine art, architecture, and iconography in Yugoslavia, medieval and Renaissance art and architecture in Dalmatia, costumes, modern painting and sculpture, Roman art, portraiture, and so forth. Such weaknesses as there are in this collection's coverage and depth are quite isolated; there is very little here on Yugoslav ceramic art. Yet this library has the *Corpus Vasorum Antiquorum,* and in it, the fascicles for Zagreb, Musée national, nos. 1-2, and Belgrade, Musée du Prince Paul, no. 1 (3).

Among the Yugoslav museums whose publications have been collected are: the National Museum, the Museum of Applied Art, the Museum of Contemporary Art in Belgrade; and the Muzej za umjetnost i obrt in Zagreb.

Periodicals in complete series in the Fine Arts Library include: *Umetnički pregled* (Belgrade, 1937-41), *Zbornik za likovne umetnosti* (Matica srpska, Novi Sad, 1965-), *Sinteza* (Ljubljana, 1964-), *Zbornik za umetnosno zgodovino* (Ljubljana, 1921-), and *Život umjetnosti* (Zagreb, 1966).

The collection of architectural photographs relating to Yugoslavia is devoted largely to traditional architecture; other arts are represented in the slide collection.

A number of titles on Yugoslavia in the Library of the Graduate School of Design supplement the holdings of the Fine Arts Library; these libraries are located only two city blocks apart in Cambridge. See the published *Catalogue of the Library of the Graduate School of Design* (Boston, 1968) for the holdings of that library relative to Yugoslavia.

The Law of Yugoslavia

After the Slavic History and Literature collection in Harvard College Library, the holdings of the Harvard Law School Library are the largest and finest in the Harvard University Library relative to Yugoslavia. The Law School Library's collection embraces several thousand titles and comprehends not only Yugoslav laws and law reviews but also a wealth of material on diverse related subjects, such as public administration, insurance, taxation, immigration and emigration, customs, governmental history, and military organization. This collection is a superb base for research into any aspect of legal order in Yugoslavia since the independence of Serbia and Croatia.

Constitutional, civil, criminal, and military law are all thoroughly covered. Publications regularly collected include those of the National Assembly (laws, statutes, rules, and procedures), the Federal Administrative Council, the Union of Societies of Attorneys of Yugoslavia, etc. Complete serials include: *Zbornik* (later *Zbirka*) *zakona, uredbi i naredbi* (Zagreb, 1927-40); the laws, handbooks, and regulations of individual republics; *Službeni list,* (Ljubljana, 1930-); and such rarities as *Povjestni spomenici slobodnoga kraljeva grada Zagreba,* v. 1-19 (Zagreb, 1889-1953), by Ivan Tkalčić *et al.*

Folklore

The most thoroughly collected subject relative to Yugoslavia in the Harvard University Library is folklore in Serbo-Croatian, particularly Serbo-Croatian popular epos. The acquisition of published matter in this subject by the Harvard College Library began a century ago, stimulated by the personal interest of the great scholar of British popular ballad and Professor of English, Francis James Child. Many of the initial acquisitions were bought with income from a bequest of Charles Minot of Somerville, Mass.

The librarians of Harvard College Library continued to foster this collection in later years, adding popular epic and other popular poetry, folktale, descriptions of custom, and ethnography, as well as monographs on these topics, as they were published. Then in 1936 the heirs of Milman Parry gave to the Library the splendid collection of editions of Serbo-Croatian popular epic poetry which Professor Parry had gathered in Yugoslavia in the years 1933-35. These holdings have since been augmented, particularly from 1945 onward. Today the collection of printed Yugoslav folklore and scholarly works on that subject, classified under Widener Library's call numbers beginning with 27234, is the best overall collection on the subject in the Western Hemisphere.

Milman Parry also left to Harvard at his death a unique collection of Serbo-Croatian, Macedonian, and Albanian oral poetry in original manuscripts and field recordings which he and his field staff made with portable sound recording equipment and by dictation in the countryside and small towns of Yugoslavia in the years 1933-35. These unique and irreplaceable materials amount to more than 3,500 sound recordings on 12-inch aluminum discs and over 12,000 individual texts, among which are texts more than 12,000 verses in length. In 1950, 1951, 1962, 1963, 1964, and 1966 the Curators of the Milman Parry Collection added new materials of the same kinds, so that the Parry Collection is now more than twice its original size. Furthermore, all the principal extant manuscripts of oral epic poetry in the chief repositories for such material in archives in Yugoslavia have been microfilmed by the Curators and the microfilms deposited in the Parry Collection. This microfilming, subsidized by the U.S. Departments of State and of Health, Education, and Welfare, has made available to American scholars through the Milman Parry Collection of Oral Literature in the Harvard College Library the monumental manuscript collections by such outstanding Yugoslav collectors as Ante Alačević, Baldo Melkov Glavić, Antun Hangi, Nikola Kašiković, Andrija Luburić, Luka Marjanović, Andro Murat, Mate Ostojić, Jovan Perović, Bogoljub Petranović, Jovan Srećković, and many others.

The Parry Collection, consisting entirely of unpublished manuscripts and sound recordings, is today an absolutely unparalleled archive, not only the best on its subject with respect to Yugoslavia, but also the best collection of oral epic poetry from any oral poetic tradition anywhere in the world.

David E. Bynum
Harvard University

Other Countries

Albania

Albanian materials have never been collected systematically, and the collection is weak; approximately 400 volumes in Widener Library are classified as Albanian history and literature, and the Harvard Law School Library reports some 60 volumes.

Most of the Widener material is in French, German, Italian, Modern Greek, Serbian, or Russian, rather than in Albanian. Popular works and travel accounts make up much of the history collection, which also includes material on Albanians in America. Of post-World War II publications on history listed in Kastrati, Harvard has little more than 5 percent. There are some works on folklore and linguistics. At least by comparison with other subjects, these fields are relatively well represented. The Harvard Law School Library has an incomplete set of the general collection of laws (*Gazeta zyrtare*) and has been receiving *Drejtësia popullore* since 1957.

Romania

Widener Library has approximately 1,750 volumes classified as Romanian history and 1,050 classified as Romanian literature. Collecting has not been systematic or intensive, but there is some strength in holdings of literary texts and history of literature. Nineteenth-century sets of historical sources are fairly well represented, and folklore is relatively strong, but geography appears to have been neglected. Economics is an area of relative strength, and most of the fundamental bibliographic tools have been acquired. Some 130 Romanian serials are currently received.

The Harvard Law School Library, with 1,200 volumes on Romania, has a good collection, which it continues to build systematically; from 1960 to date it is believed to be nearly complete. Both the official collections of general laws, *Buletinul oficial* and *Colecţie de legi i decrete,* are received, as well as the *Colecţie de hortărîri*. Law reviews and treatises are covered comprehensively.

Edwin E. Williams
Harvard University

Hebrew Union College—Jewish Institute of Religion

Klau Library

General Information

The Klau Library is located at 3101 Clifton Avenue, Cincinnati, Ohio 45220. Normal hours are Monday to Friday, 8:00 a.m. to 5 p.m., except during the summer when the Library closes at 4:30 p.m. When the college is in session, hours are extended to 11 p.m., Monday to Thursday, and Sunday from 2 to 10 p.m. During the extended hours the public may use only the open stack and the reference collection.

The Director of the Library is Herbert C. Zafren, Professor of Jewish Bibliography, who can be reached at the above address or phoned at (513) 221-1875. He is also the Director of the three other libraries (in Jerusalem, Los Angeles, and New York) which are part of the same overall institution.

The Library is very well adapted for research. Scholars are welcome to use all of its facilities and collections. Microfilm readers are available as are photocopying facilities. Nonresidents of Cincinnati are generally required to borrow materials through interlibrary loan.

In addition to a complete card catalog of all its holdings, the Klau Library has a 32-volume printed catalog of its collections, published by G. K. Hall, which covers all items entered through the end of 1963.

Beginning in November 1966, the Klau Library switched to the Library of Congress Classification System and Subject Headings, with all cards being filed in a newly established catalog. Cards for books received from 1964 to 1966 continued to be filed in the original catalog.

The Library had its beginning in 1875 when the College was founded. It recently marked the acquisition of its 250,000th book. It has, over the years, developed into one of the largest and best research libraries in the world devoted to the study of Judaism. In its collections there are about 70 Hebrew and 65 non-Hebrew incunabula, approximately 3,000 literary manuscripts (mainly Hebrew), a very extensive cumulation of 16th-century printed Hebraica, the Edward Birnbaum (Cantor in Königsberg) Music Collection, a very fine concentration in Near Eastern studies, Spinoza, Josephus, Agnon, and rarities of all kinds in every area and category of Judaica and Hebraica. The Klau Library is particularly rich in its store of materials relating to the life, history, and literature of the Jews in Europe. It publishes *Studies in Bibliography and Booklore, Some Recent Acquisitions and other Matters* (mimeographed), and the bibliographical series *Bibliographica Judaica*. It is, together with the American Jewish Archives, the parent body of the American Jewish Periodical Center.

The College itself publishes the *Hebrew Union College Annual,* which has acquired an international reputation for excellence in its field, as well as occasional monographs authored by members of its faculty. The Klau Library acquires bookplates (a large number in its collection stem from the old Austro-Hungarian Monarchy), pamphlets, stamps, maps, broadsides, microfilm, phonograph records, films, tapes, and cassettes, in addition to its primary collection of books, all of which also promote its basic aim of being a storehouse for the study of Jewish life all over the world in all ages. About 10,000 items are added annually to the Library's holdings.

The East Central and Southeast European materials are distinguishable primarily through subject entries and associated references in the various catalogs. For each country, in addition to the major entry, there are also entries for larger and smaller subdivisions as well as for scores of cities and towns, especially in the case of larger countries which had extensive and vibrant Jewish populations.

It is not possible to estimate accurately the exact percentage of the Klau Library's holdings and annual additions which are East Central and Southeast European. It is also not possible (except for entries of the last six years under the Library of Congress System) to distinguish the German Democratic Republic from Germany as a whole. Furthermore, because of previous differences in political boundaries, and resulting catalog entries, some "Poland" entries (or subdivisions thereof) are filed under "Russia" and some for "Hungary" and "Czechoslovakia" are entered under "Austria-Hungary."

The Klau Library is particularly rich in materials on Jewish life and history in Germany and Poland. It possesses complete runs of most of the important periodicals connected with Jewish life published in those countries, especially in the 19th and 20th centuries, in both Hebrew and the language of the country in question. Among its manuscripts are to be found a number stemming from areas once covered by Czarist Russia and the Austro-Hungarian Monarchy which would be useful for research into the development of Jewish life in these areas. The collection of printed secondary materials dealing with these countries from the Jewish point of view is in some cases (e.g., Germany, Poland, Czechoslovakia, and Hungary) very extensive, reaching into the thousands and tens of thousands. Among these are a very large number of volumes and studies, some of a memorial nature, as well as many analytical entries, devoted to individual cities and towns in these lands.

In other cases, in contrast to the above and probably reflecting the paucity of Jewish population and activity in these countries, there are few entries for, e.g., Yugoslavia and Bulgaria, and none at all for Albania.

Under Bulgaria the researcher will find the publications of the Institutum Historicum of the Academia Litterarum Bulgarica pertaining to Jewish life in Bulgaria in the 16th century; of the Bulgarian B'nai B'rith Lodge on microfilm; and histories of individual communities in Rustchuk, Widdin, and Yamboli. The Klau Library was fortunate to have acquired copies of a file of secret correspondence between the Gestapo and the German Embassy in Bulgaria and the Foreign Ministry in Berlin.

Under the heading "Germany," the Klau Library holds what is probably one of its richest and most extensive blocks of materials. It has all the publications of the Leo Baeck Institute of Jews from Germany, and among its runs of periodicals (emphasizing here the Eastern part of Germany) there are: Israelitische Religionsgemeinde, Dresden. *Gemeindeblatt* (1925-34); Israelitische Religionsgemeinde zu Leipzig. *Gemeindeblatt* (1925-38); *Zeitschrift fuer die Juden in Deutschland* (1887-91); *Mittheilungen vom Deutsch-Israelitischen Gemeindebunde* (1873-1903); *Deutsche Israelitische Zeitung* (1904-38); Forschungsabteilung Judenfrage des Reichsinstituts fuer Geschichte des neuen Deutschlands. *Forschungen zur Judenfrage,* v. 1-8; Office of U.S. Chief of Counsel for Prosecution of Axis Criminality, Nazi Conspiracy and Aggression, v. 1-8, suppl. 1-2; Trials of War Criminals Before the Nuremberg Military Tribunal under Central Council Law No. 10, v. 1-15.

For research into Jewish life in Hungary and Czechoslovakia, the Klau Library is fortunate to possess, among many other sources, the *Monumenta Hungariae Judaica,* v. 1-13; *Jahrbuch der Gesellschaft fuer Geschichte der Juden in der Čechoslov. Republik,* v. 1-3; and *Zeitschrift fuer die Geschichte der Juden in der Tschechoslowakei,* v. 1-3.

Among its books on the Jews in Greece, the library has monographs dealing with the Jewish communities in Corfu, Kastoria, Kos, Macedonia, Mytilene, Rhodes, Salonica, and Serres.

Poland, as stated before, has a great many entries. Under the very precise heading *Poland-Warsaw-Ghetto Uprising* there are approximately 100 entries alone. Literally scores of individual communities are included in the file of those for which there are individual monographs and there are many larger cities such as Lemberg (Lwów), Lodz, (Łódź), Cracow (Kraków), and Lublin for which there are multiple entries.

Amos Schauss
Hebrew Union College—
Jewish Institute of Religion

Hoover Institution On War, Revolution and Peace

General Information

THE HOOVER INSTITUTION collections on East Central and Southeastern Europe constitute part of a larger collection known as the *East European Collection,* which together with the Western European Collection is the foundation of the Hoover Institution Library. The East European Collection encompasses 14 country or subject-area collections: Russia/USSR (including minorities), Poland, Czechoslovakia, Yugoslavia, Hungary, Bulgaria, Romania, Albania, Greece, Estonia, Latvia, Lithuania, the International Communist Movement, and East European publications on non-East European subjects. The German Democratic Republic (GDR) is included in the Western European Collection. The East European collection is administered by a Curator, who carries direct responsibility for the development of the included country collections. The Stanford University Library holds complementary collections for the period preceding the Hoover's range, as well as humanities collections for all periods. A separate survey of that collection is included in this publication.

General Purpose

The East European Collection is intended A) to develop and maintain major comprehensive research collections of both published and unpublished primary and secondary sources from and about the countries covered; B) to collect and preserve documentation of 20th-century political, historical, and ideological developments within these countries, as well as their international and interbloc relations; C) to make these materials available, and to foster their use by the worldwide scholarly community.

Range of Collection Coverage

The basic policy is four-fold in its focus: subject coverage, chronological coverage, types of materials, and language coverage.

A) *Subject Coverage.* In general, the East European Collection places its main emphasis on documentation of the 20th-century political, historical, and ideological developments of each of the countries included therein. In addition, special emphasis is placed on the following:

1) *History:* includes general, political, social, economic, and diplomatic history; also local, regional, and national history (relatively little emphasis is placed on ethnography, though some basic items are acquired);

2) *Communism:* Substantially everything of interest, both factual and interpretive, is acquired if published in the East European Communist States, excluding only inferior mass-consumption popularizations. (Materials on Marxism and the history of the Marxist movement within these countries are selected in an attempt to develop a background collection.);

3) *Additional extensive coverage:* in the field of politics and government; international relations; material of and about political parties and opposition groups; economic policy; political

biography; foreign policy; military affairs; social developments; underground, radical, liberation, and subversive movements; and constitutional law.

4) *Selective Coverage:* Some materials in the fields of law, finance, labor, industry, and education are amassed, for the most part as they reflect the political or ideological policies of the country; some items on religion, philosophy, agriculture, and even literature are collected.

B) *Chronological Limits.* Priority in acquisitions goes to the preservation of 20th-century materials which may be lost to scholarship in a relatively short time if not collected and preserved. At the same time, accurate research on 20th-century events depends in many cases upon the material concerning the events of the 19th century, or even earlier. The time boundaries of material for each regional collection are decided on the basis of the particular research problems involved, and in many instances may be referred to as practical coverage of a problem.

C) *Principal Types of Publications Collected.* Parliamentary debates; government documents and reports; official gazettes; stenographic records of legislative bodies and political parties (especially those in power); texts of laws and statutes; directives and doctrines of political parties; party organs; periodicals and newspapers published by the various political parties and/or factions; material of or about political parties, pressure groups, special interest groups; posters; memoirs; unofficial documentary publications; émigré publications; biographies; reference works; bibliographies; indexes. Archival materials and private papers related to all social upheavals within the East European area are actively sought.

D) *Language Coverage.* Most of the holdings are in the 10 "literary languages" of the East Central and Southeastern European countries. These are followed by writings on these countries in the languages spoken in the remaining Communist-Party States, particularly Russian. These are supplemented by quite thorough coverage of scholarly works in English and the Western European languages, especially French and German.

Library Services

All the East European Collections are housed in the Tower Building. Facilities of the Library are available to all scholars and students of college level and above, and to others doing serious research. Borrowing privileges are extended to Stanford University faculty, students, and staff; to visiting scholars in residence; and to local residents and Stanford alumni. All others may use materials within the Library upon presentation of identification. Borrowing privileges are not extended to students of nearby universities and colleges, but such students may obtain materials on interlibrary loan.

Access to the stack area is limited to Stanford faculty and Hoover Institution staff. Exceptions are made when material cannot feasibly be paged.

All Archival and Special Collections are served through the Institution Archives, with reading room and administrative offices on the 10th floor of the Tower Building. The Institution also has a number of carrels in its various reading rooms which are assigned on request to Stanford faculty, doctoral candidates, and visiting scholars making intensive use of the Library. It is advisable to reserve a carrel at least a month in advance by writing to the Reference Department at the Institution.

The Library provides a complete photographic reproduction service through outside processors. Microfilm, Copyflo prints from microfilm, direct copy, and other types of reproduction are available. Information on conditions and rates may be obtained from a reference librarian or at the Photographic Service Desk.

The Hoover Institution Library itself does not maintain facilities for Xeroxing or similar forms of reproduction. Limited copying may be done at the Stanford University Library or at other campus facilities. Permission to copy Hoover material must be obtained at the Loan Desk where the material is checked.

Hours of Service

Monday through Friday, 8:15 a.m. to 5:30 p.m.; Saturday, 8:30 a.m. to 5 p.m.; closed Sunday, and on the following University holidays: New Year's Day, Washington's Birthday, Memorial Day, Independence Day, Labor Day, Thanksgiving Day and the following Friday, Christmas Eve, and Christmas Day. Hours are subject to change.

This survey of the Hoover Institution's area collections for East Central and Southeastern European countries covers approximately 150,000 of the more than 300,000 volumes, excluding newspapers and archival collections, in the East European Collections; the remainder belongs to the Russian/USSR Collection. The research potential of the various collections is demonstrated by analyzing groups of materials rather than individual items. In general, the large number of monographs in each of these collections is not treated, but may be inferred from the discussion of the documentary holdings.

The holdings are surveyed to the end of 1970. The Polish area collection is discussed in more detail than the others because of its uniqueness. An extensive survey of the East European collection was prepared by K. Maichel and is available at the Library in typed form. An abbreviated version of this survey entitled *Eastern Europe: A Survey of the Holdings at the Hoover Institution on War, Revolution and Peace* is scheduled for publication.

A description of the East German area collection can be found in A. F. Peterson's *Western Europe: A Survey of Holdings* . . . Stanford, Hoover Institution Press, [1972], pp. 22-40. An abbreviated survey of Hoover's collection on international communism, prepared by K. Maichel, was published on p. 2-4 of the 1971 Hoover Institution publication, *International and English-Language Collection: A Survey* . . . prepared by K. M. Glazier and J. Hobson.

Czechoslovakia

ALTHOUGH THE CZECHOSLOVAK COLLECTION officially begins with the creation of the Czechoslovak Republic (ČSR) in 1918, its research value starts with 1914. The ČSR collection is the second largest among the East Central and Southeastern European Collections consisting of over 21,000 volumes of books and pamphlets, 882 journal titles, and 148 newspaper titles, which does not include extensive materials relating to Czechoslovakia in other collections.

World War I

The excellent holdings of official Austrian and Hungarian governmental publications such as parliamentary papers, official gazettes, and other governmental publications constitute the backbone of this collection. For the Czech and Moravian lands, the parliamentary papers include the "stenographic" protocols of the Austrian *Reichsrat* for the *Abgeordneten-Haus*, the *Herren-Haus*, and especially of the *Delegation*, which the Library holds for the period 1891-1918. For the Slovak lands and Ruthenia there are similar records and documents of the Hungarian government and its parliament for the years 1901-18.

These are supplemented by the Empire's two official gazettes, *Wiener Zeitung* and *Budapesti Közlöny;* bulletins of the various ministries and other governmental bodies; statistical publications of the government, and various smaller collections of decrees and laws.

This group includes an extremely well-rounded collection of publications of the Austrian goverment on Austro-Hungarian relations during this period.

Among Czech and Slovak documentary publications, the Institution holds a very good collection of published documents on the activities of the Czechoslovak *Národní Rada* (National Council) established in Paris, the *Slovenská Národná Rada,* (the only Slovak Nationalist council in the Slovak territories during the war), and all major documentary publications issued by other Czech-Slovak bodies in emigration, such as the "ČSR Legions."

Another important holding on this period is the extensive collection of memoirs, reminiscences, and biographies of the leading political figures of the Czech and Slovak movement for independence, as well as individuals from every part of the Hapsburg Monarchy that had dealings with the nations that came to form the Czechoslovak Republic.

The Czechoslovak Republic (1918-1938)

The Institution's holdings on the interwar Czechoslovak Republic constitute one of the richest depositories of contemporary primary sources in the West. However, the quality of material for research varies for different periods of the First Republic. Basically, the holdings for events occurring during the first 14 years of the Republic are much stronger and more detailed than for the post-1932 years. The holdings on political developments in Czechoslovakia started to weaken in the early 1930s and by the time of the Munich Crisis, coverage by contemporary sources became comparatively weak, since the Institution concentrated on gathering material on the Nazi Party.

The second weak point of this period is that nearly all contemporary sources are in Czech; there being practically no Slovak publications. Some important internal problems that influenced the course of the Republic cannot be researched from the Slovak point of view. However, the Institution does hold a voluminous collection of post-1947 publications on the Slovak parties and their activities and on general developments in the 1932-38 period. Further, memoirs of politically active Czechs, whose publications are well represented in the collection, have often proved extremely important in the absence of other materials.

GOVERNMENT DOCUMENTS. The backbone of the interwar collection consists of unusually strong holdings of contemporary ČSR governmental documentary publications, from the birth of the Republic to the German occupation. These holdings contain ample material for research on juridical, governmental, and legislative matters. Further, there are official gazettes such as *Sbírka zákonů a nařízení* and *Úřední list ČSR,* both held in complete sets in Czech.

The activities of the National Assembly are recorded in a complete set of its official stenographic records, *Národní shromáždění. Těsnopisecké zprávy o schůzích Národního shromáždění Republiky Československé,* (Prague, 1919-39), which are supplemented by numerous other publications of the various legislative bodies, and by voluminous holdings of many of the official and semiofficial publications of the various ministries and other governmental departments. Collectively, they furnish the scholar with resources on internal and external developments that are available in but a few Western libraries.

These extensive holdings of standard works for the study of parliamentary history, supported by a collection of ephemera recalling the political atmosphere of the times, make up an excellent group of materials for research on the structure of the government well into the mid-1930s.

MEMOIRS, REMINISCENCES, AND LETTERS OF CORRESPONDENCE. From 1918 to World War II, many prominent individuals in the ČSR published their memoirs, a majority of which are at Hoover. Few works better illuminate the events of this period than the memoirs of Masaryk and his friend and successor, E. Beneš. The Institution's holdings of their writings are comprehensive and are supplemented by a rich collection of publications on them. There is also a large group of memoirs by interwar Marxist personalities, and a host of participants in the "Workers and Trade Union Movement" and the "ČSR Communist Party." Additionally, a large group of memoirs by diplomats from the United States, Great Britain, France, Hungary, Poland,

Germany, Romania, Italy, Russia, and Austria add greatly to the collection, giving yet another slant on events of this period.

DOCUMENTARY PUBLICATIONS OF POLITICAL PARTIES. The holdings of official and semiofficial documents of the various political parties are another valuable type of publication on the pre-Munich ČSR and include records of meetings, platforms, programs, newspapers, and journals, as well as published speeches of leading party members. No less than 26 parties took part in the ČSR democracy between 1918 and 1938, all having voting representatives in the Parliament; thus an understanding of the general political situation and individual parties is essential for an insight into the workings of the government.

Records of meetings of most of the major parties are quite well represented at the Hoover Institution, though not always in complete sets; however, some of the central parties are poorly represented or not represented at all in this respect.

The published speeches of leading members of these parties are generally well represented, especially for such parties as the ČSR Agrarian Party, the ČSR National Socialist Party, the Socialist Democratic Party, the ČSR Populist Party, the National Union Party, the ČSR Communist Party, and the Sudeten German Party.

Holdings on Czechoslovakia at the Paris Peace Conference and the Slovak Soviet Republic of 1919 are unique at Hoover. They are the only such Archival and Special Collection holdings in the West and, in fact, much of this material is not even contained in ČSR depositories.

PRESS PUBLICATIONS. The most complete political and nonpartisan newspaper sets for the interwar years are: *Politika; Národní listy; Národní politika; Obzor; Prager Tagblatt; Prager Presse; Prager Abendzeitung; Prager Abendblatt; Venkov;* the Agrarian daily; *Nový hlas; Sozial-demokrat,* the German Social-Democrat daily; *Die Zeit* and *Die Front,* Sudentendeutsche Partei Party organs; *Kassai Ujság,* the Carpatho-Ruthenian Political Bloc organ; and *Narodnaia gazeta,* the Russian National Party newspaper in Slovakia. All the important journals of the period are held by the Hoover Institution Library.

The Second World War

On March 14, 1938, German forces occupied Czechoslovakia, and its territories were divided into three parts: Bohemia and Moravia became a German protectorate in March, 1939, with its own government; the Slovak area was declared an autonomous state under German patronage; and all of Carpatho-Ruthenia came under Hungarian domination. During World War II, the ČSR territories were under five different governments, including the two exile governments.

THE PROTECTORATE OF BOHEMIA AND MORAVIA. Fundamental governmental documents are well represented in the law gazette, *Sbírka zákonů a nařízení Protektorátu Čechy a Morava* which contains all legal provisions enacted by the government; and in a nearly complete set of the official gazette, *Amstblatt des Protektorates Böhmen und Mähren* (Úřední list Protektorátu Čechy a Morava) which lists decrees and ordinances issued by the German Chief Commander in the Protectorate. Excellent holdings of the German law gazette, *Reichsgesetzblatt,* the only source to print laws and decrees of the central German authorities for use in the Protectorate, serve to complete the picture.

These fundamental sources on the Protectorate are supplemented by an extensive collection of postwar materials on this period including a strong collection of documentary materials on the trials of Czech collaborators. The collection also contains a large number of works written from the German point of view, among which are a great many memoirs.

The Czech publications on the war years, issued mostly between 1962 and 1970, are well represented in the Institution's holdings, especially regional histories of the occupation, the student resistance movement, the underground movement, Lidice, racial persecution, and the Prague armed insurrection.

THE SLOVAK AUTONOMOUS STATE.   Hoover's only contemporary sources on this subject are in a small but valuable collection of archival materials, the rarest of which are the hand-written memoirs of President Tiso's brother Štefan, who served as the last Slovak Prime Minister. The diaries reveal much of what went on in the last days of the Republic as well as the thinking of President Tiso. They cover the period August 30, 1944, to May 5, 1945, and are probably the only documentation on the events seen through the eyes of the government.

The documents include lengthy notes and commentary on the Slovak Anti-German Uprising of 1944, and the government's attempts to pacify the German forces, as well as Hitler's feelings on this affair.

Captured German documents are another contemporary archival source. Documents covering all aspects of Slovak life are found in holdings from the archives of the Office of the Reichsführer SS, and the German Foreign Ministry. Further contemporary documentation of the last year of the State's existence are found in the large archival collection of the ČSR Eastern Front Armies. This collection contains the only contemporary publications issued on Slovak territory during World War II, i.e., the newspapers of the ČSR Eastern Armies, published during the 1944 uprising.

Finally, while the Institution has a sizable collection of published documentation on the Slovak State, all these documents appeared in the postwar years, especially between 1962 and 1970.

LONDON EXILE GOVERNMENT.   The Institution holds a strong collection of contemporary publications of this provisional government, both in Czech and English, which can be divided into the following basic types: a) a very good file of the government's official gazette, *Úřední věstník československý* (London); b) almost complete holdings of published speeches and memoirs of its members on exile activities; c) contemporary publications of documentary materials on the activities of the exile government in such sources as *Czechoslovak Sources and Documents* (New York, 1942-45), which contains speeches by exile statesmen and reproductions of various documents, and the important publication of the government's Ministry of Foreign Affairs, *Czechoslovakia Fights Back* (Washington, D.C., 1943); d) numerous contemporary monographs of historic and propagandistic value, such as *Four Fighting Years* (New York, 1943), or R. Reichart's unofficial biography of Beneš (New York, 1943).

MOSCOW EXILE GOVERNMENT.   Following the German occupation, the Czech Communist group fled to Moscow, where, under the leadership of Klement Gottwald, it created an unofficial exile government.

The only contemporary sources on this group held by the Institution are archives of the ČSR Eastern Front Armies.

The remaining holdings relating to this group are of postwar imprint. While the holdings represent a moderate subject collection, they include nearly all documentary publications and memoirs of the members of the Moscow exile government, and selective memoirs of military personnel.

The aforementioned rare archival and special-material collection originating with the ČSR Eastern Front Armies, which were organized in the USSR, contains several hundred contemporary printed and manuscript items (mostly originals), and consists of the following major groupings: a) a collection of the army's press publications; b) numerous handwritten regimental diaries; c) a large volume of correspondence between various Brigade Commanders and the exile government in Moscow, as well as German correspondence of the Prime Minister for the *Protectorate* with SS units and other German army commanders; d) a great many telegrams and radiograms with military orders (among which are numerous ones from Stalin and Khrushchev); e) a large collection of letters, reports, memoirs, etc. written by or originated by Ludvík Svoboda, commander of the ČSR Eastern Front Armies, who subsequently became president of the ČSR; f) various reports by commanders on the outcome of their campaigns including many secret reports; and g) a large collection of military maps and plans.

The whole collection is very large, with much unique material. The above is intended to give an idea of its scope and research value.

The Post-World War II Period

Following the liberation of Czechoslovakia, a democratic government was established in Košice on April 5, 1945, with a program based on the "National Front" of four Czech parties (Communist, Social-Democrat, National Socialist, and the Catholic People's Party) and two Slovak Parties (Democrat and Communist). The Communist Party seized power in a bloodless coup in February 1948, and has been the ruling party since.

Hoover's holdings on post-World War II Czechoslovakia can be evaluated as follows: the period 1956-70 is covered comprehensively, the period 1945-55 is weaker, lacking many contemporary sources but containing documentary works (especially those published in 1945-47) which are considered rare finds, many representing a high level of scholarship without political ideology.

The Czechoslovak Communist Party is most strongly represented in Hoover's holdings, constituting an excellent research base.

GOVERNMENTAL PUBLICATIONS.   Holdings of various governmental publications of the postwar period are good to strong, although the sources of origin are not as varied as for the interwar period. This is adequately compensated by the holdings of Communist Party publications. The only major continuous documentary publications in the holdings for the period 1945-53 is the official law gazette, *Sbírka zákonů Republiky československé,* in which all acts passed by the central authorities were promulgated. The second official organ of this nature, the gazette *Úřední list Republiky československé,* which is held from 1953 on contains statutory provisions, such as decrees, directives, orders, and materials of the governmental bodies not included in *Sbírka.* Both are complete for the years indicated.

Stenographic records of the meetings of the Czechoslovak Parliament, *(Národní Shromáždění)* are in the Institution from 1955, while governmental statistical publications, especially as of 1962, are also well represented.

COMMUNIST PARTY PUBLICATIONS.   In a Communist country major decisions are officially published as joint resolutions of the Party and the Cabinet. An example of this type of joint publication is the *Usnesení strany a vlády o některých otázkách budování socialistického hospodářství* (Prague, UV KSČ, 1955).

Additionally, official Party organs as a rule provide the full text of forthcoming legislation long before it is published by the government, an example being *Sociální politika,* which is held by the Institution. Many official publications of the Party are rich supplements to the governmental sources, often being more informative, accurate, and official. Hoover's holdings of the Czechoslovak Communist Party publications are by far the largest and most comprehensive holdings in the Czechoslovak Collection.

Party decrees published by the Central Committee of the Communist Party appear in various sources, for example, in the annual *Usnesení a dokumenty ÚV KSČ*, of which the Institution holds a complete set starting with 1958. Earlier decrees are also well represented, though in separate documentary publications.

PERSONAL WRITINGS AND SPEECHES.   A third important category of documentary sources on the activities of the ČSR government within Hoover's holdings are the published writings, speeches, proclamations, etc., of the presidents of the Republic and the members of the executive branches of the legislative body, as well as the writings of some of the members of the National Assembly and leaders of the Communist Party. All are richly represented in the holdings.

SUBJECT DOCUMENTARY PUBLICATIONS.   Most of the post-World War II events are well covered by published contemporary or later documentary publications of the Czechoslovak government or the Communist Party. Hoover's holdings of the various spectacular political purges of the Stalin era are an example of the coverage of this collection. Official trial records are supplemented by extensive works by those who survived and were released during the de-Stalinization period, by works of those executed, published posthumously, by numerous volumes in defense of the tried, and by descriptions of the purges. The Institution also holds the original manuscript version of the "Kaplan Report," by the government Commission of Inquiry, established in 1968.

The Institution's collection of materials on the 1968 invasion of Czechoslovakia by the armies of the Warsaw Pact countries is extensive, containing not only works published subsequent to the events, but numerous leaflets, underground newspapers, and flyers distributed by the invading armies, leaflets from the ČSR government instructing the people in methods of passive resistance and calling for solidarity, appeals to foreigners for support, and an extensive collection of special editions of the leading newspapers.

JOURNALS AND NEWSPAPERS.   The Institution's holdings consist of some 300 political, governmental, military, historical, and other subject titles of post-World War II Czech and Slovak journals and newspapers as well as a strong collection of émigré press publications.

Poland

Introduction

THE POLISH COLLECTION is the largest and the most important of the East Central and Southeastern European country collections at the Hoover Institution and may be considered one of the strongest research collections on its period in the United States.

The collection deals with modern Poland, beginning with 1914, although there is a strong collection of works on history and economic problems published during and after the period 1863-1914. This portion of the collection is primarily background material, but owing to its strength (particularly for 1875-1914) it has been widely used for primary research into that era by both American and European scholars.

Due to the partition of Poland by Austria, Prussia, and Russia, and its subsequent absorption into three different economic systems, much of the research material concerning pre-1914 Poland is included in the Russian and Western European Collections. Taking these materials into consideration, the Polish Collection can be considered a research collection as of the mid-1870s; a strong background collection from the 1860s; and a teaching and reference level collection for the period 1830-60. There are some older publications as well, but they do not offer a continual coverage of Polish history.

As of January, 1970, the Polish Collection, representing only those works in any language devoted strictly to Poland, constituted 28,000 volumes of books; 2,130 journal titles, and 268 newspaper titles.

POLISH 19TH-CENTURY MATERIAL.   Although the collection constitutes a research collection as of the mid-1870s, its overall excellence dates from the founding of the Polish Socialist Party (Polska Partja Socjalistyczna, PPS) in Paris in 1892 and the Social Democracy of the Kingdom of Poland (Socjal-Demokracja Królestwa Polskiego, SDKP) established in 1893 in Paris.

The Hoover Institution has a wealth of materials for researching the 19th-century Polish territories, especially those under Russian rule. These materials include all types of official records such as historical and legislative (juridical) documents, collections of laws, archives, and serial publications of the various partitioning powers, and to a lesser degree, of Polish governmental institutions. Most of these are in the language of the ruling empire.

GOVERNMENT DOCUMENTS.   Official Russian Imperial publications form the mainstay of Hoover's research sources on legislative, juridical, and administrative matters concerning Russia's Polish territories of the 19th and 20th centuries. These holdings are nearly complete and form the backbone of the collection. Hoover holds most of the records of the Vienna Parliament, especially for the post-1890 period, while the German official publications are best represented for the post-1900 period.

These basic sources of the partitioning powers are supplemented by such Polish-language publications as the complete set of the semiofficial gazette for the Russian Polish provinces, *Zbiór Praw: Postanowienia i rozporządzenia rządu w guberniach Królestwa Polskiego obowiązujące, wydane po zniesieniu w 1871 roku urzędowego wydania "Dziennika Praw Królestwa Polskiego,"* covering the years 1871-1915. The Hoover Collection contains similar semiofficial and unofficial publications of this period in Polish, though far fewer than the Russian- or German-language holdings, and mostly in quite incomplete sets. The Institution's collection, however, is quite rich in post-1918 Polish governmental documents dealing retrospectively with the 19th century.

World War I

The huge volume of material covering this period comprises books, pamphlets, leaflets, posters, multigraphed prints, and manuscripts, as well as a rich collection of illegally printed pamphlets, leaflets, and other propaganda and ephemera material issued by various workers organizations of this period. Several complete files of periodicals and newspapers from this period permit the study of contemporary public opinion and firsthand accounts of current events in Poland.

The Institution holds most of the contemporary publications of the major Polish "Committees" or "Councils," which, during World War I, acted as representatives of the Polish people under the sponsorship of the Russians, the Central Powers, the Western powers, or the Polish exiles. These include: 1) the Austrian-sponsored Polish Supreme National Committee (Naczelny Komitet Narodowy, NKN) formed August 16, 1914; 2) the Russian-sponsored Polish National Committee (Komitet Narodowy Polski, KNP) formed November 25, 1914, in Warsaw; 3) the German-sponsored Temporary State Council (Rada Główna Opiekuńcza) formed January 1, 1916; 4) the Council of State (Tymczasowa Rada Stanu, TRS) set up by the Central Powers on December 6, 1916, on former Russian Polish territories; 5) the Council of Regency (Rada Regencyjna) set up in Warsaw on October 15, 1917, by the Central Powers as a successor to the TRS; 6) the Polish National Committee (Polski Komitet Narodowy, PKN), established in Lausanne on August 15, 1917, (with headquarters in Paris) by Polish exiles in the West; as well as publications of the military organizations of some of these bodies as: 7) the Polish Military Organization (Polska Organizacja Wojskowa, POW), sponsored by the NKN, established October 22, 1914, in Warsaw; or 8) the Polish Army in France (Armia Polska we Francji) also known as Armia Hallera or Błękitna Armia, which was established in June, 1917, and which later became the official army of the PKN.

The Institution's holdings of Polish publications and foreign-language publications on World War I events in Poland are extensive.

ARCHIVAL AND UNPUBLISHED DOCUMENTS AND SPECIAL COLLECTIONS.   The Institution holds a large volume of individual archival units relating either directly or indirectly to Poland in World War I, dominantly in its Russian, but also in its Austro-Hungarian and German archives. A few of these archival holdings are mentioned here.

The *Wislowski Collection* contains proclamations, leaflets, broadsides, reports in manuscript form, and memoranda in Polish, German, and Russian dealing with social, economic, political, and military conditions in Poland from the beginning of World War I through the Austro-German military occupation, including the Brest-Litovsk period, and Soviet-Polish relations, 1918-20. Material on political parties, especially the Polish Socialist Party under Piłsudski, is particularly well represented, as are the formation of the Polish Legion, Polish activities in foreign countries on behalf of independence, and the military situation of Polish armies against the Bolsheviks and the Germans.

The *Wisnicki and Reimer Collections* basically represent holdings on the military occupation of Poland during World War I. These collections provide extensive coverage of the official proclamations and regulations of the occupying powers, and include the official gazette of the Austro-Hungarian military government, Lublin, February 19, 1915-October 19, 1918; the official gazette of the German military government, Warsaw, September 11, 1915-October 30, 1918; and many related documents.

The *Karol Badecki Collection* is devoted basically to East Galicia during 1914-18. It includes broadsides, leaflets, typewritten reports, and miscellaneous documents of the Polish National Committee concerning the independence of Poland and the Polish Legion, 1914-18; posters and proclamations issued in Lemberg (Lwów) and neighboring cities and towns by the Russian and Austro-Hungarian military authorities, 1914-17; and miscellaneous Austrian, Russian, and Polish newspapers.

The *Ciechanowski Collection,* while predominantly covering the years 1918-22, includes material as early as 1916. The collection contains copies of many diplomatic reports collected from various Polish legations and embassies, as well as circulars and notes, a limited number of illegally printed leaflets from the last years of the war, and other propaganda ephemera.

The *Wilder Collection* consists of over 500 pamphlets and some books on Poland issued during World War I and the early postwar period. They are devoted to such subjects as Poland's struggle for independence, Poland and the military occupying powers, the effect of the Russian revolution on Polish affairs, the execution of the Versailles Treaty, the plebiscites, the problems of the new Polish State, and Poland's relations to the League of Nations and to individual states.

The *Polish War Posters*. A collection of approximately 753 miscellaneous posters issued in Poland during World War I.

Records of the Russian Socialist Revolutionary Party (Partia Socjalistów-Rewolucyjnerów); selected documents dealing with the program and work of that party, 1880-1923, including references to the Socialist movement of that period in Poland.

The *M. V. Rodzianko Papers*. Documents written by the former president of the Russian Duma, 1916-21, concerning Russian affairs during World War I, where much mention is made of the Polish territories, and during the Bolshevik Revolution and the Civil War.

The *General N. N. Golovine Collections*. Documents, reports, memoranda, and manuscript articles relating to the Russian armies in World War I, including those in the Polish territories.

The *Bielevskii Collection*. A small collection of Russian army documents for the period March-October, 1917, including the Polish provinces.

The *V. A. Maklakov Collection*. A collection of both handwritten and typed materials from the personal papers of Maklakov, a member of the Russian Duma, and Russian Ambassador to Paris at the time of the Russian Provisional Government. While most of this collection relates to the Russian Civil War, many references are made to conditions in Poland during World War I.

The *Russian Okhrana (or Okhranka) Archives*. Russian secret police dossiers from 1895 to 1917 on Russian revolutionaries. The whole collection consists of several hundred archival boxes of which well over 20 are devoted strictly to Polish revolutionaries of that time.

Political Parties, 1890-1918

This collection of political ephemera, second in scope and size only to the holdings of official documents, contains contemporary and retrospective documentary materials, contemporary works by the parties, and later works about them. The official press publications are especially well represented for all parties; the depth of coverage depends on the importance of the party.

The various socialist, left-wing, and radical groups are best represented. The holdings of the pre-1892 *Polish Social-Revolutionary Party* which existed as *Proletariat I* (''Wielki'') from 1882-86 and as *Proletariat II* (''Mały'') from 1888-92, include such important sources as the press publications *Przedświt* (1881-92); *Proletariat* (1883-84); and *Walka klas* (1884-89).

Holdings of the socialist groups are quite extensive beginning with 1891/92, especially for the Polska Partja Socjalistyczna (PPS), the Socjaldemokracja Królestwa Polskiego i Litwy (SDKPiL), the PPS-Lewica (PPS-L) and the PPS-Frakcja Rewolucyjna. The press publications of the PPS for the period 1891/92 to 1906 are well represented.

The Institution has most of the collected works, memoirs, reminiscences, published correspondence, biographical publications, and a good many individual works by and about the leading personalities of the predecessor parties, especially those of the World War I period.

The Library holds the published records of all party congresses and conferences (often in various printings or editions), and records of the PPS-L for, before, and after the party split in 1906, and of the SDKPiL, although only from its union with Dzierżyński's Wilno Workers group in 1900; the coverage is somewhat weaker for the years preceding their merger. There is an even richer collection of semiprimary sources (sponsored by the parties) such as party histories, circulars printed for the party members, memoirs and biographies of the leading members (though many of these appeared after 1918), and archival material, as well as party pamphlets, leaflets, and political writings of party members.

Most of these contemporary sources are in the form of pamphlets, some of which were reprinted in large collections on a particular subject. The Hoover Library has most of these inter-war publications and just about all the post-World War II publications of this type.

The collection also contains a large number of monographs on the parties and their activities, some published between the wars, but most after World War II, when the subject of these predecessors of the KPP and their opposition was treated in a flood of publications.

One of the most important political archival units in the Hoover Polish collection is the *Rosa Luxemburg Collection,* which consists of six parts:

Approximately 125 letters from Rosa Luxemburg to Mathilde Jacob.

Miss Luxemburg's pseudo-prison diary: small Soennecken daily calendars for 1915, from February 19 to the end of the year; 1917, and 1918.

Unpublished letters and postcards from Mathilde Jacob to Franz and Eva Mehring, L. Kautsky, K. Liebknecht, Anna Bresler, Hans Diefenbach, Martha Rosenbaum, M. Luxemburg, and Sophie Liebknecht.

More than 50 letters of Clara Zetkin-Zundel to Mathilde Jacob.

An unpublished memoir in manuscript form by Mathilde Jacob entitled, *Rosa Luxemburg und ihren Frienden, 1914-1919* (135 p.).

Four manuscripts by Franz Mehring.

This Archival Collection contains far more letters of Rosa Luxemburg than heretofore published. It is invaluable for any study of Miss Luxemburg and sheds considerable light on a number of other ''old'' Communists during the war years and on the origins of the Communist movement.

The Library has strong, though less extensive, holdings of press publications for:

a) the Bund. The All-Jewish Union of Workers in Lithuania, Poland, and Russia (Ogólno-Żydowski Związek Robotniczy na Litwie, w Polsce i Rosji), 1897-1917;

b) The Polish Social-Democratic Party of Galicia and Silesia (Polska Partja Socjalno-Demokratyczna Galicji i Śląska, PPSD), 1899-1914;

c) The Socialist faction publications abroad, specifically in the United States and Russia.

The remaining Socialist, left-wing, and radical parties or groups have much weaker coverage than the above, ranging from satisfactory to poor. These include The Polish People's Party-Left Wing (Polskie Stronnictwo Ludowe-Lewica), Polska Partja Socjalistyczna zaboru pruskiego, and many others, especially small splinter groups.

The Library has research collection coverage for the following parties that were neither socialist nor left-wing:

Union of the Peasant Party (Związek Stronnictwa Chłopskiego);

The People's Party (Stronnictwo Ludowe);

The Polish People's Party (Polskie Stronnictwo Ludowe; Polskie Stronnictwo Ludowe— "Piast" as of 1913);

The National Democratic Party (Stronnictwo Demokratyczno-Narodowe);

The National Peasant Union (Narodowy Związek Chłopski);

The Peasant Union (Związek Chłopski);

The Polish Democratic Party (Polskie Stronnictwo Demokratyczne);

The Polish People's Union (Polski Związek Ludowy).

Parties with representation below the standard of a research collection, but still with satisfactory holdings, are:

The Polish Catholic People's Party (Polsko-Katolicka Partia Ludowa); the Mazurian People's Party (Mazurska Partia Ludowa); and the Christian-Democratic Party (Stronnictwo Chrześcijańsko-Demokratyczne).

Independent Poland (1918-1939)

The Hoover Institution collection for this period rates as a high-level research collection. The coverage of Polish history, politics, economic developments, contemporary government documents, and statistics is excellent; the holdings for other social sciences are strong enough to qualify as research holdings.

The voluminous holdings of government documentary materials include complete sets of both law and official gazettes, and are supplemented by various retrospective collections such as the eight-volume collection of statutes and regulations published under the title *Ustawy i Rozporządzenia z lat 1918-1934* (Warsaw, Min. Sprawiedliwości, 1935-38). There are also numerous subject indices to the *Dziennik Ustaw* providing many different approaches to this important source. These strong holdings are matched by those of the "Stenographic Records" of the Sejm in its main publications, further enriched by an excellent and extensive collection of official publications of various governmental ministries and departments or their documentary publications, and publications of other governmental bodies.

The Institution also holds the most basic documents of the Sejm Śląski, including its *Dziennik Ustaw Śląskich* (Katowice, 1922-36) and its official gazette, *Gazeta Urzędowa Województwa Śląskiego* (Katowice, 1922-39), as well as the stenographic records *Sprawozdania stenograficzne Sejmu Śląskiego,* etc. This collection includes about 150 monographs and documentary compilations on the Sejm Śląski. The collection also contains sets (though incomplete) of the leading Silesian journals and newspapers.

The official governmental publications are supported by abundant semiofficial documentary issuances, principally devoted to the work of the Polish Parliament. The Hoover Library has a nearly complete collection of the memoirs of Polish statesmen, diplomats, and political leaders.

Political Parties (1918-1938)

Polish interwar political life was characterized by a profusion of political groupings. The Hoover Institution holds practically all published platforms of these parties and the speeches of the various party leaders, including almost all speeches made before the Sejm and some of those made before the Senate.

The Institution's holdings for the following party groupings and parties are most representative and rounded:

The Left, especially:

The Polish Socialist Party (Polska Partja Socjalisticzna, ZPPS);

The National Workmen's Party (Narodowa Partja Robotnicza, NPR);

The Radical Peasant Party "Wyzwolenie" (Stronnictwo Ludowe "Wyzwolenie");

The Polish Communist Party (Komunistyczna Partja Robotnicza Polski, KPRP);

The Peasant Union (Klub Związku Chłopskiego).

The Center:

The "Piast" Polish Peasant Party (Stronnictwo Ludowe "Piast").

The Right Coalition, particularly:

The National Christian Party (Stronnictwo Chrześcijańsko-Narodowe, Chrz.-N.);

The National Populist Union (Związek Ludowo-Narodowy).

The Conservative group:

The Non-Partisan Bloc of Cooperation with the Government (Bezpartyjny Blok Współpracy z Rzadem, BBWR).

Of the national-minority political groups, the Ukrainian Club (Klub Ukraiński) is best represented in the Library's collection; the others are weakly represented. Some 30 other parties are represented in the collection to varying degree.

THE POLISH SOCIALIST PARTY, PPS. The Polish Socialist Party was the largest left-wing Polish party of the interwar era and had one of the strongest representations in Parliament through the years. Its modifications of policy over the years led to the formation of opposition splinter groups, for example, the Niezależna Socjalistyczna Partja Pracy w Polsce. Other splinter groups joined the original adherents of the SDKPiL (Social Democratic Party of the Kingdom of Poland and Lithuania) to form the Polish Communist Party.

The Library's major holdings of the interwar Polish Socialist Party include:

1) Five of the six official press organs of the PPS, as well as PPS publications issued abroad;

2) Other PPS press publications issued during the interwar period, including runs of 17 important periodicals;

3) Political writings and memoirs of the Party's leading members and its representatives in the Sejm and Senate;

4) A strong collection of contemporary PPS documents; reports of its congresses, collective or individual publications of speeches, debates, etc., of the Party's representatives in the Sejm and the Senate, exemplified by such publications as H. Diamand's *Przemówienia w Sejme R. P. 1919-1930* (Warsaw, 1932).

5) This rich collection of primary sources is supported by equally strong holdings of scholarly (monographic) studies of the interwar as well as the post-World War II publications.

THE COMMUNIST PARTY OF POLAND, KPRP/KPP. In general, Hoover's holdings on the Communist Party of Poland (KPP) are excellent. Coverage of contemporary documentary and semidocumentary publications of the Party (speeches and writings of its leaders, its official press publications, et al.) is very good to the early thirties, but only fair for the later years to the

German invasion. Although many KPP publications of the 1930s are known to have been lost entirely, the collection for this period may still be regarded as a research collection, especially in conjunction with postwar documentary material on the thirties.

The Institution holds individual publications (interwar and postwar imprints) of both the better-known and the lesser-known Party members, and it has a very good collection of minutes and records of the Party congresses, supplemented by many reprints of individual reports presented to some of the congresses, numerous other publications of contemporary and post-World War II imprints concerning these congresses, publications by the Party's central committee and some of its other committees or special commissions.

The holdings include: a strong collection of diaries and monographs; less conventional publications as reprints of periodical articles on most aspects of the interwar existence of the KPP; a large number of political ephemera; and strictly propaganda material directed to the various subversive activities.

Individual Topics and Subjects

All historical, political, diplomatic, and military events of interwar Poland are well covered by contemporary and retrospective publications. Further, there are extensive holdings on minorities, the economy, social conditions, education, law, religion, et al.

The Hoover Institution has what can be considered the world's richest collection of sources, archival material, and official documents on the Paris Peace Conference (1919), comprising fairly complete files of official records of the Conference as recorded by the American Commission to Negotiate Peace, minutes of meetings of the bodies of the Conference, reports, diplomatic correspondence, and bulletins. Much documentation and several unique items for the study of Poland are not available elsewhere.

There is a complete file of propaganda material, including memoranda, pamphlets, publications, maps, leaflets, etc., distributed by the different delegations at the Peace Conference.

Partial holdings of this unique collection are listed in the work by Nina Almond and Ralph Haswell Lutz, *An Introduction to a Bibliography of the Paris Peace Conference (Collections sources, archive publications and source books)* (Stanford Univ. Press, 1935).

The Hoover Institution holds considerable additional material on the Peace Conference—a large body of material in the private archives of President Herbert Hoover, founder of the Hoover Institution, and other pertinent materials including various manuscript collections, published documents, studies, monographs, et al.

World War II

All important materials on the events in Poland during World War II will be found in the collections. Therefore, the description here will be confined to several unique collections.

The Hoover Institution has what is generally considered the largest collection of World War II "underground" publications outside Poland. These are held as originals or photostatic copies and are an extremely valuable source on the occupation years and the Polish resistance movement. The collection includes titles not known to be in Poland and individual issues missing from Polish library collections (the Institution's sets also lack individual issues).

The *Archives of the Polish National Council* (Rada Narodowa Polska), 1940-45, form another group of Archival and Special Collection materials. This collection contains a rare, complete set of the stenographic records of all meetings (plenary meetings, meetings of commissions, sub-commissions, etc.) of the Council. The entire file consists of about 8,000 typewritten pages, and approximately 2,500 additional pages on microfilm.

The *Personal Archives of General Sikorski* comprise the third large archival collection (microfilm) on World War II-Poland. They contain a large portion of important documents relating to the activities of the Polish government-in-exile during World War II, from September 1939 through the middle of 1944, and material on Polish-Soviet relations and on the organization of the Polish army in the Soviet Union (1941-43).

The fourth large archival collection is the *Collection of Papers of the Polish Ministry of Preparatory Work.* The holdings consist of a large body of memoranda and other papers prepared by the Ministry to enable the Polish government-in-exile to present its case to the future Peace Conference after World War II). It also contains a large volume of research papers prepared by the staff for the Ministry office's use only. Most of these are typewritten, with some in mimeograph or other types of multicopies.

The fifth of these World War II-Polish émigré archives is the *Archive of the Polish Information Center* (New York, 1940-45), which contains such materials as the complete sets of press releases in English and Polish prepared by the Center, and a complete set of cables received from the Polish Ministry of Information in London. The collection comprises some 8,000 single-spaced typewritten pages.

Sixth is an outstanding collection of personal accounts of Polish citizens who were deported to the Soviet Union during World War II and spent a number of years in forced labor camps. This collection of memoirs and recollections, combined with the collection on Polish and other minorities in the forced labor camps in the Soviet Union (representing a total of 60,000 pieces), supplemented by the wealth of printed and archival information in other collections, gives the Hoover Institution the most outstanding collection in the world on the various aspects of internal conditions of the Soviet Union during World War II, the question of forced labor camps, and Polish-Russian relations during the war years.

In addition, there are several smaller Polish Archives or Special Collections relating to World War II, among which are the *General Anders Archives*, which contain documents on the formation of the Polish Army in the USSR; the *Archives of the Polish Embassy in Moscow* (1941-43); the *Papers of the Polish Ministry of Industry, Commerce and Maritime Transport in London;* and the *Archives of Colonel Barkowski,* aide-de-camp to General Sikorski.

After its dissolution and movement underground in 1938, the Polish Communist Party was reestablished on January 5, 1942, as the Polish Workers Party (Polska Partia Robotnicza-PPR). By the end of 1942, the PPR had established a large network of underground cells and developed its own military organization, the People's Guard (Gwardia Ludowa), later named the People's Army (Armia Ludowa). In 1945 the Polish Communist exile group in Moscow established the Polish People's Army (Polska Armia Ludowa-PAL) and the Union of Polish Patriots (Związek Patriotów Polskich-ZPP) whose members formed the administrative and political superstructure of this army.

Hoover has a good collection of documentary sources, a large collection of memoirs, and official or semiofficial histories (including the histories of the various battalions, regiments) of these pro-Communist military organizations.

The Institution holds numerous publications in book form or articles (all with postwar imprint) by the leading representatives of the PPR during World War II and of a substantial group of members of the ZPP who attained high Party or government positions in postwar Poland, as well as Communists who joined the ZPP and the People's Guard.

Hoover has most of the postwar documentary materials on Party achievements during the war (published by the Party and others), with lacunae mostly in regional publications of the early postwar years.

The Institution's collection of wartime publications of the various important legislative and military Communist-sponsored bodies, such as the National People's Council (Krajowa Rada Narodowa, KRN) and the Polish Committee of National Liberation (Polski Komitet Wyzwolenia Narodowego, PKWN) is small, since very few sources were published at that time, although these bodies are treated in various portions of most every postwar Polish publication on World War II as well as in Western publications. The Institution has perhaps the most important contemporary source on the PKWN, the official gazette, *Dziennik ustaw,* (Lublin, 1944, nos. 1-7, 9-19 [Aug.- Dec.], and 1945, nos. 1-58 [Jan.-Dec.], which is supported by uneven holdings of the KRN Presidium's central press organs, *Rada Narodowa* (Warsaw, 1944, scattered issues), *Biuletyn Sprawozdawzy Prezydium KRN* (Warsaw, 1944), *Wolność* (Lublin, 1944), and *Informator Krajowej Rady Narodowej* (Warsaw, 1944). The other documentary sources concerned with the KRN and PKWN are of the postwar vintage. There is also a large collection of memoirs dealing directly with these official bodies.

Post-1945 Poland

The Hoover collection on postwar Poland undoubtedly rates as a high-level research collection on all historical, political, governmental, and other social science subjects. The period from 1955 to 1970 is represented more comprehensively than is the 1945-54 period, especially for provincial materials and press publications on particular subjects, but both periods are well represented.

GOVERNMENT DOCUMENTARY PUBLICATIONS. 1) *Laws, Statutes, Official Gazettes.* The Institution holds, among others, complete sets of the two most important sources on the administration of this period. The first is the law gazette of the Polish Peoples Republic, *Dziennik Ustaw Rzeczypospolitej Polskiej* (1944-), which contains all legislative acts, executive decrees, statutes, and orders issued by the Council of State, the Council of Ministers, the Prime Ministers, and the various ministries. The second source is the official gazette of the Polish People's Republic, *Monitor Polski—Dziennik Urzędowy Rzeczypospolitej Polskiej* (1945-50; 1970-), which carries the executive orders of the President, the Council of Ministers, and other high governmental authorities; and the regulations, decisions, instructions, and announcements issued by these authorities. These are supplemented by various collective volumes of Polish legislation.

2) *Parliamentary Records.* The Institution has the stenographic records of the postwar Parliament, or Sejm, which appear under various titles and are supplemented by a host of other official publications.

3) Among the important sources for the Polish postwar government, the Institution has a complete set of the directives of the Polish Communist Party, issued by its Central Committee in its various publications.

4) These major primary sources are supplemented by publications of the various ministries and government departments such as those of the *Główny* Urząd Statystyczny, of which the Institution carries most publications in its sphere of interest. The collection of publications from these various ministries, though by no means complete, offers a fairly good research potential.

PERSONAL WRITINGS. Writings by members of the Council of State and its chairman, members of the Council of Ministers, the writings of the various representatives to the Sejm, of numerous other lesser governmental officials, and of representatives of various local administrative People's Councils, are a rich supplementary source to the official publications. The Institution holds a very large collection, several thousand volumes, of the writings of these individuals.

THE COMMUNIST PARTY.   Hoover Institution holdings on the post-World War II Polish Communist Party constitute, both qualitatively and quantitatively, the most comprehensive holdings of the entire Polish collection. The collection can be broken down into the following well represented classes of sources:

1) A large collection of speeches and writings of the major Party leaders. All these sources are collected comprehensively, often in various editions: in the Party press, as contemporary pamphlets, in collective volumes of speeches presented at a particular congress, plenum, etc., or as reprints in collected works or speeches. A great many of these are also available in translation.

2) Stenographic and other official records of all PZPR congresses, and rather comprehensive (especially after 1955) collections of publications concerning these congresses. This collection includes extensive holdings of publications by and about the Party's Central Committee. Published records of the Party Plenums are complete as of 1958, while many of the pre-1958 partial records can be found in individual pamphlets and in the Party press.

3) Comprehensive special collections of Party documents such as statutes, resolutions, ideological declarations, etc., often in several successive editions.

4) Documentary material on subjects intimately connected with the development of the Party, such as economics, the armed forces, the international Communist movement, and trade unions.

5) Official and semiofficial histories of the Party from its beginnings through the most recent developments, as published in the postwar period, are comprehensively represented.

6) Scholarly monographs on the Party and its activities are covered almost completely for the period 1958-70, while the periods before and after these dates reflect strong but selective coverage.

7) A selective, but strong collection of Polish post-World War II émigré publications on conditions in Poland as well as on the Party. Many of these are memoirs or other writings of former Party members.

8) A comprehensive collection of Western works published in English, German, and French on Polish Communism.

JOURNALS AND NEWSPAPERS.   Periodicals and newspapers constitute one of the most comprehensive holdings of sources on political matters, including all the major centrally published political, governmental, trade union, and scholarly press publications. The holdings of political presses of the 1945-48 period deserve special attention; coverage for 1948-56 is slightly weaker. From approximately 1957/58 to the present, these holdings are quite comprehensive in the fields of Hoover coverage, including central as well as principal regional publications.

Yugoslavia

THE HOOVER INSTITUTION collection on Yugoslavia contains over 18,000 volumes, in addition to some 500 journal and 105 newspaper titles, covering the period from the late 19th century to the present, but the research strength of the collection rests in the post-World War II period. The topics of the pre-1918 period with the best coverage are the movements toward nationalism, socialism, and trade unionism in the various nations that today are Yugoslavia, but about 80 percent of this material is of post-World War II imprint. The subject best covered by contemporary sources is the Austro-Hungarian occupation of Bosnia and Herzegovina. Holdings include most of the official documentary material published by the occupation forces, which are supplemented by interwar and postwar published documents and scholarly works on the subject.

Small nuclei of other contemporary pre-1918 sources include stenographic records of the Croatian, Slovenian, and Dalmatian Parliament (Sabor) for 1892-1918, and of the Serbian Parliament (Skupština) for 1902-12. The overall shortages of contemporary government documents are compensated to some extent by the extensive holdings of Austrian and Hungarian parliamentary and executive body records (surveyed in the Hungarian Collection).

This type of material is further supplemented by such sources as the Serbian Interior Ministry's *Policijski glasnik* (1907-14); the Kingdom's official newspaper *Radničke novine* (1903-15); *Srbske novine* (Aug.-Nov. 1918), the official gazette of the Serbian government in exile; the official Montenegran gazette *Glas tsernogortsa* (1917-20); and such newspapers and journals as: *Rabotnishko delo* (1903-05), *Belgrader Nachrichten* (1915-18), *Beogradske novine* (1915-17); *Obzor* (1917-19), *Hrvatski dnevnik* (1915-16), *Cettiner Zeitung* (1916-18), and a number of other less complete files of additional newspapers. Hoover also holds a small collection of "trench papers."

Of the small collection of unpublished archival holdings for this early period, the most noteworthy is the manuscript of Vladimir Ćorović's memoirs, *Relations Between Serbia and Austro-Hungary in the Twentieth Century*. In addition, the Institution holds all basic scholarly histories of political life for this period.

1918-1939

The entire interwar history of Yugoslavia is well covered in the Institution by leading historians such as Šišić, Ćorović, Radošević, Horvat, Ćulinović, and Milovanović. Holdings of contemporary primary sources, newspapers, and scholarly journals for most historical and political developments cover only the period through 1925. From then until the beginning of World War II, only a very few isolated subjects are supported by primary sources, but the scholar may safely assume that post-World War II documentary publications on historicopolitical and socioeconomic developments of the interwar period are in the Hoover Collection.

Hoover's holdings of major official primary sources of the "United Kingdom of Serbs, Croats, and Slovenes" contain the complete records of the parliamentary bodies from the first Provisional National Assembly through the Constituent Assembly and the National Assembly from 1919 to October 1925. For the early years of Yugoslavia's independence this is strengthened by a complete set of the official gazette, *Službene novine* (1919-25), and by substantial holdings of various ministerial gazettes, bulletins, and annuals.

SUBJECTS WITH STRONG RESEARCH HOLDINGS.   Hoover's holdings on Yugoslavia at the Paris Peace Conference and the resulting Treaty of Rapallo in 1920 are excellent for research purposes. The Institution's unique holdings of archival and official documents include a 12-volume set of documentary materials presented by the Yugoslav delegation to the Peace Conference: *Memoranda Presented to the Peace Conference, in Paris, Concerning the Claims of the Kingdom of the Serbians, Croatians and Slovenes* (Paris, 1919), and a very strong collection of Yugoslav "delegation propaganda," consisting of such material as *Bulletin Yugoslave* (Geneva) (nos. 1-3, 5-27).

Other topics having good research holdings include Yugoslavia's role in the "Little Entente," the "Balkan Entente," and the "Sporazum" agreement of April 27, 1939, as well as German-Yugoslav relations, especially of the later 1930s, and financial and economic conditions of the whole interwar period.

The main characteristic of Yugoslavia's interwar political life was bitter strife among existing political parties, a majority of which had ethnic or religious bases. Institution holdings of primary sources on these various parties differ considerably. The strongest resources are for the Communist Party of Yugoslavia (Komunistična stranka Jugoslavije—KSJ) followed by the (Serbian) National Radical Party (Narodna radikalna stranka), in power almost continuously until 1926; and the Croatian Peasant Party (Hrvatska seljačka stranka), the largest minority party. The remaining parties are represented largely through secondary sources, with the exception of some memoirs by leading members. This is also true of these parties after 1935, when they acted as the United Opposition, organized into several loose political blocs.

Most published memoirs, autobiographies, or other works relating to interwar political developments (of interwar and postwar imprints) by the leading representatives of the above-mentioned parties are in the collection and are supplemented by almost comprehensive holdings of published scholarly histories on most of the parties.

Research resources on the Communist Party are most thorough, though practically all of them are of postwar imprint. The postwar Yugoslav government (or the Party) published a large number of interwar documents on the Communist Party in individual volumes, for example: *Komunistička partija Jugoslavije u Crnoj Gori 1919-1940* by B. Jovanović; or in series such as the *Istorijski arhiv Komunističke partije Jugoslavije, Istorijski arhiv na Komunističkata partija na Makedonija.* Thus the interwar Yugoslav Communist movement is documented by records of its congresses, conferences, a selection of the Party's individual interwar publications, and a number of its official organs.

A huge collection of speeches, memoirs, and writings of the Party leaders is also of postwar imprint. The scholar may assume that he will find most of the postwar documentary publications at Hoover.

Hoover has a fine archival collection of unpublished memoirs and political reminiscences and studies, an example of which is the typewritten manuscript *Yugoslav Communism Under the Influence of Soviet Communism During the Period 1919-1941* by Ante Ciliga, head of the "Counter-Revolutionary Trotskiism" faction which was active within the left wing of the Communist Party of Yugoslavia from 1926-28.

Another important unpublished source of information on Yugoslavia during the years 1934-41 is a manuscript by Dragiša Cvetković (prewar leader of the Serbian National party, member of the Government since 1935, and later Prime Minister) entitled, *Internal and Foreign Policy of the Regency.*

World War II

The Hoover Institution possesses an excellent collection of primary sources documenting World War II developments in Yugoslavia, from all points of view. A continuous research collection begins from this time; a selected sampling of it follows.

The primary-source coverage of the "Coup d'Etat of 1941" is especially strong. In addition to the "Documents of the German Foreign Ministry" and its sequel documentation found in the various Western Powers' Foreign Policy series, there is a large collection of published and unpublished memoirs and papers of leading participants in or observers of the events. The Hoover collection on the "Coup" was the basis for a documentary study on those events published in 1966, under the title: *Yugoslavia's Revolution of 1941,* by D. N. Ristić, aide-de-camp to General Simović, and later his executive secretary.

Yugoslavia's patriotic war against the occupying forces and their own collaborationist countrymen suffered deeply from internal strife leading to civil war: the conflict between the Royalist Chetniks under Yugoslav Army Gen. Draža Mihailović, and the Communist-oriented Partisans led by Josip Broz Tito; the deep-seated antagonism between Serb and Croat, resulting in conflicts between the Ustaša and the Chetniks; and conflicts within Communism and with a variety of anticommunists.

This "patriotic war" or "underground movement" is one of the best documented subjects in the Collection, second only to the overall holdings on the Yugoslav Communist Party.

The archival collection of the former Ambassador to Washington, Constantin Fottich, contains as full a collection of books, pamphlets, articles, manuscripts, documents, etc., on the Chetniks' point of view as one can hope to find under any circumstances. The archives include many unpublished accounts of former Chetniks, letters sent to the Yugoslav Embassy in Washington by American soldiers rescued by Chetniks, and official correspondence on the subject between the Embassy and the Exile Government in London, or the U. S. Government. The archive also documents the relations between Tito, Mihailović, and Churchill.

The overall documentary collection on the Communist-sponsored Partisan Movement consists of a sizable collection of postwar reprints of partisan publications, including 1) the leading organ of the Yugoslav Communist Party, *Borba* (1941-43), the Party's Central Committee official organ *Delo* (1941-42), and a number of regional party organs; 2) records of the various Party congresses and records of sessions of AVNOJ (Tito's provisional Government); 3) all published speeches and works of the leaders of the Party or its affiliated organizations; 4) a collection of memoirs of leading personalities and of rank and file members; 5) a strong collection of histories of the movement, the various organizations within the movement, histories of various partisan brigades, etc.

The collection includes holdings on the many other "groups" that took part in the internal strife in former Yugoslav territories, mostly the national "guards" or "armies" established by the four collaborationist regimes. While all are represented by documentary and descriptive works of postwar years, the following have the best coverage 1) the Croat "Ustaša," and Ante Pavelić, their leader; and smaller holdings on the Slovenian "Domobranstvo," or Home Guard; 2) the Serbian Ljotić Group—a Fascist organization in Serbia, and their army group, "The Serbian Volunteer Army" as well as the regular Serbian militia, the State Guard; 3) other groups as the "Ilindanci" in Macedonia, or the local Chetniks of Montenegro, are represented by much smaller holdings.

THE ROYAL GOVERNMENT-IN-EXILE. Holdings of contemporary published documentation of this body are quite complete, including complete files of their official gazette, *Službene Novine,* information bulletins, *Jugoslovenski Glasnik* (Cairo), *Yugoslav News Bulletin* (New York), et al. These are richly supplemented by memoirs of several former members of the government published both in Western exile and in postwar Yugoslavia, offering sharply differing views on the development within the Exile government. There is also a collection of "documentary" and analytical works on the exile group, published by the present government of Yugoslavia.

AVNOJ. AVNOJ (Antifašističko veće narodnog oslobodjenja Jugoslavije), the Antifascist Council for National Liberation, was the Partisan-sponsored provisional government established in 1942, which became the basis for postwar government in Yugoslavia. The Institution holds stenographic records of its three sessions, both in abridged and complete editions. The collection includes all published works and speeches of most members of its legislative and executive bodies. Though most of these are in postwar editions, some individual speeches are in first editions. In general, we may say that everything published by the AVNOJ is by now at Hoover, either in the original, in reprint, or on microfilm. These sources are supplemented by an excellent group of writings on World War II events by Allied government and military officials—by British and American officers serving as liaison officers with the Partisans or Chetniks.

Two archival collections concerning the Partisan and Chetnik movements which deserve special mention are the unpublished memoirs of M. I. Žujović, and the so-called "Goebbels Military Diaries." The first of these includes seven manuscript boxes of unpublished memoirs and other materials collected by one of the chief political advisers to Mihailović, and material dealing specifically with the struggle between Mihailović and Tito. The Goebbels diaries are a series of detailed day-by-day accounts of the general military situation including Yugoslavia in original manuscript form, comprising altogether some 26 boxes.

Post-1945 Yugoslavia

After much negotiating between the Exile government in London and Tito's AVNOJ, on March 8, 1945, the Provisional Coalition Government was established with Marshal Tito as premier. This government, based on the Šubašić-Tito agreement, however, was dissolved by October of the same year, and the Communist Party formed its own government.

The Institution holds an extensive collection of published and unpublished records on the Šubašić-Tito negotiations, complete stenographic records of the Third Session of AVNOJ (August 1945) when it was transformed into the Provisional People's Assembly *(Privremena Narodna Skupština),* and complete records for all the resulting interim bodies, up to the establishment of the Federal People's Assembly (Savezna Narodna Skupština) in 1946, and its modified bodies, until the present day.

Records of the Presidium of the National Assembly, and its official journal *Službeni vestnik . . . ,* are also fully represented for the period 1946-53, as is the official law gazette, *Službeni list (S)FRJ* from 1945 to the present. These excellent holdings are supplemented by records of official documents of the six constituent republics and the two autonomous regions. Although not all of these regional documents are in complete sets, they are substantial, and represent full holdings from the mid-1960s.

All these holdings are aided by long runs of some 20 "non-party" newspapers (from 1945/46 or 1962 to the present) representing a good cross-section of the most important central, regional, trade union, and other social science subject papers. Supplemented by numerous shorter-lived titles, these serve as a strong base for research on the entire postwar period.

All Communist Party documentation, whether published by the Party itself, or one of its affiliated institutions, as well as publications on the Party by other groups, are represented in the collection at a research level from approximately 1945, with only a slight decline in strength between 1948 and 1953. The collection includes complete sets of stenographic records of Party congresses beginning with 1948, as well as most of those for the Republic parties. Complete records of the Party's Central Committee are available beginning with 1960. All the Party's official central organs are here from the dates of their appearance, supplemented by the existing regional Party organs starting from 1963/66 to the present. Further information is provided by all the published memoirs of Party members, official Party histories, constitutions, directives, documentation of Party reorganizations, and the Party's mass "front" organizations. The best collections on front organizations are on the Socialist Alliance of Working People of Yugoslavia (Socijalistički Savez Radnog Naroda Jugoslavije), the Confederation of Yugoslav Trade Unions (Savez Sindikata Jugoslavije), and the Youth League of Yugoslavia (Savez Omladine Jugoslavije). Additionally, there is a voluminous collection of monographs treating the Party.

All subjects on the Government-Party level since 1944 are almost comprehensively covered. The new economic reforms, worker's self-management, and related subjects are carefully and fully documented in the collection. Further, Yugoslavia's foreign relations in general, and especially the two major disputes with the Soviet Union and resulting problems with other Communist countries, are extensively covered. Similarly, well documented are various internal changes, purges, and trials.

Finally, the largest collection in the Institution's Yugoslav archives is the aforementioned *Constantin Fottich Collection,* which includes many copies of official correspondence between Fottich (as ambassador) and leading diplomats of various countries, especially the United States and England. It also contains much printed material of Yugoslav émigrés in the years following World War II; such material was usually published in article form in rare, little-distributed émigré newspapers and journals. It is one of the most important archives on post-1945 émigré circles abroad.

Other Countries

Albania

The Albanian Collection is the least developed of the East European Collections at the Hoover Institution, consisting of approximately 1800 volumes of books and pamphlets, 18 journal titles, and 7 newspaper titles (in Albanian as well as in West and East European languages). Most of these holdings belong to the post-World War I period. The pre-1945 holdings consist largely (about 70 percent) of publications in West and East European languages on Albania, reflecting Albania's political situation and the unfamiliarity of American scholars with the Albanian language.

The Albanian Collection starts officially with 1912, the year Albania achieved independence from Turkey. During World War I, Albania was occupied by various foreign governments, each installing its local administration and civil services. The Institution's rich holdings of the publications of these governments (the Austro-Hungarian Monarchy, Italy, France, Germany, and Russia) along with the Institution's strong holdings on the Paris Peace Conference, provide documentary sources for the study of Albania during the period of the First World War.

The events of the turbulent interwar period (1920-39) of Albanian history are not well represented by primary sources at Hoover. Except for a small collection of West European language sources, including a quite substantial collection of treaties between Albania and Italy (in Italian), all the documentary Albanian publications in Hoover holdings were published by the Communist government after 1945; for example, the 1959 publication by Fane Veizi, *Kongresi i Lushnjes* (Tirana), which is an account of the Albanian National Congress held in 1920, or Vangjel Moisiu's *Lufta për Krijimin e Partisë Komuniste të Shqipërisë (1917-1941)* (Tirana, 1957), a documentary history of the origins of Albania's labor movement and the Communist Party in Albania.

An interesting source for the interwar period is the unusually strong collection of official governmental publications in the fields of tariffs, custom taxes, custom statistics, and statistical publications covering the fields of industry, commerce, and population. Primary sources on the military forces, especially governmental laws and regulations concerning them, are another area of unusual strength.

Inasmuch as Albania was occupied by the Fascist armies from 1939 until 1943 and by Nazi forces from 1943 to 1944, for the World War II period of Albania's history contemporary sources are in the Italian and German languages exclusively, as exemplified by such publications as *Legislazione Fascista e del Lavoro in Albania* (Naples, 1942). The Institution holds the journal *Mundimi,* which was dropped by Allied forces into Albania during World War II. This collection of contemporary material is supplemented by postwar publications of documentary works and monographic studies, on most subjects of the Second World War.

The post-1945 period is represented by far stronger and more balanced holdings of research value, as well as original Albanian documentary sources published by the post-1945 regime. (especially since 1964) on all the historical, political, and other events. Of the post-1945 subjects covered, the Albanian Communist Party is most strongly represented.

ALBANIA UNDER COMMUNIST RULE.   The Institution's weak collection of Albanian official governmental publications is counterbalanced by its strong collection of Communist Party official materials, for example: the main official organ of the Albanian Worker's Party, the monthly *Rruga e Partisë,* supplemented from 1955 on by the Party daily organ, *Zëri i Popullit,* and by publications carrying many of the Party directives cumulatively as the *Dokumenta Kryesore të Partisë së Punës së Shqipërisë* (1960), which contains resolutions and decisions of Party congresses, conferences, and committee plenary meetings, joint resolutions of the Central Committee of the Party and the government, and many other directives of Party organs, for the period

1941-54; collections of Party and governmental laws and decrees such as the specialized *Përm- bledhje Dekretesh, Vendimesh dhe Urdhëresash mbi Kooperativat Bujqësorë* (1957), which represents the text of all legislation and regulation of agricultural collectives.

Reports on the congresses of the Communist Party of Albania are represented in the Institu- tion beginning with the Third Congress in 1956, among which are translations into Russian, Polish, or English.

Bulgaria

Although the Bulgarian Collection officially begins with the Balkan Wars (1912), it also includes a selective background collection of primary and secondary sources for the earlier period, up to 1878. The whole collection consists of some 7,000 to 8,000 volumes of books and pamphlets, 236 journal titles, and 36 newspaper titles. Serious research, however, can be supported only for specific events or periods.

THE BALKAN WARS AND WORLD WAR I (1912-1918). Holdings for this period con- stitute a good research collection, the events of this period being documented by a variety of sources. To these belong such official publications as records of the proceedings of the National Assembly, *Stenografski Dnevnitsi,* and reports of parliamentary committees. There are also numerous contemporary and interwar publications of various ministries on these events. Two such sources, from the Bulgarian Ministry of War, are the seven-volume documentary collection on the Balkan Wars, *Voinata mezhdu Bŭlgariia i Turtsiia 1912-1913* (1928-30), and the nine-volume documentation of World War I, *Bŭlgarskata armiia v Svietovnata voina, 1915-1918,* (1936-43).

Such collections of documents are supplemented by both Bulgarian and foreign diplomatic documentary sources, as well as by diplomatic memoirs, (Vasil Radoslavov, I. Geshov, M. Madzharov, G. W. Buchanan, V. Nekliudov, and others), and a strong collection of interwar and post-World War II histories and scholarly monographs on this period.

THE INTERWAR PERIOD (1918-1939). The entire interwar period in Bulgaria is well covered by the best historical works of the period, by such authors as A. Girginov, A. Malinov, G. Nurigiani, N. Stanev, and K. Todorov. These are supplemented by a large collection of post- World War II histories of the interwar period, such as those of M. Dimitrov, D. Kazasov, D. Kosev, and N. D. Petkov, and a large collection of both interwar and postwar scholarly studies.

Primary sources are less fully represented. However, there are such official sources as the law gazette, *Dŭrzhaven vestnik,* which the Institution has for the period 1908-46, and the parlia- mentary stenographic records, *Stenografski dnevnitsi,* which covers this whole period. This type of major governmental source is supported by a fair collection of documentary publications of various ministries and departments, and good runs of some of the leading interwar historical journals and newspapers. These include such basic journals as the *Izvestiia* of the Bulgarian His- torical Society, or the *Bŭlgarska istoricheska biblioteka,* and others, supplemented by specialized journals, for example, *Voenno-istoricheski sbornik, Protest; anarkho-komunistichen vestnik, Rabotnicheska misŭl; anarkho-komunistichesko spisanie,* and others. Newspaper holdings include (in various degrees of completeness) such titles as *Dnevnik, Dnes, Mir, Narodno edinstvo, Rabot- nicheski vestnik, Slovo, Svoboda, Utro, Zname, Zora,* and others. However, the research value for this period lies in individual historical events, rather than in the entire period. Of these, the strongest documentation is for such topics as Bulgaria and the Paris Peace Conference, the period of government under Alexander Stambolski, the Agrarian Union, the Balkan Conferences and the Balkan Pact, the "Zveno" organization, the Internal Macedonian Revolutionary Organization (IMRO), and the Communist Party. Communist Party sources include predominantly documentary holdings published after World War II. Overall coverage of interwar events is strengthened by a moderate but good collection of political writings and memoirs of political personalities.

WORLD WAR II.   Holdings of contemporary Bulgarian publications of the World War II period are quite poorly represented in the Institution. The most important sources are the afore-mentioned stenographic records of the proceedings of the parliament. The Institution's holdings of the German- and Italian-language publications and archival materials relating to World War II events in Bulgaria are much larger, but cover the whole Southeastern "Feldzug," including the other Balkan countries, especially Yugoslavia.

The small collection of contemporary Bulgarian publications is strengthened by a quite exten-sive collection (some 300 volumes) of post-World War II published collections of documentary material, memoirs of partisans and members of the "Fatherland Front," and histories of these two groups. Although this material is of postwar issue, with a predominance of Bulgarian Com-munist publications, the collection's value is somewhat balanced by writings of Bulgarian émigrés who took part in these events.

THE POST-WORLD WAR II PERIOD.   The postwar period has the strongest representation at Hoover. The whole period is covered by a good, though not comprehensive, collection of lead-ing governmental and administrative sources; and by documentary collections of the Communist Party, the official ruling party since the last quarter of 1946. As such, many of its publications supplement and support postwar historical studies of the country.

Governmental holdings in the collection include such major sources as the National Assem-bly's *Dŭrzhaven vestnik,* its stenographic records, *Stenografski dnevnitsi,* The Assembly Presid-ium's records, *Izvestiia . . .* and *Narodni Sŭvet;* and the Council of Ministers' collection of decisions and directives, *Sbornik postanovleniia i razporezhdaniia na Ministerskiia Sŭvet.* These are supplemented by various other collections of laws, constitutions, state-administration, and the publications of selected ministries, as well as by the leading central journals relating to the legal and administrative fields.

These state publications are further supplemented by a good, though quite selective collection of Communist Party documentary publications for the period 1945-58 and quite comprehensive holdings of documentary publications since 1958. For example, a few of the more important docu-mentary holdings of the Party are the five-volume collection of Party decisions and policy state-ments adopted between 1891 and 1962, *Bŭlgarskata rabotnicheska partiia (komunisti) v rezoliutsii i resheniia na kongresite, konferentsiite i plenumite na TsK* (Sofia, 1947-65); a collection of steno-graphic records of the first five postwar Party congresses (known as the fifth—eighth) in a five-volume set published as *Bŭlgarska kommunisticheska partiia. Kongress. Stenografski protokoli* (Sofia, 1948-67).

These types of sources are further supplemented by all the published collected works of communist personalities, and by a good collection of other leading personalities, or in individual publications. Some of these works are also held in English translation. Further, there is a small but good collection of official Party histories. All these materials are further supplemented by an extensive collection of publications on the Party and a selective collection of central journals and newspapers, as the *Izvestiia* of the Institute of History of the Bulgarian Communist Party; the *Izvestiia* or the Party Higher School of the Central Committee; the Party official theoretical organ, *Novo vreme; Rabotnichesko delo; Partien zhivot; Armeiski kommunist; Partien opit,* and others.

In addition to these two major areas of source materials, Hoover has collections of research value in history (in which the largest number of scholarly journals are received) and economics.

Hungary

The Hungarian Collection consists of about 12,000 volumes, some 500 journal titles, and 60 newspaper titles. While the collection officially begins with 1918, its research value starts with the beginning of World War I.

1914-1918.   For this period, the Institution holds an extraordinary collection of all the basic official governmental publications, the core of which, *Magyar Törvénytár,* covers all laws, decrees, etc., from 1526 to 1948. This collection is supplemented by good holdings of decrees and laws published by most of the existing ministries, or cumulative collections arranged by subject. The second major source for this period is an excellent collection of records and documents of the Hungarian Parliament—the stenographic records and "documents" of the House of Representatives from 1901-18 and of the Lower House from 1910-18, and the "proceedings" of the Lower House from 1914-18.

These sources are supplemented by substantial holdings of books and pamphlets published by the executive agencies, especially the Ministries of Foreign Affairs, Interior, Agriculture, and Justice. In this category the most valuable, indeed unique, records relate directly to World War I, namely, a six-volume collection of documents from the Office of the Prime Minister, Count István Tisza, for 1914-18. The material was copied from the originals, which were destroyed during World War II, and is cataloged as part of the Tisza Collection under the title, *Abschriften aus den Staatsarchiven des Kön. ungarischen Ministerpräsidenten, 1914-1918.* Also noteworthy are the holdings of departmental and ministerial bulletins and gazettes, and the substantial collection of official statistical publications.

An important asset to research on World War I and Hungary is the Institution's unusually good collection of Hungarian newspapers of this period, for example, *Pester Lloyd* (1914-19), *Pesti Hírlap* (1913-19), *Magyarország* (1914-19), *Népszava* (1906-21), *Pesti Napló* (1914-19), *Fővárosi Közlöny* (1913-28), *Az Est* (1914-19), *Budapesti Közlöny* (1916-27), and *Neues Pester Journal* (1914-19). There is also an extremely good collection of monographic and documentary studies in Hungarian and Western languages. Austrian government statements on Austro-Hungarian relations during the First World War, such as the 7-volume *Österreich-Ungarns letzter Krieg, 1914-1918. Herausgegeben vom Österreichischen Bundesministerium für Heerswesen und vom Kriegsarchiv.* (Vienna, 1931-38); the two-volume documentary *Károly visszatérési kisérletei* (Budapest, 1921) representing Karl I's relations with Hungary are also important sources. A recent study by the Hungarian scholar, Gyula Tokody is *Ausztria-Magyarország a pángermán szövetség (Alldeutscher Verband) világuralmi terveiben, 1890–1918* (Budapest, 1963).

The Institution possesses a collection of miscellaneous manuscripts from the Royal Hungarian Ministry of Foreign Affairs. The set covers various events in Hungary from about 1915-20 including the resignation of Károlyi's government; protocols of the council of Peidl's ministry; military reports on conditions in the Army; revolutionary propaganda in the Army from 1916 through 1918; the return of war prisoners; various official plans and measures taken against the Bolshevik movement, 1916-18; documents relating to minorities, especially the Southern Slavs; and documents relating to land reform, 1918-20.

Other sources for this period are extensive holdings of memoirs and similar writings of the leading political figures.

THE HUNGARIAN SOVIET REPUBLIC.   Béla Kun's regime was the first to establish a revolutionary beachhead of Communism outside Russia. Documentation at Hoover on this event can be considered unique, including approximately 450 of the 680 leaflets published by the government, a complete file of the Republic's law gazette, *Tanácsköztársaság,* and the government's official organ, *Népszava,* as well as 11 other newspapers and numerous journal titles of that period.

This material is supplemented by such official publications as the Socialist-Communist Party's 32 issues of *Kommunista Könyvtár;* the 59-volume collection of the People's Commissariat of Education *(A Közoktatásügyi Népbiztosság) Press,* and its *Veröffentlichungen* in 20 volumes. The Institution possesses the original telegrams (347 pages) sent by the government of the Hungarian Soviet Republic to the *Leipziger Volkszeitung* for the period April-August 1919, reporting on the situation in the new regime. The seven-volume collection of Communist propaganda flyers and flyers published by the Romanian occupation forces after the fall of the Hungarian Soviet Republic are also noteworthy. In addition to some 40 volumes of Béla Kun's work, published both during and after the revolutionary period, the Institution has a rich collection of memoirs and recollections of the leading figures of the Hungarian Communist Party of that period and of other officials of the Soviet Republic.

THE INTERWAR PERIOD.   Although documentation on the interwar period does not quite come up to the excellent coverage for the World War I period, the holdings are still of research value. Governmental laws, statutes, etc., are well covered in *Magyar Törvénytár,* and stenographic records and documents of the Parliament are covered for the years 1927-47; holdings on the National Assembly, which replaced the Parliament during 1920-26, are represented for the period of its duration.

Newspaper coverage of these years is through such papers as *Pester Lloyd* (1920-21; 1931-39), *Pesti Hírlap* (1919-38), *Magyarország* (1920-39), *Pesti Napló* (1920-26), *Az Est* (1920-36), *Nemzeti Ujság* (1919-36), *Magyar Front* (1932-39), *Népszava* (1939), and *Sonntagsblatt* (1934-38; in 1936 it became *Neues Sonntagsblatt*). Journal holdings for the interwar period are rather weak. There are over 300 journal titles in the catalog for the period 1914-27; however, most consist of very incomplete sets, often (about 10-30%) only one or two numbers.

Thus, standard official publications and newspapers have good coverage for the interwar period, but holdings of contemporary scholarly works and monographs are rather poorly represented. However, the Institution has a rather large and unique collection of material published on Hungary in Western languages.

WORLD WAR II.   The Second World War is rather poorly covered for both official and scholarly contemporary publications. Best represented are newspapers and journals published during this time. Journals with the most complete coverage are: *Láthatár; Kisebbségi Kultúrszemle* (1937-44, monthly), *Külügyi Szemle, Külpolitika* (1939-44, bimonthly), and *Magyar Szemle* (1940-43, monthly). Among newspapers, the best holdings are *Pester Lloyd* (1939-44), *Pesti Hírlap* (1939-41), *Magyar Front* (1939-41), *Deutscher Volksbote* (1939-42), *Népszava* (1939-42), and *Magyarország* (1939-44).

These holdings are supplemented by a voluminous collection of postwar publications of memoirs, collections of documents, and scholarly monographs sponsored predominantly by the Hungarian Communist Party.

POST-WORLD WAR II PERIOD.   The postwar collection can be evaluated as a good to strong research collection on all historical, political, governmental, and related subjects. The period from 1960-70 is represented most comprehensively; 1945 to 1949 has the weakest representation, though it is still good enough to enable research.

BASIC OFFICIAL SOURCES.   The basic source for the promulgation of acts passed by the government was *Magyar Törvénytár,* which Hoover has complete for 1945-48. For the post-1948 period, there was a new gazette, *Magyar Közlöny.* These basic sources are supplemented by a number of cumulative collections such as the four-volume set, covering 1945-58, *Hatályos jogszabályok gyüjteménye* (1945-60). Besides this type of collective set, the Institution also possesses individual laws as they were published, many of them in English translation. National Assembly decisions, edicts, and decisions of the Presidium, etc., for the years 1945-48 are also contained in a rare four-volume collection, *Hatályos jogszabályok gyüjteménye 1945-1948. Készült a Magyar Forradalmi Munkás Paraszt Kormány 2011/1959 (LLL.18) sz. határozata alapján,* compiled by Ferenc Nezvál, Géza Szénási, and Tivadar Gál (Budapest, 1960).

After 1948, the directives of the Party are the factual source for laws. For 1956-62 the Party's publication, *Magyar Szocialista Munkáspárt határozatai és dokumentumai* (Budapest, 1962) acts as such. Further, decrees appear in such official Party monthlies as *Pártélet* (1956-70); and

Társadalmi Szemle (1957-1970); and the daily, *Népszabadság* (1952-70), which are all in the collection for the years indicated.

SELECTED CHRONOLOGICAL PERIODS AND SUBJECTS 1945-1948.   In addition to the mentioned holdings of governmental acts of this period, other documentary material in the Institution is best represented by the excellent collection of newspapers, particularly *Magyar Nemzet* (1946-49), the official organ of the Patriotic People's Front, geared to the noncommunist masses; *Szabad Szó* (1946-49) of the National Peasants' Party, *Kis Újság* (1946-49) of the Small-holder's Party; and *Szabad Nép* (1947-50) of the Hungarian Worker's Party.

THE HUNGARIAN COMMUNIST PARTY.   The Institution has large holdings of docu-mentary materials dealing with the Hungarian Communist Party in the postwar period. Among these are the published stenographic records of all Party congresses, except for the second, held in 1951. These are supplemented by the holdings of Party decrees in one form or other, published speeches, and works of all the leading Party members, and almost complete sets of official Party press publications. These are further supplemented by all post-1956 Party documentary publica-tions relating to the various political developments. Similar holdings of publications for the 1945-55 period are less complete.

THE HUNGARIAN REVOLUTION OF 1956.   Hoover has all postrevolutionary docu-mentary publications on the Hungarian Revolution published in Hungary or other countries. Con-temporary primary sources include a collection of over 400 items of original proclamations and Party programs, special issues of Party and other newspapers published during the days of the revolution, various anti-Party leaflets, etc. Among these sources are the ''First Declaration'' of the Revolutionary government; a document on the new National government listing all its repre-sentatives by name and position; orders of the Soviet military forces (after the Soviet interven-tion), for surrender of arms, work orders, curfew, etc.; numerous leaflets published by youth organizations in support of Imre Nagy; various mimeographed collections of demands, and resolu-tions of various revolutionary groups, etc.

Also included in this collection are the majority of Hungarian newspapers published during the period between October 29 and November 3.

Of special research value for the immediate postwar years as well as the interwar years are the archives of Rusztem Vámbéry, a lawyer and well-known left-wing politician of the interwar period. From 1925 to 1938 he was Vice Chairman of the Radical ''Kossuth Party.'' His importance also lay in the fact that he defended Mátyás Rákosi, the head of the Hungarian Communist Party during the interwar and post-World War II periods until 1954. After the Second World War, Vámbéry was Hungarian ambassador to the United States until 1948. The archives include his diaries, memoirs, drafts of his books and articles, letters to and from friends, and other material.

Romania

The Romanian Collection, beginning with the Balkan wars, consists of approximately 5,000 volumes, 230 journal titles, and 34 newspaper titles. The subjects that have developed research potential are treated below.

The first of these covers the period of the Balkan wars and World War I (1912-18), the backbone of the collection being the stenographic records of the House of Representatives (Adunarea Deputaţilor) for 1911-26 and of the Senate (Senatul) for 1913-26, along with a col-lection of newspapers of which the most important is *Adevărul,* supplemented by *Dimineaţa* and *Universul.* In addition there are the *Siebenbürgisch-Deutsches Tagblatt* for 1915-18, the official organ of the German Party in Romania; *L'Indépendance Roumaine* for 1914-21, official organ of the Liberal Party; and *Bukarester Tageblatt,* official organ of the German minority. Other newspapers in the collection, in varying degrees of completeness covering approximately 1914-18, are *La politique, Gazeta Bucureştilor, Gazeta Transilvaniei,* and *Rumänischer Lloyd.*

Substantial holdings of publications by individual government departments, especially for 1908-18, are an additional source of documentation and, as a rule, contain regulations issued by the various ministries. The best holdings of these publications are from the Ministry of Foreign Affairs (Ministerul Afacerilor Străine), the Ministry of Finance (Ministerul Financelor), the Bureau of Statistics (Biroul Statistic), the Ministry of Justice (Ministerul de Justiţiei), and the Ministry of Agriculture (Ministerul Agriculturii şi Domeniilor). Further, the collection contains substantial holdings of statistical publications of which the basic source is *Anuarul Statistic al Româ-niei* (for 1912-26). This is supported by an extensive volume of individual statistical publications on various subjects put out by many ministries and governmental agencies.

Both the Balkan wars and World War I are documented in a number of official and semi-official publications. For example, the involvement of Romania in the Balkan wars is documented in a publication of the Ministry of Foreign Affairs, *Documents diplomatiques. Les evénements de la péninsule Balkanique. L'action de la Roumanie, Sept. 1912-Août 1913* (Bucharest, 1913). Of the many documentary holdings on World War I, we cite the collection on Russia's involvement with Romania, *Tsarskaia Rossiia v mirovoĭ voĭne* (Leningrad, 1925).

Unique documentation on the war is provided by the Institution's outstanding collection on the Paris Peace Conference. Apart from official publications of the Conference, the Institution has extremely good holdings of materials distributed by the Romanian delegation there.

Coverage of the interwar period is voluminous, but most events are covered by secondary sources, thus few topics of this period have true research potential. The best coverage by primary official publications, as well as by individual scholarly documentary publications, is for the years 1919-26, after which coverage becomes haphazard. The best covered individual subjects are the Hungarian-Romanian hostilities of 1919 and the ensuing diplomatic relations involving Transylvania; major political parties; the economic development of Romania (an unusually good collection); and the fascist Legionar (Iron Guard) movement. The very valuable collection of contemporary propaganda leaflets published by the Legionar movement is probably the only collection of its kind in the United States.

For the post-World War II period, the strongest holdings are those of the Romanian Worker's (Communist) Party, which include almost complete records of Party Congresses from 1948, some of which are in translations into English or one of the Slavic languages. Most published decisions of the Party's Central Committee are represented in individual publications in Romanian and in English, as well as in collective volumes such as *Rezoluţii ş hotárîri ale Comitetului Central al PMR,* 2 v. (Bucharest, 1955), statutes of the Party, such as *Statul Partidului Muncitoresc Romîn* (Bucharest, 1960), and others. The holdings include Party publications on various aspects of the State, such as economic or agricultural problems, and the pre-1945 history of the Party.

The holdings also contain massive collections of published speeches and writings of all the postwar leaders of the Party. Finally, of the Party's press organs, the Institution holds the monthly *Lupta de Clasă* (1955-) and the daily *Scînteia* (1955-), as well as all the leading central newspapers (basically as of 1962) and scholarly historical journals.

Karol Maichel
Library Development Institute
Palo Alto, Ca.,
formerly of the
Hoover Institution

University of Illinois

General Information

SLAVIC AND EAST European library collections of the University of Illinois at Urbana-Champaign have grown to more than 500,000 volumes as a result of intensive efforts which began in 1958. The strength of these collections is now approximately in line with the Library's total holdings of more than 5 million volumes, first in size among state university libraries and third among all university libraries. Use of these resources was facilitated greatly by the opening in 1970 of a Slavic and East European reading room in the main library. This room is dedicated to Doris Duke in recognition of her generous support of Russian and East European studies at Illinois. It has 30 reading stations and a collection of more than 7,000 volumes, including encyclopedias, bibliographies, biographic and language dictionaries, archival guides, serial indexes and other basic reference sources for each country, and current issues of about 460 periodicals and 40 newspapers concerning the area.

A special feature of the Doris Duke Room is its immediate proximity to the staff and facilities of the Slavic and East European Division. This permits the seven professional bibliographers and catalogers of the Division to provide reference service and bibliographic help to users from 8 a.m. to 5 p.m. on weekdays. The reading room is open to the public 68 hours each week, including evening and weekend hours when classes are in session, and 45 hours per week between sessions. The room has a large microform collection, several microfilm and microfiche readers, and a listening station for foreign-language tape recordings.

Except for East European legal materials housed in the Law Library, all major collections pertaining to the area are in the general library stacks. All publications, including law, are recorded in the Library's main card catalog and public shelflist. In addition, the Slavic and East European Division maintains a shelflist for all publications in the area languages, and order files which can be used to locate titles received but not yet cataloged. Although nearly all of the East European serials are fully cataloged, more than 90 percent of the extensive Illinois holdings of older titles are not recorded in the third edition of the *Union List of Serials* because they were cataloged after the closing date for inclusion in that list. The holdings of retrospective Cyrillic monographs are also not represented in any published catalog.

Specific questions about the East European collections may be sent to the Special Languages Department, Room 225, University of Illinois Library at Urbana-Champaign, Urbana, Illinois 61801. Interlibrary loan requests should be sent on standard ALA forms to: Interlibrary Lending Division, Circulation Department, and requests for photoduplication to Photographic Services. The Library lends out-of-print books (except for rare books and reference books), volumes of monographic series, and positive microfilms. Photocopies usually are provided in lieu of periodical loans. To help visiting scholars use the Slavic and East European research resources, the University's Russian and East European Center has established a number of Summer Research Associateships. Information about this program may be obtained from the Research Director, Russian and East European Center, 1208 West California Street, Urbana, Illinois 61801.

At the end of the 1950s Western-language collections concerning East European (especially Balkan) history were good, but the major holdings in the area languages consisted of a few dozen historical, philological, and statistical sets and serials acquired during the 1920s and 1930s, mainly from Yugoslavia, Romania, Hungary, and Czechoslovakia.

Establishment of a Russian and East European Center at Illinois led in 1959-60 to the hiring of special library staff and the organization of a Slavic acquisition division for the purpose of bringing Slavic resources up to the level of the Library's long-established collections. Although the main priority was to develop comprehensive research collections on Russia and the Soviet Union (by 1972 the Russian and Soviet collections had grown to 200,000 volumes), Eastern Europe was not neglected.

For East Central and Southeastern Europe the initial emphasis was to acquire basic reference and serial publications, primarily concerning the history, literature, and culture of the Slavic countries. In 1960 the Library made the first of many large retrospective purchases, which included numerous complete runs of serials and monumental sets from Czechoslovakia, Yugoslavia, and Bulgaria. In the early 1960s members of the Library staff made acquisition trips to Yugoslavia, Czechoslovakia, Poland, and Bulgaria, and exchanges with Eastern European libraries were expanded. By 1964 serial subscriptions from Eastern Europe included nearly all substantial publications in the social sciences and humanities. Purchase of current monographs increased steadily, and in 1969 blanket orders were started for books from Poland, Czechoslovakia, Bulgaria, Hungary, Romania, and Albania to balance receipts from those countries with increased acquisitions from Yugoslavia under the PL-480 Program. Illinois is a participant in the PL-480 Program for Poland.

Beginning in 1967 the purchase of several large retrospective Romanian and Hungarian historical and legal collections was initiated and a collection of about 3,000 Slovak books published mainly between the First and Second World Wars, was acquired.

The following table indicates the size on June 30, 1972, of the major Illinois collections concerning individual countries of East Central and Southeastern Europe. The number of volumes added yearly to the collections is an average based on cataloging statistics for five years (1968-72) and includes only volumes in the area languages. Retrospective publications have constituted a major part of the annual increments. No statistics are available for Albanian, Modern Greek, and East German publications. Thus far the Library has not carried on extensive programs for these areas.

Country	Total volumes	Monograph titles	Serial titles	Volumes added annually
Bulgaria	6,200	2,300	300	600
Czechoslovakia	31,800	10,500	1,220	2,400
Hungary	15,000	4,700	425	1,400
Poland	23,700	9,200	950	1,700
Romania	12,000	3,600	315	1,000
Yugoslavia	24,200	11,000	1,240	2,730
TOTALS	112,900	41,300	4,450	9,830

The collections concerning Czechoslovakia and Romania are the subject of separate essays. Of nearly equal importance are the holdings on Yugoslavia, and there are significant areas of strength in the Hungarian, Bulgarian, and Polish collections. Some subjects extensively covered for each country are 19th-century history and politics, the nationality question, archeology, current and retrospective statistical publications, reference works, and law. Holdings on the Slavic languages and literatures are strong. All subject areas in the social sciences and humanities are well covered by current serial subscriptions and blanket orders for monographs. The Library has no manuscript collections concerning the area. Retrospective newspaper holdings either in the original or on microfilm are weak, and there are gaps in the coverage of monographs published from approximately 1948 to 1960, particularly in economics and politics. Books from émigré publishers and on East European peoples abroad are not well represented.

Laurence H. Miller
University of Illinois
at Urbana-Champaign

Czechoslovakia

CZECH AND SLOVAK collections of the University of Illinois Library numbered 31,800 volumes on June 30, 1972, and an average of 2,400 volumes in Czech and Slovak, mostly retrospective acquisitions, have been added yearly through cataloging for the past five years. This collection is substantially larger than the Yugoslav and Polish collections which are next largest for the area with 24,000 volumes each, and the Czechoslovak holdings are considerably stronger in pre-1950 serials and monographs. Until 1960 most Czech and Slovak holdings concerned science and technology. The phenomenal growth which began in 1960 was chiefly the result of efforts by Israel Perlstein, who for many years was the major supplier of Czech and Slovak publications to American research libraries. Hundreds of retrospective serial titles were acquired, most of them complete runs, at very reasonable cost. Standard reference works, historical sources, and older sets in language, literature, law, and history were also purchased steadily and in great quantity from Mr. Perlstein over a period of more than 10 years.

The major distinction of the collection is the scope and completeness of its serial files. The University of Illinois holdings are not represented in the *Union List of Serials,* and many of the titles are not in that catalog at all, or are listed with fragmentary holdings and at only one or two locations. The present description of the collection lists a number of the more than 1,200 serials at Illinois, not only to indicate the range of the holdings, but possibly also to aid scholars who may be searching for specific older journals. Titles which began publication after 1945 are not mentioned, since these are much more widely available in American libraries.

The principal weaknesses of the collection are the lack of back files of daily newspapers and significant gaps in the coverage of monographs published from about 1950 to the mid 1960s. Acquisition of current monographs increased from 1960 on, but blanket order coverage of books from Czechoslovakia began only in 1969. Periodical holdings from the same period are much stronger, but with some missing volumes. The Library formerly held substantial collections of Czech and Slovak newspapers published in the United States, but these were sent many years ago to the Center for Research Libraries in Chicago. Émigré imprints are not extensively represented yet, and there are few books on the history of Czechs and Slovaks in America. Until about 1968 Slovak holdings were disproportionately weak in comparison to the Czech resources, but at that time Illinois strengthened its Slovak collections by selecting and acquiring about 3,000 Slovak books published before 1948 in literature, education, art, philosophy, history, religion, and other aspects of Slovak culture.

The Library's Slavic and East European Division is responsible for the selection, acquisition, and cataloging of Czech and Slovak publications, and the Division's librarians provide reference service in the adjacent Slavic and East European reading room. The reference section on Czechoslovakia has a selection of about 300 volumes of bibliographies, dictionaries, seven encyclopedias (including the Masaryk and Otto encyclopedias, *Československá vlastivěda,* and *Slovenský naučný slovník*), handbooks, and biographical reference works. Except for law, music, and a special collection of Czechoslovak fine printing, all major collections on Czechoslovakia are housed in the main library stacks. Several early Czech Bibles (most notably the six-volume Kralice Bible) and other early Czech printings, as well as certain costly series of facsimile reprints, are in the Library's Rare Book Room.

The Slavic and East European Division has completed the checking of most sections of Horecky's bibliographies on *East Central Europe* and *Southeastern Europe* against the Library's holdings for selection purposes and in order to evaluate the collections. The rather extensive section on Czechoslovak history in *East Central Europe* seems to provide a good checklist, and the Illinois history collection with more than 6,000 volumes on the area has between 85 and 90 percent of the titles. Holdings on the state and law, literature, and language appear equally strong. The few missing titles are most often recent publications. Percentages of titles held in subjects such as economics, sociology, and demography are of course lower, because of their emphasis on contemporary developments.

Among the important scholarly journals, Illinois has the *Časopis* of the National Museum in Prague, the *Sborník* and *Časopis* of the Slovak National Museum, and the other major museum journals from Olomouc and Brno, as well as those from Plzeň, Prostějov, and others. Nearly all of the humanities and social science journals of the major learned societies are available. The periodicals and monographic series of the Czech Academy pertaining to history, philology, and the humanities are mostly complete, as are the similar publications of the universities of Prague, Brno, and Bratislava.

In history and archeology all of the major journals appear to be held, mostly in unbroken runs, and including the titles in military history, the history of agriculture, numismatics, genealogy, archival science, and the German-language periodicals concerning Silesia, Bohemia, and Moravia. The major journals in anthropology and ethnography such as *Český lid, Anthropologie,* and *Národopisný sborník* are in the collection, and there is a wealth of serials on regional studies, local history, and minorities. Some of these are *Bezděz, Brdský kraj, Černá země, Českolužický věstník, Jihočeský kraj, Jihočeský přehled, Kalendář česko-židovsky* (1907-38), *Kutnohorské příspěvky k dějinám vzdělanosti české, Kultúra* (Trnava), *Národnostní obzor, Naše menšiny, Od Ještěda k Troskám, Plzeňsko, Pod Zelenou Horou, Podkarpatoruská revue, Slánský obzor,* and *Věstník Poděbradska.* The study of Slovak history is greatly facilitated by the very good Illinois holdings in Hungarian history and law and the exhaustive collection of Hungarian parliamentary records. The history resources are also enhanced, of course, by extensive collections of basic sources for Austrian history.

Collections of laws and official gazettes for Bohemia, Moravia, and the Czechoslovak Republic are mostly complete and comprise more than 600 volumes. In addition, there are complete sets of the various series of decisions and other publications of the Supreme Courts. Holdings of the parliamentary records for the Bohemian and Moravian Diets and the Czechoslovak Assembly are not as complete. There is a large number of monographs on Czechoslovak law published from 1919 through 1949, including the monographic series *Sbírka spisů právnických a národohospodářských* (Brno) and other similar collections. Coverage from 1950 to 1968 is not good as yet. Among the substantial journal runs in law are *Časopis pro právní a státní vědu, Právní prakse,* and *Právník.* One of the interesting features of the historical and legal collections is a group of about 580 letters patent pertaining to Bohemia, issued by the Habsburg kings from 1583 to 1848. Most are from the 18th century. Many of the letters are in both Czech and German versions or in Czech and German in parallel columns. This collection is in the Rare Book Room, and individual items can be located by using the Library's marked copy of the published guide to the letters patent collection of the State Central Archive in Prague: *Patenty; katalog sbírky patentů Státního ústředního archiva v Praze,* Prague, 1956 *(Inventáře a katalogy, 2).* Except for the post-1948 period, which is still weak, the history collections cover most periods with about equal strength. The Hussite movement, the 19th century, and the period 1918-39 are probably covered best. The Comenius, Dobrovský, Masaryk, and Beneš collections are all sizable but not comprehensive. There are some 19th-century political weeklies, but holdings are mostly incomplete and not yet filled in with microfilm. The collections of political, economic, and social science periodicals for the Czechoslovak Republic are very rich.

Holdings of older journals in fields other than the political and social sciences are also quite extensive. Some of the files in art and architecture are *Architektonický obzor, Dilo, Drobné umění, Umělecký list, Umělecký měsíčník, Veraikon, Volné směry,* and *Život.* The music journals include *Dalibor, Hudební revue, Slavoj,* and *Tempo.* In theater there are about a dozen older titles, including *Česká thalia, Československé divadlo, Divadelní kalendář,* and *Naše divadlo.* Among the surprisingly large number of complete or long runs of religious journals are *Časopis pro katolické duchowenstwo* (1829-51), *Časopis katolického duchovenstva* (1863-1948), *Evanjelický cirkevník, Hus, Na hlubinu, Náboženská revue, Služba, Věstník Jednot duchovenstva,* and *Viera i veda.* Philosophical periodicals include *Česká mysl, Filosofická revue, Filosofie,* and *Ruch filosofický.*

Substantial and mostly complete files of Slovak titles include *Mladé Slovensko, Náš ľud Naše Slovensko, Nový svet, Prúdy, Slovenské pohľady, Slovensko, Slovenskou otčinou, Slovenský ľud,* and *Živena.* Among the large numbers of general Czech journals are *Alétheia, Athenaeum, Česká revue, Čin, Fronta, Hlídka, Květy, Meditace, Modrá revue, Moravsko-Slezská revue, Národní myšlenka, Naše doba, Naše věda, Nové Čechy, Osvěta, Pokroková revue, Pražská lidová revue, Přehled, Přítomnost, Rozhledy, Rozmach, Slovan* (Havlíček), and *Svoboda* (Prague).

The literature collections are strong in standard collected editions, reference works, and critical and biographical works, with about 5,000 volumes in Czech and 1,500 in Slovak literature. In addition to the standard scholarly journals in literature and philology, there is a very large collection of Czech literary periodicals, including *Akord, Archa, Besedy Času, Červen, Cesta, Dnešek, Kmen* (Šalda), *Kolo, Kritický měsíčník, Kvart, Listy pro umění a kritiku, Lumír, Maj, Moderní revue, Novina, Nový obzor, Pramen, Rozpravy Aventina, Šaldův zápisník, Sever a východ, Stopa, Topičův sborník, Vlast,* and *Vzlet.* Most of the Slovak literary journals have some years missing. Contemporary literature has been the latest to be developed, and there are still gaps for the post-1948 period.

Although it is not the only collection of this type in the United States, the jewel of the Illinois Czech and Slovak holdings is the I. Perlstein Collection of Czechoslovak Book Design. This includes about 750 selected volumes of limited, signed bibliophile editions of Czech literature, many in fine bindings, published mainly during the 1920s and 1930s, with numerous examples of earlier and later periods of the 20th-century renaissance of Czech fine printing. More than 90 percent of the books and all of the most outstanding specimens were acquired from Israel Perlstein. The major Czech bibliophile journals and a few pertinent bibliographies are shelved with the Perlstein collection, which is housed in a room adjacent to the Slavic and East European Division. There is a separate card catalog which indexes illustrators, designers, and binders, as well as authors, titles, and subjects.

Two of the foremost leaders in the development of modern Czech book design, Karel Dyrynk, Director of the Státní tiskárna, and Method Kaláb, Director of the Průmyslová tiskárna, are each represented by more than 60 books. Many books from the foremost private and provincial presses are also in the collection. From the early period there are several examples of the work of Vojtěch Preissig, V. H. Brunner, Slavoboj Tusar, and others. Among the artists and designers most frequently found are Cyril Bouda (50 titles), Jan Konůpek (75), and Karel Svolinský (about 80 titles). Most notable among the many outstanding Svolinský works is his elephant folio edition of Mácha's

Maj (1925), printed in 35 copies of which Illinois has copy number one. There are about 30 books printed by Jaroslav Picka and from his library, including several printed as unique copies, and Picka's copy of the monumental bibliophile edition of the *New Testament* (1939), based on the Kralice Bible. Other designers and illustrators with from 10 to 30 specimens are Jaroslav Benda, František Bílek, Adolf Kašpar, Svatopluk Klír, František Kobliha, Václav Mašek, Oldřich Menhart, Max Švabinský, and Josef Váchal. Among the several strange Váchal productions, the largest and most striking is his *D'ablova zahrádka aneb přírodopis strašidel*. Although acquisitions continue to be made for the Perlstein Collection, they are highly selective, since the collection is intended to be representative of the finest achievements in the area.

Laurence H. Miller
University of Illinois
at Urbana-Champaign

Romania

THE BULK OF the collection is located in the main University Library building and is organized according to the Dewey Classification System. The Library is open Monday through Friday from 8 a.m. to 10 p.m., Saturday 8 a.m. to 5 p.m., and Sunday 2 p.m. to 11 p.m. Scholars may also use the Slavic and East European Reading Room (225 Library) where there is a small number of reference and bibliographic works on Romania. This room is open Monday through Thursday from 8 a.m. to 5 p.m. and 7 p.m. to 10 p.m., Friday from 8 a.m. to 5 p.m., Saturday from 9 a.m. to 12 noon and 1 p.m. to 5 p.m., Sunday from 2 p.m. to 5 p.m. It offers readers the particular advantage of being adjacent to the acquisitions and cataloging departments for East European materials where librarians will assist in locating both cataloged and uncataloged materials. An important part of the law collection is housed in the Law School Library, which is open Monday through Thursday from 7:30 a.m. to midnight, Friday and Saturday from 7:30 a.m. to 10 p.m., and Sunday from 10:00 a.m. to midnight.

Information about the Romanian holdings may be obtained from Professor Laurence H. Miller, Special Languages Department, 225 Library, University of Illinois, Urbana, Illinois 61801.

Romanian items may be located in the general University Library catalog (subject, author, and title), the shelflist, and the serial catalog. A special card file of books on order and of books not yet cataloged is kept in the Slavic and East European Reading Room.

Photocopying services are available in the basement of the Main Library. There are also coin-operated copying machines in the stack area and in the undergraduate library adjacent to the main building.

Books and periodicals may be borrowed through interlibrary loan or in person by scholars who have obtained visitors privileges from the reference desk in the Main Library Reading Room.

The systematic formation of an East European collection at the University of Illinois Library is of relatively recent origin, following the establishment of the Russian and East European Center in 1960. During the period 1962 to 1972 the Slavic holdings were expanded from 37,023 fully cataloged volumes to 240,000, of which approximately 148,000 are Russian. When non-Slavic items are added, the total East European collection numbers about 300,000 volumes. The acquisition of Romanian materials on a systematic basis was begun in 1967. The collection now contains approximately 12,000 items, and the annual intake is about 700 volumes. Since 1970 the Library has had a blanket order for works of scholarly value in the humanities and social sciences and acquires about 200 volumes a year in this way. Perhaps 100 similar items are received each year through exchanges. An exchange with the Library of the Romanian Academy in Bucharest dates from the 1920s. The program has now been expanded to include the Central State Library in Bucharest, the Library of the Romanian Academy in Cluj, the University of Cluj Library, and the Brukenthal Museum in Sibiu.

The Main Features of the Collection

BIBLIOGRAPHIES AND REFERENCE AIDS.   The Library possesses a basic collection of reference works, including bibliographies such as Ioan Bianu and Nerva Hodoș, *Bibliografia românească veche 1508-1830,* 3 v. (Bucharest, 1903-12) and the current bibliographic publications from Romania, including *Bibliografia Republicii Socialiste România, cărți, albume, hărți, note muzicale* (since 1956); encyclopedias such as Cornelius Diaconovich (ed.), *Enciclopedia Română,* 3 v. (Sibiu, 1898-1904) and *Enciclopedia României,* 4 v. (Bucharest, 1936-43); and numerous general statistical works, most of which deal with the period since 1945. The collection is sufficiently large and comprehensive to permit scholarly orientation in almost every discipline of the humanities and social sciences.

History

The main strength of the Library's collection is in history. Of the major general histories of the Romanians, it has Alexandru Xenopol's *Istoria Românilor din Dacia Traiană,* 3d ed., 14 v. (Bucharest 1925-30) and the current multivolume *Istoria României,* 4 v. (Bucharest, 1960-). Older historiography is well represented by, among others, the works of Grigore Ureche, Miron Costin, and Dimitrie Cantemir and numerous editions of chronicles and other historical works published before the middle of the 19th century. There are many works by the most important modern historians: Nicolae Iorga, Ioan Bogdan, Dimitrie Onciul, and Vasile Pârvan, to name but a few.

The periodical collection contains a number of important items, among them: Academia Română, *Bulletin de la section historique,* v. 1-27 (Bucharest, 1913-46); Academia Română, *Memoriile Secțiunii Istorice,* 3d series, v. 1-18 (Bucharest, 1923-37); *Boabe de Grâu,* v. 1-5 (Bucharest, 1930-34); *Anuarul Institutului de Istorie Națională,* v. 1-10 (Cluj, 1921-45) and its successor, *Anuarul Institutului de Istorie din Cluj,* v. 1-(Cluj, 1958-); *Revue Roumaine d'Histoire,* v. 1- (Bucharest, 1962-); *Studii. Revistă de Istorie,* v. 8- (Bucharest, 1955-); *Arhiva Românească,* v. 3-7, 10 (Iași, 1939-46); *Revista Istorică Română,* v. 1-3, 8-13 (Bucharest, 1931-43); and *Studia Universitatis Babeș-Bolyai din Cluj,* History Series, v. 1- (Cluj, 1958-). There are also serial publications, including: *Studii și materiale de istorie medie,* v. 1-5 (Bucharest, 1956-62); *Studii și materiale de istorie modernă,* v. 1-3 (Bucharest, 1957-63); and *Studii și materiale de istorie contemporană,* v. 2-3 (Bucharest, 1962-63).

As for separate periods, prehistory and the Greek and Roman eras are represented by older monographs by Pârvan and others and by volumes in the current series published by the Institute of Archaeology in Bucharest, *Biblioteca de arheologie,* v. 1, 4-11, 14-16 (Bucharest, 1957-). Periodicals and serials are represented by such works as: *Dacia,* old series, v. 1-10 (Bucharest, 1924-44) and new series, v. 12-14 (Bucharest 1968-70); *Materiale și cercetări arheologice,* v. 2-8 (Bucharest, 1956-62); and *Studii și cercetări de istorie veche,* v. 17- (Bucharest, 1966-). There are numerous items on the problem of the origins of the Romanian people, including Alexandru Philippide's *Originea Românilor,* 2 v. (Iași, 1925-28) and Gheorghe Popa-Lisseanu's *Izvoarele istoriei Românilor,* 15 v. (Bucharest, 1934-39), as well as scholarly and polemical works on the subject by Iorga, Xenopol, Gheorghe Brătianu, and P. P. Panaitescu, to mention only a few.

For the so-called medieval period (about 1200 to 1821) there are a few basic collections of sources: Eudoxiu de Hurmuzaki, *Documente privitoare la istoria Românilor,* v. 1-19 + 9 v.

supplement (Bucharest, 1876-1938); *Documente privind istoria României,* series A. *Moldova,* 11 v. (Bucharest, 1951-57) and series B. *Ţara Românească,* 13 v. (Bucharest, 1951-60); Ioan Bogdan, *Documentele lui Ştefan cel Mare,* 2 v. (Bucharest, 1913); and Endre Veress, *Documente privitoare la istoria Ardealului, Moldovei şi Ţării-Româneşti,* 11 v. (Bucharest, 1929-39). Most of the monographs dealing with the period are recent publications, for example, the series published by the Institute of History in Bucharest, *Biblioteca de Istorie,* 30 v. (Bucharest, 1957-72), of which the library has a nearly complete collection.

The holdings are strongest for the modern period (1821-1944). There are major source collections dealing with the uprising of Tudor Vladimirescu of 1821, the revolution of 1848, the period of the union of Moldavia and Wallachia, and the reign of King Carol I, and there are numerous volumes of speeches and other writings of political leaders in the period 1866 to 1914, including: Lascăr Catargiu, Nicolae Filipescu, Vasile Lascăr, Titu Maiorescu, and Alexandru Marghiloman. The monographic literature is adequate and includes some important older works and most of the scholarly publications that have appeared in Romania in the last decade.

The period since 1944 is represented by only a few monographs and collections of sources, mainly the speeches and writings of Communist Party leaders. The Library also has *Lupta de clasă,* v. 35- (1955-).

Of the collections dealing with the provinces that were joined to the Kingdom of Romania after World War I, the one concerning Transylvania is the most comprehensive. There are numerous general histories in Hungarian, German, and Latin as well as Romanian from Bethlen, Benkő, Haner, Felmer, Kőváry, and Bariţiu to modern syntheses like *Din istoria Transilvaniei,* 2 v. (Bucharest, 1960-61). There are also numerous works of description and travel, especially for the 19th century, an excellent collection of multivolume monographs on local and county history in Hungarian, including, for example, Balázs Orbán, *A Székelyföld,* 6 v. (Pest, 1868-73), and important collections of sources, among them, Andrei Veress, *Fontes rerum Transilvanicarum,* 5 v. (Cluj, 1911-21) and Ioan Lupaş, *Documentele istoriei transilvane, 1599-1699* (Cluj, 1940). The collection on the Romanian national movement in Transylvania is comprehensive and includes many important monographs and collections of documents by, among others, Alexandru Papiu-Ilarian, Augustin Bunea, Silviu Dragomir, Ioan Lupaş, Ştefan Pascu, and Zoltán Tóth. Materials on the Saxons are limited but include a number of rare items published in the 19th century, for example, Johann Karl Schuller, *Umrisse und kritische Studien zur Geschichte von Siebenbürgen,* 2 v. (Hermannstadt, 1840-51), and Franz Zimmermann, *Urkundenbuch zur Geschichte der Deutschen in Siebenbürgen,* 3 v. (Hermannstadt, 1892-1902).

The collection of historical and general periodicals dealing with Transylvania is excellent. In Hungarian, there are *Erdélyi Múzeum,* first series, v. 1-9 (Kolozsvár, 1874-82), second series, v. 1-51 (Kolozsvár, 1884-1946); *Erdélyi Tudományos Intézet,* v. 1-3 (Kolozsvár, 1940-43); *Kolozsvári Szemle,* v. 1-3 (1942-44), and *Hitel,* v. 1-9 (Kolozsvár, 1936-44). Those relating primarily to the Saxons are: *Transilvania,* (1833-34, 1847, 1861-62); *Magazin für Geschichte, Literatur, und alle Denk- und Merkwürdigkeiten Siebenbürgens,* v. 1 (Kronstadt, 1844-45); *Archiv des Vereines für Siebenbürgische Landeskunde,* new series, v. 1-49 (Hermannstadt, 1853-1938); and *Korrespondenzblatt des Siebenbürgische Karpathenvereins,* v. 1-56 (Hermannstadt, 1881-1944). Those dealing primarily with the Romanians are: *Revue de Transylvanie,* v. 1-5 (Cluj, 1934-39) and many issues of *Transilvania* (Sibiu) from v. 23 (1892) to v. 75 (1944).

Law

The collection on Romanian law is large and comprehensive and numbers approximately 2,500 pieces. About 80 percent deal with the period between 1919 and 1939, 10 percent 1940-47, 5 percent before 1919, and 5 percent since 1947. The collection contains the principal collections of laws, regulations, decrees, and ministerial acts and is particularly strong in works on civil law and procedure; the organization and operation of the judiciary; bankruptcy and banking; commercial, land, and tax law. There are also some important periodicals such as: *Curierul judiciar,* v. 21-25, 28-41 (Bucharest, 1912-32); *Pandectele române* (Bucharest, 1922-32); and *Revista societăţilor şi a dreptului comercial,* v. 1-7 (Bucharest, 1924-30). The Library currently subscribes to *Revista română de drept, Revue roumaine des sciences sociales,* and *Studii şi cercetări juridice.*

Intellectual and Cultural Life

The collection is modest but contains sufficient standard works to permit a scholarly orientation. On art and architecture, besides albums of a number of major painters, there are monographs by Petru Comarnescu, Grigore Ionescu, Nicolae Iorga, George Oprescu, and Virgil Vătăşianu. The holdings on the history of education are small, but offer a general overview of the subject. Noteworthy are: V. A. Urechia, *Istoria şcoalelor de la 1800-1864,* 2 v. (Bucharest, 1892) and Nicolae Iorga, *Istoria învăţămîntului românesc* (Bucharest, 1928). There is a small collection of works on Romanian philosophy, and the two main periodicals, *Revista de filozofie* and *Revue roumaine des sciences sociales. Philosophie et logique,* are currently being received. Holdings on the history of the Romanian Orthodox Church include a number of monographs and, since 1967, runs of the principal church periodicals.

Language

The Library has a good collection of general descriptive works and grammars, by Kristian Sandfeld, Alf Lombard, Ovid Densuşianu, Sextil Puşcariu, Sever Pop, Iorgu Iordan, and Alexandru Rosetti, to mention but a few. The collection of linguistic atlases and dictionaries, many from the 19th century, is quite comprehensive. The collection of periodicals is strong and contains, for example: Timoteiu Cipariu (ed.), *Archivu pentru filologia şi istoria* (Blaj, 1867-71); *Columna lui Traian,* 4 v. (Bucharest, 1876-84); Leipzig University. *Jahresbericht des Instituts für Rumänische Sprache,* 29 v. (Leipzig, 1894-1921); University of Bucharest. *Bulletin linguistique,* v. 1-16 (1933-48); *Dacoromania,* v. 1-9 (1920-38); *Revue roumaine de linguistique,* v. 1- (Bucharest, 1956-); *Limba română,* v. 2- (Bucharest, 1953-); *Romanoslavica,* v. 1- (Bucharest, 1958-); *Studii şi cercetări lingvistice,* v. 6- (Bucharest, 1955-); *Cercetări de lingvistică,* v. 1- (Cluj, 1956-); and *Anuar de lingvistică şi istorie literară,* v. 7- (Iaşi, 1956-).

Literature

The collection contains a representative cross section of works of bibliography, history, and criticism. Besides the standard histories by Sextil Puşcariu and Nicolae Iorga, there are such specialized items as Titu Maiorescu, *Critice,* 3 v. (Bucharest, 1908-28); Eugen Lovinescu, *Critice,* 8 v. (Bucharest, 1921-23); and D. Popovici, *La littérature roumaine à l'époque des lumières,* (Sibiu, 1945), as well as an ample selection of critical studies published since 1960. There are works by and about all the major poets, prose writers, and critics of the 19th and 20th centuries, mostly in recent editions.

The Library has several important collections of documents, notably: I. E. Torouţiu and Gh. Cardaş, *Studii şi documente literare,* 13 v. (Bucharest, 1931-46), and, besides the general publications of the literary section of the Romanian Academy during the interwar period, a number of rare periodicals, including: Academia Română. *Bulletin de la section littéraire,* v. 1-3 (Bucharest, 1941-46); *Cercetări literare,* v. 1-5 (Bucharest, 1934-43); *Gând românesc,* v. 1-7 (Cluj,

1933-39); *Luceafărul,* v. 5-9 (Sibiu, 1906-10); and *Revista Fundaţiilor Regale,* v. 1-14 (Bucharest, 1934-47). There are also numerous volumes of *Convorbiri literare* and *Viaţa românească.* The Library currently receives all the important national and provincial scholarly journals and literary reviews.

The folk literature collection is small, but it does include a number of anthologies and critical studies published since 1960 and such important older items as: Moses Gaster, *Literatura populară română* (Bucharest, 1883); Nicolae Cartojan, *Cărţile populare în literatura românească,* 2 v. (Bucharest, 1929-39); Iuliu A. Zanne, *Proverbele românilor din România, Basarabia, Bucovina, Ungaria, Istria, şi Macedonia,* 10 v. (Bucharest, 1895-1903); and Simion Marian, *Sărbătorile la Români,* 3 v. (Bucharest, 1898-1901).

Keith Hitchins
University of Illinois
at Urbana-Champaign

Other Countries

Bulgaria

Of the 6,200 volumes in the Bulgarian collection, about 1,500 are in literature and 1,200 in history. Serials on language, literature, and folklore include *Bŭlgarska rech, Rodna rech, Iskra, Khiperion, Misŭl, Prosvieta,* and *Sbornik za narodni umotvoreniia i narodopis.* There are the bulletin series of the national societies (economic, geographic, historical, archeological) and the various *Godishnik* series of Sofia University. Historical serials are well represented, and the collection has several Bulgarian titles concerning Macedonia. Other Bulgarian journal titles held include *Bŭlgarska sbirka, Bŭlgarski pregled, Demokraticheski pregled, Ikonomicheska borba, Uchilishten pregled, Zaveti,* and *Zlatorog.*

Hungary

The major strength of the Hungarian collections is in history up to 1918. There are about 2,500 items on Hungarian law, and the Library has a complete collection of Hungarian parliamentary papers from 1790 to 1944. Examples of the extensive serial holdings include: on art, *Magyar Művészet, Művészet,* and *Magyar Iparművészet;* on language, *Magyar Nyelv, Magyar Népnyelv, Magyar Figyelő, Magyar Pedagógia, Magyar Pszichológiai Szemle, Magyar Szemle, Magyar Philologiai Közlöny, Irodalomtörténet, Irodalomtörténeti Közlemények,* and *Nyugat.* The major archeological titles are held along with *Genealogiai Füzetek, Magyar Gazdaságtörténelmi Szemle, Monumenta Hungariae historica, Numizmatikai Közlöny, Századok, Történeti Szemle, Turul,* and other periodicals in history and its auxiliary sciences.

Other Hungarian serial titles include *Jogállam, Kisebbségvédelem, Külügyi Szemle, Láthatár, Magyar Figyelő, Magyar Pedagógia, Magyar Pszichológiai Szemle, Magyar Szemle, Magyar Tudomány, Minerva,* and *Szocializmus.* Holdings of monographs in fields other than history and law are not outstanding, but efforts to build up the retrospective Hungarian language, literature, and social science collections are being made.

Poland

The Polish collections number about 23,700 volumes. Literature (about 4,600 volumes) and language are the subjects covered best. Reference and bibliographic resources are excellent. The

Polish history collection has about 3,400 volumes, but there are notable gaps in the coverage of older periodicals and monographs. There are sizable holdings in the social sciences, intellectual and cultural life, and law, but no subject is yet covered comprehensively. The collection includes many complete sets of yearbooks, transactions, monographic series, and other irregular serial publications from about 1950 to the present.

Among the substantially complete retrospective serial files are *Kwartalnik filozoficzny*, *Lamus*, *Marcholt*, *Neofilolog*, *Przegląd Geograficzny*, *Przegląd Kawaleryski*, *Przegląd Warszawski*, *Świat Słowiański*, and *Wiadomośći Numizmatyczno-Archeologiczne*. Serials with large, but incomplete, files include *Krytyka*, *Niepodległość*, *Pamiętnik Literacki*, *Przegląd Historyczny*, *Przegląd Powszechny*, *Przegląd Socjologiczny*, *Rocznik Krakowski*, and *Skamander* (with the missing issues on microfilm).

Yugoslavia

The Yugoslav collections are next in size to Czech and Slovak and include a wealth of retrospective serial publications in all fields. Among the titles in Croatian literature are *Dubrovnik*, *Iskra* (Zadar), *Književni jug*, *Književna republika*, *Književnik* (1864-66, 1928-39), *Slovinac*, *Savremenik*, and *Vienac*. Slovenian holdings are particularly strong, including museum, university, Slovenian Academy and Slovenska matica publications, *Razprave* (Znanstveno društvo v Ljubljani), *Čas*, *Časopis za zgodovino in narodopisje*, *Časopis za slovenski jezik, književnost i zgodovino*, *Dejanje*, *Dom in svet*, *Etnolog*, *Kres*, *Kronika slovenskih mest*, *Zvon*, *Ljubljanski zvon*, *Misel in delo*, *Narodna starine*, *Socialna misel*, *Sodobnost*, *Svoboda* (1929-36), *Zbornik za umetnostno zgodovino*, and many others.

Illinois has nearly all of the basic geographic, historical, and archeological periodicals from the Yugoslav lands. Serials from the major learned societies, universities, and academies are mostly complete, including Matica srpska publications, the historical and literary document series of the Yugoslav Academy and its *Djela, Ljetopis, Posebna djela*, and *Rad*, and the Serbian Academy *(Glas, Glasnik, Godišnjak, Posebna izdanja, Spomenik, Zbornik za istoriju, jezik i književnost*, and *Glasnik* (Srpsko učeno društvo). Among the serials in law are *Arhiv za pravne i društvene nauke*, *Mjesečnik* (Pravničko društvo, Zagreb), *Pravo* (Split), and *Zbornik znanstvenih razprav* (Ljubljana University Law School). Although religion has not been emphasized, the journal collection includes *Croatia sacra, Drobtince, Hriśćanski život, Katoliški obzornik*, and others.

Some of the other titles, mostly complete files, from the comprehensive periodical collections are *Bosanska vila, Brankovo kolo, Delo* (1894-1915), *Ekonomist* (Zagreb), *Ekonomska revija, Godišnjica Nikole Čupića, Hrvatska revija, Hrvatsko kolo, Javor, Jugoslavenski pomorac, Južnoslovenski filolog, Licejka, Makedonski pregled, Misao, Narodna odbrana, Nova Evropa, Otadžbina, Pregled, Srpski dijalektološki zbornik, Srpski etnografski zbornik, Srpski književni glasnik* (old and new series), *Starinar, Starine, Stožer, Stražlivo*, and *Život i rad*.

Other features of the collection are the nearly complete sets of laws and parliamentary papers from Croatia. Retrospective legal holdings are not as extensive as for Hungary, Romania, and Czechoslovakia, but the collections on contemporary Yugoslav law are much more comprehensive than for the other countries. Retrospective monographs on Yugoslav history and culture have been acquired quite actively for the past 10 years.

Laurence H. Miller
University of Illinois
at Urbana-Champaign

Indiana University

General Information

THE COLLECTIONS REFERRED to at Indiana University as the "Slavic Collection" actually comprise library materials relating to the Soviet Union and the countries of East Central, and Southeastern Europe.

The collections described below are the component parts of the Slavic Collection, which in the Indiana University Library denotes all library materials from, or related to, the Soviet Union, Albania, Bulgaria, Czechoslovakia, Hungary, Poland, Romania, Yugoslavia, as well as Lusatia and the German Democratic Republic. Although some books of the Slavic Collection were purchased at the end of the 19th and the beginning of the 20th century, the real buildup of the collection began after World War II and gained momentum only in 1958, when the East European Institute was reorganized as the Russian and East European Institute.

The Slavic and East European library materials can be found not only in the Main Library building but also in the Lilly Library (rare books and special collections) and in several school and departmental libraries and reading rooms. The card catalog, located on the first floor of the general collections (East Tower) of the Main Library, is divided into two sections: author-title and subject. The Library uses the Library of Congress transliteration and classification systems, except for some law materials which are classified according to the Library's own system.

The principal portion of the Slavic Collection (about 100,000 volumes) is now located on the fifth floor of the general collections, in the new, completely air-conditioned main library building. On this floor are all materials of general and European history (D through DR) and history's auxiliary sciences (C), Slavic, Baltic, and Albanian philology (PG), Slavic reference works, and current Slavic and East European newspapers and periodicals. The fifth floor also houses the office of the Librarian for Slavic Studies, who is in charge of book selection and reference work in the field of Slavic and East European studies, and a special Slavic card catalog. Except for a typescript of *Slavic and East European Serials in the Indiana University Libraries* (1974, 553 p.), there is no book catalog of the Slavic Collection in the Library. Study facilities for faculty members, doctoral candidates, and general readers are also on this floor.

Indiana University Library has open stacks; readers have direct access to the collection. The loan period for most library materials charged at the circulation desk is two weeks; for those charged through the Interlibrary Loan Office, the period is usually one month. Reference materials, bound journals, and government publications are normally not loaned for home use.

When school is in session the Library is open Monday through Saturday from 8:15 a.m. until midnight and on Sunday from 11 a.m. to midnight. During vacation periods the hours are Monday —Saturday, 8:15 a.m.—5 p.m.; Sunday, 1—5 p.m. Materials in the Lilly Library may be used only in its Reading Room, which is open Monday through Thursday from 9 a.m. to 5 p.m. and from 6 p.m. to 10 p.m.; Friday from 9 a.m. to 5 p.m.; and on Saturday from 9 a.m. until noon. Copies of Lilly Library materials may be made by special permission only.

With the exception of government publications, all microforms (microfiche, microfilm, microcard, microprint), readers, and printers are located on the ground floor. Microforms and portable readers are available for home use. Prints are made for 10 cents each.

A copying service on the fourth floor of the general collections will make copies of library-owned or borrowed materials. There are several coin-operated machines in key locations around the building where one may make copies for five cents per exposure. Microfilms are made by the University's Microfilm Department, but orders should be sent to the Library's Interlibrary Loan Office when library materials are involved.

Since library materials related to the Soviet Union and East Central and Southeastern Europe are located in various places in the Library, it is not easy to determine their exact number and distribution by countries. On the basis of the annual statistics of the Slavic Section of the Catalog Department, which in the school year 1970/71 processed 14,706 volumes of monographs and serials and 227 units of microforms, and after a count of some classes of materials, the collection was estimated in 1971 as being in excess of 180,000 volumes; there were about 99,000 volumes related to the Soviet Union, about 68,000 volumes dealing with the individual East European countries, and about 13,000 covering the area as a whole. Following is a survey of the Czechoslovak and other East Central and Southeast European collections in the Indiana University Library.

Czechoslovakia

ALTHOUGH INDIANA UNIVERSITY Library started purchasing books related to the Czech and Slovak lands some 75 years ago, its Czechoslovak collection actually is a child of the post-World War II period. Charles Maurice's *The Story of Bohemia from the Earliest Times to the Fall of National Independence in 1620,* published in New York in 1896, was the first book acquired for the present Czechoslovak collection. It was accessioned on February 17, 1897. The second book of the Czechoslovak collection, Will Seymour Monroe's *Bohemia and the Čechs; the History, People, Institutions, and the Geography of the Kingdom, Together with Accounts of Moravia and Silesia* (Boston, 1910), was purchased on October 30, 1914, when the Library already had almost 100,000 volumes in its stacks. In 1950, the Library had only 80 books on Czech and Slovak history. Now, 22 years later, the Library has almost 4,000 volumes on the history of Czechoslovakia and over 5,000 volumes on Czech and Slovak languages and literatures. The total Czechoslovak collection is estimated at about 17,000 volumes. In spite of some neglect of East European studies in comparison to Russian studies, the Czechoslovak collection has almost doubled in the last eight years. On the average, about 900 volumes are added to it annually.

The Czechoslovak collection grew to its present level through the purchase of special collections, annual acquisitions, book exchange, and gifts. The first boost to the collection was the purchase of a fine, well-preserved collection of the late John L. Payer of Cleveland through Kraus Periodicals, Inc., in 1957. It contained several thousand items and became the core of the Library's Czechoslovak collection. In 1968 an agreement between the International Affairs Center at Indiana University and the Institute of History at the Czechoslovak Academy of Sciences in Prague became effective under which the Institute of History was to send to Indiana University every year 4,000 bound copies of significant books, journals, and newspapers published in Czechoslovakia on history, the social sciences, and Czech culture and art. Although the contract was not long in force due to changes in Prague, Indiana University Library was able to increase its Czech and Slovak holdings, as well as to improve their quality. The Library has also received about 300 well-selected books, chiefly on Czech belles lettres, from the late Mrs. Edgar Bing of Seattle, Washington, known in Czech literature as Marie Jakerlová Renčová, and from her husband.

In developing the Czechoslovak collection, special attention has been paid to reference aids and serials. The reference section has nine general encyclopedias published between 1860 and 1967, namely: *Slovník naučný,* 11 v. (and its *Názorný atlas); Ottův slovník naučný,* 28 v., and its supplement *Ottův slovník naučný nové doby,* 6 v. in 12; *Malý Ottův slovník naučný,* 2 v.;

Masarykův slovník naučný, 7 v.; *Nový velký ilustrovaný slovník naučný*, 20 v.; *Komenského slovník naučný*, 10 v.; *Slovenský náučný slovník*, 3 v.; and *Příruční slovník naučný*, 4 v. The Library also has special encyclopedias on Czechoslovakia and Slovakia, namely *Československá vlastivěda* (both editions), and *Slovenská vlastiveda*. There are also many handbooks and surveys covering pre- and post-World War II Czechoslovakia, guides, and more than a score of special reference aids in biographies, such as *Album representantů všech oborů veřejného života česko-slovenského*, edited by F. Sekanina; *Kulturní adresář ČSR* of 1934 and 1936; *Česká biografie; Kdo je kdo v Československu;* a music dictionary, dictionaries of writers and their pseudonyms, directories of members of the academies, Czechoslovak officials, etc. The bibliography section includes several recent bibliographic guides to Czechoslovakia in English, as well as current bibliographies, Czech and Slovak, component parts of *Bibliografický katalog ČSSR*. The collection has the more important retrospective Czech bibliographies, but there are still some gaps in 19th-century bibliography. The Slovak retrospective bibliography is well represented by the works of L'.V. Rizner, J. Mišianik, M. Fedor, J. Kuzmík, M. Potemra, M. Kipsová, and others.

In the other fields, the Library has a majority of the titles listed in Paul L. Horecky's bibliographic guide to East Central Europe, especially those in the chapters "History," "The State," and "Intellectual and Cultural Life."

Czech literature of the 19th and 20th centuries is represented by the works of over 630 authors. There are many first editions and complete sets of the collected works of the Czech classics. Especially rich are the collections of works by and about Karel Hynek Mácha and Petr Bezruč (Vladimír Vasek). The Slovak collection is less developed. The works of about a hundred Slovak authors represent Slovak literature since 1800.

As far as statesmen are concerned, there are well-developed collections relating to Presidents Beneš and Masaryk.

One of the shortcomings of the Czechoslovak collection is a lack of newspapers. For example, the Library has *Rudé právo* only for the years 1950-59 and 1963-68. Since 1969, the Library has retained current newspapers from Czechoslovakia for only two years, relying on their availability in the Center for Research Libraries in Chicago. Of the older newspapers published in Prague, the Library has *Union,* 1909-14, *Prager Tagblatt,* 1915-16, 1924-37, and *Prager Presse,* 1922-38.

The collection of government documents includes about 300 titles, over 50 of which are serials. However, most of the serials are incomplete. The Library has, for example, the official gazette of the Czechoslovak Republic and the Protectorate of Bohemia and Moravia (*Úřední list,* 1920-37, 1940-43); the official gazette of Slovakia (*Krajinský vestník pre Slovensko,* 1929-39; *Úradné noviny,* 1939-45; *Úradný vestník,* 1945-49); the official register for the promulgation of the laws of Czechoslovakia (*Sbírka zákonů . . .* from 1918), and Slovakia (*Slovenský zákonník,* 1939-44); the stenographic records of the Bohemian Diet for the years 1861-1908; and incomplete sets of the stenographic records and the other publications of the National Assembly of the Czechoslovak Republic.

As far as serials in general are concerned, the Library is receiving more than 120 current publications for the Czechoslovak collection. However, the collection is valuable to a scholar primarily for its older publications, which now are almost unobtainable. The Library has complete sets or long runs of the publications of the Czech and Slovak museums and learned societies, such as Národní museum (*Časopis,* since 1827); Slovenské národné múzeum (*Sborník,* since 1896); Vlastenecký spolek musejní in Olomouc (*Časopis,* from v. 3, 1886); Česká akademie věd a umění (*Almanach,* 1891-1940; *Historický archiv,* 1893-1949); Matica slovenská (*Letopis,* 1864-1920; *Sborník,* 1922-42); Matice moravská (*Časopis-Sborník,* since 1869); Matice opavská (*Věstník-Slezský sborník,* since 1878); Společnost přátel starožitnosti (*Časopis,* from v. 2, 1894); Česko-slovenská společnost zeměpisná (*Sborník,* since 1895), Učená společnost Šafaříkova (*Bratislava,*

1927-37); Slovanský ústav (*Ročenka*, 1928-47); Rodopisná společnost československá (*Časopis*, 1929-46); and others.

The titles of Czech and Slovak serials published before 1949 in Czechoslovakia and abroad are numerous, but many of them are incomplete, especially those published in the United States. The Library has complete or almost complete sets of the following publications: *Akord* (J. Durych's), *Archiv český, Athenaeum, Časopis pro dějiny venkova, Časopis pro moderní filologii, Česká revue, Česká mysl, Česko-Jihoslovanská revue, Česky časopis historický, Český lid, Cesta, Cyrill, Dalibor, Filosofická revue, Filozofický sborník, Hlas* (1898-1904), *Host, Kolo, Květy* (S. Čech's, 1879-1915); *Lumír* (1851-63 and 1873-1940), *Moderní revue, Moravsko-slezská revue, Naše doba, Naše reč, Naše revoluce, Nové Čechy, Osvěta, Pokroková revue, Prager Rundschau, Pramen, Přehled, Prúdy, Přítomnost, Řad, La revue française de Prague, Rudé květy, Šaldův zápisník, Slavia, Slavische Rundschau, Slovanský přehled, Slovanský sborník, Slovenská reč, Slovo a slovesnost, Slovenské pohľady, Služba, Sociologická revue, Švanda Dudak, Topičův sborník, Var, Volné směry, Vlasť, Zahraniční politika, Ženské listy, Zlatá Praha* (1884-1930), *Zvon,* and several other, chiefly local, serials.

There are also complete sets or the first volumes of the following, generally short-lived, serials: *Časopis českého studentstva,* 1889-91, *Červen,* 1918-21, *Česká kultura,* 1913, *Dnešek,* 1946-48, *Fronta,* 1927-31, *Iskra,* 1932, *Kmen,* 1926, *Kniha,* 1895-96, *Kritický měsíčník,* 1938-42, *Kritika,* 1924-25, *Kultura doby,* 1936-38, *Lipa,* 1918-20, *Listy pro umění a kritiku,* 1933-37, *Naše Slovensko,* 1907-10, *La nation tchèque,* 1915-19, *Novina,* 1908-12, *Obrození,* 1912, *Obzor literární a umělecký,* 1899-1902, *Praha-Moskva,* 1936-38, *ReD,* 1927-29, *Ruch filosofický,* 1920-25, *Srdce,* 1901-03, *Stopa,* 1900-12, *Tak,* 1937-38, *Týn,* 1917-18, *U* (Blok) 1936-37, *Umělecký měsíčník,* 1911-13, *Země,* 1920-23.

There are many old and rare items in the Main Library and, especially, in the Lilly Library. The collection includes the first printed Czech Bible of 1488, the Bible printed in Kutná Hora in 1489, the Ecclesiasticus of 1561, a New Testament of 1568, a Czech Bible of 1570, a Czech Bible published in Kralice, 1579-1601, the *Manuálník* of 1658, and a Czech Bible of 1677-1715 (Svatováclavská). There are also works of Pope Pius II (*Historia Bohemica,* 1475 and ca. 1489, *Le historie, costumi et successi della nobilissima provincia delli Boemi,* 1545); *Hystoria . . . von den alten Hussen zu Behemen in Keiser Sigmunds Zeiten,* by Albert Krantz, 1525; *Historiae Regni Boiemiae . . .* by Jan Dubravius, bishop of Olomouc, 1552; Prokop Lupač's *Rerum Boemicarum ephemeridis historicae liber primus,* 1578 and *Rerum Boemicarum ephemeris . . .* 1584; Martin Boregk's *Behmische Chronica,* 1587; *Bohaemia pia,* by Jiří Bertold Pontanus (Georgius Bartholdus Pontanus a Braitenberg), 1608; Zacharias Theobald's *Hussiten Krieg* of 1621 and 1750; *. . . Promptuarium . . .* of Franciscus Ferdinandus de Serponte et Bregaziis, 1678; works of Bohuslav Ludvík Alois Balbin (*Epitome historica rerum Bohemicarum,* 1677; *Miscellanea historica regni Bohemiae,* decas 1-2, 1679-1687; *Verisimilia humaniorum disciplinarum,* 1710; *Historia de ducibus ac regibus Bohemiae,* 1735; *Dissertatio apologetica pro lingua Slavonica, praecipue Bohemica,* 1775; *Bohemia docta,* 1776); Václav Jan Rosa's *Grammatica linguae Bohemicae,* 1680; Václav Hajek's *Böhmische Chronik,* 1697, Jan František Beckovský's *Poselkyně starých příběhův cžeských, aneb Kronyka cžeská . . .* 1700-1880, and many others. The libraries also have works of V. M. Kramerius, A. J. Puchmayer, J. Dobrovský, V. Hanka, J. J. Jungmann, J. Kollár, J. Nejedlý, F. M. Pelcl, and P. J. Šafárik, published at the end of the 18th and during the first decades of the 19th centuries, as well as the almanacs *Wesna,* 1837, 1839; *České besedy,* 1842; *Nitra,* 1842; *Perly české,* 1855; *Máj,* 1858, 1860, 1862, *Lipa,* 1862, *Máj,* 1872; *Ruch,* 1873, and *Almanah české omladiny,* 1879. The Library also has some old serials such as *Čechoslav,* 1822, 1825; *Pražské nowíny,* 1831; *Wlastimil,* 1840; *Pautnik,* 1846-47; *Lípa slovanská,* 1848; *Národní noviny,* 1848-50; *Pražský posel,* 1848; *Pražský večerní list,* 1848-49;

Slovan, 1850-51; *Obrazy života*, 1860; *Posel z Prahy*, 1860; *Rozpravy z oboru historie, filologie a literatury*, 1860; *Hlasy*, 1868-69; *Orol*, 1871-79. There are also reprints of *Slovenskje narodnje novini*, 1845-48; *Orol tatránski*, 1845-48, and *Slovenskje pohľady na literatúru, umenie a život*, 1846-47, 1851-52.

Although relatively small, the Czechoslovak collection is nevertheless quite sufficient in scope not only to satisfy the basic needs of a general reader in the field of humanities and social sciences but also to attract scholars in the fields of Czechoslovak history and culture.

Other Countries

Albania

The Albanian collection includes about 800 volumes. A large portion of these materials, especially those on Albanian history and contemporary Albania (handbooks, general surveys, guides) is in languages other than Albanian. Recent Albanian materials were provided through the PL 480 Yugoslav Program. Currently the Library is receiving over 20 serials in the field of Albanian studies.

Bulgaria

The Bulgarian collection amounts to about 5,000 volumes. Although small in size, the collection contains most of the basic publications in several major fields of Bulgarian studies. As in all of the Library's East Central and Southeastern European collections, the quantity of materials covering language, literature, and history is the largest. Relatively well-developed general reference aids and bibliographies increase the quality of the collection. Current bibliographic serials include a complete set of *Bŭlgarski knigopis*.

Currently the collection is receiving about 70 serial publications. The Library also has complete sets or long runs of about three dozen Bulgarian serial publications (government publications, publications of learned societies and institutions, general and subject periodicals, etc.) issued in the 19th century and the first half of the 20th century, as well as recent reprints of several periodicals of the Bulgarian national revival.

Hungary

The Hungarian collection contains over 8,000 volumes. The materials covering the Hungarian language and literature amount to about 2,000 titles. The collection includes many publications issued in the 18th and 19th centuries, especially in the field of history. A large portion of the material is in West European languages. The collection currently receives over 40 serials. The Library also has about 900 volumes in complete or almost complete sets of over two dozen old serials. The Library has, for example, such serials as *Ungarisches Magazin* . . . (1781-87), *Katolikus Szemle* [Catholic Review] (1887-1944), *Huszadik Század* [The Twentieth Century] (1900-19), *Nyugat* [West] (1908-41), *Magyar Szemle* [Hungarian Review] (1927-44), *Magyar Csillag* [Hungarian Star] (1941-44), *Danubian Review* (1934-41), *Ungarische Jahrbücher* (1921-43), the Hungarian official gazette, *Magyar Közlöny* (1921-64), *Almanach* of the Hungarian Academy of Sciences for many years between 1874 and 1913, and the historical periodical *Századok* [Centuries] (since 1867); serials dedicated to studies of the Hungarian language, linguistics, and literary history such as *Magyar Nyelv* [Hungarian Language] (since 1905), *Nyelvtudományi Közlemények* [Linguistic Studies] (since 1862), *Irodalomtörténet* [Literary History] (1912-62), *Irodalomtörténeti Közlemények* [Studies in Literary History] (since 1891); ethnologic serials such as *Ethno-*

graphia (since 1890) and *Ethnologische Mitteilungen aus Ungarn* (1887-1905); and several others.

Lusatia

The Lusatian collection consists of about 600 volumes in various languages published mainly in the 20th century. Currently the Library is receiving five serials published in Bautzen, East Germany.

Poland

The Polish collection contains over 15,000 volumes. There are many old and rare publications, including, for example, a Polish Bible published in Kraków in 1577. The reference section is well developed. There are 10 general encyclopedias published between 1859 and 1970, special encyclopedias on Poland, general surveys and guides, several biographic dictionaries, including *Polski słownik biograficzny,* bibliographies of Polish bibliographies, general bibliographies, including K. J. T. Estreicher's monumental work, and some subject bibliographies.

The collection is especially strong in such fields as Polish language and literature, history, and government. Since the mid-1950s the Library has been receiving over a hundred Polish serials published in Poland and abroad. This number was increased in 1972, when the Library was accepted as a participant in the PL 480 Polish program. However, the collection is very weak in older serials.

Romania

The Romanian collection includes about 4,500 volumes. There are many old publications, including, for example, the Gospels in Church Slavic, known as *Evangheliar slavonesc,* published in Braşov in 1562. The collection is strongest in the areas of Romanian language and literature. Holdings in history include many basic sources. The Library receives about 70 current series but lacks, with a few exceptions, the older serial publications.

Yugoslavia

The Yugoslav collection contains over 20,000 volumes and grew rapidly thanks to the PL 480 Yugoslav Program. After the Russian collection, it is the largest Slavic collection in the Indiana University Library. The materials in the Yugoslav collection (old and new, monographs and serials) are well balanced.

Serious acquisition of Yugoslav materials began in the early 1950s. The collection was greatly improved through the purchase of a fine collection from Dr. Milan Ivšić of Yugoslavia.

The strongest component of the Yugoslav collection is the Serbian collection, but the Croatian collection is not far behind it, especially in the field of literature. The Slovenian collection is stronger than the Macedonian, primarily because a greater number of Slovenian materials were published before 1945.

The Yugoslav collection is highly diversified and should satisfy the basic needs not only of students but also of specialists. Much if not all of the material needed for writing a dissertation or doing serious research on Yugoslavia—its history, politics, economic and social conditions, as well as the languages, literatures, and folklore—is in the Library.

The Library receives over 600 current serials published in Yugoslavia and abroad and also has quite a good collection of publications issued before 1945. There are several series of government publications like the official gazettes, stenographic records of assemblies, official registers for the promulgation of the laws, etc.; publications of the learned societies and institutions as, for example, *Bulletin international* (1930-43), *Djela* (inc.), *Ljetopis* (since 1867), *Rad* (since 1867), and *Starine* (since 1869) of the Jugoslavenska akademija znanosti i umjetnosti; *Narodni koledar in letopis* (1867-68), *Letopis* (1869-1912), and *Zbornik* (1899-1912) of the Slovenska matica in Ljubljana; *Letopis* (since 1938) of the Slovenska akademija znanosti in umetnosti; *Razprave* (1923-1940) of the Znanstveno društvo za humanistične vede in Ljubljana; *Carniola* (1908-09, and new ser. 1910-19), *Glasnik* (1920-45), *Izvestja* (1891-1909), *Jahresheft* (1856-1862) and *Mitteilungen* (1866-1907) of the Muzejsko društvo za Slovenijo; *Glasnik* (since 1889) of the Zemaljski muzej in Sarajevo; *Glasnik* (1925-40) of the Skopsko naučno društvo; *Glas* (inc., 229 v.), *Posebna izdanja* (inc., 387 v.), *Spomenik* (inc., since 1890), and *Zbornik za istoriju, jezik i književnost srpskog naroda* (3 series) of the Srpska akademija nauka i umetnosti; *Letopis* (inc., 376 v.) of the Matica srpska in Novi Sad; complete sets or long runs of the general periodicals and serials dedicated to history, philology, ethnography, etc., such as *Makedonski pregled* (1924-42), *Čas* (1907-42), *Časopis za slovenski jezik, književnost in zgodovino* (1918-31), *Dom in svet* (1888-1944), *Kres* (1881-86), *Ljubjanski zvon* (1881-1941), *Misel in delo* (1934-40), *Novice gospodarske, obertniške in narodne* (1843-74), *Slovan* (1902-17), *Slovenski glasnik* (1858-68), *Sodobnost* (1933-41), *Zvon* (1870-80); *Arkiv za povjestnicu Jugoslavensku* (1851-75), *Bosanska vila* (1885 1910), *Brankovo kolo* (1897-1912), *Brastvo* (1921-40), *Delo* (1894-1914), *Godišnjica Nikole Čupića* (1877-1941), *Građa za povijest književnosti hrvatske* (since 1897), *Hrvatska revija* (1928-45), *Hrvatska smotra* (1933-44), *Hrvatsko kolo* (1905-46), *Južnoslovenski filolog* (since 1913), *Kolo* (1842-53), *Matica* (1866-70), *Misao* (1919-33), *Monumenta spectantia historiam Slavorum meridionalium* (since 1868), *Nada* (1895-1902), *Narodna starina* (1922-35), *Naš jezik* (1933-40, and new ser.), *Naše gore list* (1861-66), *Otadžbina* (1875-92), *Prosvjeta* (1893-1911), *Srpski etnografski zbornik* (since 1894), *Srpski književni glasnik* (1901-14, and new ser., 1920-41), *Vienac* (1869-1944), and numerous other serials, including many short-lived ones.

Andrew Turchyn
Indiana University

Jankola Library

American-Slovak Research Center

The Jankola Library in Danville, Pa., is an American library which specializes in Slovakiana and related Slavic interests. It is housed in the complex of structures that include Villa Sacred Heart, St. Cyril Academy, and the Motherhouse of the Sisters of Sts. Cyril and Methodius, Maria Hall, and the Villa Conservatory.

The collection, which now numbers over 10,000 works fully cataloged under Dewey Decimal classification with two Cutter numbers, together with many more recent acquisitions which await processing, had grown over the years since about 1922, but the Library began to be formally organized by Sister M. Martina Tybor in July 1968. The holdings are being steadily expanded through purchased acquisitions, through gifts, and through library exchange activity with various libraries and learned institutes abroad as well as with the Slovak Institute of Cleveland and the libraries of the Slovak Jesuit Fathers in Cambridge, Ontario, Canada, the Slovak Franciscans of Pittsburgh, and the Slovak Dominicans of Oxford, Mich.

The holdings of Jankola Library include many American Slovak publications. Among them are the annuals or yearbooks *Jednota, Furdek, Národný kalendar, Sokol sborník, Bratstvo,* and a small representation of *Sion*. There is also a complete file of *Literárny almanach, Most, Slovakia*. Besides writings in Slavic tongues there are relevant English works concerned with Slovak and Slavic history, literature, linguistics and grammar, and culture. The shelflist cards are color coded to indicate: a) works published in Slovakia and Hungary; b) Slovak works published in the United States; c) Slovak works published outside Slovakia and the United States (e.g., in Rome, Canada, South America, Australia, etc.); and d) English works.

One of the main objectives of Jankola Library is to serve research scholars who are engaged in developing projects that are more or less Slovak oriented. Anyone who is interested is welcome to use resource materials by visiting Jankola Library in person. Convenient housing facilities are readily available in Danville, even within walking distance, but it may be advisable to arrange reservations for housing if an extended stay is planned and it may be well to come to the library by appointment in order to be assured that the librarian in charge will be at hand to offer guidance or assistance. Ample working hours can be arranged for study and exploration. Short-term visitors are also welcome at all times.

Understandably, it is not always easy for students and researchers to come to Danville in person, and for this reason Jankola Library is engaged in brisk interlibrary loan activity. This involvement has already reached out to Lisbon, Rome, Padua, and Bern in Europe, and from coast to coast in the United States. Jankola Library policies are liberal.

This center is interested primarily in documentary references and in works of recognized scholarship. It would like to increase its collection of standard titles from abroad as well as representative American publications that have historical, literary, art form, or research value. Works that reflect ecumenism in attitudes as well as in intellectual activity and perspectives are sought on behalf of scholars who seek substance for exploration. Jankola Library will house works of diversified background, excepting only what may be offensive to sound morals or standard proprieties.

A program of analytical cataloging from periodical literature and a project of filing clippings is under way as a futher expedient to assist scholars. New acquisitions include phonograph records, tapes, and slides.

This is a private, unendowed library that is occasionally favored with some modest gifts.

Sr. M. Martina Tybor
Jankola Library

University of Kansas

The Slavic collection at the University of Kansas numbers well over 100,000 volumes (including materials on the Soviet Union). The collection has grown partly according to a conscious plan and partly as a response to the interests of scholars at the University. Within the areas covered by the present survey, the focus has been on Poland and Yugoslavia. Reference and bibliographic materials relating to these two countries are well balanced and varied. Those on Czechoslovakia, Greece, East Germany, and Hungary are fair and holdings on Albania, Bulgaria, and Romania are weak. Collections on individual countries include various national bibliographies, encyclopedias, dictionaries (biographic, geographic, and etymological), atlases, and statistical yearbooks. Among the many bibliographies are Estreicher's *Bibliografia Polska,* the most recent edition of Korbut's *Literatura Polska . . ., Bibliografija Jugoslavije,* Novaković's *Srpska bibliografija* (1869, reprint 1967), and *editio princeps* of Kukuljević-Sakcinski's *Bibliografia Hrvatska,* dio prvi (1860). Important reference works and bibliographies are located in the Slavic Reference Alcove adjacent to the Slavic Department in Watson Library.

These and numerous other important works on Poland, Russia, Lithuania, and Eastern Europe were acquired by the distinguished scholar Professor Oswald P. Backus, who is the founder of Slavic and Soviet area studies at the University. Rare materials are housed in the Department of Special Collections in Spencer Library. Persons to be consulted for rare materials are the Assistant Director of Libraries (for Special Collections), and the Associate Special Collections Librarian.

All fields of the humanities are covered in the Library's holdings on Poland. The collection includes sources of general information on the country, its people, society, civilization, culture, and progress. Works by Władysław Kazimierz Kumaniecki, Józef Kostrzewski, Witold Hensel, and many others are included. Of particular interest are Stanisław Sarnicki's *Statuta y metrika przywilejów koronnych . . .* (Kraków, 1594), which treats manners, customs, kings, religions, and related topics, and *The ancient and present state of Poland . . .* (London, 1697).

Archival materials include an important work on the Sanguszko family, *Archiwum książąt lubartowiczów Sanguszków w Sławucie . . .,* 7 v. (Lwów, 1887-1910), of which the University of Kansas possesses the only complete set in the Western Hemisphere. The collection is strong in medieval and modern Polish history, with about 80 rare works published from the 16th to the 19th century. Among these are *De origine et rebus gestis Polonorum Libri XXX* (Basile, 1558), *Ad regem, proceres* (1557), *Polonia, sive de situ, populis, moribus, magistratibus et republica Regni Polonici . . .* (1577), and several other items by the well-known chronicler, writer, bishop, and diplomat, Marcin Kromer (Cromerius). There are also works by Maciej z Miechowa, Salomon Naugebauer, François Baudouin, Filippo Buonaccorsi, Bernardino Mariscotti, Joachim Pastorius, Samuel Kuszewicz, Stanisław Kobierzycki, Michel David La Bizardière, J. G. Jolli, Hugo Kołłątaj, Jan Długosz, Joachim Lelewel, Jędrzej Moraczewski, and others. The late 19th and early 20th centuries, the interwar period, and the period since 1945 are represented by works of Julian Ursyn Niemcewicz, Szymon Askenazy, Marceli Handelsman, Stanisław Bukowiecki, Jan Stanisław Bystroń, Stanisław Smolka, Ernest Kalinka, Tadeusz Korzon, Tadeusz Jędruszczak, Oskar Halecki, and others.

A collection of books and pamphlets written by members of the Polish Socialist Party (Polska Partia Socjalistyczna), ca. 1890-1914, has great potential for scholars, incorporating works of Bolesław Limanowski, Witold Jodko-Narkiewicz, Adolf Warszawski, Stanisław Szpotański, Ludwik Waryński, Leon Wasilewski, and others. Several military training manuals, designed to prepare officer cadres for a war against Russia, are included.

A particular strength of Kansas' Polonica lies in its source materials on Polish laws, the constitution, and the *Sejm* (Parliament) in the 17th and 18th centuries. Relations between the Vatican and Poland are also well documented, in manuscripts as well as in published works. The constitutional laws of Lithuania and Galicia are also represented.

The University's comprehensive collections in Polish language and literature include most of the standard materials as well as much unusual material. Early Polish literature, humanism, romanticism, positivism, realism, futurism, and émigré literature are all well represented, although in the early humanist period works by Clemens Janicki are lacking and holdings on the 17th-century Latin poet Maciej Kazimierz Sarbiewski (Casimir) are scanty. All pre-1801 American imprints of Nicholas [Mikołaj] Rey, with whom modern Polish literature began, are available in microform. The major works of the great 16th-century poet Jan Kochanowski are well represented.

Among the many 17th-century Polish writers covered are Twardowski, Potocki, Opaliński, and Kołłataj. Holdings on the romantic period are well balanced, with works by Mickiewicz and his rival Słowacki as well as by Krasiński and Norwid. The positivist movement and the historical novel are represented by the works of Kraszewski, Łoziński, Sienkiewicz, Prus (Głowacki), and Orzeszkowa.

The late 19th and early 20th centuries, characterized by realism, romantic realism, and neo-romanticism, are reflected in the works of Żeromski and the Nobel prizewinner Reymont, as well as those of the Tatraists (represented by Tetmajer, Asnyk, and Kasprowicz) and the modernists such as Przybyszewski, Wyspiański, and Żeleński. Two other movements, futurism and Ska-mander, include works by many writers, from Ważyk to Kosidowski and from Lechoń to Iwasz-kiewicz. Finally, representing realism, the postwar period, and émigré literature, the Library has such authors as Maria Kuncewicz (Szczepańska), Maria Dąbrowska (Szumska), Miłosz, Andrze-jewski, Różewicz, and many more.

The Library's Polonica also include literary criticism by Juliusz Kleiner and works on Polish culture by Alexander Brückner and Zygmunt Gloger. Coverage of art, political science, foreign relations, and geography is only moderate, although the last is augmented by a number of maps of Poland and Lithuania. The Music Library has works by Chopin and recordings of his most significant compositions. The contemporary composers Penderecki and Lutosławski are repre-sented in scores and recordings.

The Library's collection on Yugoslavia is both rich and diversified. All periods of Yugoslav history are well covered, the interwar period in particular. For more detailed coverage of holdings on Yugoslav history, see "A Survey of Source Materials on Yugoslav History" in *Books and Libraries at the University of Kansas*, v. 9, no. 1 September 1971, from which this survey is drawn.

The collection includes some 200 rare pamphlets and books dealing with Balkan history, 1912-20: the Balkan War of 1912; World War I and the creation of the Yugoslav state; social con-ditions of Serbs, Slovenes, and Croats; the question of Fiume and Istria; minority group prob-lems, etc.

Yugoslavia's individual republics are likewise well represented. In the collection on Serbia one finds important "Žitija" (Russian models), such as *Životi kraljeva i arhiepiskopa srpskih* by Archbishop Danilo II *(1270- ca. 1337)* (Zagreb, 1866) and similar works; on Croatia there are prominent works in Latin and Croatian, including Kukuljević-Sakcinski's *Jura Regni Croatiae, Dalmatiae, et Slavoniae; Monumenta Spectantia Historiam Slavorum Meridionalium; Codex*

Diplomaticus Regni Croatiae, Dalmatiae et Slavoniae; Monumenta Historica Lib. Regiae Civitatis Zagrebiae Metropolis Regni Dalmatiae, Croatiae et Slavoniae; Laszowski's *Codex Turopoljensis,* and Šišić's *Enchridion Fontium Historiae Croatiae.*

Yugoslav literature actually comprises four distinct literatures: Serbian, Croatian, Macedonian, and Slovenian. These literatures are proportionately represented in the South Slavic collection, which now exceeds 20,000 volumes. See "The Library's South Slavic Collection" in *Books and Libraries at the University of Kansas,* v. 4, no. 3 December 1966. The early beginnings of Serbian literature are represented by a few hagiographic works. The strength of the collection is in the 19th and 20th centuries, with works by Obradović, Karadžić, Njegoš, Radičević, Marković, Ilić, Kostić, Nobel prizewinner Ivo Andrić, Davičo, and the literary critics Skerlić, B. and M. Popović, Gligorić, and others.

Croatian literature has flourished since its Renaissance beginnings in Dubrovnik (Ragusa). Stress has been placed on the Dalmatian poet and Latinist Marko Marulić (Marulus), works on Protestantism in Slovenia and Croatia; the golden period of the 17th century, in particular works by Gundulić; and the 18th century movement led by secular writer Reljković and his contemporaries Grabovac, Miošić, and Brezovački. Other movements and periods are well covered: the Illyrian movement, which began about 1830; romanticism, which flourished in the first half of the 19th century; realism, from the second half of the 19th century; Croatian Moderna, from 1895 to 1945; and the postwar period, with its new political waves and ideologies. Included are works by Gaj, Mažuranić, Botić, Kranjčević, Nazor, Ujević, and Krleža, as well as by the literary critics Barac, Palavestra, Vučetić, and Pavletić. Recent publications were regularly received under the PL 480 Program for Yugoslavia.

The collection on Macedonia is neither large nor comprehensive, since the development of the literary language, which is closely related to Bulgarian, is relatively recent, as is the literature. Although sketchy, the Library's coverage does include basic works in literature, history, and political science.

The Slovenian literary tradition is rich and the University of Kansas holdings include the works of Trubar, Kopitar, Vodnik, Prešeren, Kersnik, Župančić, Prijatelj, Finžgar, Gradnik, Gruden, Voranc, Pregelj, Kranjec, Kreft, Vidmar, and others.

The collection on Yugoslavia also contains a fair number of linguistic, historical, and ethnographic atlases and maps. Some 1,000 periodicals, primarily in the humanities, supplement the Yugoslav collection.

The Library's collection on Czechoslovakia contains basic reference works, as well as some materials on linguistics and literature. History in general is well covered, with emphasis on the period 1918-38. Rare and noteworthy titles on early history and national rulers include *Historia Bohemica* (Rome, 1475), by Pope Pius II; *Historia Regni Bohemiae* (Prossnitz, 1552), by Johannes Dubravius; *Bohemiae regnum electiuum . . .* (London, 1620); *The manifest of the most illustrious, and sovereign Prince, Charles Lodowick . . .* (London, 1637), by Karl Ludwig, *Elector Palatine; Histoire de la dernière guerre de Bohème* (Amsterdam, 1750), by Eleazar de Mauvillon; *Series chronologica rerum Slavo-Bohemicarum . . .* (Vetera Pragae, 1768) by František Pubička, and a work dealing with the Czechoslovak borders entitled *O mezech, hranicých . . .* (Prague, 1600), by Iakub Menšik z Menšteina. The collection includes a considerable number of maps and city plans of Bohemia, Moravia, and Slovakia.

The collection on the German Democratic Republic emphasizes geography, history, economic conditions, and economic policy since 1945. Social and economic changes under Communism are well documented.

For Hungary, the Library has collected sources pertaining to Hungarian rule over Croatia (1102-1526), the War of 1848, the *Sabor* (the Croatian Diet) during the period of the Hungarian-Croatian agreement of 1868, the Hungarian Empire as a whole, World War I, and the Hungarian revolution of 1956. Equally important is a collection of sources on the politics and government of the Hungarian People's Republic. Geography is represented by some maps, atlases, and travelers' accounts such as Edward Browne's *A Brief Account of Some Travels in divers parts of Europe, viz. Hungaria, Servia* . . . (London, 1687), Abel Boyer's *A Description* . . . (London, 1702), *Ignaz Born's Travels Through the Banat of Temiswar, Transylvania, and Hungary, in the year 1770* (London, 1770), and Robert Townson's *Travels in Hungary* (London, 1797). In music, there are some scores and recordings of major works by Bartók and Kodály. As a whole, however, the Hungarian collection is rather weak.

The relatively small collection on Romania emphasizes history, politics, and government, with some basic works on language and literature. One noteworthy item in geography should be mentioned, *Marele dicţionar geografic al Romîniei* . . . , 5 v. (Bucharest, 1898-1902) by George Ioan Lahavari.

Bulgarian materials include literary works by Vazov, Iavorov, Kristov, Dimov, Todorov, and Pelin. Literary history and criticism are represented by works of Arnaudov, I. Georgiev, Bogdanov, Tsanev, L. Georgiev, Markov, Pinto, Manning, and Smal-Stocki. Philological festschrifts dedicated to Miletich, Teodorov-Balan, and Shishmanov are included as is the *Bulgarski dialekten atlas.* The first major literary journal in Bulgaria, *Misŭl,* is one of about 60 periodicals covering language, linguistics, Balkan studies, and history.

Emphasis in the Greek collection is placed on prehistoric, early, classical, Hellenistic, and Byzantine history. Primary sources relating to Greek history include Jacques Paul Migne's *Patrologiae cursus completus* . . . *(Patrologia graeca),* 161 v. (Paris, J. P. Migne, 1857-66) and Giovanni Domenico Mansi's *Sacrorum conciliorum nova et amplissima collectio* . . . , 38 v. (Paris, H. Welter, 1901-04). Also included are numerous *codices manuscripti graeci* in the Biblioteca Vaticana series. Maps and atlases are represented by such rare items as Mercator's *Italie, Sclavoniae, et Graeciae geographicae* . . . (Duysburgi, 1589) and Wheler's *A Journey into Greece* . . . (n. p., 1682). Millard's *Incidents of Travel in Greece, Turkey, Russia and Poland* . . . , 2 vols. (New York, 1838).

The Library's small Albanian collection contains a few sources on the 15th century and works dealing with the national hero Georg Kastrioti or Skenderbeg. Some material is available on the Albanian Workers' Party, on relations with Yugoslavia, China, Greece, and Bulgaria, and Albania's historical, cultural, linguistic, and social ties with the West and the East. Travel accounts and maps in the Department of Special Collections include *A Journey Through Albania,* 2d ed. (London, 1813) by J. C. Hobhouse, and *A Tour in Dalmatia, Albania, and Montenegro* (London, 1859) by F. W. Wingfield.

In spite of certain gaps, the Library's collections offer rich holdings of primary sources and complementary materials, particularly in Poland and Yugoslavia, and contain a wealth of information for research in the history, religion, culture, and economics of these two countries.

George C. Jerkovich
University of Kansas

The Library of Congress

General Information

THE LIBRARY OF Congress, address 10 First Street S, E., Washington, D.C., telephone (202) 426-5000, is primarily a library for the use of Congress; it is at the same time a general reference and research library for public use.

The Library's collections of Slavic and East European materials are of considerable strength and scope. In recent years the development of the collections has particularly benefitted from the initiation of the National Program for Acquisitions and Cataloging (NPAC) and the Public Law 480 (PL 480) program. Under the former program, the Library has established special procedures for acquiring, from abroad, all monographic publications of value to scholarship, including those reported by other research libraries, along with the pertinent bibliographic data for these publications. Within the scope of this survey, these arrangements are in effect with Bulgaria, Czechoslovakia, the German Democratic Republic, Romania, and Yugoslavia. Under the latter cooperative program, the Library administers a multicopy acquisitions program for American research libraries, using excess currencies accrued from the sale of surplus agricultural commodities to foreign countries to purchase monographs and serials from those countries. The Library of Congress is one of the participating libraries. Yugoslavia was included in this arrangement from 1967 to 1973 (when the available funds were exhausted) and Poland has been in the program since 1971.

The general book collection is accessible to readers through the Main Reading Room or through the Annex Reading Room, which are open Monday through Friday, 8:30 a.m. to 9:30 p.m., Saturdays 8:30 a.m. to 5 p.m., and Sundays and some holidays 1 p.m. to 5 p.m. A schedule of hours of public service in all reading rooms and offices offering service to readers is available from the Information Office.

Study desks are provided for full-time scholars and researchers doing advanced work, and typing and recording devices are permitted in specific areas. A booklet, *Special Facilities for Research in the Library of Congress,* is available from the Stack and Reader Division.

Catalogs

The principal catalog is the Main Catalog, in the Main Building. The portion of the National Union Catalog of pre-1956 imprints not already published is maintained as a card catalog adjacent to the Main Reading Room. The Main Catalog is further supplemented by catalogs maintained by special divisions of the Library of Congress. Printed catalogs of the Library are also available.

Requests for Books and Serials

Books in the general collections may be requested at the circulation desks in the Main and Annex Reading Rooms. Bound volumes of periodicals are included in the general collections.

The Newspaper and Current Periodical Room (Annex, Room 1026) services unbound serial publications in Western languages, unbound newspapers in Western languages, and all bound and microfilmed newspapers in the Latin and Cyrillic alphabets.

Most of the microforms in the collection are kept in the Microform Reading Room (Main Building, Room 140-B).

Materials in the special collections may be requested in the corresponding reading rooms.

Loan Regulations and Photocopying Facilities

Most monographic materials are available on interlibrary loan when they cannot be obtained in the reader's local libraries.

The Photoduplication Service provides photoreproduction, in a variety of forms, of materials in the Library's collections, subject to copyright or other restriction. Price lists and order forms are available on request.

Self-service coin-operated machines are available in some of the reading rooms.

Special Area and Subject Divisions and Services

The Slavic and Central European Division
Annex Building, Room A-5246
Telephone: (202) 426-5413
Service Hours: Monday through Friday, 8:30 a.m. to 4:30 p.m.
Division Chief: Paul L. Horecky

The Slavic and Central European Division, established in 1951, is responsible for the Library's reference and biographical services and programs pertaining to the cultural, political, social, and economic life of Albania, Austria, Bulgaria, Cyprus, Czechoslovakia, Estonia, Finland, Germany (Federal Republic, Democratic Republic, Berlin), Greece, Hungary, Latvia, Lithuania, Poland, Romania, the Soviet Union, Switzerland, and Yugoslavia. The Division's staff provides specialized reference services in all areas covered by the Division.

Public reading facilities and reference service for the Slavic and Baltic countries are available in the Slavic Room (Main Building, Room G-147). The Slavic Room also houses basic reference collections for Albania, Cyprus, East Germany, Finland, Greece, Hungary, and Romania. Service hours are: Monday through Saturday, 8:30 a.m. to 5 p.m.; Sunday and some holidays, 1 p.m. to 5 p.m. The Slavic Room maintains a reference collection of about 9,000 volumes on these countries and has custodial and servicing responsibilities for current unbound Slavic and Baltic newspapers and periodicals.

The Division has prepared a number of published reference aids as well as lists and bibliographic surveys for facilitating access to certain categories of materials in the collections. A list of these publications is available without charge, on request from the Division office.

The following special reference aids are available to readers through the Slavic Room:

A microprint copy of the Cyrillic Union Catalog, which records holdings in the Cyrillic alphabet for the Library and 185 other major libraries in the United States and Canada. With some exceptions, this catalog has entries for holdings received by or reported to the Library prior to April 1956. (The Catalog itself is accessible through the Main Reading Room.)

Subject card file on recent German-language books.

A clippings file of *New York Times* articles on the Soviet Union and Eastern Europe, begun in mid-1971.

Available through the Division Office (Annex, Room 5246) are:

The Division area reference file on the Soviet Union and Eastern Europe: a card file arranged by country and within country by subject, containing primarily references to recent Western-language books and articles.

A vertical file of pamphlet materials on the Soviet Union and Eastern Europe.

The following divisions, which maintain specialized collections of relevance to this survey, provide reading room facilities, catalogs, and, in some cases, printed guides to their collections.

The *European Law Division* of the Law Library (Main Building, Room 230) provides specialized reference assistance. The Law Library collects materials on all aspects of law, for all countries and all periods, and is the most complete foreign law library in the country.

The *Manuscript Division* (Annex, Room 3005) with some exceptions collects only Americana, some of which are related to foreign areas. Of special interest to Central and East European specialists is the large and important body of material pertaining to the Paris Peace Conference of 1919.

The *Geography and Map Division* (Pickett Street Annex, 845 South Pickett St., Alexandria, Va. 22304) houses the largest and most comprehensive cartographic collection in the world. The Bibliography of Cartography, maintained since the 1880s, is an analytic card catalog based on the collection; it is available on microfilm and in book form, both versions to be kept up to date with supplements. A list of the bibliographies and reference aids prepared by the Division is available on request.

The *Music Division* (Main Building, Room G-144) has custody of books on music, sound recordings of all kinds, and other related materials. The collection is the most comprehensive in the world, both in quality and quantity, and provides resources for research on almost all aspects of Western music. Special strengths of the collection are opera and chamber music. Parts of the collection are organized in two special units, the Archive of Folk Song and the Recorded Sound Section.

The *Prints and Photographs Division* (Annex, Room 1051) collects drawings and fine prints, posters, photographs, and motion pictures. The holdings are by far strongest in Americana, but collecting extends to all countries. The huge photograph and poster collections in particular contain material relating to Central and Eastern Europe.

The *Rare Book Division* (Main Building, Room 256) has custody of early, important, rare, and fine books, including the largest collection of 15th-century books in the United States.

The Library's collections of documents and other materials captured at the end of the Second World War in Germany contain many unique and significant items pertaining to Eastern Europe before 1945, in particular, materials dealing with German relations with this area. These items are to be found in various parts of the Library, including the Manuscript Division, the Prints and Photographs Division, and the Recorded Sound Section. Much of the material in the Library's collection is described in Gerhard L. Weinberg, *Guide to Captured German Documents* (Maxwell Air Force Base, Alabama, 1952) and in its *Supplement . . .* (Washington, National Archives and Records Service, 1959).

Anita R. Navon
Library of Congress

Selected Bibliography of Publications on the Collections Described

Childs, James B. *German Democratic Republic Official Publications, With Those of the Preceding Zonal Period, 1945-1958; a survey.* Washington, Library of Congress, 1960-1961. 4 v.

Cyrillic Union Catalog in Microprint. New York, Readex Microprint, 1962.

East European Accessions Index. v. 1-11, 1951-1961. Washington, Library of Congress, 1951-1961. Monthly.

Fischer-Galati, Stephen A. *Rumania; a Bibliographic Guide.* Washington, Library of Congress, 1963. New York, Arno Press, 1968. 75 p.

Grzyboswki, Kazimierz. *Poland in the Collections of the Library of Congress; an Overview*. Washington, Library of Congress, 1969. 26 p.

Harrsen, Meta Philippine. *The Nekcsei-Lipocz Bible, a Fourteenth Century Manuscript from Hungary in the Library of Congress . . . a Study*. Washington, Library of Congress, 1949. 99 p.

Horecky, Paul L. "The Slavic and East European Resources and Facilities of the Library of Congress." *Slavic Review*, v. 23, no. 2, June 1964: 309-327.

Hoskins, Janina W. *Polish Books in English*. Washington, Library of Congress, 1974. 163 p.

Mid-European Law Project. *Legal Sources and Bibliography of . . .* Vladimir Gsovski, general editor. New York, Praeger (for the Free Europe Committee) [1956-1964] A series of bibliographies for the following countries: Bulgaria, Czechoslovakia, Hungary, Poland, Romania, and Yugoslavia.

Milojević, Borivoje Z. *Geography of Yugoslavia; a Selective Bibliography*. Washington, Library of Congress, 1955. 79 p.

Petrovich, Michael B. *Yugoslavia; a Bibliographic Guide*. Washington, Library of Congress, 1974. 270 p.

Pundeff, Marin V. *Bulgaria; a Bibliographic Guide*. Washington, Library of Congress, 1965. New York, Arno Press, 1968. 98 p.

Sturm, Rudolf. *Czechoslovakia; a Bibliographic Guide*. Washington, Library of Congress, 1968 [Also available in hard-cover from Arno Press, 1968] 157 p.

Union List of Serials in Libraries of the United States and Canada. Edited by Edna Brown Titus. 3d ed. New York, H. W. Wilson Co., 1965. 5 v. Coverage after Jan. 1, 1950, continued by *New Serial Titles*, issued monthly by the Library of Congress. Years 1950-1970 cumulated in *New Serial Titles 1950-1970* (Bowker, 1973. 4 v.).

U.S. Bureau of the Census. *Bibliography of Social Science Periodicals and Monograph Series: . . .* Washington, D.C. [1961-1965] A series of bibliographies for the following countries and periods: Albania, 1944-1961; Bulgaria, 1944-1960; Czechoslovakia, 1948-1963; Poland, 1945-1962; Hungary, 1947-1962; Romania, 1947-1960; Yugoslavia, 1945-1963.

U.S. Library of Congress. *Hungarians in Rumania and Transylvania*. A Bibliographical List of Publications in Hungarian and West European Languages Compiled from the Holdings of the Library of Congress, by Elemer Bako and William Solyom-Fekete. Washington, U.S. Govt. Print. Off., 1969. 192 p. (91st Congress, 1st Session. House Document no. 91-134)

U.S. Library of Congress. *Library of Congress Publications in Print*. Washington, Library of Congress. Annual. Includes data on the Library of Congress printed catalogs and general bibliographic aids relating to the countries under discussion.

U.S. Library of Congress. *Quarterly Journal*. v. 1- July-Sept. 1943- Washington, D.C. Quarterly. Includes regular surveys of new acquisitions on the countries of East Central and Southeastern Europe, and contains, *inter alia*, the following articles of specific area interest: "The Czech Renaissance, Viewed Through Rare Books" (v. 14, May 1957: 95-107); "The Glagolitic Missal of 1483" (v. 20, March 1963: 93-98); "The Hungarian Constitutional Compact of 1867" (v. 24, October 1967: 287-308); "The Image of America in Accounts of Polish Travelers of the 18th and 19th Centuries" (v. 22, July 1965: 243-45); "The Matica Hrvatska and Croatian Literature" (v. 23, July 1966: 251-56); "The Matica Srpska and Serbian Cultural Development" (v. 22, July 1965: 259-65); "Printing in Poland's Golden Age" (v. 23, July 1966: 204-17); "Sources for Bulgarian Biography" (v. 24, April 1967: 97-102).

U.S. Library of Congress. Division of Bibliography. *The Balkans; a Selected List of References*. Compiled by Helen Conover. Washington, D.C., 1943. 5 v.

U.S. Library of Congress. Division of Bibliography. *Greece: A Selected List of References*. Compiled by Ann Duncan Brown and Helen Dudenbostel Jones. Washington, D.C., 1943. 101 p.

U.S. Library of Congress. European Affairs Division. *War and Postwar Greece: an Analysis Based on Greek Writings*. Prepared by Floyd A. Spencer. Washington, D.C., 1952. 175 p.

U.S. Library of Congress. Periodicals Division. *A Check List of Foreign Newspapers in the Library of Congress*. Compiled under the direction of Henry S. Parsons. Washington, D.C., 1929. 209 p.

U.S. Library of Congress. Serial Division. *Newspapers Received Currently in the Library of Congress*. 4th ed. Washington, D.C., 1972. 45 p.

U.S. Library of Congress. Slavic and Central European Division. *East Germany; a Selected Bibliography*. Compiled by Arnold H. Price. Washington, D.C., 1967. 133 p.

U.S. Library of Congress. Slavic and Central European Division. *Newspapers of East Central and Southeastern Europe in the Library of Congress*. Edited by Robert G. Carlton. Washington, D.C., 1965. 204 p.

U.S. Library of Congress. Slavic and Central European Division. *The USSR and Eastern Europe: Periodicals in Western Languages*. Compiled by Paul L. Horecky and Robert G. Carlton. 3d ed. Washington, D.C., 1967. 89 p.

Anita R. Navon
Library of Congress

Albania

General Information

THE ALBANIAN COLLECTIONS of the Library of Congress are by far the smallest of its East European holdings. In mid-1972, for example, the Library's Albanian book holdings made up less than one-half of one percent of its total East European book collection. Nonetheless, this collection of Albanian materials is the largest and most comprehensive in the United States.

The limited size of the Library's Albanian holdings stems from two major factors. First, until recently relatively few works on Albania were published either within or outside Albania. As late as 1938 only 61 books were published in Albania in the entire year. A random examination of several Albanian bibliographies indicates that, on an average, less than 20 book-length studies dealing with Albanian life or culture were published annually in foreign languages during the interwar period. Following the establishment of the present regime in November of 1944, both scholarly and literary output increased markedly. According to official Albanian statistics, 628 books were published in 1967. By the early 1970s approximately 20 newspapers and 40 periodicals were published in Albania.

Second, except for newspapers and periodicals, it was exceedingly difficult to obtain publications from Albania until the mid-1960s. Consequently there are some gaps in the Library's holdings of post-World War II Albanian materials.

Since 1969 the Library of Congress has conducted a limited exchange of publications with the Albanian National Library and the Library of the State University of Tirana, but most of the Library's Albanian acquisitions have been obtained through private dealers.

In the late 1960s, under the PL 480 Program with Yugoslavia, the Library began receiving Albanian publications produced by the Rilindja Publishing House of Priština, Yugoslavia. As the lot of the Albanian minority in Yugoslavia and the state of Yugoslav-Albanian relations have continued to improve, the Rilindja Publishing House has been increasing its output of literary and scholarly works originally published in Albania.

In June 1972 the Albanian collections of the Library of Congress comprised approximately 1,800 books, about 80 percent of which were fully cataloged. Of the Library's holdings, about 60 percent are in the Albanian language, about 30 percent in West European languages, and the remainder in Russian, East European, and other languages. About 15 percent of the works were published before 1914, another 15 percent between 1914 and 1945, and approximately 70 percent since 1945. During the late 1960s the Library added an average of approximately 100 books annually to its Albanian holdings.

In June, 1972, the Library was receiving 35 Albanian periodicals and 11 newspapers. All but three of the periodicals and three of the newspapers regularly received were published in Albania. In addition, there are about 20 discontinued Albanian periodicals of varying degrees of importance. With few exceptions, the newspapers and periodicals are in the Albanian language. The post-World War II collection of newspapers and periodicals constitutes one of the most important and valuable portions of the Library's Albanian collections.

Research and Bibliographic Aids

Most of the Albanian materials in the Library of Congress are cataloged under the major entries for Albania, sometimes with cross-references, and under author or corporate entries. The Library also has relatively rich Albanian bibliographic materials. Among the more useful of these are *Southeastern Europe: A Guide to Basic Publications,* ed. Paul L. Horecky, (Chicago, 1969), pp. 73-115); Emile Legrand's *Bibliographie albanaise* (Paris, 1912); Library of Congress, Division of Bibliography, *Albania* (Washington, 1943); Library of Congress, *East European Accessions List* (Washington, 1951-61); and Jup Kastrati, *Bibliografi Shqipe: 29/XI/1944-31/XII/1958* [Albanian Bibliography: 29/11/1944-31/12/1958] (Tirana, 1959). The quarterly *Libri Shqip* [Albanian Books] lists and briefly discusses books published in Albania. The monthly publication *Artikujt e Periodikut Shqip* [Albanian Periodical Articles] lists the major articles published in journals and newspapers in Albania. Periodical articles published in non-Albanian sources are listed in the standard guides to periodical literature.

Documentary Collections

The Library of Congress' holdings of published documents relating to Albania are fairly strong for the 19th and 20th centuries, especially in the areas of politics and diplomacy. Its holdings for the earlier periods of Albanian history are limited and will be of only marginal value to the specialist. It should be noted, however, that the most significant primary sources for the study of pre-19th century Albania will be found in the Ottoman, Vatican, Venetian, French, and other European archives. Since the mid-1950s Albanian scholars have been identifying, classifying, microfilming, translating, and publishing what they deem to be the most important of this archival material. In June 1972 the Library had five of the volumes of published documents in this series, *Burime dhe materiale për historinë e Shqipërisë* [Sources and Materials on the History of Albania], prepared by the staff of the Institute of History and Linguistics of the State University of Tirana. These volumes pertain to developments in 17th- and 18th-century Albania. The fruits of this project will render obsolete most of the pre-19th century Albanian documentary materials in the Library of Congress, but a project of this magnitude requires time and it will be some time before the Library's holdings will be adequate for research on pre-19th century Albania.

The situation is more promising for those working in 19th- and 20th-century Albanian history, politics, and international relations. Inasmuch as the Albanian question was an important issue in European diplomacy at various times between 1878 and 1914, there are valuable data regarding both domestic and international developments in such major documentary collections as *Die grosse Politik der europäischen Kabinette: 1871-1914; Documents diplomatique français: 1871-1914;* and *I Documenti diplomatici italiani.*

An indispensable source for the initial period of Albanian independence (November 1912-January 1914) is Dhimitër Kotini, et al. (eds.), *Qeveria e përkohëshme e Vlorës dhe veprimtaria e saj* [The Provisional Government of Vlorë and Its Activity] (Tirana, 1963).

Among the most useful non-Albanian sources, apart from the Italian documents, for the study of developments after World War I are the *Documents on British Foreign Policy: 1919-39* (especially their coverage of the Italian invasion of Albania in April 1939) and *Foreign Relations of the United States* (especially the reporting on the Albanian situation between 1944 and 1946). There is also some worthwhile information regarding the internal and external problems that confronted Albania during the 1920s in the *Official Journal and Records of the Assembly* of the League of Nations for that decade.

Two of the most valuable items in the Library's collection of Albanian documents are *Bisedimet e Dhomes së Deputetvet . . . 1925-26* [Deliberations of the Chamber of Deputies . . . 1925-26] and *Bisedimet e Parliamentit: 1928-36* [Parliamentary Debates: 1928-36]. These materials constitute one of the most valuable primary sources on Albanian politics during the Zog regime (1925-39) available outside Albania. Another important documentary account of the interwar period is Veli Dedi, et al., eds., *Dokumenta e materiale historike nga lufta e popullit Shqiptar për liri e demokraci: 1917-1941* [Documents and Historical Materials from the Struggle of the Albanian People for Freedom and Democracy: 1917-1941] (Tirana, 1959).

Since the late 1950s a number of significant documentary collections of material dealing with the World War II and post-World War II periods have been published in Albania. The Library's holdings of these items, especially those published since the mid-1960s, are sufficiently strong to support substantial in-depth research into this crucial period of Albanian history.

The Library, for example, has been receiving the *Vepra* [Works] of Enver Hoxha, First Secretary of the Albanian Party of Labor, since its establishment in 1941. Nine volumes of Hoxha's *Vepra,* covering the period November 1941-August 1952, were published between 1968 and 1972. These documents, some of which have been made public for the first time, are indispensable for serious research in the post-1941 period. The Library also possesses the four volumes published by mid-1972 of *Dokumenta kryesore të Partisë së Punës të Shqipërisë* [Principal Documents of the Party of Labor of Albania] (Tirana, 1960-70) as well as the proceedings of the Third (1956), Fourth (1961), and Fifth (1966) Congresses of the Albanian Party of Labor. In addition, the collection contains individual volumes of documents concerning such topics as the Albanian War of National Liberation (1941-45), the mass organizations, and Soviet-Albanian relations. With few exceptions these materials are in the Albanian language.

While there are some serious gaps in the Library's holdings of post-1941 published documents, the absence of these sources is somewhat offset by the Library's comprehensive collection of Albanian newspapers and periodicals of this era.

Newspapers and Periodicals

Newspapers and periodicals are an important source for the study of Albania. The modern Albanian press, however, dates back only to the last half of the 19th century. Prior to that the Ottoman political authorities and the Greek Orthodox hierarchy had discouraged the use of the written Albanian language.

One of the most significant manifestations of the emerging Albanian nationalist movement during the late 19th and early 20th centuries was the establishment of Albanian language newspapers and journals in such countries as Italy, Romania, Bulgaria, Belgium, and the United States. These Albanian publications played a major role in the achievement of Albania's independence in 1912 and in the preservation of her territorial integrity and sovereignty following World War I. Because of the unsettled state of affairs prevailing within Albania between 1912-20 the materials published in the Albanian press both abroad and later at home are among the most important sources of information regarding developments at this time.

The only Albanian publications for this period available in the Library are a complete collection of the monthly *Albania*, published in Brussels and London between 1897 and 1909, and *The Adriatic Review*, published in Boston during 1918-19. However, the content of *Albania*, edited by the gifted writer Faik Konitza, is representative of most of the nationalist periodicals of this era and is superior to them in quality.

A valuable source for developments both within Albania and in the Albanian community in the United States is the newspaper *Dielli*, published continuously in Boston since 1909 by the Pan Albanian Federation of America. The Library has extensive holdings of this important newspaper, in part on microfilm.

For the years 1920-39, the Library's newspaper and periodical holdings comprise only broken runs of several Albanian periodicals, the most important and extensive of these being *Fletorja Zyrtare* [The Official Gazette], which published the texts of laws, decrees, and official statements of the Albanian government. The Library's holdings of this item cover the years 1931-36 only.

The Albanian newspaper and periodical collections are stronger for the period extending from the 1940s to the present. These collections are somewhat spotty for the later 1940s and early 1950s, but improve in quality thereafter. The Library's Albanian newspaper holdings up to the early 1960s are described in Robert G. Carlton's (ed.), *Newspapers of East Central and Southeastern Europe in the Library of Congress* (Washington, 1965).

All of the major national newspapers which circulate in Albania today (e.g., *Zëri i Popullit*, organ of the Albanian Party of Labor, *Bashkimi*, organ of the Albanian Democratic Front; and *Drita*, organ of the Albanian League of Writers and Artists) are received by the Library of Congress. However, the Library does not receive any of the local newspapers established during the late 1960s (apparently these do not circulate outside the country), but the Library does receive *Laïko Vima*, the Greek language organ of the Greek minority in southern Albania. Although there is a degree of repetition in the coverage of Albanian newspapers, they are one of the most important research tools for the study of contemporary Albania.

In addition to newspapers published in Albania, since 1962 the Library has received the Albanian-language newspaper *Rilindja*, published in Priština, Yugoslavia. This newspaper is the organ of the Albanians of the Autonomous Province of Kosovo-Metohija.

For the most part, the Library's holdings of post-World War II Albanian periodicals extend back to the mid-1950s. With the exception of the State University of Tirana's medical journal, which is maintained in the National Library of Medicine, the Library of Congress currently receives all the major scholarly periodicals produced in Albania. These are all published in the Albanian language. For the benefit of those scholars who do not read Albanian, since 1964 the Institute of History and Linguistics of the State University of Tirana has published *Studia Albanica*, which contains translations (into Russian and Western European languages) of articles in the social sciences and humanities that had originally appeared in the leading Albanian scholarly journals. English translations of selected articles from Albanian newspapers and periodicals appear in the *Translations on Eastern Europe* series of the U.S. Joint Publications Research Services. Indexes to these materials are available in the Newspaper and Current Periodicals Reading Room of the Library of Congress.

Of the Albanian periodicals published in Yugoslavia, the Library receives only *Jehona*, printed in Skopje, and, irregularly, *Gjurmime Albanologjike*. This latter journal, issued in Priština

(1962-), contains some of the most significant contributions made to Albanological studies by the new generation of Albanian specialists in Yugoslavia.

Most of the periodicals dealing with Albania published in the West since 1945 have been the organs of the various anticommunist émigré political groups. In recent years most of these have encountered financial difficulties and have either expired or appear infrequently. The Library has a representative collection of these publications. Among the nonpolitical periodicals of the post-World War II era *Shêjzat: Le Pleiad* and *Studi Albanesi,* both published in Italy, have made noteworthy contributions to the study of Albanian society and culture.

Special Collections

There are two special collections of Albanian materials worthy of mention: the Law and Map collections.

The Law collection, which is housed mainly in the Law Library, comprises approximately 275 items. As is the case with the main body of the Library's Albanian holdings, this collection is richest for the period since 1945 and is of sufficient depth to support meaningful research in Albanian and comparative law.

For the pre-World War II period, the Law collection includes the complete compilations of the 1928 Civil Code, 1929 Penal Code, and 1929 Commerical Code. There are also several dozen monographs and commentaries on the law codes and contemporary legal questions.

In addition to the civil and criminal codes of the post-1945 regime, the Law Library has the 11 volumes and supplements of the *Kodifikimi i përgjitheshme i legjislacionit në fuqi të Republikës Popullore të Shqipërisë: 1945-57* [The General Codification of the Legislation in Force in the People's Republic of Albania: 1945-57] (Tirana, 1958-63), and a number of important works dealing with the Albanian constitutional system. The collection includes a complete run of the successor to the *Fletorja Zyrtare,* the *Gazeta Zyrtare,* which began publication in 1944. The Law Library has an Albanian specialist who provides expert assistance.

The Albanian map collection, which is housed in the Geography and Map Division, consists of approximately 160 maps and 3 atlases. The individual maps in the collection date from 1786 to 1969. There are, however, no rare maps among the Albanian holdings. About 90 percent of the maps were prepared in the period following World War I, mostly by non-Albanian cartographers. Many of the more important items in the collection were prepared by the Istituto Geografico de Agostini.

Most of the maps are physical and economic. They reflect the interest of the European powers in developing Albania's economic and mineral resources during the interwar period. Consequently, the maps are of greatest value to economic historians and physical geographers. The aerial maps of the cities of Tirana, Durrës, and Vlorë, prepared in 1963-64, should be of use to the urban geographer and social historian.

On the whole, the items in this collection appear to be of high quality and superior to those available to scholars on an unrestricted basis in any other institution in the United States.

Books

The Library holds almost all books of any consequence on Albania that have appeared either in Europe or the United States during the 20th century. Most of the Library's collection of books issued in Albania have been obtained through purchase or gifts, thus it is less systematic and selective than the aforementioned collection.

The book holdings are very weak in art, music, science and technology, sociology and anthropology, education, and geography, in part because only limited work relating to Albania has been done in these fields by either Albanian or non-Albanian scholars.

In mid-1972, the main strengths of the book holdings lay in the areas of history (including travel accounts), literature, law, language and linguistics, politics, diplomacy, and economics. There is sufficient material in each of these categories, when used in conjunction with the other components of the Albanian collection, to sustain original and significant research.

Nicholas C. Pano
Western Illinois University

Bulgaria

THE DEVELOPMENT OF the Bulgarian collection in the Library of Congress parallels the evolution of the Library itself and the development of publishing in Bulgaria. The first contacts of the Library with Bulgarian agencies appear to date from 1904 when an exchange of official government publications—law sources, records of the National Assembly, census and other statistical compilations, etc.—was initiated. In the ensuing years the Library also began to acquire the publications of the Bulgarian Academy of Sciences, the University of Sofia, and learned societies, as well as individually published works of Bulgarian scholars, publicists, and literati. The volume of acquisitions, reaching the present excellent level in 1969, has made the Library by far the richest repository of materials from and about Bulgaria in the United States.

In assessing the nature, strengths, and weaknesses of the Library's collection, the history and pattern of Bulgarian publishing must be taken into account. Since printing in Cyrillic did not become possible in the Ottoman Empire until the middle of the 19th century, very few Bulgarian books appeared before the country's liberation in 1878 and most of them were printed outside the Empire in Vienna, Belgrade, Bucharest, and Budapest. The first book in modern Bulgarian appeared in 1806, the first periodical in 1844. According to the most recent bibliography of publications from this period of the Bulgarian "renaissance," *Bŭlgarska vŭzrozhdenska knizhnina; analitichen repertoar na bŭlgarskite knigi i periodichni izdaniia, 1806-1878,* compiled by Man'o Stoianov, 2 v. (Sofia, 1957-59), only 1,910 books (in a loose sense of the word) were printed during those years, most of them being translations and compilations from foreign sources for use in the newly established Bulgarian churches and schools. In 1950, the Library succeeded in acquiring about 700 of these books through the purchase of the private collection of Todor D. Plochev. The collection was analyzed and described in the May, 1957, issue of the Library's *Quarterly Journal of Current Acquisitions* by Charles Jelavich, who found in it some 40 titles not listed in the earlier bibliography of Bulgarian "incunabula," *Opis na starite pechatani bŭlgarski knigi, 1802-1877,* by V. Pogorelov (1923). [Here and hereafter Sofia is the place of publication, unless otherwise indicated.] The books in the Plochev collection are kept as a self-contained unit in the Rare Book Division. A few titles of that period, which were acquired separately, are cataloged and have been placed in the general collections.

Thus, Bulgarian publishing of other than purely historical interest dates from the liberation of the country and the decade of the 1880s when the Bulgarian Literary Society, founded in 1869 in Brăila, Romania, resumed its activity in Sofia, the State Printing Office was set up, and the Higher School was opened. The annual rate of publishing was slightly over 200 books in 1878-85, 350 in the ensuing decade, and 800 in 1895-1905, so that when the first comprehensive bibliography, *Bŭlgarski knigopis za sto godini, 1806-1905,* was produced by A. Teodorov-Balan (1909), it showed some 15,000 titles. The sources of the principal publications were the Literary Society, which in 1911 took the name Bulgarian Academy of Sciences, the Higher School, which became the University of Sofia in 1904, and the various government agencies. A large proportion of the individually published books continued to be translations and compilations and their average size remained small (under 80 pages). In fact, another Bulgarian bibliographer, Nikola Nachov, asserted at the time that "many of them are rubbish and Bulgarian letters would have lost nothing, on the contrary, would have gained if they did not exist." According to the national bibliography, *Bŭlgarski knigopis,* issued since 1897 when the National Library in Sofia became by law the deposit library, the book production, especially by private publishers, rose substantially after 1905 to some 1,500 titles per year and, after a slump in the wars of 1912-18, to 2,300 until 1942. Since World War II, following another slump in 1943-45, it has averaged about 3,000 titles per year.

The substantial body of some 180,000 titles, which these figures indicate, contains a high percentage of publications of dubious value in the case of selective acquisition. For example, in an average interwar year (1930) over 35 percent of the titles published were pamphlets under 33 pages, or 55 percent if those under 65 pages are added. Books of more than 160 pages amounted to slightly over 10 percent. In content, the annual production has included numerous translations, textbooks for the lower grades, children's books, repetitive propaganda materials, works of popularization, minor publications of government agencies for internal use, instructional manuals and "How To" books, calendars, and the like, most of which are of little or no consequence to Bulgarian studies pursued outside Bulgaria. The publications of importance thus appear to be not more than 50 percent of the total production, and those of central importance about 10 percent.

In this light the Library's collection can be rated as very good and, in comparison with collections in other great libraries outside Bulgaria, as superior. By the end of 1968, when the present program of comprehensive acquisition was initiated, the Library had, in addition to works in Russian and Western languages on Bulgarian subjects, approximately 16,500 Bulgarian books which for the most part are of central importance to Bulgarian studies. Most of these (some 65 percent) have appeared since 1945, reflecting the postwar increase in Bulgarian publishing as well as the intensification of the Library's acquisition effort.

Under the arrangements negotiated as part of the National Program for Acquisitions and Cataloging and in effect since January 1, 1969, the Library currently receives from the National Library in Sofia at least one copy of each book (monograph or volume in monographic series) appearing in Bulgaria, with these exceptions: textbooks below the university level; children's books; translations into Bulgarian, unless the translation is accompanied by introductions, comments, or other material adding to the original and, in the case of translations of works of outstanding American authors, unless specifically requested by the Library; materials not available in the book trade or for exchange purposes and publications intended for internal use only; materials of little importance such as pamphlets, leaflets, publications with a small circulation, and the like; and music and maps, which continue to be acquired on a more selective basis. The books are shipped by the National Library in Sofia by airmail every week, as soon as possible after it receives the legal deposit copy, and are accompanied by the catalog cards printed in Sofia, to facilitate the Library's cataloging. The Library also receives each week by airmail the printed cards for all other publications listed in *Bŭlgarski knigopis* (which is currently issued every two weeks), so that additional selections can be made by its own recommending officers.

The monographic holdings in the Library's collection by and large reflect the main fields of publishing in Bulgaria since the 1880s. The largest block is formed by publications in the general domain of philology (PG 801-, ca. 5,500 v.), which encompasses works of literature, criticism, literary history, linguistics, and folklore and has traditionally been the country's most fertile intellectual field. The collection contains, with minor exceptions, the works of the Bulgarian writers, critics, and literary scholars listed in *Bŭlgarski pisateli; biografii, bibliografiia,* by Georgi Konstantinov and others (1961), *Bibliographische Einführung in das Studium der neueren bulgarischen Literatur (1850-1950),* by Peter Gerlinghoff (Meisenheim am Glan, 1969), and other bibliographies of Bulgarian literature. Among the now rare works is the four-volume *Istoriia na novata bŭlgarska literatura* of Boian Penev (1932-36). The early grammars in the collection include the small publication of the American missionary Elias Riggs, *Notes on the Grammar of the Bulgarian Language* (Smyrna, 1844), the first attempt by a Westerner to establish the rules of the uncodified speech of the Bulgarians in the Ottoman Empire. There are numerous studies of medieval Bulgarian, as well as bilingual and multilingual dictionaries, translations of Bulgarian literary works, publications on the Bulgarian theater, and other subfields of philology.

The second-largest block consists of publications on Bulgarian history, which as a field of study in Bulgaria shares with philology the longest academic traditions and many of the country's finest scholars. The subject classification (DR 51-) includes land descriptions and travel accounts. Together with Bulgarian publications on Macedonia and other regions historically linked with Bulgaria, Class D contains approximately 3,000 Bulgarian books. The collection contains the great series *Sbornik za narodni umotvoreniia i narodopis*, 53 v. to date (1889-), *Izvori za bŭlgarskata istoriia,* 20 v. to date (1954-), and other publications of sources and documents as well as the general and period histories and the major monographic investigations of Bulgarian historians.

The Library holds a fine collection of Bulgarian legal publications (KB 3000-), numbering some 2,850 volumes, including the annual runs of the official law gazette, *Dŭrzhaven vestnik,* since 1944, collections of Bulgarian laws enacted since 1879, indexes, textual analyses, textbooks, and monographs of Bulgarian experts. A useful guide is *Legal Sources and Bibliography of Bulgaria,* by Ivan Sipkov (New York, 1956), which identifies the Library's holdings as of 1955 and is supplemented by current files in the European Law Division. Related materials are classified in Class J which contain the earlier runs of *Dŭrzhaven vestnik* dating back to 1879 and the records of the Bulgarian legislature, *Stenografski dnevnitsi na Narodnoto Sŭbranie,* since 1879. Books on Bulgarian politics (JN 9600-), most of which deal with the history and organization of the Bulgarian Communist Party, comprise a substantial group of some 750 volumes. The Library also has about 200 books on the party's ideology, in Class H (HX 361-).

The collection contains numerous publications on Bulgarian economic and social history, economic development, transportation, communication, commerce, finance, etc., but they are mostly books published after 1945 and include only a fraction of what is listed in the comprehensive bibliography, *Stopanska i sotsialna knizhnina v Bŭlgariia; bibliografiia na bŭlgarskite knigi i statii ot nachaloto do dnes, 1850-1945,* edited by Todor Vladigerov (Svishtov, 1948). In this class, among the large number of statistical publications received from Bulgaria over the years, are sets of *Statisticheski godishnik na Tsarstvo Bŭlgariia* (1909-42) and its successor, *Statisticheski godishnik na Narodna Republika Bŭlgariia.*

Another substantial group of some 700 volumes (AS 343-) consists of publications of the Bulgarian Academy of Sciences, which are reflected to 1953 in *Opis na izdaniiata na Bŭlgarskata akademiia na naukite, 1869-1953,* by Emiliia Sŭbeva and Mariia Stancheva (1956), and those of the University of Sofia, listed to 1965 in *Bibliografiia na Sofiiskiia universitet "Sv. Kliment Okhridski," 1904-1942,* by Asen Kovachev (1943) and its continuations. Publications by and on the Bulgarian Orthodox Church (BX 650-) comprise a much smaller group, less than 100 volumes. Small collections on Bulgarian geography, anthropology, education, music, arts, architecture, bibliography, and other subjects are scattered throughout the Library. A substantial reference collection of books, some 400 volumes, is assembled in the Slavic Room. Bulgarian reference works and a select number of principal publications in various fields are discussed in a publication of the Slavic and Central European Division, *Bulgaria: A Bibliographic Guide,* by M. Pundeff (1965; reprinted by Arno Press, New York 1968), which lists the Library's holdings with call numbers. Reference files maintained in the Slavic and Central European Division supplement this information. Noteworthy acquisitions have also been indicated in annual surveys and articles in the Library's *Quarterly Journal.* Its April, 1967, issue has a discussion of the main sources for Bulgarian biography by M. Pundeff, identifying the Library's holdings in this field.

The Library's acquisitions of journals and serials reveal a similar pattern to that of books. At first the efforts were directed to acquiring the official Bulgarian serials reflecting legislative activity and statistical data as well as the serials and journals of various government departments and agencies, the academy, the university, and leading learned societies. The early collection of government materials is indicated in *List of the Serial Publications of Foreign Governments, 1815-1931,* by Winifred Gregory (New York, 1932). In addition to the publications of the Academy and the University, the Library acquired *Spisanie na Bŭlgarskoto ikonomichesko druzhestvo, Godishnik na Bŭlgarskoto prirodoizpitatelno druzhestvo* and its *Trudove, Izvestiia na Bŭlgarskoto istorichesko druzhestvo, Izvestiia na Narodniia etnografski muzei,* and other learned journals and serials. However, a comparison of the Library's acquisitions with the exhaustive bibliography of pre-1945 Bulgarian periodicals, *Bŭlgarski periodichen pechat, 1844-1944; anotiran bibliografski ukazatel,* by Dimitŭr P. Ivanchev, 3 v. (1962-69) reveals that the Library lacks a number of the important journals from these years, notably *Bŭlgarska misŭl* (1925-44), *Bŭlgarska sbirka* (1894-1915), *Demokraticheski pregled* (1902-28), *Iuridicheski pregled* (1893-1933), *Khiperion* (1922-31), *Novo vreme* (1897-1923), *Obshto delo* (1900-05), *Otets Paisii* (1928-43), *Prosveta* (1935-43), *Uchilishten pregled* (1896-1949), *Voenno-istoricheski sbornik* (1927-), *Zlatorog* (1920-43), and *Zveno* (1928-34). Moreover, in numerous instances it has only a few issues of the periodicals it does hold.

In contrast, the acquisitions of periodicals since 1945 leaves relatively little to be desired. At present the Library receives, by purchase or exchange, some 300 choice titles among the 839 titles in this category listed by Bulgarian statistical sources in 1970. The annual *Bŭlgarski periodichen pechat; bibliografski ukazatel,* issued in Bulgaria since 1967 (for 1965), lists all current periodicals, including newspapers. A partial list of the Library's holdings indicating call numbers is *Bibliography of Social Science Periodicals and Monograph Series: Bulgaria, 1944-1960,* compiled by the Bureau of the Census in 1961. Another useful list is the Library's *The USSR and Eastern Europe: Periodicals in Western Languages,* 3rd ed. (1967).

In regard to newspapers, the Library's acquisitions before 1944 are negligible, as evidenced by its bibliography *Newspapers of East Central and Southeastern Europe in the Library of Congress* issued in 1965, and are limited to occasional issues of *La Bulgarie, Bulgarische Wochenschau, Dnes, L'Echo de Bulgarie, Nova vecher, La Parole Bulgare* (fairly complete), *Slovo, Vita Bulgara, Zaria, Zora,* and *Zornitsa.* The volume and regularity of acquisition improved after 1944 to the point that the Library now has nearly complete sets of such principal newspapers as *Otechestven front, Rabotnichesko delo,* and *Zemedelsko zname,* and in general a substantial collection of central and local newspapers. At present it receives 13 central and 21 local newspapers. The Library's current subscriptions are listed in its *Newspapers Received Currently in the Library of Congress,* 4th ed. (1974).

The Manuscript Division of the Library houses papers of a number of American statesmen, diplomats, and others who have dealt with Bulgarian questions since World War I: President Wilson, Secretaries of State Lansing and Hull, Ambassador Lawrence Steinhardt, among others. The papers and the records of the American Peace Commission in 1919 are held by the Manuscript Division, which has developed finding aids for most of them. Bulgarian manuscripts are described in *Opis na slaviansite rŭkopisi v Sofiiskata narodna biblioteka,* issued by the National Library in Sofia, 3 v. (1910-64) and *Pŭtevoditel na Tsentralniia dŭrzhaven istoricheski arkhiv* (1970), and other guides to manuscript collections in Bulgaria.

The Library's prints and photographs pertaining to Bulgaria are limited. The Prints and Photographs Division holds about 500 photos, stereos, and reproductions of paintings with historical subjects from the Russo-Turkish war of 1877-78 and the Balkan wars of 1912-13, as well as views of streets, buildings, and people in Sofia and the provinces in that period. Some of the pictures, including a few of leading Bulgarian personalities in the 1920s, were taken by American Red Cross personnel and reflect Red Cross activities in Bulgaria.

The Library's Geography and Map Division holds a substantial number of maps of Bulgaria in single sheets, map sets, and atlases made in various countries and periods. The earliest is Antonio Zatta's *Le provincie di Bulgaria e Rumelia tratte dalla carta dell'Impero Ottomano del Sig^r Rizzi Zanoni* (Venice, 1781). The single sheets classified under "Bulgaria" fill eight map cabinet drawers and include historical, physical, political, military, geological, agricultural, local (region and city), and other maps. In addition, there are numerous single sheets under "Balkan States" and "Turkey," as well as map sets and atlases from various periods which include Bulgaria and the Bulgarian lands.

Marin Pundeff
California State University, Northridge

Czechoslovakia

THE RATE OF acquisition of Czech and Slovak books and periodicals has increased since the Second World War with the improvement of exchange programs. Through an agreement between the Library of Congress and the State Library of the Czechoslovak Socialist Republic (1969) the Library of Congress acquires everything of research value that is currently published in Czechoslovakia. An exchange of official publications, government documents, and microfilms is also in force. All told, the Library has some 150 exchange partners in Czechoslovakia, including museums, research institutes, libraries, and universities. The State Library is, however, the main partner. In addition, the Library receives most books and serials of significance dealing with Czech and Slovak matters published abroad.

As of this writing, the Library has approximately 75,000 books dealing with Czechoslovakia: about 82 percent of which are in Czech or Slovak, 17 percent in Western languages, and one percent in Russian. The periodical holdings amount to 2,400 titles, with about 1,000 current subscriptions. The newspapers total 174 titles, with 25 current subscriptions. About 30 percent of all holdings describe the period before World War I, 30 percent cover the years 1914-45, and 40 percent the events since 1945. The Library's Czechoslovak holdings have been treated in several Library of Congress publications: Rudolf Sturm's *Czechoslovakia; A Bibliographic Guide* (1967); *Newspapers of East Central and Southeastern Europe in the Library of Congress* (1965); *The USSR and Eastern Europe; Periodicals in Western Languages* (3d ed., 1967) by P. L. Horecky and R. G. Carlton; the *East European Accessions Index* (for the years 1951-61); and in *Bibliography of Social Science Periodicals and Monograph Series: Czechoslovakia, 1948-1963,* of the U.S. Department of Commerce.

Bibliographies and General Reference Works

CZECH BIBLIOGRAPHIES. The Library has 40 bibliographic works covering the entire production of books and serials, starting with *Knihopis československých tisků od doby nejstarší až do konce XVIII. století.* The national bibliography of the Czechoslovak Republic *Bibliografický katalog ČSR* (since 1960, ČSSR) began publication in 1922 and its entire run is at the Library.

Several bibliographies and catalogs are devoted exclusively to serials, such as Miroslav Laiske's *Časopisectví v Čechách, 1650-1847* and subsequent bibliographies by František Roubík. Since 1956 current bibliographies are listed in the annual *Soupis českých bibliografií.*

SLOVAK BIBLIOGRAPHIES.   Among a dozen works devoted solely to things Slovak is the massive *Bibliografia slovenského písomníctva* by L'udovít V. Rizner, and subsequent bibliographies compiled by Michal Fedor. Since the 1950s, *Bibliografický katalog* has listed current Slovak materials separately in *Slovenské knihy* (later *Knihy)* and *Slovenské hudobniny.* The Library also has several bibliographies by Jozef Kuzmík listing Slovak books in Western, Eastern, and Slavic languages; the more recent volumes on translations from and into Slovak by Libor Knězek; and Michael Lacko's *Slovak Bibliography Abroad 1945-1965* (v. 7 of *Slovak Studies*).

Slovak serials are covered in several volumes listed above under Czech Bibliographies, in Michal Potemra's *Bibliografia slovenských novín a časopisov; Súpis novín a časopisov na Slovensku,* by Matica slovenská, and its monthly *Články v slovenských časopisoch.*

REFERENCE WORKS.   The coverage of Czech and Slovak encyclopedias is comprehensive, including *Ottův slovník naučný* and its *Dodatky, Masarykův slovník naučný,* both editions of *Československá vlastivěda* as well as *Slovenský naučný slovník* and *Slovenská vlastiveda.* Handbooks and surveys, both prewar and postwar, are also well represented.

Biographies include *Album representantů všech oborů veřejného života československého* (1927), *České biografie* (1936-41), *Kdo je kdo v Československu* (1969-). Statistical materials issued by the Státní úřad statistický (since 1961, Ústřední komise lidové kontroly a statistiky) abound in the Library of Congress, the most comprehensive being the periodical publications *Zprávy* and its German version *Mitteilungen, Statistický obzor,* and *Statistická ročenka.*

THE LAND.   The collection contains several dozen general books on geography, both physical and human. Lists of inhabited places can be found in *Statistický lexikon obcí Republiky československé* (circa 1930) and *Administrativní lexikon obcí Republiky československé* (1955). Several works cover the climate, e.g., *Atlas podnebí Československé republiky* and *Bulletin československých seismických stanic.* For the flora there are, among many others, *Studia botanica Čechoslovaca* and *Flora ČSR,* and for the study of animal life, *Fauna ČSR,* Josef Kratochvíl's massive *Soustava a jména živočichů,* and several others. Geology and geodesy can be studied in a dozen works, including the two-volume *Regional Geology of Czechoslovakia,* edited by Josef F. Svoboda, and the periodical *Studia geophysica et geodaetica.*

Books and guides describing the country and its main cities for the tourist in Czech, Slovak, and all principal foreign languages are plentiful.

The People

The reader will find a description of the population in general in a number of books. The Czechs can be studied in such basic periodicals as *Český lid* and *Československá etnografie;* the Slovaks, in *Slovenská vlastiveda* and in the periodical *Slovenský národopis.* The holdings on the German, Jewish, Hungarian, Polish, and Ukrainian minority groups are rich, including both prewar and postwar publications.

The coverage of materials dealing with the Czechs and Slovaks living abroad is comprehensive. Books on those living in the United States seem to be here *in toto,* from the studies on the 17th-century immigrant Augustin Herrmann to the most recent immigration wave after 1968.

History

TO WORLD WAR I.   At the time of this writing, the Library has nearly 700 titles listed under Czech or Slovak history or the history of Czechoslovakia. Among them are the five volumes of *Bibliografie české historie,* by Čeněk Zíbrt, and its continuation *Bibliografie české* (and later *československé) historie;* the periodical *Průvodce po státních archivech,* issued by the Ministry of the Interior; *Soupis archivní literatury v českých zemích, 1895-1956,* by Otakar Bauer and

Ludmila Mrázková; and Teodor Lamoš's *Bibliografia k archívom na Slovensku*. Histories of the country include first editions of František Palacký's five-volume *Geschichte von Böhmen* and the 10-volume *Dějiny národu českého;* L'udovít Holotík's massive *Dejiny Slovenska*. Contemporary historians are well represented. The Habsburg monarchy and its dissolution are treated in numerous studies.

The Library has most of the works dealing with the Czech and Slovak involvement in World War I and the Czechoslovak military units (legions) in Russia, France, and Italy.

1918 TO THE PRESENT.   Most of the publications on the first 20 years of the Czechoslovak Republic are in the Library of Congress, in Czech and Slovak, English, German, and other languages. The Little Entente and other diplomatic activities are covered in a dozen books, and works on major personalities are well represented. Two dozen newspapers and other general periodicals current in 1918-38 are here, including the dailies *Prager Tagblatt, Prager Presse,* the Bratislava-based *Grenzbote,* and incomplete runs of several newspapers in Czech and Slovak.

The Library has nearly everything of substance on the Munich crisis and World War II.

The Czechoslovak political and military activities at home during World War II, including those of the Slovak state, are covered amply. Further, there is a nearly complete run of the Prague daily *Der neue Tag* and a file of the Bratislava biweekly *Slowakische Rundschau,* as well as a half dozen books on the Subcarpathian Ukraine (Podkarpatská Rus).

For research on Czechoslovak activities abroad, there are the files of the Paris-based weekly *Československý boj* (1939-40), the London weekly *Čechoslovák* (1939-45), many publications of the Czechoslovak Information Service in New York, the Czechoslovak National Council of America (Chicago), and the Czechoslovak Government in exile in London, as well as numerous books and memoirs.

Politics and Government

STATE ADMINISTRATION, ARMED FORCES, AND POLITICAL PARTIES.   There are over 500 titles in the Library dealing with politics and government, most of them listed under "Czechoslovak Republic" or "Slovakia." Some of the more important volumes on the administrative structure are the official collection of decrees and announcements called *Úřední list* (since 1920), *Organisace politické správy v Republice československé* (1928), and the two-volume *Organisace československého státního zřízení* (1946-48). The armed forces in 1918-38 and the prewar political parties are described in various books. The activities of the Communist Party in particular, both before and after the war, are the subject of a vast amount of literature.

POLITICAL DEVELOPMENTS SINCE 1945.   The events of 1945-48 and the Communist coup are abundantly represented in the Library. Michael Parish's *The 1968 Czechoslovak Crisis: a Bibliography,* as well as the listing of books printed since 1968 in the quarterly *Svědectví* provide nearly complete coverage for the "Czechoslovak Spring" and its aftermath. About one-half of the 300-odd publications in question are in the Library of Congress. The atmosphere of the period is well reflected in the current issues of the Czech and Slovak daily newspapers, in the weeklies *Literární noviny, Literární listy, Kultúrny život,* and others.

FOREIGN RELATIONS.   The Library has over 100 titles devoted to foreign relations. Those covering the period before 1945 or the diplomatic activities were discussed above. Treaties, conventions, agreements, and settlements between Czechoslovakia and foreign countries are listed under the names of the Presidents of Czechoslovakia. There are many books on relations with Germany and even more on relations with Russia and the Soviet Union, in Czech, Slovak, and Russian. There are fewer books on relations with Poland, Hungary, England, the United States, and Canada, probably in that order.

Works on the mass media and public opinion include *Výberová bibliografia článkovej odbornej literatúry o novinároch, novinách, rozhlase a televízii* (annual, since 1959), books by Jozef Darmo, Karel Zieriss, Anthony Buzek, et al., and a critical study by Vladimír Reisky-Dubnic, *Communist Propaganda Methods*. Weekly schedules of radio and television programs are listed in *Rozhlas a televízia*. Other periodicals at the Library include *Novinářský sborník, Filmové a televizní noviny, Československá televize,* and *Československý rozhlas*.

The Economy

GENERAL WORKS.   The researcher has over 300 titles at his disposal in the general category of economy or economics, including basic bibliographies, all of which contain statistical data on the Czech and Slovak economy. There are many pertinent bilingual dictionaries. One may cite the three-volume *Velký anglicko-český technický slovník,* compiled by Otakar Pekárek, et al.; and there are other economic glossaries for French, German, Italian, Russian, et al. Some of the current periodicals are the annual *Czechoslovak Economic Papers* and the monthlies *Politická ekonomie* and *Czechoslovak Co-op News*.

AGRICULTURE AND INDUSTRY.   The periodical *Česká zemědělská bibliografie* (since 1941) and the monthly *Přehled zemědělské literatury zahraniční i domácí* (since 1959), and *Soupis nejnovějších zemědělských bibliografií* are useful tools. Other works on agriculture and forestry are the multivolume *Velká encyklopedie zemědělská* (the Library has only v. 2, part 3) and *Naučný slovník lesnický*. Prewar and postwar conditions are the subject of a dozen publications each. Indispensable for the study of the developments since 1945 is the daily *Zemědělské noviny*.

Bibliographic control of literature on industry and technology, at best spotty before World War II, is nearly complete for the postwar period, thanks to *Přehled technické literatury* for 1947-50 and its successor *Přehled technické a hospodářské literatury* (semimonthly, since 1951). *Adresář československého průmyslu* is a directory of industry published annually since 1946. Periodicals received by the Library cover virtually all fields of industrial theory and production.

FINANCE, COMMERCE, AND TRANSPORTATION.   The Library has over 100 volumes on Czechoslovak finance and commerce, including foreign trade. The basic work is the annual *Státní rozpočet* (since 1919). There are several books by the foremost prewar economists Alois Rašín and Karel Engliš; important postwar publications include those by Miloš Horna, Boris Pešek, and Ladislav Veltruský, and the annual *Adresář československého obchodu*. The periodicals include the monthly *Czechoslovak Foreign Trade,* the quarterly *Czechoslovak Exporter,* and several others in Czech and Slovak.

Transportation holdings include *Úřední jízdní řád,* the annual official railroad timetable since 1919, the weekly *Přepravní a tarifní věstník, Pravidla silničního provozu,* and several periodicals in Czech or Slovak devoted to transportation and communications.

Social Conditions

GENERAL WORKS AND LABOR.   About 300 titles are listed under labor; welfare, health, and housing; women, children, and youth, recreation, and sports. An overview of Czechoslovak society can be found in *Československá vlastivěda* and *Slovenská vlastiveda*. Shorter works reflecting the developments since World War II are those by Lidmila Balcárková, Bedřich Václavík, and Jaroslav Šíma.

Labor in the prewar period can be studied in *Labor Legislation in Czechoslovakia,* by Esther Bloss. The developments since 1945 are discussed in many books, including *The Labor Force of Czechoslovakia,* by Andrew Elias. Other useful publications are the monthlies *Information Bulletin* of the Revolutionary Trade Union Movement and its successor, *Czechoslovak Trade Unions*.

WELFARE, HEALTH, AND HOUSING.   The system of social and health insurance and public welfare is discussed in several works. An important source of information is the quarterly *Social Security in Czechoslovakia*. Valuable reference sources on public health are: *Bibliographical Review of the Czechoslovak Literature on Communal, School, and Food Hygiene*, an annual, Josef Vyšohlíd's *The Training of Doctors and Other Health Workers, Malý biografický slovník československých lékařů*, by Miroslav Matoušek, the annual *Bericht des Staatsgesundheitsanstalt in Prag*, and half-a-dozen Czech or Slovak periodicals.

WOMEN, CHILDREN, YOUTH; SPORTS.   Several periodicals at the Library treat these topics, e.g., *Czechoslovak Women, Czechoslovak Youth, Pionierské noviny, Tělesná výchova a sport* (for 1950-54), the monthly *Bibliografie tělovýchovné literatury* (since 1955), and *Czechoslovak Sport*. The Sokol movement is the subject of a number of books, e.g., by F. A. Toufar, Charles Bednar, and Jarka Jelinek.

Religion and Philosophy

RELIGION.   Many general surveys mentioned above contain chapters dealing with religion. In addition, one can consult Míla Liscová's *The Religious Situation in Czechoslovakia* for the prewar period, and for the postwar years, the two publications of the Mid-European Law Project: *Czechoslovakia; Churches and Religion* and *Church and State Behind the Iron Curtain*. Both the Catholic and Protestant versions of the Bible are represented by many volumes.

Basic works on Czech and Slovak Catholicism are available, such as the five-volume *Bibliografie české katolické literatury*, by Josef Tumpach and Antonín Podlaha, the six-volume *Dějiny křesťanství v Československu*, by Ferdinand Hrejsa, as well as treatments of specialized aspects of the Catholic Church. The Library of Congress subscribes to the Czech *Katolické noviny* and the Slovak *Katolícke noviny*.

The Library's monographic coverage of Czechoslovak Protestantism is extensive. Jan Hus and the religious aspects of the Hussite movement are discussed in many scholarly works. Among the several periodicals that the Library receives in this field are *Český bratr, Evanjelický posol*, and *Hlas pravoslaví*.

In addition to previously mentioned works on the Jewish population, the Library has *Czechoslovak Jewry, Past and Future, Die Ausschaltung der Juden aus der Wirtschaft des Protektorats, Der slowakische Judenkodex*, and many others. The only current Jewish periodical from Czechoslovakia is *Věstník židovských náboženských obcí*.

PHILOSOPHY.   A basic work is Andreĭ Pavlov and Boris V. Iakovenko's *Kurze Bibliographie der neuen tschechoslowakischen Philosophie* and *Československá filosofie; nástin podle vývoje disciplin*, by Josef Král. The history of Slovak philosophy is discussed in the massive *Prehľad dejín slovenskej filozofie*, edited by Elena Várossová. On Marxist philosophy there is an excellent source in *Marxismus-Leninismus in der ČSR*, by Nikolaus Lobkowicz. There are various other publications under this subject heading, as well as periodicals such as *Filosofický časopis* and *Studies in Soviet Thought*.

Education and Culture

EDUCATION.   The collection includes books giving the overall picture of the educational system, as well as many books on Charles University. Other useful publications in the Library are the monthly *World Student News, Učitelská ročenka, Učitelské noviny*, and several other periodicals in Czech or Slovak.

SCHOLARLY ACTIVITIES; LIBRARIES.   The Library of Congress has nearly all the publications of the Czechoslovak and Slovak universities and academies, as well as various works on the organization of research in Czechoslovakia. Several surveys of public libraries are available.

Current bibliographies include *Bibliografie české knihovědy, Bibliografie československého knihovnictví,* and Matica slovenská's *Bibliografia slovenskej knihovníckej literatúry.* The Library has most of the works of the foremost library-science writers and bibliographers. Current periodicals from the ČSSR include *Knihovník* and *Knižní kultura.*

Languages

CZECH.   The Library of Congress has over 600 titles on the Czech language, including the seven-volume *Bibliografie československých prací filologických* and *Bibliografie české lingvistiky.* Phonology, morphology, and syntax as well as their various subdivisions are fully covered in the Library's holdings. There is an abundance of textbooks, old and new, published in America as well as in Czechoslovakia. The wealth of vocabulary of modern Czech is contained in the nine volumes of *Příruční slovník jazyka českého* (1937-57) and its successor, the four-volume *Slovník spisovného jazyka českého* (1960-71). Bilingual and polyglot dictionaries cover most written languages; the prize items are Josef Jungmann's five-volume *Slovnjk česko-německý* (1835-39) and *Dodatky* (1851) by F. L. Čelakovský. Several periodicals from the ČSSR include *Naše řeč* and *Slovo a slovesnost.*

SLOVAK.   The holdings on the Slovak language comprise about 250 titles, among them Vincent Blanár's *Bibliografia jazykovedy na Slovensku v rokoch 1939-1947* and its continuation, the current *Bibliografia slovenskej jazykovedy* of Matica slovenská, Eugen Pauliny's *Slovenská gramatika, Morfológia slovenského jazyka,* by Ladislav Dvonč, Ján Stanislav's *Slovenská historická gramatika* and a new edition of his three-volume *Dejiny slovenského jazyka,* recent editions of *Pravidlá slovenského pravopisu,* the six-volume *Slovník slovenského jazyka,* many bilingual dictionaries, several textbooks for the teaching of Slovak, several Czech-Slovak and Slovak-Czech glossaries, *Slovenská reč,* and several other periodicals from the ČSSR.

Literature and Folklore

CZECH LITERATURE.   In addition to basic bibliographic sources mentioned above, the researcher has at his disposal several specialized tools such as *Základní bibliografie k dějinám české a slovenské literatury,* issued by Charles University. The history of literature is covered in numerous works in Czech, Slovak, and other languages, including the multivolume *Dějiny české literatury* (1959-). Several Czech-language anthologies provide examples of nearly the entire literary production from the early times to the present. Studies of special aspects of literature are well represented and the Library also has many individual books by major writers that were published in Czechoslovakia.

The available materials include books and booksize bibliographies on all major and many minor literary figures. The belles lettres in translation can be found in a number of anthologies. Many single literary works, from Jaroslav Vrchlický to Josef Škvorecký, are translated into English and some other languages. Translations of writings by Hus, Comenius, Karel Čapek, and Egon Hostovský are particularly well represented. The Library also has the principal postwar literary magazines, but lacks some of the prewar periodicals.

SLOVAK LITERATURE.   Bibliographical control over Slovak belles lettres is provided by the general bibliographies listed at the beginning of this study. There are several histories of literature and the multivolume *Dejiny slovenskej literatúry* (1958-). There are also monographs on the major writers. Anthologies of Slovak writings, both in the original and in translation, are also available.

Holdings of works by individual writers in the original are at best selective. Those authors whose works have been published in the ČSSR since 1945 are adequately represented. Those who published abroad are absent more often than not. Periodicals at the Library of Congress include *Kultúrny život, Slovenská literatúra,* and *Slovenské pohľady.*

FOLKLORE.   The Library holds several bibliographies of Czech folklore as well as many collections of legends and tales, folksongs, and dances. Periodicals at LC include *Národopisný věstník československý, Český lid,* and several others, although their runs are not complete.

Slovak folklore can be studied here in a score of volumes. An important source is the bimonthly *Slovenský národopis.*

The Arts

THEATER AND CINEMATOGRAPHY.   The Library has about 100 publications in these fields. The history of the theater is well covered and there are several important bibliographies and current periodicals from the ČSSR. Cinema publications are also well represented and the half-dozen film periodicals LC receives from the ČSSR include *The Czechoslovak Film, Film a divadlo,* and *Film a doba.*

THE FINE ARTS.   For art literature one can consult several bibliographies, dictionaries of artists, and a number of surveys. Books are available on the various periods in painting (Gothic, Renaissance, Baroque, 19th and 20th centuries). The history of cartoons is told by Adolf Hoffmeister in *Sto let české karikatury,* and there are monographs on a number of painters, from Magister Theodoricus to Max Švabinský, as well as many surveys of architecture.

The Library holds several Czechoslovak publications on urban planning. The collection contains monographs on sculpture by leading Czechoslovak authors and works on individual sculpture, such as Matyáš Bernard Braun and Josef Václav Myslbek.

Folk art (material culture) is described and illustrated in various publications. The subject matter includes the Subcarpathian Ukraine.

Periodicals on the fine arts are plentiful and include *Architektura ČSSR, Československý architekt, Umění, Umění a řemesla,* and *Výtvarné umění.*

Specialized Collections

GEOGRAPHY AND MAP DIVISION.   The earliest original maps at the Library showing the areas of present-day ČSSR are the portolan maps of the 15th century. A set of maps representing Prague since the 12th century, dates from 1892. The Library's collection of 16th-century atlases includes the 1545 Münster edition of Ptolemy's *Geographia,* the first atlas with the first Czech map of Bohemia (Nicholas Claudian, 1516-18). The first independent map of Moravia (Fabricius, 1568) appears in Ortelius' *Theatrum orbis terrarum* (Antwerp, 1573), and the first Ortelius atlas with Lazius and Sambucus maps showing Slovakia (1579) is also in the collection.

Versions of Comenius' map of Moravia appear in the atlases from 1633 on. Some notable works of the 18th century include Homann's *Atlas regni Bohemiae* (Nüremberg, 1776) and Marsigli's *La Hongrie et le Danube* (The Hague, 1741). Maps of Slovakia by the Slovak cartographer Samuel Mikovinyi are in Matej Bel's *Notitia Hungariae novae historica geographica* (Vienna, 1735-42), and in reproduction in the handsome volume on Mikovinyi published in Bratislava in 1958, *Samuel Mikovini, 1700-1750; život a dielo.* Two 17th-century émigrés from Bohemia who made maps abroad are also represented in the collection: the maps of the artist Václav (Wenceslas) Hollar appear in a number of contemporary atlases, and Augustin Heřmann's extremely rare map of Virginia and Maryland (London, 1673), a priceless item indeed, was acquired by the Library in 1960. Maps from the 19th century include a complete set of the special maps of the Czech lands and Slovakia (1:75,000).

The collection for the period between the wars is quite good, including the *Atlas Republiky československé* (1935). The period since World War II is well represented by a number of good maps and atlases from Czechoslovakia. The Library holds the impressive relief map *Geologická mapa ČSSR* (1968). The Division also has maps produced by the U.S. Army Map Service, which cover all of Czechoslovakia on a scale of 1:25,000.

THE LAW LIBRARY. Most of the 4,700-odd books and bound periodicals in the Czechoslovak collection were acquired after World War II. Currently the Library receives 19 periodicals of a legal nature from Czechoslovakia.

The Library has all the basic bibliographies; the stenographic minutes from the meetings of Národní shromáždění from 1918 to the present; both penal and civil codes of law; volumes on criminal and civil court procedures; several books dealing with the history of law; collections of the decisions of the Supreme Court, the Supreme Military Court, and the Supreme Administrative Court, as well as many editions of the constitutions of 1920, 1948, and 1960 in Czech, Slovak, Russian, English, and other languages.

THE MANUSCRIPT DIVISION. The Library of Congress has four categories of manuscript materials in which resources on the ČSSR are significant: 1) Collections pertaining to the Paris Peace Conference of 1919, including the papers of President Woodrow Wilson that document the creation of the Czechoslovak state; 2) the Thomas Čapek (1861-1950) collection of nearly 5,000 pieces of manuscripts, letters, documents, books, and periodicals assembled over many years by this Czech-American writer; 3) the papers (about 3,000 items) of Edward O. Tabor, a Pittsburgh lawyer prominent in Czechoslovak-American affairs from 1918 to 1948; 4) a collection of manuscripts, in Czech, of writings on the history of Prague by the art historian Antonín Novotný (about 15 of these manuscripts have never been published).

Other materials to be found here include the correspondence of American ambassadors to Prague, e.g., Wilbur J. Carr, William E. Dodd, Lawrence Steinhardt; vast collections of captured German documents; and sizable files on the Czechoslovak National Socialist and the German Social Democratic Party (in Czechoslovakia).

THE MUSIC DIVISION. The Library's collection covers all fields and periods of music, vocal and instrumental, from the early hymns to last year's popular music and songs. For such major figures as Smetana, Dvořák, and Janáček, for example, there are manuscripts of letters and music, many first editions, numerous recordings, a large body of literature pertaining to them, and many editions of their works. While the receipt of records from Czechoslovakia has been spotty, much Czech and Slovak music appears on records manufactured in western Europe and the United States, and is acquired by the Library.

The collection of operas includes an impressive set of scores by Smetana, Dvořák, Janáček, Zdeněk Fibich, Eugen Suchoň, et al. Another special strength of the collection is chamber music, represented by several baroque and early classical figures such as Jan Dismas Zelenka, Josef Mysliveček, Jan Stamitz, and Jiří Benda, up through the modern period (Bohuslav Martinů).

The Library also owns a number of rare hymnals of the 16th and 17th centuries, including, in facsimile, the important collection by Jan Roh, *Piesně chwal Božských* (Prague, 1541), and an original copy of Comenius' hymnal printed in Amsterdam in 1659. The collection of hymn books has continued to the present. Also deserving special mention here is the material pertaining to the large body of folk music. Standard and scholarly printed collections of the 19th and 20th centuries are supplemented by recorded music in the Recorded Sound Section and the Archive of Folk Song. The Recorded Sound Section also has custody of a set of 23 tapes of the 1952 trial of Rudolf Slánský as broadcast by Radio Praha; the CBS tapes with the network's entire coverage of the September 1938 crisis; the Office of War Information broadcasts in Czech and Slovak; speeches by Edvard Beneš, Jan Masaryk, et al.

All the general reference works on music and a half-dozen current periodicals from the ČSSR are in the collection.

THE PRINTS AND PHOTOGRAPHS DIVISION.   This division possesses photographs of people and places in Czechoslovakia which date from the late 19th century and cover all decades, although unevenly. Most of the photographs are filed by subject (often in ''lots'') or by name rather than by geographical area, so that it is hard to find everything that may pertain to Czechoslovakia. The following materials stand out among the holdings: 1) A substantial number of photographs of Czechoslovakia in the 1920s and 1930s; 2) Many pictures of Czechoslovak subjects in the large stereograph collection dating from about 1900 to 1930, mainly illustrating folk art and folkways; 3) Photographs in the Red Cross Collection, taken in the Subcarpathian Ukraine in 1920-22 during relief work there, and pictures of the Czechoslovak legions in Siberia; 4) About 130 photographs of important architectural monuments in Czechoslovakia taken by the Germans in 1943-44; 5) Official Eastfoto photographs, mainly from recent decades. Some important Czech and Slovak figures can also be located in the Portrait Collection.

A scattering of Czech and Slovak artists from several centuries can be found in the prints collection, with the 20th century best represented. An important exception is a group of some 70 individual prints by Václav (Wenceslas) Hollar. During the past decade, fine prints from Czechoslovakia began to be bought on a regular basis, and LC now has the beginnings of a fine collection of the best works of modern printmakers.

The holdings contain several hundred posters from Czechoslovakia, most of them from the 1930s and 1960s. At present they are being acquired steadily, but quite selectively and not in large quantity.

Most of the Library's motion pictures pertaining to the ČSSR are either documentary, or in the newsreel collection, or in the collection of German films—newsreels, documentaries, and some features—of the 1930s and 1940s. The nonfilm, ''Descriptions'' collection, a large and useful collection of movie reviews, summaries, and still pictures, provides good coverage of Czechoslovak feature films.

The largest group of German films on Czechoslovakia consists of 40-50 short documentaries on news and cultural themes, mainly from the late 1930s.

THE RARE BOOK DIVISION.   The principal holdings on Czechoslovakia consist of an important collection of 15th-17th century imprints, mainly from the Czech lands, which illustrate and illuminate the Czech Renaissance.

The Library's seven known incunabula from this area include one of the first Bibles printed in Czech (Kutná Hora, 1489). Another is the extremely rare anti-Hussite work by Augustinus Moravus, *De secta Waldensium,* printed in Olomouc in 1500. Other important Bibles include a one-volume edition of the Kralice Bible (1596) and a copy of the Melantrich Bible of 1570. The collection contains legal, linguistic, historical, and household literature, as well as many religious writings. Among the especially rare works are Jan Hus' *Postilla* (Nüremberg, 1563), the *Kalendář hystorycký* published by Melantrich in 1578, early grammars, including a fine Donát grammar published in Litomyšl in 1647, and a Veleslavín edition of Jan Kocín's *Abeceda pobožné manželky a rozssaffné hospodyně* (1585).

Among the rare editions of Comeniana are several volumes of his pansophical and pedagogical works printed in London during his lifetime, and the first American edition of *Orbis sensualium pictus* (New York, 1810).

For a discussion on the rare books from the Czech Renaissance, see Paul L. Horecky's ''The Czech Renaissance, Viewed through Rare Books,'' *Library of Congress Quarterly Journal of Current Acquisitions,* May 1957, pp. 95-107.

Rudolf Sturm
Skidmore College

East Germany

General Information

Contemporary East Germany dates back to 1945, when this region was occupied by the Soviet Union in accordance with wartime Allied agreements. The present survey addresses itself to the postwar period of this area and focuses in particular on the development of the German Democratic Republic. A separate section deals with the special problems of East Berlin.

The Library's holdings reflect the intense interest the U.S. Government had in the reconstruction of postwar Germany, not only during the initial stage of occupation but also during the subsequent period characterized by the organization and development of the Federal Republic of Germany and the German Democratic Republic.

Over the years the Library has refined and enlarged its acquisitions program, and current purchase policy calls for the procurement of all new East German titles that appear in the book trade and are relevant to the study of this area. This effort is further supplemented by exchange relationships maintained directly by the Library with over 200 East German libraries, universities, learned societies, and other institutions. The substantive aspects of this acquisitions program have been guided in regard to the social sciences and humanities by an area specialist for Central Europe, a position established in the Slavic and Central European Division in the mid-1950s. Science and technology, geography, art, music, and law are the responsibility of other units within the Library.

It is estimated that the Library has over 50,000 monographs that have been published in East Germany since 1945. Of these about 30,000 pertain to subjects within the purview of this survey. In addition, the collections contain about 2,500 books that deal with East Germany but were published elsewhere. At present the Library receives over 3,000 titles annually that fall within the scope of this study.

The Library of Congress currently subscribes to about 400 East German serials and receives an additional 400 from East Germany through exchange or gift. Approximately one-half of these publications deal with the social sciences, humanities, and general subjects.

The size of the Library's East German collections may be described in terms of sufficiency, i.e., the percentage of items that should be acquired and that are normally available for procurement. The desideratum in this context is very broadly conceived; it includes all treatises of any merit dealing with East Germany, excluding obvious duplications, other editions, translations, extracts, and the like; it also allows for acquiring all materials that can be classed as basic sources (e.g., documents, statistics, legislation) with other publications of a popular, instructional, or propaganda nature being acquired only to the extent necessary to permit an effective analysis by sampling.

The following is a tabulation of the estimated relative strength of Library of Congress holdings by category:

Category	Selective (1% to 50%)	Representative (51% to 75%)	Comprehensive (76% to 100%)
Books in the book trade			x
Books not in the book trade		x	
Serials in the book trade			x
Serials not in the book trade		x	
Maps in the book trade			x
Maps not in the book trade	x		
Pamphlets	x		
Dissertations	x		

Category (Continued)

Graphics	x	
Films	x	
	(or less)	
Posters	x	
	(or less)	
Sheet music and music scores		x

Treatises and basic sources in the book trade, the core around which such a collection must be developed, are estimated to represent over 90 percent of the Library's needs in respect to such publications.

The Slavic and Central European Division maintains extensive subject files on books that have been published since 1960 in and on East Germany and pertain to the social sciences, humanities, and general subjects, but excluding law, geography, art, and music. There is also an alphabetical working file on serials published in East Germany. In view of the limited differentiation between East German and other German materials in treatment and cataloging at the Library, the subject book files are of particular value for conducting work in the field of East German area studies.

With the emergence of both the Federal Republic of Germany and the German Democratic Republic, the Library's subject cataloging practice began to differentiate between publications pertaining to West and East Germany. The system has been worked out to the point that books dealing primarily with conditions and developments closely identified with East Germany as a whole are given the appropriate geographic notation in the subject heading. Publications, however, that deal with all of Germany or with cultural aspects such as German literature or language usually lack such a specific geographic reference to East Germany. This holds true even for books that deal, for example, only with the development of the German language in East Germany since 1945. In addition, many publications of the early postwar period and works whose exclusive treatment of East German aspects is not readily recognizable have received similar treatment.

The Collections

REFERENCE WORKS AND GENERAL PUBLICATIONS.   East Germany has its own set of reference works many of which date back to the pre-1945 period and do not limit their coverage to East Germany. This applies particularly to the national bibliography, which continues to include both East and West German imprints. Conversely, East Germany is in many instances fully covered by West German reference works, often even better than by East German counterparts, since East German publications of this type have frequently been slower in coming out and have in many cases been smaller in size. Encyclopedias are a case in point. In contrast to the extensive bibliographic efforts made in East Germany, the field of biographical handbooks is neglected and one has to rely on West German publications. The Library is particularly strong in reference works pertaining to East Germany, including a broad spectrum of samples of local statistical yearbooks.

In addition to these reference tools the Library has a comprehensive collection of East German general research publications, such as academy reports or the scholarly journals *(Wissenschaftliche Zeitschriften)* issued by the various universities and colleges.

The Library subscribes to 12 East German newspapers (nine of which are on microfilm) published in the major cities and addressing themselves to various audiences.

LAND AND PEOPLE.   The Library has pertinent census publications, related statistical works, and treatises pertaining to East German demographic developments. The number of analytical studies in this field has been relatively small.

In addition to the large body of pre-1945 works, which still retain much of their validity for contemporary studies, the Library has an extensive and diversified collection of recent guides, studies, and handbooks dealing with the regional and local geography of East Germany. These holdings are supplemented by a collection of East German atlases which are in the custody of the Library's Geography and Map Division.

The Geography and Map Division has a large, up-to-date collection of specialized maps on the German Democratic Republic. Since 1969 all current acquisitions are fully cataloged and maps dealing with East Germany as a whole are listed in the map catalog under a special heading pertaining to this area and can thus be readily located. Pre-1969 acquisitions of regional maps are also substantial, as can be seen from the following tabulation of holdings by state:

State	Number of Maps (Estimate)
Brandenburg	280
Mecklenburg	240
Saxony	560
Saxony-Anhalt	280
Thuringia	640
Total	2,000

In addition, there are comparable collections of city plans.

The holdings of pre-1945 large-scale survey maps are excellent, but East German official publications of such material have not been available for the postwar period.

HISTORY.   The core of the Library's holdings of East German historical developments since 1945 is classified under "DD261," a group of about 700 titles. Reference works and serials that record or analyze current events, such as *Dokumentation der Zeit* (since 1949) or *SBZ-Archiv* (1950-68), as well as a small collection of individual biographies (the latter in subclass "DD261.7") can be found here. In addition, the Library has all the major (and some local) East German historical journals, including the annual list of writings in German history, as well as a comprehensive collection of historical treatises published in East Germany, supplemented by a solid body of publications providing guidance on East German archival holdings.

POLITICS AND GOVERNMENT (INCLUDING MILITARY AND NAVAL AFFAIRS). The Library's holdings on East German political and military developments are both diversified and extensive, including a better than average collection of materials not in the book trade and covering such subjects as civil administration, local government, components of the armed forces, Marxist theory, and the various political parties. Materials in the last of these categories total about 300 titles and are classed under "JN3971.5."

SOCIETY AND ECONOMY.   The bulk of the very extensive East German publications on East Germany's society and economic life describe the accomplishments made in specific fields or the immediate problems under consideration. This material is highly diversified as far as subject cataloging is concerned, although a fair proportion can be located in the Library under such headings as "Germany (Democratic Republic, 1949-)—Economic Conditions" or "—Economic Policy." The comparable catalog citation for East German society is less rewarding.

Similarly, the rather large number of critical overall appraisals of the economy (mostly published in the West) is contrasted by the dearth of studies analyzing East German society.

The only purely ethnic minority of any size in the area—that of the Sorbs—is extensively covered in the Library's collections in regard to language, literature, history, social and economic conditions, and related developments.

LAW.   The Law Library has a comprehensive collection of law gazettes, journals, statutes, codes, court decisions, commentaries, and treatises pertaining to the East German legal and constitutional system. At present these publications are intershelved with other German Law Library holdings, including those for West Germany. It is expected that with the reclassification of this collection, East German material will be shelved separately from other German law items.

EXTERNAL RELATIONS.   The Library's holdings on East German external affairs are extensive and can be grouped both under foreign relations specifically and under the problem of a *modus vivendi* inside Germany generally. About 200 publications pertaining to the first group, including basic East German serials, have been classified under "DD261.4," while some 400 titles (mostly published in the West) on the latter aspect are shelved under "DD257.25" and "DD257.4."

LANGUAGE.   The Library has an excellent collection of the substantial contribution made by East German philologists to the field of German linguistics through their work on general dictionaries (including the completion of Grimms' *Deutsches Wörterbuch*) and by their regional studies of the dialects in the German Democratic Republic. Standard reference works on modern German usage, as practiced in East Germany, are also available. Studies on other aspects, especially on linguistic relations with Slavic languages, round out the collection.

LITERATURE AND FOLKLORE.   The Library has an extensive collection of East German contemporary literature, in particular works of the well-known writers (sometimes mostly in West German editions) but also those of other authors, as well as some fiction published primarily for popular consumption. These holdings are supplemented by East and West German reference works and monographs on the postwar literary scene.

Postwar works in the field of East German folklore available in the Library are particularly strong in regional studies of such aspects as customs, place-names, and folktales.

EDUCATION AND SCHOLARSHIP.   East German publications in the field of education available in the Library of Congress are mostly didactic in approach, being designed for the use of students, teachers, or administrators. The holdings, which are at least representative, are supplemented by Western studies designed to provide a critical evaluation of East German developments in the fields of education and scholarship.

RELIGION AND PHILOSOPHY.   East German religious works are issued primarily by the respective denominational publishing houses. They cover a wide range of theological, historical, ecumenical, and other subjects. The Library of Congress has a comprehensive collection of publications representing original contributions (including West German analyses) which is supplemented by a representative sample of popular works.

East German philosophical publications reflect the regime's overriding interest in Marxism-Leninism. Serious works (as distinguished from popular expositions and the like) in this field are well represented in the Library.

ARTS.   The Library has made a consistent effort to obtain all East German books that make contributions to the fine arts and music and it would appear to have comprehensive holdings of such publications. The collection also includes such materials as exhibit catalogs and music instruction guidebooks. Since neither LC catalogs nor LC custodial practices differentiate in regard to provenance of fine arts and music publications issued in West and East Germany, the reader wishing to identify East German materials may have to use pertinent bibliographic tools.

The Prints and Photographs Division has but a negligible collection of East German graphics, posters, and films.

The Music Division's holdings of music scores and sheet music from East Germany is quite extensive.

MASS MEDIA. The Library has a small but solid collection of books and journals dealing with East German mass media, mostly East German didactic or informative publications and primarily West German critical evaluations.

PAMPHLETS. The Library has a significant collection of uncataloged East German pamphlets. Subject references in the catalog direct the researcher to the special "X" call number through which this material can be requested. The following entries and the corresponding holdings are noted as examples of this system:

Subject Heading	Call Number	Number of Boxes
Germany (Democratic Republic)	X DD261	7
Germany (Democratic Republic)—		
Politics and Government	X DD261.4	1
Propaganda—Germany (Democratic		
Republic)	X DD261.4.Z9	3

The main strength of this collection lies in material dating from the 1950s.

EAST BERLIN. Only publications by or on East Berlin municipal agencies are cataloged in the Library under "Berlin (East)." All other publications dealing with East Berlin or with East Berlin institutions (such as museums, colleges, and the like) are under the heading "Berlin" together with comparable entries relating to West Berlin.

The Library's holdings include books that deal specifically with that part of the city, as well as publications on Berlin as a whole providing adequate treatment of East Berlin aspects. The material in these collections is primarily descriptive in nature, but it also contains the East Berlin legal gazette *(Verordnungsblatt)* and basic studies on the status of East Berlin.

The Geography and Map Division has some 600 maps on Berlin as a whole.

Arnold H. Price
Library of Congress

Greece

General Information

The Greek collections of the Library of Congress constitute a major corpus of literature. They are probably the most comprehensive in the United States and are certainly among the two or three best collections of Hellenica in the country.

The Library's Ancient Greek, Byzantine, and Modern Greek collections comprise well over 150,000 volumes.

This survey of Hellenica in the Library is the first to have been conducted in the 157-year history of the Library's Greek collections. It focuses on the Modern Greek collection, about 50,000 volumes which cover the history and culture of Modern Greece from the fall of Constantinople in 1453 to the 20th century. About half of the material is in Greek and the remainder in Western languages. There is a large number of Greek incunabula, early prints, and rarities. Accessions to the Modern Greek collection, by purchase, exchange, gift, and copyright, have risen to over 1,000 volumes per year. The Library has more than 1,000 Greek serial titles, including government publications, and about 100 newspapers.

The Library's holdings include important special collections on Modern Greece: maps and charts; manuscripts; music; prints, photographs, and motion pictures; and law.

The Library's Modern Greek collections offer a comprehensive and balanced coverage of all aspects of Modern Greek history and culture.

The Greek area specialist in the Library's Slavic and Central European Division provides specialized reference and consultant services (in person, by telephone, or by correspondence).

The history of the Library's Hellenica dates back to the Founding Fathers of this country, who had a deep respect for the Greek legacy. Thomas Jefferson was an ardent admirer of Hellenism and considered Greek the "most beautiful of all languages" and the "finest of human languages." He read, wrote, and spoke Ancient Greek and could read Modern Greek "with the aid of a few words from a modern Greek dictionary," to quote one of his letters.

Jefferson's library became the nucleus of the Library of Congress, when it was purchased by an Act of Congress in 1815 to replace the original library lost in the burning of the Capitol in 1814.

An analysis of the five-volume *Catalogue of the Library of Thomas Jefferson* (Washington, D.C., 1952-59) indicates that of 4,931 entries listed, about 300 titles (in more than 500 volumes) are works by Ancient Greek, Byzantine, and Modern Greek authors, or books about Greece, including Modern Greece. The entire Jefferson library, when acquired by the Library of Congress in 1815, comprised more than 6,000 volumes; thus every 12th volume in the Jefferson collection was a Greek book or a book about Greece. Jefferson's Greek books were among the most valuable materials in the collection; over a third of these books were published in the 16th and 17th centuries, and almost two-thirds were 18th-century imprints. They covered an extraordinary range of subjects, including not only all the major Ancient Greek authors, but also such varied materials as the books of Byzantine historians and of the Eastern Church Fathers, Greek dictionaries, the Bible in Greek, and several works by Modern Greeks or about Modern Greece.

The subsequent growth of the Library's Greek collections parallels that of the rest of the Library; that is, a slow but steady increase in the 19th century, a quickened pace in the early part of the 20th century, and a rapid growth in the post-World War II era.

In the 1820s, with the Greek War of Independence raging, a wave of philhellenic enthusiasm swept over America, reaching both the White House and Congress. James Monroe, John Quincy Adams, and Daniel Webster, among others, eloquently expressed America's deep sympathy for the cause of Modern Greece. American missionaries from the American Board of Commissioners for Foreign Missions contributed to the regeneration of the Greek nation in the 1820s and early 1830s by distributing, in Greek areas, Greek Bibles, grammars, and textbooks in Modern Greek. They also prepared numerous reports on their work. One of the earliest groups of materials in the Library's Modern Greek collection reflects the educational activities of these American missionaries. From the late 1830s on and for the rest of the 19th century Greek acquisitions came to the Library primarily through United States diplomatic contacts with that country.

The Library's strong collection of Greek Government publications has been acquired mostly via exchange. In his annual report for the year ending December 1, 1867, the Librarian of Congress, A. R. Spofford, stated that the Government of Greece was "among the governments which have responded affirmatively to the circular proposing an exchange of government publications." In the 20th century the exchange program was expanded to include publications of Greek institutions of higher learning and learned and scientific societies.

In 1901, Herbert Putnam, the Librarian of Congress, reported that in the field of literature the Library had 383 volumes by or relating to Homer alone. The Library also had 704 volumes primarily on Ancient Greek history and geography. It is estimated that at the turn of the century, the Library's Hellenica, including the Ancient Greek collection, totaled well over 10,000 volumes, of which no less than a third were books pertaining to Modern Greece.

During the first four decades of the 20th century, the growth of the Greek collections continued at an accelerated pace, through exchange arrangements, gifts, and copyright deposits, an increasingly important source of English-language publications on Greece. In recent years, a special effort has been made to increase current receipts of Greek materials and to fill gaps in the Library's retrospective holdings. Since 1965, over 5,000 current and retrospective Greek books and periodical volumes have been acquired and added to the Modern Greek collection.

The importance of the Library's Hellenica is qualitative as well as quantitative. They cover all fields of Greek thought and learning from ancient times to the present and include the most outstanding and representative works.

The Collections

GREEK TREASURES IN THE LIBRARY OF CONGRESS. The Library of Congress has 44 of the 86 Greek incunabula with definite dates listed in Legrand's standard *Bibliographie hellénique*. Each of these titles is a treasure. Among them is the first Greek printed book, Konstantinos Laskaris' *Epitomē tōn oktō tou logou merōn* (Milan, 1476).

One group of Greek incunabula in the Library consists of Greek grammars and dictionaries. Besides K. Laskaris' Greek grammar, cited above, this category includes: the 1495 Venice edition of Theodorus Gaza's Greek grammar, and Manuel Chrysoloras' *Erōtēmata* (Florence, c. 1496), another grammar probably edited by Janus Lascaris; Suidas' *Lexikon* (Milan, 1499) edited by Demetrios Chalkokondyles (Chalkondyles); and the magnificent *Etymologikon Mega* (Venice, 1499), the largest of the existing medieval Greek dictionaries, edited by Marcus Musurus and printed by the Cretan Zacharias Callierges. Another group of Greek incunabula in the Library consists of *editiones principes* of Greek authors, edited by Greek scholars. Classical Greek authors are included here only if edited by modern Greek authors. The Library has many other editions by Western scholars. These are the superb edition of Homer's works in two volumes (Florence, 1488) edited by Demetrios Chalkokondyles; Musaeus' *Ta kath' Hērō kai Leandron* (Venice, c. 1494-95) with a Latin translation by Marcus Musurus; the *Anthologia Graeca* (Florence, 1494) edited by Janus Lascaris; Euripides' *Mēdeia. Hippolytos. Alkēstis. Andromachē* (Florence, c. 1495) edited by Janus Lascaris; Apollonius *Rhodius' Argonautika* (Florence, 1496) edited by Janus Lascaris; Aristophanes' nine plays (Venice, 1498) edited by Marcus Musurus; *Epistolai diaphorōn philosophōn rhētorōn sophistōn*, 2 v. (Venice, 1499) also edited by Marcus Musurus; and Orpheus' *Argonautika* (Florence, 1500) generally thought to have been edited by Janus Lascaris.

In addition to the categories of grammars and dictionaries (five titles) and *editiones principes* (8 titles), the Library has a third major group of incunabula, consisting of 31 titles, which includes works by 15th-century Greek scholars in Latin, works of ancient Greek authors in Latin edited or translated by Greek scholars, and other editions or translations by Greeks.

The Library's holdings of early modern Hellenica include a rare collection of 30 titles for the 16th century, over 20 for the 17th century, and about 30 for the 18th century. Thus, the Library's Greek collections are not confined to 18th- and 19th-century publications, important as they may be. They include an outstanding collection of Greek incunabula and a considerable number of Greek books printed in the 16th, 17th, and 18th centuries. Together these materials constitute the backbone of the Greek collections.

Most of the Greek incunabula are not listed in the Library's general card catalogs, but can be located by checking F. R. Goff's *Incunabula in American Libraries; a Third Census* (New York 1964). The Library's Greek incunabula are in the custody of the Rare Book Division, but many rare Greek books or books about Greece of the 16th, 17th, and 18th centuries are still shelved in the Library's general collections.

MODERN GREEK HISTORY. The Library of Congress has a magnificent collection of more than 30,000 volumes illustrating Greek history and civilization from ancient times to the present. About 10,000 volumes deal with the history of Modern Greece from the fall of Byzantium to the present. The modern section is particularly strong in published accounts of travelers who visited Greece and the Near East from the 15th century onward, general works as well as source and documentary materials on the Greek War of Independence, 1821-29, the rule of Kapodistrias, 1827-31, the life and reign of King Otho I, 1833-62, and the reign of King George I, 1863-1913. The Library has an outstanding collection of works, particularly in Western languages, on the history of Greece in the 20th century, with particularly rich materials on the Greek statesman Eleutherios Venizelos, and the controversy between him and King Constantine I over the policy to be followed by Greece during World War I; the interwar period of the Republic, 1924-35; the rule of General Ioannes Metaxas, 1936-41; the struggle of Greece against the Axis powers in 1940-41, during enemy occupation, and subsequent Communist insurrection.

America's increasing interest in Greece, following the enunciation of the Truman Doctrine in 1947, is reflected in the Library's excellent collections on Greek contemporary history and politics from the 1950s to the present. For example, the Library has over 40 monographic titles, in various European languages, analyzing the genesis, development, and policies of the present Greek Government.

Greeks have had an attachment to their birthplace. In the 19th century and especially in the 20th century, research in local and regional Greek history has been assiduously pursued by the Greeks. The Library has a rich collection of monographs and Greek scholarly journals dealing with the history of Greek regions and localities, such as the Ionian Islands, Crete, the Cyclades, the Peloponnesus, Sterea Hellas, Thrace, Macedonia and Epirus, and their subdivisions. Recent acquisitions in the field of Modern Greek history include complete sets of all series published by the Society for Macedonian Studies, in Salonika.

The Library has made a special effort in recent years, following the establishment of the Republic of Cyprus in 1960, to strengthen its collections dealing with this Mediterranean island. The Cypriot materials, including government publications, number over 2,000 volumes covering a wide range of subjects in the humanities and social sciences.

LAW.   The Library's Modern Greek law collection is one of the best in the United States. It numbers approximately 2,500 volumes and has expanded at the rate of 50-100 items per year. About 95 percent of the material is in Greek and the remainder in Western languages. It includes numerous editions of Greek constitutions and codes, collections of laws and statutes, court decision reports, over 600 treatises, including many multivolume works, on all branches of law, and an excellent collection of Greek legal periodicals and serials.

Although the collection is particularly strong in legal publications issued during the last 50 years, it also contains many important and rare 19th-century imprints. The Library's Greek law treatises cover constitutional and administrative law, criminal law and criminal procedure, civil law—before and after the coming into force of the civil code of 1940, civil procedure, commercial law, private international law, public international law, ecclesiastical law, labor law, and legal theory. All important Modern Greek legal scholars are represented.

Fourteen selected titles indicate the strength of the Law Library's Greek serial and periodical collection. The Library has the following (unless otherwise indicated, the place of publication is Athens): *Ephēmeris tōn Hellēnōn nomikōn, v. 1-38 (1934-71); Themis,* v. 1-65 (1890/91-1954); *Kōdix nomōn,* 38 v. (1934-71); Akadēmia Athēnōn. Kentron ereunēs tēs historias tou Hellēnikou dikaiou. *Epetēris,* no. 1-14, (1948-67); *Archeion ekklēsiastikou kai kanonikou dikaiou,* v. 6-25 (1951-70); *Archeion idiotikou dikaiou,* v. 1-17 (1934-54/59); *Deltion ergatikēs nomothesias,* v. 1-27 (1945-71); *Deltion phorologikēs nomothesias,* v. 5-25 (1951-71); *Epitheōrēsis ergatikou dikaiou,* v. 1-30 (1941/42-70); *Epitheōrēsis tou emporikou dikaiou,* v. 1-9 (1950-58); *Harmenopoulos,* Thessalonikē, v. 1-25 (1946/47-71); *Neon dikaion,* v. 1-27 (1945-71); *Poinika chronika,* v. 1-21

(1951-71); *Revue hellénique de droit international et étranger,* v. 1-24 (1948-71). The titles cited above account for almost 400 volumes of Greek legal serials. These together with other legal serials with long runs and the 500-volume Greek official gazette, containing laws, decrees, and other enactments, the *Ephēmeris tēs Kybernēseōs* (which is classified with political science materials) form a collection, unique in the United States, of over 1,000 volumes of Greek legal serials and periodicals.

MODERN GREEK GOVERNMENT AND POLITICS.   Among the Library's rich materials on Modern Greek government and politics is a collection of official Greek Government documents and publications, amounting to several thousand volumes unique in this country. It includes a complete set of the first Greek Government gazette, *Genikē ephēmeris tēs Hellados* (October 7, 1825-March 23, 1832) and an almost complete set of the present Government gazette *Ephēmeris tēs Kyberneseōs* (no. 1, February 16, 1833-1970-). There are also long runs of the *Cyprus Gazette,* nos. 578-3662 (1898-1952) and its various supplements, and of the Government gazette of the Republic of Cyprus, *Episēmos ephēmeris tēs Kypriakēs Dēmokratias* (no. 1, August 16, 1960, to the present) and its six groups of supplements.

The collections include over 100 volumes of the *Praktika* (Minutes) and of the *Ephēmeris tōn syzētēseōn* (Journal of Discussions) of the Greek parliament in the 19th and 20th centuries. Many works on Greek political parties, elections and electoral systems, and studies on Greek local government are also available to scholars.

Students of Greek politics and contemporary Greek history can find an extensive collection of Greek newspapers. Only a selected number of titles can be cited here: *Akropolis, Eleutheria, Ethnos, Hestia, Kathemerinē, Le Messager d'Athènes, To Vēma, Hē Vradynē, Hellēnikos Vorras,* and *Makedonia.* Holdings for Greek newspaper titles usually start with the early or middle 1940s, although there are also substantial sets (with some years missing) of *Akropolis* for the first two decades of the 20th century, and of *Le Messager d'Athènes* for the 1920s and 1930s.

Among newspapers published outside Greece, long, but incomplete, sets of *Eleutheria* and *Cyprus Mail,* published in Nicosia, Cyprus, and *Atlantis* and *National Herald* (Ethnikos Kēryx) issued in New York are available.

GREEK LANGUAGE AND LITERATURE.   The Library's collection of over 45,000 volumes on Greek philology and language and Greek literature is remarkable. Works are grouped as classical, medieval, or modern, with the classical and modern materials being the richest and most comprehensive.

The Modern Greek language section includes several hundred important Greek grammars and dictionaries as well as many works on the language question in Greece and on Greek dialects.

The collection on Modern Greek literature—individual works, anthologies, translations into English and other European languages, literary history and criticism—is strong. The Library has many of the works of Greek writers who flourished between 1453 and 1800. There are also several recent editions of 17th-century Cretan literature and almost all the standard collections of Greek folk literature, which reached the height of its development during the period of Ottoman occupation and, particularly, in the 17th and 18th centuries.

All major Greek writers of the 19th and 20th centuries, and the various literary forms, trends, and schools are well represented in the Library. Included are Solomos and Kalvos, the Phanariots and the Athenian School, Greek romanticism, the Heptanesian School, Palamas and the generation of 1880, prose at the end of the 19th century, Kavaphes, Sikelianos, Kazantzakes and poetry to 1930, George Seferis and the generation of 1930, and the post-World War II writers.

In recent years systematic efforts have been made to strengthen the holdings of Modern Greek literature. Recent acquisitions in this field include the collected works of various Modern Greek authors issued by the "Hetaireia Hellēnikōn Ekdoseōn," over 150 publications of the important

Greek publishing house "Ikaros," complete sets of the Greek Cypriot literary periodicals *Kypriaka grammata*, 21 v. (1934-56) and *Philologikē Kypros* (1960-67-68-), and a long run of the general periodical *Kypriakai Spoudai*, v. 7-33 (1943-69) which contains significant contributions on Greek Cypriot literature, history and culture.

MANUSCRIPTS.   A special relationship between Greece and the United States has existed since the founding of the American Republic. The manuscript collections, which center on American history and civilization, offer opportunities for the study of relations between America and Greece in the last 200 years. To illustrate the variety of this material and its importance for Greek-American studies, some of the collections and papers bearing upon Greece in the custody of the Manuscript Division should be mentioned.

The Thomas Jefferson papers contain the Jefferson-Koraes correspondence, consisting of four letters from Koraes to Jefferson and one letter from Jefferson to Koraes. In 1823 Adamantios Koraes, the renowned Hellenist and patriot, wrote to his friend Thomas Jefferson for guidance in drawing up the most desirable constitution for liberated Greece. Jefferson responded with a long letter "on the subject of national government," pointing out, *inter alia,* that the limited geographical boundaries of independent Greece made it imperative that, unlike the United States, she adopt a centralized government with wide executive authority equipped to cope with the "warring powers of Europe."

Other 19th-century collections of interest to students of Greek-American affairs are: the papers of the financier Nicholas Biddle (1786-1844), whose journal (at the Historical Society of Pennsylvania) and letters (at the Library of Congress) contain the earliest surviving account of extensive travel in Greece by an American; he journeyed to Greece in 1906); and the papers of Daniel Webster, who played a leading role in the Philhellenic movement in the United States during the Greek War of Independence (other of Webster's papers are to be found in the New Hampshire Historical Society and Dartmouth College).

Pertinent 20th-century manuscript collections include: the Woodrow Wilson papers, with numerous documents on Greece for the period from 1913 to 1920; the papers of Robert Lansing, Wilson's Secretary of State from 1915 to 1920 (in particular, the 1919 papers on Greek claims in Eastern Thrace); the papers of Charles Evan Hughes, who was Secretary of State from 1921 to 1925; the papers of Mark L. Bristol, U.S. High Commissioner to Turkey (1919-27), particularly the documents on the Greeks in Asia Minor; the papers of Henry Morgenthau, Sr., Vice Chairman of Near East Relief, Inc. from 1919 to 1921 and Chairman of the Greek Refugee Settlement Commission in 1923, describing his achievement in expediting the transfer of almost 1,500,000 Greek refugees from Asia Minor and Eastern Thrace to Greece; the papers of Arthur Sweetser, League of Nations and United Nations official; the papers of President Calvin Coolidge, which contain several documents on Greece for the period 1923-29; and the papers of Cordell Hull, Secretary of State from 1933 to 1944, with many memoranda on Greece for this period.

MAPS, CHARTS, AND ATLASES.   The Geography and Map Division houses an outstanding cartographic collection on Greece. It includes five of the eight sheets of what is believed to be the earliest extant map of Greece (exclusive of those in Ptolemy's *Geographia*), that by Nikolaos Sophianos from before 1543 in the edition issued in Basel in 1545 by Johannus Oporinus.

Greek materials are found in each of the three principal segments of the map collection and include approximately 2,000 single-sheet maps, some 100 multisheet map series, and about 200 nautical charts. The first category contains rare maps of mainland Greece and the Greek islands published in the 16th, 17th, and 18th centuries, modern maps of the entire country, maps of Greek regions and provinces, the Greek islands, and Greek cities, and thematic or subject maps.

Following the formation of the modern Greek state in the 19th century, and particularly in the early part of the 20th century, official map surveys of Greece were undertaken. This official mapmaking activity is reflected in the Library's multisheet map collection. These sheets of large and medium-scale official sets provide full or partial coverage of the Greek mainland and islands. Holdings include series executed by the Greek Army Geographical Service, the U.S. Army Map Service, the German Army General Staff, and the Geographical Section of the British General Staff. Most of these declassified series date from World War II or earlier periods.

The nautical or hydrographic charts embrace all major Greek harbors, Greek coastal charts, and charts of Greek gulfs, bays, straits, and canals. In addition to charts prepared by the Greek Hydrographic Service, the Library has a complete set of British Admiralty charts, many of which cover Greek coasts and harbors.

There is also a significant collection of modern Greek atlases, such as the two-volume *Atlas of Municipalities and Communities of Greece* (Athens, 1951), the *Industrial Atlas of Greece* (Athens, 1966), and the *Kayser-Thompson Economic and Social Atlas of Greece* (Athens, 1964). An excellent Greek atlas, prepared under the direction of the Greek architect Konstantinos Doxiades, is entitled *The Sacrifices of Greece in the Second World War* (Athens, 1946). An interesting 19th-century item is an atlas entitled *A Trigonometrical Survey of the Island of Cyprus* (London, 1885), executed under the direction of Horatio Herbert Kitchener.

PRINTS, PHOTOGRAPHS, AND MOTION PICTURES.   The collection of fine prints housed in the Prints and Photographs Division includes several works by Greek artists living abroad. Demetrios Galanis, an important painter and engraver who worked in Paris, is represented by a mezzotint still life. The Library has six works by George Constant, an American artist of Greek origin, including his drypoint *Portrait of John Sloan*.

The monasteries of Meteora and the temples of Greece are the subjects of a collection of 27 lithographs and 11 etchings by the American artist Joseph Pennell. Other holdings include an extensive collection of Modern Greek posters published from the 1930s to the 1960s.

Among the photographic collections dealing entirely or in part with Greece, the following are of special interest: the Holland collection of Views of Greece, 1919-21; the Riggs collection, geographic and art-historical in character, with a large section on Greece; and the Carpenter collection of photographs concerning human geography, with a strong Greek representation. The rich portrait collection includes pictures of Greeks prominent in various fields of human endeavor from ancient times to the present.

The Library has about 600 stereographic views of Greece, most of which were produced at the turn of the century. Characterized by striking photographic detail, they depict a wide range of subjects, such as public buildings, archeological sites, churches and monasteries, and scenes in Athens and various other localities and areas of Greece.

The achievements of Greeks who have been prominent in the field of cinematography especially in the United States during the last 30 years can be studied in the Motion Picture Section. Of particular interest are several motion pictures released by Twentieth Century-Fox Film Corporation while Spyros P. Skouras was its chief executive.

Elia Kazan won two Academy Awards for his direction of the feature films *Gentleman's Agreement* (1947) and *On the Waterfront* (1954); both of these are in the Library's collections, along with over a dozen other films directed by him. In *America, America* (1964), written, produced, and directed by Mr. Kazan and based on his novel of the same title, he deals with the theme of emigration, so crucial for Greeks.

The Greek actress Katina Paxinou won an Academy Award for best performance by a supporting actress, in *For Whom the Bell Tolls* (1943); the Greek-American actor George Chakiris was awarded an "Oscar" for best performance by a supporting actor, in *West Side Story* (1961). John Cassavetes is another important Greek-American actor and director.

Other feature films in the Library's motion picture collection which should be mentioned are: *Boy on a Dolphin* (1957), set in Greece with Alexis Minotis in the cast; *He Who Must Die* (1958), *Never on Sunday* (1960), *Phaedra* (1962), and *Topkapi* (1964), all starring Melina Mercouri;

Electra (1962) and *Zorba the Greek* (1964), both directed by Michael Cacoyannis and both starring Irene Papas. Manos Hadjidakis wrote the music for *Never on Sunday* and *Topkapi* while Mikis Theodorakis composed the music for *Zorba the Greek, Electra,* and *Phaedra.*

The Motion Picture Section also houses a group of Italian newsreels on the Greek-Italian War of 1940-41 and the preparations by Italy for that war in Albania. A group of German wartime newsreels depict the German invasion and occupation of Greece in 1941.

Finally, there is an interesting collection of educational films, shorts, and documentaries on Greek history and culture.

MUSIC.   The Music Division has custody of a noteworthy collection of the works of Modern Greek composers, ranging from the 19th-century Ionian school to the post-World War II Greek avant-garde school.

The first important representative of the Ionian school, Nikolaos Mantzaros, set to music Solomos' *Hymnos eis tēn eleutherian,* which was adopted in 1861 as the Greek national anthem. The Library also has music scores by the Corfiote composers Napoleon Lambelet and Georges Lambelet.

Among the early 20th-century Greek works are those by Manoles Kalomoires, the founder of the so-called "national school," George Sklavos, including a holograph score of his symphonic poem *Aiglē,* Marios Barbogles, Aimilios Riades, Demetrios Levidis, Petros Petridis, Giorgos Ponerides, and Antiochos Evangelatos.

Greek composers of the post-World War II era are particularly well covered. Nikos Skalkottas, a student of Arnold Schoenberg, is represented by over two dozen major works, including photocopies of holograph scores of several of his Greek dances. The Library also has works of several other Greek modernists, such as Anestis Logothetis, Theodor Antoniou, and Iannis Xenakis, including a holograph score of his composition *Akrata,* commissioned by the Serge Koussevitzky Music Foundation in the Library of Congress. The Library's holdings also include a group of 12 letters from Dimitri Mitropoulos to Arnold Schönberg.

The varied holdings of Modern Greek popular music encompass hundreds of Greek songs in the sheet music collection, and numerous compositions by Manos Hadjidakis and Mikis Theodorakis who are also known for their serious music. The Music Division also houses a wealth of Modern Greek folk music, which flourished in the period of the Ottoman occupation of Greece as well as in modern times. The Archive of Folk Song has many recordings of Greek folk music. Its best field collection on Greece is that of the late Professor James A. Notopoulos, which includes 645 songs he recorded in 1952-53 on field trips to Greece and Cyprus. These are classified as follows: 149 traditional heroic oral poems (*Akritan, Klephtica,* etc.); 63 songs and short epic poems on events of the Second World War; and 433 nonheroic folk songs, and dances, instrumental pieces, folktales, and works of Byzantine church music. In addition, this collection contains tape recordings of 339 songs from the Folklore Archives of the Academy of Athens and 15 recordings from the Archives of the Radio Station of Athens. Thus, the Notopoulos Collection, totaling about 1,000 songs, constitutes a definitive collection. The Archive of Folk Song houses voluminous manuscript material by the Federal Writers' Project, WPA, in the fields of folklore and ethnic studies, some of which deals with the Greek communities in the various states.

Most of the musical and nonmusical recordings pertaining to Modern Greece or by Greek composers or musicians which have appeared in the United States over the past 25 years are included in the collections housed in the Recorded Sound Section. Prominent among these, for example, are numerous recordings by the conductor Dimitri Mitropoulos.

George E. Perry
Library of Congress

Hungary

General Information

The first books about Hungary and Hungarians (or by Hungarian authors) came to the Library of Congress with the Thomas Jefferson Library. Among them was a 6-volume work by Domnok Brenner, entitled *Histoire des révolutions de Hongrie* (1735), which dealt mainly with the Hungarian war of liberation under the leadership of Prince Francis Rákóczi II in the early 18th century.

The collection was expanded at the time of the Hungarian war of independence (1848-49) when works on the modern history, existing conditions, and prospects of Hungary were purchased. The resulting collection was further enlarged by publications concerning the Hungarian leader Lajos Kossuth, especially after his visit to the United States in 1851-52.

Following the 1867 "Compromise" between Austria and Hungary, by which Hungary was raised (at least nominally) to an equal partner in the Austro-Hungarian Monarchy, Hungarian institutions established broad contacts with their counterparts abroad. Many of these institutions, e.g., the Library of the Hungarian Parliament and the National Museum began sending their publications to the Library of Congress. In 1906 the Library of the Hungarian Parliament gave the Library of Congress several hundred volumes on Hungarian general and constitutional history and in 1909 sent the Library a selected collection, almost 700 pieces, of belles lettres and works on literary history "to form a foundation in the general literature of Hungary."

Transfers from the Smithsonian Institution and the increasing number of direct contacts with Hungarian government agencies and libraries ensured a steady growth of the Hungarian holdings until the eve of World War II. However, the real expansion occurred in the 1950s when budgeted appropriations for systematic acquisitions programs and the purchase of the Hungarian Reference Library of New York (consisting of more than 13,000 pieces of rare books, research monographs, and scholarly journals) laid the foundations for a modern area collection

The Library's present Hungarian holdings, within the subject areas of this survey, constitute more than 55,000 monographs and other works and some 2,000 serials, including about 100 newspapers. The following tabulation, based on rough estimates, reflects the relative strength of the materials in the various categories.

The Collections

GENERAL REFERENCE WORKS. The Library's holdings in these areas consist of general bibliographies, encyclopedias, directories, statistical works, general handbooks, and periodicals.

Among the bibliographies, the current national bibliography, *Magyar Nemzeti Bibliográfia* (1946-) is the most important. Hungary's past literary and scholarly endeavors are documented in earlier editions, which, under changing titles (*Magyar Könyvészet, Magyarország Bibliográfiája,* etc.) provide bibliographic data beginning with 1473, the date of the printing of the first book in Hungary. Early works of the biobibliographic type include *Specimen Hungariae literatae* (1711), by Dávid Czwittinger and *Magyar Athénás* (1766), by Péter Bod. The most prominent 19th-century work is József Szinnyei's 14-volume handbook *Magyar írók élete és munkái* (1891-1914), now replaced by *Magyar életrajzi lexikon* (1969), edited by Ágnes Kenyeres.

The Library holds several excellent older encyclopedias as well as the new, authoritative 6-volume *Új Magyar Lexikon* (1959-62). Local gazetteers and directories begin with János Lipszky's *Repertorium locorum . . . regnorum Hungariae, Slavoniae, Croatiae, . . . Transylvaniae,* etc. (1808), and with a 1920 edition of Hungary's 1773 topographic lexicon. The works of András Vályi, Elek Fényes, Károly Keleti, and other statisticians and documentalists cover the 18th and 19th centuries. Hungary's counties and cities are treated in *Magyarország vármegyéi és városai* (1896-1928) and a parallel set issued in the 1930s.

The Hungarian Collections of the Library of Congress

	Monographic vols. et al*	Serials titles	Serials vols.	Pre-World War I %	Interwar Period %	1945- %
GENERAL COLLECTION						
General Publications	2,400	190	1,200	30	20	50
Land and People	1,900	80	1,200	15	10	75
History	4,000	50	600	30	20	50
Politics & Govt.	4,500	420	5,000	25	30	45
Society	5,000	240	3,000	10	15	75
Economy	4,000	300	2,000	15	15	70
Law	3,500	50	1,200	40	20	40
Foreign Affairs	300	18	80	20	20	60
Language	1,700	60	1,300	15	15	70
Literature	8,000	160	1,700	10	20	70
Folklore	1,500	50	700	20	20	60
Religion, Philosophy	350	32	200	10	10	80
Education & Scholarship	3,200	100	1,000	10	15	75
Fine Arts, etc.	2,000	60	600	10	25	65
Media of Communication	1,800	30	300	10	20	70
Hungarians Abroad	200	30	300	10	20	70
Sub-Totals	44,350	1,870	20,380			
SPECIAL COLLECTIONS						
Rare Book Division	40	5	10	90	5	5
Manuscript Division	300	—	—	80	20	—
Music Division	3,150	9	100	15	15	70
Geography & Map Div.	7,400	—	—	25	25	50
Prints & Photographs Div.	350	—	—	60	10	30
Sub-Totals	11,240	14	110			
Grand Totals	55,590	1,884	20,490			

TOTAL NUMBER OF VOLUMES (pieces, sheets): 75,964

*Figures in this column include monographs, documents, manuscripts, sheet music, phonograph records, maps, broadsides, motion pictures, and other pictorial materials.

The Library has all important statistical handbooks and pocketbooks about Hungary and Budapest; they are supplemented by large holdings of statistical journals, monographic series, and special issuances.

Among the general handbooks of current imprints, *Information Hungary* (1968), edited by Ferenc Erdei, Elemer Bako's *Guide to Hungarian Studies*, 2 v- (1974), *A Guide to Hungarian and Foreign Reference Works* (1963), compiled by János Szentmihályi and Miklós Vértes form the core of a basic selection. General scholarly and reference tools are *The New Hungarian Quarterly* (1959-), *The Hungarian Quarterly* (1936-42), and the handbook *A Companion to Hungarian Studies* (1942).

THE LAND AND PEOPLE.   Publications about the land of Hungary include the geographic bibliographies: *Magyar földrajzi könyvtár* (1893) by Rezső Havass and *A magyar földrajzi irodalom, 1936-1940* (1938-42) by István Dubovitz. A handbook, *Földrajzi zsebkönyv*, published annually by the Hungarian Geographic Society since 1942, and two geographic journals, *Földrajzi Értesítő* (1952-) and *Földrajzi Közlemények* (1873-) are the basic bibliographic sources in this area. Holdings include comprehensive works about Hungary's geography and related environmental studies by Gyula Prinz (1942), László Szabó (1954), Márton Pécsi (1964), and Béla Bulla (1964).

Publications are also available in English and other Western languages, e.g., *A Geographical, Economic and Social Survey of Hungary* (1919), edited by Lajos Lóczy, *The Geography of Hungary* (1964), by Márton Pécsi and Béla Sárfalvi; the journal *Acta Geographica* (1955-), issued by Szeged University, and the monographic series *Studies in Geography* (1964-), published by the Institute of Geography of the Hungarian Academy of Sciences.

Publications about the people of Hungary (Hungarians as well as others) cover the areas of archeology, anthropology, ethnography, demography, and various subjects related to Hungarians outside Hungary. Holdings include archeological bibliographies and publications series such as the *Folia Archaeologica* (New Series, 1954-) and the quarterly *Acta Archaeologica* (1951-).

The Library possesses multivolume editions of various Hungarian censuses, fundamental demographic works by Lajos Bartucz, József Kovacsics, Pál Lipták, István Szabó, by the Finn Toivo Vuorela, the American Jacob S. Siegel, and others. The journal *Demográfia* (1958-) treats current Hungarian demographic research.

HISTORY.   Major bibliographies in this field include Domokos G. Kosáry's *Bevezetés a magyar történelem forrásaiba és irodalmába* (1951-56), Zoltán I. Tóth's *Magyar történeti bibliográfia, 1825-1867* (1950-59), and the *Bibliographie d'oeuvres choisiés de la science historique hongroise*, issued periodically by the Institute of Historiography of the Hungarian Academy of Sciences for the years 1945-59 (in 1960) and for 1960-63 (in 1965). The quarterly *Századok* (1867-), and the Academy's foreign language journal, *Acta Historica* (1951-) top the list of current periodicals in this area; the *Revue d'histoire comparée* (1923-48) and the *Ungarische Jahrbücher* (1921-43) are classic publications.

The Library's holdings of rare and valuable monographic series include, among others, Georgius Fejér's *Codex diplomaticus Hungariae*, 42 v. (1829-55), *Magyar történelmi tár*, 136 v. (1855-1920), *Monumenta Vaticana* (1887-91), *Archivum Rákóczianum* (1871-79).

Among the general handbooks of Hungarian history are Sándor Szilágyi's *A magyar nemzet története* (1895-98), the standard post-World War I work *Magyar történet*, 2nd ed. (1935-36), by Bálint Hóman and Gyula Szekfű, and the works of the British scholar Carlyle Ailmer Macartney.

The Library has nearly all publications of the Hungarian National Archives, the Academy of Sciences, and the various university institutions. It has strong collections in Hungarian archeology and ancient history, on the history of the Principality of Transylvania, the Hungarian Soviet Republic (1919), the Treaty of Trianon (1920) and its aftermath, and the revolution of 1956, as well as works by and about Hungarian political leaders of the 19th and 20th centuries.

GENEALOGY AND LOCAL HISTORY.   The Library of Congress has, in addition to Sibmacher's classic work on Hungarian and Transylvanian nobility, a microfilm copy of Iván Nagy's 13-volume work, *Magyarország családai, czimerekkel és nemzedékrendi táblákkal* (1857-68), a set of Béla Kempelen's 11-volume *Magyar nemes családok* (1911-32), a partial set of *Turul*, v. 1-57 (1883-1943), journal of the Hungarian Heraldic and Genealogical Society, Budapest, as well as several minor or supplementary works.

Works on local history include well over 300 monographic and periodical volumes, among them circa 150 volumes in the Budapest collection.

POLITICS, GOVERNMENT, MILITARY AFFAIRS.   The best guide to the older literature is the catalog of the House of Representatives of the Hungarian Parliament, entitled *A Képviselőház könyvtárának katalógusa* (1891), and its supplements issued in 1891 and 1929. The special bibliographies of political and social sciences compiled by the staff of the Municipal Library of Budapest (1909) and the Hungarian Institute of Social Studies (1925-26) cite not only literature published in Hungary (including periodical articles, statistical and legislative materials, pamphlets, reports, etc.) but a number of relevant foreign publications and book reviews.

The Library possesses proceedings, in several hundred volumes, of the two houses of the Hungarian Parliament for the period 1868-1944, as well as comprehensive histories, and handbooks of various institutions, offices, and branches of central and local administration relating to Hungarian history from the 10th century to the present time.

The "Haus-, Hof-, and Staatsarchiv" collections released by Austrian authorities and research centers contain many references to Hungary and its institutions, policies, and personalities. The Library has abundant documentary collections and other publications about Hungary's political parties and movements, especially for the last two centuries, administrative and political directories and handbooks, guides, and similar materials.

The Library does not have a full set of any Hungarian military journal, organizational handbook, or training manual, but works such as the 22-volume *A magyar nemzet hadtörténelme* (1929-41) by József Bánlaki provide substantial information in this field.

Hungary's participation in the Warsaw Pact is well documented in both Hungarian and Western sources.

SOCIETY.   The Library has basic bibliographic sources on the history of Hungarian society and its problems. The periodical bibliographies of Hungarian social science literature, compiled by the Institute of Social Sciences of the Hungarian Academy, cover current publishing activity in these fields. Retrospective bibliographies of Hungarian social science publications can be found under the various subject headings in the Library's catalogs. Important topical monographs include works by Ignác Acsády (history of serfdom), Kálmán Benda (history of Jacobinism in Hungary), Baron József Eötvös (nationalities problems), Oszkár Jászi (social reform), and Gyula Szekfű (state administration and domestic policy). The Library subscribes to all important periodicals in this area.

Publications of the United Nations Organization and its agencies are very important sources of information on Hungarian topics in this field.

ECONOMY.   The Library has excellent economic maps by Aladár Edvi Illés and Albert Halász (1921 and 1926 editions), and a volume of historical maps and charts presenting the statistical aspects of Hungarian social and economic history. This work, entitled *Magyarország társadalma és gazdasága, 1867-1967* (1967), was compiled by the Hungarian Central Statistical Office. The Library also has a directory, by Gyula Rubinek, of agricultural landowners (1911), a directory of state cooperatives and state-owned companies for the post-World War II era, a 5-volume historical bibliography of Hungary's economic literature issued by the Library of the Agricultural Museum in Budapest (1934-61), a guide, compiled by György Rózsa, to economic research literature (1959), the annual bibliographic compilations of the Institute of Economy of the Hungarian Academy of Sciences, most of the publications of the Hungarian National Bank, and most economic monographs and journals published in Hungary in the past twenty years.

Information on finance, the economy, and other nontechnological aspects of industry, transportation, communications, etc., may also be found in various technological publications, both monographic and serial.

LAW.   The Hungarian law collection of the Library of Congress is the largest such collection in the United States, and the most comprehensive and useful collection outside Hungary.

Collections of customary law, one of the main sources of Hungarian civil law before 1945, were first published in István Werbőczi's *Tripartitum opus juris consuetudinarii inclyti regni Hungariae* (1517), commonly called *Tripartitum*. The Library has original copies of several editions of this great work (the largest Werbőczi collection outside Hungary), in Latin as well as in Hungarian.

Holdings include royal decrees and diplomas dating back to the 11th century (in the original, in first prints, or in facsimile prints), general collections of Hungarian law, and court decisions. They begin with the *Decretum seu articulorum aliquot priscorum Ungariae regum* (1581), published by János Zsámboki as an appendix to Antonio Bonfini's work on the history of Hungary, and *Decreta, constitutiones et articuli regum inclyti regni Hungariae* (1584), by Zacharias Mosóczy and Miklós Telegdi.

Subsequently updated compilations by individual scholars such as Márton Szentiványi (1696), János Szegedi (1761), Márton György Kovachich (1790, 1799-1801), József Miklós Kovachich (1815, 1818), and Dániel Gegus (1866) were followed by officially compiled collections, e.g., *Országos Törvénytár* (1896-1948) and others, issued by the Ministry of the Interior.

Post-World War II editions available in the Library include legislative provisions issued before the assumption of power by the Communists in 1948 and an almost complete run of Communist publications which include laws published in the official gazette *Magyar Közlöny* and in periodically issued law collections; resolutions issued by the Presidial Council and by the Council of Ministers; decrees issued by the Council of Ministers. Decrees are also published in the official gazette. The Library has partial sets of ministerial decrees and of directives issued by the ministers and top-level national agencies. These are printed in the various ministerial gazettes. The voluminous body of court decisions can be accessed through special indexes. *Legal Sources and Bibliography of Hungary* (1956), compiled by the Law Library staff and based on the holdings of the Library of Congress, is available.

The Library has many hundreds of volumes of Hungarian constitutional and administrative law, in Hungarian and in other languages, including English. The most important of these publications are the proceedings of the two houses of the Hungarian Parliament prior to 1945. The Library has a sizable collection of Hungarian publications on international law. This material, both monographic and serial, is to be found in the General Collection.

Hungarian scholarly journals in the various fields of legal thought and interest include *Magyar Jogi Szemle* (1885, 1920-44), the foreign language publication entitled *Acta Juridica* (1953-), and many others.

FOREIGN AFFAIRS.   Earlier periods of Hungarian diplomatic history are relatively well presented in numerous publications (Hungarian and non-Hungarian) in the fields of general Hungarian, Austro-Hungarian, and European history, governmental, political, and economic affairs.

The Library has most of the text editions of treaties, diplomatic correspondence, war reports and notes, personal diaries and memoirs of diplomatic personnel, as well as post-1950 analytical studies of the foreign policies of the various Hungarian governments. Such materials may be found under author entries or under the established subject and corporate headings in the Library catalogs. Lists of papers and collections such as *Magyarország államszerződéseinek jegyzéke. Catalogue des traités de la Hongrie, 973-1526* (1921), compiled by Jenő Horváth, or editions of diplomatic papers relating to specific historical periods of events are also available, as are memoirs of foreign diplomatic and military personnel, for example, the diary kept by United States Army General Harry H. Bandholtz in 1919 while stationed in Budapest, and the diplomatic notes and reminiscences of United States Minister to Hungary John F. Montgomery for the period of his service there (1933-41).

LANGUAGE.   The Library's extensive collection of Hungarian dictionaries comprises general, historical, etymological, and special dictionaries for scholarly purposes as well as for the practical needs of the language teacher, the translator, the interpreter, or the tourist. These include monolingual, bilingual, and multilingual dictionaries.

Earliest among these is Ambrosio Calepino's *Dictionarium duodecim linguarum* (1585) which contains the first extensive vocabulary of the Hungarian language in a work published outside Hungary. Several works by early Hungarian lexicographers are represented by recent facsimile editions. Among the Library's holdings are *Magyar tájszótár* (1881), an Academy publication; *A magyar nyelv szótára* (1862-67), the first comprehensive dictionary of the Hungarian language, by Gergely Czuczor and János Fogarasi; and *Magyar nyelvtörténeti szótár* (1890-93), the first historical dictionary of Hungarian, by Gábor Szarvas and Zsigmond Simonyi.

The fine collection of linguistic bibliographies, journals, and monographic series includes the annual *A magyarországi nyelvtudomány bibliográfiája. Bibliographie linguistique de la Hongrie*, (1961-), *Nyelvtudományi Pályamunkák* (1834-64), *Magyar Nyelvészet* (1856-61), *Nyelvtudományi Közlemények* (1862-), *Magyar Nyelvőr* (1872-), *Magyar Nyelv* (1905-), *Acta Linguistica* (1951-).

American publications in this field appear mainly in the *Uralic and Altaic Languages Series* of *Indiana University Publications*. Journals and monographs containing materials on Hungarian and related languages, published in Hamburg, Helsinki, Munich, Paris, Vienna, and elsewhere, are also available in the Library.

LITERATURE.   The Library's holdings in Hungarian literature are among the most comprehensive in the United States. They include original works of fiction, poetry, drama, literary history, and criticism, literary journals published in Hungarian or in foreign languages, general and special bibliographies, and English translations of Hungarian literature. The holdings also include publications of Hungarian émigrés in Hungarian and foreign languages.

Major sources of information about Hungarian literary life include the 8-volume *Pintér Jenő magyar irodalomtörténete* (1930-44), József Szinnyei's 14-volume *Magyar írók élete és munkái* (1891-1914), the annual bibliographies of Hungarian literature prepared by Sándor Kozocsa for the years of 1932 through 1960, the Academy's 3-volume *Magyar irodalmi lexikon* (1963-65), Albert Tezla's *An Introductory Bibliography to the Study of Hungarian Literature* (1964), and its supplement *Hungarian Authors: a Bibliographical Handbook* (1970).

The collection includes the most important special periodicals: *Irodalomtörténeti Közlemények* (1891-), *Irodalomtörténet* (1912-62), and the foreign language annual *Acta Litteraria* (1957-). General journals with a rich literary content, such as the *Budapesti Szemle* (1857-1943), and literary journals such as the conservative *Napkelet* (1923-40) and the radical *Nyugat* (1908-41) are also available. The Library also holds the most recent comprehensive histories of Hungarian literature and works by literary scientists and essayists.

Hungary's poetry is represented by Bálint Balassa (1524-94), Mihály Csokonai Vitéz (1773-1805), Sándor Petőfi (1823-49), János Arany (1817-82), Endre Ady (1877-1919), Attila József (1905-37), and many others. Among the novelists, the works of Mór Jókai (1825-1904), Kálmán Mikszáth (1847-1910), and Zsigmond Móricz (1879-1942) are available both in the original and in translation. The collection includes the works of prominent Hungarian dramatists, such as József Katona (1791-1830), Imre Madách (1823-64), Ferenc Molnár (1878-1952), and László Németh (1901-). The post-World War II collection of belles lettres is particularly strong and is being developed systematically.

The holdings include numerous works about special aspects of metrics, stylistics, the art of translation, comparative literary science, as well as histories of literary societies, groups, movements, prizes, and awards.

FOLKLORE.   Among publications on folklore, ethnography, and cultural anthropology, the Library has almost complete sets of the most important journals, *Ethnologische Mitteilungen aus Ungarn* (1885-1905), *Ethnographia* (1890-), *Néprajzi Értesítő* (1900-), as well as István Sándor's basic bibliography of post-World War II literature entitled *A magyar néprajztudomány bibliográfiája* (published periodically since 1965 to cover the whole period since 1945), the 4-volume *A magyarság néparjza* (1941-43), and numerous valuable research monographs by Béla Bartók (Hungarian and European folk music), Béla Gunda (ethnography of the Finno-Ugrians and of the Carpathian Basin), István Győrffy (village culture, folk architecture), Zoltán Kodály (folk music, folk songs), Mária Kresz (peasant costumes), János Kriza and Gyula Ortutay (folktales), Dezső Malonyai (folk arts), Elisabeth Rearick (folk dances), Károly Viski (peasant customs). The Library has a complete set of the multilingual *Acta Ethnographica* (1950-).

RELIGION AND PHILOSOPHY.   Among the publications held are the bibliography of the medieval manuscripts of the National Széchényi Library, Budapest, entitled *Codices manuscripti Latini* (1940), by Emma Bartoniek, the excellent *Catalogus incunabulorum quae in bibliothecis publicis Hungariae asservantur* (1970), by Géza Sajó and Erzsébet Soltész, several bibliographies and catalogs related to ecclesiastic history and studies, as well as the representative Roman Catholic journal, *Katolikus Szemle* (1887-1914). Almost all post-World War II journals issued by the various religious denominations are available.

Publications on philosophy are represented by some general historical outlines and several sound, scholarly works such as those of Béla Brandenstein, Gyula Kornis, Ákos Pauler, and József Halasy-Nagy. Writings by Communist philosophers Béla Fogarasi and György Lukács are available as is Hungary's antireligious journal, *Világosság* (1960-).

EDUCATION AND SCHOLARSHIP.   The Library's holdings in this area cover a wide variety of related topics, including all periods of Hungarian educational history since the 11th century and the development of educational institutions and curricula from the Middle Ages to the present. The Library has several encyclopedias, special dictionaries, and other materials on special aspects of education and scholarship, as well as the representative periodicals in this field. A sample collection of current (or recent) textbooks used on various levels of the educational and school system is also available.

FINE ARTS, ARCHITECTURE, THEATER, AND MOTION PICTURE ARTS.   Holdings include special encyclopedias, dictionaries, biographic and membership directories in several fields of the arts, as well as histories of societies, schools of thought among creative artists, academies, and special educational institutions. Art journals include *Acta historiae artium* (1953-), several bulletins published by the Hungarian National Museum of Fine Arts, the National Gallery, and other institutions, and yearbooks issued by societies, museums, and art education institutions.

Hungarian architecture, its history, monuments, and prominent builders, are amply covered. The Library has the publications of the Institute of Theatre and Motion Picture Arts in Budapest. The indexes of literature in these fields, compiled by Géza Staud, Elemér Hankiss, and others, are available, as are the standard histories of the Hungarian National Theater, the Opera House in Budapest, and other cultural institutions.

MEDIA OF COMMUNICATION.   The holdings are strong in works about publishing and printing history, radio and television, especially for the period since World War II, but weak in newspapers published prior to the first World War and between the wars. The periodical press is well represented for all periods, but especially since the initiation of the subscription and acquisition programs of the Library in the early 1950s. The Library has all important bibliographies and special monographs on the history of the press, publishing, and printing in Hungary, as well as a nearly complete set of *Magyar Könyvszemle* (1876-).

Newspaper holdings, in Hungarian as well as in languages of the various ethnic groups in Hungary, number over 100 titles, but only about half of them are represented by long runs. The Library holds more than 2,000 periodical titles, about half of which are held in more than one volume.

HUNGARIANS ABROAD.   Materials of this type are scattered through the collection; thus it is difficult to arrive at a satisfactory count of them. The Library subscribes to several Hungarian newspapers published abroad, mainly in countries neighboring Hungary and in the United States. The bibliographic directory, *Hungarians in America* (the 1963 and 1966 editions, the latter being the most recent one in print) lists thousands of professionals of Hungarian origin in the Americas. Library holdings include statistical reports and surveys on the Hungarian emigration, beginning with the 1870s, about a dozen almanacs published by the editorial staffs of various American newspapers issued in Hungarian, and some studies of social customs, educational institutions, and church life.

RARE BOOKS.   Custodial materials in the Rare Book Division include the richly illuminated 14th century Latin codex, the *Nekcsei Lipócz Bible* commissioned by Demeter Nekcsei-Lipócz, a royal treasurer. A copy of Meta P. Harrsen's study of this treasure is also in the Rare Book Collection. There are 12 Hungarian incunabula, among them two editions of the second printed history of the Hungarian nation, the *Chronica Hungariae* (Augsburg and Brünn, both in 1488), by János Thuróczy, royal judge and historian. Its precursor, the *Chronicon Budense* (Buda, 1473), the first book printed in Hungary, is represented by facsimile editions of later dates.

Assertio vera de Trinitate (Geneva, 1573), by the Calvinist Theologian István Szegedi Kiss, and a fine first edition copy of the first Hungarian translation of the Roman Catholic (Vulgate) version of the Bible by the Jesuit György Káldi, entitled *Szent Biblia* (Vienna, 1626), are examples of the Library's holdings on the Reformation and Counter-Reformation periods in Hungary.

First or rare early edition copies of works by reform statesman Count István Széchenyi (1791-1860), poets Sándor Kisfaludy (1772-1844), Sándor Petőfi (1823-49), János Arany (1817-82), and other leaders of Hungary's 19th-century political and literary movements are included among the rare books of the Library.

MANUSCRIPTS.   The earliest manuscript materials in the Library related to Hungarians consist of service reports and relevant correspondence between George Washington and Colonel Michael de Kovats, Hungarian-born commandant of the Pulaski Legion, dated June, 1778.

A much larger volume of manuscripts originated with the American interest in the events, issues, and personalities of the Hungarian ''Age of Reform'' and the subsequent war of independence in 1848/49. The Zachary Taylor Papers and the correspondence files of Daniel Webster, William H. Seward, Hamilton Fish, and other leading men of the period contain hundreds of letters, notes, instructions, programs, etc. related to the Hungarian war of independence and to the recognition of the independent government led by Lajos Kossuth. The manuscripts describe activities of the Committees for Hungary, formed in the United States in the late summer of 1849. (Abraham Lincoln was one of the active members of the committee in Springfield, Illinois.) Later, the fate of the Hungarian emigration, especially of Kossuth and his entourage, their release from exile in Turkey, Kossuth's memorable journey to the United States in 1851/52, and other related events are discussed or reported in many letters and documents.

Beginning with the 1870s, Hungarian immigration to the United States became the subject of numerous communications, official or private. The Woodrow Wilson Papers contain considerable material relating to Hungary and the Paris Peace Conference (1919): correspondence, reports of various delegations and commissions, treaty drafts, intelligence reports from the President's field agents, letters from various Hungarian-American groups, et al.

The manuscript collection also contains documents relating to the refusal of Congress to ratify the peace treaty with Hungary, signed by other powers on June 4, 1920, and the related activities of Eugene Pivány.

MUSIC.   The approximately 300 publications on Hungarian musicology and music history include two special encyclopedias and more than 100 volumes of 9 special journals. The reference collection covers all periods and topics of Hungarian musical history. There are also more than 2,000 pieces of sheet music, cataloged under the names of the composers, and numerous letters by Hungarians on music, musical instruments, and related topics. Selected holdings of phonograph records begin with 1950. The Library has several Hungarian classics (operas and concerto pieces) on long-playing Qualiton records, and Hungaroton's *Complete Bartók,* issued between 1968 and 1971. Among the serials are *A magyar népzene tára. Corpus musicae popularis Hungaricae* (1951-) and *Studia musicologica* (1961-).

The Liszt collection includes 114 autographs by Franz Liszt and 200 of his letters. There are also two Bartók autographs: the *Concerto per Orchestra* and the *Fifth String Quartet.* Unique is the collection of photographic replicas of 75 music autograph manuscripts of Joseph and Michael Haydn and other 18th-century composers known as the "Esterházy Collection." It was procured from Prince Paul Esterházy on the eve of World War II.

The Archive of Folk Song, a unit within the Music Division, has 36 10-inch discs of Hungarian folk music and a 7-inch reel DT tape of Hungarian folk music originally recorded on cylinders by Béla Bartók during the 1910s and duplicated by the Hungarian Academy of Sciences. American Hungarian folk songs are represented by 130 12-inch records made in California by Sydney Robertson Cowell and by 248 12-inch acetate records made in Michigan and Wisconsin by Alan Lomax.

GEOGRAPHY AND MAPS.   While most of the works published about the geography of Hungary are in the General Collection, maps and atlases are in the custody of the Geography and Map Division.

The first map of Hungary (1528), compiled by a certain Lázár, secretary to the Prince Primate of the Roman Catholic Church in Hungary, is part of the *Theatrum orbis terrarum,* first issued by Abraham Ortelius in 1570 and subsequently published in 41 editions. The Geography and Map Division has many copies of this great work.

The first modern topographic survey of Hungary was completed between 1763 and 1785, resulting in a 1:28,800 scale map. It served as the reference base for many later editions, some of which are available at the Library.

Pre-World War I Hungary is represented by two comprehensive atlases: the *Nagy magyar atlasz* (1906), by Károly Brózik, which contains 158 color maps and 257 monochrome maps, and the *Teljes földrajzi és történelmi atlasz,* 5th rev. and enl. ed. (1911), by Manó Kogutowicz, which has 130 main and 80 supplementary maps.

There are also four general and school atlases for the period between the two world wars. Post-World War II materials have been received irregularly, mostly in the past decade, and comprise approximately 450 single-sheet maps and 15 atlases.

The Library holds some 7,400 individual maps (about 80 percent of the pre-World War I maps are listed under the Austro-Hungarian Empire) of counties, districts, cities (including Budapest), their administrative, environmental, transportation, and other aspects.

PRINTS AND PHOTOGRAPHS.   Prominent members of the first group of Hungarian immigrants to the United States appear in the photographs taken by Matthew B. Brady and his associates during the American Civil War. Portrait collections and group photographs include Generals Asbóth and Stahel, Major Zágonyi, commander of Fremont's Body Guard, and others. The same military leaders figure among the 300 drawings by Civil War artist Edwin Forbes which appeared in *Leslie's Illustrated Weekly Newspaper;* a card file of this material is available.

The Library has approximately 400 posters designed by Hungarians, ranging in time from the First World War through the 1930s. The designers are of varying artistic and political persuasion such as Mihály Bíró (1886-1948), István Farkas (1887-1944), György Konecsni (1908-), Tibor Pólya (1886-1937), and Marcel Vértes (1895-1961), to mention only those who are currently referred to in Hungarian publications. The subject matter includes government war loans, postwar political events, travel, theater, and miscellaneous advertisements.

Custodial holdings of the Prints and Photographs Division's Motion Picture Section include 15 documentary films on Hungary related to the life and customs of the Hungarians, political and military events during and after the two world wars, and the Hungarian revolution in 1956. In addition, there are several motion pictures from Communist Hungary. The Library has a number of American motion pictures made by producers Adolph Czukor, Alexander Korda, Ivan Tors, and motion pictures employing the talents of composers Miklos Rozsa, actresses Vilma Banky and Ilona Massey, and actors Michael Varkonyi, Paul Lukas, and Stephan Bekassy, all of whom came from Hungary.

Elemer Bako
Library of Congress

Poland

General Information

THE ORIGINS OF the Polish collection in the Library of Congress can be traced to Thomas Jefferson's library, which included copies of A. L. Caraccioli's *La Pologne, telle qu'elle a été, telle qu'elle est, telle qu'elle sera* (Paris, 1775) and G. B. Mably's *Du gouvernment et des loix de la Pologne* (Paris, 1781). Early American interest in Polish affairs was somewhat sporadic, however, and development of the Library's Polish collection proceeded quite slowly during the 19th century. In 1901 Herbert Putnam, the Librarian of Congress, reported that there were only 97 Polish books in the Library.

The 80,000-volume Yudin collection, acquired by the Library in 1907, contained about 200 items of Polonica, largely in Russian, and included a 17th-century Polish work by Jakub K. Haur, *Skład abo skarbiec znakomitych sekretów oekonomiey ziemiańskiey.*

After 1918 Poland received considerably more attention in the United States, and productive exchanges of scholarly publications were initiated with Polish institutions. The Library also received a number of books on Poland from the collection of the American Legation in Riga.

Interest in Central and Eastern Europe increased further after World War II, and in 1951 the Library established a special Division to effect a systematic expansion of its Slavic collections. A Polish Area Specialist was assigned to the Division, and the Library now maintains a network of 290 exchange arrangements with governmental and scholarly institutions in Poland. Books dealing with Poland in English, French, German, and other languages have been received in substantial quantities in recent years through the various acquisition channels of the Library and increasingly so through the operations of the Library's shared cataloging program. By 1972 approximately 90,000 books in Polish or relating to Poland were available in the social sciences and humanities. The Polish serials collection includes roughly 130 newspapers, as well as about 5,000 periodicals. In recent years the average annual accrual of new books in Polish or about Poland has been over 2,000, and it is expected that acquisitions under the Library's Public Law 480 Program initiated in Poland in 1971 will significantly increase this rate.

The Collections

GENERAL REFERENCE WORKS.   Poland has a distinguished bibliographic tradition, and the Library's collections in this area span some three and a half centuries. Included among the many significant items are the earliest Polish bibliographic work, prepared by Szymon Starowolski and covering a hundred Polish writers (1625), the multivolume *Bibliografia Polska,* compiled by the Estreicher family and covering the period from the 15th century to 1900, and the Polish national bibliography, *Przewodnik Bibliograficzny.* Holdings of bibliographies for various subjects and regions, as well as those recording research on Poland conducted outside that country, are comprehensive. Indexes to periodical articles and printed catalogs of Polish newspapers and periodicals also provide coverage extending from the earliest items available through those most recently published.

Handbooks published in Poland and in other countries range from the 17th-century *Respublica; sive, Status Regni Poloniae,* by the Elzevir Press, to modern surveys in Polish, English, French, and German. Polish biographical research remains incomplete, but reference works such as the *Polski Słownik Biograficzny* and various biographical dictionaries are available. Genealogical records, from Okolski's 17th-century *Orbis Polonus* or K. Niesiecki and A. Boniecki's "herbarze" [armorials] to the postwar *Genealogia* of Włodzimierz Dworzaczek are included. A considerable body of statistical information issued by the Main Statistical Bureau and by local and municipal governments is available. The few gaps in this area are gradually being filled.

THE LAND AND PEOPLE.   Geographic descriptions of Poland range from the 16th-century studies of Maciej of Miechów to the most recent geographic dictionaries, tourist guides, and gazetteers. Physical, political, and economic geographies, as well as scholarly journals such as *Czasopismo Geograficzne* and *Przegląd Geograficzny,* are also represented. An impressive geographic dictionary of the Polish Kingdom and other Slavic lands, published in 16 volumes between 1888 and 1914, is among the rare items in the collections.

Poland's population is treated in many studies, including the censuses of 1921 and 1960, analyses of Poland's population history, and works on war losses, population composition and distribution, and post-1945 resettlements caused by shifting political borders.

The problem of nationalities (minorities) is discussed in various publications of the Nationality Research Institute in Warsaw and in the journal *Sprawy Narodowościowe* (1927-39). Studies issued abroad are also available.

The background of the Polish people and the early migrations of the Slavs are the subject of many scholarly investigations, among which are Jan Czekanowski's anthropological studies. Many works on ethnography and ethnology are also available, including those of Jan S. Bystroń, Ludwik Krzywicki, Kazimierz Moszyński, and Adam Fischer.

MAPS.   The Geography and Map Division houses a rich collection of maps pertaining to Poland, including a number of early original maps of Eastern Europe showing the Polish-Lithuanian Commonwealth. Poland first appeared as a geographic entity on Cusanus' printed map of 1491, a version of which, revised by Marcus Beneventanus, can be found in the 1507 Rome edition of Ptolemy's *Geographia,* under the title "Tabula moderna Polonie . . ." Reproduced fragments of a map dating from 1526 by Polish cartographer Bernard Wapowski, with longitudes and latitudes supposedly determined by Copernicus, are available. A map by the cartographer Wacław Gro-decki, originally printed in Basel around 1560, is contained in the first edition of Ortelius' *Theatrum Orbis Terrarum* (Amsterdam, 1570) under the title "Poloniae locorumque viciniorum descriptio."

Seventeenth-century maps of the Polish-Lithuanian Commonwealth are included in numerous contemporary atlases of Jodocus Hondius, Willem Janszoon Blaeu, Jan Jansson, and Frederick de Wit, Sanson and Jaillot, and Johann Baptist Homann. Among significant items are a map of the Grand Duchy of Lithuania and adjoining countries, drawn by Tomasz Makowski (Amsterdam, 1613), and a map of the Polish Commonwealth by the French military surveyor Guillaume le Vasseur de Beauplan.

Important 18th-century items include Rizzi Zannoni's *Carte de la Pologne, divisée par provinces et palatinats et subdivisée par districts* (Londres, 1772).

The influence of Homboldt and Ritter on 19th-century Polish cartographers can be seen in the topical maps of that period. The collection also contains such old-school examples as Joachim Lelewel's *Géographie du moyen âge* (Bruxelles, 1850-52), and *Atlas do dziejów polskich* (Warszawa, 1830).

Among the numerous maps printed between 1918 and 1939 are excellent examples of the work of Eugeniusz Romer, the founder of a new school of cartography in Poland. The period since 1945 is represented by a great number of maps and atlases. These include a 1946 administrative map (1:500,000), showing the new boundaries, many physical maps, and various special atlases. Some 50 sets of American, British, and German maps of Poland from the Second World War are also available.

The Library has plans and views of many cities, many of great artistic merit. Panoramic views of Kraków, Warsaw, Lublin, Poznań, and numerous towns appear in *Civitates Orbis Terrarum*, published from 1572 to 1618 by Georg Braun and Franz Hogenberg of Cologne, in Braun's *Théâtre des cités du monde* (Bruxelles, 1620), and Jan Jansson's *Illustriorium principumque septentrionalium Europae* (Amsterdam, 1657). Among the city maps is a particularly fine 18th-century colored map of Warsaw by P. F. Tardieu.

The collection as a whole comprises 2,500 single-sheet maps relating to Poland, of which about 500 are city maps; many others are filed under Austro-Hungary and Russia.

HISTORY.   Historical materials constitute some 30 percent of the Library's Polonica. All aspects of the historical literature from the Middle Ages through the present are well represented, including the basic and specialized historical bibliographies, most of the important catalogs of publications of the Polish Academy of Sciences and the learned societies, and numerous reference works in auxiliary fields. Of great importance are the extensive published medieval and modern archival sources, from the oldest chronicles included in the *Monumenta Poloniae Historica* to documents on Polish-Soviet relations since 1917. Among these are *Acta Historica,* covering the period between 1507 and 1795; *Monumenta Medii Aevi Historica; Acta Tomiciana,* containing important sources on the Polish Renaissance; the 22-volume *Scriptores Rerum Polonicarum; Monumenta Poloniae Vaticana,* selected documents from the Vatican archives on the Polish-Papal relations; a compilation of documents relating to the Polish-Lithuanian Union from 1385 to 1791; documents on the Kościuszko insurrection in 1794; and materials pertaining to the regaining of Poland's independence in 1918.

Polish historiography may be traced from the 15th-century *Historiae Polonicae Libri XII* of Jan Długosz through Adam Naruszewicz's *Historya narodu polskiego* and numerous works of Joachim Lelewel to the present. General comprehensive histories constitute a chronicle of alternating independence and subjugation.

The positivistic historians, and the so-called Kraków school of thought, are well represented. Considerable material is available on the period of renewed optimism at the turn of the century.

The period after 1918 is covered by many specialized studies in such fields as political, constitutional, military, diplomatic, social, and cultural history.

Post-1945 historical studies, as exemplified by the multivolume Marxist *Historia Polski* (1957-), have emphasized social history and economic conditions. Current historical research also extends to the medieval and Renaissance periods.

Special fields such as constitutional history are covered in great detail. Economic and social history is likewise represented by many publications including those of Jan Ptaśnik, Franciszek Bujak, and Jan Rutkowski. Materials in political and diplomatic history are adequate for most research, and cultural history is represented by works of Aleksander Brueckner and others.

The Library has such leading periodicals as *Kwartalnik Historyczny, Przegląd Historyczny,* and the specialized and regional periodicals *Archeion, Biuletyn Żydowskiego Instytutu Historycznego, Kwartalnik Historii Kultury Materialnej, Roczniki Dziejów Społecznych i Gospodarczych, Rocznik Krakowski,* and *Przegląd Zachodni.*

MANUSCRIPTS.   Although the Library's manuscript collections include material relating to Poland and the Poles, the extent of these holdings cannot be precisely estimated since many of the collections have not been analyzed for their relevance to Polish affairs. Most of the Library's manuscripts relating to Poland are American in origin. One of the few collections from Poland is the record of the Confederation of Bar, a movement formed in 1768 by Polish gentry led by Kazimierz Pułaski's father and, later, by Kazimierz himself, in defense of Poland's independence.

Several references to the earliest Polish immigrants to America, who arrived in Jamestown in 1608, can be found in the *Records of the Virginia Company of London.* The George Washington papers contain 17 letters from Pułaski and seven from Kościuszko (two as photostats), as well as 22 letters from Washington to Pułaski and six to Kościuszko. The Jefferson papers include his 12 letters to Kościuszko and approximately 40 about him, as well as nine letters from Niemcewicz and copies of seven letters to him from Jefferson.

The Polish participation in the American Civil War is documented in numerous manuscripts, including records on Brigadier General W. Krzyżanowski and other Union officers.

The papers of the American statesman Caleb Cushing include many documents relating to the Polish Emigration Land Company, established in Virginia in 1869 for the benefit of Polish immigrants. The Minnie Maddern Fiske papers and the Ellen Louise Moulton (Chandler) papers contain correspondence from Helena Modjeska, the Shakespearean actress so popular with the American public.

The Woodrow Wilson and Robert Lansing papers provide information on the reestablishment of the Polish State in 1918, as do the papers of Henry White, a member of the U.S. delegation to the Versailles Peace Conference. The papers of William Orr who wrote on education in Poland, and of Charles S. Dewey, who served as financial adviser to the Polish Government, contain valuable information on post-1918 Poland.

RARE BOOKS.   Early and rare Polonica in the Library of Congress include a score of incunabula, among which is Cardinal Matthaeous' *Dialogus rationis et conscientiae,* printed in Mainz in 1460, probably by Gutenberg. There are also books by Polish printers working abroad before permanent presses were established in Poland, the most distinguished of whom was Stanislaus Polonus in Seville. The Library has several works from the first permanent press in Poland, established in Kraków by Jan Haller and Kasper Hochfeder around 1503. Jan of Stobnica's commentary on Ptolemy's *Cosmographia,* printed in 1512, is the first work printed in Poland to mention America.

Books relating to or printed in Poland during the 16th and 17th centuries cover such subjects as history, science, theological polemics, religion, and law. The Library's fifty 16th- and 17th-century legal volumes also provide insight into the early Polish language and political and economic life. A volume of laws and decrees compiled by Jan Januszowski and printed in Kraków in 1600 includes the 15th-century "Neminem captivabimus nisi iure victum" statute, a parallel to the Magna Carta.

Early historical works include Marcin Kromer's *De origine et rebus gestis Polonorum* (1558), Krzysztof Warszewicki's *Turcicae quatuordecim* (Kraków, 1595), and Reinhold Heidenstein's *De bello Moscovitico* (1588).

Science is represented by the 1543 and 1566 editions of Copernicus' *De revolutionibus orbium coelestium,* and theological polemics by *Bibliotheca Fratrum Polonorum* (1656-92).

The Library also possesses some fifty 16th- and 17th-century books of Hebrew Polonica, including Moses Isserles' *Torat ha-ḥatat,* printed in Kraków in 1569. The struggles of the 18th century are reflected in a manifesto of the Dzików Confederation, issued by the supporters of Stanisław Leszczyński against Augustus III during the War of Polish Succession (1735). Broadsides contain manifestoes and proclamations of Tadeusz Kościuszko. Also available is Felix P. Wierzbicki's *California as It is, and as It may be, or a Guide to the Golden Region* (San Francisco, 1849), the first book in English of an original nature to be printed in California.

GOVERNMENT AND POLITICS.   Coverage of government and politics ranges from the 16th century to the present and from international relations, revolutionary movements, and local governments to émigré groups, international conferences, and political leaders. The collection is particularly strong in publications on the 20th century, including the various efforts of the Western Allies, the Central Powers, and the Poles themselves to settle upon a unified policy, the restoration of the Polish state in 1918, the relationship between Poland and the Free City of Gdańsk (Danzig), and the various internal political affairs and parties. Stenographic reports of the Parliament for the years 1922-39 are included, together with discussions of its activities and composition. The current political scene in Poland is discussed in numerous works, as are the Constitutions of 1921, 1935, and 1952.

Poland's military affairs are adequately represented. The events of the Second World War, the Polish uprisings of 1943 and 1944, are discussed in many works, including those by Polish authors living abroad. Coverage of the First World War and earlier military accounts is not complete, although the campaigns of Marshal Piłsudski are covered extensively. Military science and history are also discussed in various periodicals (*Bellona,* and *Wojskowy Przegląd Historyczny*).

LAW.   The Law Library houses some 6,000 books on Polish Law, as well as sets of about 80 periodicals, providing information on the various legal systems applied during Poland's complex political history, from the days of the early Kingdom to today's Peoples' Republic.

An original edition is available of *Volumina Legum,* containing all Polish legislation from 1347 to 1793. The laws in force in the Lithuanian part of the Commonwealth can be studied in an 18th-century Church Slavic edition of the Lithuanian Statutes, enacted in 1529 and subsequently modified in 1566 and 1588. A Polish translation of this work is also available. Of interest is the *Akta grodzkie i ziemskie* (Lwów, 1868-1935), a 25-volume collection dealing with local city and provincial statutes from 1244 to 1768. Two complete sets of official gazettes from the partition period are available, the 76-volume *Dziennik Praw Królestwa Polskiego,* containing laws and decrees of the Duchy of Warsaw and the Congress Kingdom of Poland, and the 16-volume *Dziennik Praw Rzeczypospolitej Krakowskiej* (1815-46) for the Free City of Kraków. The collection includes laws enacted by the Central Diet of the Polish-Lithuanian Commonwealth, as well as codes of enactments of the provincial diets (sejmiki) and statutes and regulations adopted by the provincial synods of the Church. Also represented are legal provisions for city government derived from the laws of Magdeburg, which became known as the *ius municipale.*

The collection is strong in post-World War I materials, reflecting efforts to codify the legal systems inherited from the partition period. Complete sets are available of the official *Dziennik Ustaw* and *Monitor Polski,* as well as *Dziennik Ustaw* (1939-45), published in France and later in England by the Polish Government in Exile. Also of interest is a comprehensive set of *Dziennik Ustaw Śląskich* (1922-39), the official legislation of Upper Silesia.

Equally comprehensive are holdings of contemporary legislation and legal literature. The civil code of 1964, the family code of 1964, the code of criminal procedure of 1969, and many specialized codes are all available.

The numerous modern legal and parliamentary studies in the collection include volumes by Oswald Balzer, Joachim Bandtkie, Stanisław Kutrzeba, Julius Bardach, Bogusław Leśnodorski, and Stefan Rozmaryn.

THE ECONOMY.   Various general surveys and detailed studies of the Polish economy are available, particularly for the period since 1918. The economic problems that faced Poland between the wars are covered in the works of such leading economists as Feliks Młynarski, Tadeusz Brzeski, and Edward Taylor. The great depression in Poland (1930-35) produced investigations of business cycles in industry and agriculture, and the Library has the studies of such specialists as Edward Lipiński and Michał Kalecki, as well as theoretical works produced at the economic research centers.

Since 1945 emphasis has been placed on industrialization and economic planning. Holdings in these areas are quite strong, and numerous statistical publications are available. The writings of such economic scholars as Oskar Lange, Bronisław Minc, Włodzimierz Brus, Stefan Kurowski, Andrzej Karpiński, Jósef Pajestka, and Kazimierz Secomski may be consulted, as may the studies of scholars living outside Poland. The holdings of Polish periodicals in economics are likewise strong.

LANGUAGE.   Works on the Polish language reflect every aspect of the philological and linguistic studies conducted during the 19th and 20th centuries in Poland, the collection being especially strong in publications issued since World War II.

Bibliographies covering research on the Polish language have been published in *Prace Filologiczne* (Warsaw, 1885-1937), *Zeitschrift für slavische Philologie,* and since 1945, in monographic form. Basic works offering a historical synthesis of the development of the language include studies by A. Brueckner, J. Baudouin de Courtenay, Zenon Klemensiewicz, and Tadeusz Lehr-Spławiński. Polish orthography is discussed in numerous works, both popular and scholarly.

Extensive lexicographic publications include the monumental national dictionaries of Samuel Linde, the so-called "Warsaw dictionary" of Karłowicz, Kryński, and Niedźwiedzki, and the recent 11-volume dictionary of the Polish language as spoken during the last 200 years, sponsored by the Polish Academy of Sciences. The oldest dictionary in the Library to include the Polish language is A. Calepino's *Dictionarium undecim linguarum* (Basel, 1598). Specialized dictionaries cover synonyms, special terminology, and etymology. The collection of bilingual and polyglot dictionaries is particularly rich.

Holdings of historical and descriptive grammars of the Polish language are comprehensive, including works by Jan Łoś, Z. Klemensiewicz, J. Szober, W. Doroszewski, H. Gaertner, H. Grappin, A. Meillet, C. Verdiani, and many other authorities.

The dialectology of the Polish language is represented not only by analyses of the results of numerous contemporary studies but also by dictionaries of dialects and maps which indicate the areas in which specific dialects are spoken. Of particular value in this field are the works of Kazimierz Nitsch. American research on the Polish language is fully covered, and almost all of the current scholarly materials on the teaching of the Polish language to native speakers of English are available. The collection also includes several Polish-language primers published in the United States during the 19th century for American children of Polish descent.

LITERATURE.   A wide variety of materials is available for the 16th century, during which literature in the vernacular as well as in Latin flourished, including various modern editions of the

Polish works of Mikołaj Rej and Jan Kochanowski and of the Latin poetry and prose of Klemens Janicki, and Łukasz Górnicki. The extensive collection of critical studies is sufficient to satisfy the requirements of the most penetrating research.

The transitional period to Polish Baroque literature of the 17th century is covered in considerable detail. The 17th-century memoirs of Jan Pasek are available in several editions. Other items of that era include works by Haur in Polish and by Warszewicki and Andrzej Fredro in Latin. The lyrics of Maciej Sarbiewski are represented in 19th- and 20th-century editions. Overall coverage of 17th-century Polish literature is, however, still somewhat uneven.

The 18th-century Polish literature is highlighted by the works of Ignacy Krasicki, Bishop of Warmia (Ermland). The Library has various editions of his novel *Mikołaja Doświadczyńskiego przypadki,* the 19th-century Paris and Leipzig editions of his collected works, and a rare 1794 Russian translation of his *Historia na dwie księgi podzielona.* Works of other gifted poets and writers of the period include the satires of Stanisław Trembecki and of Kajetan Węgierski, who is also the author of a diary about his travels in America in 1783, and the poetry, plays, and patriotic songs of Julian Ursyn Niemcewicz, as well as memoirs covering his travels in America and his recollections of George Washington and Thomas Jefferson.

Polish Romantic literature is extensively represented in the collections, including the complete works of Adam Mickiewicz, Juliusz Słowacki, and Zygmunt Krasiński, in many editions. The first editions of Mickiewicz's *Konrad Wallenrod* (Petersburg, 1828) and *Pan Tadeusz* (Paris, 1834) are available.

Positivist writing of the period 1863-1918 is reflected in the novels of Bolesław Prus (Aleksander Głowacki) and Eliza Orzeszkowa, the complete works of Nobel laureate Władysław Reymont, the works of Maria Konopnicka, the poetry of Adam Asnyk, and numerous other writings.

For the period between the First and Second World Wars, the literary group known as "Young Poland" is particularly well represented; the complete works of Stanisław Przybyszewski, for example, are available in several languages. Almost all the poets of independent Poland are represented in the collections. Holdings of Polish literature since World War II are quite strong, although gaps remain for the period from the end of the war to 1956.

Works by Polish authors began to be translated into English as early as the 16th century. During the 1840s translations of Polish poetry appeared in the *North American Review* in the United States. Holdings of Polish literature in English are extensive and include the novels and short stories of Henryk Sienkiewicz, various works of Mickiewicz, and the plays and novels of Sławomir Mrożek, Witold Gombrowicz, and Jerzy Andrzejewski. An unusual item is Joseph Conrad's English translation (1931) of Bruno Winawer's comedy *Księga Hioba.*

The Library has the most extensive collection of Polish children's books in the United States, including both classics and modern Polish works, many of which won international awards for their content or illustrations.

EDUCATION AND SCHOLARSHIP.   Polish educational history, reforms, organization, programs, and legislation are all treated adequately in the Library's collections. Extensive resources are available in the fields of educational theory and the contemporary educational system and curricula. Histories of Polish learned organizations and institutions, studies on contributions to learning, guides to archives and libraries, recent series of Polish research guides, university catalogs, and accounts of scholarly congresses provide an introduction to the world of Polish scholarship. A complete set of *Nauka Polska, jej potrzeby, organizacja i rozwój* (1918-47) and other pertinent periodicals are also available. Studies on intellectual and scholarly activities of Poles living abroad will be found on the shelves.

PHILOSOPHY AND RELIGION.   Polish philosophy is documented in the Library's collection from the 15th century to the present. The influence of the philosophies of Christian Wolff and

Immanuel Kant upon Polish thinkers may be traced in detail, as may the relationship between the works of Stanisław Staszic, Hugo Kołłątej, and Jan Śniadecki and those of Reid, Condillac, and most of all, Rousseau. Polish 19th-century idealistic philosophy is developed in the writings of B. F. Trentowski, Karol Libelt, and August Cieszkowski. Polish Messianism exerted a deep influence on the literature of the period, especially on the writings of Andrzej Towiański, Adam Mickiewicz, and Słowacki. The works of the precursor of Romanticism and Polish Messianism, Hoene-Wroński, and other philosophers of that period are also well represented.

Positivist philosophy developed in Poland after the unsuccessful uprising of 1863 and is represented by a number of works, including those of Aleksander Świętochowski and Stanisław Brzozowski. Polish psychologists, among whom Kazimierz Twardowski was most prominent, exerted a great influence on Polish logicians. This research, as well as numerous studies by Polish logicians and estheticians (Ajdukiewicz, Kuratowski, Chwistek), is covered adequately. Works by the younger generation of Polish philosophers, including Stanisław Ossowski, Maria Ossowska, and I. Bocheński are also available. Recent acquisitions include works by the Marxist philosophers Adam Schaff and Leszek Kołakowski.

Periodicals in the field include *Przegląd Filozoficzny* (1898-1949), *Kwartalnik Filozoficzny* (1923-50, with some gaps), and the current *Studia Filozoficzne* and *Studia Logica*.

A bibliography of Polish philosophical writings for the period 1750-1864, anthologies, a biographical dictionary of Polish philosophers, and several histories of the discipline provide an extensive introduction to studies in this field.

The history of the Catholic Church in Poland is thoroughly documented. A number of publications contain statutes in force in various ecclesiastical provinces. Other denominations are covered in historical studies.

The numerous Church histories include Józef Umiński's *Historia Kościoła;* the legal status of the Church is covered in writings of Przemysław Dąbkowski, Sadok Barącz, Jan Fijałek, and Adam Vetulani; and cultural aspects of religion are discussed in the works of Kazimierz Morawski, Zdzisław Kaczmarek, and Aleksander Brueckner, among others. The status of Jews in Poland, first defined in 1264, is adequately documented. The many works dealing with the Jewish religion in Poland range from collections of "responsa" printed in Kraków and Lublin in the 16th and 17th centuries to modern studies by Majer Bałaban, Ignacy Schiper, and Zbigniew Pazdro.

THE ARTS. The reference collection on the arts in Poland includes biographical dictionaries of Polish artists, art histories, guides to museums and art galleries, and exhibition catalogs. The holdings are sufficiently comprehensive for the most sophisticated research on Romanesque architecture, Gothic styles, Renaissance and Baroque churches, palaces, and buildings.

Sources for the development of Polish painting and sculpture from the Middle Ages to the present are numerous, including several editions of Canaletto's 18th-century scenes and views of Warsaw, which were used by Polish architects in restoring the city after its almost complete destruction during World War II.

Sculpture in Poland may be traced from the Middle Ages to the present. Several reproductions of the famous 15th-century sculptured altar by Wit Stwosz (Stoss) are available, as are works on Ksawery Dunikowski's Polish national style of the early 20th century and contemporary sculpture. The collection is strong in folk arts. The last decade has produced a number of good reference works in these fields.

PRINTS, PHOTOGRAPHS, AND MOTION PICTURES. The Library's fine prints collection includes works by various Polish artists as well as many pictures relating to Poland. For example, Jean Pierre Norblin, the court painter of the Czartoryski family in Warsaw, is represented by some 65 prints. The nucleus of the Polish collection was formed by the engravings received in the Gardiner Greene Hubbard Collection, which include representations of Polish Kings and other notable personalities by artists of Flemish, French, and German schools. Modern Polish prints by some 20 contemporary artists, ranging from the rather traditional landscapes of Edmund Piotrowicz to the abstract studies of Ryszard Otręba, reflect the high quality of contemporary Polish art. Numerous portraits and historical prints in the collection relate to Poland, and some 500 Polish posters illustrate modern graphic art.

Abundant photographic materials include a small group of stereo photographs from the period 1897-1939. Several hundred photographs depict the activities of the American Red Cross in Poland during the years 1918-21. Life in Poland in the 20th century is also portrayed by a pictorial record of the German invasion in 1939, aerial photographs of Poland taken in 1943, and Soviet photographs taken in 1964. The photographic records of the U.S. Farm Security Administration and of the Office of War Information include extensive coverage of Polish immigrants in America. A recently acquired collection comprising the complete photographic files of *Look Magazine* for 1937-71 contains much valuable material for the study of Polish affairs.

The outstanding motion picture collection includes German newsreels and documentaries from the period 1939-45 as well as pre-1939 German films of Poland and anti-Polish propaganda films, educational films on Poland produced in the United States, short films prepared by the Polish Government in exile during the war, and contemporary short films made in Poland.

MUSIC.   The music collection embraces publications on the history and theory of Polish music and biographical data on composers, by such scholars as Maurycy Karasowski, Józef Suszyński, Aleksander Poliński, Zdzisław Jachimecki, and Adolf Chybiński. Coverage of Polish music extends from the Middle Ages to the modern compositions by Tadeusz Bird, Wojciech Kilar, and Bogusław Schäffer.

Facsimiles and reprints of the principal sources of Polish music of the medieval, Renaissance, and Baroque eras are available, including the earliest chants as well as monographic music of the 16th and 17th centuries. Jan of Lublin's *Tablatura* is an important source for 16th-century organ music, and Mikołaj Zieliński's *Offertoria* and *Communiones* (Venice, 1611) are significant Polish examples of the Venetian style of the early Baroque.

Among the numerous sources are reprints of the first Polish operas, many editions of Stanisław Moniuszko's *Halka* and *Straszny Dwór* and of Szymanowski's *Harnasie,* and there is an extensive collection of chamber music.

Of the individual composers represented, Chopin is perhaps outstanding. There are first editions of some of his mazurkas and waltzes, as well as his collected works. Modern music is represented by the compositions of Zygmunt Noskowski and his pupils and of the "Young Poland" group, including Mieczysław Karłowicz, Karol Szymanowski, Ludomir Różycki, Grzegorz Fitelberg, and Apolinary Szeluto. Works by Witold Lutosławski, Grażyna Bacewicz, and Andrzej Panufnik are available, as are the compositions of such avant-garde musicians as Krzysztof Penderecki, Stanisław Skrowaczewski, and Kazimierz Serocki.

Polish classical and modern music, as well as folk music and operas, may be heard on recordings. The collection of ethnic music and lore in the Archive of Folk Song contains some 400 items recorded in Polish communities in Michigan, Wisconsin, and California. The Archives also has printed texts of songs and music from almost all of the regions of 19th-century Poland, primarily in Oskar Kolberg's multivolume collection entitled *Lud.*

Correspondence and autograph scores by Polish composers encompass many rare items, including Paderewski's second draft of the Minuet in G, Opus 14, which was rewritten by Paderewski for the benefit of the Red Cross and auctioned off in London during World War I. Among the many other autograph scores are those of Chopin's *Mazurka* in B minor for piano, Opus 33, no. 4, Karol Szymanowski's opera *Król Rogier,* and Tadeusz Kassern's opera *Annointed,* Henryk Wieniawski's *Polonaise Brillante* in A major, Opus 21, and Tadeusz Jarecki's prizewinning string quartet

Quatuor. Other holographs include compositions by Leopold Godowski, Józef Hofman, and Moritz Moszkowski.

POLES ABROAD.   Political and economic conditions in Poland have forced many Polish citizens to live abroad, and their life and activities in foreign countries are extensively documented. Legal materials, general histories of Polish emigration such as Gadon's *Emigracya polska* and Retinger's *Polacy w cywilizacjach świata,* histories of Poles in various countries, published letters and memoirs, periodicals such as *Polacy Zagranicą* and *Przegląd Emigracyjny,* and catalogs of the Polish immigrant press are all available.

Polish immigration to the United States is treated in U.S. Government publications, general works on immigration, individual studies, and in newspapers and periodicals. The cultural and religious activities of the immigrants are documented in numerous publications, including the classic work of Thomas and Znaniecki on the transplanted peasant community. One can also find pertinent works by the historian M. Haiman, W. Kruszka's *Historya polska w Ameryce,* and Wachtl's *Polonja w Ameryce*. Efforts are being made to acquire various Polish-American newspapers to fill gaps in the collection. Most of the Polish immigrant publications listed in the bibliographies compiled by Alfons S. Wolanin, and Janina Zabielska and Maria Danilewicz, are found in the collections. The activities of the leading Polish-American cultural, educational, and religious institutions and organizations are also well documented.

Janina W. Hoskins
Library of Congress

Romania

THE BULK OF the Romanian collection is housed in the Main Building (general periodicals, economics, political science, language and literature), and in the Annex (history and geography). Romanian law books and related materials are located in the Law Library in the Main Building. Romanian maps are housed in the Geography and Map Library in Alexander, Virginia. Information about the Romanian collections may be obtained from the Slavic and Central European Division.

Besides the general author and subject catalogs and the shelflist, the Library of Congress has a special shelflist containing cards for all the Romanian titles received under the Shared Cataloging Program with Romania, which began in January, 1971. The Library has prepared or published a number of bibliographies and finding aids relating to its Romanian collections, the most interesting of which are cited below.

The Romanian collections of the Library of Congress, which are strongest and most comprehensive in history, political science, economics, law, and geography, are described in several works published by the Library of Congress: Stephen A. Fischer-Galaţi, *Rumania, a Bibliographic Guide* (1963); *Newspapers of East Central and Southeastern Europe in the Library of Congress,* ed. by R. G. Carlton (1965); *East European Accessions Index,* 10 v. (1951-61); Helen F. Conover's *The Balkans: IV. Rumania* (Washington, 1943); and in *Bibliography of Social Science Periodicals and Monograph Series. Rumania, 1947-1960* of the U. S. Department of Commerce. Bureau of the Census (1961).

There are also representative cross sections in language and literature, intellectual and cultural life, and social conditions. Taken as a whole, the collection is excellent for research purposes because of its size and diversity. It will be most useful to scholars who are working on the late 19th and the 20th centuries.

The collection now numbers about 40,000 volumes. Approximately 70 percent are in Romanian, 25 percent in Western languages, and 5 percent in Russian. There are over 800 periodical titles, including current subscriptions to about 400 titles. There are 70 newspaper titles, 27 of which are currently being received. About 50 percent of the collection deals with the period since 1945, 35 percent with the period between 1914 and 1944, and 15 percent with the period before 1914. The estimated intake for calendar year 1971 was 5,500 pieces, many of which were acquired through the Library's extensive exchange programs with some 45 partners, including the Romanian Academy and the newly founded Academy of Social and Political Sciences as well as their respective branches and research institutes, other institutes under various government ministries, the universities of Bucharest, Cluj, Iaşi, and Timişoara, and national and local museums. Since January 1971, when the Library of Congress extended the National Program for Acquisitions and Cataloging (NPAC) to Romania, receipts have been extensive. Under the terms of NPAC the Library receives all monographs and periodicals of scholarly value. Approximately 2,150 pieces were received under this program during calendar year 1971. Exchanges and NPAC together now account for most of the Library's annual acquisitions of Romanian materials.

The Main Features of the Collection

BIBLIOGRAPHIES AND REFERENCE AIDS.   The collection of bibliographies and reference works is comprehensive and contains most of the standard titles. In addition, there are numerous inventories and descriptions of major archive holdings, especially those of the Library of the Romanian Academy in Bucharest and the branches of the State Archives in Bucharest, Iaşi, Sibiu, Timişoara, and other cities. The collection of general statistical materials is excellent and includes: *Anuarul statistic* (Bucharest, 1904-); *Comunicări statistice,* nos. 1-19 (Bucharest, 1945-48); and *Buletinul statistic al României* (Bucharest, 1892-1940).

GEOGRAPHY.   The Library has several fundamental bibliographies, among them: Victor Tufescu and A. Toşa, *Bibliografia geografică sumară a României* (Bucharest, 1947) and Vasile Cucu, *Bibliografie geografică, 1944-1964* (Bucharest, 1964), and a number of major descriptive works from the older *Marele dicţionar geografic al României,* edited by George Ioan Lahavari, 5 v. (Bucharest, 1898-1902) to the monumental work in progress, *Monografia geografică a R.P.R.,* 2 v. (Bucharest, 1960-). There is also a good collection of periodicals, containing, among others: Societatea Regală Română de Geografie. *Buletinul,* v. 4-59 (Bucharest, 1883-1940); *Lucrările Institutului de Geografie al Universităţii din Cluj,* 6 v. (Cluj, 1924-38); *Probleme de geografie,* v. 1- (Bucharest, 1954-); and *Revue roumaine de géologie, géophysique et géographie. Série de géographie,* v. 1- (Bucharest, 1957-).

These important works notwithstanding, the uniqueness of the Library's collection rests upon an outstanding map collection. There are approximately 3,000 topographic and physical maps in sets or series dating from the beginning of the 19th century to the present. Many are detailed German military maps used in World Wars I and II, which are especially useful for the study of transportation networks and human geography, and up-to-date geologic and soil maps indispensable for the study of agriculture, forestry, and mining. There are also about 900 single maps, the oldest of which, a map of Moldavia and Wallachia by Vindel, dates from 1596. The collection contains a series of maps of Transylvania from 1596 to World War II, including an ethnographic map made during World War I, and a large number of maps on Romania as a whole: physical (1877-1966), population and railroads (1920s-1950s), administration (1926-64), ethnography (1919-40), industry and mines (1923-63), and cities, mostly of Bucharest and Timişoara. The entire collection has been carefully indexed.

HISTORY.   The Library has large holdings in history, but the main strength lies in works published since 1945. Nonetheless, there is an extensive collection of sources containing numerous fundamental works for the medieval and modern periods, beginning with Eudoxiu de Hurmuzaki, *Documente privitoare la istoria Românilor,* 31 v. (Bucharest, 1887-1938) and including items on the reigns of Stephen the Great and Michael the Brave, the Revolution of 1848, the period of the union of Moldavia and Wallachia, peasant uprisings and agrarian conditions in the 19th century, and Romanian diplomacy during the reign of King Charles I. The Library also has the major general histories of Romania by Alexandru Xenopol, Nicolae Iorga, Constantin C. Giurescu, and the neglected, but still valuable *Istoria Românilor,* 14 v. (Bucharest, 1891-1902) by V. A. Urechia. The Library has nearly complete holdings of the two most important monograph series, *Biblioteca Istorică* and *Bibliotheca historica Romaniae,* both sponsored by the ''N. Iorga'' Institute of History in Bucharest.

The Library holds representative works on the Greek and Roman eras, including most of the monographs published since 1960. On the medieval period (1200-1821), there are standard monographic studies on the most important reigns and a number of general studies of the period, mostly recent publications such as: Mihai Berza (ed.), *Cultura moldovenească în timpul lui Ștefan cel Mare* (Bucharest, 1964) and Gheorghe Cronț, *Instituții medievale românești: Înfrătirea de moșie, Jurătorii* (Bucharest, 1969). The collection is strongest in the 19th and early 20th centuries (1821-1918), including almost all the important works in English, French, and German, as well as a representative selection of older works in Romanian. They are concentrated on the same topics as the documentary collections mentioned above. For the interwar period there are a few older standard works, but the holdings consist mainly of recent publications. The collection contains valuable items on economic development, especially agriculture, Romania's diplomatic relations with other Balkan states and France and Germany, and the socialist and working-class movement. Most of the works on the post-World War II period deal with the history of the Romanian Communist Party, the working-class movement, and socialist reconstruction.

The Library of Congress has modest holdings on the provinces that were joined to Romania after World War I. Works on Transylvania are the most abundant, encompassing general surveys by Iorga and László Makkai, among others, an occasional older monograph such as Nicolae Densușianu, *Revoluțiunea lui Horia în Transilvania și Ungaria 1784-1785* (Bucharest, 1884), and runs of important periodicals like *Archiv des Vereines für Siebenbürgische Landeskunde,* (Hermannstadt, 1853-1931) and *Revue de Transylvanie,* v. 1-5 (Cluj, 1934-39). The collection contains significant works on three topics, in particular: the Romanian national movement from the Enlightenment to 1914; the nationality problem, i.e., the status of the Magyars in Greater Romania between the two World Wars; and the Saxons.

Materials on Bukovina and Bessarabia are less abundant, but they do include a number of indispensable works dealing with various aspects of the Romanian national movement. In addition, there are valuable, but incomplete runs of statistical and official publications on Bukovina such as the *Stenographische Protokolle* of the diet; the *Gesetz- und Verordnungsblatt* in 48 v. (Czernowitz, 1850-1918); and the *Mitteilungen* of the *Statistisches Landesamt,* v. 1-2, 4-6, 8-14, 17 (Czernowitz, 1892-1913). On Bessarabia there are a few older monographs such as the classic *Basarabia în secolul XIX* (Bucharest, 1898) by Zamfir Arbure, and Gheorghe Bezviconi, *Boierimea Moldovei dintre Prut și Nistru,* 2 v. (Bucharest, 1940-43). In addition, the collection contains a number of books and pamphlets in both Romanian and Russian published during the Paris Peace Conference and between the two World Wars asserting rival claims to Bessarabia and a fairly complete series of general histories, collections of documents, and monographs published in Russian since 1945 on ''Moldavia'' and dealing mainly with the 19th and 20th centuries.

The collection of scholarly journals is excellent. There are, for example: Academia Română. *Bulletin de la Section Historique,* v. 1-26 (Bucharest, 1912-45); *Revista istorică română,* v. 4-16 (Bucharest, 1934-46); *Studii. Revistă de istorie,* v. 4-5, 7- (Bucharest, 1951-52, 1954-); *Materiale*

şi cercetări arheologice, v. 1- (Bucharest, 1955-); *Studii şi cercetări de istorie veche,* v. 2, 7, 9-
(Bucharest, 1951, 1956, 1958-); *Dacia,* old series, v. 1-12 (Bucharest, 1924-47), and new series,
v. 1- (Bucharest, 1957-); *Ephemeris Dacoromana,* v. 1-10 (Rome, 1923-45); *Revista arhivelor,*
v. 1- (Bucharest, 1924-); *Hrisovul,* v. 1-5, 7 (Bucharest, 1941-47); and *Revista istorică,* edited
by Nicolae Iorga, v. 2-20 (Bucharest, 1916-34). The library currently receives all important
national and provincial periodicals.

POLITICS AND GOVERNMENT.   There is a small collection on institutions in the interwar period, but most of the holdings deal with the period since 1945. Almost all the items on
political parties in the collection have been published since 1945, and, consequently, except for
a few émigré publications, they deal with the Communist and working-class movements. (The
principal exception is the Iron Guard, on which the Library has the writings of Corneliu Zelea
Codreanu.) The collection permits a manifold analysis of the Communist Party and its policies.
Significant subjects covered are: The development of socialism in Romania in the 19th and early
20th centuries; the formation of the Romanian Communist Party in 1921 and the history of the
Party since then; the socialist and working-class press; Party organization and the youth move-
ments; strike movements of the interwar period; and the influence of the Bolshevik Revolution and
Lenin on Romanian Communists. The Library holds *Lupta de clasă,* v. 30- (Bucharest, 1950-).
Newspapers are an important source of information on Party policy and day-to-day events. The
Library receives 27 daily newspapers from 16 cities; most titles since 1962 are on microfilm.
Scînteia, the organ of the Central Committee of the RCP, is available since 1956.

There are many older works in French, German, and English, as well as in Romanian, on
Romania's foreign relations during the interwar period. Monographs in Romanian published since
1945 stress Romania's relationship with the Soviet Union, inter-Balkan cooperation between the
two World Wars, the activities of Nicolae Titulescu, and relations with Germany. In addition,
there is an extensive collection of treaties and works about treaties concluded by Romania with
foreign countries, mostly European, between 1881 and 1964.

LAW.   The collection is comprehensive and contains fundamental works on every aspect
of the law: collections of laws and legal decisions; civil and criminal law and procedure; constitutional law; administrative law; corporation law; labor law, forensic medicine; land law; domestic
relations; legal theory and philosophy of law, and international law. Although the bulk of the
collection deals with the period 1900 to 1944, there are also works on civil and labor law, legal
theory, and property in the Romanian Socialist Republic.

The collection of legal periodicals is excellent. Noteworthy are: *Buletinul curţilor de apel*
(Bucharest, 1924-39); *Dreptul, jurisprudenţa, doctrina, legislaţie* (Bucharest, 1873-74, 1880-
1900, 1902-16, 1923-33); *Pandectele române* (Bucharest, 1921-47); *Revista de drept comercial*
(Bucharest, 1934-46); *Revista de drept public a institutului de ştiinţe administrative ale României*
(Bucharest, 1926-39); *Revista penală* (Bucharest, 1922-41); and *Studii şi cercetări juridice* (Bucha-
rest, 1956-).

A useful guide to the LC's holdings is Virgiliu Stoicoiu, *Legal Sources and Bibliography
of Romania* (New York, 1964).

ECONOMICS.   The collection as a whole is very strong. It contains a large number of older,
fundamental surveys of Romanian economic development and theoretical works such as: Virgil
Madgearu, *Evoluţia economiei româneşti după războiul mondial* (Bucharest, 1940) and Mitiţa
Constantinescu, *Politica economică aplicată,* 3 v. (Bucharest, 1943); many monographs published
since 1960 on all aspects of economic history; and numerous editions and re-editions of the writings
of Romanian economists from the early 19th century to the present.

There are long runs of indispensable periodicals rare in the United States: *Buletinul institutului economic românesc,* v. 2-3, 9-13, 18-21 (Bucharest, 1923-42); *Buletinul Ministerului
agriculturei, industriei, comerciului şi domeniilor,* first series, v. 1-27 (Bucharest, 1885-1916)

and second series, v. 1-11 (Bucharest, 1920-30); Banque Nationale de Roumanie. *Bulletin d'information et de documentation,* v. 2-18 (Bucharest, 1930-46); *Correspondance économique,* v. 2-22 (Bucharest, 1920-40); and *Statistica agricolă a României,* v. 1-8 (Bucharest, 1937-47). The collection includes the censuses of 1899, 1912, 1913, and 1930, the latter a massive work in 10 volumes, as well as analyses for 1941, 1948, and 1956.

Of the several main branches of economic activity, agriculture is by far the best represented. The Library has almost all the numerous monographs and collections of documents published since 1960 on the history of Romanian agriculture and traditional agrarian organization. There are numerous works, many in Western languages, dealing with agriculture between the World Wars, especially agrarian reform and its consequences. The holdings are also strong for the period after 1945, particularly on the socialist organization of agriculture, the organization of collective farms, and agricultural law. The Library has a nearly complete run of *Buletinul informativ al Ministerului Agriculturii și Domeniilor,* v. 5-17 (Bucharest, 1934-46), and currently receives the weekly *Agricultura* and *Gazeta cooperației* and the monthly *Gospodariile agricole de stat.*

There is little on industrialization before 1950, except for a few general works on the oil industry and the investment of foreign capital. Besides the statistical works and periodicals already mentioned, which contain useful data on industrial development in the interwar period, there are several valuable source books such as: *Contribuțiuni la problema materiilor prime în România,* 5 v. (Bucharest, 1939-41). The bulk of the collection deals with the development of industry since 1945. In addition to general surveys, there are numerous monographs and booklets on such specialized topics as the productivity of labor, the costs of production, and the organization and activities of labor unions.

The holdings on Romania's foreign commerce during the period 1900 to 1944 are extensive, including a number of periodicals and statistical publications for the 1930s and early 1940s, among them, *Comerțul exterior al României* (Bucharest, 1906-43) (incomplete), and many works on Romanian-German trade relations. Most of the items on the post-1945 period deal with internal (socialist) commerce. The small collection on finance supplements the holdings on other aspects of economic development. The Library has several major periodicals, including *Budget general de venituri și cheltuieli,* 33 v. (Bucharest, 1871-1909), and a series of monographs dealing primarily with government monetary policy, taxation, and tariffs between the two World Wars.

SOCIAL CONDITIONS.   Although the collection of works on this specific topic is small, if used in conjunction with legal studies, censuses, statistical works, and periodicals on economic development, it offers the possibility of fruitful preliminary research. The holdings on the peasantry are by far the strongest and include important sociological studies of the village by Dimitrie Gusti, Henri H. Stahl, and Anton Golopenția. Such works reflect the traditional preoccupation of Romanian sociologists. The collection contains a number of recent theoretical works on sociology as well as a steadily increasing number of monographs and surveys of contemporary problems such as the condition of the new working class and urbanization. Periodical holdings are modest: Besides the invaluable *Buletinul informativ al muncii,* v. 1-28 (Bucharest, 1920-47) and the more recent *Rumanian Journal of Sociology,* 5 v. (Bucharest, 1962-), the Library has a few volumes of Dimitrie Gusti's *Arhiva pentru știința și reforma socială,* v. 8, 10-12, 14 (Bucharest, 1929-36).

INTELLECTUAL AND CULTURAL LIFE.   On education there are several older monographs by Urechia and Iorga and a few specialized monographs on the Romanian school during the interwar period. The collection includes more important works published in Romania since 1960 on the history of Romanian education and currently receives the two most important periodical publications, *Revista de pedagogie,* v. 5- (Bucharest, 1956-) and *Gazeta învățămîntului.*

Art and architecture are represented by a large number of albums of the work of modern and contemporary painters and sculptors, most of the major recent monographs, and such classic works as I. D. Ștefănescu's *L'évolution de la peinture religieuse en Bucovine et en Moldavie depuis les origines jusqu'au XIXe siècle,* 2 v. (Paris, 1928), and a sufficient number of works on architecture to provide a good overview from medieval times to the present. The Library currently receives the most important periodicals: *Studii și cercetări de istoria artei, Arta plastică,* and *Arhitectura R.P.R.*

In its Music Division the Library has a large collection of materials dealing with Romanian music and musicians, including: Viorel Cosma, *Compozitori și muzicologi români; mic lexicon* (Bucharest, 1965); P. Brincuș and N. Călinoiu, *Muzica în Romînia după 23 August 1944* (Bucharest, 1965); and Mihail Poslușnicu, *Istoria musicei la Români . . .* (Bucharest, 1928). Serials include *Muzica,* v. 6- (Bucharest, 1956-) and *Studii de muzicologie,* v. 1- (Bucharest, 1965-). An author, subject, and title catalog of music materials may be found in the Music Reading Room. Printed music is listed in three other Music Division card catalogs: scores and sheet music by title; composers; a Classed Catalog of Music. The library holds nearly 90 cards for works by George Enescu and there are 159 cards for Romanian national music under the "National Music" classification, with strong emphasis on folk songs and folk music.

LANGUAGE.   The Library has a good general research collection in this field. All the major branches of philology and linguistic study are covered, but the bulk of the holdings consists of works published since 1945. There are standard descriptive works and grammars by Ovid Densu-șianu, Sextil Pușcariu, Alexandru Rosetti, Iorgu Iordan, Sever Pop, Kristian Sandfeld, and Alf Lombard, an ample selection of dictionaries beginning with the *Lexicon de Buda* (1825), including all the important publications of the Romanian Academy and all the linguistic atlases published since 1945. The Library has a good collection of periodicals, mostly recent publications: *Limba română,* v. 1- (Bucharest, 1952-); *Studii și cercetări lingvistice,* v. 3- (Bucharest, 1952-); *Cercetări de lingvistică,* v. 1- (Cluj, 1956-); *Revue roumaine de linguistique,* v. 1- (Bucharest, 1956-); and Societatea de științe istorice și filologice din R.S.R., *Limba și literatura,* v. 1- (Bucharest, 1955-).

LITERATURE.   Besides the most important bibliographies, the Library of Congress collection contains a number of general histories ranging from older works by Nicolae Iorga and Sextil Pușcariu to the most recent survey by George Ivașcu, *Istoria literaturii române* (Bucharest, 1969). Of the pre-World War II works of criticism, the Library has Eugen Lovinescu, *Istoria literaturii române contemporane,* 6 v. (Bucharest, 1926-29) and a few other classics. The collection of general criticism and works by and about individual authors of the 19th and 20th centuries published since 1960 is comprehensive.

The collection of periodicals published before 1945 is small and incomplete, but the Library receives all important national and provincial scholarly journals and monthly and weekly literary reviews.

Keith Hitchins
University of Illinois at Urbana-Champaign

Yugoslavia

THE LIBRARY OF Congress collections on Yugoslavia have been developed chiefly as a result of exchange programs since the Second World War. The Yugoslav collection as a whole now stands at over 75,000 volumes, with an annual intake of about 5,000 volumes, about 2,000 periodical titles, with current subscriptions at 786 titles, and approximately 78 newspapers, including 15 current subscriptions to the best known and most comprehensive newspapers. The collections are rich in all areas of the humanities, but coverage is strongest in the fields of history, politics and government, economic conditions, and the cultural plurality of Yugoslav society.

Owing to the Public Law 480 Program, by which the Library of Congress received substantial resources from Yugoslavia from 1967 to 1973, the collection of materials from this period is particularly varied.

Sources such as *Bibliografija jugoslovenskih bibliografija, 1945-55,* and the national bibliography, *Bibliografija Jugoslavije,* covering articles, literary criticism, serials, etc., are fundamental to any scholarly research and the strength of a sound collection. Of no less importance are statistical yearbooks and biographies—for example, *Ko je ko u Jugoslaviji* (Belgrade, 1970); *Znameniti i zaslužni Hrvati te pomena vrijedna lica u hrvatskoj povijesti od 925-1925* (Zagreb, 1925) by Ivan Kukuljević-Sakcinski; *Znameniti Srbi XIX veka,* 3 v. (Belgrade, 1901-04), by Andra Gavrilović; bilingual and multilingual dictionaries listed in *Southeastern Europe: A Guide to Basic Publications,* edited by Paul L. Horecky (Chicago and London, 1969; items 2080-2146), most of which are in the collection. Deserving of mention here are significant works such as *Znameniti crnogorski junaci; po istoriskim podacima, tradiciji i narodnoj pjesmi* (Cetinje, 1951-), by Mirko A. Vujačić; *Portreti srpskih vladara u Srednjem veku* (Skopje, 1934), by Svetozar Radojčić; and *Specimen bibliographicum de Dalmatia et agro Labeatium . . .* (Venice, 1842), by Giuseppe Valentinelli. A great asset to the collection as a whole are publications by the Matica of Novi Sad, of Zagreb, and of Ljubljana. Useful sources include publications of bibliographic institutes, directories of various types of libraries, and archive and museum sources, as well as those relating to the history of printing and publishing: to mention only a few, the notable work *Südslavische Rara und Rarisima . . .* (Vienna-Leipzig-Zurich, 1937), by the well-known bibliophile, Mirko Breyer; *A Study of Slavic Incunabula* (Zagreb, 1968) by Mladen Bošnjak; many other works are available.

Some sources on Yugoslavs in the United States that merit attention are *Hrvati izvan domovine* (Zagreb, 1967), by Većeslav Holjevac, *Americans from Yugoslavia* (Gainesville, 1961), by Gerald Gilbert Govorchin; and above all, *The Croatian Immigrants in America* (New York, 1971), by Prof. George J. Prpić.

The collection contains more than 400 works on Yugoslavia in general—description, travel, guidebooks, etc.—in English, French, German, and other languages. In addition, the collection contains numerous beautifully illustrated folios depicting the country and its cities. *Gradovi Jugoslavije* (Belgrade, 1965) and *Jugoslavija—zemlja i ljudi* (Zagreb, 1967), among others, also treat folklore—costumes and dances, mores and customs.

Besides many valuable sources dealing with Yugoslavia in general, the collection includes indispensable materials on the Republics which comprise it. *Osnove za geografiju i geologiju Makedonije i Stare Srbije,* 3 v., (Belgrade, 1906-11), by Jovan Cvijić; *Dalmacia and Montenegro with a journey to Mostar and Herzegovina . . . ,* 2 v. (London, 1848); *Zemljopis i poviestnica Bosne* (Zagreb, 1851), by Slavoljub Bošnjak (pseud.); *Compendiolum regnorum Slavoniae, Croatiae, Dalmatiae . . .* (Posonii, Sumptibus J. M. Landerer, 1792) by Matej Bel; *Travels into Dalmatia . . .* (London, 1778) by Alberto Fortis; and *A tour in Dalmatia, Albania, and Montenegro with a historical sketch of the Republic of Ragusa* (London, 1859), by William F. Wingfield. A work of much broader scope and depth (general and specific) is *Croatia: Land, People, Culture* (Toronto, 1964-), two volumes of which have been published so far, edited by Francis H. Eterovich and Christopher Spalatin, and a detailed work *Slovenija: geografski opis,* 2 v. in 5 (Ljubljana, 1935-60), by Anton Melik.

Many geographic and historical maps are housed in the Geography and Map Division, whose holdings are excellent. The oldest map in this collection is a 1541 Ptolemaic map of the Dalmatian coast. Among the many 17th-century maps are a Mercator, ca. 1638, covering Slavonia, Croatia, and Dalmatia; a beautiful color map, *Illyricum hodiernum: Slavonia, Croatia, Bostnia, et Dalmatia,* printed by Joan Blaeu in Amsterdam in 1663; a map of Belgrade printed in Paris in 1692-95; numerous military maps covering cities in Serbia, Bosnia, Pannonia, Dalmatia; and a series of maps of the Istrian Peninsula. The beginning of the 20th century is marked by Jovan Cvijić's work *Velika jezera Balkanskog poluotoka* (Belgrade, 1902). Military maps of the Balkan Wars of 1912 and World War I, as well as recent ones showing waterways, natural resources, demography, communications, soil, and ethnography are in the collection. The geographic collection is generally rich both in monographs and maps. For monographs and periodicals published by geographic institutes and societies of the Republics, dealing with demographic changes—statistics, changes in population since World War II, the radical and structural change in the village, and the rapid increase in urban population which creates the great problem of rural-urban balance, nationally and regionally—the collection is rather moderate. Basic publications on the material, social, and spiritual culture of Yugoslavia are included in the collection, as are reference works and other sources such as *Demografska bibliografija radova iz demografije objavljenih 1945 do 1961* (Belgrade, 1963) compiled by Vera Đorđjević; *Rečnik-imenik mesta kraljevine Jugoslavije . . .* (Belgrade, 1930) by Vladimir Marinković, with the latest edition of the *Abecedni spisak naselja, 1-I-1971.god.* (Belgrade, 1971); *Zakoni porasta stanovništva: prilog biosocijalnoj teoriji o razvitku naroda* (Belgrade, 1929), by Dinko Antun Tomašić; *Dinamika i struktura gradskog stanovništva Jugoslavije: demografski aspekt urbanizacije* (Belgrade, 1967), by Milenko S. Filipović; *La Péninsule balkanique* (Paris, 1918), by Jovan Cvijić; *La Macédoine: Études ethnographiques et politiques* (Paris, 1919), by Aleksandar Belić, and numerous periodicals issued by various ethnographic institutes and museums.

In this necessarily brief account of an enormous collection on Yugoslavia it will be possible to mention only some of the most important works pertaining to its complicated and intricate history, its invasions by Romans, Goths, Huns, Franks, Magyars, Byzantines, Normans, and especially Turks, whose domination lasted for centuries. An essential source for the country as a whole, which treats the settlement of the Slavs and their life in the seventh and eighth centuries, is *De administrando imperio,* by the Byzantine Emperor Constantine Porphyrogenetus, edited by Moravesik-Jenkins (Budapest, 1949). Other essential ancient sources in the collection are *Ljetopis popa Dukljanina,* by an anonymous priest from Duklja in the editions of Šišić and Mošin, published in Belgrade (1928) and Zagreb (1949), respectively, and *Il regno degli Slavi hoggi correttamente deti Schiavoni,* by Mavro Orbini, known also as *Kraljevstvo Slovena.* More recent are *Arhiv za povestnicu jugoslavensku,* and *Godišnjica Nikole Čupića.* Moreover, *Građa o stvaranju jugoslavenke države; Dokumenti o Jugoslaviji: historijat od osnutka zajedničke države, do danas,* by Ferdo Čulinović; *Jugoslavenska bibliografija,* 2 v. in 1 (Belgrade, 1934-38); *Jugoslavica usque ad annum MDC* (Belgrade, 1955; Baden-Baden, 1966), by Josip Badalić; *Ten Years of Yugoslav Historiography 1945-1955;* and numerous journals which contain a wealth of data in this field.

The collection is rich in works of a general character treating topics such as the history of Yugoslav peoples, the creation of the Yugoslav state, fundamentals of contemporary Yugoslavia, history of South Slavs, etc. Items 2373-94 in Horecky's *Guide* provide a sampling.

For the period from 1918 to 1941, space permits the mention only of *Slom stare Jugoslavije* (Zagreb, 1958), by Čulinović, and the rare *Nova Srbija i Jugoslavija. Istorija nacionalnog oslobodjenja i ujedinjenja Srba, Hrvata i Slovenaca od Kočine Krajine do vidovdanskog ustanka (1788-1921) . . .* (Belgrade, 1923), by Đurđe Jelenić. The chronology of the national movement in the Second World War is presented in a voluminous (1265 pp.) and informative work *Hronologija oslobodilačke borbe naroda Jugoslavije 1941-1945* (Belgrade, 1964), issued by the Historical Institute. Among other useful data for the period, this source includes personal and geographic names. Besides the multivolume collected works *Zbornik dokumenata i podataka o narodnooslobodilačkom ratu Jugoslovenskih naroda* (Belgrade, 1949-), there are numerous works treating contemporary Yugoslavia, fluctuating in interpretation of facts according to the political, social, and economic changes in the country and abroad. Therefore, most of the works of the postwar period fit equally well into the fields of history and political science.

The history of Yugoslavia as a whole is well represented in the collection, as is the history of Serbia, Macedonia, and Montenegro. In addition to sources such as *Monumenta Serbica spectantia historiam Serbiae . . .* (Vienna, 1858), by Franz Miklosich, *Spisi bečkih arhiva o prvom srpskom ustanku,* compiled by Aleksa Ivić, and items 2316-2342 in the Horecky *Guide,* considerable material is available on the period of the Battle of Kosovo (1389). This event and the years up to 1456 are covered by many authors, notably Stojan Novaković, Nikola Radojčić, and Dušan J. Popović. The period from 1456 to 1804 is not particularly well covered, but that from 1804 to the Balkan War of 1912-13 is well represented by rare works such as *Grada za istoriju Kraljevine Srbije. Vreme pre vlade Kneza Miloša Obrenovića,* 2 v., (Belgrade, 1882-84), by Vukašin J. and Nikola Petrović; *Vlada ustavobranitelja 1842-1853* (Belgrade, 1932), by Dragoslav Stranaković; *Srbi i Turci u XIV veku. Istorijske studije o prvim borbama s najezdom turskom pre i posle boja na Kosovu* (Belgrade, 1893) and other works by Stanoje Stanojević. Of importance also are *Srbija pre sto godina* (Belgrade, 1946), by Tihomir R. Đorđević; *Druga vlada Miloša i Mihaila, 1858-68* (Belgrade, 1928); *Vlada Aleksandra Obrenovića,* 2 v. (Belgrade, 1929-31), *Ustavobranitelji i njihova vlada (1838-1858)* (Belgrade, 1912), and other works by the very prolific Serbian writer Slobodan Jovanović.

With over 200 entries on the Balkan War of 1912-13, one can easily find a variety of treatments and approaches. Most notable, however, are *Prvi balkanski rat, 1912-1913 . . .* (Belgrade, 1959), published by the Historical Institute of the National Army; *Srbi i Bugari u balkanskom savezu i u međusobnom ratu* (Belgrade, 1913), by Aleksandar Belić; *Balkanski rat is Srbija,* 2d ed. (Belgrade, 1912), by Jovan Cvijić; *Srpskoturski rat 1912 godine* (Belgrade, 1928), by Stanoje Stanojević.

The collection on Macedonia in general and on its history in particular is strong in comparison with the coverage of the other Republics. Over 1,000 works are available on this subject, including numerous items in Bulgarian, Greek, Italian, and other languages. Among the many rare books are *Stara Srbija i Makedonija . . .,* 2 v. in 1 (Belgrade, 1890), by Spiridion Gopčević, translated from the original *Makedonien und Alt-Serbien* (Vienna, 1889) by Milan Kasumović; and *O Makedoniji i Makedoncima,* 2d ed. (Belgrade, 1928), by Stojan M. Protić.

Coverage of the history of Montenegro is not particularly strong, yet mention should be made of the rare *Dva Petrovića Njegoša—vladika Danilo Petrović i Knez Nikola I* (Belgrade, 1896) and of a recent comprehensive source, *Istorija Crne gore* (Titograd, 1967-), three volumes of which have been published so far.

The fact that Bosnia and Herzegovina did not attract historians as early as other states is attributed to the lack of sources. Their long history of invasions by Romans, Gauls, Vandals, Goths, and Huns is attested to by such well-known works as *Geschichte Bosniens von den ältesten Zeiten bis zum Verfalle des Königreiches . . .* (Leipzig, 1885), by Vjekoslav Klaić; *Historija Bosne* (Belgrade, 1940-) by Vladimir Ćorović; and *Povijest Bosne u doba osmanlijske vlade,* 2 v. (Sarajevo, 1924?), by Milan Prelog. Besides these and *Poviest hrvatskih zemalja Bosne i Hercegovine od najstarijih vremena do godina 1463* (Sarajevo, 1942), by Krunoslav Draganović, et al.; *L'annexion de la Bosnie et la question Serbe* (Paris, 1909), by Jovan Cvijić; and *Herceg-Bosna prigodom aneksije* (Zagreb, 1908), by Ferdinand Šišić, the collection includes many recent works.

As a result of centuries of foreign domination by Romans, Hungarians, Venetians, and Turks, the resources on over a millennium of old Croatian history are to be found in Latin, Hungarian, Italian, German, and other European languages, as well as in the vernacular. Many of the most important documents on Croatian history are collected in *Monumenta Spectantia Historiam Slavorum Meridionalium,* v. 1-44 (Zagreb, 1868-1948), a very important item in the Library's collection. Some other works of great value for a historian are *Codex Diplomaticus Regni Croatiae, Dalmatiae et Slavoniae* (Zagreb, 1904-17), edited by Tadija Smičiklas; *Enchiridion Fontium*

Historiae Croaticae (Zagreb, 1914); *Geschichte der Croaten I (bis 1102)* (Zagreb, 1917); *Kralj Koloman i Hrvati godine 1102* (Zagreb, 1907); *Povijest Hrvata za kraljeva iz doma Arpadovića, 1102-1301* (Zagreb, 1944), and *Vojvoda Hrvoje Vukčić Hrvatinić i njegovo doba (1350-1416)* (Zagreb, 1902), by Ferdinand Šišić. Also present and important are *Hiljadugodišnjica hrvatskoga kraljevstva g. 925-1925* (Split, 1925), by Marko Perojević; *Bribirski knezovi . . .* (Zagreb, 1897); and *Krčki knezovi Frankopani* (Zagreb, 1901), by Vjekoslav Klaić.

The collection contains several important works on the history of the Croatian capital, Zagreb. These are: *Monumenta Historica liberae et regiae civitatis Zagrabiae (1889-1953); Stari Zagreb* (Zagreb, 1941), by Gjuro Szabo; *Prošlost grada Zagreba* (Zagreb, 1942), by Rudolf Horvat; and *Zagreb—Past and Present* (Zagreb, 1937), by Stjepan Srkulj. Similar works on other major cities of Yugoslavia are also available and the coverage of sources listed in Horecky's *Guide* (items 2343-62) of Croatian history is thus quite extensive.

The history of Slovenia, which goes back to the Slovenes' first settlement in the upper Sava River Valley and vicinity in the sixth century, is presented, for instance, in *Zgodovina Slovenskega naroda,* 2 v. (Ljubljana, 1964-65), by Bogo Grafenauer, and in works by such well-known Slovenian historians and literary historians as Josip Gruden, Milko Kos, Josip Malik, and Ivan Prijatelj (see Horecky's *Guide,* items 2363-67). Moreover, the collection includes *Gradivo za zgodovino Slovencev v srednjem veku,* 5 v. (Ljubljana, 1902-28), by Franc Kos, and *Viri za zgodovino Slovencev,* v. 1- (Ljubljana, 1939-), as well as works covering history and cultural history. On the whole, Slovenian history is well represented in the collection, particularly in works dealing with the period since 1848 and the period of the Austro-Hungarian Monarchy.

As might be expected, the collection of materials on the politics and government of Yugoslavia is, without doubt, the largest and the most impressive. Although the period 1914-45 is well covered, the collection of the post-World War II period is much richer. Works published between 1918 and 1945 deal primarily with the creation of Yugoslavia and the political problems between the two World Wars. These and similar issues are treated in works such as *Jugoslavija između dva rata,* 2 v. (Zagreb, 1961), by Ferdo Čulinović; *Yugoslavia at the Paris Peace Conference; a Study in Frontier Making* (New Haven, 1963), by Ivo J. Lederer; *La dictatur du roi Alexandre . . .* (Paris, 1933), by Svetozar Pribičević, and works by Danilo Gregorić, Lazar Marković, Wendel Hermann, and others. In addition, one finds a wealth of information in the records of parliamentary proceedings, legislation, speeches, laws, decrees, regulations, etc., published in *Službene novine.* Other important primary sources in the collection are *Politika, Novosti,* and *Arhiv za pravne i društvene nauke,* a significant publication which covers political issues and affairs and also treats current economic conditions.

Writings of the post-World War II period tend to emphasize such aspects as the building of the country, economic conditions, labor laws, the democratization of society, the struggle for self-government, workers' management, and the Communist Parties of Yugoslavia's Republics. Included among the many sources available are *La Yugoslavie* (Paris, 1967); *Društveno-političke zajednice,* 4 v. (Belgrade, 1968); *25 godina socijalističke Jugoslavije* (Belgrade, 1968), by Jovan Đorđević. The collection also has numerous works by political leaders and writers. Foreign language sources are also well represented.

Works on individual Republics which deserve special mention are: *Političke i pravne rasprave,* 3 v. (Belgrade, 1932-33), by Slobodan Jovanović; *L'annexion de la Bosnie et la question Serbe* (Paris, 1909), by Jovan Cvijić; and *La Serbie d'hier et de demain* (Paris, 1917), by Nikola Stojanović.

Other important works are *Političke prilike u Bosni i Hercegovini* (Belgrade, 1939), by Vladimir Ćorović; *Stranke kod Hrvata i njihove ideologije* (Belgrade, 1939); *Politička povijest Hrvatske, 1918-1929* (Zagreb, 1938), by Josip Horvat; *Politika u Hrvatskoj* (Zagreb, 1953), by

Frano Supilo, edited by Vaso Bogdanov; *Hrvatska državna i pravna poviest,* Part I (Zagreb, 1940), by Antun Dabinović; *Fundamente des Staatsrechtes des Königreiches Kroaten* (Zagreb, 1918), by Nikola Tomašić, a bibliographic rarity; *Uspomene na ljude i dogadjaje* (Buenos Aires, 1961), by Ivan Meštrović (Knižnica Hrvatske revije, knj. 5); and finally, on Slovenian politics and government, works by Dušan Biber, Edvard Kocbek, and Edvard Kardelj.

On questions of national culture and character, works of value are *Karakterologija Jugoslovena* (Belgrade, 1939), by Vladimir Dvorniković; *Antologija jugoslovenske misli i narodnog jedinstva, 1390-1930* (Belgrade, 1930), by Viktor Novak; *Južnoslovensko pitanje . . .* (Zagreb, 1943), by Südland (pseud. Ivo Pilar); *La question jugoslave* (Paris, 1918), by Vuk Primorac; *Südslawische Studien* (Munich, 1965) by Josef Matl; and *Serbia between East and West* (Stanford, 1954), by Wayne S. Vucinich. This latter also discusses the Macedonian question, a subject represented by more than 300 other entries in the catalog. Works are mainly in Serbian, Bulgarian, Greek, and Italian; many were published between the two wars, but most date from after World War II.

Economic conditions and Yugoslav society are also covered in considerable depth. The collection contains many basic sources for the period between the two wars, but for the years from 1945 on numerous sources are available—both monographs and serials. Among the monographs principally devoted to the history of economics, mention should be made of Mijo Marković's *Ekonomska historija Jugoslavije* (Zagreb, 1958); *Ekonomika FNRJ . . .* (Zagreb, 1951), by Rudolf Bičanić; *The Economy of Yugoslavia* (Belgrade, 1961), by Milutin Bogosavljević; and *Ekonomika FLRJ* (Ljubljana, 1959), by Franc Černe. Numerous monographic and collective works titled *Ekonomika Jugoslavije* are also available.

No less impressive is the collection of books on social planning, where one finds an abundance of titles. Moreover, there are many works dedicated to laws on economic policies passed by the National Assembly, e.g., the laws on Five-Year Plans; and the standard doctrinal monographs discussing the ever-present themes of current problems in sociopolitical and democratic development, such as *Aktuelni idejno-politički problemi daljeg demokratskog razvoja u Jugoslaviji* (Belgrade, 1968). Of similar nature are the monograph *Aktuelni problemi sadašnje etape revolucije* (Zagreb, 1967), by Vladimir Bakarić, and many other monographs by contemporary writers dealing with regional problems of economic development, social conditions, unemployment, etc. Information on Yugoslav society and its economic conditions can be found in works such as *Naši socijalni problemi* (Belgrade, 1932), by Slobodan Z. Vidaković; *Promene u strukturi jugoslovenskog društva i Savez Komunista* (Belgrade, 1967); *Socijalna politika* (Belgrade, 1960), by Mihailo S. Stupar; *Jugoslavia, a Multinational State . . .* (San Francisco, 1966), by Jack C. Fisher; *Peasants, Politics, and Economic Change in Yugoslavia* (Stanford, 1955), by Jozo Tomasevich; *Peasant Renaissance in Yugoslavia, 1900-1950* (London, 1952), by Ruth Trouton; *Peasant Life in Yugoslavia* (London, 1942), by Olive Lodge; *Kako živi narod: život u pasivnim krajevima* (Zagreb, 1936), by Rudolf Bičanić; and *Les problèmes agraires en Yougoslavie* (Paris, 1926) by Milan Ivšić. The collection is not strong on the history of agriculture, although there are adequate sources on the present structural changes in the village and on the changes in agricultural development.

Besides monographs, serials on economics are well represented. Most of these have been launched since the early fifties by the various Economic Institutes. Many of the above sources include literature discussing economic setting and planning, decentralized socialist planning, the increase of labor efficiency and productivity, the reduction of unemployment, etc.

Although the collection of lawbooks and other legal resources is not exceptionally large, its strength in rare materials makes it one of the best in the country. From the 17th century onward the collection is rich in holdings on law, statutes, customs, and decrees. The oldest code of law, written in 1349 by the eminent Tsar Dušan and known as *Zakonik Stevana Dušana*, is represented by Stojan Novaković's edition of 1898. Also noteworthy is *Zakon czarkovni . . .,* 2 v. (Venice, 1787) on church law, by Costa Dalla Angela, head priest in the cathedral of Split. The real greatness of the collection is in the legal literature of the 19th century, works such as *Ustav Kniažestva Serbie, Sultanski Hatišerif iz 1254-1838* (Belgrade, 1840) in Serbian and Turkish; *Zapisnik Sabora trojedine Kraljevine Dalmatiae, Hrvatske, Slavonie . . .* (Zagreb, 1848) and compilations of Italian tariff laws for Dalmatia and Istria, civil and court procedures, and construction laws, as well as interpretations of laws by many European legal scholars. This distinctive collection is also ample in legal periodicals and official gazettes. Some outstanding and comprehensive collections are *Raccolta delle leggi ed ordinanze per Dalmazia,* 56 v. (Zara, 1830-48); *Sbornik ugarsko-hrvatskih skupnih zakona* (Budapest), irregular; *Zemaljsko-vladni list za kraljevine Hrvatsku i Slavoniu, 1850-1858* (Zagreb); *Hrvatsko-Ugarski ustav ili Konstitucija* (Zagreb, 1861 and 1882), and *Naše pravice: izbor zakonah, poveljah i spisah, znamenitih za državno pravo Kraljevine dalmatinsko-hrvatsko-slavonske od g. 1202-1868* (Zagreb, 1868), by Bogoslav Šulek; *Sbornik ugarsko-hrvatskih skupnih zakona . . .* (This source includes legislation of Hungary, Croatia, and Dalmatia); *Saborski dnevnik kraljevinah Hrvatske, Slavonije i Dalmacije,* 14 v. (Zagreb, 1862-1903); *Nagodba. Svi zakoni o nagodbi* (Zagreb, 1906), and *Statuti primorskih gradova i općina . . .* (Zagreb, 1911), compiled by Ivan Strohal. Particular mention must also be made of a very rare, complete, and significant source on Serbian laws, statutes, etc., *Sbornik zakona i uredaba i uredbeni ukaza izdani u Knjažestvu Srbskom, od vremena obnarodovanog ustava zemaljskog,* 64 v. (Belgrade, 1840-1912). Of great value are also *Sprske novine; Službeni dnevnik Kraljevine Srbije,* 1834-56 and 1861-1918, published in Krf, Belgrade, and Niš, which was superseded by *Službene novine* of Yugoslavia. Lastly, *Deželni zakonik za Vojvodino Kranjsko* (Ljubljana, 1868-1917) *(Landesgesetzblatt für . . . 1849-1918),* and *Mjesečnik* (Zagreb, 1875-1937) are included. Over 30 legal periodicals are regularly received, and the collection includes numerous monographs by prominent Yugoslav legal scholars. Law Library holdings on Yugoslavia are discussed in detail in Government, Law, and Courts in the Soviet Union and Eastern Europe, edited by Vladimir Gsovski and Kazimierz Grzybowski (item 2395 in Horecky's *Guide*).

The Library's collections on diplomacy and foreign relations are also comprehensive. Noteworthy among 20-century sources published before World War II are: *Političke i pravne rasprave,* 3 v. (Belgrade, 1932-33), by Slobodan Jovanović; *Borba za narodno ujedinjenje, 1914-1918* (Belgrade, 1934); *Serbia and Europe 1914-1920 . . .* (London, 1920), by Lazar Marković; *Odnosi izmedu Srbije i Austro-Ugarske* (Belgrade, 1936); and *Kralj Koloman i Hrvati god. 1102* (Zagreb, 1907), by Ferdo Šišić.

The period after World War II, particularly after the break of Tito with Stalin in 1948, is the richest in sources. One finds a vast literature in the form of addresses and speeches by Milovan Đilas, Edvard Kardelj, and Marshal Tito. The collection also contains the texts of treaties with numerous countries. However, the strongest holdings relate to Yugoslav relations with Hungary, Italy, and the Soviet Union (in particular, the problems resulting from Tito's defection).

In the multinational state of Yugoslavia, with its great ethnic variety and cultural diversity, there are four major languages in which materials are acquired by the Library of Congress—Serbian, Croatian, Slovenian, and Macedonian. In addition, many minority groups in Yugoslavia speak the language of neighboring countries and maintain their cultural heritage. The Library acquires some of the materials in Hungarian published in Yugoslavia, as well as material published in Albanian in the province of Kosmet.

Among many dictionaries, glossaries, vocabularies, and other reference works, the *editio princeps* of *Srpski rječnik* (1818), and other editions, as well as other important works by Vuk Karadžić, are in the collection. Further, there are important dictionaries as *Rječnik iz književnih starina srpskih,* 3 v. (Belgrade, 1863-64), by Đuro Daničić; *Rječnik hrvatskoga ili srpskoga jezika,* published by the Yugoslav Academy of Arts and Sciences in Zagreb from 1880 on; *Rječnik hrvatskoga jezika,* 2 v. (Zagreb, 1901) by Franjo Iveković and Ivan Broz; *Slovar slovenskega jezika* (Ljubljana, 1936) by Joža Glonar; and numerous dictionaries published after World War II.

The history of these four languages, their grammars, dialectology, and related topics are treated in many works. Older materials in the collection include *Grammatik der illyrischen Sprache* (Vienna, 1845), by Andrija Torkvat Brlić; *Mala srpska gramatika (1850),* by Đuro Daničić; *Ilirska slovnica* (Zagreb, 1854), by Vjekoslav Babukić.

The works of the leading linguists and scholars are well represented. All aspects of language are represented in the collection. In spite of the recency of the official "birth" of Macedonian in 1945, the collection includes grammars and dictionaries for this language.

The collection is also rich in dozens of important periodicals for language study: *Južnoslovenski filolog, Srpski dijalektološki zbornik, Hrvatski dijalektološki zbornik, Filologija, Makedonski jazik, Slavistična revija,* etc., and a wealth of publications of the Academies in Yugoslavia.

"Yugoslav literature" comprises four distinctive literatures: Serbian, Croatian, Slovenian, and Macedonian. As a result of centuries of exposure to different political, socioeconomic, and cultural conditions, these literatures have taken different courses of development. Thus, Serbian literature is hagiographic, legendary, apocryphal, and biographic. It flourished under Saint Sava, the founder of the Serbian Church, King Dušan, and the monks Domentian and Theodosius. But after Dušan's death in 1355 and the conversion of the last remnant of a free Serbia into a Turkish *Pašaluk* in 1459, creative literary work virtually halted. The exposition of Serbian literature in the Library's collection might begin with the first edition of Dositej Obradović's translation of Aesop's fables, *Ezopove i prochikh raznikh basnotvortsev basne,* published in Leipzig in 1788. For the same century the collection includes works by Lukijan Mušicki, Milutinović-Sarajlija and Milan Vidaković. The rich 19th century is represented by works of such famous writers as Njegoš (Petar II, Prince Bishop of Montenegro), with many editions of his *Gorski vijenac,* Radičević's *Pesme,* Karadžić's *Srpske narodne pjesme; Srpske narodne pripovijetke,* etc. The period of Romanticism is represented by many works of Zmaj, Jakšić, Kostić, etc., and that of Realism by Ignjatović, Lazarević, Sremac, Matavulj, Ilić, Ranković, and Kostić. The beginning of the 20th century is extensively covered by works of poets and short story writers: Dučić, Šantić, Rakić, Domanović, Kočić, Stanković, Nušić, Andrić, and others. Literary criticism is also well covered, with works of Skerlić, B. and M. Popović, and many more.

The periods of Humanism and the Renaissance produced quite a number of works in poetry in the Croatian language. Dalmatian cities—Hvar, Split, Trogir, Zadar, Senj—had nourished the old West European cultural traditions, as had the city of Dubrovnik (Ragusa). The end of the 15th and the beginning of the 16th century are represented in the collection by works of the two famous Dubrovnik poets Šiško Menčetić and Džore Držić. In 1501 Marko Marulić (Marcus Marulus), the father of Croatian literature, wrote his *Judita,* of which several editions are in the collection. Moreover, the collection includes works of Petar Hektorović and Hanibal Lucić. The 17th century is represented by the rare *Osman, spjevagne vitescko Giva Gundulichja . . .,* 3 v. (Dubrovnik, 1826), by Ivan Gundulić, and his *Diela* (Zagreb, 1847); works of Bunić, Zrinski, Frankopan, Vitezović, and others; for the 18th century, works of Đorđević, Kačić, Reljković, and Brezovački are among the many available items. The 19th-century "Illyrian movement" of about 1830 is represented by *Danica Ilirska* (Zagreb, 1835-46), Gaj, Mažuranić, Vraz and Preradović; the Romanticism of the first half of the century, by Šenoa, Marković, and others; the Realism of the later half, by works of Kumičić, Kovačić, Đalski, Leskovar, Harambašić, Novak, and Kranjčević; and the Croatian "Moderna," by Marjanović, Begović, Nehajev, Vidrić Vojnović, Matoš, Nazor, and, most notably, Miroslav Krleža and his numerous contemporaries.

The Protestant movement that originated in Germany spread to Croatia and Slovenia, almost coinciding with the peasant uprisings in Slovenia in 1515 and in Croatia in 1573. All are well covered not only in works dealing with history but also in literary sources. Most works of the representatives of Protestantism—Matija Vlacić (Flacius Illyricus), Primož Trubar, and his supporters Juraj Dalmatin and Adam Bohorič—are included in the collection, as are sources dealing with the literary criticism of the period. Major representatives of the Slovenian literature of the 18th century are Linhart and Vodnik. The first half of the 19th century includes works of Kopitar, Prešeren, and others. The periods of Romanticism and Realism are covered with works of Levstik, Stritar, Jurčić, Jenko, Gregorčić, Kersnik, Aškerc, Tavčar, and others, and for the modern movement the collection includes the works of Prijatelj, Kidrič, Cankar, Kette, Murn, Župančić, Finžgar, Voranc Prežihov, and others.

In sum, Serbian, Croatian, and Slovenian literatures are well represented not only with most of the collected works of classical authors and of literary criticism, but also with numerous literary journals such as *Književnost* (Belgrade), *Republika* (Zagreb), *Novi svet* (Ljubljana), *Brazda* (Sarajevo), etc. The field of folklore is also strongly represented, especially with the epic genre which flourished in Serbia, nourished by its tumultuous history. Macedonian literature, which is relatively recent, is well represented with works published from the 1960s onwards.

The collection on education and culture, in comparison with the fields so far surveyed, is not voluminous. Nonetheless, there are more significant works than can be cited. A few might be singled out, as *Istorija škola u Srbiji 1700-1850* (Belgrade, 1935), by Živojin Đorđević; *Povijest školstva i pedagogije u Hrvatskoj* (Zagreb, 1958), written by a team of Croatian scholars and edited by Dragutin Franković; and *Šolski sistemi na Slovenskom od 1774-1963* (Ljubljana, 1964), by the staff of the Slovenian School Museum. Moreover, there are works in education and sources dealing with the main currents of culture and thought. From the nation's most important cultural centers come *Matica srpska, 1826-1926* (Novi Sad, 1927); and *Matica hrvatska, 1842-1962* (Zagreb, 1963), by Jakša Ravlić and Marin Somborac. Moreover, the Library owns *Kultura Hrvata kroz 1000 godina*, 2 v. (Zagreb, 1939-42), by Josip Horvat; *Kulturna historija Hrvatske* (Zagreb, 1962), by Zvane Črnja (also translated as *Cultural History of Croatia*, Zagreb, 1962), and the comprehensive *Kulturna in politična zgodovina Slovencev, 1848-1895* (Ljubljana, 1938-40), edited by Anton Ocvirk.

The four major religious denominations in Yugoslavia—Orthodox, Roman Catholic, Moslem, and Protestant—are covered by a wealth of literature which includes periodicals, the standard major reference works, and basic monographs. These latter include *Istorija Srpske Pravoslavne Crkve*, 2 v. (Munich, 1962-66), by Đoko M. Slijepčević; *Sveti Sava, pregled života i rada* (Belgrade, 1900), by Andra Gavrilović; *Croatia sacra* (Zagreb, 1949), a rare source by Dragutin Kniewald; various other works, including those listed in Horecky's *Guide* as items 2919-41, are available. Such historically important religious splinter groups as the old Bogumils of the Church of Bosnia, known in the West as "Ecclesia Sclavonie," or "Ordo Sclavonie," are discussed in many sources in the collection. Recent large, beautifully edited and illustrated works in the field are *Srpska Pravoslavna crkva, 1219-1960. Spomenica o 750-godišnjici autokefalnosti* (Belgrade, 1969); *Srpska Pravoslavna crkva, 1920-1970. Spomenica o 50-godišnjici vaspostavljanja Srpske patrijaršije* (Belgrade, 1971); and a book dedicated to the first Croatian saint, *Nikola Tavelić prvi hrvatski svetac* (Zagreb, 1971), edited by Hrvatin Jurišić, et al.

The Library's collections on art, architecture, music, and theater are not extensive. There are, however, basic works on the history of early and medieval art, mural paintings and decorative Christian art and symbolism, and iconography in Serbia and Macedonia. Coverage of the 17th to 20th centuries is adequate with the Baroque and Romanesque periods most complete.

The history of music is best treated in works like *Historijski razvoj muzičke kulture u Jugoslaviji* (Zagreb, 1962), by Josip Andreis, et al.; *Pregled povijesti hrvatske muzike* (Zagreb, 1922), by Božidar Širola; and *Zvuk: jugoslovenska muzička revija* (Belgrade). Included in the collection are sources on Classicism in music and on regional music. Music scores will be referred to later.

Although weak for the periods predating World War II, the collection contains enough monograph and serial material on the history of theater in general and on modern Yugoslav theater, history of the stage, history and criticism of drama, and theatrical performances in Yugoslav theaters for research. Among the leading periodicals in the collection are *Scena* (Zagreb), *Scena* (Novi Sad), and *Pozorišni život* (Belgrade). Most of the sources in Horecky's *Guide* (items 2969-3008) are in the collection, as are Branko Gavela's *Književnost i kazalište* (Zagreb, 1970), edited by Nikola Batušić, et al.; Arturo Cronia's *Teatro serbo-croatico . . .* (Milan, 1955); and *Bibliografija hrvatske dramske i kazališne književnosti* (Zagreb, 1948), by Josip Badalič.

The Library's Manuscript Division contains extensive correspondence between Woodrow Wilson and his Secretary of State Robert Lansing and the Serbian Prime Minister Nikola Pašić. The correspondence of the latter with French Premier Georges Clemenceau, relating to the peace settlements after World War I, is also in the collection. Information on the creation of Yugoslavia is included in the papers of the American Peace Commission to Versailles (1917-19). There are also documents relating to United States-Yugoslavian relations, as well as the correspondence of the famous scientist Nikola Tesla and the papers of Mrs. Thorp Boadman, President of the American Red Cross Organization. Captured German documents containing information on the activities of the occupation forces in Yugoslavia, Yugoslav underground movements, and the Allied forces in World War II are incorporated in the holdings.

In the collection of the Rare Book Division there are four prominent items which call for a brief exposition. The oldest and most important landmark of the cultural and spiritual legacy of the Croatian people is *Missale Glagoliticum,* printed in 1483. Until recently it was held that the missal was published in Venice. Zvonimir Kulundžić, however, in his book *Kosinj-kolijevka štamparstva slaven-skog juga* (Zagreb, 1960) argues persuasively that it was published in Kosinj in Lika, which was a strong center of glagolitism. The next oldest source in the collection is the *Psalterion,* printed in Venice in 1638. For a detailed discussion of this missal, which is the first Croatian printed book, see Barbara Krader's "The Glagolitic Missal of 1483," *Library of Congress Quarterly Journal of Current Acquisitions,* 20 (April 1963), pp. 93-98. This is supposedly one of the last books set in Cyrillic type in Venice. Also in the collection is an account of military successes of the armies of Leopold II against the Turks in Croatia and Transylvania. This work, entitled *Ungria restaurada compendiosa noticia, de dos tiempos: del passado. Baxo el jugo la tirania othomana, del presente: Baxo el dominio catholico di leopoldo II. de Austria. Felices succesos de sus armas cesareas, en el reyno de Croatia, y principado de Transylvania . . .* was originally written in Italian by Simpliciano Bizzozero. Treating the early history of Hungary, Croatia, and Transylvania, it is perhaps one of the earliest sources in Spanish referring to any Croatian historical event. A fourth gem in the collection is *De litteraria expeditione per pontificiam ditionem ad dimentiendos meridiani gradus et corrigendam mappam geograficam . . .* (Rome, 1755), by Ruđer Bošković, the famous Croatian astronomer and mathematician, also known as Rogerio Josepho Boscovich. There are also many examples of beautifully illustrated Yugoslav books, mainly from the 1930s, as well as several broadsides, posters, etc., which were printed in 1941 by the German occupation authorities.

The Music Division owns an excellent collection of music by modern Yugoslav composers, ranging from Stevan Mokranjac (1856-1914) to Vojislav Kostić (1931-). Librettos and scores of major composers, e.g., Jakov Gotovac, Petar Konjović, Stevan Hristić, and Krešimir Baranović, are well represented. However, the real strength is in Yugoslav folklore, folk music, and works drawn on folklore themes, particularly epics based on the hardship of centuries of Turkish invasions. Available recordings include Yugoslav folk songs, the oral epic tradition of Moslems in Bosnia, Macedonia, Serbia, and Montenegro; as well as Yugoslav folk music in America, and Yugoslav dances. Serbian printed church music of the 1920s and 1930s, and basic reference tools in the field —*Muzička Enciklopedija, Yugoslav Music, Zvuk,* and other first-rate sources—are in the custody of the Archive of Folk Song of the Library.

In the Prints and Photographs Division the collection on Yugoslavia consists of tourist photographs, war pictures, and portraits of prominent Yugoslavs. Several kinds of photographs are listed in the so-called "lot" catalog, which includes scenes of devastation of the country during the two World Wars, photographs of museum exhibits ranging from Roman sculpture to national costumes, and ethnographic studies important both for their beauty and as records of a national heritage. Furthermore, there are photographs, numerous postcards on major Yugoslav cities, and events such as Jacqueline Kennedy Onassis' visit to Dubrovnik in 1963. The Library also owns the Carpenter collection of photographs depicting the life of Serbian, Montenegrin, Bosnian, and Macedonian peasants, as well as urban life in Belgrade in the 1920s and early 1930s.

George C. Jerkovich
University of Kansas

University of Michigan

he collections of material on East Central and Southeastern Europe are an integral part of the
eneral book collection of the University of Michigan Library, which currently includes over four
million volumes. The total for the Slavic and East European area in the vernacular languages inclu-
ve of Russia is estimated at 157,000 volumes. The main part of the collection is located in the
Harlan Hatcher Library.

There is no special Slavic collection or Slavic reading room maintained as a separate unit;
l books and periodicals are intershelved with other library material. There is a Slavic Division
ithin the Technical Services Department designating the staff responsible for book selection,
cquisitions, and cataloging of material in the vernaculars of Eastern Europe. The staff members
clude four professional librarians who process the material and who are available to assist in
ference service.

There are no separate catalogs or finding aids prepared for the East European collection. The
eneral catalog and the guides of the special reading rooms for periodicals, newspapers, and micro-
int may be consulted. The collection is arranged for the most part in the Library of Congress
assification. Most of the books in the field of literature remain in an adaptation of the Dewey
ecimal Classification. The stacks are open to qualified users. Regular loans are limited to the
culty, staff, and students of the University. Photocopying facilities are available at numerous
in-operated machines. Special photocopying is also done by the Photoduplication Department
cated in the main library building.

The University of Michigan collection of material on East and Central Europe took shape
conspicuously as the general resources of the Library were being gradually developed. During
e 1920s a concerted effort was made to complete and round out the Library's sets of transactions
learned societies, including societies from the Slavic and East European area, and the Library
s been able to acquire quite complete sets not only of the Russian academy, but of the Czech,
lish, and Serbian academies as well, with emphasis on publications in the humanities and social
iences. Some Slavic and East European titles were included in the lists of notable acquisitions
the annual reports of the Director of Libraries during the 1930s and 1940s. The "Oriental
nguages" section of e Library, which evolved in connection with the establishment of the
enter for Japanese Studies in 1947/48, handled Slavic and East European material as well, but
thin a few years a separate section to handle only Slavic and East European titles was estab-
hed. Mr. Rolland C. Stewart, retired Associate Director of the Library, was closely involved
th collection development over the last three decades, and during the early 1950s was respon-
le for extensive valuable acquisitions of Czech, Polish, and Serbo-Croatian material. During this
ne exchange agreements with East European partners were expanded significantly. After Novem-
r 1957 and the upsurge of interest in Russian material, the pace of acquisitions quickened. In
58 for the first time a staff member in the Acquisitions Department was assigned to deal exclu-
ely with Russian and East European material. Funds for both material and library personnel
re made available with the establishment of the University's Center for Russian and East Euro-
an Studies in 1960.

While the continuous growth of the collection emphasized Russian material an effort was
de to acquire important titles in other East European languages. The staff now comprises four

professional librarians together with clerical assistants devoted exclusively to the selection and cataloging of Slavic and East European material. For the past few years an average of 5,000 to 6,000 volumes of vernacular material has been cataloged annually. In addition, titles in Western European languages have been added. About 75 to 80 percent of the 157,000 volumes in the Slavic and East European collection in the languages of Eastern Europe are in the Russian language. Estimates of holdings for individual Eastern European languages other than Russian are given in the sections below.

Yugoslavia

The largest collection other than Russian is the collection of Serbo-Croatian, Slovenian, and Macedonian material totaling about 12,000 volumes. The Library participated in the PL 480 Program for Yugoslavia from 1968 to 1972. However, apart from this program, concentrated effort has been made to acquire antiquarian material, chiefly in Serbo-Croatian. Corresponding to curriculum offerings, emphasis has been placed on material covering language and literature, political and social history, ethnology, and art. The Library has many complete or almost complete runs of Academy publications, and a large portion of monographs in series are analyzed. The annual intake over the last few years for this area has averaged about 900 titles.

Notable titles representative of the collection include: Belgrad. Narodni muzej. *Srpski spomenici,* v. 1-7 (Belgrade, 1922-34); *Bosanska vila; list za zabavu, pouku i književnost* (Sarajevo, 1885-1914; some volumes lacking); Đorđević, Tihomir. *Naš narodni život,* 10 v. (Belgrade, 1930-34); Dvorniković, Vladimir. *Karakterologija Jugoslovena* (Belgrade, 1939); Jovanović, Slobodan. *Sabrana dela,* 16 v. (Belgrade, 1932-36); *Ljubljanski zvon,* 61 v. (Ljubljana, 1881-1941); Megiser, Hieronymus. *Annales Carinthiae,* 2 v. in 1 (Leipzig, 1612); Milaš, Nikodim, Bishop of Dalmatia. *Pravoslavna Dalmacija* (Novi Sad, 1901) and *Pravoslavno crkveno pravo* (Zadar, 1890); Ninčić, Momčilo. *La crise bosniaque, 1908-1909,* 2 v. (Paris, 1937); Novak, Viktor. *Magnum crimen; pola vijeka klerikalizma u Hrvatskoj* (Zagreb, 1948); Novaković, Stojan. *Najnovija balkanska kriza i srpsko pitanje* (Belgrade, 1910); Popović, Dušan. *O hajducima,* 2 v. (Belgrade, 1930) and *Srbi u Vojvodini,* 3 v. (Novi Sad, 1957-63); *Prilozi za književnost, jezik, istoriju i folklor* (Belgrade, 1921-); Ruvarac, Dimitrije. *Opis Fruškogorskih manastira 1753 g.* (Sremski Karlovci, 1903); Šišić, Ferdinand. *Dokumenti o postanku Kraljevine Srba, Hrvata i Slovenaca, 1914-1919* (Zagreb, 1920); Strossmayer, Josip Juraj. *Dokumenti i korespondencija,* knj. 1 (Zagreb, 1933); *Zbornik za narodni život i običaje Južnih Slavena* (Zagreb, 1896-).

Poland

The second largest non-Russian collection is Polish, totaling about 9,500 volumes, with particular strengths in general history, language, and literature. Academy publications are well represented, many in quite complete runs with a large proportion of monographic series analyzed. Long runs of the serials of major universities are cataloged and analyzed. The Copernicus first edition listed below is the outstanding title in the collection. The average annual intake currently is about 900 titles. The Library participates in the PL 480 Program for Poland.

Representative titles include: *Akty powstania Kościuszki,* 3 v. (Kraków, 1918-55); *Biblioteka krakowska,* v. 1-112 (Wrocław, [etc.], 1897-1958); Copernicus, Nicolaus. *De revolutionibus orbium coelestium* (Norimbergae, 1543); Hartknoch, Christoph. *De Republica Polonica* (Lipsiae, 1698); Jocher, Adam Benedykt. *Obraz bibliograficzno-historyczny literatury i nauk w Polsce od wprowadzenia do niej druku po rok 1830 włącznie,* 3 v. (Wilno, 1840-57); Kochowski, Wespazjan. *Annalium Poloniae ab obitu Vladislai IV,* 3 v. (Cracoviae, 1683-98); Kromer, Marcin. *Polonia* (Coloniae Agrippinae, 1589); Kuropatnicki, Ewaryst Andrzej. *Wiadomość o kleynocie szlacheckim oraz herbach domów w Koronie Polskiey i Wielkim Xięstwie Litewskim* (Warsaw, 1789); Machiowita, Maciej. *Chronica Polonorum* (Craccouuie, 1521); Mukhanov, Pavel Aleksandrovich. *Podlinnyia svidietel'stva o vzaimnykh otnosheniiakh Rossii i Pol'shi, preimushchestvenno vo vremia samozvantsev* (Moscow, 1834); Niesiecki, Kasper. *Herbarz polski,* 10 v. (Leipzig, 1839-46); Pastorius, Joachim. *Historiae Polonae plenioris partes duae,* 3 v. in 1 (Dantisci, 1685); Poland. Sejm, 1830-1831. *Dyaryusz Sejmu,* 6 v. (Kraków, 1907-12); Pologne. *Guerre pour la succession* ([n.p., 1735] [48] p.). A journal in manuscript of the campaign of the Austrian Army under Count Seckendorff during September and October, 1735; Starowolski, Szymon. *Polonia* (Wolferbyti, 1656); Wierzbowski, Teodor. *Bibliographica polonica XV ac XVI ss.,* 3 v. (Warsaw, 1889-94).

Czechoslovakia

Czechoslovak books total about 7,000 volumes with strengths in history, from medieval to modern times, language, and literature. There are more Czech items in the Rare Book Room than those of any other Slavic or East European language. The most prominent titles are the two Czech Bibles noted below. The Rare Book Room also has a collection of about 500 limited editions, outstanding examples of the art of Czech bookmaking. Quite complete runs of the monographic series of the Czech Academy are analyzed. The average annual intake is about 300 titles.

Notable titles include: Bible. Czech. 1506. *Biblij cžeská* (W Benátkach tisstena [1506]); Bible. Czech. 1579-1593. *Biblj české djl prwnj [-ssestý],* 6 v. (V Kralicích 1579-93); Balbin, Bohuslav Alois. *Syntagma historicum* (Pragae, 1665) and *Vita venerabilis Arnesti, primi archiepiscopi Pragensis* (Pragae, 1664); *Bibliofil; časopis pro pěknou knihu a její upravu,* 17 v. (Uherské Hradiště, 1923-40); Bohemian Brethren. *Kancyonal* (W Amsterodame, 1659); Czechoslovak Republic. Narodní shromáždění (Almost complete sets of the *Těsnopisecké zprávy, Tisky,* and *Zapisy* of the Poslanecká snemovna and of the Senat, 1918-39); Hus, Jan. *Epistolae quaedam piissimae & eruditissimae* (Vitembergae, 1537); Krofta, Kamil. *Byli jsme za Rakouska; úvahy historické a politické* (Prague, 1936); *Literární listy* (Prague, 1967-68; some issues lacking); Maly, Jakub Josef Dominik. *Vlastenský slovník historický* (Prague, 1877); Palacký, František. *Dějiny narodu českého w Čechach a w Morawě; dle původnich pramenů,* 5 v. in 10 (Prague, 1848-76); *Památky archaeologické,* v. 1- (Prague, 1855-); Pešina, Jan Tomáš, z Čechorodu. *Mars Moravicus* (Pragae, 1677); Pius II, Pope. *Aeneae Silvii senensis de Bohemorum origine ac gestis historia* (Coloniae, 1524); Rosa, Václav Jan. *Grammatica linguae bohemicae* (Micro-Pragae [1672]); Sedlaček, August. *Hrady, zámky a tvrze Království Českého,* 15 v. (Prague, 1927-36) and *Mistopisný slovník historický Kralovství Českého* (Prague, [pref. 1908]); Winter, Zikmund. *Český průmysl a obchod v XVI věku* (Prague, 1913) and *Dějiny řemesel a obchodu v Čechach v XIV a XV století* (Prague, 1906); Zap, Karel Vladislav. *Česko-moravská kronika,* new ed., 8 v. (Prague, 1880-1905); Zíbrt, Cenek. *Bibliografie české historie,* 5 v. (Prague, 1900-12).

The remaining collections total far fewer volumes than those noted above. The collections on Bulgaria (about 1,600 titles), Hungary (about 1,500 titles) and Romania (about 1,500 titles) also have subject concentrations in history and philology, with perhaps a slightly higher percentage of material on the economy of the country. The current average annual intake is: Bulgaria, 200 titles; Hungary, 125 titles; and Romania, 150 titles.

Prominent titles from each of these countries include:

Bulgaria

Arnaudov, Mikhail Petrov. *Bŭlgarski pisateli; zhivot, tvorchestvo, idei,* 6 v. (Sofia, 1929-30); Bŭlgarska akademiia na naukite, Sofia. *Sbornik za narodni umotvoreniia i narodopis* (Sofia,

1889-); *Bŭlgarsko narodno tvorchestvo,* 13 v. (Sofia, 1961-65); Derzhavin, Nikolai S. *Istoriia Bolgarii,* 4 v. (Moscow, 1945-48); Duĭchev, Ivan. *Iz starata bŭlgarska knizhnina,* 2 v. (Sofia, 1943-44); Kanitz, Felix Philipp. *Donau-Bulgarien und der Balkan; historisch-geographisch-ethnographische Reisestudien aus den Jahren 1860-1879,* 2nd ed., 3 v. (Leipzig, 1882); Kesiakov, B. D. *Prinos kŭm diplomaticheska istoriia na Bŭlgariia,* 3 v. (Sofia, 1925-26); Kompleksna nauchna Rodopska ekspeditsiia, 1953. *Dokladi i materiiali* (Sofia, 1955); Kompleksna nauchna Dobrudzhanska ekspeditsiia, 1954. *Dokladi i materiiali* (Sofia, 1956); Kompleksna nauchna Strandzhanska ekspeditsiia, 1955. *Dokladi i materiiali* (Sofia, 1957); Kompleksna nauchna ekspeditsiia v Severozapadna Bŭlgariia. *Dokladi i materiiali* (Sofia, 1958); Mikhov, Nikola V. *Naselenieto na Turtsiia i Bŭlgariia prez XVIII i XIX v.; bibliografsko statistichni issledovaniia,* 5 v. (Sofia, 1915-67); Seton-Watson, Robert William. *The Southern Slav Question and the Habsburg Monarchy* (London, 1911).

Hungary

Bél, Matěj. *Compendium Hungariae geographicum* (Posonii et Cassoviae, 1777) and *Hungariae antiquae et novae prodromus* (Norimbergae, 1723); Bethlen, Farkas, gróf. *Historia de rebus Transsylvanicis,* 6 v. (Cibinii, 1782-93); Dilich, Wilhelm Schäffer. *Ungarische chronica* (Cassel, 1606): Fraknói, Vilmos. *Magyarország egyházi és politikai összeköttetései a Római Szent-Székkel,* 3 v. (Budapest, 1901-03); Gebhardi, Ludwig Albrecht. *Geschichte des Reichs Hungarn und der damit verbundenen Staaten,* 4 v. (Leipzig, 1778-82); Hungary. Központi Statisztikai Hivatal. *A Magyar Szent Korona Országainak helységnévtára, 1907* (Budapest, 1907); Irányi, Daniel. *Histoire politique de la revolution de Hongrie, 1847-1849,* 2 v. (Paris, 1859-60); Lampe, Friedrich Adolf. *Historia ecclesiae reformatae in Hungaria et Transylvania* (Trajecti ad Rhenum, 1728); Lukinich, Imre. *Documenta historiam Valachorum in Hungaria illustrantia usque ad annum 1400* (Budapest, 1941); Szabó, László, bártfai, ed. *Adatok gróf Széchényi István és kora történetéhez 1808-1860,* 2 v. (Budapest, 1943); Szentiványi, Márton. *Summarium chronologiae Regni Hungariae* (Viennae, ca. 1750).

Romania

Bianu, Ioan. *Bibliografia românească veche, 1508-1830* de Ivan Bianu şi Nerva Hodoş, 4 v. (Bucharest, 1903-44; Nendeln/Liechtenstein, 1968-69); Iorga, Nicolae. *Histoire des relations russo-roumaines* (Jassy, 1917); Kogalniceanu, Mihail, ed. *Cronicele României,* 2d rev. ed., 3 v. (Bucharest, 1872-74); Laurian, August Treboniu. *Istoria Românilor,* 3 v. in 1 (Iaşi, 1853); *Magazinu istoricu pentru Dacia,* v. 1-5 (Bucharest, 1845-47); Ştirbei, Barbu Dimitrie, *Mărturii istorice* (Bucharest, 1905).

The collections on Albania, Modern Greece, and East Germany number below 1,000 volumes each, with only a small percentage in the language of the country, particularly in the case of Albania and Greece.

Representative titles include:

Albania

Albania; revue d'archeologie, d'histoire, d'art et des sciences appliquées en Albanie et dans les Balkans, no. 1-6 (Paris, etc., 1925-39); Galanti, Arturo. *L'Albania; notizie geografiche, ethnografiche e storiche* (Rome, 1901); Giannini, Amedeo. *La formazione dell'Albania,* 3d ed. (Rome, 1930) and *La questione albanese,* 2d ed. (Rome, 1925); Godin, Marie Amelie Julie Anna, Freiin von. *Aus dem neuen Albanien; politische und kultur-historische Skizzen* (Vienna, 1914).

East Germany

Germany (Democratic Republic, 1949-). Zentralinstitut für Bibliothekswesen. *70 Jahre DDR; ein Bücherverzeichnis* (Leipzig 1959); Jänicke, Martin. *Der dritte Weg; die antistalinistische Opposition gegen Ulbricht seit 1953* (Koln 1964); Halle, Universität. Rechts- und Staatswissenschaftliche Fakultät. *Staat, Recht, Wirtschaft; Beiträge* (Halle, 1964); Moscow. Vsesoiuznyĭ institut nauchnoĭ i tekhnicheskoĭ informatsii. Otdel ėkonomiki promyshlennosti. *Razvitie narodnogo khoziaĭstva Germanskoĭ Demokraticheskoĭ Respubliki* (Moscow, 1959); Ulbricht, Walter. *Referat: das Program des Sozialismus und die geschichtliche Aufgabe der Sozialistischen Einheitspartei Deutschlands* (Berlin, 1963).

Modern Greece

Bujac, Jean Leopold Emile. *Les campagnes de l'armée hellenique, 1918-1922* (Paris, 1930); Bybilakis, E. *Neugrichisches Leben, vergleichen mit dem Altgriechischen zur Erläuterung beider* (Berlin, 1840); Ideville, Henri Amedee Le Lorgne, comte d'. *Journal d'un diplomate en Allemagne et en Grèce* (Paris, 1875); Vaudoncourt, Frederic François Guillaume, baron de. *Memoirs on the Ionian Islands considered in a commercial, political and military point of view* (London, 1816); Ventiris, Georgios. *Hē Hellas tou 1910-1920; historikē meletē,* 2d ed., 2 v. (Athens, 1970).

Joseph A. Placek
University of Michigan

Michigan State University

The East European collection of the Michigan State University Library is small, but in the process of a fairly rapid expansion to fill the demands of the growing university community. The collection is housed in the graduate wing of the Michigan State University Library in East Lansing, Michigan. Each floor of the graduate library has reading areas and individual desks set up for researchers. Photocopying facilities and coin-operated electric typewriters are available. During the academic year the Library is open from 8 a.m. to 11 p.m. weekdays; from 9 a.m. to 11 p.m. on Saturdays, and from 1 p.m. to 11 p.m. on Sundays. Between terms it is open from 8 a.m. to 6 p.m. weekdays; from 9 a.m. to 5 p.m. on Saturdays; and is closed on Sundays.

The East European collection is cataloged together with the Library's regular collection. The books are accessible to the general public with permission from the head of the Library, but are loaned only to students for four weeks and to faculty and staff for 70 days.

The following report covers only Bulgaria, Czechoslovakia, Hungary, Poland, Romania, and Yugoslavia. Materials relating to or emanating from the eastern parts of prewar Germany are housed with, and are inseparable from the Library's extensive German collections. The collections relating specifically to postwar East Germany, and to modern Greece and Albania, are inconsequential.

The Michigan State University Library has been collecting seriously from the East European countries for approximately five years, although a number of antiquarian acquisitions antedate 1968. Since the middle of 1969 the Library has received on regular order, and in considerable quantities, the important reference publications, monographic publications of academic-research interest, literature, and other materials in the official language of each country. The Library subscribes to the major historical and political journals of each country, to a few literary journals, and to major statistical and scientific reports, especially those pertaining to forestry and agriculture. In addition faculty members regularly submit requests for special acquisitions.

As of 1971 the approximate size of the collection in volumes by country was: Bulgaria, 400; Czechoslovakia, 700; Hungary, 700; Poland, 950; Romania, 600; Yugoslavia, 600. The approximate annual increment in volumes since 1971 by country has been: Bulgaria, 95; Czechoslovakia, 125; Hungary, 250; Poland, 650; Romania, 190; Yugoslavia, 365. These figures cover general literature, history, related cultural areas, et al. They do not include scientific and technical material, which is shelved separately.

Generally speaking the Library owns the most important bibliographic and reference materials relating to these countries, and it now possesses adequate materials to support the undergraduate and graduate Liberal Arts teaching programs of the University and to service the science departments. The Library possesses certain important blocs of research material, for example, parliamentary records from Hungary, Austria, and Bulgaria. Further, the Library has been collecting, on a substantial scale, German, Russian, and Ottoman history; and the faculty and students working on Eastern Europe can draw on the extensive nearby collections of the University of Michigan and the Orchard Lake (Michigan) Center for Polish Studies.

Bulgaria

In the reference rooms the Library has various standard bibliographic registers and periodicals from the past 20 years, but among encyclopedias only the *Kratka bŭlgarska entsiklopediia* (1963).

The Library is relatively weak in history and literature, but possesses several volumes of the Bulgarian National Assembly debates running from 1899 to 1929; and a complete collection of the annual official *Statisticheski godishnik na Tsarstvo Bŭlgariia* from 1910 to 1942. the Library subscribes to several of the Bulgarian Academy of Sciences's scientific *Izvestiia* series, and to most of its abstracts of scientific literature.

Czechoslovakia

The reference rooms have the standard bibliographic works and periodicals of the post-1950 era; such pre-1939 publications as the *Bibliografický katalog Československé republiky* (1922-46), Zíbrt's *Bibliografie české historie*, and the *Mazarykův slovník naučný*. For several years the Library has been steadily buying works on Czech history and literature, and possesses a substantial collection of works on Austrian history and related topics. It owns complete sets of the *Český časopis historický,* the *Archiv für Oesterreichische Geschichte,* and the *Mitteilungen für Oesterreichische Geschichtforschung.* It has the complete records of the Austrian *Reichsrath,* runs of such interwar periodicals as *Naše doba* and *Zahraniční politika;* a collection of the *Statistisches Handbuch* of the city of Prague; the complete *Statistický obzor (Statistická ročenka Republiky československé);* the philological journal *Slavia* from 1922 to date; and a considerable collection of Czech scientific periodicals going back to the turn of the century.

Hungary

The reference rooms have the standard bibliographic registers and periodicals published since 1950, and such older works as Petrik's *Magyar könyvészet* and the *Révai nagy lexikona.* The Library is acquiring strength in secondary literature about Hungarian history and political affairs. Further, it has the 105 volumes of the *Monumenta Hungariae historica,* the records of the Austrian *Reichsrath* for the Dual Monarchy period; the records and papers of the Hungarian Parliament for the interwar period, the *Magyar Pénzügyi Compass* from 1877 through 1948; and the *Budapest statisztikai évkönyve* from 1894-1936. In addition the collection contains a few linguistic and literary serials, and a substantial holding of the Hungarian Academy's mathematical and natural science publications, some of them dating back to the 1890s.

Poland

The reference rooms have the standard bibliographic registers and periodicals published from 1947 to the present; the historical bibliographies by Estreicher and Ziffer; Orgelbrand's older *Encyklopedja Powszechna,* and the recent *Wielka Encyklopedia Powszechna.* The collection of secondary historical works and of literature shows well compared to the other East European collections. There are holdings of scientific and technical periodicals, especially in agriculture and ethnography.

Romania

The reference rooms have the standard recent bibliographic publications and the *Bibliografia românească veche 1508-1830;* but among encyclopedias only the *Dicţionar enciclopedic român* (1966). The Library is relatively strong in Romanian literature and in Romanian history. It has Hurmuzaki's basic documentary collection, *Documente privitoare la istoria românilor,* 34 v. (1887-1913), the Academy's *Documente privind istoria României,* and some smaller documentary collections.

Yugoslavia

The reference rooms have standard bibliographic periodicals published since the war, and the *Hrvatska enciklopedija* of 1941. The collection is beginning to show strength in history and politics; less so in literature. The Library owns a few source collections, for example, the *Diplomatički zbornik . . . hrvatske;* and it has certain significant serials, for example, the *Srbski književni glasnik* from 1901-41; the *Zbornik za istoriju, jezik i književnost srpskog naroda* from 1919-32; the *Vjesnik Hrvatsko-slovensko-dalmatinsko zemalskog arkiva* from 1899; and the *Hrvatsko kolo* from 1905 to 1943. The holdings of scientific and technical periodicals, especially current publications, are relatively strong.

Lara Zakoworotny
and William O. McCagg
Michigan State University

University of Minnesota
Immigration History Research Center

General Information

The University of Minnesota's Immigration History Research Center (IHRC; formerly the Immigrant Archives/Center for Immigration Studies) is located at 826 Berry Street, St. Paul, Minnesota 55114. The IHRC Library and Archives are open for scholarly research from 8 a.m. to 4:30 p.m., Monday through Friday, and from 9 a.m. to 1 p.m., Saturdays. The collection is non-circulating, except for interlibrary loan of some microfilms. Limited quantities of printed and manuscript material may be photocopied at the discretion of the Curator.

The Collections

The Immigrant Archives were organized within the University of Minnesota Library in 1964 as a repository for the historical records generated by those immigrants and their descendants who came to North America from Eastern and Southern Europe and the Middle East. Following the formation of the Archives, the Center for Immigration Studies was established by the University to direct the collection of material and to develop academic and research programs in the field of ethnic and immigration studies. In 1974 the Center for Immigration Studies and the Immigrant Archives were brought together under the single name of the Immigration History Research Center.

The Archives consist of published matter, including books, periodicals, "calendars" (annual publications issued by religious, fraternal, and other organizations outlining the year's activities, and often containing literary and historical writings), and newspapers, as well as manuscript material (personal papers, organizational archives, and church records) produced by the immigrants themselves following their arrival in North America. There is also material originating in Europe which provides information on background conditions under which emigration took place. Although many of the IHRC's holdings are in the immigrants' mother tongues, a sizable portion is in English.

Virtually all of the material found in the archives has been donated by members of the various ethnic groups or by their organizations.

Scholars in the fields of anthropology, folklore, geography, history, linguistics, literature, political science, and sociology may all find the Archives valuable to their research.

The IHRC is organized by ethnolinguistic groups, among which are Albanian, Arab, Armenian, Bulgarian/Macedonian, Byelorussian, Carpatho-Ruthenian, Croatian, Czech, Estonian, Finnish, Greek, Hungarian, Italian, Jewish (East European), Latvian, Lithuanian, Polish, Romanian, Russian, Serbian, Slovak, Slovenian, and Ukrainian.

The published material is being cataloged according to Library of Congress rules, while the manuscript collections are controlled through the use of finding aids which provide a detailed description of each collection. Guides to the IHRC manuscript and microfilm collections are available upon request. For more information on the holdings, history, and organization of the

IHRC, see Rudolph J. Vecoli, "Immigration Studies Collection of the University of Minnesota," *The American Archivist*, v. 32, no. 2, April 1969: 139-145.

The IHRC's holdings include over 25,000 monographs, 1,700 periodical titles, 250 newspaper titles, some 200 manuscript collections (nearly 2,000 linear feet, or more than 2 million items), and 2,500 reels of microfilm.

Certain of the ethnic collections maintained by the IHRC are outside the scope of this handbook (e.g., Finnish, Italian, Ukrainian, etc.), and other collections are extremely small (e.g., Albanian and Jewish). Therefore, the following is a description of the IHRC's larger, pertinent collections.

CARPATHO-RUTHENIANS.   The Carpatho-Ruthenian Collection is small, but in the near future it promises to become sizable, as a consequence of a recent cooperative project of the IHRC and the Byzantine Catholic Archdiocese to microfilm and preserve as much as possible of the Carpatho-Ruthenian American press.

Presently the collection consists of about 45 monographs, six serial titles and six runs of newspapers, including *Nauka* (Užhorod, 1897-1921); *Listok* (Užhorod, 1887-1900); and *Svit* (Wilkes Barre, Pa., 1911-, with some gaps). The single manuscript collection for this group is a microfilm of the *Marriage Records of the Holy Ghost Greek Catholic Church,* Cleveland, 1909-67.

CZECHS.   The monograph portion contains some 650 volumes documenting the religious, cultural, and fraternal-organizational life of Czech Americans on both the local and national level. Among the volumes are the poetic works of Josef Martínek, the prose works of Benďrich Moravec, and many textbooks used in Czech-American schools. Accounts of immigrant life in the U.S. by the immigrants themselves include Tomáš Čapek's *Naše Amerika* (Prague, 1926), a general account of Czech immigration; Jan Habenicht's *Dějiny Čechův amerických* (St. Louis, 1910), a state-by-state description of Czech-American communities; and several guides to Czech national parishes in local regions, such as *Průvodce po českých katolických osadách v Archidioecesi St. Paulské* (Chicago, 1910). There are many publications dealing with the Czech-American Sokol organization as well.

The periodical section is made up of some 90 titles, with a few of the most important runs being: *Amerikán národní kalendář* (Chicago, 1910-57, nearly complete); *Svojan* (Chicago, 1894-1924); *Hospodář* (Omaha and West Texas, 1950-73); and *Katolík kalendář* (Chicago, 1915-49, nearly complete).

Seventeen Czech-American newspaper titles are held by the IHRC (seven titles currently received). Some of the longer runs are: *Hlasatel* (Chicago, 1944-72, incomplete); *Kewaunské listy* (Kewaunee, Wisconsin, 1892-1917); and *Slavie* (Racine, Wisconsin, 1870-1918).

Three collections of personal papers form the manuscript holdings: the papers of Joseph S. Roucek, 1931- (a Czech-American author and sociologist interested in immigration studies); the papers of *Joseph Pavlíček,* 1923-59 (consisting mainly of records of the Northern District of the Czech American Sokol); and the papers of *Rev. Edward Kassal,* 1924-65 (a Czech immigrant priest in southern Minnesota).

GREEKS.   The Greek-American Collection consists of about 150 monographs, including such titles as Thomas Burgess' *Greeks in America* (New York, 1913); Seraphim Kanoutas' *Hellēnismos en Amerikē ētoi Historia tou Hellēnismou Amerikē* (New York, 1918); G. Oikonomidas' *Historia tēs Hellēnikēs Orthodoxou Koinotētos, Peabody-Salem, Massachusetts, 1897-1936* (Boston, 1936); and Elias Ziōgas' *Ho Hellēnismos tēs Amerikēs* (Athens, 1948).

In addition, the collection contains some 25 periodical titles. Most of these are recent, short runs, with the exception of the organ of the American Hellenic Educational Progressive Association, *AHEPA* (Washington, D.C., 1929-present, with some gaps). The IHRC is currently receiving nine Greek-American newspapers, but none of the runs go back more than ten years.

The *Department of Laity of the Greek Orthodox Archdiocese of North and South America* has been depositing its records in the IHRC archives since 1965. There is also a large selection of Greek church newsletters from all parts of the United States.

HUNGARIANS.   The IHRC's Hungarian-American Collection is rapidly becoming substantial. The monograph section contains approximately 700 volumes, ranging from a representative selection of belles-letters to comprehensive histories of the Hungarians in North America, e.g., Jenő Ruzsa's *A kanadai magyarság története* (Toronto, 1940) and Géza Kende's *Magyarok Amerikában*, 2 v. (Cleveland, 1927). Numerous anniversary albums of churches and other organizations containing literary and photographic records of Hungarian community life in all parts of the country are an important adjunct to these histories.

The serial portion of the collection, consisting of more than 50 titles, includes *Bethlen Naptár* (Ligonier, Pa., 1943-75); *Képes Világhíradó* (Toronto, 1959-69); and *Előre,* a Hungarian-language socialist journal (New York, 1917).

Fifteen Hungarian-American newspaper titles are currently received, for the most part encompassing only the past 15 years.

The manuscript holdings are made up of a dozen separate collections. The three largest and most important are: *Hungary. Országos Levéltár. Miniszterelnökségi Levéltár, 1895-1917* (those portions of the Hungarian Prime Minister's archives dealing with emigration, on microfilm); the papers of *Association of Hungarian Students in North America* (Cambridge, Mass., 1956-67); and the *Hungarian Evangelical Reformed Conventus* (Budapest, 1904-60, on microfilm).

POLES.   Within the Polish-American Collection there are more than 3,700 monographs documenting the broad spectrum of the life of Poles in America, i.e., culture, society, religion, and organizational life. There is also an important collection of books and articles on microfilm concerning demographic changes, migration patterns, and emigration policies in pre-World War I and in interwar Poland, e.g., Józef Buzek's *Pogląd na wzrost ludności ziem polskich w wieku 19-tym* (Kraków, 1915); Leopold Caro's *Staystyka emigracyi polskiej i austro-węgierskiej do Stanów Zjednoczonych Ameryki Północnej* (Kraków, 1907); and Krystyna Duda-Dziewierz' *Wieś Małopolska a emigracja amerykańska: studium wsi Babica Powiatu Rzeszowskiego* (Warsaw, 1939).

The rich collection of Polish-American serials, amounting to nearly 175 titles, serves as another source for the scholar. A few of the most noteworthy titles are: *Dzień Święty* (Chicago, 1884-1909); *Postęp* (Baltimore, 1916-20); *Jaskółka* (Stevens Point, Wis., 1927-35); *Kalendarz Ameryki-Echa* (Toledo, 1925-59); *Skarb Rodziny* (Erie, Pa., 1917-55); and *Polka* (Scranton, Pa., 1935-present).

Twenty Polish-American newspapers are currently received in the Archives, and there are holdings of back issues for more than 50 titles. The Polish Microfilm Project (PMP; a part of the IHRC Ethnic Records Microform Project) has, since 1971, filmed the extant files of the following 14 newspapers: *Czas* (Brooklyn, 1906-71); *Dziennik Związkowy* (Chicago, 1908-71); *Gazeta Polska Narodowa* (Chicago, 1873-1917); *Głos Polek* (Chicago, 1902-73); *Górnik* (Wilkes-Barre, Pa., 1922); *Naród Polski* (Chicago, 1897-1971); *Nowy Świat* (New York, 1920-70); *Ognisko Domowe* (Detroit, 1929-30); *Orzeł Polski* (Union, Mo., 1870-72); *Wiara i Ojczyzna* (Chicago, 1891, 1894, 1896); *Wici* (Chicago, 1916-17); and *Zgoda* (Chicago, 1887-1971). The ultimate goal is to film 40 Polish-American titles. The files of these PMP titles are located at the Center for Research Libraries in Chicago, but can be rapidly borrowed for use at the IHRC.

The manuscript holdings in the Polish-American area are vast in size and in value for scholarly research. The 20 separate collections total nearly 350 linear feet. Six of the major collections are: the papers of *Rev. Paul Fox,* ca. 1890-1961 (Polish-American clergyman, editor, and social worker); the papers of *Józef L. Zawistowski,* 1914-67 (important figure in the Polish National Catholic Church); the papers of the *Paryski Publishing Co.,* Toledo, ca. 1930-60 (publisher of *Ameryka-Echo);* the papers of the *Polish American Congress, Illinois Division,* ca. 1944-73; the papers of *Edward C.*

Różański, 1940- (prominent figure of the Chicago Polonia); and the papers of *Karol T. Jaskółski,* 1939-72 (editor of the Boston newspapers *Kuryer Codzienny* and *Gazeta Polonii*).

ROMANIANS.   The IHRC has a collection of 130 Romanian-American monographs. This relatively small, but highly select group contains such titles as Ioan Schiopul's *Românii din America* (Sibiu, 1913); Christine Galitzi's *Assimilation of Romanians in the United States* (New York, 1929); S. Drutzu and A. Popoviciu's *Românii în America* (Bucureşti, ca. 1925); Şofron S. Fekett's *Istoria Uniunii şi Ligii Societăţilor Româneşti din America* (Cleveland, 1956); Nicolae Iorga's *Scrisori către Românii din America 1921-24* (Cleveland, n.d.); Rev. Vasile Hategan's *Fifty Years of the Romanian Orthodox Church in America* (Jackson, Mich., 1959) and Bishop Valerian Trifa's *Solia: istoria vieţii unei gazete româneşti în America* (Jackson, Mich., 1961). There are many volumes dealing with the music and liturgy of the Romanian Orthodox Church and publications of the Union and League of Romanian Societies in America.

Calendarul Solia (Detroit, 1936-75) and *Calendarul America* (Cleveland, 1912-74, nearly complete) are the two longest runs among the 20 serial titles.

Six titles form the Romanian-American newspaper holdings: *America* (Cleveland, 1906-66, 1974-); *Drum* (Grosse Pointe Woods, Michigan, 1966-); *Românul* (Cleveland, 1906-28); *Românul american* (Detroit, 1939-60, scattered issues); *Solia* (Detroit, 1936-); and *Steaua noastră* (New York, 1912-31).

The IHRC currently has three Romanian-American manuscript collections, but the papers of the *Union and League of Romanian Societies in America, 1900-1958,* are easily the largest and most important for research.

SLOVAKS.   The body of monograph material relating to Slovak Americans numbers approximately 700 volumes. It is especially rich in religious and church-related publications, publications of fraternal societies, local histories, and studies on the Slovak national cause. Important titles are: Milan Getting's *Americkí Slováci a vývin československej myšlienky* (New York, 1933); Imrich Mazar's *Dejiny Bighamptonských Slovákov* (Binghampton, New York, 1919); *Slovak Catholic Parishes and Institutions in the United States and Canada* (Cleveland, 1955); Jozef Paučo's *Slovenskí priekopníci v Amerike* (Cleveland, 1972); and the same author's *75 Rokov Prvej Katolíckej Slovenskej Jednoty* (Cleveland, 1965).

The serial portion of the collection is made up of more than 80 titles, some of the longer runs being: *Slovenské pohľady* (Martin, Slovakia, 1881-1947); *Sborník Matice slovenskej* (Martin, Slovakia, 1923-37); *Kalendár Jednota* (Middletown, Pa., 1908-75); *Národný kalendár* (Pittsburgh, 1899-); and *Sborník Slovenského Katolíckeho Sokola* (Passaic, N.J., 1913-60, with some gaps). There are, in addition, long runs of annual reports and minutes of annual meetings for both the First Catholic Slovak Union and for the National Slovak Society.

The IHRC possesses a particularly broad collection of Slovak-American newspapers. Altogether there are holdings for 23 titles (12 currently received), including such extensive files as: *Jednota* (Middletown, Pa., 1893-1940, 1965-); *Národné noviny* (Pittsburgh, 1910-); *Slovák v Amerike* (Middletown, Pa., 1894-, with some gaps); and *Slovenská obrana* (Scranton, Pa., 1914-72).

The four most outstanding examples from the IHRC's 13 Slovak-American manuscript collections are: the papers of the *First Catholic Slovak Union,* Cleveland, 1890-1958 (largest Slovak benefit society in the U.S.); the papers of *Adam Podkrivacky,* ca. 1920-65 (former chief officer of the First Catholic Slovak Union); the papers of the *National Slovak Society,* Pittsburgh, 1913-69 (another nationwide Slovak society); and a two-reel microfilm collection of *Correspondence of U.S. Slovaks with Leaders in Slovakia, 1890-1940* (a selection of "America Letters" held by the Matica slovenská in Martin, Slovakia).

SOUTH SLAVS. The South Slavic Collections encompass materials for four individual ethnic groups, Slovenians, Croatians, Serbians, and Macedonians/Bulgarians. The majority of the IHRC's South Slavic holdings deal with Slovenians and Croatians, whereas the other groups are represented in only a limited way.

Within the 530-volume monograph collection some titles worth mentioning are: Jože Zavertnik's *Ameriški slovenci* (Chicago, 1925); Jože Bajec's *75 let Slovenskega Časnikarstva v ZDA* (Ljubljana, 1966); Vjekoslav Meler's *Hrvatske kolonije u Chicagu i St. Louisu* (Chicago, 1928); nearly complete collections of the writings of Louis Adamic, Ivan Molek, and Etbin Kristan; and many local histories of South Slavs in various regions of the United States.

Included in the collection of more than 140 serial titles are the following: *Ave Maria* (Lemont, Ill., 1910-); *Ameriški družinski koledar* (Chicago, 1915-50); and *Hrvatski list & Danica hrvatska koledar* (New York, 1926-44, with some gaps).

From the 46 files of South Slavic-American newspapers held by the IHRC, the following are among the longer runs: *Zajedničar* (Pittsburgh, 1907-40, 1962-); *American Srbobran* (Pittsburgh, 1906-12, 1918-40, 1965-); and *Amerikanski Slovenec* (Cleveland, 1907-).

The South Slavs are among the best represented in the manuscript collections of the IHRC. In total there are some 25 separate collections, covering a broad range of experiences in America. A few examples are: the papers of *Zlatko Balaković*, 1942-55 (Croatian-American musician who was active in Yugoslav relief efforts as well); the papers of *Francis R. Preveden*, 1924-59 (Croatian-American professor and author of *History of the Croatian People*); the papers of the *Jugoslav Socialist Federation*, 1905-52 (South Slav section of the American Socialist Party); the papers of the *Slovene National Benefit Society*, 1904-66; and the records of many South Slavic national churches on microfilm.

In addition to the various specific ethnic collections, the IHRC has a large body of material on the general topics of immigration and ethnic groups in America. These materials are often multi-ethnic in character. In this area there are about 600 monographs, more than two dozen serial titles, and 16 manuscript collections. A sampling of the manuscript collections includes: the papers of the *American Council for Emigrés in the Professions*, 1938-54; the papers of the *American Council for Nationalities Service*, 1918-present; the papers of the *Assembly of Captive European Nations*, 1954-present; a microfilm collection of consular reports dealing with emigration taken from the Austrian *Allgemeines Verwaltungsarchiv;* and the records of two of the many international institutes which have aided immigrants throughout the United States.

Joseph D. Dwyer
University of Minnesota
Immigration History Research Center

University of Missouri at Columbia

Although courses on Eastern Europe have not been offered in the Department of History at Missouri, the Library's holdings are surprisingly developed. No attempt at systematic analysis of the East European collections has been made, thus an arrangement by specific categories will not be followed. The most recent bibliographies on various East European countries have been used to measure the collection, and they reveal about one-third to one-fifth of the items listed in the bibliographies to be present in the Library.

More interesting than the Library's completeness or breadth are some of the individual collections of documents and other such basic items which form the heart of a research library. In Romanian history, for instance, the Library has the Hurmuzaki collection of documents from 1199 to 1836 and the *Documente privind istoria Romîniei* (38 v.). For Yugoslavia, the *Codex diplomatus regni Croatiae, Dalmatie et Slavoniae* (15 v.). While the collection for Eastern Europe has not been built systematically, essential research tools for the history of each country of Eastern Europe are present. The collection on Byzantium is very strong, and some important sets of Turkish-language documents and periodicals exist for the study of the Ottoman Empire.

One index of the collection of materials on Eastern Europe is the holdings of publications of learned societies. A check of that group reveals the following: Česká akademie vĕd a umĕní, (1952-, Českoslovenksá akademie vĕd), *Rozpravy,* Třída 1, 98 v. (1891-1946); Třída 2, 62 v. (1891-1952); Třída 3, 76 v. (1892-1938); Česka akademie vĕd a umĕní, *Vĕstník,* 62 v. (1891-1953); Česká akademie vĕd a umĕní. [Academie des Sciences de l'Empereur François Joseph I.], *Bulletin international,* 53 v. (1896-1952); Brno. Moravské Museum. *Časopis*, 43 v (1901-58); Polska Akademia Umiejętnośсi, Kraków, *Rozprawy,* 23 v. (1874-88). Also included are publications of the Academie Polonaise des Sciences et des Lettres, Kraków, 10 v. (1929-39); Slovenska Akademija. Ljubljana, 9 v. (1948-63); and the Hungarian Academy of Sciences. *Akademiai Értesítő,* Budapest, 76 v. (1859-). Other series published by these learned societies in multivolume sets are also widely represented in the University of Missouri Library. Clearly, a firm foundation upon which to build in the area of East European history exists in the collections in Columbia, Missouri.

Charles E. Timberlake
University of Missouri at Columbia

The National Archives

General Information

The National Archives Building is located at 8th Street and Pennsylvania Avenue NW., Washington, D.C. 20408. It is open to researchers from 8:45 a.m. to 10 p.m., Monday through Friday, and from 8:45 a.m. to 5:15 p.m. on Saturdays. Access to documents may be restricted, and authorization may be required for use of post-World War II files.

The Collections

Among the holdings of the National Archives are many records relating to Albania, Bulgaria, Czechoslovakia, Greece, Hungary, Poland, Romania, and Yugoslavia. These documents reflect the particular interests of the U.S. Government agencies that created or received them. The bulk of the material is dated 1919-45; most such records of the post-World War II period remain closed to research.

GENERAL.   The State Department served as the main conduit for information on foreign countries to other U.S. agencies. Until 1906 the State Department records were arranged by type of communication (notes, despatches, and instructions) and by country, and thereunder chronologically; after 1906 they were arranged by subject. Prior to the establishment of diplomatic relations with Eastern European countries, the State Department sent special agents during the 19th century to investigate possibilities of trade and patent and property rights, to negotiate consular conventions, and to report on local conditions. For example, several agents went to Greece to further trade relations; A. Dudley Mann investigated Hungary's laws on emigration in 1849; John A. Kasson visited Romania and Serbia in 1879 to determine what type of diplomatic intercourse would be most appropriate; and Eugene Schuyler negotiated a trade treaty and consular and trademark conventions with Serbia in 1881.

Despatches from diplomatic officers to the State Department from Greece began in 1834, from Austria-Hungary in 1837, from Romania in 1880, from Serbia in 1882, from Bulgaria in 1889, and from Montenegro in 1905. Most of the letters are dated after 1880 and relate to such diverse subjects as politics and geography; trade and finance; ethnic, linguistic, and religious boundaries; brigandage and persecution of minorities; military supplies and personnel; development of mines and industries, railroads, and ports; insurrections in Herzegovina, Crete, and Macedonia; and the Congress of Berlin and the Eastern question. In addition to the diplomatic despatches there are despatches from consular officers in Salonika starting in 1832, Athens in 1837, Zante in 1853, Galatz in 1858, Chios in 1862, Piraeus in 1864, Bucharest in 1866, Prague in 1869, Warsaw in 1871, Patras in 1874, Budapest in 1876, Breslau in 1878, Belgrade in 1883, Liberec (Reichenberg) in 1886, Sofia in 1901, and Carlsbad in 1902.

The National Archives also makes available the captured records of the German Foreign Office, which date from 1855 and are now on microfilm. They closely parallel the U.S. State Department records, although the Germans had a much keener interest in Eastern Europe. The German despatches include a broad spectrum of data on political, diplomatic, military, economic, and social matters. They date from 1867 in Poland; 1868 in Greece; 1869 in Hungary; 1879 in Bulgaria, Romania, and Montenegro; 1901 in Bohemia; and 1914 in Albania.

With the exception of commercial and political notes in the correspondence and logs of the Mediterranean Squadron, 1843-60, and the European Squadron, 1865-1900, documentation on Eastern Europe in the 19th century by the U.S. Navy and War Departments is insignificant. American military and naval observers in the area began reporting on local conditions extensively during the Balkan wars and World War I. Their reports describe the military situation, coastal defenses, border disputes, economic relief, communication and transportation, industry and finance, and health and public laws. Significant military files on Eastern European countries are also found in the following War Department offices: the Adjutant General, the Chief of Staff, the Army War College, and beginning in 1918 in the War College Historical Section and the War Plans Division. The General Staff Map Collection includes topographic, political, and military maps of the area, and the Major F. T. Colby Collection contains photographs of Balkan scenery and people.

WORLD WAR I AND AFTER.   During World War I several U.S. agencies began studying Eastern European areas. In 1917 ''The Inquiry'' was organized to prepare reports for the American delegation to the Paris Peace Conference. These ''Inquiry Documents'' include material on Eastern European geography, ethnography, language, religion, boundaries, industry, agriculture, and political history. Among other civilian agencies reporting on Eastern Europe were the War Trade Board, whose records deal with shipping, trade, and finance; the American Relief Administration (with field offices in Warsaw, Belgrade, Prague, Salonika, and Bucharest); and the Office of Foreign Agricultural Relations, which began receiving reports from agricultural attachés in 1911 concerning commodity prices, trade, business regulations, and consumption.

During the Paris Peace Conference the independent nations of Albania, Czechoslovakia, Hungary, Poland, and Yugoslavia were established. The records of the American Commission To Negotiate Peace and the Supreme Allied War Council include documentation of the major and minor conferences, meetings, and decisions relating to the political and economic configurations of Eastern Europe in the crucial period 1918-20. They concern such questions as boundary adjustments, population movements, relief work, debts, reparations, and the establishment of political representation. The United States recognized these newly independent nations and opened legations there during 1919 and 1920.

After 1910 internal memorandums and correspondence of the State Department with its diplomatic and consular officers, with other Government agencies, and with foreign embassies and legations were arranged according to a decimal-subject classification system. The first digit of the file number represents the primary subject class, such as protection of interests, claims, international conferences, commercial relations, political relations between states, and internal affairs of states. The remaining digits represent country names and/or more specific subjects. The numbers assigned to the Eastern European countries are: 75 for Albania, 74 for Bulgaria, 60f for Czechoslovakia, 68 for Greece, 64 for Hungary, 60c for Poland, 71 for Romania, and 60h for Yugoslavia (before 1920, Serbia is 72 and Montenegro, 73).

Among the thousands of subject files of State Department records in the interwar period are the following: 371.115 St 2, protection of the interests of the Standard Oil Co. in Romania; 464.11, claims of American citizens against Hungary; 550.S1 Washington, opinions and aims of Eastern European countries regarding the 1933 World Economic and Monetary Conference; 611.6831, American commercial relations with Greece; 760f.62, the Sudetenland controversy between Czechoslovakia and Germany; 860c.6373, the potash industry in Poland; 860f.51, Czech financial affairs; 860h.4016, minority problems in Yugoslavia; 864.00, Béla Kún's Communist regime in Hungary; 868.48, relief measures for Greek refugees from Asia Minor; 871.15, public works in Romania; 874.77, development of railroads in Bulgaria; and 875.404, negotiations for an autonomous Albanian Church.

There are also separate conference records concerning American participation in the Lausanne Conference, 1923, the Reparations Commission, 1919-30, and the Tripartite Claims Commission with Austria and Hungary, 1924-29, all of which include documents of Eastern European boundaries, debts, and reparations claims. Among the records of the Commerce Department are weekly reports from trade commissioners and commercial attachés. The Bureau of Foreign and Domestic Commerce has files on Eastern Europe covering such subjects as industrial development, iron and steel, import duties, agricultural machinery, livestock, and crops. Among the records of the Department of the Treasury are country files in the Bureau of Accounts, 1917-41, providing in-depth analysis of war debts, loans, currencies, and reparations. The Public Health Service has reports from posts in Eastern Europe, 1921-36, concerning diseases, hygiene, and medical practices.

In addition to extensive German Foreign Office records of Eastern Europe for the interwar period, the National Archives has the following captured records: those of the Reich Ministry for Public Enlightenment and Propaganda, 1936-44, and of the Reich Ministry of Economics, which inventoried the resources of Eastern Europe; the papers and diaries of German diplomats, Count Ciano, and Mussolini, which cover diplomatic, military, and economic relations with Eastern Europe; the Hungarian Collection of military and political documents for 1909-45, including the files of the pro-Nazi Arrow Cross Party; and Italian military records, 1934-43, including plans for the attacks on the Balkans.

The U.S. Naval Records Collection and the Records of Naval Intelligence attachés include reports from Eastern Europe on the Montenegrin revolt, the Fiume controversy, plague and disease quarantines, naval maneuvers in the Mediterranean and Black Seas, and country studies of political, military, and economic conditions in the early 1920s. General records of the Navy include material on blockades, communications systems, equipment, and military training. The records of the War Department's Military Intelligence Division, which include the military attaché reports from Eastern Europe, cover in addition to military topics personalities, politics, geography, minorities disputes, foreign affairs, trade, finance, agriculture, and transportation. Similar but less concentrated material is found among the files of the Adjutant General, the Army Chief of Staff, and the American Expeditionary Forces in Europe, especially among the files of the American Polish Relief Expedition.

WORLD WAR II.   State Department records for Eastern Europe during World War II are voluminous. For specific subject and country references, the Department's documentary publication *Foreign Relations of the United States* serves as a supplementary finding aid. The National Archives' two-volume guide *Federal Records of World War II* (1950-51) also assists the researcher in understanding the organization and records of wartime agencies that were involved with Eastern Europe.

Among the emergency agencies set up to gather and transmit information on Eastern Europe and the European war in general were the Office of War Information (OWI), 1942-46, the Foreign Broadcast Intelligence Service (FBIS), 1941-46, and the Foreign Economic Administration (FEA), 1943-45, which inherited lend-lease, economic warfare, and relief functions. The records of the OWI include reports, news releases, bulletins, and letters under the headings Central Europe, Czechoslovakia, Greece, Hungary, Poland, and Yugoslavia; there are also geographic, photographic, and radio survey files for the region. OWI's weekly bulletin "Inside the Axis" describes personalities, resistance movements, military supply and production, sabotage and propaganda, and events of political, military, and economic significance. FBIS records include tapes and transcripts of intercepted broadcasts from underground, Communist, and pro-Nazi stations. FEA records include economic studies of occupied and pro-Axis areas; copies of British Ministry of Economic Warfare intelligence reports, 1942-44; and lend-lease records for projects in Czechoslovakia, Greece, Poland, and Yugoslavia, 1940-45.

The German, Italian, and Hungarian captured records are especially significant for World War II research. In addition to the above-mentioned diplomatic, military, economic, and political document collections are the following: the Von Rohden Collection on the German Air Force, including intelligence reports and target sheets for Eastern Europe, war journals and correspondence, reconnaissance maps and charts, and reports on aircraft and raw materials output in Hungary, Slovakia, Croatia, and Romania; records of the German Air Force and Armed Forces High Command concerning plans and strategy; records of the German Army Field Commands in charge of the occupation and administration of Eastern Europe; records of Rosenberg's Einsatzstab, which looted artworks; papers of Himmler, Reichsleader of the S.S., on espionage, race studies, and repression; records of the Office of the Reich Commission for Strengthening Germandom, which was responsible for resettling Germans and for nationality policies in Poland and Yugoslavia; records of the Reich Plenipotentiary for the Serbian Economy, which confiscated and administered Jewish properties and assets; and records of the German Air Force Mission to Romania, 1940-44, particularly concerning the oil, defense, and airplane industries. Finally, the records of the Nuremberg trials and subsequent proceedings contain pretrial interrogations, extensive testimony, and complete documentation of Nazi aggression, exploitation, and genocide in Eastern Europe. In addition to the main trials of the International Military Tribunal there are several important cases in subsequent proceedings: *United States* v. *Erhard Milch* exposes Nazi medical experiments and slave labor policies in Poland, and *United States* v. *Wilhelm List et al.* details the brutal treatment of hostages in Yugoslavia.

The records of the Joint Chiefs of Staff (JCS) include files of the Combined Chiefs of Staff and the Combined Civil Affairs Committee, which contain reports on enemy targets, equipment, and loans for underground organizations, relief work, armistice negotiations, and planning for the control commissions in Bulgaria, Hungary, and Romania. The Office of Strategic Services (OSS), which came under the jurisdiction of the JCS, collected and analyzed intelligence data for the prosecution of the war against the Axis. Correspondence, pamphlets, and reports from the OSS Research and Analysis Branch and the European-African Division cover, among other subjects, economic affairs, resistance movements, propaganda and psychological warfare, living conditions, concentration camps, movement of populations, forced labor and military conscription, competing political factions and governments-in-exile, institutions and laws under pro-Nazi regimes, religion and education, the press, public health, social classes, German business penetration and exploitation, agriculture, and relations with the Soviet Union, 1942-45.

Records of the U.S. Strategic Bombing Survey include bombing targets, aerial views, and reports on Nazi economic activities in Eastern Europe. In the files of the Adjutant General for this period are medical and sanitary reports; handbooks on labor, agriculture, industry, and enemy armed forces; reports on relief and rehabilitation of Nazi-occupied areas, communications and transportation systems, and the purchase and production of war materials. There are similar records in the Military Intelligence Division, the Operations Division, and the Civil Affairs Division (all offices of the War Department General and Special Staffs), the Headquarters of the U.S. Army Air Forces, the Allied Force Headquarters in the Mediterranean, and the Supreme Headquarters, Allied Expeditionary Forces. The records of the U.S. contingent to the Allied Military Liaison Headquarters in the Balkans provide documentation from Albania, Greece, and Yugoslavia on agriculture and fisheries, economics and finance, relief and public health, fine arts and antiquities, labor and industries, transportation and military intelligence, and justice and government.

Gibson Smith
National Archives

Newberry Library

General Information

The Newberry Library is open throughout the year from 9 a.m. to 6 p.m. Monday through Saturday. It is closed only on Independence Day, Labor Day, Thanksgiving, Christmas, and New Year's Day. The Library issues grants-in-aid for periods of study ranging from one to three months, at a stipend of $350.00 monthly. Address: The Newberry Library, 60 W. Walton St., Chicago, Ill. 60610.

The Collections

The Newberry Library is a privately endowed research library possessing well over a million manuscripts and printed books. In the field of European history and literature it concentrates almost exclusively on western Europe, roughly from the High Middle Ages through the 18th century, and to 1914 for England. Nevertheless, there are significant pockets of Central and Eastern European materials scattered among the collections. There are two principal reasons for this. First, because the Library's present acquisition policy, with its exclusion of Eastern European material, has only been practiced for the last two decades it is possible for the Eastern European specialist to encounter such relatively uncommon collections of sources as the *Monumenta spectantia historiam Slavorum meridionalium* (46 v.), the *Documente privitóre la istoria Românilor* (28 v.), or such periodicals as *Le Polonais* (a run which begins at the year 1833). Second, the Library's fields of specialization lend themselves to the collection of Eastern European material.

Thus, because of the Newberry's strong interest in Renaissance historiography, one finds the first humanist histories of Hungary; János Thuróczy, *Chronica Hungariae* (Augsburg, 1490; Vienna, 1534); Antonio Bonfini, *Rerum Hungaricarum decades quatuor* (Frankfurt, 1581); G. N. Doglioni, *L'Ungheria* (Venice, 1595), etc. Similarly, for Poland, the Library possesses such early histories as: Macriej, *Chronica Polonorum* (Kraków, 1521); Marcin Kromer, *De Origine et rebus gestis Polonorum* (Basel, 1568); and Jan Herburt, *Histoire des Roys et Princes de Pologne* (Paris, 1573). For Bohemia, one encounters such works as Aeneas Sylvius Piccolomini's *De Bohemorum origine* (in several editions); Albertus Krantz, *Hystoria von den alten Hussen zu Behemen* (Strasbourg, 1523) and P. Lupac, *Rerum Boemicarum* (Prague, 1584), among others.

The Newberry's interest in the Protestant Reformation (especially its Italian manifestations), has led it to collect Socinian material, including the rare Racovian imprints of the writings of Faustus Socinus and his followers. Due to the Library's strength in bibliography, a number of rare and important bibliographies and biobibliographies are encountered, for example, Christopher Sand, *Bibliotheca Anti-trinitariorum* (1684). The Wing collection, devoted to the history of printing, contains such unusual items of Eastern European interest as the Croatian-language edition, in Glagolitic type, of the *Trattato Utilissimo del Beneficio di Cristo* printed in 1563 at Tübingen (Urach) by Primus Truber and Hans Ungnat von Sonneck. The Newberry possesses the only copy in the United States of this little booklet intended to advance the doctrines of the Reformation among the Slavs. The Bonaparte Library, acquired at the turn of the century, is one of the great linguistics collections—see V. Collins, *Attempt at a Catalogue of the Library of the Late Prince*

Louis-Lucien Bonaparte, 2 v. (London, 1894). It contains well over a thousand works (roughly 10 percent of the entire collection) devoted to the origin and development of Slavic alphabets and tongues—many of them rare examples of 17th- and 18th-century scholarship. Although the Bonaparte books are primarily concerned with the question of language, there are among them a fair number of historical works not frequently encountered in American libraries, e.g., George Papanek, *Historia gentis Slavae* [Fünfkirchen, n.d.]; J. Ch. de Jordan, *De originibus Slavicis* (Vindobonae, 1745); and J. P. Koh, *Introductio in historiam et rem literariam Slavorum* (Altonaviae, 1729).

John Tedeschi
Newberry Library

New York Public Library

General Information

MATERIALS RELATING TO East Central and Southeastern Europe at the Research Libraries of the New York Public Library are contained within the buildings at Fifth Avenue and 42d Street, the Library and Museum of the Performing Arts at Lincoln Center, and, in the case of most newspapers in the Roman and Greek alphabets and all patents, at the Annex to the Research Libraries at 521 West 43d Street in New York City. The Research Libraries' materials do not circulate and are restricted to use within the buildings noted.

At present most of the collections of the Research Libraries are open five days a week, but this is subject to change and scholars planning in-depth research should write in advance for information.

All materials in the Research Libraries are available to the public upon request, with the exception of those in the Special Collections, i.e., the Arents Collection of Books in Parts; the Arents Tobacco Collection; the Berg Collection of English and American Literature; the Manuscript Division; the Prints Division; the Rare Book Division; and the Spencer Collection of Illustrated Books and Manuscripts and Fine Bindings. Access to these Special Collections is open to qualified scholars, experienced researchers, and students engaged in programs of graduate study, who may obtain a card of admission for a limited period by making application to the Research Libraries Administrative Office, Room 214 in the Central Building; further information may be obtained by writing directly to the Executive Assistant in Room 214. It should be noted that cards of admission to the Special Collections do not guarantee access to specific items within the collection. The curators in consultation with the reader have final responsibility for determining which materials can be made available for use.

The Research Libraries contain both subject and language divisions, so the user of East Central and Southeastern European materials may have to consult materials in different divisions for the same project. The Library will attempt to meet any reasonable request of a reader who must work simultaneously on materials from more than one division. Normally the work should be done in the division having the greater amount of material to be used by the reader. The borrowing division shall be responsible for determining the reasonableness of the reader's need and initiating the request for items to be brought to him from other divisions. Certain types of materials cannot be transferred, for example, vertical file materials, current periodicals, materials on reserve in the division (i.e., bearing the classmark *R-), materials in the Special Collections (vide supra), and materials considered rare by the transferring division. In such cases the reader must go to the division itself to consult the materials.

Information on specific aspects of the collections under review can be obtained from a qualified librarian in any of the aforementioned buildings or in the case of the Special Collections initially from the Executive Assistant of the Research Libraries.

The reader's attention is directed to the numerous special indexes and files maintained by most of the divisions and collections of the Research Libraries which often contain unique information. Librarians in the divisions and collections concerned can give further information on specific details.

General Catalogs and Finding Aids

For materials in the Balto-Slavic languages and in Balto-Slavic studies the most productive search is started at the Slavonic Division card catalog. For all other materials in the Roman and Greek alphabets the proper starting point for a search is the great Public Catalog of the Research Libraries in Room 315 of the Central Building. Public documents except those in Balto-Slavic or oriental languages or in Hebrew should first be searched in the Documents Catalog of the Economics Division in Room 228 of the Central Building. Materials in Hebrew must be searched in the Jewish Division catalog, and materials in oriental languages must be searched in the Oriental Division Catalog. Only after these basic approaches to the holdings of The Research Libraries have been explored should the researcher go to the other divisional catalogs.

The above paragraph refers to the so-called "Retrospective Catalog" of the Research Libraries which was phased out during 1971. Recently cataloged materials and all materials bearing a 1972 or later imprint will be found in a new book catalog published by the New York Public Library entitled *Dictionary Catalog of The Research Libraries*. The book catalog is cumulated periodically into basic bound volumes which are updated by monthly cumulative supplements. Non-Roman alphabets will be included in romanized form using the Library of Congress transliteration system. Thus, for some time to come the main Public Catalog, consisting of over ten million cards, will continue to serve as the primary research tool for the materials which have been added to the collections of the Research Libraries during the almost 125 years of its existence ending December 31, 1971.

In 1966, the Library established a Central Serial Record which is a single central record of all the serial holdings of the Research Libraries including newspapers and gazettes. Cards in the public catalogs of the Library will bear the notation—"Full Record of Holdings in Central Serial Record." The Library staff will give further assistance.

Many of the divisional catalogs, containing cards for books and booklike materials have also been reproduced by a photographic process and issued in book form by G. K. Hall & Co. of Boston, Mass. Among the catalogs available that are applicable to this area of studies are:
Dictionary Catalog of the Jewish Collection, 14 v. (1960)
Dictionary Catalog of the Music Collection, 33 v. (1964-) *Supplement 1,* 1 v. (1966)
Dictionary Catalog of the Oriental Collection, 16 v. (1960)
Dictionary Catalog of the Rare Book Division, 21 v. (1972)
Dictionary Catalog of the Slavonic Collection, 2d ed., rev. and enl., 44 v. (1974)
Catalog of the Theatre and Drama Collections, 21 v. (1967)
Subject Catalog of the World War I Collection, 4 v. (1961)

The above represent titles available at this time; other titles are in production, most notably the *Catalog of Government Publications. Economics Division.*

Nonbook Materials

A record of the manuscripts in the Research Libraries is found in the Manuscript Division, with the exception of most manuscripts in the performing arts which appear in the card catalogs of the divisions of the Research Library of the Performing Arts at Lincoln Center. Maps as well as atlases are listed in the catalog of the Map Division. Prints and drawings must be searched in the Print Division with the exception of the divisions at Lincoln Center which are rich in other pictorial material relating to their subjects. Phonorecords and tapes are in the Rodgers and Hammerstein Archives of Recorded Sound at Lincoln Center and sheet music in the Music Division there. The Rare Book Division in the Central Building contains, in addition to books and booklike material, ephemera, and miscellaneous items as coins, medals, and paper money. The researcher should consult the divisional librarians for further assistance. The following divisional catalogs containing listings of nonbook materials have been published by G. K. Hall & Co.:

Dictionary Catalog of the Manuscript Division, 2 v. (1967)
Dictionary Catalog of the Map Division, 10 v. (1971)
Dictionary Catalog and Shelf List of the Spencer Collection of Illustrated Books and Manuscripts and Fine Bindings, 2 v. (1971)

Size of the Collections

The size of the collections of the Research Libraries for each of the countries of East Central and Southeastern Europe is expressed below in volumes (i.e., each separate book and pamphlet and each bound volume of a serial):

Albania	2,000
Bulgaria	8,300
Czechoslovakia	28,000
German Democratic Republic	27,300
Greece	16,000
Hungary	20,000
Poland	35,000
Romania	13,000
Yugoslavia	25,500

The above figures represent the estimated holdings as of June 30, 1972; they include both cataloged and uncataloged materials. In the case of Yugoslavia the total is swollen by extensive receipts through the PL 480 program. Government documents are also included in all the totals.

The Library maintains exchange relationships with most of the important institutions of East Central and Southeastern Europe. It participated in the Public Law 480 Program for Yugoslavia from 1968 till its conclusion (1973) and has participated in the Program for Poland since 1972. The Library subscribes to the ARL Foreign Newspaper Project at the Center for Research Libraries in Chicago, through which it receives a loan positive microfilm of about 200 of the most important newspapers published outside the United States.

Loan Regulations

The Research Libraries do not make material available for use outside the Library. Patrons visiting the Library are given access to the general collections. Access to and use of the Special Collections are restricted. Patrons should apply to the Research Libraries Administrative Office. In addition to on-site use of materials, the Research Libraries provide the following services:

PHOTOCOPYING SERVICE. The Photographic Service of the Library in Room 316 makes photographic, photostatic, electrostatic, and microfilm reproductions of materials in the collections available for a set fee. In some instances permission to reproduce materials will depend upon the condition of the materials involved, or other restrictions, e.g., copyright protection. Books in the Slavonic Reserve, the Jewish Reserve, and in the Rare Book Division, because of their rarity, may only be reproduced by photostat or microfilm, if permission to reproduce them is given.

PHOTOCOPYING IN LIEU OF INTERLIBRARY LENDING. The Research Libraries participate in the New York State Interlibrary Loan Network (NYSILL) and will, upon request and subject to the restrictions of the program, supply full-size copy from serial publications and in the case of monographs, positive microfilm.

BOOK RESERVE SERVICE.   Persons intending to visit New York City may reserve any title listed in the catalog by notifying the Library in advance, and on special request forms available through libraries subscribing to the *Dictionary Catalog of The Research Libraries.*

Bibliography of Publications on the Collections Described

BIBLIOGRAPHIES OF PRINTED AREA CATALOGS.   The general encyclopedic work covering all aspects of the Library's holdings is Karl Brown's *A Guide to the Reference Collections of The New York Public Library* (New York, New York Public Library, 1941); it is to be republished in revised and updated form as *A Guide to the Research Collections of The New York Public Library.*

Several other bibliographic studies have been published in the *Bulletin of The New York Public Library* or by the Library:

Allen, Walter, "The four Corvinus manuscripts in the United States," *BNYPL,* XLII (1938): 315-323.

Freimann, Aron. *A Gazetteer of Hebrew Printing,* 1946 (first published in the *BNYPL,* XLIX (1945): 355-374 f.)

Lewański, Ryszard. *A Bibliography of Slavic Dictionaries.* 1959-63. V. I, Polish; V. II, Belorussian, Bulgarian, Czech, Kashubian, Lusatian, Old Church Slavic, Macedonian, Polabian, Serbocroatian, Slovak, Slovenian, Ukrainian; V. III, Russian.

———. *Literatures of the World in English Translation: A Bibliography.* 1967. V. II, *The Slavic Literatures*

———. *The Lusatians: A Bibliography of Dictionaries,* 1959

"List of works in The New York Public Library relating to the Near Eastern Question and the Balkan States including European Turkey and Modern Greece," *BNYPL,* XIV (1910): 7-55 f.

The Research Libraries. Slavonic Division. "A bibliography of Slavonic bibliography," *BNYPL,* LI (1947): 200-208.

Swanson, Donald Carl Eugene. *Modern Greek Studies in the West: A Critical Bibliography.* 1960

Yarmolinsky, Avrahm. "Tomáš Garrigue Masaryk: A list of works by and about . . . in The New York Public Library," *BNYPL,* XLV (1941): 989-996 f.

Viktor Koressaar and Sam P. Williams

Czechoslovakia

Bibliography

The Library has an almost complete run of the various sets of the *Bibliografický katalog ČSR* beginning with the year 1922.

The majority of the titles listed in such guides as those of Rudolf Sturm or Jiří Kábrt are in the holdings. Note should also be made of the presence of the major and indispensable bibliographies as those of Zíbrt, and Kunc, as well as the *Knihopis československých tisků od doby nejstarši až do konce XVIII století.*

The collection includes a few catalogs of manuscripts and incunabula. The Library can furnish bibliographical coverage for books published in Czechoslovakia from 1774 to 1925 in such works as František Doucha's *Knihopisný slovník československý; seznam knih, map, obrazů a hudebnin 1774-1864* (1865) and the compilation of Karel Nosovský and Vilém Pražák *Soupis československé literatury za leta 1901 až 1925.* For a listing of the war years' publications, Vlastimil Kybal's mimeographed *Standard Czechoslovak Publications Published During the German Occupation* (New Haven, 1947) can be used.

From 1922 on, books in the Slovak language are included in the *Bibliografický katalog ČSR* and many of the sources listed above also include publications in the Slovak language. The major Slovak bibliography by Rizner is in the Library. A relatively complete list of publications of Matica slovenská from 1863 to 1953 is the *Vydavatel'ské dielo Matice slovenskej* by Peter Liba. A bibliography of Slovak bibliographies is being published by Matica slovenská in the *Bibliografia slovenských bibliografii 1961/62-*.

The Library's holdings of Austrian bibliographies for the pre-1919 period are incomplete and in poor condition.

Biographies

A substantial representation of the standard collected biographies is available. Among them are Heinrich Kuhn's *Biographisches Handbuch der Tschechoslowakei*, a contemporary work, and its predecessor, *Československo*. Other collective works available are the *Album representantů všech oborů veřejného života Československého* (1927); František Kulhánek's *Kronika československá;* and *Slavín* (1870). Obituaries are to be found in the *Nekrolog* of the Česka Akademie věd a uměni, Prague, and women's participation in the political life of the past is reflected in Karel Stloukal's *Královny, kněžny, a velké ženy* (1940). A rarity is the biography of the Archbishop Arnošt of Pardubice by Bohuslav Balbin, the *Vita venerabilis Arnesti* (1664).

The Libraries have representative holdings of individual biographies.

Genealogy and Heraldry

The Genealogy Division has a one hundred and one volume set, the *Siebmacher's Wappenbuch* (Nürnberg, 1885-1900). *Der Boehmische Adel, Der Maehrische Adel,* and *Der Schlesische Adel* in parts of v. 57-59 contain tables of coats of arms and family backgrounds. For Slovakia, *Der Ungarische Adel,* v. 63 and 64, will be useful. Other works to be consulted are *Der Adel von Boehmen, Maehren und Schlesien* by Král z Dobré Vody (Prague, 1904), and Béla Kempelen's *Magyar nemes családok* (Budapest, 1911-32).

The Slavonic Division has a two-volume set of *Staromoravští rodové* [Old Moravian Families] by Joseph Pilnáček.

Dictionaries and Encyclopedias

The Czech and bilingual dictionaries are well represented and easily accessible. Main sets are on the open shelves in the Reading Room of the Slavonic Division. Most of the dictionaries and encyclopedias mentioned in the bibliographies of Horecky and Sturm are in the Library.

Libraries and Archives

The Research Libraries receive most of the leading publications of the libraries in Czechoslovakia.

Library science in Czechoslovakia is well represented in the holdings. A bibliography of library science can be found in the *Časopis Československých knihovníků*, of which the Library has v. 1-10, 1929-38. Currently a bibliography is being published in a special supplement to the Bibliografický katalog ČSSR, *Bibliografie československého knihovnictví*. A number of manuals and dictionaries of library science as well as sets of *Knihovna* and *Knižničný sborník* are available.

The Library has a good collection of published archival literature. In addition to publications of most of the central archives, the Library has the published records of the archives of about 12 cities and towns in Czechoslovakia, among them Brno, Košice, Plzeň, and Kutná Hora.

Printing

The Library has a solid collection of books on the history of printing. The earliest printed books in the Rare Book Division relating to Czechoslovakia are two Bibles printed in Prague in 1488 by Jan Kamp (one of them from the Lenox Collection), and János Thuróczy's *Chronica Hungarorum* printed in Brno in the same year (name of the printer unknown). There is also a Bible printed in Kutná Hora in 1489 by Martin of Tischinowa. Samples are available of the presses of Somerhowsky, Pawel Seweryn, Melantrich, and Daniel Adam of Veleslavín, and of books in Hebrew produced by the Gershom ha Kohen Press.

Serials

Currently, the Library subscribes to approximately 200 periodicals and newspapers from Czechoslovakia. However, many of the sets are incomplete or poorly represented. Furthermore, many subscriptions are comparatively new and are received irregularly. The years of the German occupation of Czechoslovakia, 1939-45, and the years immediately following are represented sparingly.

Among the newspapers in the holdings are *Rudé Právo* (1948-) published by the Czechoslovak Communist Party. The Slovak leading daily *Pravda* (1963-) is represented by a few years only. *Lidové noviny* (1929-51) and *České slovo* (1934-43) are on microfilm.

Národní noviny marks the beginning of modern Czech journalism. The Library has the first 226 issues of this very scarce newspaper. When the Austrian authorities suppressed *Národní noviny* in January of 1850, Karel Havlíček, its editor, started to publish *Slovan*. Only the 1850 issues are in the Library. Both newspapers played an influential role in the political life of the Czech people.

The periodical holdings from Czechoslovakia are divided by subject matter in four divisions of the Library: Economics, Periodicals, Slavonic, and Science and Technology. The Library has *Plamen* (1959-), *Květy* (1961-), and *Slovenské pohľady* from the latter part of the 19th century. *Kronika* (1901-11) contains a chronological list of important events on a monthly basis. In the holdings are such titles as *Lumír* (1873-1936), *Květy* (1879-1915), *Osvěta* (1873-1920), and *Naše doba* (1894-1932) among others.

The Library has only a small percentage of the serials mentioned in V. N. Duben's *Czech and Slovak Periodical Press outside Czechoslovakia*. The most complete holdings are those of the *New Yorské listy* (1890-1962), followed by *Americké listy* (1963-). Slovak newspapers are represented by *New Yorský deník* (1913-) and *Slovák v Amerike* (1968-).

Monographs and serials of learned societies are well represented and regularly received. They include the publications of the Československá Akademie věd a umění and Slovenská Akadémia vied a umení, those of the Královská česká společnost nauk (1775-), those of the Matice moravská and Matica slovenská, and those of the Akademie der Wissenschaften (Vienna, 1850-).

Transactions from Karlova universita, Prague; Masarykova universita, Brno; Palackého universita, Olomouc; and Komenského universita, Bratislava, pertain to the social and political life of Czechoslovakia.

Public Documents

The Library has a standing order for publications issued by government departments and is strong in holdings of documents. Some of its major sources in the field of statistics, statutes, parliaments, official gazettes, and local government will be mentioned specifically.

STATISTICS. A 180-volume set of *Československá statistika* [Czechoslovak statistics] published by the Státní úřad statistický, 1922-48, is the most comprehensive document in the field of statistics for Czechoslovakia. It covers 19 series. A supplementary source, the *Zprávy*, includes summaries of statistical investigations. French and German editions, the *Rapports* and *Mitteilungen*, are less complete. *Zprávy Zemského statistického úřadu* and its German counterpart, *Mitteilungen*, published by the Statistisches Landesamt, Bohemia, 1899-1918, precede this source. Statistical data for Bohemia, Moravia, and Silesia are included in the 93-volume set on microfilm, the *Oesterreichische Statistik,* published by the Statistische Zentralkommission, Austria, 1882-1916.

The years 1842-1921 are well covered in statistical sources from the Austrian Ministerium des Innern and the Statistische Zentralkommission. Statistics before 1840 were collected, but by a royal decree could not be distributed. Data for this period can be found only through indirect sources, of which there are many available. A good introduction to statistical publications in the Austrian Empire is the *Denkschrift der K.K. Statistischen Zentralkommission,* published by the Austrian Central Statistical Commission.

STATUTES. Statutes of Czechoslovakia from 1918 to date will be found in *Sbírka zákonů* [Compilation of Statutes], largely on microfilm. A German edition, *Sammlung der Gesetze und Verordnungen des Čechoslovakischen Staates,* 1918-45, and a French edition, *Exposé sommaire des travaux legislatifs,* 1918-38, are available in bound volumes.

Statutes for Bohemia from 1848-1918, in Czech and German, are in *Zákonník zemský království českého.* The *Provinzial-Gesetzsammlung des Koenigreiches Boehmen* is available for the years 1819-48.

Statutes for Moravia from 1861 to 1906 are in *Usnešení sněmu markrabství moravského.* A German edition, covering the same years, can be found under Moravia, Landtag, *Beschluesse des Landtages der Markgraftschaft Maehren.*

The Provinces of Silesia and Moravia formed a single unit between 1763-1849, and after 1928. Publications for these dates are entered under Moravia. The Library's holdings for Silesia are incomplete.

Documents for Slovakia before 1918 will be found in Hungarian sources.

The Library's Spencer Collection has an illustrated 15th-century edition of *Die Güldin Bulle.* This book of laws was issued by Charles IV and governed the elections of the German king. The only other known copy in the United States is at the Library of Congress.

The Library has a complete set of Parliamentary papers from 1918 to 1938 and from 1946 to date in *Těsnopisecké zprávy o schůzích* and in *Tisky k těsnopiseckým zprávám o schůzích,* issued by both Chambers, the Poslanecká Sněmovna and Senát and by the Národní Shromáždění.

Reports in Czech and German on the administration of Moravia, 1864-1918, are in a 100-volume set, *Zprávy,* and *Rechenschaftsberichte,* issued by the Zemský Výbor.

Resolutions of the Bohemian Landtag between 1567 and 1811 are recorded in its *Artickel.* The 16th-century documents were printed by the great humanist printer Melantrich. The Research Libraries' set is incomplete and in poor condition; some of the documents, however, were reprinted in *Sněmy české od leta 1526 až po naši dobu* [Bohemian Diets from 1526 Till Our Times]. This 15-volume set was published by the Landesarchiv of Bohemia and ends with the year 1611. Domestic and foreign archives were searched for documents pertaining to Czech history and were then reprinted in modern Czech and German spelling.

The early history of Bohemia can be traced through the *Calendar of State Papers,* from the Public Record Office, Great Britain.

OFFICIAL GAZETTES. The official gazette of Czechoslovakia, *Úřední list republiky Československé* (Amtsblatt) is available for the years 1927-47 and 1952-61. Beginning with 1962 this publication merged with *Sbírka zákonů,* mentioned under statutes. The Library has *Úřední věstník Československý,* 1939-45, issued by the exiled Czechoslovak government in London. Slovakia's *Úřadné noviny* are available for the years 1940-45.

LOCAL GOVERNMENTS. The Library has statistical and administrative material for the city of Prague for the years 1885-1937.

Almanach hlavního města Prahy from 1898 to 1935 contains information on political and local activities and lists of city representatives and officials. *Věstník hlavního města Prahy,* 1905-37, and *Administrační zprávy hlavního města Prahy,* 1885-1911, are other sources in the Library.

Statistical data and data on births and deaths can be found in *Wochenberichte ueber die Geburten und Sterbefaelle in Prague,* 1897-1924, and in *Statistická zpráva hlavního města Prahy,* 1873-1933, published by the Statistická Komise, Prague.

For the Moravian metropolis, Brno, a population count for the years 1343-65 can be found in a publication by Matice moravská, *Prameny dějin Moravských,* v. 5. An administrative and statistical source, *Gemeinde-Verwaltung und Gemeindestatistik der Landeshauptstadt Bruenn,* is available for the years 1897-1917.

Another statistical source for Brno and other cities is in the *Oesterreichisches Staedtebuch* Austria, 1887-1918.

Language

Representative works in the field of linguistics are in the Library under the subject headings: "Czech Language," "Slovak Language," and "Slavonic Languages," and include publications of the Linguistic Departments of the Czech and Slovak Academies of Science.

Literature

Czech literature in the vernacular is about 700 years old. Of the 14th-century writings, the Library has the Dalimil Chronicle, the legends of St. Catherine and St. Procopius, *Alexandreida,* and works by Emil Flaška z Pardubic, Tomáš ze Štítného, and Jan Hus. For the 15th century, there are the treatises on Christianity and social order by Petr Chelčický. Of the 16th-century writings, Jan Blahoslav's *Grammatika česká* and *Vady kazateluv* should be mentioned. Works by and about Jan Amos Comenius are well represented in the Library, as are the 18th-century writers Josef Dobrovský, Antonín Jaroslav Puchmajer, and Josef Jungmann.

Karel Jaromír Erben, Karel Hynek Mácha, and Božena Němcová are the Czech romanticists of the 19th century. Their individual and collected works, as well as some English translations, are available.

Svatopluk Čech, Jan Neruda, and Julius Zeyer are among the leading Czech authors of the 19th century well represented in the holdings. Jan Kollár's first edition of *Sláwa Bohyně* (1839) is in the Library. Works by the leading Slovak writers Pavel Josef Šafarik, Ľudovít Štúr, Ondřej Sládkovič, Svetozar Hurban Vajanský, Pavel Országh-Hviezdoslav, Josef Miloslav Hurban, and Jan Botto can be consulted.

Writings by the Czech realist Vladimír Vašek (Petr Bezruč) and the Czech symbolist Otakar Březina are on the Library's shelves. There are English translations as well as the original Czech versions of the works of Karel Čapek. Works by Janko Jesenský, Ján Smrek, Milo Urban, Laco Novomeský, Petr Karvaš, and Andrej Plávka represent 20th-century Slovak literature. Czech literary periodicals include *Host do Domu* (1960-), *Květy* (1879-1915), *Literární noviny* (1934-47) and *Lumír* (1873-1938); while the Slovak literary titles include *Slovenská literatura* (1958-) and *Slovenské pohľady* (1889-95, 1922-65).

Religion

The history of the religious movements is recorded in the general history of the country. Special subject headings for Reformation, Church and State, and Church History can be checked for additional works.

The Library has a *Catalogue of books* (at the Malin Library, Bethlehem, Pa.) *relating to or illustrating the history of the Unitas fratrum, or United brethren, as established in Bohemia and Moravia by followers of Jan Hus,* by William Gunn Malin. However, only a few items from this bibliography are in the Library. The first edition of the *Biblj České,* a version printed for the use of the Moravian Brethren at their private press in the Žerotín castle at Kralitz in 1579 is in the Library. This is the famous *Kralice Bible* which James Lenox, the founder of the Lenox Library, bought from the Duke of Sussex. Jan Hus' works, including his sermons printed in 1524, and other rare prints by and about Jan Hus are in the holdings.

Fine Arts

Books on art and architecture are located partly in the Slavonic Division and partly in the Art and Architecture Division. Both card catalogs include all titles. The holdings are truly comprehensive. Almost all the listings of books and periodicals in Horecky and Sturm are on the shelves and for those not in the Library many other titles can be substituted. The Prints Division has a selective representation of prints from the late 19th and for the 20th century by Czechoslovak artists. Included are works by Kupka, Mucha, F. Simon, and Svolinský.

Music

There are strong holdings in the field of ethnomusicology. The Library can show comprehensive holdings of the published scores of major Czechoslovak composers as well as critical works about them. Since so much of importance appears in the musical journals of the world, the strong holdings of the Research Libraries here give added importance. For example, there are runs of the *Allgemeines europäisches Journal* (1794-98) and the *Neue musikalische Rundschau* (1896-97), the former title being one of only two recorded sets in the United States. Current titles include *Hudební rozhledy* (1948-) and *Tempo* (1946-). Manuscripts of Czechoslovak composers in the Music Division include three letters and an article written by Antonín Dvořák.

The Library's Rodgers and Hammerstein Archives of Recorded Sound contain fairly extensive holdings of 78-rpm and LP phonorecords and catalogs for the Ultraphon, Supraphon, and Esta labels, as well as Gramophone Co., Ltd. recordings produced in Czechoslovakia from about 1930 onward. In addition there are fairly extensive holdings of recorded performances from the country as released on the major western European labels such as Angel, RCA, Columbia, and Gramophone Co., Ltd. and their affiliates from the early years of the century as well as the post-World War II years, including 78-rpm, 45-rpm, and LP-recordings.

Theater; Cinema; Dance

The holdings are comprehensive for all periods and cover not only the theater and cinema, but also radio and television, the circus, puppetry, and other aspects of the performing arts. The resources include extensive clipping files, theatrical photographs, movie stills, programs, etc., with emphasis on performances in the United States. Periodicals received include *Divadlo* (1953-), *Československá divadla* (1963-), *Československý loutkář* (1953-), and *Film a divadlo* (1963-). The Dance Collection has book material on folk and theatrical dance. Periodicals of the dance include *Taneční listy* (1934-) and *Terpsichora* (1930-47). There is also some material on specific dances, such as the Kalamaika, and on professional companies.

Political Science

There are about 300 cards under "Czechoslovakia—Politics" and a great many cards under "Kommunistická strana československá." The Library has two bibliographies in the field: *Novinky literatury. Společenské vědy. Řada III. Stát a právo,* 1964- and *Řada V. Politika,* 1965-.

The reader may also want to consult: *Čáda, František, Československá literatura právnická a státovědecká . . . v letech 1918-1925. Soupis knižní literatury a důležitých článků právnických a státovědeckých s doplňky za rok 1926* (Prague, 1926).

The following periodicals are also on the shelves: *Československý přehled* (1954-58); *Naše doba* (1945-47); *Nová mysl* (1947); *Novinářský sborník* (incompl.) (1947-); *Parlament* 1921/22-1928/29); *Stát a právo,* (1957-); *Zahraniční politika* (1922-39); *Pravda* (Bratislava) (on film, 1963-).

The Library does not collect books and commentaries in the field of law. Statutes and Codes, however, are in the collection as part of the official documents.

Economics

Apart from official sources, there are gaps in the collection in the field of economics and the social sciences in the Czech and Slovak languages before the early 1960s, when the Economics Division began systematic collecting. However, economic conditions in Czechoslovakia both before and after it became an independent country are well represented in languages other than Czech. The catalogs of the Economic and Public Affairs Division should be checked under the following headings: "Economic history-Bohemia," "Economic history-Austria," "Economic history-Czechoslovakia."

The Economic and Public Affairs Division collects comprehensively in the field of economic planning, with special emphasis on published plans on all levels. Books and periodicals in the field of statistics and demography are also collected comprehensively and the collection is very good, particularly for recent years. The Library's holdings of periodicals in the fields of economics, demography, and statistics, both official and unofficial, current and retrospective, are comprehensive.

Education

The Library collects only selectively in the field of education with emphasis on the history of education.

Works by and about Johann Amos Comenius are well represented. The Rare Book Division has Comenius's *Ianva avrea reserara qvatvor lingvarvm* (1640), *Janua linguarum* (1665), both printed by Elzevier in Amsterdam, and *Orbis sensualium pictus-Visible world* (1700) printed in London.

Reports from the Department of Education are available from 1919 through 1940: Czechoslovakia. Ministerstvo školství a národní osvěty *Věstník.*

Sociology

Sociology in Czechoslovakia has been short-lived and its development interrupted by political changes in the 1940s. The Library's holdings are thin in scope. Perhaps the only figure of note in the field for which the holdings are strong is Tomáš Garrigue Masaryk.

Leading serials in the Library are *Sociologická revue* (1930-39), *Sociologický časopis* (1965-), and the *Sborník prací* of the Philosophy Faculty of the University of Brno.

The Land and the People

For basic material on the land and the people, the bibliographies of Horecky and Sturm should be used, as most of the titles listed are in the resources of the Library. In addition the Library can meet most requirements for a study in depth.

The historical view of the Czechs under Austrian rule is well represented, and the Library is rich in publications for the years after World War I, and all points of view can be studied. Among other titles there are the publications of the Verein der Deutschen in Boehmen, and those of the Institut fuer Statistik der Minderheitsvoelker an der Universitaet Wien. The publications of the Sudeten Germans and Slovaks abroad after 1945 can be found in the card catalog under the headings: "Germans in Czechoslovakia," and "Slovakia-Politics." Strong holdings giving the Czech side of the story can be found in the card catalog under the headings "Nationalism and Nationality-Czechoslovakia;" "Germans in Bohemia," "Germans in Czechoslovakia." There is a very good collection of publications under the headings Ethnography, Folklore, Folk Art, and Folk Songs. Complete sets of *Český lid* (1891-date), also *Československá etnografie* (1953-62), *Narodopisný sborník československý,* and the *Časopis* of Brno. Moravské zemské museum are available. From the Slovenské národné múseum in Turčiansky Sv. Martin, the Library has the *Zbierky národopisného odboru* and a few volumes of its *Sborník. Slovenský národopis* is also available. For folklore of the Germans in Bohemia a good source is also available in the *Beitraege zur sudetendeutschen Volkskunde* under various titles. The card catalog under the headings "Czechoslovakia-Description and Travel," and "Czechoslovakia-Views" will furnish a good collection of books in that field and the reader will find most of the books mentioned in Horecky and Sturm. The microfiches of the Human Relations Area Files are located in the Economic and Public Affairs Division.

With some 12 atlases, 111 maps, and four sets, the Map Division holdings cover various aspects of Czechoslovakia's society from 1894 to 1967. Extensive set collections cover in some depth the geology, toponymy, and topography of the country. Two national atlases, one for 1929-35 and one for 1966 provide for comparative studies. Additional resources are available via numerous eastern European materials within the Division, along with the U.S. Army Topographic Command's 1:250,000 western European maps.

History

The selection policy for Czechoslovakian history is comprehensive. The leading historical periodical is the *Český časopis historický* now called the *Československý časopis historický*. The Library's holdings start with 1895, the year this periodical was founded by Jaroslav Goll. *Historica slovaca* (1940-) and *Historický časopis* (1953-) formerly *Historický sborník* (1950-52) are leading Slovak periodicals in the resources. Works published by the Československá akademie věd, Prague. Historický ústav are also available.

The entire range of Czechoslovak history can be studied in the Research Libraries from the works of the father of Czech history, František Palacký, particularly his *Dějiny národu českého,* called the national Czech bible. Other historians represented in the holdings include Jaroslav Goll, Josef Pekař, Robert J. Kerner, Zdeněk Tobolka, and Otakar Odložilík. For the formative years of the Czechoslovak Republic, established in 1918, and its development, works by Tomáš Masaryk are important (the Library's holdings of his works are strong). Edvard Beneš' works extend the development in Czechoslovakia through the Munich crises and World War II. The Munich period is also documented in the parliamentary debates of the House of Commons and House of Lords of Great Britain during that period, extensive holdings of which are in the Economic and Public

Affairs Division. Later history of Czechoslovakia is covered in works by K. G. Ronnefarth, Stephen Borsody, John Brown, Josef Josten, Hugh Seton-Watson, Paul Zinner, and others. United Nations documents can also be consulted in the Library.

For history devoted to Slovakia, works by František Bokeš, František Hrušovský, Václav Chaloupecký, Josef M. Kirschbaum, Josef Lettrich, Josef Mikuš, Daniel Rapant, Juraj Slavik, Branislav Varsik, and by the Slovenská akadémia vied, Bratislava, Historický ústav are important.

Historians of other nationalities contributed significantly to Czech history. Ernest Denis, a French historian, assisted by Palacký and Vrchlický, mastered the language of the Czech people and wrote about Czech history from the 15th through the 19th century; Robert Seton-Watson, a British historian, turned his attention to the *History of Czechs and Slovaks,* up to 1943. Sir Robert Hamilton Bruce Lockhart, a former British diplomat, covered the Communist takeover of 1948. Works by these historians are well represented in the Library.

Alice Plowitz and Milada Klátil
New York Public Library

East Germany

THE LIBRARY HAS collected extensively in both the book-trade and non-book-trade outputs of East Germany.

Reference Materials

East German reference works, together with Russian, West German, and other titles covering East Germany, can be described as almost complete within the framework of the Library's collecting practices. Bibliographies of books, periodicals, and government documents are virtually complete in the Research Libraries' collections. Worthy of special note are the six-volume (to date) *Ostdeutsche Bibliographie* of Herbert Marzian; the *Katalog des Schrifttums ueber den deutschen Osten,* 5 v. (1958-68), published by the Niedersaechsische Landesbibliothek in Hanover; the bibliographic works of Herbert Rister, Librarian of the Johann-Gottfried-Herder Institut in Marburg; and that Institute's *Zeitschrift fuer Ostforschung,* which is strongly bibliographical.

The Library's holdings vis-à-vis the Horecky list are comprehensive and almost complete, including handbooks, encyclopedias, statistical compilations, and documents.

The Library's holdings of periodicals are extensive and far-ranging. The collection also includes a union list of the periodical holdings of some 125 libraries in Thuringia, "Thüringer Zeitschriftenkatalog" in *Claves Jenenses,* v. 8, in 2 v. (1960); a subject index of 36 East German literary-political journals and two newspapers, *Neues Deutschland* and *Taeglische Rundschau* is provided in *Beitraege zur Literaturkunde; Bibliographie ausgewaehlter Zeitungs- und Zeitschriftenbeitraege,* (Leipzig, VEB Verlag fuer Buch und Bibliothekswesen, 1945/51-). The Library's holdings of this index, on microfilm, are not complete.

The Library also collects material on East Germany published elsewhere, e.g., *Ostdeutsche Wissenschaft; Jahrbuch des Ostdeutschen Kulturrates* (Munich, Oldenburg, 1954-).

No East German newspapers are being received currently by the Research Libraries; however, *Neues Deutschland* can be made available through the Center for Research Libraries, Chicago, on microfilm (1946-).

Biography

The Library's collections include many volumes of historical and current biographies published in East Germany. Many biographies which list contemporary East German personalities are limited to one professional group, while others are propagandistic in nature, for example, Friedrich Martin's *SED-Funktionaere in Offiziersuniform* . . . (Cologne, Markus-Verlag, 1962) and *Nationalpreistraeger* (Berlin, Aufbau, 1953).

Libraries, Press, and Publishing

The Library's holdings in these fields are strong. An important new work in this area is: Kurt Koszyk's *Presse der deutschen Sozialdemokratie, eine Bibliographie* (Hannover, Verlag fuer Literatur and Zeitgeschichte, 1966).

Intellectual and Cultural Life

This is another subject area in which the Library's holdings are generally quite strong, with the exception of education and pedagogy, in which fields the Research Libraries have not collected aggressively. The holdings of documents, bibliographies, and learned-society series in education are extensive enough to be regarded as selective.

The basic bibliographic guide in the field of philosophy is Hellmuth G. Buetow's *Entwicklung der dialektischen und historischen Materialismus in der Sowjet Zone,* 3 v. (Berlin, Freie Universitaet, 1960-63). The Library's collection of East German belles lettres is highly selective rather than comprehensive and is intended to represent the literature that will be useful to the critical literary scholar. Selection tools are relatively scarce. Some recently published works on East German literature in the holdings are: *Lexikon deutschspraechiger Schriftssteller . . .,* 2 v. (Leipzig, VEB Bibliographisches Institute, 1967-68) by Günter Albrecht, et al.; Konrad Franke's *Die Literatur der DDR* (Munich, Kindler, 1971); and Theodore Huebner's *The Literature of East Germany* (New York, Unger, 1970).

The other selections in the Horecky list are comprehensively represented, as are language studies, with such recent titles as Herbert Bartholome's *Bruder, Buerger, Freund und Genosse und andere Woerter der sozialistischen Terminologie* (Goeteborg, 1970, being Goeteborger Germanistische Forschungen, Nr. 11).

Religion treated as Socialism-and-Christianity, or Socialism-and-Religion, is patchily represented in The Research Libraries, as are Socialism-as-Aesthetics polemics. The Library practices some selective collecting in this area, especially when bibliographical in scope, for example: Hans Koch's *Marxismus und Aesthetik* (Berlin, Dietz, 1961); and the Deutsche Akademie der Kuenste's *Zur Tradition der sozialistischen Literatur in Deutschland* (Berlin, Aufbau, 1962).

Music, cinema, and the performing arts are widely collected and well represented. The basic Horecky list is supplemented by Heinz Kersten's *Filmwesen in SBZ Deutschlands,* 2d ed. (Bonn, Bundesministerium fuer Gesamtdeutschen Fragen, 1963) and *Deutsche Musikbibliographie* (Leipzig, Hofmeister, 1943-). The Music Division has extensive holdings of the published scores of the major composers of East Germany. The Rodgers and Hammerstein Archives of Recorded Sound contains a good representation of catalogs as well as some discs bearing the Eterna label of the post-World War II period. In addition there are fairly extensive holdings of recorded performances from East Germany as released on the major Western European labels, i.e., Angel, RCA, Columbia, Gramophone Co. Ltd., and their affiliates.

The State

Much has been collected at the Research Libraries on political conditions in postwar Germany, the occupation period, and reunification; the Library's subject entries on the German reunification question number some 200 cards, including an East German appraisal of reunification by Guenter

Heyden, *Grundwiderspruch in Deutschland,* 2d ed. (Berlin, Dietz, 1962). The East German Staatssekreteriat fuer Westdeutsche Fragen publishes widely on a variety of subjects and much of their book output is being collected by The Research Libraries. An example of its publications is Juergen Kuczynski's *So war es wirklich* (Berlin, 1969).

East German statutes are being kept at the Library, but law is not a strong subject area for Germany in the Library. The legal journals and the history of law are poorly represented. An exception is the active collecting in the field of criminology.

The political reports and periodicals of the official Communist Party of East Germany, the SED (Sozialistische Einheitspartei Deutschlands) are received and maintained in the Economics Division. The titles noted in Horecky are all available, many having been converted to microform. Hermann Weber's *Demokratischer Kommunismus?* (Hannover, J. H. W. Dietz, 1969) is an attempt to compare German and Russian experiments with Bolshevism and includes many bibliographical references.

Diplomacy and foreign relations are extensively represented in the Research Libraries.

The Economy

The East German economy has made great strides toward recovery from the ruin of the Second World War and much has been published to document these advances. The Library's holdings on the East German economy may be termed comprehensive for the researcher.

The Society

Most of the books on social conditions of East Germany come from West German or non-German publishers. The *SBZ-Archiv* (Bonn, Bundesministerium fuer Gesamtdeutsche Fragen, 1954-68), for example, concentrated on social aspects of East German life. East German authors, whose work and critical capacities are strong when examining society historically, publish relatively little that is critical of their own current social conditions. The Library's holdings reveal both sides of the picture. The public catalog lists, among others, six items on social policy planning, a dozen or so items on German social conditions since 1945 (those published in East Germany), an oddment on the position of women in the East German state, and Walter Ulbricht's announcement of a seven-year plan to improve the living conditions of the East German populace: *Siebenjahrplan des Friedens, des Wohlstands und des Gluecks des Volkes* (Berlin, Dietz, 1959).

The Land and the People

The Library's collections have always been strong in descriptive and travel materials from throughout the world. Given the long-established proclivities of German writers to assess—and publish—their impressions as travelers, and of the New York Public Library to collect them, the Research Library's holdings may be said to be comprehensive. The Library holds eight maps of East Germany and three atlases, dating from 1949.

The Research Library's holdings are strong in all aspects of geographic research and publishing. Maps, monographs, and periodicals in this field have been collected steadily over the years and this tradition has been extended to East Germany. All the selections in the Horecky list are available. Gazetteers published in East Germany are also available in the holdings.

The Library has comprehensive holdings with respect to the selections by Horecky. Occasional gaps in East German documents may be attributed in part to the Library's arrears in cataloging; accordingly the researcher should consult the Documents Librarian in the Economic and Public Affairs Division.

As regards displaced Germans, both during and after World War II, the Library has actively collected political-refugee materials, including bibliographies, monographs, newspapers, as well as old and current telephone directories.

History

Historiography and the writing of history have long held a high place in German scholarship. Since World War II, new directions have been apparent in East Germany, where historians have devoted special attention to economic developments since the 18th century. East German historians have documented well the rise of Socialism and the roles of German workers' movements and of German theorists of the 18th and 19th centuries. Worker's movements were strong in 19th- and early 20th-century German industrial history. Many of their newspapers and periodicals were collected by the Library (mostly now on microfilm), and are being reprinted in both Germanies. The public catalog's subject entries under Labor-Germany run to almost a tray of cards by themselves; thus, the holdings are to be considered comprehensive, with perhaps many unique items in New York City. Two general surveys of labor history are Juergen Kuczynski's *Die Geschichte der Lage der Arbeiter unter dem Kapitalismus* (Berlin, Akademie-Verlag, 1960-) and the SED's *Geschichte der deutschen Arbeiter Bewegung* (Autoren-kollektiv), 8 v. (Berlin, Dietz, 1966).

Historiography reflects a broadening interest in social history. For an annotated bibliographic account in English, see Arnold H. Price, "German History, a Review of Some Recent Publications," in the *Quarterly Journal of the Library of Congress* (April 1966).

The Library's collecting policies in the field of history are quite broad and the collections comprehensive. The field of local history is especially strong and emphasized at the Research Libraries; it is one of the Library's Farmington Plan commitments.

Among other significant titles the Library has the annual *Jahresbericht fuer deutsche Geschichte*, N.F., v. I-, 1949-, published by the Deutsche Akademie der Wissenschaften in Berlin. A relevant example of local history bibliography is: *Berlin Bibliographie bis 1960* (Berlin, de Gruyter, 1965). The state of historical research in East Germany is the subject of an essay by Albrecht Tim: *Das Fach Geschichte in Forschung und Lehre in der sowjetischen Besatzungszone seit 1945* (Bonn, Bundesministerium fuer Gesamtdeutsche Fragen, 1961). A fine example of the kind of historical research associated with German specialists is being published by the Saxon Academy of Sciences, viz., Martin Jahn's *Bibliographie zur Vor- und Fruehgeschichte Mitteldeutschlands* (Berlin, Aufbau, 1955-).

Zenos F. Booker
New York Public Library

Greece

General Bibliographies

The Library's holdings are fairly complete. They include the only hitherto published bibliography of bibliographies on Modern Greece, G. G. Phousaras', *Vivliographia tōn hellēnikon vivliographiōn 1791-1947* (Athens, 1961). The 11-volume monumental work of E. Legrand, *Bibliographie hellénique . . .*, which covers Greek books from the beginning of printing through 1790, remains the major achievement in general bibliography. The Library's holdings include several additions to Legrand which appeared in periodical literature, the most significant of which is the work by

G. G. Ladas and A. D. Chatzēdēnos, *Hellēnikē vivliographia, symvolē sto dekato ogdoo aiōna* (Athens, 1964).

Two bibliographies cover the years 1791 through 1799. The first (in mimeograph form) is that of V. E. Raste, *Hellēnikē vivliographia . . . 1791-1799* (Athens, 1969). The second and by far the most important contribution is by G. G. Ladas and A. D. Chatzēdēmos, *Hellēnikē vivliographia tōn etōn 1791-1795* (Athens, 1970).

The next major bibliography in the collection is that of D. S. Ghinēs (Nkinēs) and V. Mexas, *Hellēnikē vivliographia, 1800-1863 . . .,* 3 v. (Athens, 1939-57). Additions to the above, made by various scholars who researched both in Greece and abroad, were published under the title "Hellēnikē vivliographia 1800-1863. Prosthēkes," in *Ho Eranistēs* between 1963 and 1970. Two other works connected with the Ghinēs-Mexas bibliography are an alphabetical list of titles in the main bibliography and its additions: E. I. Moschonas, *Alphavētikē anagraphē tōn titlōn tēs vivliographias Nkinē-Mexa . . .* (Athens, 1968) and indices of publishers and places of publication: D. S. Pikramenou and I. Zampaphtē, *Hellēnikē vivliographia D. Nkinē-V. Mexa . . . Pinakes ekdotōn kai topōn ekdoseōs* (Athens, 1971).

The years between 1864 and 1907 remain unrecorded although there are projects under way to cover this period. The period 1907 through 1920 is covered by the bibliography of Nikolaos G. Politēs, *Hellēnikē vivliographia. Katalogos tōn en Helladi ē hypo Hellēnōn allachou ekdothentōn vivliōn apo tou etous 1907 . . .,* 3 v. (Athens, 1909-32). The next useful bibliographic tool in the collection is the *Bulletin analytique de bibliographie hellénique,* v. 6-, 1945- (Athens, 1947-).

Finally, M. Richard's *Répertoire des bibliothèques et des catalogues de manuscrits grecs,* 2d. ed. (Paris, 1958) and its *Supplément I, 1958-1963* (Paris, 1964) also belong in this category.

Library Catalogs

Here, one should single out the main library catalogs, published in book form, of important collections, such as the catalogs of the Greek Patriarchate of Alexandria compiled by Th. D. Moschonas, *Katalogoi,* 3 v. (Alexandria, 1945-47), which include both the manuscript and book holdings of the Library, and the *Catalogue* of the Gennadius Library at Athens, 7 v. (Boston, 1968). Other library catalogs to be cited here should include the catalog of *The Modern Greek collection in the Library of the University of Cincinnati . . .* (Athens, 1960); the catalog of the library of G. Zaviras in Budapest, edited by G. András, *Jeórjiosz Zavírasz budapesti könyvtárának . . .* (Budapest, 1935); the catalog of the library of Olympiotissa Monastery edited by A. Lazarou, *Katalogos entypōn vivliothēkes Olympiotissēs* (Athens, 1964); and the catalogs of the library of Kozani, N. P. Dialēs, *Katalogos entypōn . . .,* 2 v. (Thessalonike, 1948-64), which lists its Greek holdings from 1494 to 1912.

The Research Libraries have a number of catalogs put out periodically by the Library of Parliament (Vivliothēkē tēs Voulēs tōn Hellēnōn) the most important of which are cited here: *Katalogos Vivliothēkēs Voulēs* (Athens, 1900) listing Greek newspapers and periodicals in the library's collections; and *Katalogos tōn eisachthentōn syngrammatōn kai periodikōn kata to etos 1958-[1962],* 3 v. (Athens, 1959-63). One must point out the recently published catalog of incunabula, and 15th and 16th century imprints in the collections of the Library of Parliament, *Archetypa kai ekdoseis XV & XVI aiōnos,* 2 v. (Athens, 1971). The Library's holdings on the catalogs of the National Library of Greece (Ethnikē Vivliothēkē tēs Hellados) are less comprehensive.

Subject Bibliographies

The Library's collection is extensive and varied, including most of the important subject bibliographies; even theology, not ordinarily a strong subject in the Research Libraries, is fairly well covered.

Regional Bibliographies

The Library has most of the published bibliographies in this area, either by region, province, or island. Such works as P. P. Argenti, *Bibliography of Chios . . . to 1936* (Oxford, 1940); N. Maurēs, *Dōdekanēsiakē vivliographia* (Athens, 1965-) in progress; E. Legrand, *Bibliographie ionienne . . .*, 2 v. (Paris, 1910), and its addition by N. Pierris, *Bibliographie ionienne. Suppléments . . .* (Athens, 1966) form but a small sampling in this field.

Encyclopedias

The New York Public Library possesses the most important Greek encyclopedia in both the first and second editions, e.g., *Megalē hellēnikē enkyklopaideia,* 2d. ed., 24 v. (Athens, 1956-65), its *Symplērōma,* 4 v. (Athens, 1957-63), and K. Eleutheroudakēs, *Enkyklopaidikon lexikon,* 12 v. (Athens, 1927-31). However, the Library does not hold its second edition (also in 12 volumes, 1962-65), nor does it hold either of the two editions of the *Neōteron enkyklopaidikon lexikon,* 2d ed., 18 v. (Athens, 1957-62) or the most important encyclopedia of the Orthodox Church, *Thrēskeutikē kai ēthikē enkyklopaideia,* 12 v. (Athens, 1962-68).

Biographies

GENERAL BIOGRAPHIC DICTIONARIES. The New York Public Library has what is probably the first "Who's Who" ever published in Greece, *Poios einai poios eis tēn Hāllada,* 1st ed. (Athens, 1958). It also has the *Hellēnikon who's who, 1962* (Athens, 1962); however, it does not have the second edition of the above (Athens, 1965) or its supplement, *Hellēnikon who's who: kypros* (Athens, 1965).

A comparatively recent attempt to compile a comprehensive biographic dictionary is among the Library's holdings: *Mega hellēnikon viographikon lexikon,* dieuthynsis: Sp. A. and K. A. Vovolinēs, 5 v. (Athens, 1958-62).

Although the biographical dictionary by K. Sathas, *Neoellēnikē philologia: Viographiai tōn . . . 1453-1821* (Athens, 1868) is now over a century old, it remains the most important general biobibliographic dictionary of its type. The Library also has the additions and corrections to Sathas found in A. Dēmētrakopoulos, *Prosthēkai kai diorthōseis eis tēn Neoellēnikēn philologian . . .* (Leipzig, 1871, facsim. repr. 1965) and his *Epanorthōseis sphalmatōn . . . en tēi Neoellēnikē philologiai K. Satha* (Trieste, 1872, facsim. repr. 1965).

SPECIAL BIOGRAPHIC DICTIONARIES. Several specialized biographic works fall within this category, for example, A. N. Goudas, *Vioi parallēloi tōn epi tēs Anagennēseōs tēs Hellados diaprepsantōn andrōn,* 8 v. (Athens, 1872-76, facsim. repr. 1971); and A. Stasinopoulos, *Lexiko tēs Hellēnikēs Epanastaseōs tou 1821* (Athens, 1970-   ), still in progress. There are several regional biographic dictionaries in the Library's holdings which deserve mention here: Two of these deal with Epirus, P. Aravantinos, *Viographikē syllogē logiōn tēs Tourkokratias* (Ioannina, 1960) and *Ēpeirōtikon mnēmeion: Viographikē syllogē eklipontōn epiphanōn Ēpeirōtōn,* 2 v. (Ioannina, 1927-28).

Genealogy and Heraldry

Very little has been published in these fields. The Library has the work of E. Rizos Rangabé, *Livre d'or de la noblesse ionienne,* 3 v. (Athens, 1925-27); and Ph. P. Argenti, *Libro d'oro de la noblesse de Chio,* 2 v. (London, 1955). One can also consult G. Gerola, "Gli stemmi cretesi dell' Università di Padova," *Atti del R. Istituto veneto discienze, lettere ed arti,* v. 88, 1928-29: 239-78.

Libraries and Archives

The most useful and up-to-date guide to libraries and archives in Greece is that of Sp. Kokkinēs, *Vivliothēkes kai archeia stēn Hellada* (Athens, 1970). With regard to archives alone one should consult such articles as Peter Topping, "The Public Archives of Greece," in the *American Archivist*, v. 15, 1952:249-57; N. V. Tōmadakēs, "Peri archeiōn en Helladi kai tēs archeiakēs hypēresias," *Deltion tēs Historikēs kai Ethnologikēs Hetaireias tēs Hellados*, v. 11, 1956:1-42; and M. Manousakas, "Ekthesis peri tōn en Kephallēnia kai Zakynthō vivliothēkōn kai archeiōn . . .," *ibid.*, v. 11, 1956:43-58. For other regional archives see I. K. Vasdravellēs, *Historika archeia Makedonias*, 3 v. (Thessalonike, 1952-55), and E. Kourilas, "Ta hagioreitika archeia kai ho katalogos tou Porphyreiou Ouspenskē," *Epetēris Hetaireias Vyzantinōn Spoudōn*, v. 7, 1930:180-222 and v. 8, 1931:66-109.

For a survey of the published documents and bibliographies of manuscripts of the Athos monasteries see M. Manousakas, "Hellēnika cheirographa kai engrapha tou Hagiou Orous: vivliographia," *Epetēris Hetaireias Vyzantinōn Spoudōn*, v. 32, 1963:377-419.

Serials

The Research Libraries have a good representation of works published on the history and bibliography of the Greek press. Some key works can be cited here: A. Daskalakēs, *La presse: néohellénique . . . Journaux et journalistes . . .* (Paris, 1930); K. Mager, *Historia tou hellenikou typou*, 3 v. (Athens, 1957-60); D. Nkinēs, *Katalogos hellēnikōn ephēmeridōn kai periodikōn, 1811-1863* (Athens, 1967); Ph. Mpoumpoulidēs, *Symvolē eis tēn Heptanēsiakēn vivliographian: periodika kai ephēmerides Zakynthou* (Athens, 1955); D. Margarēs, *Ta palia periodika, hē historia tous kai hē epochē tous* (Athens, 1954); A. Koumarianou, *Ho typos ston Agōna, 1821-1827*, 3 v. (Athens, 1971), and A. Gavatha-Panagiōtopoulou, *Ta hellēnika proepanastatika periodika . . .* (Athens, 1971).

The Library currently receives some 75 journals covering archeology, classics, and Byzantine and Modern Greek studies. Efforts are constantly being made to fill the gaps. Aside from the various journals already cited elsewhere one should single out a few older sets such as *Hermēs ho Logios* (Vienna, 1811-21; the Library has only the volume for 1819); *Iōnios Anthologia* (Kerkyra, 1834-35; only the volume for 1834); *Ho Astēr tēs Anatolēs*, etos 13-17 (Athens, 1870-74); *Hellēnomnēmon* (Athens, 1843-53); *Byrōn* (Athens, 1874-79); Hellēnikos Philologikos Syllogos Kōnstantinoupoleōs. *Syngramma periodikon* (Konstantinoupolis, 1863-1910); *Parnassos* (Athens, 1877-95).

The Library receives a great many regional journals: *Archeion Pontou; Dōdekanēsiakon Archeion; Mikrasiatika Chronika; Krētika Chronika; Kerkyraika Chronika; Kypriakai Spoudai; Ēpeirōtikē Hestia,* and many others.

Monographs and serials of learned societies are also acquired in good number. They include the publications of the various archives of Akadēmia Athēnōn, those of the Hetaireia Makedonikōn Spoudōn, the Historikē kai Ethnologikē Hetaireia tēs Hellados, Ethnikon Hidryma Ereunōn, as well as the publications of the Universities of Athens and Salonika.

Public Documents

The New York Public Library holdings of government documents are not comprehensive and there are many gaps in the series the Library does receive.

In statistics the Library has *Mēniaion statistikon deltion*, 12 v. (Jan. 1929-May 1940), which ceased publication with the 1943/44 volume and resumed publication in 1956. The Library receives it on a more or less continuous basis as it does the *Statistikē epetēris tēs Hellados,* v. 1- (1954-), which superseded the *Annuaire statistique de la Grèce,* 10 v. (1930-39) that was suspended between 1940 and 1953.

The Library also has the *Bulletin mensuel du commerce spécial de la Grèce avec les pays étrangers* from 1898 to date with gaps. Statistics on foreign trade with Greece can also be obtained from such sources as France. Ministère du Commerce. *Annales du commerce extérieur. Faits commerciaux. Grèce* (1847-   ) and Great Britain. Foreign Office. Diplomatic and Consular Reports. *Finances of Greece* (1887-   ).

Statistics on education (elementary and higher) are very spotty. The Library has some items as *Pinakes synkritikoi kai statistikoi tēs stoicheiōdous ekpaidauseōs en tō kratei apo tou etous 1894 mechri tou etous 1897* and *Statistique de l'enseignement pendant l'année scolaire* (1926-60 with many gaps). The same holds true for population statistics such as the *Statistikē tēs physikēs kinēseōs tou plēthysmou tēs Hellados* (1884-1965) and for population censuses.

The Library has the official gazette of the Government of Greece, the *Ephēmeris tēs Kyvernēseos tēs Hellados,* beginning with 1899, but without the indices, *Heuretērion nomōn kai diatagmatōn 1833-1924* (Athens, 1924) compiled by A. Malagardēs. For the holdings of the proceedings of Parliament (Voulē) it has the *Ephēmeris tōn syzētēseōn tēs Voulēs,* 38 v. (1865-1936) and the *Praktika tōn synedriaseōn tēs Voulēs kai Gerousias* (1929-33).

Among publications of the various constitutional assemblies, the Library has the Greek text and English translation of the constitution of Epidaurus of 1822 in *Provisional constitution of Greece translated from the second edition of Corinth . . .* (London, 1822). This item is very rare today (perhaps the only copy in the United States). Of other documents on the constitutional assemblies which met between 1822 and 1950 the Library has facsimile reproductions of the proceedings of the original editions of the constitutions of 1822, 1823, and 1827. The text of the Athens constitutional assembly of 1843-44 is recorded in A. C. Heinze, *Die hellenische National-congress zu Athen in den Jahren 1843 und 1844 nach der Originalausgabe der Congressverhandlungen . . .* (Leipzig, 1845). The Library possesses the proceedings of the Syneleusis of 1862-64 in the *Episēmos ephēmeris tēs Syneleuseōs . . . ,* 6 v. (Athens, 1863-64) with supplements and its *Praktika tōn synedriaseōn tēs en Athēnais B' tōn Hellēnōn Syneleuseōs* (Athens, 1864). The Library has v. five only. For the Syntaktikē Syneleusis of 1920-22, see *Ephēmeris tōn syzētēseōn tēs 3es en Athēnais . . . ,* 3 v. (Athens, 1932-33). For the Syntaktikē Syneleusis of 1924-25, see *Ephēmeris tōn syzētēseōn tes 4es . . .* 5 v. (Athens, 1924-27), and its *Praktika tōn synedriaseōn . . . ,* 5 v. (Athens, 1924-26). For the Ethnikē Syneleusis of 1935, see *Episēma praktika tōn synedriaseōn tēs Ethnikēs Syneleuseōs,* 1 v. (Athens, 1935).

The only official text of the various constitutions of Greece held by the Library is the French edition of the constitution of 1927. However, the Library does have two early local constitutions of the Ionian Islands, *Constituzione della Republica Settinsulare* (Corfù, 1803) and *Le tre costituzioni (1800, 1803, 1817) delle sette isole Jonie . . .* Corfù, 1849).

Language

The Library's collection of grammars and dictionaries of Modern Greek is very rich, including almost everything mentioned in Horecky on grammars and syntax. Some early and little known grammars in the collection are singled out here: J. A. E. Schmidt, *Neugriechische Sprachlehre* (Leipzig, 1808); H. Robertson, *A concise grammar of the modern Greek language* (London, 1818); D. Alexandridēs, *Grammatikē graikiko-tourkikē* (Vienna, 1812), and the first grammars of modern Greek published in the United States (the first in the katharevousa, the other in the romaic or dhimotikē): A. Negris, *Grammar of the modern Greek language* (Boston, 1828) and E. A. Sophocles, *A romaic grammar* (Hartford, 1842).

The Library has all but one of the dictionaries mentioned in Horecky; in addition, some earlier basic dictionaries should be noted, namely those of Alexis de Sommevoire, *Tesoro della lingua greca* . . . , 2 v. (Paris, 1709); D. Vyzantios Skarlatos, *Lexikon tēs kath' hēmas hellēnikēs dialektou* (Athens, 1835); K. Weigel, *Lexikon haploromaikon* . . . (Leipzig, 1796); F. D. Dehèque, *Dictionnaire grec moderne-français* (Paris, 1825); G. Ventotēs, *Lexikon tēs grai-kikēs* . . . (Venice, 1816 and 1820); I. Lowndes, *A modern Greek and English lexicon* (Corfù, 1837); D. Alexandridēs, *Lexikon procheiron tēs graikikēs* . . . (Vienna, 1812). Several of these are quite rare today.

Surveys of the language problem and the polemics it invoked are not as well represented, but the Library does have the works of M. Triantaphyllidēs, G. Psycharēs, B. Vlastos, E. Giannidēs, D. Glēnos, and the older works of K. Sathas, A. Koraēs, and G. Chatzidakēs, among others.

The Library has a good sampling of works on the various dialects of Modern Greek as well as assorted other special studies and books, some of which are rare today. An example is the rare little Greek primer compiled by S. S. Wilson and published by the London Missionary Society at Malta: *The Anglo-Greek primer, or First step to a practical knowledge of the English and Greek languages* (Malta, 1829).

Journals which are predominantly linguistic are *Athēna* (Athens, 1889-); *Lexikographikon deltion Akadēmias Athēnōn* (Athens, 1939-); and *Lexikographikon archeion tēs mesēs kai neas hellēnikēs* (Athens, 1915-23).

Literature

Medieval and modern Greek literature are collected comprehensively. The Library has many of the complete works, poetical works, or other collected works of the major Greek literary figures. It can also boast a very good collection of the histories of modern Greek literature. In addition to the works cited in Horecky, one may add such works as D. C. Hesseling, *Histoire de la littérature grecque moderne* (Paris, 1924); A. Rizos Rankavēs, *Histoire littéraire de la Grèce moderne* (Paris, 1877); I. Rizos Neroulos, *Cours de la littérature grecque moderne* (Geneva, 1828); A. Kampanēs, *Historia tēs neas hellēnikēs logotechnias* (Athens, 1948), G. Kordatos, *Historia tēs neoellēnikēs logotechnias,* 2 v. (Athens, 1962); M. Vitti, *Storia della letteratura neogreca* (Turin, 1971); and many others. The collection includes a rare item, the first history of modern Greek literature written in English, A. Negris' *An outline of the literary history of modern Greece* (Edinburgh, 1833).

The collection has strong holdings in literary studies of special periods or areas such as the works of M. Manousakas and St. Alexiou on the literature of Crete, of G. Zōras and Ph. Mpoum-poulidēs on the literature of the Ionian Islands, of I. M. Chatzēphōtēs on the modern Greek culture of Alexandria. It also has a strong collection of studies devoted to special genres such as Greek drama and theater, poetry, and prose. The same holds true for anthologies of modern Greek literature. These include both general anthologies and anthologies restricted by genre, area, or special topic. Some of the older anthologies of medieval and modern Greek literature in the collection are the complete series of E. Legrand, *Collection de monuments pour servir à l'étude de la langue néo-hellénique,* 27 v. (Paris, 1870-1907) and his *Bibliothèque grecque vulgaire,* 10 v. (Paris, 1880-1913); K. Sathas, *Krētikon theatron* (Venice, 1879) and his *Mesaiōnikē vivliothēkē,* 7 v. (Venice, 1872-94); W. Wagner, *Carmina graeca medii aevi* (Leipzig, 1874) and his *Alpha-vētos tēs agapēs* (Leipzig, 1879). The Library also has the 48 volumes of the *Vasikē vivliothēkē* (Athens, 1952-58). The Library holds many first editions and other fine editions of individual authors, among which the first two editions of Andreas Kalvos, *Hē lyra. Ōdai* (Geneva, 1824) and his *La lyre patriotique de la Grèce* (Paris, 1824) are very rare.

The Library's holdings are not strong on bibliographies of single literary figures. For example, the Library has only four of the 25 bibliographies of prominent Greek writers by G. K. Katsimpalēs.

The collections include many journals devoted primarily to literature: *Nea Hestia* (Athens, 1934-); *Kainouria epochē* (Athens, 1956-65); *Diagōneios* (Thessalonike, 1958-); *Nea Poreia* (Thessalonike, 1955-); *Kritika phylla* (Athens, 1971-); *Hellēnikē dēmiourgia* (Athens, 1948-55); *Iōnios anthologia* (Zakynthos, 1927-41); *Philologikē prōtochronia* (Athens, 1943-); *The Charioteer* (New York, 1960-), *Kochlias* (Thessalonike, 1946-48), as well as journals devoted to Greek drama and the theater.

Folklore

The general works on folklore available include N. Politēs, *Meletai peri tou viou kai tēs glossēs tou Hellenkou laou,* 6 v. (Athens, 1965) and his *Neoellēnikē mythologia,* 2 v. (Athens, 1871-74); all but two of the items cited in Horecky (Politēs and Rōmaios), and many more.

The Library has a very good representation of Greek folklore by region or island such as the works of G. Georgeakis and L. Pineau, *Le folklore de Lesbos* (Paris, 1894); G. F. Abbott, *Macedonian Folklore* (Cambridge, 1903); Ph. Argenti, *The Folklore of Chios,* 2 v. (Cambridge, 1949); G. Papacharalampous, *Kypriaka ēthē kai ethima* (Leukosia, 1965); K. Rōmaios, *Cultes populaires de la Thrace* (Athens, 1949); G. Rēgas, *Skiathou laïkos politismos,* 4 v. (Thessalonike, 958-70), to cite but a few. This is also true of works by type such as folktales, linguistic folklore, proverbs, folk narrative, myth, etc.

The Research Libraries have particularly rich collections of folk songs and ballads, including almost all the early basic pioneer collections and a good many others. A small sampling is given here: Cl. Fauriel, *Chants populaires de la Grèce moderne,* 2 v. (Paris, 1824-25) and its German and English adaptations: *Neugriechische Volkslieder,* 2 v. (Leipzig, 1825); *Songs of modern Greece* (London, 1825); A. Passow, *Popularia carmina Graeciae recentioris* (Leipzig, 1860).; Th. Kind, *Anthologie neugriechischen Volkslieder* (Leipzig, 1861); N. Politēs, *Eklogai apo ta tragoudia tou Hellēnikou laou* (Athens, 1932); G. Apostolakēs, *Ta dēmotika tragoudia* (Athens, 1929), and numerous other such collections. It is also rich in collections of ballads and songs by region particularly the Dodecanese, Crete, Macedonia, Epirus, and Mani.

History of Thought and Culture

The Library has all the books and journals cited in Horecky under the subheading "Byzantium and Medieval Greece," and has a richer and more varied collection than the one mentioned in Horecky under "Modern Greece." Materials on the life and achievements of the Greeks of the Diaspora had a great influence on the shaping of the intellectual and cultural life of the Greeks at home during the Turkish Occupation. Works dealing with the Greeks of Venice and Italy are: A. Firmin-Didot, *Alde Manuce et l'hellénisme à Venise* (Paris, 1875); D. J. Geanakoplos, *Greek Scholars in Venice* (Cambridge, Mass., 1962); I. Veloudēs, *Hellēnōn Orthodoxōn apoikia en Venetia* (Athens, 1964); A. P. Stergellēs, *Ta dēmosieumata tōn Hellenon . . . Panepistēmiou tēs Padovas . . .* (Athens, 1970); Z. N. Tsirpanlēs, *Hoi Makedones spoudastes tou Hellēnikou Kollegiou Rōmēs . . .* (Thessalonike, 1971); J. Irmscher and M. Mineemi, *Ho Hellēnismos eis to exōterikon* (Berlin, 1968).

The Greek community of Vienna is discussed in such works as A. Pallatidēs, *Hypomnēma historikon . . . tou en Viennēi Hellēnikou Synoikismou* (Athens, 1965); P. Enepekides, *Symvolē eis tēn mystikēn pneumatikēn . . . tōn Hellēnōn tēs Viennēs . . .* (Berlin, 1960); and E. Turczynski, *Die deutsch-griechischen Kulturbeziehungen . . .* (Munich, 1959).

Books on the Greek Enlightenment include the works of K. Dēmaras, *La Grèce au temps des Lumières* (Geneva, 1969); A. Papaderos, *Metakenōsis. Griechenlands Kulturelle Heraus-forderung durch d. Aufklärung* . . . (Meisenheim, 1970); G. P. Henderson, *The Revival of Greek Thought 1620-1820* (Albany, 1970).

Journals which emphasize the study of modern Greek intellectual history are *Ho Eranistēs* (Athens, 1963-), a journal devoted to the Greek Enlightenment, and *Thēsaurismata* (Venice, 1962-), published by the Hellēnikon Institouton Vyzantinōn kai Metavyzantinōn Spoudōn in Venice, which is devoted to the Greeks of the Diaspora and especially of those active in Venice and elsewhere in Italy.

Art and Architecture

The holdings are very strong in Byzantine art but not as strong in modern Greek art and artists, and folk art. There is the collection of Greek national costumes published by the Benaki Museum and some of the works of A. Chatzēmichalē. Two art periodicals in the holdings are *Nees morphes* (1957-62) and *Zygos* (1959-). Modern Greek architecture is not particularly well represented. The writings of Kōnstantinos A. Doxiadēs appear mostly in English. The Library currently receives the periodical *Oikistikē* (1962-) published by the Doxiadis Institute and two other Greek architectural periodicals: *Architektonika themata* (1967-) and *Architektonikē* (1957-).

Music

The Library receives the published scores of such modern Greek composers as Manolis Kalomiris, Spiro Samara, and Iannis Xenakis. Modern Greek folk songs are quite well represented, with over 60 titles from 1826 to the present. The Rogers and Hammerstein Archives of Recorded Sound has several catalogs and discs of both pre- and post-World War II Greece largely comprising folk music.

Dance and Theater

Most of the books in the Dance Collection relate to the ancient and the "revived" Greek dance. There are some clippings and photographs on the Greek dance as well as a tape on theatrical dance and three films on folk and two on theatrical dancing. In addition, the Collection has materials on specific Greek dances such as the Kalamatianos and on Greek professional dance companies. The Theater Collection holdings cover all aspects of the performing arts as radio, television, motion pictures but excluding music and the dance. These holdings are representative for the Greek performing arts. The generally extensive holdings of clippings, programs, theatrical photographs, movie stills, etc., are related mostly to United States performances. Of the journals devoted to Greek drama and the theater, the Library has *Thespis* (Athens, 1964-65); *Theatro* (Athens, 1957-), an annual; *Theatro* (Athens, 1961-67); and *Theatrika* (Athens, 1971-).

The State; the Economy; the Society

The Library has comprehensive holdings in this field and very strong holdings in sociology, including the publications of the Kentron Koinōnikōn Epistēmōn and virtually all of the titles mentioned in Horecky. In economics, the holdings are comprehensive, with almost all the titles noted in Horecky available. In addition, there are all the series published by various agencies in Greece in this field. Some of these are: the Kentron Oikonomikōn Ereunōn (Center for Planning and Economic Research); the publications of the Athens Center for Economic Research, and the

National Center for Economic Research. The Library also has a series of pre-World War II bibliographies on the Greek economy entitled *Oikonomikē vivliographia tēs Hellados* (Athens, 1935-38) and receives all monographs on economics and books on economic development published by such government agencies as the Ministry of Coordination (Hypourgeion Syntonismou). Other titles of interest are the *Quarterly Review* (1957-) of the National Bank of Greece and the *Daily Official List* of the Athens stock exchange (current issues only). The Economic and Public Affairs Division has very strong representations of statistical and demographic materials from before and after World War II.

General and Descriptive Works

The most important aspect of the travel literature on Greece, the one which can offer a great deal of research material to many disciplines, is the collection of travel accounts written between the fall of Constantinople (1453) and the Greek Revolution (1821). Outside these travel accounts there are very few sources of information about the education, customs, daily, and intellectual life of the Greek people. Much information in these areas and in many others (such as information on population, toponymics, etc.) can be provided by a systematic study of the early travel literature on Greece.

The Library has a good collection of bibliographical aids available in this area, some of which are cited below: S. M. Weber, *Voyages and Travels in the Near East* . . . (Princeton, 1952) and his *Voyages and Travels in Greece . . . to the Year 1801* (Princeton, 1953); J. M. Paton, *Chapters on Medieval and Renaissance Visitors to Greek Lands* (Princeton, 1951); E. Malakis, *French Travellers in Greece 1770-1820* . . . (Philadelphia, 1925); P. P. Morphopoulos, *L'image de la Grèce chez les voyageurs français du xve au début du xxiiie siècle* (Baltimore, 1947), and B. M. Silvestro, *Western European Travellers to Mainland Greece 1700-1800* (Madison, Wis., 1959).

The strength of the Library's collection in this field lies in its numerous early books of travel literature on Greece. Besides the works mentioned in Horecky, the Library collection includes 16th-, 17th-, and 18th-century works, as well as numerous later ones, e.g., P. Belon, *Les observations de plusieurs singularitez et choses mémorables trouvées en Grèce* . . . (Paris, 1553, and Anvers, 1555); G. Wheler, *A journey into Greece* . . . (London, 1682); J. Spon, *Viaggi . . . per la Dalmazia, Grecia* . . . (Bologna, 1688) and his *Italiänische, dalmatische, griechische . . . Reise* . . . (Nürnberg, 1690); M. V. Coronelli, *Mémoires historiques et géographiques . . . de la Morée* . . . (Amsterdam, 1688); his *Description géographique et historique de la Morée* . . . (Paris, 1687) and his *Isola di Rodi* (Venice, 1695); O. Dapper, *Naukeurige beschrywing in de Archipel* . . . (Amsterdam, 1688); P. Lucas, *Voyage . . . dans la Grèce* . . . (Paris, 1712); Fr. Piacenza, *L' Egeo redivido* . . . (Modena, 1688); Cl. 'Et. Savary, *Letters on Greece* . . . (London, 1788); A. L. Castellan, *Lettres sur la Morée et les îles de Cérigo, Hydra et Zante* (Paris, 1808); J. Stuart and N. Revett, *The antiquities of Athens*, 5 v. (London, 1762); Wm. Gell, *The itinerary of Greece* . . . (London, 1810); M.-G. F. A. Choiseul-Gouffier, *Voyage pittoresque de la Grèce* (Paris, 1780-1826).

History

The most important Greek historian of the past century was K. Paparrēgopoulos, who wrote the monumental *Historia tou Hellēnikou Ethnous*. The Library has the fifth edition of this work (Athens, 1925) in 5 v., a reissue of the first edition of 1853 with commentary by K. Dēmaras in 1970, and a French abridged edition *Histoire de la civilisation hellénique* (Paris, 1878). Other Greek historians represented are P. Karolidēs, *Historia tēs Hellados apo tēs hypo tōn Othomanōn*

Halōseōs . . . (Athens, 1925); E. K. Kyriakidēs, *Historia tou synchronou Hellēnismou* . . . *1832-1892,* 2 v. (Athens, 1892). The most important history of Greece written by a Greek scholar to date is the work now in progress by A. Vakalopoulos, *Historia tou Neou Hellēnismou* (Thessalonike, 1961-). Three volumes have appeared, covering the late Byzantine and Ottoman periods up to 1669. (v. 1 of this work has appeared in an English translation, *Origins of the Greek Nation* . . . New Brunswick, 1970.) This work is accompanied by a supplementary volume of source materials entitled *Pēges tēs historias tou Neou Hellēnismou* (Thessalonike, 1965). The Library lacks G. Kordatos, *Historia tēs Neoterēs Hellados,* 5 v. (Athens, 1957-58), which gives the Marxist interpretation of Modern Greek history. The Library has all the important histories on Modern Greece written by foreign scholars and cited in Horecky. The same holds true of political and diplomatic histories of Greece. To the list in Horecky add the work of A. F. Frangoulis, *La Grèce, son statut international, son histoire diplomatique,* 2 v. (Paris, 1954).

The period of the Turkish Occupation (1453-1821) is well represented in the Library's holdings, with a few notable exceptions, in particular D. Zakythēnos, *Hē Tourkokratia* (Athens, 1957). Although the Library lacks some items on the Philikē Hetairia (the secret society founded in 1814 which played an important role in preparing the Greek Revolution), it has all but two of the items on the Hetairia mentioned in Horecky, as well as other works not mentioned in Horecky, such as A. Xodilos, *Hē Hetairia tōn Philikōn* . . . (Athens, 1964).

The Library has all but five of the items mentioned in Horecky on the Greek Revolution, as well as other works. It also has a good sampling of the memoirs of those who took part in the war, and many works by foreign observers who wrote about it. The same holds true of works on Philhellenism, especially American, English, and French. The Library has a good many pamphlets consisting of appeals, collections, creation of committees to aid the Greek cause, etc.

The collection has a good representation of books covering later history. All but one or two of the books mentioned in Horecky are to be found in the Library, but the Library has many not cited there. It also has a good sampling of regional histories, by province, island, or other geographical subdivision as well as books and reports on the wars which took place after the Greek Revolution such as the various Cretan uprisings, the Greco-Turkish War of 1897, the Balkan Wars, the disputes over Northern Epirus, Macedonia, the Asia Minor campaign of 1922, Greece's involvement in the two World Wars, the German Occupation, the Civil War, the Cyprus question, down to the present time.

Journals devoted almost exclusively to history are *Neos Hellēnomnēmōn,* v. 1-21 (Athens, 1904-27) and Index (1930). *Historikē kai Ethnologikē* Hetaireia tēs Hellados. *Deltion.* (1883-), and *Mnemosynē.* (Athens, 1967-).

Evro Layton
Modern Greek Studies Association
Cooperative Library Project
Setauket, N.Y.

Hungary

General Bibliographies

The Hungarian bibliography collection of the New York Public Library is one of its extensive bibliography collections. The Library has the current national bibliography and its companion series for Hungarian periodical articles, as well as the two series of annual volumes: *Magyar Könyvészet*

[Hungarian Bibliography], 1961-, and the *Általános Könyvjegyzék* [General Booklist], 1950/51-55, 1966-.

Retrospectively, the earliest period (1473-1711) is covered by Károly Szabó's *Régi magyar könyvtár,* and by the addenda published since 1959 in the yearbook of the National Széchényi Library. The *Magyar Könyvészet* lists books from 1712 to 1910, and again from 1936 to 1960. The aforementioned annual cumulation of the national bibliography covers the period from 1961. Gaps are taken care of in part by a 1925 *List of All Hungarian Books in Trade,* and more importantly, by the monthly *Magyar Könyvészet,* which was included as a monthly supplement to *Corvina,* the bulletin of the National Association of Hungarian Publishers and Bookdealers, from 1898 to 1940. There is an earlier *Magyar Nemzeti Bibliográfia* (Ungarische National-Bibliographie), which covers October 1941 to March 1944.

Another interesting aspect of Hungarian bibliography is the listing of foreign language publications dealing with Hungary. In German there are four studies, two by Károly Kertbeny, one by Count Sándor Apponyi, and one by the Berlin University's Ungarisches Institut. Together they cover the period from 1454 to 1921. In French there is Ignác Kont's *Bibliographie française de la Hongrie, 1521-1910,* and in Italian, Klára Zolnai's *Magyarországi olasz nyomtatványok (1699-1918) (Bibliografia della letteratura italiana d'Ungheria).*

There is a two-volume work listing the publications of the Hungarian Academy of Sciences from 1830 to 1910. For the original library of Count Széchényi, the basis of the National Széché nyi Library, the Library has the *Catalogus Bibliothecae Hungaricae* (Sopron, 1799-1807). Another unique item is an illustrated history of the University of Budapest press, *A királyi magyar egyetemi nyomda története, 1577-1927.*

Another item of interest is a 1958 publication of the Hungarian Parliamentary Library, *A Magyar Tanácsköztársaság kiadványai és az első kommunista kiadványok* (ed. György Vértes), which lists publications during the short-lived Communist government of Béla Kún in 1919, and earlier Hungarian Communist Party publications.

General guides to sources in Hungarian studies are also available. An equivalent to the American librarians' Winchell is János Szentmihályi and Miklós Vértesy's *Útmutató a tudományos munka magyar és nemzetközi irodalmához, A Guide to Hungarian and Foreign Reference Books* (1963). In 1943 the *Hungarian Quarterly* published a helpful *Companion to Hungarian Studies,* comprising introductory essays and bibliographies. Since 1956, there has been a Hungarian bibliography of bibliographies, the *Magyar bibliográfiák bibliográfiája.*

Some excellent bibliographic guides are also available in specific subject fields. There is the exceptionally thorough *Bibliography of Hungarian Dictionaries, 1410-1963* by I. L. Halasz de Beky (1966) and equally thorough studies by Albert Tezla, *An Introductory Bibliography to the Study of Hungarian Literature* (1964) and its companion volume *Hungarian Authors* (1970). These volumes serve as union lists for all references cited, which include general reference sources as well as specifically literary citations.

Encyclopedias and Dictionaries

The holdings of Hungarian dictionaries are extensive. Of particular interest is the large collection of bilingual dictionaries, from Hungarian into some 15 languages, including the languages of countries of this survey. Biographic dictionaries are well represented.

Serials

NEWSPAPERS.   The Library's holdings of Hungarian newspapers are extremely poor, for example, no newspapers are currently received from Hungary. The Library's holdings of older newspapers are very incomplete. The one 19th-century paper is *A Hon* (Pest, 1866-67). Prior to and including World War II there are *Az Est* (1914-24), *Budapesti Hirlap* (1926-39), *Pester Lloyd* (1935-41), *Népszava* (1938-41), and *Magyarország* (1943-44). This weakness is offset somewhat by two microfilm collections of sample Hungarian newspapers, one of issues for 1946, and the other of miscellaneous issues of newspapers published in Budapest and other Hungarian cities during the 1956 revolution, from October 24 through December 31. There are also two extensive summaries of the Hungarian press: one by the French Ministère des Affaires étrangères, *Bulletin périodique de la presse hongroise* (March 10, 1917-October 1933), and the other by the British Legation in Hungary, *Hungarian Press Summary* (July 1, 1958-April 30, 1968).

PERIODICALS.   The holdings of general periodicals from and about Hungary are much more satisfactory. Of the six general periodicals received currently the Library has complete runs of *Books from Hungary, Hungarian Review,* which supersedes the *Hungarian Bulletin, Magyarországi Hirek* [Hungarian News], and the *New Hungarian Quarterly.* The Library has all but the first two volumes of *Könyvtáros* and the first 12 volumes of *Magyar Könyvszemle* [Hungarian Book Review], one of the oldest library periodicals in the world.

Of the older general periodicals perhaps the most interesting is a rare copy of *Hazánk* (Pest, 1858-60), an illustrated collection of articles of primarily historical interest. There are complete runs of the *Hungarian Quarterly,* the *Revue de Hongrie,* the *Ural-altaische Jahrbuecher* and its predecessor, the *Ungarische Jahrbuecher.* The Library lacks some earlier years of *Csillag* and *Corvina,* and the holdings of the Hungarian Academy of Sciences' publication, *Magyar Tudomány,* begin only with 1956, although the Library holds 1901-11 of an earlier title, *Akadémiai Értesítő,* and the index volume, compiled by Pál Gergely and Zoltán Molnár, covering 1840-1960. The Library has *Budapesti Szemle* from 1857 to 1918 and all but the last three years of Magyar Szemle [Hungarian Review].

LEARNED SOCIETIES.   The serial publications of the learned societies and the universities are extremely well-represented. Except in those fields in which the Library does not buy, there are complete sets of all the currently published sets of *Acta* of the Hungarian Academy of Sciences, e.g., *Acta antiqua* and *Acta litteraria.* The holdings of university publications are also quite extensive, usually with complete sets of the serial publications of the universities at Budapest, Debreczen, and Szeged.

Genealogy and Heraldry

The collection of general sources in this field is quite extensive, although there are very few individual family histories. There are two excellent sources for locating family histories, Kálmán Baán's bibliography, *Magyar genealógiai és heraldikai forrásmunkák 1561-1932,* and the index to the Hungarian volumes of the set of Johann Siebmacher's *Grosses und allgemeines Wappenbuch.*

Two general sets for Hungarian genealogy are the 11-volume work by Béla Kempelen, *Magyar nemes családok* and the 12-volume work by Iván Nagy, *Magyarország családai, czimerekkel és nemzékrendi táblákkal.* A possibly unique item is Carolus Franciscus Palma's *Heraldicae regni Hungariae specimen* (Vindobonae, 1766); another rare item is Károly Wagner's *Collectanea genealogico-historica illustrium Hungariae familiarum* (1802). For heraldry, there is the richly illustrated *Heraldika kézikönyve* of Oszkár Bárczay, and the beautiful color plates of *Magyar czimeres emlékek* of the Magyar Heraldikai és Genealogiai társaság. The Library has the periodical *Turul,* Magyar Heraldikai és Genealogiai társaság közlönye, for its entire run, 1883-1942.

Public Documents

The collection of Hungarian government documents at the Library is extremely selective, but the collection of Hungarian statistical documents is extensive. Perhaps the outstanding set of government documents is the Hungarian parliamentary proceedings, which go back to 1790. This includes the *Irásai* [Writings], beginning with 1843, and the *Jegyzőkönyve*, [Debates], beginning 1836. The Library has all three parts—the *Irom, ányok* [Documents], the *Napló* [Journal], and the *Jegyzőkönyvek* [Debates] of the Proceedings of the Lower House (1861-1944) and of the Upper House (1884-1918). Two parts of the Proceedings, the *Napló* and the *Irom ányok*, are available for the renamed Upper House, from 1927-36.

From 1920 to 1926 there was a single house, the Nemzetgyűlés, for which the Library has the *Irományai* and the *Naplója*, but only the 1920-21 volume of the *Jegyzőkönyvei*. Since World War II, the Library has apparently acquired only the *Országgyűlési Értesítő* [Parliamentary Gazette], which is available from 1963 to date. This is supplemented by the *Budapesti Közlöny . . . Journal officiel*, the official government gazette for laws and official decrees, from 1906 to date.

Of interest also are the *Működése*, and its successor the *Magyar kiralyi kormány*, which are the condensed reports and statistics from each ministry and department from 1877 to 1941.

There are also, in some cases, the reports of individual ministries, such as the *Igazságügyi Közlöny* [Judicial Gazette] of the Ministry of Justice from 1894 to 1948, and the decrees, or *Magyarországi Rendeletek*, of the Ministry of Internal Affairs from 1920-45.

For the Hungarian National Bank, the Library has the English-language *Monthly Reports* from 1926-49, and the *Annual Reports* from 1925 to date. Copies of the Hungarian constitution are available as early as 1861 and as late as 1949. The constitution of the Hungarian People's Republic and the 1961 *Criminal Code* are available in English. Two important legal sets are the *Magyar Törvénytár*, or *Corpus juris hungarici*, from 1000 to 1938, and the *Országosítörvénytár*, or *Corpus juris*, from 1869 to 1948.

MUNICIPAL DOCUMENTS.   Holdings of city documents are extremely spotty but include *Ungarns Handel u.Industrie*, from 1870/72 to 1940, published by the Budapest Chamber of Commerce and Industry.

STATISTICS; DEMOGRAPHY.   Statistical documents are much more complete. Perhaps the most interesting is a set of volumes covering almost all counties for 1956, the year of the Hungarian Uprising, followed 12 years later by another equivalent set.

Many statistical yearbooks, periodicals, and special publications are represented, usually listed under the Statisztikai hivatal [Bureau of Statistics]. The yearbook coverage begins in 1875 with the *Magyar Statisztikai Évkönyv* (Statistisches Jahrbuch für Ungarn), continued by the *Magyar Statisztikai Évkönyv*, new series, and finally by the *Statisztikai Évkönyv* to 1964. These are supplemented by the *Ungarisches statistisches Jahrbuch* (1893-1915), the *Annuaire statistique hongrois* (1901-41), the *Commerce extérieur* (1901-39); the *Statistical Yearbook* (1949-), and the *Statistical Pocket Book of Hungary* (1960-).

Periodical coverage begins with 1899, the monthly *Statisztikai Havi Közlemények*, to 1964; the monthly *Magyar Statisztikai Szemle*, continued by the *Statisztikai Szemle*, from 1923 to date. Its quarterly supplement, *Statistical Review*, is available from 1962 to date.

The Library has a complete set of the *Statisztikai Időszaki Közlemények* since 1957. There are also the *Publications statistiques hongroises* (1900-39), and the *Ungarische statistische Mittheilungen* (1893-1940).

In demography the first census is 1784-87. Then beginning in 1870, and except for 1880, there are the census volumes at approximately 10-year intervals to 1960. The quarterly *Történeti Statisztikai Közlemények* [Historical Statistics Publications] (1957-59), was followed by the yearbook, *Történeti Statisztikai Évkönyv*, which the Library has to 1967/68. There is also a quarterly magazine, *Demográfia* (1960-), and a yearbook, *Demográfiai Évkönyv* (1965-).

Other more specialized material includes a 1956 publication, *Economic Accounts and Real Income in Hungary*, a monthly *Statement on Financial Conditions in Hungary* (1926-38), *Állami Költségvetés* [State Budget] (1882-1938/39), and the *Mezőgazdasági Statisztikai Zsebkönyv*

[Pocketbook of Agricultural Statistics] (1959-). Among the statistical publications of the city of Budapest are the *Statisztikai Közlemények* (1871-1940), the *Budapest Statisztikai Évkönyve* (1959-), and the *Budapest főváros statisztikai havi füzetei* (1894-1949). One of the early significant gifts to the Library was a 600-volume collection of Hungarian statistical economic and scientific works donated by the city of Budapest.

Language

Language and literature are two of the strongest fields of collection at the Library. Under the catalog heading, "Hungarian language," there are some 250 entries, with special strengths in the sub-headings for Dialects, Exercises and readers, and Grammar.

The grammars and histories include a number of antiquarian and rare volumes. They are Mátyás Bél, *De vetere litteratura Hunno-Scythica exercitatio* (Leipzig, 1718); Joannis Sajnovics, *Demonstratio idioma Ungarorum et Lapponum idem esse* (Nagy-Szombath, 1770); Miklós János Révai, *Antiquitates literaturae Hungaricae* (Pest, 1803); and his *Elaboratior grammatica Hungarica* (Pest, 1806). Of the more modern works the Library has almost all of the titles cited in Horecky, as well as Aurélien Sauvageot's *Esquisse de la langue hongroise* (1951). There is a nearly complete set of the Indiana University Publications, Uralic and Altaic Series. Further, the Library has received volume one of a long-announced atlas of Hungarian dialects.

There are complete sets of the periodicals cited by Horecky, except for *Nyelvtudományi Közlemények*, of which the holdings begin with 1928. Additional periodicals are the *Révue des études hongroises et finno-ugriennes* (1923-48), and the *Acta universitatis Szegediensis . . . Sectio philologica. Nyelv és irodalom*, and its successor . . . *Sectio ethnographica et linguistica. Néprajz és Nyelvtudomány*, since 1955. The Library also has the Szeged University's series of linguistic monographs from 1924 to 1949.

The Library owns an excellent collection of the language and literature of the Ostyaks and Voguls, Ugric peoples living near the Arctic Circle, ranging from a "description of the Ostiaks" in Friedrich Christian Weber's *The Present State of Russia* (1722), to Robert Austerlitz's *Ob-Ugric Metrics* (1958). Some possibly unique items are: Serafim Patkanov, *Irtisi-osztják szójegyzék;* H. Paasonen, *Ostjakisches Wörterbuch;* Antal Reguly, *Osztják hősénekek;* and Bernát Munkácsi, *Vogul népköltési gyüjtemény*.

Literature

The Library has always collected literature extensively, even in the minor languages. The Hungarian collection includes all the better-known authors, their collected and individual works, and much of the critical and biographic material. The Library also buys translations of the more important works, and holds many of the historical and critical works, both general and specific studies.

In addition to the bibliographies listed in Horecky, the Library has a bibliography of peasant revolts in Hungarian prose and poetry by László Geréb, and Magda Czigány's *Hungarian Literature in English Translation Published in Great Britain (1830-1968)*.

Hungarian authors publishing in the United States are collected as fully as possible. Of interest is Leslie Konnyu, *A History of American Hungarian Literature*, a "presentation of American Hungarian authors of the last 100 years and selections from their writings" (1962). There is a surprising number of sources on the foreign influence of and on Hungarian literature. Examples are: Emro Gergely, *Hungarian Drama in New York*, American Adaptations, 1908-1940; Alexandre Eckhardt, *De Sicambria a Sans Souci, histoires et légendes franco-hongroises;* Zoltán Haraszti, *Shakespeare in Hungary;* and Ignace Kont, *Étude sur l'influence de la litterature française en Hongrie*.

Two sets of monographic studies published by the Hungarian Academy of Sciences are *Irodalomtörténeti könyvtár* (1958-) and *Értekezések* (1867-). In addition to the periodicals listed in Horecky, most of which the Library has, three others of interest are *Revue des études hongroises* (1923-48); Szeged University's *Acta historiae litterarum Hungaricarum* (1961-), and Debrecen University's *Studia litteraria* (1963-).

Manuscripts

The Manuscript Division has unique source material available for both Ferenc Molnár and Lajos Kossuth. There are the outlines, notes, and first versions of four Molnár plays: *Esküvő, A Cukraszné, Szivdobogás,* and *A Császár.* Kossuth materials include letters to the Honorable Dudley Mann, to Horace Greeley, and a series of 13 letters to Henry J. Raymond, editor of the *New York Times.* These were for publication, and were an analysis of American foreign policy. An additional letter considers England's relations with Russia, and there are some miscellaneous letters as well.

Also available through the Manuscript Division is the Schwimmer Lloyd Collection. Rosika Schwimmer (1877-1948) was a Hungarian feminist and pacifist. The Collection includes extensive files of her correspondence, particularly from 1890 to 1920; her diplomatic files as Hungarian Minister to Switzerland; and diaries and press clippings. The Collection also contains books, pamphlets, and periodicals in the general fields of woman suffrage and political affairs. Material on the 1913 International Woman Suffrage Congress, held in Budapest, is available, as are Hungarian newspapers of World War I and later.

The Spencer Collection's Corvinus manuscript is described under HISTORY.

Religion

Religious publications are acquired very sparingly by the Library. The Hungarian material does not include books on theology, but does have histories of various churches, especially in their political and social connections. Examples are the Cardinal Mindszenty materials and such books as György Bauhofer's *History of the Protestant Church in Hungary,* and József Galánti's *Egyház és politika, 1890-1918.* In periodicals, the only significant run is the *Katolikus Szemle,* since 1953.

However, the Library does have a very extensive collection of Bibles. Two very rare Hungarian Bibles, both from the Lenox Library, are a 1626 Catholic translation by György Káldi, Vienna, and a 1730 Protestant translation by Károli Gáspár, Utrecht.

Folklore

The Library buys generously in the field of folklore, so that it has most of the Horecky listings. In addition, there are such specialized journals as the *Alba regia* from Székesfehérvár, and such special area studies as János Berze Nagy's *Baranyai magyar néphagyományok,* and Gyula Ortutay's *Bátorligeti mesék* and *Székely népballadák.*

Art

The collection on Hungarian art at the Library is representative, rather than comprehensive. Although the Library has most of the titles cited in Horecky, the holdings over the years have been acquired on a highly selective basis, emphasizing scholarly materials in languages other than Hungarian.

Of monograph series there is a possibly unique set of 12 volumes of *Ars Hungarica* (1932-38), and the later set, *L'Art hongrois* (1944-49). In addition to the two Horecky periodicals, another set of interest is the *Bulletin du Musée hongrois des beaux arts* (1947-).

The other great treasure of the Hungarian collection in the Library is the painting by Mihály Munkácsy, "Blind Milton Dictating 'Paradise Lost' to his Daughters." Painted in 1877/78, it was exhibited at the Paris Exposition of 1878, where it was awarded the Grand Gold Medal and the Cross of the Legion of Honor. In the following year it was bought by Robert Lenox Kennedy, nephew of James Lenox, and presented to the Lenox Library. It is a large painting, some 7 by 9 feet, and is an excellent example of Munkácsy's large historical paintings.

The Library also possesses a Munkácsy landscape, "Shepherdess at the Forest's Edge," and a bronze bust of the painter by the French sculptor Louis Barrias. The Prints Division has a portrait of Franz Liszt, painted from life by Munkácsy and etched by Rippl-Rónai. The catalog has some 50 entries for Munkácsy. Two items of particular interest are the heavily illustrated life and works by Lajos Végvári, and also his *Katalog der Gemaelde und Zeichnungen Mihály Munkácsys.*

Music

The Music Division has strong holdings in the field of ethnomusicology, and the published scores of the major composers, with many arrangements by Béla Bartók and Zoltán Kodály. The Library has extensive files of music journals. Currently the Division receives four periodical titles from Hungary: *Film, Szinház, Muzsika* (1968-); *Magyar Zene* (1962-); *Muzsika* (1961-); and the *Közlemények* (1951-) of the Hungarian Academy of Sciences. The Special Collections of the Music Division have some Hungarian musical autographs, most notably 25 letters, notes, and cards, and five musical manuscripts of Franz Liszt. The iconography of Hungarian musical figures is also available.

The Rodgers and Hammerstein Archives of Recorded Sound has phonorecords and catalogs for the Qualiton and Hungariton labels from 1965 onwards, both classical and folk. There are, in addition, scattered holdings of 78-rpm recordings from Gramophone Co., Ltd., and Patria labels, from 1935 onward, with many recordings of Béla Bartók at the piano.

Dance and Theater

The Dance Collection has works on Hungarian folk and theatrical dance, some clippings, and two videotapes of Hungarian theatrical dancing. Additional information is found under the names of specific dances, as the Csardas.

The holdings are comprehensive in published works on the theater, cinema, radio and television, circuses, etc., supplemented by extensive clipping files, and files of theatrical programs, photographs, movie stills, etc., with emphasis on performances in the United States. Periodical titles currently received include *Filmvilág* (1961-), *Színházi Tanulmányok* (1960-), and *Szinháztörténeti Könyvtár* (1961-).

The State; the Economy; the Society

Except for history and anthropology, the Library's holdings in the social sciences are representative rather than comprehensive.

There are excellent standard bibliographic sources. The more specialized bibliographies include volume I of the *Bibliographia oeconomica Hungariae,* covering 1505-1805, and *Magyar közgazdasági és statisztikai irodalom* from 1960/62 to 1966.

Other basic reference tools include M. Szilágyi's *Ötnyelvü áruszótár* and two yearbooks: *Ungarisches Wirtschafts-Jahrbuch* (1925-43) and *Volkswirtschaft Ungarns* (1926-40). Economic atlases range from a post-World War I *Magyarország gazdasági térképekben* (1920) to volume

I of the *Oxford Regional Economic Atlas* (1956), covering the USSR and Eastern Europe. Of special interest in economic history are three studies by Ferenc Eckhart: *A Magyar közgazdaság száz éve, 1841-1941, A Bécsi udvar gazdasági politikája Magyarországon Mária Terézia korában,* and a parallel title for the period 1780-1815. The postwar Hungarian economy is surveyed in an excellent Yale study by Béla A. Balassa, *Hungarian Experience in Economic Planning.*

The most extensive run of a Hungarian economic periodical is *Közgazdasági Szemle* (1874-). Other periodicals are *Acta oeconomica* (in English) since 1966, *Pénzügy és Számvitel* [Finance and Accountancy] under varying titles, since 1954, the *International Bibliography of Political Science* (1953-), and Ervin László's *The Communist Ideology in Hungary, Handbook for Basic Research* (1966), which includes a 200-page bibliography. There is also a *Yearbook on International Communist Affairs* (1966-) by the Hoover Institution on War, Revolution and Peace, Stanford University.

Another Hoover Institution publication of special interest is Rudolf L. Tőkés, *Béla Kún and the Hungarian Soviet Republic,* which includes a biographic directory of leading figures of the 1919 Soviet Republic and an extensive bibliography. Other historical studies include Count Julius Andrássy's *Development of Hungarian Constitutional Liberty,* and Charles d'Eszlary's *Histoire des institutions publiques hongroises.*

The prewar structure of Hungary is surveyed in the 1932 *Magyar közigazgatás tükre,* including a "Synopsis of the public administration of Hungary." Present coverage includes *Communism in Europe,* v. I, edited by William E. Griffith, and various collections of the speeches and articles of János Kádár. The periodical of the Hungarian Communist Party is the *Társadalmi Szemle* [Social Review] (1947-56; 1966-).

Another section of the *International Bibliography* covers sociology since 1951. Also valuable is *East Europe; a Bibliography of . . . Translations in the Social Sciences Emanating From . . . Hungary,* begun in 1962, and its continuation, *Transdex.* A further publication of interest is the Hungarian Geographical Institute's five-volume *Bibliography of Social Sciences,* based on the acquisitions of the Budapest Public Libraries in 1924-28.

The Library has a number of the classic studies of Hungarian society such as Gyula Illyés, *People of the Puszta,* Lajos Kiss, *Szegény ember élete* [Life of the Poor Man], and Géza Féja, *Viharsarok,* a study of the land and people of the lower Tisza region. Observations of social conditions by travelers range from John Paget's *Hungary and Transylvania; with remarks on their condition, social, political and economical* (1850), to *Choses vues en Hongrie, 1957-1960* by Guy Hostert. And a 1961 Princeton University thesis by Andrew C. Janos covers *Hungary: 1867-1939, a Study of Social Change and the Political Process.*

Hungarian publications in these subject fields include *Huszadik Század* [Twentieth Century], which contains literary as well as sociological and political articles. This title is available from 1900 to 1919 and, when it resumed publication, from 1947 to 1949. The gap is partially covered by *Századunk* (1926-39). Two final titles noted are *Társadalomtudomány* (1921-44; 1960-) and *Magyar pszichológiai Szemle.*

The Land and the People

The Library has an excellent collection of Hungarian maps ranging from rare 16th-century maps to current historical, economic, ethnographic, geologic, and road maps. There are also city plans of Hungarian towns and cities and war maps.

Among the rarities are a 1559 copper engraved map by Antoine Lafréry, several exquisitely hand-colored maps by Ortelius as early as 1570, a number of Ptolemy maps as early as 1578, and engravings of Buda and other Hungarian cities, as well as maps of Ungheria, *Regno di Ungheria* (1707), by the Venetian geographer Coronelli. The Map Division has some 180 maps from the 18th century to 1969 illustrating Hungarian geography as a whole, and covering localized areas from Aggtelek to the Zempléni mountains. Some 21 sheets cover Budapest from 1870-1963. Five atlases of the country from 1802-1968 cover such topics as water supply and geology, economics, and meteorology. Nine sets include postal maps from the 1830s, topographic maps, geologic maps, and a 25-sheet ethnographic map. Another set covering portions of the former Austro-Hungarian Monarchy on a scale of 1:75,000 has proven invaluable for place-name research.

The Library has the best-known geography, *A Kárpát-medence földrajza* by Béla Bulla and Tibor Mendöl, as well as such more recent studies as *The Geography of Hungary* (1964), by Márton Pécsi, and Den Hollander's *The Great Hungarian Plain.* The periodical coverage is excellent. There is the Hungarian Geographical Society's *Földrajzi Közlemények* (1873-), which includes the *Bulletin internationale.* Of more recent periodicals, the Library has *Földrajzi Értesítő* (1955-), the Szeged *Acta geographica* (1955-), and the monograph series *Studies in Geography* (1964-) of the Hungarian Academy of Sciences.

The fields of archeology, anthropology, and ethnology are very well represented at the Library. There is the *International Bibliography of Social and Cultural Anthropology* (1955-), and three archeological bibliographies by János Banner: *Bibliographia archaeologica Hungarica, 1793-1943; A Közép-Dunamedence régészeti bibliográfiája a legrégibb időktől a XI századig,* and a supplementary volume for 1954-59.

Most of the standard works are available, such as Béla Balogh and Ludwig Bartucz, *Ungarische Rassenkunde,* and Gyula László, *A honfoglaló magyar nép élete.* Works on the Finno-Ugric problem include Péter Hajdú's *Finnugor népek és nyelvek* and Toivo Vuorela's *Finno-Ugric Peoples.*

There is also an excellent collection of periodicals: *Archaeologiai Értesítő* since 1869, *Ethnologische Mitteilungen* (1887-1911), and of more recent periodicals, complete runs of *Anthropologia hungarica* and its predecessor *Crania hungarica; Acta archaeologica,* the yearbook of the Hungarian National Museum; and *Műveltség és Hagyomány.*

For years, the Library has collected material on foreigners in the United States, so that there is an excellent collection of both books and magazines on Hungarians in the United States. Whenever possible, the Library also collects books in the Hungarian language published in America.

History

History is one of the strongest collections in the Library, comprising 1,500 entries under the catalog heading, "Hungary—History," and its various subdivisions. There is an excellent spread of material for all periods, with the possible exception of the pre-896 A.D. period. The holdings are especially good not only for the Revolution of 1918-20, but for the uprisings of 1848-49 and 1956. The subheading "Sources," for printed collections of primary source materials, has some 50 entries.

One of the features of the holdings is the large number of early and rare histories printed in the 15th, 16th, and 17th centuries. The Library has two of the 1900 facsimile editions of the first book printed in Hungary, *Chronica Hungarorum,* printed by Andreas Hess in 1473. This anonymous history covers the period from legendary times to King Matthias, the famous Renaissance ruler of 15th-century Hungary.

The Library's Spencer Collection has two original examples of this period. The first, probably commissioned by King Matthias, is the *Chronica Hungarorum,* written by a Hungarian nobleman, János Thuróczy, and printed at Brno in 1488. It emphasizes Emperor Sigismund and the Hunyadi rulers of Hungary, illustrated with woodcuts and portraits of Hungarian kings.

A treasure of the Library's Hungarian collection is a Corvinus manuscript. This is one of the four known Corvinus manuscripts in the United States. The Spencer Collection's Corvina by

Titus Livius, *De Secundo Bello Punico,* books XXI-XXX, was illuminated in Florence by Ioannes Franciscus Martinus Geminianensis about 1475 or 1480.

In the Rare Book Division, the Library holds both the Latin and the German versions of Antonio Bonfini's *Rerum Ungaricarum decades,* commissioned by King Matthias, but not completed until after his death. The German version, *Ungarische Chronica,* was printed in Frankfurt in 1581. Its woodcut illustrations are by Jobst Amman. A third 16th-century book of special interest is *Il Turco vincible in Ungaria* by Archille Tarducci, published in Ferrara in 1597.

In both the Rare Book Division and the general stacks, there is a surprising number of histories of Hungary printed in the 17th century. Among those of most interest are: *Respublica et status regni Hungariae* (Leyden, 1634); Péter Révai, *De monarchia et sacra corona regni Hungariae centuriae septem* (Frankfurt, 1659), beautifully printed with fine initials; Hieronymus Oertel, *Ortelius redivivus et continuatus* (Nürnberg, 1665), with woodcuts and portraits; Giovanni Bontempi, *Historia della ribellione d'Ungheria* (Dresden, 1672); M. Johannes Poltzius, *Ein klein Ungarisches Chronicon* (Rostock, 1685); and Márton Szent-Iványi, *Dissertatio paralipomenonica, rerum memorabilium Hungariae* (Nagy-Szombat, 1699).

The most interesting printed editions of archives, in addition to those cited in Horecky, are the three-volume *Scriptores rerum Hungaricarum minores* of Márton G. Kovachich (1798); the two-volume *Catalogus fontium historiae Hungariae* of A. F. Gombos, (1937); and a collection of printed archives of the 1919 Béla Kún regime, *A magyar tanácsköztársaság művelődéspolitikája* of Katalin Petrák and György Milei (1959).

Bibliographies of special interest, in addition to those cited in Horecky, include: George Fejér, *Index codicis diplomatici Hungariae ecclesiastici ae civilis;* Emeric Lukinich, *Les éditions des sources de l'histoire hongroise, 1854-1930;* the *Bibliography of the Hungarian Revolution, 1956,* by I. L. Halasz de Beky and its "Supplement 1956-1965," published in Francis S. Wagner's *The Hungarian Revolution in Perspective.*

The collection of histories is quite extensive. Two somewhat unusual primary sources might be mentioned. One is a possibly unique copy of an 1857 study, *Esquisses de la vie populaire en Hongrie,* by Gabriel de Pronay, which is a collection of full-page color lithographs of peasants at work in their environment, an unusual work for this period of Hungarian history. The other source is a microfilm edition, since 1951, of the influential literary gazette, *Irodalmi Újság.* The collection of university and learned society periodicals in the field of history is quite complete.

Norma A. Balsam
New York Public Library

Judaica

General Information

The holdings of the Jewish Division now number more than 140,000 items, which include material in all languages on subjects relating to the Jews and works in the Hebrew alphabet (Hebrew, Yiddish, Judeo-Spanish, etc.) on all subjects. About 40 percent of the collection consists of Hebrew alphabet materials and approximately 60 percent of works in the Roman alphabet, with some Cyrillic alphabet materials. The Division's card catalog also contains listings of works important to the subject field but housed in other parts of the Library. The existence of such a distinct collection within a general research library makes it especially useful for the study of the place of the Jews in world civilization.

In many ways Jewish life over the ages has transcended national or even regional boundaries, so that the geographic limitations of this survey inevitably lead to some distortion through exclusion of important research tools, including encyclopedias, whose scope is broader than the region, and permit only spotty coverage of subjects of general Jewish interest. Therefore, it is recommended that researchers outside the New York metropolitan area consult the *Dictionary Catalog of the Jewish Collection, the New York Public Library, Reference Department,* 14 v. (Boston, G. K. Hall & Co., 1960), its supplements in 8 v. (Boston, G. K. Hall & Co., 1975), and the *Dictionary Catalog of The Research Libraries.*

A basic research tool for any aspect of Jewish life is Shlomo Shunami's *Bibliography of Jewish Bibliographies,* 2d. ed. (Jerusalem, 1965), which contains over 4,700 entries in various languages and includes bibliographies issued separately as well as those published as parts of other works. Two basic reference works in the field are Herbert C. Zafren's annotated "Jewish reference books: a select list," (in: *Jewish Book Annual,* v. 28, 1970/71: 56-71) and *Judaica Reference Materials; a Selective Annotated Bibliography,* preliminary ed., compiled and annotated by Joshua Rothenberg (Waltham, Mass., 1971). The *Encyclopaedia Judaica,* 16 v. (Jerusalem, 1972), in English, contains many articles on Jewish communities.

Some important biographical dictionaries are Salomon Wininger's *Grosse jüdische National-Biographie,* 7 v. (Cernauţi, 1925-36), Zalmen Zylbercwaig's *Leksikon fun Yidishn teater,* 6 v. to date (New York, 1931-), the *Leksikon fun der nayer Yidisher literatur,* 7 v. to date (New York, 1956-), and Getzel Kressel's two-volume *Leksikon ha-safrut ha-'ivrit ba-dorot ha-aharonim* (Merhavya, Israel, 1965-67).

The literature which has grown up in the wake of the Holocaust (1939-45) comprises a special category. Although more will be said about this later, certain works which are all-European in scope should be mentioned. The Bibliographical Series of the Joint Documentary Projects of the Yad Washem Martyrs' and Heroes' Memorial Authority, Jerusalem, and the YIVO Institute for Jewish Research, New York, now includes:

1. Robinson, Jacob and Philip Friedman. *Guide to Jewish History under Nazi Impact.* (New York, 1960). 3,841 entries in 24 languages.
2. Friedman, Philip. *Bibliography of Books in Hebrew on the Jewish Catastrophe and Heroism in Europe* (Jerusalem, 1960). 1,246 entries.
3. —— and Joseph Gar. *Bibliography of Yiddish Books on the Catastrophe and Heroism* (New York, 1962). Over 1,700 entries.
4. Braham, Randolph. *The Hungarian Jewish Catastrophe; a Selected and Annotated Bibliography* (New York, 1962). Over 750 entries.
5-8. Piekarz, Mendel. *The Jewish Holocaust and Heroism through the Eyes of the Hebrew Press: a Bibliography* (Jerusalem, 1966). 4 v. Over 23,000 entries.
9-10. Gar, Joseph. *Bibliography of Articles on the Catastrophe and Heroism in Yiddish Periodicals* (New York, 1966-69). 2 v. (Jerusalem, 1966-69). Over 93,000 entries.

'Arim ve-imahot be-Yisara'el, 7 v. to date (Jerusalem, 1945/46-), edited by Judah Leob Fishman, includes material in Hebrew on such Jewish communities as those of Ostrog, Eisenstadt, Lwów, Mukachevo, Budapest, Kraków, Warsaw, Ungvár (Uzhgorod), Czernowitz (Chernovtsy, Cernauţi), Brody, Bratislava, et al. The *Entsiklopediyah shel galuyot* (Jerusalem, 1953-), of which v. 11 appeared in 1971, is a series in Hebrew devoted to various Jewish communities, including those of Warsaw, Tarnopol, Lwów, Lublin, Carpathian Ruthenia, Bulgaria, Bessarabia, et al.

Especially promising is the new *Pinkas ha-kehillot, Encyclopaedia of Jewish Communities* (Jerusalem, 1969-) of which one volume in Hebrew, the first of two planned to deal with the Jews in Romania, has appeared. The scholarly articles deal with sections of the country or with individual communities. Bibliographies and records of archival materials in various languages are included.

A useful work in progress is the *Guide to Unpublished Materials of the Holocaust Period; Specimen Pages* (Jerusalem, 1965) by Jacob Robinson and Shaul Esh. Statistics of Jewish residents are included in the *Blackbook of Localities Whose Jewish Population was Exterminated by the Nazis* (Jerusalem, 1965), issued by Yad Washem. A particularly valuable study is Isaiah Trunk's *Judenrat: the Jewish Councils in Eastern Europe Under Nazi Occupation* (New York, 1972). *Jews in the Communist World; a Bibliography, 1945-1962* (New York, 1963), by Randolph L. Braham and Mordecai M. Hauer, a general bibliography dealing with the postwar period, contains 845 entries representing material in many languages.

Early Printing

Information in Hebrew on the early Hebrew presses in this part of Europe is contained in the writings of Bernard Friedberg, especially his *Toledot ha-defus ha-'ivri ba-'arim ha-eleh shebe-Eropa ha-tikhonah . . .* (Antwerp, 1935) and *Toledot ha-defus ha-'ivri be-Polanyah* (Tel-Aviv, 1950). Other works on Hebrew typography in Poland are Isaac Rivkind's *le-Toledot ha-defus ha-'ivri be-Polin* (Jerusalem, 1934), and, in Yiddish, Emmanuel Ringelblum's *Tsu der geshikhte fun Yidishn bukh un druk in Poyln in der tsveyter helft fun 18tn y''h* (Vilna, 1936) and *Pinkes fun Yidishe druker in Poyln* (Warsaw, 1949). Naphtali Ben-Menachem's *mi-Sifrut Yisra'el be-Ungaryah* (Jerusalem, 1957/58) is a Hebrew work on Jewish literature and bookmaking in Hungary.

The main locations of 16th-century Hebrew printing in East Central and Southeastern Europe were Salonica, Prague, Kraków, and Lublin. The collection has about 85 specimens of the work of these presses for this period and many of these books are by 16th-century authors. *Hanhagat ha-hayim* or *Regimiento de la Vida* (Salonica, 1564), a work on the moral life, with a chapter added on dreams, by Moses b. Baruch Almosnino (1510-80), a rabbi in Salonica, is an early example of Judeo-Spanish printing. His exposition of the Talmudical treatise "Abot" [Ethics of the Fathers], entitled *Pirke Moshe,* and an apologetic work on the Pentateuch, called *Tefilah le-Moshe,* both in Hebrew, were published in Salonica in 1563. A leading Talmudist of Salonica and a schoolmate of Almosnino's was Samuel b. Moses di Medina (1505-89). *She'elot u-teshuvot ha-shayakhot ba-tur hoshen mishpat* (Salonica, 1595) constitutes part of the enlarged second edition of his responsa, which are recognized as an important source for the study of the period.

The work of the great codifier Joseph Caro (1488-1575) is represented in this group by the first published volume of his responsa, *She'elot u-teshuvot* (Salonica, 1597). One of the major works of Moses Cordovero (1522-70), a pupil of Caro's and an important kabbalist, *Pardes rimonim,* was first published in Kraków in 1591. *Torat ha-olah* (Prague, 1569?) by Moses Isserles (ca. 1520-72), who was considered by his contemporaries as "the Maimonides of Polish Jewry," is a philosophic discussion of the symbolism of the Temple and the sacrificial system. His *Zot torat ha-hatat,* 2d. ed. (Kraków, 1577) deals with forbidden foods and related topics. The critical notes of Solomon Luria (1510-73) on 19 tractates of the Talmud were published in Kraków in 1582 as *Hokhmat Shelomo,* also known as *Hidushei Maharshal.* Moses b. Abraham Mat (ca. 1550-1606), a disciple of Solomon Luria, was the author of *Mateh Moshe* (Kraków, 1590-91), a compendium of rites and ceremonies.

A number of works by the celebrated Prague rabbi Judah Loew (Liwa, Loeb) ben Bezalel (also known as Der Hohe Rabbi Loew and Maharal mi-Prag, ca. 1525-1609) first appeared in Prague or Kraków during the 16th century and are found in the collection. These include *Gur Aryeh* (Prague, 1578-79), on Rashi's Pentateuch commentary; *Gevurot A[donai]* (Kraków, 1581-82), on the Exodus and on Passover; *Masekhet Avot* (Kraków, 1589), his commentary on the talmudic tractate Abot; *Netivot 'olam* (Prague, 1595), on ethics; *Be'er ha-golah* (Prague, 1598), on difficult talmudic passages; and *Netsaḥ Yisra'el* (Prague, 1599), on exile, messianic redemption and repentance.

Levush pinat yekarot (Lublin, 1594) of Mordecai Jaffe (ca. 1530-1612) is a commentary on Maimonides' Guide to the Perplexed. *Levush eder ha-yakar* (Lublin, 1594) deals with the laws of the Jewish calendar according to Maimonides and *Levush ha-buts veha-argaman* (Kraków, 1599) concerns itself with the writ of divorce. *Imre shefer* (Lublin, 1590-97) is a work on the Pentateuch by Nathan Nata b. Samson Spira (d. 1577).

Poland

The section on the history of the Jews in Poland now numbers over 600 volumes. Important classes of literature which contribute to the continuing growth of this section are memorial volumes recalling Jewish life in cities, towns, and regions, and personal narratives of Holocaust survivors. The Division strives to collect as exhaustively as possible in these fields. Coverage is not complete in the absolute sense, but it is extremely thorough. The basic work in English on the history of the Jews in Poland, despite the chronological limit of its coverage, is Simon Dubnow's three-volume *History of the Jews in Russia and Poland* (Philadelphia, 1916-20). To this may now be added *The Jews of Poland: a Social and Economic History . . . from 1100 to 1800* (Philadelphia, 1973) by Bernard D. Weinryb. Another work in English is Israel Friedlaender's *The Jews of Russia and Poland* (New York, 1915). In Polish, the work of Majer Balaban is important. The collection includes *Historja i literatura żydowska,* 3 v. (Lwów, 1924-25), *Studja historyczne* (Warsaw, 1927), and *Zabytki historyczne żydów w Polsce* (Warsaw, 1929). Other works in Polish include *Rozprawa o żydach i karaitach* (Kraków, 1860) by Tadeusz Czacki; *Kultura i sztuka ludu żydowskiego na ziemach polskich* (Lwów, 1935) by Maksymiljan Goldstein and K. Dresdner; *Żydzi w kulturze polskiej* (Paris, 1961) by Aleksander Hertz; *Historja żydow w Polsce . . .* (Lwów, 1934) by Jakób Schall. In German there is a work by the Nobel Prize winner S. J. Agnon and A. Eliasberg, *Das Buch von den polnischen Juden* (Berlin, 1916). A work in Hebrew by a leader of prewar Polish Jewry is Isaac Grünbaum's *Milḥamot Yehudei Polin, 1905-1912* (Warsaw, 1922).

Other works in Hebrew and Yiddish are *Bet Yisrael be-Polin* (Jerusalem, 1948-53), a collection in two volumes edited by Israel Halpern; *Di geshikhte fun Yidn in Poyln bizn sof fun XV y. h.,* v. 1- (Warsaw, 1957-) by Ber Mark and the source book *Te'udot le-toledot ha-kehilot ha-Yehudiyot be-Polin* (New York, 1950) compiled by B. D. Weinryb.

Other works dealing with earlier periods include *The Jews of Poland, Their Political, Economic, Social and Communal Life in the 16th Century as Reflected in the Work of Rabbi Moses Isserls* (London, 1944) by Myer S. Lew; *Mikhtevei bikoret be-'inyenei ha-va'adim de-arba' aratsot* (Kraków, 1891) by Hayyim Dembitzer; *Di virtshaftsgeshikhte fun di Yidn in Poyln be-esn mitlalter* (Warsaw, 1926) by Ignaz Schipper. Essential to the study of Jews in Poland during the 16th-18th centuries is the *Pinkas va'ad arba' aratsot* (Jerusalem, 1945), added title: Acta Congressus generalis Judaeorum regni Poloniae (1580-1764), edited by Israel Halpern, which contains the resolutions of the Council of Four Lands, the autonomous central organization of Polish-Lithuanian Jewry. A Hebrew chronicle of the pogroms of 1648-49 is *Yeven metsulah* by Nathan Nata Hannover (ca. 1620-83). This is available in a number of Hebrew editions as well as in

English, German, and Russian translation. A socioeconomic history of the Jews in Poland between the World Wars is Raphael Mahler's *Yehudei Polin beyn shtei milḥamot 'olam* (Tel-Aviv, 1968).

Among other works by Mahler are *Yidn in amolikn Poyln in likht fun tsifern* (Warsaw, 1958), a socioeconomic study of 18th-century Polish Jewry in two volumes, including a supplement consisting of tables, and his *Divrei yemei Yisra'el; dorot aharonim* (Merhavya, 1952-) of which volume 1, books 1-4 and volume 2, book 1 have appeared, a general history with strong emphasis on Eastern Europe. An abridged version of part 1, books 1-4 is available in English as *A History of Modern Jewry, 1780-1815* (London, 1971).

The economic situation of Jews in prewar Poland is the subject of Jacob Lestschinsky's *Di ekonomishe lage fun Yidn in Poyln* (Berlin, 1931). This distinguished economist and demographer also wrote *Oyfn rand fun opgrunt; fun Yidishn lebn in Poyln, 1927-1933* (Buenos Aires, 1947) and *La situation économique des Juifs depuis la guerre mondiale; Europe orientale et centrale* (Paris, 1934), which is also available in Hebrew.

The collection includes many books on the Holocaust period. Two examples are *The Black Book of Polish Jewry* (New York, 1943) edited by Jacob Apenszlak and *Sefer milḥamot ha-geta'ot* (Tel-Aviv, 1954), dealing with the Ghetto uprisings, edited by Isaac Zuckerman.

In addition to material on Poland as a whole, the collection contains historical works on Jewish life in individual cities, as Warsaw, Kraków, Łódź, Lublin, Lwów, and works dealing with entire regions, as Galicia.

Hungary

A valuable collection in English on the Jews in Hungary is the two-volume *Hungarian Jewish Studies* (New York, 1966-69) edited by Randolph L. Braham. A few books in Hungarian are *A magyar zsidóság története; a honfoglalástól a világháború kitöréséig* (Budapest, 1922) by Lajos Venetianer; *A zsidók története Magyarországon,* v. 1- (Budapest, 1884-) by Samuel Kohn; *A magyarországi zsidók statisztikája* (Debrecen, 1907) by K. Weszprémy; the collection of source materials *Magyar-Zsidó Oklevéltár* (Budapest, 1903-63), the later volumes of which are edited by P. Grünvald and A. Schreiber; and, dealing with the Holocaust period, *Fekete könyv* (Budapest, 1946) by Jenő Lévai, available in English as *Black Book on the Martyrdom of Hungarian Jewry* (Zurich and Vienna, 1948).

Some works in German are *Geschichte der ungarischen Juden* (Leipzig, 1879) by J. Bergl; *Ungarn während und nach der Kreuzzugsperiode* (New York, 1909) by Samuel Buechler; *Der jüdische Kongress in Ungarn, historisch beleuchtet* (Pest, 1871) by L. Loew; *Die geistige und soziale Entwicklung der Juden in Ungarn in der ersten Hälfte des 19. Jahrhunderts* (Berlin, 1934) by Nikolaus László. Two works of biographic interest are Sigmund Schwartz's *Shem ha-gedolim me-erets Hagar* (Paks, 19--?-1918) and Leopold Greenwald's *ha-Yehudim be-Ungariya* (Vác, 1912). Also by Greenwald is the Yiddish *Toyznt yor Idish lebn in Ungarn* (New York, 1945). Additional books are Benjamin Schreiber's *Zechor yemos olam. Remember the Early Days. Incorporating Stories of Jewish Life, Customs and Folklore* (New York, 1969) and Jenő Lévai's *Hungarian Jewry and the Papacy* (London, 1968) and his *Eichmann in Hungary; Documents* (Budapest, 1961). Within the collection there is a substantial group of books on Eichmann and the Eichmann trial as well as the transcript of the trial itself in nine volumes.

Two other important collections of documents relevant to Hungarian Jewry during the Holocaust are *Vádirat a nácizmus ellen,* v. 1-3 (Budapest, 1958-67) and *The Destruction of Hungarian Jewry* 2 v. (New York, 1963) edited by R. Braham. A recent study in Hebrew on antisemitism in Hungary is *Antishemiut be-Hungariyah, 1867-1914* (Tel-Aviv, 1969) by Nathaniel Katzburg. A regional history is *le-Korot ha-Yehudim be-Transilvaniyah* (New York, 1950-) by Eugene

Abraham. Also dealing with Transylvania is *A kolozsvári zsidóság emlékkönyve* (New York, 1970) by Moshe Carmilly-Weinberger.

Czechoslovakia

The long history of the Jews in the regions which became Czechoslovakia is thoroughly represented in the collection. Some general works are Markus H. Friedländer's *Materialen zur Geschichte der Juden in Böhmen* (Brünn, 1888) and his *Kore haddoroth; Beiträge zur Geschichte der Juden in Mähren* (Brünn, 1876); Bertold Bretholtz's *Geschichte der Juden in Mähren im Mittelalter,* v. 1- (Brno, 1934-); Gottlieb Bondy's two-volume *Zur Geschichte der Juden in Böhmen, Mähren und Schlesien, von 906 bis 1620* (Prague, 1906) and Hugo Gold's *Die Juden und Judengemeinden Böhmens in Vergangenheit und Gegenwart* (Brno, 1934-) and his *Die Juden und Judengemeinden Mährens in Vergangenheit und Gegenwart* (Brno, 1929). Gold is also the author of *Die Juden und die Judengemeinde Bratislava in Vergangenheit und Gegenwart* (Brno, 1932).

The *Jahrbücher* of the Gesellschaft für Geschichte der Juden in der Čechoslovakischen Republik, v. 1-9, (Prague, 1929-38) contain many useful contributions to the history of these communities. An important work in English is *The Jews of Czechoslovakia; Historical Studies and Surveys,* 2 v. (Philadelphia, 1968-71) issued by the Society for the History of Czechoslovak Jews. In English, too, is Ernst Rychnovsky's *Thomas G. Masaryk and the Jews* (New York, 1941), a collection of essays.

Two books on the Holocaust in Slovakia are *be-Tsel ha-mavet; ha-ma'arakhah le-hatsalat Yehudei Slovakiyah* (Tel-Aviv, 1958) by Oskar Neumann and *Hurban Yahadut Slovakiyah; te'ur histori be-te'udot* (Jerusalem, 1961) edited by Livia Rotkirchen. Several books deal with the Theresienstadt [Terezín] ghetto. A thoroughly documented two-volume study is H. G. Adler's *Theresienstadt 1941-45* (Tübingen, 1955-60). The names of the survivors are listed in *Terezín-Ghetto* (Prague, 1945) issued by the Ministerstvo ochrany práce a sociální péče of Czechoslovakia.

The rich history of Prague Jewry is well represented in the Division's collection. A key to the literature is Otto Muneles' *Bibliographical Survey of Jewish Prague* (Prague, 1952). Of historical interest is *Die Juden in Prag; Bilder aus ihrer tausendjährigen Geschichte* issued by the B'nai Brith in Prague in 1927. Books on the old Jewish cemetery are Simon Hock's *Mishpehot k"k Prag 'al pi matsevoteihen* (Pressburg, 1882) and Lubomir Jerabek's *Der alte Prager Judenfriedhof* (Prague, 1903). The Zidovské Museum in Prague has issued some noteworthy volumes including *The Pinkas Synagogue* by Hana Volavková in 1954 and *Prague Ghetto in the Renaissance Period* in 1965.

Romania

There is a considerable group of writings on the Jews in Romania. A general work in Yiddish is *Rumenye; geshikhte, literatur-kritik, zikhroynes* (Buenos Aires, 1961) by S. Bickel. Some histories are *Les Juifs en Roumanie depuis le traité de Berlin (1878) jusqu'a ce jour* (London, 1901) by Elias Schwartzfeld; *Shtudies tsu der geshikhte fun Rumenishe Yidn* (New York, 1944) by Joseph Kissman; *Korot ha-Yehudim be-Rumaniya* (Jassy, 1871-73) by Jacob Psanter and *L'histoire des Israélites roumains et le droit d'intervention* (Paris, 1913) by Bernard Stambler. Gabriel Schäffer's *Istoricul problemei evreești din România* (Bucharest, 192-?) contains a useful bibliography. The history of the Jews in a region which was a part of Romania before World War II is Hugo Gold's *Geschichte der Juden in der Bukowina* (Tel-Aviv, 1958-62) in two volumes. Manfred Reifer's *Ausgewählte historische Schriften, Dokumenten-Sammlung* (Cernăuți, 1938) contains historical essays and source materials, mainly on Bukowina, but also on Romania in general.

Greece

A study of the history of the Jews in Greece might well begin with antiquity and, in fact, the collection possesses a wealth of material on the Hellenistic period. The Hebrew *Megilat Aḥima'ats,* a medieval family chronicle, which presents a picture of life in Byzantine times, is available in two editions (Jerusalem, 1945 and New York, c. 1924, reprinted in 1966), the New York edition with English translation and notes by Marcus Salzman. Historical works on the period are *The Jews in the Byzantine Empire, 641-1204* (Athens, 1939) by Joshua Starr, issued as number 30 of *Texte und Forschungen zur byzantinisch-neugriechischen Philologie,* and *Byzantine Jewry from Justinian to the Fourth Crusade* (London, 1971) by Andrew Sharf. A major work on the Karaites is *Karaites in Byzantium* by Zvi Ankori.

On the modern period there is *In memoriam; hommage aux victimes juives des Nazis en Grèce* (Salonica, 1948-53) by Michael S. Molho and Joseph Nehama, also issued in Hebrew as *Sho'at Yehudei Yavan, 1941-1944* (Jerusalem, 1965). Joseph Nehama wrote the history of the important Jewish community in Salonica, *Histoire des Israélites de Salonique* (Salonica, 1935-59). Isaac S. Emmanuel composed a two-volume work, *Matsevot Saloniki* (Jerusalem, 1963-68), on tombstone inscriptions. He is also the author of *Histoire de l'industrie des tissus des Israélites de Salonique* (Paris, 1935). A work on customs is Michael S. Molho's *Usos y costumbres de los Sefardíes de Salonica* (Madrid, 1950). *Saloniki, 'ir va-em be-Yisra'el* (Jerusalem, 1967) is a memorial volume dealing with many aspects of the community's life. An interesting memoir in English is *Farewell to Salonica* (New York, 1946) by Leon Sciaky.

Yugoslavia and Bulgaria

Material on the Jews in Yugoslavia and Bulgaria is less abundant than are sources for the study of Jewish life elsewhere, but both countries are represented in the collection. A work encompassing both communities is *Jevreji u Jugoslaviji i Bugarskoj* (Zagreb, 1930) by Ljubomir Stefan Kosier. A local history is *Jevreji u Beogradu* (Belgrade, 1926) by Ignjat Šlang. Another is *Jevreji u Dubrovniku* (Sarajevo, 1937) by Jorjo Tadić. Two Hebrew works, the first on Bulgaria's Jews under Nazi rule and the second on illegal emigration from Bulgaria to Palestine during the mandate period, are Benjamin Arditi's *Yehudei Bulgariyah be-shenot ha-mishtar ha-Natsi, 1940-1944* (Holon, 1962) and Barukh Konfino's *Aliyah b' mi-ḥupei Bulgariyah, 1938-1940, 1947-1948* (Jerusalem, 1965). Of biographic interest is *Evrei-zaginali v antifashistkata borba* (Sofia, 1958) issued by the Tzentralna Konsistoriya na Evreite v Bŭlgariya. A source book based on rabbinic responsa, with summaries in Russian and French, is *Evreiski izvori* (Sofia, 1958), issued by the Bŭlgarska Akademiya na Naukite.

Special Subjects

The dynamics of Jewish life in the area cannot really be grasped without the study of certain special nongeographic subjects which are abundantly covered by the Division's collection, among which are redemptive movements, as Frankism and Shabbathaeanism, Hasidism, and, later, Zionism and socialism; movements toward political emancipation and enlightenment (Haskalah); sects, as the Karaites, and antisemitism, blood-accusations, as the one at Tisza Eszlar in Hungary in 1882, and the Holocaust. Of immediate relevance are the languages and literatures of the Jews. In addition to Hebrew, Yiddish is extremely important for most of East Central and Southeastern Europe. Judeo-Spanish or Ladino was the everyday language of much of Balkan Jewry. The rabbinic responses represent another category of literature which reflects the social, economic, and religious life of the Jews. The Division's collection consists of about 1,300 volumes, of which many are relevant to East Central and Southeastern Europe. The life of the area also found expression in art and music. Related material is also found in other units of the Research Libraries. The field is vast in the cases of Hasidism, Hebrew and Yiddish literature, and Zionism.

A work of great erudition is Gershom Scholem's *Sabbatai Sevi; The Mystical Messiah, 1626-1676* (Princeton, N. J., 1973), a revised and augmented translation of the 1957 Hebrew edition. A pseudomessianic figure of the 18th-century was Jakob Frank, who is the subject of Majer Balaban's *le-Toledot ha-tenu'ah ha-frankit* (Tel-Aviv, 1934-35) and Aleksander Kraushar's *Frank i frankiści polscy, 1726-1816* (Kraków, 1895). Although other individual essays are not cited here, Professor Scholem's "Redemption through sin," in his *The Messianic Idea in Judaism* (New York, 1971, pp. 78-141) is an original and significant contribution to the study of Frankism.

Eliezer Steinman's multivolume *Be'er ha-ḥasidut* is a major series on Hasidism. A good anthology of Hasidic thought is *Me-otsar ha-mahshava shel ha-ḥasidut* (Tel Aviv, 1961), compiled by Shabtai Weiss. The struggle between Haskalah, or enlightenment, and Hasidism in Galicia and Congress Poland is the subject of Raphael Mahler's *ha-Ḥasidut veha-haskalah* (Merhavyah, 1961), the first of which is also available in Yiddish. A study of Hasidism and its opponents is M. Wilensky's *Ḥasidim u-mitnagdim*, 2 v. (Jerusalem, 1970).

A history of Zionism in Galicia is Nathan M. Gelber's *Toledot ha-tenu'ah ha-tsiyonit be-Galitsiyah, 1875-1918* (Jerusalem, 1958). The story of a proto-Zionist movement as it flourished in Romania is *Ḥibat Tsiyon be-Rumaniyah* (Jerusalem, 1958) by Israel Klausner. A Jewish socialist labor party which stood for diaspora nationalism is treated in Bernard K. Johnpoll's *The Politics of Futility; the General Jewish Workers' Bund of Poland, 1917-43* (Ithaca, N.Y., 1967).

Naphtali Ben-Menachem's *mi-Sifrut Yisra'el be-Ungariyah* (Jerusalem, 1958) deals with the literature of the Jews in Hungary, and the literature of Haskalah in Galicia is the subject of *Die neuhebräische Aufklärungs-Literatur in Galizien* (Leipzig, 1898) by Meir Weissberg. Yiddish literature in Poland between the World Wars is treated by Dov Sdan in *Sifrut Yidish be-Polin beyn shtei milḥamot* (Jerusalem, 1964) and by Jehiel Isaiah Trunk in *Di Yidishe proze in Poyln in der tekufeh tsvishn beyde velt-milḥomes* (Buenos Aires, 1949). Trunk and Aaron Zeitlin are the compilers of *Antologiye fun der Yidisher proze in Poyln* (New York, 1946). A special kind of study is William Glicksman's *In the Mirror of Literature; the Economic Life of the Jews in Poland as Reflected in Yiddish Literature, 1914-1939* (New York, 1966). Tales from Bessarabia form the substance of *Shtetelekh mit Yidn* (Tel-Aviv, 1971) by Yehoshua Gureviçi. *Di umgekumene shreiber fun di getos* (Warsaw, 1954) by Ber Mark is a volume on Yiddish authors who perished in the Ghettoes.

The Judeo-Spanish language and literature in southeastern Europe are represented by C. M. Crews' *Recherches sur le judéo-espagnol dans les pays balkaniques* (Paris, 1935), by Michael S. Molho's *Literatura sefardita de Oriente* (Madrid, 1960), Julius Subak's *Judenspanisches aus Salonikki* (Trieste, 1906) and Max A. Luria's *A Study of the Monastir Dialect of Judeo-Spanish* (New York, 1930).

The study of Jewish art may be approached through Leo Mayer's *Bibliography of Jewish Art* (Jerusalem, 1967). Relevant to Poland in particular are *Holzsynagogen in Polen* (Vienna?, 1934) by Alois Breier and *Plastishe kunst bei Yidn in Poyln* (Warsaw, 1964) and *Yidishe motivn in der Poylisher kunst* (Warsaw, 1954) both by Józef Sandel.

An acquaintance with materials on Jewish music may be gained through Albert Weisser's *Bibliography of Publications and Other Resources on Jewish Music* (New York, 1969). Hasidic music and dance are treated in Meir Simon Geshuri's *Neginah va-ḥasidut be-veyt Kuzmir u-venoteha* (Jerusalem, 1952) and *ha-Nigun veha-rikud ba-ḥasidut*, v. 1-3 (Tel-Aviv, 1954-59). Joachim

Stutschewsky wrote *Folklor musikali shel Yehudei Mizraḥ-Eropah* (Tel-Aviv, 1958) and *ha-Kleyzmerim; toledoteyhem, oraḥ-ḥayeyhem vi-ytsiroteyhem* (Jerusalem, 1959). *Sefer ha-nigunim; nigunei ḥasidei ḤaBa"D*, 2 v. (Brooklyn, 1957) by Samuel Zalmanoff deals with the music of the ḤaBa"D movement within Hasidism. A work on music in Poland between the World Wars is Isaschar Fater's *Yidisher muzik in Poyln tsvishn beyde velt-milḥomes* (Tel-Aviv, 1970). *Shirei 'am Yehudiim mi-Rumaniyah* (Tel-Aviv, 1970) compiled by Emil Sàculet is a collection of Jewish folk songs from Romania.

Serial Publications

The periodical holdings of the Jewish Division have long been considered a remarkable resource, despite gaps and inconsistencies which are inevitable in a collection of this kind. The titles mentioned below constitute no more than a skimming of the surface, and some of the runs for which inclusive dates are given are incomplete.

The collection contains over 70 Jewish periodicals of a general nature and some of a special nature (outside the scope of this survey), which were published in Poland. In Polish are the assimilationist *Jutrzenka* (Warsaw, 1862-63) and its successor *Izraelita* (Warsaw, 1866-1913); *Miesięcznik Żydowski* (Warsaw, 1930-34), a monthly review, and the postwar *Biuletyn* of the Żydowski Institut Historyczny (Warsaw, 1951-). Hebrew publications include *ha-Magid* (Lyck, 1856-1903); the weekly, then daily, *ha-Tsefirah* (Warsaw, 1862, 1874-1931); the Haskalah monthly *ha-Boker or* (Lemberg, Warsaw, 1876-86) published by Abraham Baer Gottlober; the proto-Zionist literary annuals *ha-Asif* (Warsaw, 1884-93) edited by Nahum Sokolov and *Keneset Yisra'el* (Warsaw, 1886-88) edited by Saul Phinehas Rabinowitz; the weekly *ha-Dor* (Warsaw, 1900-04) edited by David Frischmann and the cultural Zionist monthly *ha-Shiloaḥ* (1897-1927), first edited by Ahad Ha-Am (Asher Ginzberg), which began its existence in Berlin, ended it in Jerusalem, but which appeared in Kraków for several years.

Noteworthy in Yiddish are the popular Warsaw dailies *Haynt* (1914-39) and *Moment* (1910-32, 1938). *Hoyzfraynd* (Warsaw, 1888-96) edited by Mordecai Spector, and *Yudishe bibliotek* (Kraków, 1904), *Perets's bleter* (Warsaw, 1903) and *Yudish* (Warsaw, 1910), all edited by I. L. Peretz, were literary collections. *Literarishe bleter* (Warsaw, 1924-39) was a major weekly.

A few of the principal Hungarian holdings are the weekly *Egyenlőség* (Budapest, 1928-37) and the long-lived monthly, then quarterly review *Magyar Zsidó Szemle* (Budapest, 1884-1940). Another important Hungarian monthly found in the collection is the literary *Mult és Jövő* (Budapest, 1912-44), edited by J. Patai. A German-language periodical is *Ben Chananja* (Szeged, 1858-67). The annual reports (*Jahresberichte*, 1878-1946) of the rabbinic seminary, entered as Ferencz József országos rabbiképző intézet, Budapest, contain many important studies. A Hebrew periodical is *ha-Tsofeh le-ḥokhmat Yisra'el* (Budapest, 1911-31). *Új Élet* (Budapest, 1945-) is received in the Jewish Division on a current basis.

A Jewish weekly which appeared in Czechoslovakia was *Selbstwehr* (Prague, 1917, 1923-38). *Jüdisches Familienblatt* (Bratislava, 1926-33) was a religious Zionist publication. Two annuals are *Kalendář česko-židovský* (Prague, 1928-35) and *Židovský kalendář* (Prague, 1921-38). Currently the *Věstník židovských náboženských obcí v Československu* (Prague, 1945-) is received in the Division.

Serial publications from Romania include the Yiddish *D"r Birnboym's vokhnblat* (Czernowitz, 1908), the Hebrew *Zimrat ha-arets* (Jassy, 1872-76), the Romanian *Cultura* (Bucharest, 1937-40), and the current *Revista cultului mosaic* (Bucharest, 1967-), which includes contributions in all three languages.

Among titles from Yugoslavia are *Jevrejski almanah* (Belgrade, 1925-) and *Omanut* (Zagreb, 1936-40), and the current *Jevrejski pregled* (Belgrade, 1959-). Ladino holdings from Salonica include *el Lunar* (1864-65), *el Avenir* (1897-1900), and *Guerta de istoriya* (n.d.).

Leonard Gold
Assisted by
Edward Goldstein
New York Public Library

Poland

Bibliographies

The bibliographical holdings of the Polish collection are quite varied and rich, containing approximately 90 percent of the titles listed in Horecky and many additional works from various fields of bibliography. The Library has all the bibliographies of bibliographies listed in Horecky as well as other works in this field, e.g., *Bibljografja bibljofilstwa i bibljografji polskiej* (1924) and *Wykaz bibliografij retrospektywnych* (1953). Thus, emphasis here is placed on older works, not listed by Horecky, such as W. Rafalski, *Katalog ogólny książek polskich drukowanych od roku 1830 do 1850* (1852); H. Wilder. *Katalog* (1909-30); *Książka* (1901-22). (The complete set of this periodical is to be found only in the Library.); *Przegląd Bibljograficzny* (1912-29); and *Bibliografia Polska* (1914-19).

A special feature of the Library is its very rich collection of bibliographies of incunabula and manuscripts in Polish libraries, including numerous works published before 1914, e.g.: *Incunabula typographica bibliothecae Universitatis Jagellonicae Cracoviensis inde ab inventa arte imprimendi usque ad a. 1500* (1900); *Catalogus librorum saec. XV impressorum, qui in bibliotheca Leopoliensis asservantur;* and modern works on the subject, e.g.: A. Kawecka. *Inkunabuły w bibliotekach polskich* (1970). Such sources permit a comprehensive comparative study of incunabula in Polish libraries before and after the two World Wars. Polish regional bibliographies and bibliographies of serials are well represented in the Library.

General Periodicals

The Library has a comprehensive collection of Polish general periodicals, current and discontinued. There is also a good collection of periodicals about Poland in English, the most important of which are: *Poland* (1954-), and *The Review* (1956-).

Reference Aids

The Library holds a great variety of reference aids; its holdings may be considered comprehensive with respect to the data in the corresponding chapter in Horecky. Two titles deserve particular attention: T. Bystrzycki, *Skorowidz miejscowości Rzeczypospolitej Polskiej* (1933) and *Spis miejscowości Polskiej Rzeczypospolitej Ludowej* (1967); they provide the reader with lists of Polish place-names before and after the territorial changes in postwar Poland.

Statutes, Laws, and Official Gazettes

Polish statutes constitute one of the most comprehensive holdings of the Library, particularly noteworthy for their historical aspects. The Library owns several rare collections of Polish legislation, the foremost of which are the 11 volumes of *Volumina legum* (1732-92), apparently constituting the only complete set in the country.

Other important sources in this field are: *Konstitucie Seymu Walnego Koronnego Warszawskiego* (1624-40); *Statuta Regni Poloniae* (1693); S. Konarski. *O skutecznym rad sposobie* (1760-63); *Epistole, legationes, responsa, actiones, res geste serenissimi Sigismundi, regis Poloniae* (better known as *Acta Tomiciana*) (1852-66); and *Dziennik praw* (1815-71).

The Library ·also has comprehensive holdings of 20th-century statutes, important among which are the *Dziennik Ustaw* (Warsaw, 1918-) and *Monitor Polski* (Warsaw, 1918-), the official organ of the Prime Minister of Poland. The Library holds all but the first two years (nos. 1-154) of *Monitor Polski*.

The Library's set of the minutes of the sessions of the Sejm (Lower House), *Sprawozdania stenograficzne Sejmu* (1919-) lacks only the year 1939. The *Sprawozdania stenograficzne Senatu* from 1932-38 are incomplete.

The English-speaking reader will find a very helpful source of information in the serial publication, *Legislation of Poland; Laws, Decrees, Orders, Ordinances* (1955-).

The Library holdings include numerous texts of Polish constitutions as well as their translations into various languages, beginning with the oldest, the *New Constitution of the Government of Poland* (1791), to the present day.

In addition to general statutes, the Library has a comprehensive collection of the public documents of the various Polish ministries, in particular a collection of international treaties, published for the most part by the Ministry of Foreign Affairs. The oldest text of an international treaty in the Library is *Articuli pactorum conventorum inter status serenissimae Reipublicae Polonae & Magni Ducatus Lithuaniae*, published in 1697. The public documents of municipal governments are selective.

Statistics

Material on Polish statistics has been allocated partly to the Slavonic Division and partly to the Economic Division. The Library has a rich collection of these materials in various fields of the national economy and social life in Poland. In order of frequency of publication, they are: *Wiadomości Statystyczne* (1923-), *Biuletyn Statystyczny* (1957-), *Kwartalnik Statystyczny* (1924-), *Rocznik Statystyczny* (1920-), and *Statystyka Polski* (1932-). The most important collection of regional statistics is *Statystyka Regionalna* (1965-).

Polish statistical material is also available in languages other than Polish, e.g.: *Concise Statistical Yearbook of Poland* (1930-); *Statistique de la Pologne* (1919-); *Kratki statisticheski yezhegodnik* (1959-).

The Library has several statistical atlases: *Rzeczpospolita Polska; atlas statystyczny* (1930); *Statistical Atlas of Poland* (1945); *La Pologne contemporaine* (1926); et al.

An important work for the history of Polish statistics is A. Pawiński's *Polska XVI wieku pod względem geograficzno-statystycznym* (1883). There are few publications on vital statistics and censuses, but the above-mentioned *Rocznik Statystyczny* contains the most recent official data on population, as well as a brief summary of the censuses taken in 1921, 1931, 1946, 1950, and 1960.

Language

There are approximately 900 entries in this category, with a preponderance in the areas of grammar, dialects, and dictionaries. Bibliographical sources are well covered, with such examples as: Polska Akademia Umiejętności, *Katalog wydawnictw, 1873-1947* (1948); A. Kryński, *Bibliografia polskich prac językoznawczych za lata 1915-1931* (1926-34); E. Stankiewicz, *A Selected Bibliography of Slavic Linguistics* (1966-69); and R. Lewanski, *A Comprehensive Bibliography of Polish Dictionaries* (1958).

The Library also owns a considerable number of philological periodicals and serials. Among the authors of monographs in this field, the reader may find the names of such eminent Polish linguists as A. Brückner, W. Doroszewski, J. Karłowicz, Z. Klemensiewicz, A. Kryński, T. Lehr-Spławiński, J. Łoś, J. Rozwadowski, Z. Stieber, S. Szober, W. Taszycki, J. Tokarski, and S. Vrtel-Wierczyński.

The Polish collection contains more than 100 dictionaries.

Literature

One of the strongholds of the Polish collection is literature. This is equally true of scholarly works (history of literature, criticism) and of literary texts in their three principal genres: poetry, prose, and drama. Translations from and into foreign languages are least well represented. The catalog entries in literature comprise about 3,500 entries, of which approximately 1,500 pertain to prose.

The Library has numerous bibliographic sources, older as well as contemporary. The oldest of them is: A. Załuski, *Nachricht von denen in der Hochgräflich-Zaluskischen Bibliothek sich befindeten raren polnischen Büchern* (1747).

Although the holdings in literary periodicals and serials are not extensive, they do include complete sets of the most important publications, such as: *Pamiętnik Literacki* (1902-); *Twórczość* (1945-); *Kultura* (1947-); *Pamiętnik Teatralny* (1952-); et al.

Literary history and criticism are well represented by the works of such scholars as K. Budzyk, P. Chmielowski, R. Dyboski, K. Górski, J. Jakubowski, J. Kleiner, G. Korbut, J. Kott, M. Kridl, J. Krzyżanowski, W. Lednicki, W. Maciejowski, Cz. Miłosz, W. Taszycki, T. Terlecki, W. Zawadzki, and others.

The Library owns many editions of the collected and single works of the old, modern, and contemporary periods of Polish literature. There are numerous editions of the works of the three leading poets of the Romantic period, A. Mickiewicz, J. Słowacki, and Z. Krasiński, and of other eminent poets J. Kochanowski, S. Trembecki, Cz. Miłosz, K. Wierzyński, et al. It should be mentioned that the Rare Book Collection of the Library contains the first edition of the major work of Poland's greatest poet, Adam Mickiewicz, *Pan Tadeusz* (1834), and the 1583 edition of J. Kochanowski's poem *Iezda do Moskwy.*

There is a good selection of classical and contemporary novelists and playwrights: I. Krasicki, B. Prus, W. Reymont, H. Sienkiewicz, S. Żeromski, M. Dąbrowska, W. Gombrowicz, M. Hłasko, M. Kuncewiczowa, J. Mackiewicz, J. Wittlin, A. Fredro, S. Wyspiański, J. Niemcewicz, S. Witkiewicz, S. Przybyszewski, and others.

A considerable number of anthologies is available and may be found in the catalog under the subheading Polish literature—Collections; some of these are translated into foreign languages.

The Library holds nearly all the publications of the most active Polish émigré publishing center, the Instytut Literacki in Paris, which to date has published 300 issues of the literary monthly *Kultura,* and 222 book titles.

Folklore

The collection of folklore is small and fragmentary, comprising 135 entries that include several related subjects (Social life, Rites and ceremonies, Folk songs, Folk tales, et al.). No specific bibliographic sources are available, except those in general bibliographies. Two periodicals are worthy of mention: *Polish Folklore* (1956-) and *Literatura Ludowa* (1957-).

Religion

In the field of religion, the Library collects only Church History. Therefore, the Polish collection has only a very limited and random selection of works on religion. Noteworthy among these are the following monographs and periodicals: S. Witkowski. *The Roman Catholic Church in People's Poland* (1953); K. Chodynicki. *Kościół Prawosławny a Rzeczpospolita Polska* (1934); *Monumenta Poloniae Vaticana* (1913-); *Elementa ad Fontum Editiones* (1960-); A. Brückner, *Różnowiercy polscy* (1962); *Znak* (1946-); *Euhemer* (1960-).

Education

A significant event in the history of Polish education was the founding of Komisja Edukacji Narodowej in 1773, which Polish sources consider as being the first Ministry of Education in Europe. The activities of this Commission resulted in a great number of works, published by and about the Commission. Interest in this Commission continues, as is evidenced by many publications, e.g., S. Tync. *Komisja Edukacji Narodowej* (1954), and M. Mitera-Dobrowolska. *Komisja Edukacji Narodowej* (1966). This subject is quite well covered in the Library, including a special bibliography on the Commission, *Bibliografja druków odnoszących się do Komisyi edukacyi narodowej* (1907) by J. Lewicki.

The problems of education are of paramount importance to the present leadership of Poland. Therefore, many publications appear on this subject, especially on adult education. A good number of them can be found in the Library.

Between the two above-mentioned periods there are considerable gaps, which are only partially filled by the works of such outstanding Polish educators as S. Staszic, H. Kołłataj, and A. Dygasiński. Thus, the holdings of the Library in the field of education are representative rather than comprehensive.

Philosophy

In this field, the Library owns almost all of the works listed in Horecky, as well as philosophical works of over 40 other authors. Several bibliographies and periodicals are also available, e.g., *Bibliografia Filozofii Polskiej* (1955-); *Bibliograficzny obraz polskich publikacji filozoficznych* (1957); *Przegląd Filozoficzny* (1897-); *Kwartalnik Filozoficzny* (1922-); *Studia Filozoficzne* (1957-).

Therefore, the holdings of the Library in philosophy may be considered comprehensive.

Art

Materials on Art are located in both the Art and the Slavonic Divisions. The Prints Division also has a selection of contemporary prints. These holdings are selective. Bibliographic sources are lacking, but periodicals are quite well represented, including *Sztuka* (1911-), *Biuletyn Historii Sztuki* (1934-), and *Przegląd Artystyczny* (1946-), among others.

In general art history and surveys, the Library holds the works given in Horecky, as well as numerous other works, but the individual genres are less strongly represented. The best among the genres is Painting, but its subdivisions (Illustration of Books, Portraits, Painters, etc.) are poorly represented.

The Architecture and Sculpture collections are small. The only exception is the sculptor Veit Stoss (Wit Stwosz); the catalog contains 58 entries about his life and work.

Minor arts (Embroidery, Engraving, Furniture, Goldsmithing, etc.) have only a few catalog entries each.

Music

The Library preserves materials on Polish music in the Slavonic Division (books and periodicals, mostly in Polish), in the Music Division (music, scores, and other materials), and in the Rogers and Hammerstein Archives of Recorded Sound (recordings).

The number of bibliographies, periodicals, and serials is significant. Theoretical studies as well as the history of Polish music are also well represented by the following authors: J. Chomiński, A. Chybiński, Z. Jachimecki, A. Janta, S. Jarociński, S. Łobaczewska, K. Michałowski, B. Schäfer, and others. The oldest of these works is S. Felsztyński's *Opusculum musice mensuralis* (1517).

The holdings on individual composers are uneven, e.g., F. Chopin has an excellent coverage—there are more than 1,000 entries in the catalog under his name—and the second ranking Polish composer, K. Szymanowski, has more than 100 entries. But the well-known composers M. Karłowicz and S. Moniuszko are less thoroughly covered. The world-famous pianist and composer I. Paderewski has 83 entries (31 works by him and 52 about him). It is also worth mentioning that several manuscripts of I. Paderewski and K. Malcużyński are deposited in the Library. The holdings on contemporary Polish composers are unsatisfactory, even for such composers as K. Penderecki, W. Lutosławski, and B. Szabelski, who are well known not only in Poland, but abroad.

In the Rodgers and Hammerstein Archives of Recorded Sound there are Polish catalogs and scattered holdings of recordings from 1930 onward, comprising both classical and folk music. The archives also have fairly extensive holdings of recorded performances from Poland released on the major Western labels (RCA, Columbia) from the early years of this century.

Theater; Dance; Cinema

The theater is so closely linked with music and literature that some overlapping of materials in these three fields is inevitable. For example, the bibliography K. Michałowski. *Opery polskie; katalog* (1954) comprises not only materials on Polish opera music, but also on stage production. Similarly, the quarterly *Pamiętnik Teatralny* (1952-) provides information on Polish drama as a literary genre, and also about the history and contemporary state of the Polish stage.

The holdings on Polish theater should be considered representative. Their most distinctive characteristic is the great abundance of bibliographic sources.

The reader may also find a sufficient number of works on the contemporary Polish theater and on its history. However, the collection is not properly balanced in the area of special aspects and personalities; while there is good coverage of such personalities as King Stanisław August Poniatowski, benefactor of the Polish theater, or the actress Helena Modrzejewska (Helena

Modjeska, also known for her tours of the United States), and others, literature on "the father of Polish theater," W. Bogusławski, the creator of the so-called "monumental theater" in Poland, L. Schiller, and the famous director, J. Grotowski, are poorly represented.

The Dance Collection has several books on folk dance and theatrical dance (in English, French, and Polish).

The Library has only a few of the books listed in Horecky under the chapter on Cinema, but it has other books in this field. Still, the collection on Cinema is small, lacking bibliographies, and comprising only two periodicals: *Kwartalnik Filmowy* (1952-) and *Film* (1952-).

Law

The Library does not collect much in the field of law, though the history and bibliography of the subject are collected, as are codes of law. Among the periodicals and serials, the Library has the leading monthly journal *Państwo i Prawo* (1946-); among the older publications *Czasopismo Prawnicze i Ekonomiczne* (1901-39) and Polska Akademia Nauk. Komisja Prawnicza, *Archiwum* (1895-1938).

Politics

Works on political theory, i.e., on the theory of state, are entered under Political science–Poland, while works on the practical aspects of politics appear under the heading Poland–Politics. The theoretical works are not numerous and cannot be considered representative, but the field of practical politics is better covered, encompassing about 300 catalog entries, and may be described as selective. There are practically no bibliographic sources in the area of politics, but the number of periodicals is significantly higher than that given in Horecky.

Diplomacy and Foreign Relations

The holdings of the Polish collection on Diplomacy may be described as selective and include most of the works quoted by Horecky. The holdings in Foreign Relations are exhaustive; the catalog shows about 600 entries under this heading. The Library also owns all of the periodicals in this area given by Horecky.

A rare find in this field is a volume preserved in the Rare Book Division, viz., the collected works of the 16th-century Polish diplomat, K. Warszewicki, *Christophori Varsevicii Turcicae Quatuordecim.* (Cracoviae, In Officina Lazari, 1595).

Military Affairs

The Library has a medium-sized but selective collection on Polish military affairs. There are comprehensive bibliographical sources: *Wojskowe Wiadomości Bibliograficzne* (1922-33), *Wojskowy Przegląd Wydawniczy* (1926-39), and *O walkach Ludowego Wojska Polskiego, 1943-1945; poradnik bibljograficzny* (1963), and other titles.

The same can be said of periodicals. The oldest of them is *Bellona; Kwartalnik Wojskowo-Historyczny* (1918-63). In addition, the Library has *Broń i Barwa* (1949-62); *Wojskowy Przegląd Historyczny* (1959-), *Żołnierz Polski* (1945-), *Polska Walcząca* (Kingsway, Eng., 1939-45), et al.

World War II and the associated events of the struggle of the Polish people to liberate themselves from the Nazi occupation are reflected in numerous Polish and foreign language works published in Poland and abroad. The reader will find the most important of them in The Research Libraries, along with the works of numerous prewar authors, such as W. Dziewanowski, W.

Gąsiorowski, K. Górski, W. Hupert, T. Korzon, M. Kukiel, S. Kutrzeba, O. Laskowski, J. Piłsudski, and others.

Economy

The holdings in this field are comprehensive and appear in the catalog chiefly under the headings Economic History and Economics, but also under related subheadings: Business, Cost, Economic Development, Economic Policy, Finance, Income, Industries, Investments, Prices, Production, Wages.

A serious shortcoming of this collection is the lack of satisfactory bibliographic sources. The Library owns only such fragmentary bibliographies as: *Bibliografia polskiej myśli ekonomicznej, 1831-1871* (1958-61); *Bibliografia za lat dziesięć, 1926-1935* [A Bibliography of Ten Years]— a supplement to the quarterly *Ekonomista* for the year 1935, or the pertinent chapters in bibliographies of Polish bibliographies (e.g., in W. Hahn or H. Sawoniak for 1951-60). These sources cover relatively limited periods of time. Systematic coverage begins only with the acquisition of *Przegląd Bibliograficzny Piśmiennictwa Ekonomicznego,* a bimonthly publication which is now current in the Slavonic Division. The Library has this periodical only from 1958, i.e., its 12th year of publication.

The Polish economics collection of the Library affords a comparison among diverse academic points of view, including those of the most eminent Polish pre-World War II economist, J. Supiński, and other noteworthy authors, e.g., A. Cieszkowski, J. Lewiński, and A. Zakrzewski, as well as Marxist authors such as W. Brus, O. Lange, E. Lipiński, B. Minc, and M. Pohorilly. A second valuable characteristic of the Library's holdings is the availability of works by foreign authors. The Library has almost all of the works given in Horecky. In addition, the following titles available in The Research Libraries are of interest: among the older works Nicolaus Copernicus, *Rozprawy o monecie* (1923) (the Latin text of the original work *De estimatione monete* (1519) with a Polish introduction and translation); Józef Supiński, *Pisma* (1883); and Stanisław Kempner, *Badania i szkice ekonomiczne* (1902). Contemporary works include Józef Zawadzki (ed.), *Teorie wzrostu ekonomicznego a współczesny kapitalizm* (1962); and Bronisław Minc, *Ekonomia polityczna socjalizmu* (1961). Among the works published outside Poland are Jan Rutkowski, *Histoire économique de la Pologne* (Paris, 1927); and John Foster Dulles (comp.), *Poland; Plan of Financial Stabilization* (1928). Serials and periodicals in economics include: *Badania z Dziejów Społecznych i Gospodarczych* (1928-67); *Ekonomista Polski* (London, 1941-); *Roczniki z Dziejów Społecznych i Gospodarczych* (1931-62); and the *Studia Ekonomiczne* (1959-) of the Polska Akademia Nauk. Zakład nauk ekonomicznych.

The Society

Although the Library's holdings in this field are scattered and are found under various subject headings and subheadings in the catalog, in toto they can be considered comprehensive, including most of the entries in Horecky, as well as many other works. Bibliographic sources are least well represented. The Library has little beyond the bibliographies given in Horecky.

Holdings in periodicals and serials, however, are more extensive: the leading journal, *Przegląd Socjologiczny* (Poznań, Polski Instytut Socjologiczny, 1930-), and the English-language organ of the Polish Sociological Association, the *Polish Sociological Bulletin* (Warsaw, Ossolineum, 1961-), and others.

The collection is particularly rich in monographs. The Library owns the works of such eminent Polish sociologists as F. Bujak, J. Chałasiński, W. Gumplowicz, L. Krzywicki, B. Limanowski, and F. Znaniecki. In addition to these, the reader will readily find many other authors, older as well as contemporary.

On related subjects, the holdings are most complete under the headings Labor relations, Social welfare, and Women. Materials on Psychology, Family, Youth, and Urban and Rural conditions are selective, while they are scanty on Mass media and Public opinion, and comprise only a few books and periodicals on Radio and Television, but are rather extensive under Journalism and the Press.

The Land

The Library's holdings in this area are exceptionally rich. The student will find numerous valuable materials pertaining to both the contemporary and the historical aspects of the question. For the most part Horecky lists 20th-century works, almost all of which are to be found in The Research Libraries. In addition there is a goodly number of other works of considerable interest. For example, the fundamental publication, *Bibliografia Geografii Polskiej* (1936-60), published by the Polska Akademia Nauk in Warsaw, the *Polska Bibliografia Analityczna: Geografia* (1956-) and the *Centralny Katalog Zbiorów Kartograficznych w Polsce* (1961-68), as well as other bibliographical sources.

In addition to *Czasopismo Geograficzne* and *Przegląd Geograficzny,* the Library has the following periodical titles among others: *Wiadomości Geograficzne* (1923-34), *Ziemia* (1928-), and *Polski Przegląd Kartograficzny* (1923-34), as well as the *Prace* (1923-32) of the Instytut geograficzny uniwersytetu Jagiellońskiego.

All of the basic general works listed in Horecky are in the holdings as well as many others. Special attention must be drawn to the works of the famous Polish geographer Eugeniusz Romer. In addition there are numerous works on special topics or problems such as geology, cartography, city and regional planning, etc. The most prominent of the handbooks and travel guides is the *Słownik geograficzny Królestwa Polskiego* (1880-1914), edited by F. Sulimierski. Also noteworthy in this field is the periodical *Turysta* (1957-).

A special feature of this collection is an extensive literature on the regions of Poland. No attempt at an exhaustive listing will be made here. To take just one of these regions—the Western Territories—as an example, the following works may be noted: *Polish Western Affairs* (1960-), *Ziemie Zachodnie* (1957-); *Studia nad Zagadnieniami Gospodarczymi i Społecznymi Ziem Zachodnich* (1960-); Z. Jordan, *Oder-Neisse Line* (1952); J. Dylik, *Geografia ziem odzyskanych* (1946); and B. Gruchman, et al., *Polish Western Territories* (1959).

Fourteen atlases with a variety of material reveal Poland's history, geography, economic, and political development from 1772 to 1959. Two gazetteers supplement the 236 maps and 2 automobile road guides. Sixty-one of the maps show, in some detail, localities from Białystok to Wrocław. Set maps illustrate Poland's topography and geology at 1:25,000; political division and minerals at 1:300,000, airways in 1938 at 1:500,000 (published in Berlin). Not all sets are complete. Willem Janszoon Blaeu's *Toonneel des aerdriicx . . . ,* v. 1 (1664) provides historical information on 17th-century Poland. The Library also offers a wide selection of materials in English, French, German, and Russian.

Older works of a historical character are of particular value in this area. To give a general idea of their nature, the following rare publications may be mentioned: Emilio Maria Manolesso, *La Fausta et Felice Elettione in Re Di Polonia* (Venice, 1573); Johann Pistorius, ed., *Polonicae Historiae Corpus* (Basileae, 1582); Szymon Starowolski, *Simonis Starovolsci, Polonia* (Coloniae, 1632); Philipp Hartman, *Memorabilia inclytae reipublicae Polonae* (Regiomonti, 1675); and Robert Johnston, *Travels through Part of the Russian Empire and the Country of Poland* (London, 1815), among others.

Anthropology and Archeology

Although anthropology is not one of the stronger points of the Polish collection of the Library and the holdings in this field can be described as selective, there are several basic serials and periodicals which cover the general developments of anthropological studies in Poland. In this category is *Materiały i Prace Antropologiczne* (1953-) which encompasses the works of the most distinguished of the Polish anthropologists and includes the most comprehensive systematic bibliography on this subject: Adam Wrzosek, *Bibliografia Antropologii Polskiej do Roku 1955* (v. 41-42). Among the older publications is *Zbiór Wiadomósci do Antropologii Krajowej* issued by the Polska Akadamia Umiejętnósci in Kraków from 1878 to 1895 and superseded by its *Materiały Antropologiczno-Archeologiczne* (1896-1919). The most important of the periodicals is the *Przegląd Antropologiczny* (1926-) and the information gap of the period from 1919 to 1926 is partially filled by *Archiwum Nauk Antropologicznych,* an irregular serial issued from 1921 to 1923. The collection of monographs in anthropology is insufficient, but does include all of the basic titles noted in Horecky.

Archeology is better represented than anthropology, with particularly rich holdings of serials and periodicals. In addition to *Archeologia Polona* and *Przegląd Archeologiczny,* the Library has *Wiadomości Archeologiczne,* first published in Warsaw in 1873 by the Państwowe muzeum archeologiczne, *Światowit* (1899-), and several other titles.

Ethnography; Demography

The bibliographic sources available in the Library facilitate an easy access to ethnographic materials. Noteworthy among these sources are: Franciszek Gawałek, *Bibliografia ludoznawstwa polskiego* (1914) and Halina Bittner, *Materiały do bibliografii etnografii polskiej* (1955-58). Serials in the holdings are *Lud* (1895-); *Prace Etnograficzne* (1934-39) superseded by *Prace i Materiały Etnograficzne* (1947-); *Archiwum Etnograficzne* (1951-); and *Etnografia Polska* (1958-).

The resources in demography are selective. The Library does not have an exhaustive collection of bibliographies or periodicals, while the catalog lists approximately 50 percent of the titles in Horecky. The holdings on population data are richer and have been described in the Statistics section.

Nationalities

The materials available on nationalities are somewhat more extensive, mainly due to such works as: Piotr Grzegorczyk, *Bibliografja mniejszości narodowych w Polsce* (1932-37), Arthur Goodhart, *Poland and the Minority Races* (1920), and Tadeusz Koźminski, *Sprawa mniejszości* (1922), among other works.

Poles Abroad

The Library has numerous examples of publications from all parts of the world on the religious, cultural, political, and economic aspects of the life of Polish immigrants in all countries, in particular, the collection of pertinent Polish periodicals is extensive.

History

The subject Poland–History is one of the most extensively documented in the Polish collection of the Library. This subject, which is divided into numerous subheadings, encompasses approximately 3,500 catalog entries. In the field of bibliographies, the reader may find not only all of the bibliographic sources listed by Horecky, but many others, contemporary as well as older, for example: D. Braun, *De scriptorum Poloniae et Prussiae historicorum, politicorum et JCtorum typis* (Coloniae, 1723); W. Recke, *Buecherkunde zur Geschichte und Literatur des Koenigreichs Polen* (1918), *Bibliografia historii polskiej* (1939); J. Muennich, *Historja Polski; katalog systematyczny dzieł XVI-XX w.* (1930); A. Wojtkowski, *Bibljografja historji Wielkopolski* (1934-36); and *Polonica vetera Upsaliensia* (Uppsala, Universitet, 1958).

Historiography is equally well represented. The Library owns the rare work of the famous 15th-century Polish historian Jan Długosz, *Historiae polonicae libri XII.* (Lipsiae, 1711-12), which has been described as the first eminent synthesis in Polish historiography and which holds a distinguished place in European historiography. The Library has other works by the same author, among which is the *Opera omnia* (Cracoviae, 1863-87).

The Library's holdings also include a rich periodical literature. Aside from the principal and oldest historical journal, *Kwartalnik Historyczny* (1887-), there is also *Studia Historyczne* (1958-), and an important historical annual publication in foreign languages *Acta Poloniae Historica* (1958-). Special attention must be drawn to the émigré historical periodicals, such as: *Niepodległość* (1929-), *Teki Historyczne* (1947-), and *Zeszyty Historyczne* (1962-).

The Library offers access to various editions of the most eminent Polish historians: S. Askenazy, O. Balzer, F. Bujak, O. Halecki, H. Kołłątaj, S. Konarski, L. Kubala, S. Kutrzeba, J. Lelewel, A. Naruszewicz, K. Szajnocha, K. Tymieniecki, and others. In addition to works in Polish there are many in other languages. The Rare Book Division contains unique editions in the field of Polish history: Jan Herburt *Chronica, Sive Historiae Polonicae Compendiosa* (Basileae, Ex Officina Oporiniana, 1571); Alessandro Guagnini *Rerum Polonicarum Tomi Tres* (Francofurti Excudebat ioann, Wechelus, 1584); Johann Pistorius *Polonicae Historiae Corpus* (Basileae, Per Sebastianum Henriceptri, 1582); and *Codex Diplomaticus Poloniae* (Varsaviae, Typis S. Strąbski, 1847-87).

Roman Malanchuk
New York Public Library

Yugoslavia

MOST FIELDS AND DISCIPLINES in the humanities are excellently covered by the Yugoslav collection of the New York Public Library. The strength of the collection lies in reference materials, old serials and periodicals, the history of Yugoslavia from 1945 to the present, and the history of pre-Yugoslav Serbia and Croatia. Other fields with excellent coverage are vital statistics, foreign relations and affairs of 19th-century Serbia, languages, literatures, and literary criticism as well as all genres of South Slavic folklore, particularly the epic. On the other hand, the resources dealing with geography, politics and government, social conditions and social life, and education are moderate, while those on Yugoslavs in the United States, military affairs, national questions, religion, and the performing arts tend to be rather weak.

In all, the collection exceeds 30,000 volumes. Among many excellent reference works of general scope there are *Bibliografija Jugoslavije* (Belgrade, 1950-); *editio princeps* of *Srpska bibliografija za noviju književnost, 1741-1867* (Belgrade, 1869) by Stojan Novaković; *Essai de bibliographie française sur les Serbes et les Croates, 1540-1900* (Belgrade, 1900); *Ogled bibliografije o Crnoj Gori na stranim jezicima* (Belgrade, 1948) by P. Šoc; *Bibliografija knjiga i periodičnih izdanja štampanih u Hercegovini, 1873-1941* (Mostar, 1958), compiled by Lina Štitić [et al.]; *Bibliografia della Dalmatia e del Montenegro: saggio.* (Zagreb, 1855, cover 1856) by Giuseppe Valentinelli; *Bibliografija rasprava, članaka i književnih radova* of the Lexicographical Institute of Zagreb (Zagreb, 1956-); *Hrvatska bibliografija,* 9 v. (Zagreb, 1941-44) and the first edition of *Bibliografija Hrvatska I.* (Zagreb, 1860) by Ivan Kukuljević-Sakcinski. Reference and research aids are numerous in the collection, ranging from encyclopedias, directories, and yearbooks to many old and new bilingual and multilingual dictionaries, and biographies for figures prominent in Yugoslavia and the constituent republics, as: *Ko je ko u jugoslaviji* (Belgrade, 1957 and 1970); *Životi srpskih vojvoda i ostalih znamenitih Srba* (Belgrade, 1963) by Vuk Karadžić; *Znameniti Srbi XIX veka* 3 v. (Belgrade, 1901-04) by Andra Gavrilović; *Album zaslužnih Hrvata XIX stoljeća,* 2 v. (Zagreb, 1898-1900) by Milan Grlović; *Glasoviti Hrvati prošlih vjekova . . .* (Zagreb, 1868) by Ivan Kukuljević-Sakcinski; *Slovenski biografski leksikon* (Ljubljana, 1925-); et al.

Though the Library's holdings of monographs and bibliographies on and by the academies and learned societies are moderate, they offer a wealth of information in many fields of learning as do resources on and by the library institutions and museums. There are ample works treating the history of printing in the country as a whole and in the individual Republics. Included in the collection are works by Mladen Bošnjak, Josip Badalić, Vjekoslav Štefanić, Zvonimir Kulundžić, Božidar Vuković, Žarko Muljačić, Dušan D. Vuksan, Lazar Plavšić, and others.

Serial and periodical holdings lend great strength to the collection. Most of the 182 titles currently received (newspapers included) are in the humanities. Most of the first-rate items which follow are either complete or have good runs: *Glas* and *Posebna izdanja* of the Serbian Academy, and *Ljetopis* Matice srpske (Belgrade); *Ljetopis, Starine,* and *Rad* of the Yugoslav Academy of Arts and Sciences of Zagreb; *Građa za povijest književnosti hrvatske; Stari pisci hrvatski* and *Danica Ilirska* (Zagreb, 1835-46; Reprints, Zagreb, 1970-71). A bibliographic rarity, *Gajret* (Sarajevo) for the years 1926-36, which is dedicated to cultural and economic development of Moslems, is also in the collection as are numerous publications such as *Jezičnik; Ljubljanski zvon; Dom in svet; Letopis* Matice slovenske; *Zbornik za umetnostno zgodovino; Jugoslovenski istorijski časopis* of Ljubljana; and *Časopis za zgodovino in narodopisje* of Maribor.

Besides these excellent sources, the Library harbors more than one hundred carefully selected recent serial publications which were regularly received through the PL 480 Program for Yugoslavia of which the New York Public Library was a participant. Of the newspapers and weeklies, the Library receives *Borba, Politika,* and *Službeni glasnik* of Belgrade; *Oslobođenje* of Sarajevo; *Vjesnik* of Zagreb, and *Delo* of Ljubljana.

The collection also includes two rare titles which might be classified as *curiosa: Licejka* (Belgrade, 1862-64) and *Leptir: zabavnik za godinu 1859* (Zagreb), supported by Ljudevit Gaj and edited by Ljudevit Vukotinovič. Primarily dedicated to youth, these journals contain selections chosen to promote moral behavior and good manners.

The Library's collection of literature on Yugoslavs in the United States is very selective. Almanacs, serials, and monographs provide some information on the Serbian Orthodox Church in America and its history and interpret the life of Serbs in America, e.g., *Sloboda* (Pittsburgh), *The American Serb* (Chicago). Works by Chedomir Pavich, Pero Slijepčević, and Luka Pejović are included. Recently published materials dealing with Croatians are *Hrvati izvan domovine* (Zagreb, 1967) by Većeslav Holjevac with an excellent chapter "Hrvati u Sjedinjenim Američkim Državama" (pp. 63-162), and *The Croatian Immigrants in America* (New York, 1971) by George J. Prpič, which provides information on Croatians in all walks of life in the United States. The best source on Slovenians is *Američki Slovenci . . .* (Chicago, 1925) by Joseph Zavertnik. There are a few other works focused on Slovenian folklore. The land, the people, and the geography of Yugoslavia have been described not only by authors writing in the vernacular, but also by those writing in English, French, German, Polish, Czech, and other languages. A few sample sources are given to indicate possibilities for research: *Zemljopis Jugoslavije, Kraljevine Srba, Hrvata i Slovenaca* (Zagreb, 1925) by Ivo Juras; *Jugoslavija: zemljopisni pregled,* 2 v. (Ljubljana, 1923) by Anton Melik; *Geografija Jugoslavije* (Belgrade, 1970) by Dragan Rodič; *The Beauties of Yugoslavia* (Ljubljana, 1966) by Ivan Raos; *Yugoslavia* (Belgrade, 1969) by Sir Fitzroy Maclean; *Yugoslav Life and Landscape,* (London, 1954) by Alec Brown; *La Yougoslavie* (Paris, 1967) by André Blanc; the rare book *Serbien und die Serben I. Das Land* (Leipzig, 1888) by Sprirdion Gopčević; *S.H.S. szkice z Jugosławji* (Warsaw, 1921) by Stanisław Roszkowski; and *Kralovstvi S.H.S. (Srbů, Charvatů a Slovinců): historický, politický, kulturní, hospodářský a zeměpisný přehled* (Prague, 1926), edited by H. Ripka. Additionally, the collection includes works by Tomislav Krizman, Brian Wilson Aldis, Oto Bihalji-Merin, Rebecca West, Hubert Deacon Harrison, Jack Fisher, George Kish, and others.

The collection in the New York Public Library offers the scholar adequate to excellent research materials for the history of Yugoslavia from the formation of the nation in 1918 to the present, and fair to excellent coverage for the histories of the various republics prior to their union in 1918.

In addition to the serials and periodicals previously mentioned, most of which contain essential data on history, the following fundamental archival sources should be mentioned. Among the best in the collection are *Arhivist* (Belgrade, 1951-); *Prilozi za orientalnu filologiju i istoriju jugoslovenskih naroda pod turskom vladavinom* (Sarajevo, 1950-); *Državna arhiva N R Srbije, 1900-1950* (Belgrade, 1951-); *Vodić arhiva Srbije* (Belgrade, 1967-); *Glasnik arhiva i Društva arhivskih radnika Bosne i Hercegovine* (Sarajevo, 1961-); *Arhivski vjesnik* (Belgrade, 1959?-); *Vjesnik zemaljskog arhiva* (Zagreb, 1899-); *Vjesnik za arheologiju i historiju Dalmatinsku* (Zagreb, 1922-); *Narodna starina* (Zagreb, 1922-33), and *Viri za zgodovino Slovencev* (Ljubljana, 1939-63).

While coverage of the history of Yugoslavia from 1918-45 is not strong, that for the period 1945-present is very solid. However, for the first period mention should be made of basic publications such as *Dokumenti o postanku Kraljevine Srba, Hrvata i Slovenaca 1914-1919* (Zagreb, 1920) by Ferdo Šišić; *Istorija Srba, Hrvata i Slovenaca* (Belgrade, 1924) by Stanoje Stanojević; *Istorija Jugoslavije* (Belgrade, 1933) by Vladimir Ćorović; *Jubilarni zbornik života i rada Srba, Hrvata i Slovenaca, 1918-1928,* 3 v. (Belgrade, 1928-29); and *Osnovi savremene Jugoslavije: političke ideje, stranke i ljudi u XIX i XX veku* (Zagreb, 1935) by Mijo Radošević. *Der Kampf der Südslawen um Freiheit und Einheit* (Frankfurt am Main, 1925) by Hermann Wendel, *Die Jugoslawen einst und jetzt,* 3 v. (Leipzig-Vienna, 1936-38) by Gilbert Maur, and *Fifty Years of War and Diplomacy in the Balkans* (New York, 1940) by Carlo conte Sforza, are also useful for study of this period.

The post-World War II period holdings are comprehensive in both vernacular and foreign sources. Among many included are *Istorija naroda Federativne narodne republike Jugoslavije sa osnovima opšte istorije,* 2 v. (Sarajevo, 1952-53) by Fuad Slipičević; *Pregled historije narodnooslobodilačke borbe Jugoslavije* (Zagreb, 1956) by Tomo Čubelić, and a standard work *Zbornik dokumenata i podataka o narodno-oslobodilačkom ratu jugoslovenskih naroda,* 9 v. (Belgrade, 1949-56) of the Vojnoistorijski institut. Other important works are *The Truth About Yugoslavia* (New York, 1952) by P. D. Ostović with an introduction by Ivan Meštrović; *Tito's Yugoslavia* (Washington, 1955) by Eric L. Pridonoff; *Balkan Caesar: Tito Versus Stalin* (New York, 1951) by Leigh White; *Histoire de la Yougoslavie* (Paris, 1955) by Marcel de Vos; *Le procés Tito-Mihailovitch* (Paris, 1950) by Evgueniye Yourichitch; and *Yugoslavia, storia e ricordi* (Milan, 1948) by Carlo conte Sforza.

Materials on the Yugoslav lands before the creation of Yugoslavia are found in the catalog under the names of the individual republics and regions.

The history of Serbia is well covered. Only a few rare items are cited here: *Monumenta Serbica spectantia historiam Serbiae, Bosnae, Ragusii* (Vienna, 1858), edited by Fr. Miklosich; *Istorija naroda srbskog,* which was printed in Vienna in 1821, and reprinted in Belgrade in 1846, by Dimitrije Davidović; *The History of Servia, and the Servian Revolution* (London, 1853) by Leopold von Ranke; *Kraljevina Srbija . . .* (Belgrade, 1884) by Milan Duro Milićević; *Geschichte der Serben* (Gotha: F. A. Perthes A.-G., 1911) by Konstantin Jireček, also published in Serbian as *Istorija Srba,* 4 v. (Belgrade, 1922-23); *Zbornik Ilariona Ruvarca* (Belgrade, 1934); *Srbija i Crna Gora* (Ontario, 1917?) by Mićun M. Pavičević; *Serbia's War of Liberation* (London, 1916?) by R. W. Seton-Watson; *History of Serbia* (London, 1917) by Harold W. V. Temperley; and *Sabrana dela,* 16 v. (Belgrade, 1932-36) by Slobodan Jovanović. Moreover, there are works by Stojan Novaković, Vladan Dordević Stojan Protić, Jovan Cvijić, Grgur Jakšić, Jovan Radonić, Dušan Pantelić, Nikolaj Velimirović, Vaso Čubrilović, Miroslav Đorđević, and others.

The history of Macedonia in general, both the Bulgarian and Serbian periods, is adequately covered. The collection includes archival publications, monographs, and bibliographies, e.g., *Izvori za starata istoriia i geografiia na Trakiia Makedoniia . . .* (Sofia, 1915), edited by Gavril I. Katzarov and D. Dechev; *Makedonija* (Belgrade, 1929) by Tihomir R. Dordević; *Materiali za istoriiata iz makedonskoto osvoboditelno dvizhenie,* 10 v. (Sofia, 1925-31); *La Macédoine et la renaissance bulgare au XIXe siècle* (Sofia, 1918) by Simeon Radeff; *Makedonien und Alt-Serbien* (Vienna, 1889) by Spiridion Gopčević; *Serbian Macedonia: An Historical Survey* (London, 1916) by Pavle Popović, and *Makedoniia i makedonskiiat vŭpros* (Sofia, 1933) by Ivan Stoianov. For the history of the People's Republic of Macedonia 1945-present, the researcher can consult works of Dimitar I. Vlahov, Dančo Zografski, Ljuben Lape, et al.

The history of Montenegro, Bosnia, and Herzegovina is also adequately covered. To mention only most important authors, these collections include works by Milbrad Medaković, Pavel Apollonovich Rovinski, Vladan Dordević, Spiridion Gopčević, Jovan N. Tomić; Vjekoslav Klaić, Milan Prelog, Vladimir Čorović, Vaso Čubrilović, Veselin Masleša, and Krunoslav Draganović.

The strong collection on the history of Croatia includes basic sources such as *Jura Regni Croatiae, Dalmatiae et Slavoniae,* 3 v. (Zagreb, 1861-62), edited by Ivan Kukuljević-Sakcinski; *Monumanta Ragusina,* 3 v., which are volumes 10, 13, and 29 of *Monumenta Spectantia Historiam Slavorum Meridionalium* (Zagreb, 1868-1918); *Codex Diplomaticus Regni Croatiae, Dalmatiae et Slavoniae,* 14 v. (Zagreb, 1904 onwards); *Codex Diplomaticus Comitum de Frangepanibus,* 2 v. (Budapest, 1910-13), edited by Lajos Thallóczy, and *Zbornik kralja Tomislava* (Zagreb, 1925). Several outstanding monographs in the collections are *Pregled povijesti hrvatskoga naroda od najstarijih dana do god 1873* (Zagreb, 1916), and *Geschichte der Croaten* (Zagreb, 1917) by Ferdo Šišić; *Povijest Hrvata od najstarijih vremena do svršetka XIX stoljeća,* 5 v. (Zagreb, 1899-1911) by Vjekoslav Klaić, and the encyclopedic work *Croatia: Land, People, Culture,* 2 v. thus far (Toronto, 1964-), edited by Francis H. Eterovich and Christopher Spalatin. Works of other notable historians—Franjo Rački, Radoslav Lopašić, Stjepan Srkulj, Lovre Katić, Milan Marjanović, Ljubo Karaman, Grga Novak, Robert William Seton-Watson, Francis R. Preveden—are also in this excellent collection.

In addition to works cited earlier, by Ćorović, Šišić, Srkulj, Melik, et al., in which the history of the Slovenes is treated with other nationalities of Yugoslavia, the collection has basic materials and important monographs for research on the entire sweep of Slovenian history. Noteworthy sources with excellent presentation and varying interpretations are the following: *Gradivo za zgodovino Slovencev v srednjem veku,* 5 v. (Ljubljana, 1902-28) compiled by Franc Kos; *Zgodovina Slovencev od naselitve do reformacije* (Ljubljana, 1933) by Milko Kos; *Zgodovina slovenskega naroda,* 2 v. (Celovec, 1912-28) by Josip Gruden; *Spomenica tisočletnice Methodove smrti* (Ljubljana, 1885) by Franc Kos; *Slovenski knez Kocelj* (Ljubljana, 1938) by Franjo Grivec; *Slovenci in 1848 leto* (Ljubljana, 1886) by Ferdo Gestrin. Materials of the post-World War II period in the collection are those of Ivan Prijatelj, Edvard Kardelj, F. Pétré, Boris Kidrič, et al., and works by contemporary historians received through the PL 480 program.

The fields of politics and government in the Library's collection are not well covered, but there are works dealing with the history of Yugoslavia from its creation to the present, including sources treating the Croatian question and socioeconomic and political questions for the country as a whole, for example, *Dokumenti o Jugoslaviji* (Zagreb, 1968) by Ferdo Čulinović; *Politika i korupcija u kraljevskoj Jugoslaviji* (Zagreb, 1968) by Zvonimir Kulundžić; *Stara Jugoslavija i komunizam . . .* (Zagreb, 1967); *Tito's Promised Land, Yugoslavia* (New Brunswick, N.J., 1954) by Alex N. Dragnich; *Ogled o jugoslovenskom društvu* (Zagreb, 1969) by Branko Horvat; *Osnovi državnog i društvenog uređenja FNRJ* (Belgrade, 1961); *Osnovi društveno-političkog sistema Jugoslavije* (Belgrade, 1967); *Problem odnosa između federacije i federalnih jedinica sa posebnim osvrtom na Jugoslaviju* (Belgrade, 1967); *Uspomene na političke ljude i događaje* (Buenos Aires, 1961) by Ivan Meštrović, and lastly *Contemporary Yugoslavia: Twenty Years of Socialist Experiment* (Berkeley, 1969), edited by Wayne S. Vucinich [et al].

In addition to the materials mentioned above and the official Yugoslav periodical *Službeni glasnik,* the Library holds important works on the individual republics. On Serbia: *Politička istorija Srbije u drugoj polovini devetnaestog veka,* 4 v. (Belgrade, 1923-25); *Politička istorija Srbije XIX i XX veka* (Belgrade, 1956-) by Miroslav Dordević; as well as works of Milan S. Piročanac, Dimitrije Marinković, and N. Dukanović. Among selective resources on Croatia and Slovenia, *Ideologija hrvatskog seljačkog pokreta* (Zagreb, 1935) by Ivo Šarinić; Ante Starčević's *Izbrani spisi* (Zagreb, 1945) edited by Blaž Jurišić; *Borba Hrvata: kronike dvaju desetljeća političke povijesti (1919-1939)* (Zagreb, 1940) by Mirko Glojnarić; *Političko življenje Slovencev (od 4. januarja 1917. do 6. januarja 1919. leta)* (Ljubljana, 1921) by Dragotin Lončar; and *Politička istorija Slovenačke* (Belgrade, 1939) by Vekoslav Bučar deserve mention.

The Library's collection is scanty on both military affairs and national questions. The collection on constitutional history, while not comprehensive, includes some out-of-print sources referring to the Kingdom of Yugoslavia and materials pertaining to the basic law of social and political organization of the present Federal People's Republic. The titles that deserve underscoring are *Étude sur la constitution du royaume des Serbes, Croates et Slovènes du 28 juin, avec texte officiel intégral . . .* (Paris, 1924) by Nikodim Jovanović; *La constitution du royaume de Yougoslavie du 3 septembre 1931, avec le texte intégral* (Paris, 1933); several recent works by Ferdo Čulinović, most notably his *Državnopravna historija jugoslovenskih zemalja XIX i XX veka* (Zagreb, 1956-59), and *Novi ustavni sistem* (Belgrade, 1964) by Jovan Dordević. The Library also has a representative collection of publications of the National Assembly such as *Stenografske beleške.*

Although the collection of materials in the field of economics is not comprehensive, it contains some important monographs treating the economy in general, for instance, *Ekonomska geografija Jugoslavije* (Belgrade, 1952) by N. Dragičević; a work of the same title by Rude Petrović, *Ekonomska geografija Jugoslavije* (Sarajevo, 1966); and *Prirodna bogatstva Jugoslavije* (Zagreb, 1958) by Stevo Vojnović. There are more specific works devoted to the economy and economic relations with foreign countries by economists and politicians such as Rudolf Bičanić and Petar Stambolić. In addition, the collection includes several pertinent journals such as the *Journal [of] Economic Information* (Belgrade, 1957-); *Ekonomska politika* (Belgrade, 1952-), *Ekonomski pregled* (Zagreb, 1950-), and similar serial resources published by Yugoslav economic institutes.

The interrelated disciplines—social conditions and social life—are adequately covered, particularly in regard to rural life. The sources at the disposal of the researcher cover various aspects of rural life, the history of peasants and their migratory habits, work organization, land tenure, and agricultural techniques. In addition, socioeconomic and political circumstances are covered by such works as *Naše selo* (Belgrade, 1929) by Miloslav Stojadinović; *Kako živi narod* (Zagreb, 1939) of "Gospodarska sloga"; *Social and Cultural Change in a Serbian Village* (New Haven, 1956) and *A Serbian Village* (New York, 1958) by Joel Martin Halpern; *Women in a Village . . .* (London, 1957) by Louisa Rayner; *Društveni razvitak Hrvata: rasprave i eseji* (Zagreb, 1937); *Personality and Culture in Eastern European Politics* (New York, 1948) by Dinko Tomašić, and *Socijalni problemi slovenske vasi* (Ljubljana, 1938) by Ivo Pirc and Franjo Bas.

Besides the irregular periodical *Socijalni arhiv* (Belgrade, 1935-) which is primarily dedicated to labor matters, there are works by Olive Lodge, John R. Morris, Hallam Tennyson, et al. For the last decade as a whole, and particularly the period from 1967 to date (partly due to the PL 480 Program), the collection is richer in materials dealing with rural and urban life, and with the imbalance between social strata of society in larger Yugoslav cities. At least two sources are worth mentioning, *Dinamika i struktura gradskog stanovništva Jugoslavije: demografski aspekt urbanizacije* (Belgrade, 1967) by Ivanka Ginić, and *Socijalna struktura i pokretljivost radničke klase Jugoslavije* (Belgrade, 1963) by Miloš Ilić.

While the collection of statistical source materials and yearbooks is sketchy, the coverage of statistics pertaining to foreign economics and trade is moderate. Among the works referring to the latter are *Statistique du commerce extérieur 1918-1939* (Belgrade, 1920-40) of the Ministry of Finance; *Statistika spoljne trgovine* of Savezní zavod za statistiku, and *Glasnik Zavoda za unapreðenje spoljne trgovine* (Belgrade, 1930-).

Vital statistics, however, are well covered. Included are the rare census publications *Definitivni rezultati popisa stanovništva od 31 januara* and *Statistički godišnjak (Annuaire statistique) od 31 marta, 1931* of the Direkcija državne statistike (Belgrade). Recent works of importance are the census publications *Popis stanovništva* of 1953, 1959, 1960, and 1961; *Statistički bilten,* 1950- , and *Statistički godišnjak,* 1954- of the Savezni zavod za statistiku.

The size of the collection on Yugoslav foreign relations and domestic policies and issues exceeds 200 entries. This is a select collection presenting a balanced picture of Yugoslavia's ever fluctuating foreign policies. Most of the materials in the collection discuss Yugoslav-Soviet relations, primarily on Stalin's break with Tito in 1948. Works also treat the events in Hungary in 1956, and in Czechoslovakia in 1968, and Yugoslavia's stand in these matters vis-à-vis Moscow. Several representative sources are the *White Book on Aggressive Activities by the Governments of the U.S.S.R., Poland, . . .* (Belgrade, 1951) published by the Ministry of Foreign Affairs, *Tito and Goliath* (New York, 1951) by Hamilton Fish; *La Yougoslavie sous la menace intérieure et extérieure* (Paris, 1952) by Ante Ciliga; *The Triumphant Heretic* (London, 1958) by Ernst Halperin; *Yugoslavia in World Affairs* (Urbana, Ill., 1960) by George Klein; *Tito Between East and West* (London, 1961) by Ilija Jukić; and *Yugoslavia* (Berkeley, 1949) by Robert Joseph Kerner. Works of Edvard Kardelj, Tito (his visits, speeches, etc.), Dilas, and others are included in this balanced collection.

A sizable block of material is devoted to the conflicts and relations between Yugoslavia and Italy, particularly the centuries-old problem of boundaries. Among such sources are *Frontiers Between the Kingdom of the Serbians, Croatians, and Slovenes, and the Kingdom of Italy* (Paris, 1919); *Opis granične linije izmeðu Kraljevine Jugoslavije i Kraljevine Italije* (Belgrade, 1935) by the Ministry of Foreign Affairs; and *Le conflict de Trieste, 1943-1954* (Brussels, 1966) by Jan Baptiste Duroselle.

The core of the collection on foreign affairs comprises sources treating the foreign relations of Serbia, including dozens of rare items, for example, *Rossiia i Serbiia*, 2 v. (Moscow, 1869) by Nil Aleksandrovich Popov; *Spoljašnji odnošaji Srbije novijega vremena, 1848-1872*, 3 v.

(Belgrade, 1887-1901) by Jovan Ristić; *Vlada ustavobranitelja* (Belgrade, 1932) by Dragoslav Stranjaković; *Odnosi izmedu Srbije i Austro-Ugarske u XX veku* (Belgrade, 1936) by Vladimir Ćorović; *Belgrad-Berlin, Berlin-Belgrad 1866-1871* (Berlin, 1936) by Johann Albrecht von Reiswitz; *Die Habsburger und die Südslawen Frage* (Belgrade, 1924), and *Bismarck und Serbian im Jahre 1866* . . . (Belgrade, 1927) by Hermann Wendel, and *La Yougoslavie.-La France et les Serbes.-Les crises de 1908 à 1916* . . . (Paris, 1916) by Pierre de Lanux. The rare works in the collection include several by Spiridion Gopčević, and Vladan Đordevic. Thus, Serbia's relations with Austria, Hungary, and particularly Russia, are well covered.

The Library has more than 300 entries on the four major languages spoken in Yugoslavia—Serbian, Croatian, Slovenian, and Macedonian—under the subject heading Serbo-Croatian. All aspects of the language are covered, from basic dictionaries, e.g., *Rečnik srpskohrvatskoga književnoga jezika,* 3 v. (Novi Sad-Zagreb, 1967-69) to important works of a linguistic nature, such as *Oko našeg književnog jezika* . . . (Belgrade, 1951) by Aleksandar Belić and his *Savremeni srpskohrvatski književni jezik* (Belgrade, 194-?). Accentology and dialectology are also well represented by, e.g., *Izabrana djela iz slavenske akcentuacije* (Munich, 1971) by Stjepan Ivšić, the important periodicals *Južnoslovenski filolog* and *Srpski dijalektološki zbornik,* works by Pavle Ivić, Andre Vailant, and others.

The Croatian language is not as comprehensively covered as is Serbian, although the Library owns works of Petar Skok, Mate Hraste, Ljudevit Jonke, Dalibor Brozović, Drago Ivanišević, and Thomas Magner. From the historical and lexicographical points of view this collection is particularly strong in holdings of rare dictionaries and grammars. Of the former, the oldest is *Blago jezika slovinskoga (Thesaurus linguae Illyricae)* (Lavreti, 1649-51) by the well-known Jesuit lexicographer and missionary, Jacopo Micaglia (Jakov Mikalja). Other significant dictionaries are *Dizionario italiano-latino-illirico* . . . 2 v. (Ragusa, 1785) by the Jesuit Ardelio Della Bella, dedicated to the Senate of the Dubrovnik Republic, and containing a wealth of quotations from the old literature of Dubrovnik. *Ričoslovnik iliričkoga, italianskoga i nimackoga jezika, s pridpostavljenom gramatikom* (Vienna, kod Kurzbeka, 1803) by Giuseppe Voltiggi, known also as Josip Voltigji from Istria; *Rečnik ilirskoga i nemackoga jezika,* 2 v. (Vienna, 1853-54) by Radovan A. Veselić; *Ilirsko-nemačko-talijanski mali rečnik sa osnovom gramatike ilirske (protumačenem nemački i talijanski)* od Věkoslava Babukića (Vienna, Tiskom jermenskoga manastira, 1846-49) by Josip Drobnić; *Vojnički rječnik* . . . , 2 v. in 1 (Budapest, 1900-03) by Teodor Toth [et al], and *Rječnik hrvatskoga jezika,* 2 v. (Zagreb, 1901) by Franjo Iveković and Ivan Broz. Some examples of older grammars are *Grammatik der illirischen Sprache* (Zagreb, 1850) by Ignaz Al. Brlić; *Ilirska slovnica* (Zagreb, 1854) by Věkoslav Babukić; and *Skladanja ilirskoga jezika za nižu gimnaziju* (Vienna, 1859) by Adolf Weber (Adolfo Veber Tkalčević). The oldest item is *De afflictione tam Captivorum quam etiam sub Turcae tributo viuentium Christianorum* . . . (Anuerp, Typis Copenij, 1544) by Bartolomej Dordević, which contains a discussion of the Croatian language.

The collection on the Slovenian language is adequate for a study of the language in general. Besides the rare *Slovar slovenskega jezika* (Ljubljana, 1936) by Joža Glonar, there are dictionaries by Janko Kotnik, France Tomšić, Stanko Škerlj, and others. In the field of grammar particular attention should be paid to *Pravila, kako izobraževati ilirsko narječje i u obće slavenski jezik* (Ljubljana, 1848) by Matia Majar (pseud. Ziljski). This work strongly influenced the formation of the Slovenian literary language in the 1850s. There are also works dealing with the history of the language and the dialects, for example, *Kratka zgodovina slovenskega jezika* (Ljubljana, 1936) by Franc Ramovš, and *Narječje vasi sele na Rožu* (Ljubljana, 1939) by Alexander V. Isačenko. The field of dialectology is rather strong in holdings. Two other works deserve mention, *Borba za individualnost slovenskega jezika v letih 1848-1857* (Ljubljana, 1937), and the rare periodical *Jezičnik* (covering the years 1863-68, 1873-92) which deals with both the language and the literature.

The collection on the Macedonian language is not large but includes basic grammars and works dealing with orthography. Periodicals dedicated to study of the language and its history are also included.

The Library's Yugoslav literature collections are divided into seven subject headings: Yugoslav, Serbo-Croatian, Serbian, Macedonian, Croatian, Dalmatian, and Slovenian literature. The Yugoslav literature section comprises only about 50 entries, but includes the interesting *Bibliografija knjiga ženskih pisaca štampanih u Hrvatskoj Slavoniji, Dalmaciji, Bosni i Hercegovini do svršetka godine 1935* (Zagreb, 1936), sponsored by the Society of University Educated Women in Yugoslavia, and compiled by Branka Dizdarić and Jelka Nušic-Jambrešić.

Under Serbo-Croatian literature are classified books by prominent writers and literary critics such as Đuro Daničić, Vatroslav Jagić, David Bogdanović, Dragutin Prohaska, and Arturo Cronia. Here one also finds the periodical *Dubrovnik: zabavnik Narodne štionice dubrovačke*, 4 v. (Dubrovnik, 1866-76).

The coverage of Serbian literature is excellent. All periods are well covered—from the late 18th century, i.e., from Dositej Obradović, through the 19th century, represented by Vuk Karadžić, Petar Petrović Njegoš, Branko Radičević, Zmaj Jovan Jovanović, Đura Jakšić, Jakov Ignjatović, to the 20th century, represented by Jovan Dučić, Milan Rakić, Petar Kočić, Branislav Nušić, the Nobel Prize-winner Ivo Andrić, and others. Literary criticism is also richly represented. Many important literary periodicals, both new and old, are part of the collection, as *Zbornik za istoriju, jezik i književnost srpskog naroda* (1st, 2d, 3d sections) and similar works; subject bibliographies covering literature for the period of 1741-1867; and *Pregled izdanja* of the Serbian Academy of Arts and Sciences for the years 1847-1959 (Belgrade, 1961) and 1960-62 (Belgrade, 1963) which includes literature.

The Macedonian literature collection is small, reflecting the recent nature of this literature.

Croatian literature is well covered. The outstanding series *Stari pisci hrvatski* (Zagreb, 1869-) includes works of major literary figures of the 16th and 17th centuries—Marko Marulić, the celebrated poet and Latinist and the father of Croatian literature, Šiško Menčetić, Đore Držić, Petar Hektorović, Hanibal Lucić, Petar Zrinjski, Pavao Ritter Vitezović, and others. The 18th century is represented by works of such notable writers as Ignjat Đurđević, Andrija Kačić Miošic, Antun Reljković, and Tito Brezovački. The distinctive literary periods of the 19th century—the "Illyrian movement," Romanticism, Realism—are represented respectively by Ljudevit Gaj, Ivan Mažuranić, Stanko Vraz, et al.; August Šenoa and Franjo Marković; Eugen Kumičić, Ksaver Šandor Đalski, Vjekoslav Novak, and Silvije Strahimir Kranjčević. The 20th century, with the best coverage of all, is represented by Cihlar Milutin Nehajev, Vladimir Vidrić, August Matoš, Vladimir Nazor, Miroslav Krleža, and others. The collection of sources on literary criticism is extensive.

Under the subject heading Dalmatian Literature there are four works which deserve to be singled out for their importance. *Die Dichtungen Gundulics und ihr poetischer Stil* (Bonn, 1952) by Wsewolod Setschkareff, devoted to the celebrated Croatian poet of the "Golden" period, Ivan Gundulić, author of the famous epic *Osman; Dubrovačka književnost* (Dubrovnik, 1900) by Ivan Stojanović; *Zbornik iz dubrovačke prošlosti* (Dubrovnik, 1931), and *Ilirska antologija, književni dokumenti hrvatskog preporoda* (Zagreb, 1934) by Slavko Ježić. Other Dalmatian, i.e., Croatian writers are mentioned under Croatian literature.

Although the collection on Slovenian literature is not very comprehensive, it is excellent in quality. It includes works of the most important writers as Anton Tomaž Linhart, Fran Levstik, Bartolomej Kopitar, Josip Stritar, Josip Jurčić, Simon Jenko, Simon Gregorčić, and Ivan Tavčar.

The modern movement is represented by all important writers, Ivan Prijatelj, Franc Kidrič, Oton Župančić, Prežihov Voranc, et al. The sources on literary criticism are few in number, but well selected. Notable are *Geschichte der südslawichen Literatur*, 3 v. (Prague, 1864-65) by Paul Jos. Šafařik, edited by Josef Jireček; *Zgodovina slovenskega slovstva od začetkov do Zoisove smrti*, 5 pts. (Ljubljana, 1929-38) by Franc Kidrič, and other important works treating the history of Slovenian literature, notably those of Lino Legiša, Anton Ocvirk, and the recent voluminous and impressive *Zgodovina slovenskega slovstva*, 8 v. (Maribor, 1968-72) by Jože Pogačnik. (Volume 8 includes a very useful bibliography, compiled by Štefka Bulovec, which covers all periods.) Serial publications in the subject include such rare titles as *Časopis za slovenski jezik, književnost in zgodovino*, 8 v. (Ljubljana, 1918-31). Thus, despite certain gaps, the Serbian, Croatian, and Slovenian literatures are well covered. The materials received through the PL 480 Program, particularly the well-edited series of *Srpska književnost u sto knjiga* (Novi Sad, 1962, and other editions), *Pet stoljeća hrvatske književnosti* (Zagreb, 1962-), reprints as *Danica Ilirska*, as well as works of noted authors, various well-edited anthologies of poetry and other genres of belles lettres have greatly enriched the collections and their potential as a research source.

The Yugoslav folklore collection in the New York Public Library is one of the great strengths of its South Slavic holdings. All cycles and genres of this folklore, from oral epic to folk songs, folktales, proverbs, customs, mores and beliefs, are well covered, including a comprehensive collection of folk songs and tales. In this section *Južno-slovjenske narodne popievke*, 5 v. (Zagreb, 1878), *Slawische Volkslieder aus dem Süden . . .* (Zagreb, 1882) by Franjo Kuhač, and *Das Volkslied im Süden der Monarchie . . .* (Vienna, 1911) by Milan R. Rešetar deserve mention.

Among many sources dealing with Serbian folksongs, customs, and tales, some rare materials are: *Narodne srpske pjesme*, 4 v. (U lipisci, 1823-33) by Vuk Stefanović Karadžić; *Pievaniia cernogorska i hercegovačka (Volkslieder du Montenegriner und Herzegowiner Serben)* (Buda, 1833, also, in Leipzig in 1837) by Sima Milutinović; *Ilustrovana velika srpska narodna lira najveća i najpotpunija od sviju dosadašnjih, sa 2000 pesama koje se u srpskom narodu pevaju* (Novi Sad [191-?]), and *Srpske narodne pesme* (Belgrade, 1922) by Vojislav M. Jovanović. Included are also several studies on folk poetry and customs as, for instance, *Studije o srpskoj narodnoj lirici* (Skopje, 1921) by Dim. P. Đurović, *Stari život i običaji u Južnoj Srbiji* (Belgrade, 1926) by Jeremija M. Pavlović; *Beleške o našoj narodnoj poeziji* (Belgrade, 1939), *Naš narodni život*, 10 v. (Belgrade, 1930-34) by Tihomir R. Đorđević; the very rare *Obychai i piesni Turetskikh Serbov* (S. Peterburg, 1886) by Ivan Stepanovich Iastrebov; and an important source on ethnology, folklore, population, etc., titled *Srpski etnografski zbornik* (Belgrade, 1894-). The sources on Serbian folktales are of good quality such as *Kraljević Marko; zbirka 220 pesama i 90 pripovedaka narodnih, pokupljenih iz svih krajeva srpskih i ostalih jugoslovenskih zemalja* (Novi Sad, 1922), edited by Sreta J. Stojković; *Volksmärchen der Serben . . .* (Berlin, 1854) by Vuk Stefanović Karadžić, and *Narodne pripovijesti i presude iz života po Boki Kotorskoj, Hercegovini i Crnoj Gori* (Dubrovnik, 1890) by Vuk Stefan Vrčević. Sources on Macedonian folklore include *Makedonsko-slavianskii sbornik* (S. Peterburg, 1894) by Piotr Danilovich Draganov, and *Zbirka na makedonski narodni pesni* (Skopje, 1945), edited by Blaže Koneski.

Although the collection on Croatian folklore is not as strong as Serbian, there are some collected works that cover specific regions and discuss the history of the folk poetry, e.g., *Hrvatske narodne pjesme kajkavske* (Zagreb, 1950); *Hrvatske pučke popijevke iz Međumurja* (Zagreb, 1921), and *Razvoj hrvatskog pjesništva: književno poviesne razprave* [sic] (Zagreb, 1944) by Petar Grgec. The representative materials dealing with customs and other genres of folklore are the rare *Narodni slavonski običaji, sabrani i popisani po Luki Iliću Oriovčaninu* (Zagreb, 1846), and the monumental, multivolume publication of the Yugoslav Academy of Arts and Sciences, *Zbornik za narodni život i običaje Južnih Slavena* (Zagreb, 1896-).

Of similar scope and importance for Slovenian folklore studies are *Slovenske narodne pesni iz tiskanih in pisanih virov,* 4 v. (Ljubljana, 1895-1923) by Karl (Karel) Štrekelj; the leading journal, *Etnolog* (Ljubljana, 1926-44), which was succeeded by *Slovenski etnograf, časopis za etnografijo in folkloro* (Ljubljana, 1948-); and *Slovenske pripovedke o kralju Matjažu* (Ljubljana, 1951), edited by Ivan Grafenauer. The collection includes many recently published anthologies, bulletins, and works published by the Institute for the Folklore Studies in Sarajevo.

The sources on education are only fair. However, certain fields such as the history of scholarship, the cultural history of the 19th century, and even the history of education are investigated in such basic works as *Srbija pre sto godina* (Belgrade, 1946) by Tihomir R. Đorđević and *Spomenici kulture* (Belgrade, 1951), edited by M. Panić-Surep.

Much more comprehensive and detailed works are *Kultura Hrvata kroz 100 godina,* 2 v. (Zagreb, 1939-42) by Josip Horvat; *Stogodišnjica hrvatskoga preporoda* (Zagreb, 1936) by Vladimir Gudel; *Kulturna historija Hrvatske: ideje, ličnosti, djela* (Zagreb, 1964) by Zvane Črnja; *Sveslavenski zbornik. Spomenici o tisućugodišnjici hrvatskoga kraljevstva* (Zagreb, 1930) with contributions in all Slavic languages; and *Kulturna in politična zgodovina Slovencev, 1848-1895,* 4 v. (Ljubljana, 1938-40) by Ivan Prijatelj.

Sources on the leading cultural societies of Serbia and Croatia that deserve mention are *Matica srpska, 1826-1926* (Novi Sad, 1927) and *Matica hrvatska, 1842-1962. Povijest Matice hrvatske. Bibliografija izdanja Matice* (Zagreb, 1963) by Jakša Ravlić and Marin Somborac.

While the collection of materials on religions in Yugoslavia as a whole is sketchy, the holdings dealing with the Serbian Orthodox Church contain some basic works.

The collections on the performing arts, music, and the theater are dependent on donors and are fragmentary, though growing. The map collection includes some of the basic sources, among others, *Geografski atlas Jugoslavije* (Zagreb, 1961) by Petar Mardešić; *Historical Atlas of the Liberation War of the Peoples of Yugoslavia, 1941-1945* (Belgrade, 1957), works by the Geographical Society of Belgrade, and the valuable *Atlas de la Societé de géographie de Beograd,* 13 v. (Belgrade, 1929-35).

In the Department of Special Collections there are several noteworthy items dealing with statutes and codices, for example, the code of Tsar Dušan. Items of research value include works on the liturgy and rituals of the Roman Catholic Church, the printing of the Croatian manuscripts, and Glagolitic works in sources such as *Hrvatska književnost od početka do danas, 1100-1941* (Zagreb, 1944) by Slavko Ježić, and *Kolunićev zbornik, hrvatski glagolski rukopisi od god. 1486* (Zagreb, 1892), which was edited in Latin characters by the Yugoslav Academy of Arts and Sciences (*Djela* JAZU, knj. 12). The Zbornik of Broz Kolunic (fl. 1486) also deals with sermons and Glagolitic alphabet. While the manuscript collection is not comprehensive, the literature on the subject is very well represented with works of such prominent bibliophiles and scholars as Vatroslav Jagić, Tomo Maretić, Ivan Kukuljević-Sakcinski, J. Vajs, I. Miletić, Lj. Stojanović, D. S. Radojičić, Mirko Breyer, and Vladimir Mošin.

George C. Jerkovich
University of Kansas

Other Countries

Albania

Bibliographic holdings are spotty; the Library does not currently receive the quarterly national bibliography published by the Biblioteka Kombëtare.

The Library receives such periodicals of general interest as *Nëndori* (1960-), *New Albania* (1967-), and *Shêjzat* (1967-) currently as well as the expatriate publications *Besa* (Istanbul, 1953-), *Flamuri* (Rome, 1950-), and *Shqiptari i lire* (New York, 1958). The Library also receives the newspaper *Rilindja* (Priština) published in the Albanian-speaking autonomous province of Kosovo-Metohija in Yugoslavia, as well as *Bashkimi* (Tirana, 1956-).

The only documents received with any regularity are the *Gazeta zyrtare* (1959-) [the Library also has a file of its predecessor the *Fletorja zyrtare* (1927-40)] and the *Anuari statistikor i.R.P.Sh.* (1959-). Some commercial statistics are available for the 1920s and 1930s and the *Qarkoret* (1920-29) of the Ministrija e puneve të mbrendshme.

Language is a strong subject in the Library and the holdings are comprehensive in published works from Albania and other countries, but literature receives only representative treatment. Two literary periodicals are received: *Shêjzat* (Le Pleiadi) (1957-) and *Studi albanesi* (1965-). The folklore holdings include not only the standard published works but such early texts as J. G. von Hahn's *Griechische und albanesische Maerchen* (1864-). Ethnomusicology is the strongest aspect of the holdings in Albanian music. In all of the cultural and intellectual aspects of the Library's Albanian collection, the extensive holdings of general learned society publications and journals from other countries are of the greatest importance. Religion is not a strong subject in the Library thus only a few studies are available, mostly historical and bibliographical.

Law is not a strong subject with the Research Libraries. Though there is a scattering of codes and published constitutions of the country, perhaps the most notable item is the file of *Drejtësia popullore* (1967-). There is also the journal of the Parti punës shqiptare, *Rruga e partisë* (1967-). Statistical publications are the most remarkable among the economics holdings. Though there are gaps, adequate documentation can be furnished for the economic history of Albania.

The Library can furnish the standard printed sources for the geography and geology of the country. Maps and atlases provide documentation from the 17th century onward. Description and travel are strongly represented for most periods. The most significant aspect of the holdings in anthropology and ethnology lies in the extensive resources of learned society publications and journals from the countries of the world.

The holdings for Albanian history are comprehensive, including most of the references given in the Horecky bibliography and many others; titles in Greek, Russian, and Serbo-Croatian are also available. Among the historical journals currently received are *Albanische Forschungen* (1964-) and *Studime historike* (1966-) of the Universiteti shtetëror. Historical sources for Albania appear in the Hungarian *Archivum Europae centro-orientalis* (Budapest, 1935-44) and the Italian *Fonti per la storia d'Albania*. A wealth of additional material is found in the rich files of historical journals from all countries in The Research Libraries. About 200 references in the dictionary catalogs of the General Research and Humanities Division and in the Slavonic Division refer to Albanian history—the subject is arranged by date. The earliest among a number of biographies of Giorgio Castriota, called Scanderbeg, is that of Jacques de Lavardin entitled *The historie of George Castriot, surnamed Scanderbeg, king of Albanie* (London, 1596).

Bulgaria

The collection of bibliographies may be described as spotty; although both volumes of *Bŭlgarski periodichen pechat* are present, other key titles are not. The Library has the standard encyclopedias as well as other handbooks of general information. The holdings of bilingual dictionaries, while strong in numbers, are not always up to date. No biographical dictionaries of works on genealogy were noted.

The 50 retrospective files of Bulgarian periodicals in the Library include a number of titles which are unique in the United States according to the *Union List of Serials*. Some of the earlier titles are *Mirozreniye* (1850-51) and *Zornitza* (1874-81); others include *Chitalishte* (1944-65, with gaps), *Sŭvremennik* (1921-23), and *Zvezda* (1922-33). Currently the Library receives 54 periodical titles in Bulgarian in a number of fields. The Slavonic Division has always had a particular interest in collecting émigré publications and has on its current shelves *Borba* (1965-) published in New York as the organ of the Bulgarian National Front, the *Bŭlgarsko emigrantsko druzhestvo* (1960-65) published in Paris, and the *Bulgarian Review* (Rio de Janeiro, 1965, 1966, 1971-) published by the Foyer Bulgare in Brazil. Six newspaper titles are received currently, among them *Literaturen front* (1955-), *Narodna armiya* (1961-), and *Otechestven front* (1946-49, 1959-).

The public documents collection is most complete for the period of the constitutional monarchy. The official gazette, the *Dŭrzhaven vestnik,* is available from 1881 to 1931 with only a few years missing—1890, 1894, 1911, 1917, and 1920. The journals of the Grand National Assembly, the *Veliko narodno sŭbraniye,* extend from the 1st sobranie of 1879 to the extra session of the 17th sobranie of 1914. There is a gap in such records from 1914 until the *Izvestiya na prezidium* (1950-60).

The laws of Bulgaria are available in the Research Libraries in a number of separate publications from 1899 to the present time. The collected statutes of the country date from 1958 in an incomplete film edition. There are copies of treaties from 1910 to the 1948 pact of friendship with Albania. Provincial or municipal documents are represented in the holdings by only a few items from Sofia.

Resources on the Bulgarian language are comprehensive and include the first Bulgarian grammar in English, by Elias Riggs (Smyrna, 1844). Bulgarian literature also forms a comprehensive collection with most of the classic authors of the literature represented by collected editions of their works with a good selection of single editions and critical works. Folklore is another strong subject with extensive holdings of folk songs, folktales, folk costume, and folk dancing. The Library does not collect in the field of religion except for the history of the subject; the holdings are selective. Thought, philosophy, and learning are fairly well represented. Bulgarian art of the earlier periods is emphasized in the holdings where the overall holdings in the field of art lend much additional strength. This is also the case with music where the emphasis is on ethnomusicology. The Dance Collection reports some holdings on the Bulgarian dance with clippings and one film on theatrical dance. The holdings for the theater, cinema, radio, and television are comprehensive for published works supplemented by extensive clippings files, and files of programs, theatrical photographs, movie stills, etc., with emphasis on performances in the United States.

The Research Libraries do not collect in the field of law with the major exceptions of the bibliography and history of law, and statutory law. The holdings include *Abstracts of Bulgarian Scientific Literature. Economics and Law* (1958-) as well as the *Izvestiya* (1960-) of the Bulgarian Academy of Science's Institut na pravni nauki. Politics of the later 19th century are best represented in the holdings, though there is some strength in recently received periodical titles on the subject as, for example: *Chitalishte* (1944-65), *Otechestven front* (1946-48, 1962-), and the *Novo vreme* (1948-) of the Bŭlgarska komunisticheska partiya. Though there are no collections, there are texts of individual treaties. There is also some material on Bulgarian foreign relations during the World War I period.

There is no particular strength in the field of Bulgarian economics either in bibliographies or in the standard texts. Periodicals and Bulgarian government statistical publications form a representative collection.

The holdings in geography are representative only. The Map Division on the other hand can show a number of gazetteers, atlases, and maps outlining Bulgarian history, geography, and topography.

Of about 400 titles noted under the heading BULGARIA—HISTORY in the dictionary catalogs over half, or about 260 titles, are equally divided between general history and 19th-century history. Fifty titles relate to the Middle Ages; the history of the 20th century is covered in 60 titles. The holdings are comprehensive with most of the titles listed in the Horecky bibliography available. Historical source material includes the *Fontes Historiae Bulgaricae* (1954-68) of the Bulgarian Academy of Sciences. Periodicals received include the *Izvestiya* (1951-) of the Bulgarian Academy of Sciences. The resources on Bulgarian history are strengthened by holdings relating to the Ottoman Empire in the Oriental Division. The Manuscript Division holds material relating to the earthquake of 1928 in its Finley papers.

Romania

The Library's holdings in the important area of bibliography are comprehensive including the national bibliography and special catalogs of Kubon and Sagner. The standard encyclopedias are all available but biographic material is scanty and materials on genealogy and heraldry, a strong subject in the Library, are practically nonexistent. An extensive collection of handbooks, surveys, and guidebooks is perhaps most remarkable for the earlier titles of the 19th century and before. Holdings of bilingual dictionaries cover a period from 1861 to the present day.

The Romanian-American periodicals in the Research Libraries are of particular interest, many being held by few other institutions in the United States. Some of the runs are short, as *Roumania; American Roumanian Review* (Chicago, 1917-18), or *Roumania: A Quarterly Review* (New York, 1929-32), or the *Roumanian Bulletin* (New York, 1932-35). A slightly longer run is available for *Steaua noastră* (New York, 1920-27); currently the Library receives *America; Roumanian News* (Cleveland, Ohio, 1942-), *Calendarul solia* (Detroit, 1958-), organ of the Romanian Orthodox Episcopate of America, and the *Colecţia dacia* (Rio de Janeiro, 1962-).

Holdings of public documents for the period from 1860 to the outbreak of World War II are good. The Library has an incomplete file of the official gazette, *Monitorul oficial* (1894-1916, 1920-44), which is continued by the *Buletinul oficial* (1958-) published by the Marea adunarea naţională. These have been filmed as a part of the Gazettes Microfilming Project of the Library. Parliamentary proceedings begin with the *Analele parlamentare ale Românei* (1893-1902) which are journals with documents of the assemblies of Wallachia and Moldavia compiled from various archives and covering the period 1833 to 1843. The *Desbaterile* of the Adunarea generală are available from 1861/62 to 1863/64 and those of the Senatul from 1874 to 1933, although from 1883 these documents were also issued as a part of the *Monitorul oficial*. The *Desbaterile* of the Adunarea deputaţilor are available from 1866 to 1933. The Research Libraries do not have post-World War II parliamentary proceedings.

The statutes of Transylvania, *Compilatae constitutiones* (Claudiopoli, 1671) are the earliest Romanian imprint in the library.

Texts of treaties and codes of law are also available. Statistical publications are fairly complete from the early 1900s to the present day.

The Research Libraries have strong holdings in language and linguistics, but only a representative collection of literature. The periodicals include a rare file of *Convorbiri literare* (1907-40). Religion, philosophy, and education in Romania are represented by only selective collections. Romanian folklore as a subject is substantially reinforced by the strong overall holdings in folklore of all lands in the Library, including folk costume, folk songs, etc. Art and architecture are good collections with a number of catalogs of the important museums and collections. Music is strongest in the field of ethnomusicology. There are holdings of recorded performances from Romania on the major western labels (Angel, RCA, et al.) in the Rodgers and Hammerstein Archives of Recorded Sound. Theater and dance are also well represented.

The Research Libraries acquire only selectively in the field of law, government, and politics. Diplomacy and foreign relations, on the other hand, form a representative collection including the diplomatic correspondence published by the Ministerul afacerilor străine dating from the late 19th century, as well as substantial important holdings of learned journals and society publications.

The Research Libraries are especially strong in statistical publications of the Direcţia Centrală de Statistică, and its parent bodies before World War II. Not only are national statistics available but also the regional statistics for 1960 for such areas as Bacau, Baia-Mare, Cluj, Timişoara, Ploeşti, Braşov [Stalin], and others, in all 14 regions. Periodical publications in economics are another area of strength.

The holdings on the Romanian land and people are comprehensive with particular strength in periodical and society publications. In addition materials on geography in general including publications of learned societies and the proceedings of international geographical congresses, etc., add considerable depth. The Library has always emphasized collecting in the area of geographic place-names; the catalogs contain a listing of books in the field as well as index references to periodical articles. Maps and atlases are available from 1664 to the present day. The Library has the results of censuses from 1905 onward.

The Library has comprehensive coverage in the major collections of historical source material. For example there is the Hurmuzachi *Documente privitóre la istoria Românilor* (1887-1938) supplemented by the *Documente privind istoria României: (Serie nouă)* (1962-) and the less pretentious *Acte şi fragmente cu privire la istoria Romînilor* (1895-97) which cover Romanian history in general. Collections of source materials for Moldavia, Transylvania, and other areas are also represented, as, for example, *Documente privind istoria României: Moldova* (1951-). Periodical holdings are extensive, but the holdings of monographs in history only representative.

Sam P. Williams
New York Public Library

Fan S. Noli Library

General Information

The Metropolitan Fan S. Noli Library of Albanian and Eastern Orthodox Culture is housed in the Religious Education Building of the St. George Albanian Orthodox Cathedral, 529 East Broadway, South Boston, Mass. Dedicated in September 1970, the Library contains the papers and memorabilia of Metropolitan Fan S. Noli (1882-1965), prominent Albanian churchman, writer, scholar, and statesman. In addition, the Library has a small collection of Albanian and Eastern Orthodox books, newspapers, and periodicals.

The Noli Library does not maintain regular hours. Its resources can be examined and utilized by scholars and students upon application to the Reverend Arthur Liolin, the Library administrator. There is no fee for the use of the Library. Work space for researchers is limited and there are no photocopy facilities available. Except for some periodicals and books, Library materials must be used on the premises.

Collections

The most significant items in the Noli collection are the correspondence, manuscript, archive, and "working" files. There are approximately 3,000 letters received by Noli between 1930 and 1965 in the correspondence file. As of 1972, only about 100 copies of letters written by Noli were on deposit. These date mainly between 1960 and 1964. The Library encourages members of the Albanian-American community and other friends of Metropolitan Noli to deposit correspondence originating with him in its collection. Approximately 55 percent of the correspondence is in Albanian, 20 percent in Greek, 20 percent in English, and 5 percent in other languages. Aside from personal communications from relatives and friends, the bulk of the correspondence deals with matters pertaining to the administration of the Albanian Orthodox Church in America. There are also several hundred letters concerning Albanian political and diplomatic issues during the period from 1930 through the early 1950s. The correspondence is arranged chronologically, and an index to the collection is in preparation.

The manuscript file contains the typescripts of Noli's literary and ecclesiastical publications and several folios of his unpublished musical compositions. The archives file consists mainly of press clippings concerning Noli and the Albanian Orthodox Church in America and Albania. The "working" file contains reports of meetings and activities of the Diocesan Council of the Albanian Orthodox Church in America and of the individual churches of the Diocese, as well as Noli's ledgers. There are also copies of Noli's published works in the Library.

In addition to the Noli materials, the Library possesses two complete unbound sets of the Albanian language newspaper *Republika,* published in Boston between November 1930 and June 1932. These are apparently the only unbroken runs in existence of this liberal, antimonarchist newspaper, which served as the sounding board for Noli's views in the United States during the early 1930s. Since 1970, the Library has received and preserved the Albanian-American weekly newspapers *Dielli* and *Liria.* It also currently receives and maintains approximately two dozen religious (mostly Eastern Orthodox) publications.

In summary, the Noli Library is a most important research source for those scholars interested in the life and activities of Metropolitan Noli, the Albanian Orthodox Church in America, and the Albanian-American community. Its holdings will also be of value to those researchers working in the field of 20th-century Albanian history, politics, and culture.

Nicholas C. Pano
Western Illinois University

The University of North Carolina

General Information

Most of the University's East European holdings are located in the general stacks of the Main Library. These stacks are open, and all faculty and students at the University have free access to them. The usual operating hours are as follows: Monday through Friday, 8 a.m. to 11 p.m.; Saturday, 8 a.m. to 7 p.m.; Sunday, 2 p.m. to 11 p.m. General works in English may be found in the Undergraduate Library, which is open daily from 8 a.m. to 2 a.m. (Saturday to 7 p.m.). Certain specialized items are located in the Art Library, Music Library, Library School Library, etc., according to their subject content.

The University employs a Slavic bibliographer, who is assisted by a relatively small staff. He is responsible for the acquisition of new materials and the maintenance of the collection. The Main Library has a dictionary catalog for the entire University holdings. Each branch library has a catalog for its specific collection, as of now, there is no specialized catalog for the European or Slavic collection.

The Main Library (officially known as the Louis Round Wilson Library) maintains an "area studies room" wherein are located the Slavic encyclopedias, dictionaries, and Slavic national bibliographies. In addition, Wilson Library has three main reading rooms, 450 stack carrels for students, and 50 individual study rooms for faculty members. There is also a reading room in each of the branch libraries.

Books may be borrowed by faculty members or students for a period of four weeks. Certain volumes are restricted to building use only. Periodicals may be taken from the building with special permission, but the loan period is restricted to 24 hours.

Four Xerox machines for public use are located next to the periodicals room in the Main Library. There is also a photoreproduction service located on the ground floor of the building.

The Collections

The intensive collecting of materials dealing with Eastern Europe is of fairly recent origin, dating back to the 1950s. Since then it has followed closely the development of the University faculty's teaching and research programs.

In 1968 Library operations in the field of Russian and East European studies were greatly advanced by establishing the position of a Slavic bibliographer. In 1971 a full Slavic Biblio-Center was established, combining acquisition operations with cataloging and reference work under the direction of the Slavic bibliographer. Book exchanges with East European libraries have been intensified since then. A compact reference and bibliographic section for Slavic studies was established in a Library reading room, and advisory service to faculty and students seeking bibliographic information has been expanded. In 1972 a computer-produced catalog of periodicals and other serial publications in the Russian and East European area was issued, and a list of reference and bibliographic aids is forthcoming.

In 1972, the total size of the Library collections dealing with Albania, Bulgaria, Czechoslovakia, East Germany, Greece, Hungary, Poland, Romania, and Yugoslavia amounted to approximately 25,800 volumes, of which some 13,400 represent monographs and some 12,400 serial publications. Annual intake in a normal year can be estimated perhaps at 2,000 volumes. If publications relating to more than one of these countries or to such blocs as the Slavic nations, the Balkan Peninsula, the Austrian Empire, the Communist bloc, or to Eastern Europe as a whole were to be included in the count, the given figures would be substantially higher: 39,700 for the total (18,900 for the monographs; 17,800 for the serial publications) and 3,000 for the annual intake.

A recent numerical count of holdings in the field of East European studies yielded the following figures:

	Monographs (volumes)	Serials (volumes)	Total
Albania	48	0	48
Bulgaria	280	94	374
Czechoslovakia	6,941	4,843	11,784
East Germany	189	1,880	2,069
Greece	527	174	701
Hungary	680	749	1,429
Poland	2,531	2,034	4,565
Romania	369	448	817
Yugoslavia	1,860	2,161	4,021
Subtotal	13,425	12,383	25,808
Eastern Europe (as a whole)	5,472	5,453	10,925
Total	18,897	17,836	36,733

The Albanian collection, by far the smallest of the groups, consists of 48 monographs. Of these 18 volumes concern language and literature and are mainly linguistic tracts written in German. The 24 volumes dealing with history also cover such subjects as Albania's relations with other European countries and with China and the Soviet Union.

The University's Bulgarian collection is quite modest. The books in English tend to be surveys of Bulgarian history and political tracts. The more specific aspects of history and the works of Bulgarian economics are generally written in Russian or Bulgarian. The language and literature section contains a few general grammars and very specific linguistic analyses of Bulgarian. The literature section has approximately 50 general surveys and histories of Bulgarian literature and about 50 volumes by or about specific authors.

Most aspects of Czechoslovak studies are well covered; indeed, the Czechoslovak collection is larger than that for any other single country. To be noted are the many bibliographies (over 200 volumes) and archival catalogs. There are hundreds of basic lawbooks, including series such as: Bohemia. Laws, Statutes, etc. *Provinzialgesetzsammlung des Königreichs Böhmen* (32 v.); Moravia. Laws, Statutes, etc. *Landes-Gesetz- und Verordnungsblatt für die Markgrafschaft Mähren* (80 v.); Czechoslovak Republic. Laws, Statutes, etc. *Sbírka zákonů Československé socialistické republiky* (51 v.); Czechoslovak Republic. Nejvyšší soud. *Rozhodnutí Nejvyššího soudu Československé republiky ve věcech občanských* (30 v.); *Právnická knihovna* (67 v.); *Sborník věd právních a státních* (39 v.); *Prager Archiv für Gesetzgebung und Rechtsprechung* (24 v.). Collections on legislative proceedings are available too; for example: Bohemia. Zemský sněm. *Stenografické zprávy sněmu království českého* (50 v.); Czechoslovak Republic. Národní shromáždění. Poslanecká sněmovna. *Těsnopisecké zprávy o schůzích* (141 v.).

Certain Czech and Slovak institutional publications are also quite complete. For example the Library has a complete collection of serials published by the Czech Academy of Sciences and Arts (Česká akademie věd a umění) and most of those published by the Slovak and Czechoslovak academies of sciences (Slovenská akadémia vied, Československá akademie věd). University publications are also well represented; for example: Prague. Universita, Filosofická fakulta. *Práce z vědeckých ústavů* (53 v.); Brünn. Universita. Filosofická fakulta. *Spisy* (72 v.). Important museum series include: Prague. Národní museum. *Časopis* (115 v.); Brünn. Moravské zemské museum. *Časopis* (56 v.). The Library also has Matice moravská, *Časopis* (83 v.) and Matica slovenská, *Sborník* (18 v.).

In linguistics *Naše řeč* and *Slovenská reč* total 95 volumes. The literature section of some 1,500 volumes includes a complete collection of Czech and Slovak classics, including those of Němcová (14 v.), Neruda (33 v.), Baar (30 v.), Hermann (44 v.), Frída (pseud. Vrchlický, 64 v.), Mužáková (Světlá, 30 v.), Zeyer (35 v.), Bencúr (Kukučín, 32.), Országh (Hviezdoslav, 12 v.), and others. A collection of literary journals and series include *Lumír* (63 v.), *Zvon* (41 v.), *Máj* (12 v.), and all subseries of Česká akademie věd a umění, Prague. Třída III. *Sbírka pramenů k poznání literárního života československého* (49 v.). The holdings also include some authoritative basic works on the development of Czech and Slovak music, both as folk art and the creations of individual composers. Subscriptions to large-scale editions of outstanding composers' works (e.g. Dvořák) have been maintained from the start.

The larger collections in history are *Archiv český* (36 v.); Prague. Česká akademie věd a umění, Třída I. *Historický archiv* (52 v.); *Český časopis historický* (50 v.); *Časopis katolického duchovenstva* (58 v.); *Historica* (15 v.); *Vlastivěda moravská* (62 v.). Serial publications in other social sciences include *Obzor národohospodářský* (47 v.); Národní banka československá, *Bulletin* (70 v.); and several series of statistical publications, especially: Czechoslovak Republic. Státní úřad statistický. *Československá statistika* (174 v.). The Library also has several important political reviews and newspapers, such as *Přítomnost* (16 v.); *Prager Presse* (18 v.); *Slovenský denník* (20 v.), and others.

The German Democratic Republic is represented by two large sets of law collections: *Sammlung von Gesetzen und Verordnungen aus der sowjetischen Besatzungzone* (80 v.), and *Gesetzblatt der Deutschen Republik* (20 v.). No books on literature, linguistics, art, or music have been included in this survey, for here the distinction between the works of the two Germanys would be too difficult to establish. Any serial published in what is now the German Democratic Republic, but which ceased publication before 1949 has not been included in the above-given count.

The works on modern Greece are mainly monographs, with about equal representation in language, literature, and history. An additional 100 volumes are made up by encyclopedias, bibliographies, and statistical compilations.

The Hungarian section (apart from works devoted to the Austrian Empire) is of fairly modest dimension but contains the most important reference and bibliographic aids, among the latter the *Könyvtár a Magyar Tudományos Egyetem* (59 v.). For historical studies, two series are significant, the *Magyarország Vármegyéi és Városai* (20 v.) and Hungary. Laws, Statutes, etc. *Magyar Törvénytár* (13 v.). In literature—which takes up approximately half as much shelf space as history—nearly 50 percent of the titles are translations into English. Certain aspects of Hungarian folk and artistic music are relatively well represented in the Music Library which has, from the outset, maintained subscriptions to the collected editions of Bartók and Kodály as well as to the series *Musicologica Hungarica* and the journal *Studia musicologica*.

As to the Polish section, the situation is similar to the Hungarian. It, too, is stronger in teaching than in research materials. Almost 1,200 of the 1,400 Polish language and literature books are either monographs or small sets of individual authors' collected works. There are numerous small sets in history, bibliography, and encyclopedias. The departmental libraries hold 36 different serial titles, totaling 434 volumes. The Music Library has the complete edition of Chopin's works and all items published thus far in the series *Antiquitates musicae in Polonia*.

In their present state of development, the holdings in Polish literature and, to a somewhat lesser degree, in history (both mainly concentrated on the 19th and 20th century) can be considered adequate to support study up to the M.A. level but not beyond.

Most of the works in the Romanian collection are in the fields of language and history. The latter includes a few short runs of serial publications: *Revue roumaine d'histoire* (10 v.), *Revista istorică română* (7 v.), *Acta historica* (12 v.), and 37 volumes of publications by the Academia Republicii Populare Romîne.

The Yugoslav section contains some very large and impressive serial collections. Most of these are institutional in nature, such as Jugoslavenska akademija znanosti i umjetnosti, Zagreb. *Ljetopis* (51 v.); and its *Rad* (265 v.); Matica srpska, Novi Sad. *Letopis* (317 v.); Srpska akademija nauka, Belgrade. *Posebna izdanja* (318 v.); and its *Spomenik* (92 v.). In language and literature, aside from the *Hrvatsko kolo* (27 v.), and *Dom in svet* (56 v.), there are numerous sets of an author's collected works. For example: Skerlić (13 v.), Baranin (12 v.), DaviČo (20 v.), Nušic (25 v.), Šenoa (12 v.), Novak (12 v.). There are almost 100 volumes in the geography section.

As is the case with the Polish section, the Yugoslav material cannot yet support serious research beyond the level of the master's degree.

After these brief comments on the holdings classified as dealing primarily with individual countries, it must be emphasized that an additional strength of the collection is to be found in the group classified as Eastern Europe (as a whole). It is indeed sufficiently strong to support serious research leading to the master's and doctor's degree or to scholarly publication in the fields of Slavic linguistics and the history of the Austrian Empire. A distinguished feature in the former area is an almost complete collection of periodicals and other serial publications relating to Slavic languages and cultures published in all East European countries, as well as in the West. A distinguished feature in the latter area is found in the various collections of laws and ordinances relating to the Austrian Empire, as well as additional publications of government agencies and other multi-volume sets that have been added to the earlier collections on the Austrian Empire cited above.

Bibliographies Pertaining to The Collections Described

Anderle, Josef. "Major Research Collections on Austrian History in the University of North Carolina Library," *Austrian History Newsletter,* 4 (1963): 124-128.

Anderle, Josef. "Major Research Collections in Austrian History Acquired by the University of North Carolina Library in 1963-1964." *Austrian History Yearbook,* 1 (1965): 308-311.

Anderle, Josef. "Research Materials in the Field of Austrian History Acquired by the University of North Carolina Library in 1964-1965," *Austrian History Yearbook,* 2 (1966): 354-356.

Josef Anderle and †František Jeník
University of North Carolina

Ohio State University

General Information

The Ohio State University Libraries have total holdings in excess of 3,000,000 volumes and 1,300,000 items of nonbook materials (microforms, maps, sheet music, records, etc.). About one-half of the collection (including virtually all materials in the social sciences and humanities, the rare book collection, and the older works in all fields) is housed in the Main Library located on the Central Campus; the 21 department libraries contain the remainder of the collection in open stack collections.

The Main Library is open from 8 a.m. to 12 midnight Monday through Friday, and from 8 a.m. to 10 p.m. on Saturdays. Sunday hours are 1 p.m. to 12 midnight. The interquarter schedule generally omits the late evening hours. The stacks are open to faculty, graduate students, undergraduate honors students, and library staff. All others require a special permit.

Requests for information on special aspects of the Slavic collection should be addressed to the Senior Slavic Bibliographer or the Senior Slavic Cataloger.

The Ohio State University Libraries have most of the national and trade bibliographies including East Central and Southeastern Europe. The current bibliographies are either in the Bibliography Room or in the Reference Department, and the older ones, or those used less frequently, are housed in the stacks. The bibliography collection comprises approximately 1,500 titles in Slavic languages and pertaining to Slavic problems. Printed catalogs of special collections in other libraries, such as the New York Public Library Slavonic Catalog and the Harvard University Shelf List, are available.

The Slavic collection is integrated into the general collection. There is no separate Slavic Reading Room at present. The most frequently used reference materials are housed in the Modern Languages Graduate Reading Room in the Main Library. Microfilm and microfiche readers, reader/printers, and the microform collections are housed in the Special Materials Room in the Main Library. A precataloging system for Slavic and East European materials introduced in 1966 guarantees immediate access to all monographs as soon as they are received by the Library. The temporary entry recorded in the Public Catalog lists author, title, place of publication, publisher, and date of publication. A chronologic East European accession number is used prior to formal and full cataloging. There are no subject or added entries. Despite obvious bibliographic shortcomings, the system does give patrons immediate access to the available material, regardless of cataloging status. All items are also incorporated into a computer-based circulation system which has been in operation since December 1970. If the author and title or title only is known, anyone can call (614) 422-3900 (the Circulation Department Telephone Center) and the staff will be able to inform the caller whether the Library owns an item and if it is in circulation or not. When querying concerning Slavic materials, one should bear in mind that entries are transliterated, in general, using the Library of Congress system, and be prepared to request searches under variant spellings.

The Ohio State University Libraries are members of the Midwest Research Libraries Center in Chicago, Illinois, and have at their disposal teletype facilities for communication with other members. The Inter-University Library Council Reference and Interlibrary Loan Service provides rapid access to 13 state universities in Ohio. In addition, the Ohio State University Libraries are active members of the Ohio College Library Center, through which information on holdings of 400 member libraries is made available via computer. At present, this information is limited primarily to monographs in English, but gradually other types of material and other languages using the Roman alphabet will be included. Non-Roman alphabets, e.g., Cyrillic, will eventually be incorporated into this system when the Library of Congress MARC system provides such.

Anyone is privileged to use the University Libraries for reference, but books may be drawn for home use only by faculty, staff, and registered students of the University or members of the faculties of institutional members of the Ohio College Library Center. The Libraries will issue "courtesy cards" to visiting scholars. Interlibrary loan services are available to all scholars. In addition to coin-operated copying machines located at various places in the Libraries, a staffed copy service is provided on the second floor of the Main Library.

Publications and informational material describing the Slavic and East European Collection include: *A Provisional List of Microform Holdings,* prepared by the Slavic Department; *The Shelf-list of Titles in the Cyrillic Alphabet;* a card bibliography on Polish medieval poetry, Polish folk-lore, and certain aspects of cultural development (prehistoric and the early Middle Ages) on Western Slavs that formed the Polish nation; and *The Hilandar Slavic Manuscripts, A Checklist of Slavic Manuscripts from the Hilandar Monastery* (available on microfilm at The Ohio State University Libraries), compiled by Mateja Matejić and Predrag Matejić (145 p.) and published by the Department of Slavic Languages and Literatures, 1972.

The Collections

HISTORICAL SKETCH.   In 1960, when the University decided to develop its academic programs in Slavic languages and literatures and in area studies, a decision was also made to develop library holdings to support these programs. From the very beginning, it was planned to develop first Russian, then Polish, and finally Yugoslav holdings. The other Slavic and East European countries were given a much lower priority, with the understanding that if the high-priority collections developed sufficiently, then a fourth or fifth country might be selected for development, based on the needs of the University and the country at that particular time.

In 1960, total Slavic and East European holdings consisted of approximately 3,000 volumes, mostly in Russian. Today, there are approximately 145,000 volumes and 65,000 nonbook items that pertain to the USSR, East Central, and Southeast Europe. The largest collection is in Russian, with approximately 80,000 volumes. About 60,000 volumes in the humanities and in the social and behavioral sciences relate to East Central and Southeastern Europe, with an annual acquisition rate of about 6,500 items. The largest non-Russian collection deals with Poland (32,000 volumes, with an annual increase of about 3,000 items), followed by the Yugoslav collection (20,000 volumes, with an annual increase of 2,500 items). Much of the Yugoslav material was received under the PL 480 Program, which was in force from 1968-72.

Holdings for the other countries in East Central and Southeastern Europe are in the developmental stage, and must await the further development of the Polish and Yugoslav collections before major progress can be made. Eventually, it is planned to have approximately 3,000-5,000 volumes for each minor collection and to include the basic reference tools, dictionaries, encyclopedias, and standard literary works. The present holdings and annual rate of increase for each of the "minor" East Central and Southeast European collections is listed in the following table.

Country	Holdings as of 1972 (volumes)	Annual Increase (volumes)
Albania	500	25
Bulgaria	800	50

Country	Holdings as of 1972 (volumes)	Annual Increase (volumes)
Czechoslovakia		300 total
Czech	2,200	
Slovak	300	
German Democratic Republic	2,000	300
Greece (Modern)	500	20
Hungary	1,200	100
Romania	700	30

As the data listed above indicate, none of the low-priority collections has yet reached even the minimal planned size, but should the need arise, any given collection could be built up very quickly to equal or surpass the Polish and Yugoslav collections.

For Poland, Yugoslavia, and virtually all of the countries of East Central and Southeastern Europe, the major strength of the collections is in the disciplines of literature, linguistics, and history.

LITERATURE.   The best developed is the collection of Polish literature. It comprises an almost uninterrupted sequence covering developments from the Middle Ages to the present, both in prose and in poetry. The history, theory, and criticism of literature are also very well developed, including the press, theater, and folklore. In the field of belles lettres, major literary figures are represented by several scholarly editions of complete works, but in addition, many multivolume editions of "secondary" writers are also available. In the rare book category, i.e., editions published before 1800, the OSU Libraries have only a few titles, the most noteworthy being a Catholic Bible translated into Polish and published in 1599.

In addition to official bibliographies and bibliographies of individual authors, the Library has, among other sources, A. B. Jocher's *Obraz bibliograficznohistoryczny literatury i nauk w Polsce,* 3 v. (1840-47); J. Lelewel's *Bibliograficznych ksiąg dwoje;* G. Korbut's *Literatura polska* (4 v. only); K. J. T. Estreicher's *Bibliografia polska;* and L. Finkel's *Bibliografia historyi polskiej.*

Of note is the first edition of Kolberg's *Lud* (23 v.) and almost all of his other works. Periodical holdings include *Wisła* (on microfilm), *Pszczółka Krakowska* (1819-23); Pawlikowski's *Lamus* (4 v.); and *Chimera* (10 v.). There is also a very well developed collection of memoirs. Most of the items acquired are those sponsored by scholarly institutions such as the Polish Academy of Science, Wrocławskie Towarzystwo Naukowe, Universytet Jagielloński, etc.

The Yugoslav collection on literature (primarily Serbo-Croatian) can generally be described in much the same way as the Polish collection, with the following qualifications: it is smaller, and the disciplines such as folklore, theater, history, and to some extent literary criticism, although sufficient to support research and doctoral programs, are not as developed as their Polish counterparts. The Library does have complete runs of several important literary periodicals from the 19th and 20th centuries, such as *Srpski književni glasnik* (1901-41), *Letopis matice srpske* (1867-), and such minor literary journals as *Nova Evropa* (1920-40). Major authors are well represented in prewar and postwar editions. Minor authors are represented by a few hundred titles published in 1825-80. These constitute a unique feature of the collection, since many names do not appear in the National Union Catalog or in any other general catalogs and bibliographies readily available. Of note is a 1583 Croatian edition of the *Ledesma Catechism* (in Cyrillic), a unique item in the United States. The only other copy listed is at the Biblioteque nationale in Paris and differs somewhat from the 1583 edition.

By far the most important collection held by the Library is the Hilandar Collection, which will be dealt with separately.

Collections of the other literatures in the East Central and Southeast European countries are still very much in the developmental stage. The strongest collection is that in Czech literature, but even so, apart from bibliographies, encyclopedias, and dictionaries, it still includes only the better known authors.

LINGUISTICS.   The Polish materials encompass most aspects of the Polish language. Such authorities as Łoś, Baudouin de Courtenay, Taszycki, and Kuraszkiewicz are represented. There are several works on the old Polish language, including texts and facsimile editions of some of the oldest Polish texts.

There are good collections in Serbo-Croatian, Czech, and Bulgarian, with the Serbo-Croatian collection the strongest of the three. All three are strong in works on the history of the development of the language as well as on Old Slavonic.

Of interest is the collection on Sorbian (Lusatian, Wendic), approximately 120 volumes, including a number of works in German on the evolution of Lusatian geographic and personal names into German, which are useful in mapping out the frontiers of early Lusatian settlements.

HISTORY.   The Polish history collection is very strong. It begins with the medieval chronicles, including German Thietmar's, Polish Gallus's, Kadłubek's, Długosz's, and goes through to the contemporary historians. All periods of Polish history are well represented, as well as numerous collections of documents (published in book form). Source materials include the *Acta historica res gestas Poloniae illustrantia; Monumenta Mediiaevi historica . . . ; Pomniki dziejowe Polski;* Theiner's *Vetera monumenta Poloniae et Lithuaniae . . .* (on microfilm); the Russian *Akty izdavaemye Komissieiu dlia razbora drevnikh aktov v Vilne* (on microfiche); *Słownik geograficzny Królestwa Polskiego;* etc.

The collection on the history of Czechoslovakia is very well developed and is fairly strong on Palacký (i.e., the Czech movement in the 19th century) and on Hus.

The Yugoslav history collection is substantial. The Library has a special collection of several hundred volumes dealing with the Serbo-Croatian question.

ECONOMICS.   The Yugoslav economic collection is the strongest among those included in the survey, owing to the acquisitions received under the PL 480 Program.

FINE ARTS.   The Fine Arts collection contains rather substantial material on museums, architecture, sculpture, and folk art covering Poland, Yugoslavia, and Byzantine art in the Slavic, East and South European countries.

THE HILANDAR COLLECTION.   The photographic archive on microfilm of the complete holdings of all Slavic manuscripts held by the Hilandar Monastery on Mount Athos in Greece is undoubtedly the most significant collection in the Slavic and East European holdings of the Library and may even be the most important collection in the entire library. The collection consists of 802 complete manuscripts (approximately 300,000 pages). In addition, the archive contains hundreds of Byzantine, Russian, Serbian, Bulgarian, Wallachian, and Turkish edicts and charters dating from 1009 through the 19th century.

There are 555 complete manuscripts dating from the 14th century to the 17th century, 83 from the 18th century, and 230 from the 19th century. Some 735 of the manuscripts are in the Serbian version of Church Slavonic, but some are in the Bulgarian, Russian, or Wallachian version. Other languages represented are Albanian, Bulgarian, Greek, Romanian, Latin, and Turkish.

This is the only complete photographic archive of Hilandar Slavic manuscripts in the world. Only a few of these Hilandar manuscripts have previously been studied, photographed, or published. Now, for the first time, this material is truly accessible to the scholarly world. Not all manuscripts are of a religious nature. Legal, medical, and historical works are represented also, so that the collection is of interest to scholars in fields other than language and literature.

The Hilandar Collection is the nucleus of a much larger projected collection of Byzantine, Slavic, and East European manuscripts which will soon come into existence at the Ohio State University. The Hilandar Collection is described in *Hilandar Slavic Manuscripts,* compiled by Matejić and Matejić, reference to which was made earlier.

Feliks Jablonowski
and Eryk Talat-Kielpsz
Ohio State University

University of Pennsylvania

General Information

The East Central and Southeastern European collections at Penn are almost entirely located in the Van Pelt-Dietrich Library complex (the University's central library). A few items are in the Fine Arts Library or at other locations.

The Van Pelt-Dietrich Library's hours during the normal school year are from 8:45 a.m. to 12 midnight Monday through Friday, 9 a.m. to 5 p.m. Saturday, and 12 noon to 12 midnight Sunday.

The University of Pennsylvania has an open-stack collection, and the materials may be used in the Library by Penn's faculty, students, and staff, as well as by faculty members and students at other institutions of higher education. Borrowing privileges are open to Penn faculty, students, and staff and faculty members of other institutions. Other students and visitors may request permission to borrow materials at the main circulation desk. Rules regarding the granting of such permission vary from time to time.

Xerox copy machines are available to anyone using the Library, at a rate of five cents per page. Xerox copies from microfilm copy may be made on the microfilm reader-printer for 15 cents a frame.

Assistance in using the Slavic and East European collections may normally be obtained between 9 a.m. and 5 p.m. from either the Slavic Bibliographer or the Slavic Cataloger.

The Library of Congress and National Union Catalogs, the New York Public Library Slavonic Catalog, the J. G. Herder Institut Catalog, the national bibliographies of all the East Central and Southeastern European countries, and hundreds of other subject bibliographies and reference books are available in the Reference Room of Van Pelt Library. In addition, the Union Library Catalog of Pennsylvania, in which the holdings of all the major libraries in the state are combined, is located in the same building.

Almost all of the Slavic materials are located in the general stacks of the Van Pelt Library or in its Reference Room. There is no special "Slavic" room or section with a physically separate collection. The only exception is the "Slavic Seminar Room" on the 4th floor. This room contains about 2,000 volumes of reference materials and frequently used bound journals. It serves as a reading room for students of the Department of Slavic Languages at the University.

A list of periodical titles in the field of Slavic Studies (ca. 270 titles, including holdings) received by the libraries at the University of Pennsylvania may be obtained from the Slavic Bibliographer.

The Collections

The University of Pennsylvania Libraries have a Slavic and East European Collection of more than 40,000 volumes, nearly three-quarters of which relate to the Soviet Union. The strongest single collection is that for Lithuania. Other areas in which Penn has heavy concentrations are Poland (all fields), Czechoslovakia (history), and Yugoslavia (linguistics.)

Following is the distribution of monograph volumes in the collections:

Poland	**4,548** titles
Czechoslovakia	**2,238**
Hungary	**938**
Romania	**1,259**
Yugoslavia	**2,494**
Bulgaria	**1,030**
Total	**12,507** titles

Albania, Greece, and East Germany are covered in this survey. Penn's Albanian and Modern Greek collections are quite small. East Germany is not treated because it is nearly impossible to separate East German materials from other German materials. Penn's German collection is extremely strong, however, and includes much East German material.

Poland

Language and Literature	**2,560** titles
Social Sciences	**1,821**
Reference and Bibliography	**112**
Fine Arts	**15**
Religion and Church History	**40**
Total	**4,548** titles
Journals currently received	**34** titles

The Polish collection is particularly strong in linguistics, the classics of Polish literature, medieval and early modern history (especially the period of union with Lithuania, 1569-1795), heraldry and genealogy, archeology and antiquities, and Polish-Lithuanian diplomatic relations of the 1930s. The majority of the materials are in the Polish and Lithuanian languages.

The Polish collection has benefited greatly by the acquisition of the Šaulys collection. Jurgis Šaulys was a Lithuanian diplomat who served during the interwar independence period as ambassador to Warsaw and Berlin, among other places. In 1952, after the death of Šaulys, the University of Pennsylvania acquired his entire personal library, including all books, correspondence, notes, memoranda, etc. A full description of the collection can be found in the article "The Šaulys Collection," by V. Maciūnas and K. Ostrauskas, in the *University of Pennsylvania Library Chronicle,* v. 20, no. 1, 1954; 35-46.

The average annual rate of additions to the Polish collection is about 500 titles. In the field of the Polish language, virtually all publications are purchased. Most new publications are acquired from Ars Polona-Ruch, Warsaw; the majority of older materials are purchased from Kubon & Sagner, Munich, or from local American out-of-print dealers. Exchange agreements are maintained with several Polish academic libraries, including the Library of the Polish Academy of Sciences and the university libraries of Warsaw, Kraków, Poznań, etc. The number of acquisitions obtained from these exchanges, however, is relatively small.

It would be difficult to cite many specific examples of important titles in such a short survey, but nearly all of the 914 entries in the Polish section of Paul Horecky's *East Central*

Europe: A Guide to Basic Publications, can be found in Penn's collection. In addition, there are Polish items in the Rare Book collection. Some older Polish works which are of particular interest are: M. Kromer's *De origine et rebus gestis Polonorum libri XXX* (Basel, 1568); *Dziejów polskich ksiąg dwanaście,* by Jan Długosz (Kraków, 1867-70); *Annales Stanislai Orechovii Okszii,* Stanisław Orzechowski (Poznań, 1854); *Der Königlichen Polnischen Wahl und Krönung Staats-Maxim* (1697); *Mandatum Monitorium Potentissimi Regi Poloniae &c. Ad Jesuitas,* (Kraków, 1620); *Letters on the subject of the concert of princes, and the dismemberment of Poland and France . . .* (London, 1793); *Kronika polska, litewska, żmódzka, i wszystkiej Rusi . . . ,* by M. Strykowski (Warsaw, 1846); and in the field of linguistics, S. M. Linde's *Słownik języku polskiego,* 1st ed., 6 v. (Warsaw, 1807-14). The collection of modern and literary works is also quite extensive.

Czechoslovakia

Language and Literature	**906 titles**
Social Sciences	**1,008**
Reference and Bibliography	**76**
Fine Arts	**14**
Religion and Church History	**34**
Comenius Collection	**200**
Total	**2,238 titles**
Journals currently received	**15 titles**

The University of Pennsylvania's Czechoslovak collection was begun many years ago but has grown slowly, since interest in Czech and Slovak languages, literatures, and cultures per se has never been as great as in the Polish and Lithuanian areas. The relatively small number of titles belies the strength of the collection, however.

In the field of history the collection is quite strong, primarily owing to the University's interest in medieval and Central European history in general. For Czechoslovakia the main emphases are on the early modern history of Bohemia, especially the Hussite period, and on relations with the Holy Roman Empire. Many of the books in this area fall into the rare book category, e.g., *Liber egregius de unitate Ecclesiae,* by Jan Hus (Basel, 1520); Jan Hus' *Opuscula* (Strassburg, 1524-25); *Historiae Hussitarum libri duodecim . . .* by Johannes Cochlaeus (Mainz, 1549); M. Boregk's *Behmische Chronica . . .* (Wittenburg, 1587); Melchior Goldast's *Commentarii de Regni Bohemiae . . .* (Frankfurt, 1719); and two works by František Palacký, *Dějiny národu českého w Čechach a w Morawě,* 5 v. (Prague, 1876-78) and *Urkundliche Beiträge zur Geschichte des Hussitenkrieges vom Jahre 1419 an* (Prague, 1873).

In addition, the libraries maintain a special collection of more than 200 titles pertaining to Jan Amos Komenský (Comenius), many of which are rare books.

The collection of materials on modern history, languages, and literatures contains all the chief reference tools but cannot be called comprehensive.

The average current intake of Czech materials is about 100 titles per year. The majority of acquisitions are either purchased from Artia in Prague or Kubon & Sagner in Munich, or are obtained through exchanges with Czech and Slovak university libraries.

Yugoslavia

Language and Literature		1,305 titles
Social Sciences		1,076
Reference and Bibliography		93
Fine Arts		11
Religion and Church History		9
	Total	2,494 titles
Journals currently received		39 titles

The Yugoslav collection is quite recent at the University of Pennsylvania. Ten years ago Penn had virtually nothing in this field, but the collection has since grown rapidly, due to increased interest in the area on the part of the Department of Slavic Languages.

At least one-third of all the Yugoslav materials are in the field of linguistics, with particular emphasis on dictionaries, works of lexicography, and periodicals devoted to South Slavic languages.

The chief classics of Yugoslav literature (especially Serbian and Croatian) are available, but the collection is not exceptionally strong. In the field of Yugoslav folklore there is a reasonably good collection.

About 1,000 titles are spread across the entire area of the social sciences, but only political science (comparative Communist governments) has any real strength.

The rate of growth for the Yugoslav collection is about 300 titles annually. Most acquisitions are in the field of linguistics—nearly everything published in the field of Yugoslav linguistics is purchased. The major sources of these materials are Jugoslovenska Knjiga in Belgrade and Kubon & Sagner in Munich.

Bulgaria

Language and Literature		686 titles
Social Sciences		294
Reference and Bibliography		42
Fine Arts		6
Church History and Religion		2
	Total	1,030 titles
Journals currently received		18 titles

The Bulgarian collection includes a small but quite good selection of materials in linguistics; all the major dictionaries, grammars, and linguistic reference tools, as well as the main linguistic periodicals, are available. Nearly everything currently published on the Bulgarian language is purchased by Penn. The collection is quite weak in other areas.

The average growth rate of the collection is about 100 titles per year, mostly in linguistics. Most of the materials are purchased from Kubon & Sagner in Munich or received on exchange from the Library of Sofia University.

Romania

Language and Literature	**712 titles**
Social Sciences	**482**
Reference and Bibliography	**58**
Fine Arts	**5**
Religion and Church History	**2**
Total	**1,259 titles**
Journals currently received	**6 titles**

A good collection in Romanian linguistics was built up in the past through the efforts of Romanian-language specialists in the Department of Romance Languages. In other fields the collection is very weak. Today only the most basic reference tools (dictionaries, encyclopedias, statistical yearbooks, etc.) are purchased for Romania. Perhaps 50 titles per year at most are added to the collection, and the majority of these are gifts of linguistics materials from institutions in Romania through contacts established many years ago.

Hungary

The Hungarian collection consists of 938 titles, most of which are not in Hungarian. Nearly all the materials are reference materials or are in the field of history. The historical materials have been acquired mostly because of their significance to Austrian or medieval history, rather than for any interest in Hungary itself. In the field of literature, even the works of the major Hungarian authors are lacking. The standard Hungarian reference tools are available, however.

Joseph D. Dwyer
University of Pennsylvania

Józef Piłsudski Institute

General Information

The Józef Piłsudski Institute of America for Research in the Modern History of Poland is situated at 381 Park Avenue South (corner of 27th St.), New York, N.Y. The Library, Archives, and the office are located in Room 701. Regular office hours are Monday to Friday, 10 a.m. to 3 p.m., but it is recommended that an advance appointment for a first visit be made with either the Executive Director or the Chief of Library and Archives. The Library and Archives are under the direction of Dr. Wacław Jędrzejewicz.

The Library is well adapted for research. Scholars are invited to use the collection of documents, books, periodicals, and newspapers. A microfilm reader and a photocopying machine are available on the premises.

Books are not loaned to individuals, but they are made available to educational institutions on interlibrary loan.

The Institute has a card catalog of its collections, but no printed book catalog. Each year it issues a printed bulletin (in Polish and English) containing an activities report, financial report, list of officers, membership list, and information on its most recent publications.

The Józef Piłsudski Institute of America for Research in the Modern History of Poland is a continuation of an institute of the same name (minus the words "of America") that existed in Warsaw before World War II. Re-established in New York in 1943, the Institute is devoted to the collection and storage of and research into documents relating to the modern history of Poland from 1863 to the present time; the publication of scholarly works; the administration of scholarships; the organization of lectures; and the support of other scholarly activities in its subject area.

The Collections

ARCHIVAL DOCUMENTS.   A large portion of the Archives consists of original documents removed from Poland at the time of the German invasion of 1939, and now cataloged and available for research. Among them are the so-called "Belvedere Archives"—the original papers of the Military Chancellery of Marshal Piłsudski as Head of State and Commander-In-Chief of the Polish Army. They cover the period from 1918 to December 1922 and consist of more than 40,000 pages of documents, divided into 7 groups: military documents (13 folders); Czechoslovakia, the Ukraine, Lithuania, and Russia (32 folders); Germany and Austria (eight folders); France (Polish National Committee) (six folders); England, United States, Italy, Romania, and neutral countries (15 folders); Hungary and part of Czechoslovakia (three folders); and internal affairs (four folders). In addition, there are several folders of miscellaneous materials, among them four folders of records of the French Military Mission in Poland pertaining to war activities during the summer of 1920.

This is an especially rich collection of documents that has been used by various researchers in the preparation of historical work such as John Bradley's *Allied Intervention in Russia, 1918-1920* (London, 1968); M. K. Dziewanowski's *Joseph Pilsudski, A European Federalist, 1918-1922* (Stanford, 1969); Piotr Wandycz's *Soviet-Polish Relations, 1917-1921* (Cambridge, 1969); and numerous articles.

Especially valuable for the researcher are three folders of the papers of Gen. Tadeusz Roz-wadowski, Chief of the General Staff in 1920. These consist of original correspondence with the French Military Mission in Poland, letters and telegraphic communications with Marshal Piłsudski, and several handwritten documents of General Weygand with his suggestions and advice on the conduct of the Battle of Warsaw in August 1920, together with his dispatches from Warsaw to Marshal Foch in Paris.

Pertaining to the same period are the papers of the Ukrainian Military Mission in Poland. These five folders contain the correspondence of Hetman Petlura with Polish authorities and the original text of the Polish-Ukrainian Military Convention of April 1920, as well as materials on Ukrainian Army organization in Poland and other pertinent subjects. Virtually all of these papers are in Ukrainian.

A large group of documents—876 folders—relates to the Upper Silesian uprisings of 1919-21, most of them dealing with the third uprising of May-June 1921. The Polish authorities were espe-cially anxious to remove these documents from Poland when Germany attacked in September 1939; not only do they treat political, military, and organizational issues, but they also contain lists of insurgents which could have been used by the German occupation forces for purposes of repression. This collection is cataloged and well preserved.

There are many folders of the records of the Office of the Minister of War under Marshal Piłsudski, containing, inter alia, the annual reports of the Marshal when he was Inspector General of the Armed Forces. In addition, some 22 folders hold records of the Supreme Military Consulta-tive Commission of 1920, which examined the activities of generals and other high officers. Attached to many of these are original documents on operations during the Polish-Bolshevik War of 1919-1920. These rich source materials were intensively researched for a study by Wacław Jędrzejewicz, *Sprawa Wilna w Lipcu* 1920 (Paris, 1970; Zeszyty Historyczne no. 17).

The documents of General Śmigły-Rydż for operations on the Dvinsk (Latvia) in the winter of 1919-1920 were researched by Prof. Taras Hunczak for his article "'Operation Winter' and the Struggle for the Baltic" in *East European Quarterly,* v. 4, no. 1, 1970.

The Aleksander Prystor Archives (five folders) are valuable documents on Central Lithuania of 1920-22. They contain reports of all departments of the Provisional Ruling Commission of General Żeligowski and many posters dealing with the autumn 1922 elections to the Sejm.

Several documents describe the activities of the 1st Brigade of Polish Legions, and there is some material on the Polish Military Organization (Polska Organizacja Wojskowa) of 1914-18.

Additional important materials are the 25 folders of "Documents of the Commission to Investigate the Military Events of the Coup of 1926" with a detailed list of all the documents on this important event. This unique collection of well-preserved original documents served as source material for Prof. Joseph Rothschild's monograph *Pilsudski's Coup d'Etat* (New York, 1966).

There is also a large group of the papers for the years 1936-39 of Marshal Edward Śmigły-Rydż, Marshal Piłsudski's successor as Inspector General of the Armed Forces.

On the 1863 Polish Uprising the Institute has the archives of Valerian Platonov, member of the Russian Council for Poland and Minister for Polish Affairs in the St. Petersburg government. The Platonov archives, which the Piłsudski Institute obtained with the help of the wife of General Denikin, consist of 11 folders of documents on the 1863 uprising and 34 printed records from the years 1837-85 on the economic, financial, and legal issues of the Kingdom of Poland. Among these are appeals of the Polish Government and individual leaders of the uprising and letters of Counts Berg, Gorchakov, Gerstenzweig, Sievers, Paskiewicz, and Murav'ev, Margrave Wielopol-ski, and others, in French, Polish, and Russian.

The archives of Ambassador Michał Sokolnicki (60 folders) contain materials on the Polish underground movement before and during World War I. Sokolnicki was very active in this movement. The archives also contain papers on his activities when he was ambassador to Turkey in 1937-45. There are also 24 books of coded correspondence between the Polish Embassy in Ankara and the Ministry of Foreign Affairs during 1923-45, as well as four folders dealing with the political activities of the Polish Legation in Copenhagen, where Sokolnicki was the envoy during 1931-36.

The archives of Michał Mościcki are also priceless. These documents from the years 1918-19 relate to the Polish problem at the Paris Peace Conference in 1919, where Mościcki was the Secretary of the Polish delegation. The 17 folders contain some 785 documents and many clippings from French and Polish newspapers.

Many documents pertaining to Poland's foreign relations are in the collection "Archives of the Polish Embassy in London," for the years 1920-37. There are 91 folders of reports from the London Embassy and other diplomatic posts as well as instructions from the Ministry of Foreign Affairs in Warsaw.

This group also contains 31 folders of records from the Polish Ambassador in Berlin, Józef Lipski. These were used as source materials for Wacław Jędrzejewicz's book *Diplomat in Berlin, 1933-39. Papers and Memoirs of Józef Lipski, Ambassador of Poland* (New York, 1968). There is also much material pertaining to Lipski's political activities as an exile during 1939-58.

Another similar group is the seven folders of papers of the Polish ambassador in Paris, Juliusz Łukasiewicz. These were the basis of Wacław Jędrzejewicz's book *Diplomat in Paris, 1936-39. Papers and Memoirs of Juliusz Lukasiewicz, Ambassador of Poland* (New York, 1970). Łukasiewicz also left many records from his political activities as an exile during 1939-51.

For the World War II period there are many documents on the Polish Government-in-Exile in London. Among these are the original documents (11 folders) of General Kazimierz Sosnkowski for the years 1939-41 on the uprising and activities of the Armed Struggle Union (Związek Walki Zbrojnej), the predecessor of the Home Army in occupied Poland. Another large group of documents deals with the Warsaw Uprising of 1944.

There are many original documents on the prisoner-of-war camps in Murnau and Ingelstadt. The Syndicate of Polish Journalists in Germany, founded immediately after the war ended in 1945, presented its large collection to the Institute. The Institute also has records of "Poles in Germany" for the immediate post-World War II period, particularly relating to Polish organizations, education, and welfare.

As to the activities of Poles in America, the Institute has all the archives of the political organization Committee of National Defense (Komitet Obrony Narodowej) for the years 1913 to 1920 and following. For the World War II period the Institute has all the materials of the National Committee of Americans of Polish Descent—several thousand documents. The well-known Polish statesman and journalist Ignacy Matuszewski was closely connected with this committee. His many papers and writings while in exile during 1939-46 are at the Institute.

The archives of J. Weinstein (60 folders) contain original documents, extracts, and photocopies from the European archives, especially, materials on the problems of Polish-Czechoslovak and Polish-Romanian relations during the Second World War and concerning the person and policy of Józef Beck.

The archives of W. Studnicki comprise unpublished works on various politicohistorical subjects, on Polish-German relations, and on the Danzig problem.

The archives of L. Orłowski contain documents related to the Polish Legation in Budapest (1933-41) and documents from the years 1831 and 1863.

Since the Institute bears the name of Józef Piłsudski, it carefully collects all available materials on his life and activities. The Piłsudski collection contains his letters, notes, records of conversations with him, and many iconographic items. There are 22 letters in Piłsudski's own handwriting, written during his trip to Tokyo in 1904, as well as 46 letters written during the same period by

Stanisław Wojciechowski (later president of Poland) and many other letters of contemporaries in the Polish Socialist Party.

There are also other souvenirs and keepsakes of Piłsudski, such as his death mask, a mold of his hand, portraits, photographs, etc.

This survey is an indication of the rich collection of documents relating to the history of modern Poland rather than a comprehensive listing.

LIBRARY.   The Library has over 7,000 books and pamphlets on the history of Poland from 1863 to the present time, mostly in Polish and English. There is a card catalog arranged by author and by subject (some 68, including Katyn Forest Massacre, Minorities, Occupation, Concentration Camps, Warsaw Uprising of 1944, etc.). Many of these titles are rare items now out of print.

There are also over 3,500 pamphlets, uncataloged but arranged by subject. During the two World Wars, when it was not possible to publish books (due to paper and other limitations), pamphlets were the only vehicle for political publishing. Today, these small brochures, not usually collected by the large libraries, are priceless source materials for historians.

There is a file of over 1,500 periodicals. Mostly in Polish, they cover the period from before World War I to the present time. Not all sets are complete. Especially worthy of mention are original and photostatic copies of the underground press in Poland for 1939-44, and a very large—perhaps complete—collection of the Polish press in Germany during the period immediately following World War II.

PHOTOGRAPHIC COLLECTION.   Over 10,000 photographs are arranged by personal name (I. Mościcki, J. Piłsudski—a very large collection—W. Sikorski, E. Śmigły-Rydż, A. Zaleski, etc.); by subject (September 1939 Campaign, Polish Army in France, Warsaw Uprising, War devastation, etc.); and by city (Warsaw, Wilno, Lwów, Zamość, etc.).

MAP COLLECTION.   This large collection consists mostly of operations maps on the scale of 1:300,000. They are often used in studies of army operations in Poland during World War I, the Polish-Bolshevik War of 1919-20, and World War II.

PUBLICATIONS.   Despite limited financial resources the Institute has published numerous scholarly works.

The periodical *Niepodległość* [Independence] is issued as the organ of both Piłsudski Institutes (New York and London). It is a continuation of a journal with the same title published before World War II in Warsaw. Publication was revived in London in 1948, and nine volumes of about 300 pages each have now been issued. It contains articles, memoirs, book reviews, and other information for the period 1863-1939.

The Institute has published the following monographs and collections:

Gromada, T., ed. *Essays on Poland's Foreign Policy, 1918-1939* (New York, 1970, 75 p.; reprint from *The Polish Review*).

Jędrzejewicz, W., ed. *Józef Piłsudski, Wybór pism* (New York, 1944, 386 p.).

Jędrzejewicz, W., ed. *Poland in the British Parliament, 1935-1945* (New York, 1946-62, 3 v.).

Jędrzejewicz, W. *Polonia Amerykańska w Polityce Polskiej* (New York, 1954, 303 p.).

Kasprzycki, T. *Joseph Pilsudski and His Ideas on International Peace* (New York, 1967, 40 p.).

Kasprzycki, T. *Polityka pokoju i mocy zbiorowej w epoce Józefa Piłsudskiego* (New York, 1967, 40 p.).

Konstytucja Rzeczpospolitej Polskiej (New York, 1944. 69 p.).

Korczyński, A., and T. Świętochowski, eds. *Poland between Germany and Russia, 1929-1939. The Theory of Two Enemies* (New York, 1975, 72 p.; reprint from *The Polish Review*).

Piłsudski, J. *O Powstaniu 1863 roku* (New York, London, 1963, 276 p.).

Piłsudski, J. *The Year 1920: The Battle of Warsaw and the Polish-Soviet War of 1919-20* (New York, London, 1971, 292 p.).

Sokolnicki, M. *Dziennik ankarski, 1939-43* (New York, 1965, 540 p.).

Sokolnicki, M. *Rok czternasty* (New York, London, 1961, 387 p.).

Sosnkowski, K. *Materiały historyczne* (New York, London, 1966, 688 p.).

Wandycz, D. S. *Polish-Americans and the Curzon Line* (New York, 1953, 31 p.).

Wandycz, D. S. *Zapomniany list Piłsudskiego do Masaryka* (New York, 1953, 21 p.).

In addition, the Institute has provided assistance for the publication of works by other institutions, either by financing them in part or by guaranteeing to purchase a fixed number of copies.

The Institute also sells duplicates of items in its collections. A printed price catalog, issued irregularly, announces availability.

Wacław Jędrzejewicz
Józef Piłsudski Institute

University of Pittsburgh

General Information

The Hillman Library at the University of Pittsburgh is open Monday through Thursday from 7:50 a.m. to 1 a.m.; on Friday from 7:50 a.m. to 11:30 p.m.; on Saturday from 8:30 a.m. to 5 p.m.; and on Sunday from 12 noon to 1 a.m. Inquiries concerning the East Central and Southeastern European collections should be addressed to the East European Bibliographer, G-27 Hillman Library (telephone: 624-4423). The public catalog, located on the ground floor, includes all East Central and Southeast European materials. A catalog of all serials and periodicals is available at the reference desk and at other locations throughout the library. The Slavic collection is an integrated part of the general library collection. There is no special location, separate catalog, or shelflist to this collection. Loans are for two weeks, with renewal for two more weeks, upon request. Photocopying facilities are also available. The charge for books, newspapers, and magazines is 10 cents per page. That for microfilm and microfiche is 15 cents per page. Minimum charge $1.00 plus postage and handling.

Many members of the Pittsburgh community have East Central or Southeast European ethnic origins. The active involvement of ethnic groups in the affairs of the University of Pittsburgh began during the physical expansion of the University in the 1920s and 1930s. Nationality Committees were formed which participated in the planning and financing of specially decorated Nationality Rooms in the main building. Encouraged by their success, they continued to express interest in many areas of the University, including the University's Hillman Library. In 1930 the first major book collection in this area was received from the Ministry of Education of Yugoslavia. Another early contribution was a gift of books from the National Slovak Society. These, plus the contributions of individuals, were the basis of the Library collection until 1960.

In 1959-60, the University instituted a Slavic Department which offered courses in the Russian, Polish, and Serbo-Croatian languages and literature. The Department expanded rapidly, offering a Masters Degree in 1962 and a Ph.D. in Russian in 1964; the courses in Polish and Serbo-Croatian remained on the intermediate level. Although major acquisition efforts centered on Russian materials, the strong interest of some faculty members encouraged the University to purchase significant linguistic materials in all the Slavic languages. The Library has over 3,000 titles in East European linguistics and literature (other than Russian), with materials representative of all the languages of the area. The largest number of titles is in Serbo-Croatian, followed by Romanian and Polish.

In 1965-66 the University expanded the scope of its interests to include a program of Russian and East European Studies. In 1967-68 a special Program in Comparative Communism was developed involving five colleges and universities in the Pittsburgh area. Teaching is done by teams of faculty from all the schools, and the library resources of all the schools are available to all members of the program. Since 1960 library materials have been chosen to support the curriculum of these programs, with emphasis on Russian and Soviet studies. For the area covered by this survey, the monograph collection (exclusive of the materials in literature and linguistics mentioned earlier) can generally be characterized as: 1) recently published material, 2) more often concerned with the area as a whole than with a specific region or country, 3) reflecting Western

European and U.S. scholarship about the area to a greater extent than works written within the area, 4) selected to meet general curriculum needs of undergraduates and beginning graduate students. Retrospective holdings are largest for Yugoslavia and Poland, with Czechoslovakia and Romania second and Albania, Bulgaria, and Hungary third. The Library has very little material on Modern Greece. The East German collection is quite extensive but could not be covered in this survey because of limitations in staff time.

General policy is to provide basic reference and research aids such as atlases, statistical yearbooks, guides, encyclopedias, dictionaries, and biographic and bibliographic tools for all the countries of Eastern Europe. Most of these materials should also be available in the collections of other universities.

The Library subscribes to the major periodicals concerning the area in all languages. In addition, exchange agreements are maintained with learned institutions throughout Eastern Europe, including the academies of sciences, universities, museums, and libraries. Current publications, including periodicals, irregular series, and monographs, are obtained through these exchanges. Approximately 450 journals and irregular series relating to the area are received currently through both subscription and exchange. This number should increase greatly in the coming year due to new titles being received on exchange for the journal *Canadian-American Slavic Studies,* which is now located at the University of Pittsburgh.

The Library receives 12 newspapers from the Eastern European countries, excluding the Soviet Union, and 10 published by émigré groups from the area. A special collection called the Archives of Industrial Society, sponsored by the History Department, contains basic source material on local history, including some related to the ethnic origins of the area's population.

In 1974, the Hillman Library received, as a gift, the library and papers of the late distinguished professor of Slavic and general linguistics, Charles Bidwell. A substantial portion of this 1,200 volume collection on philology and linguistics is devoted to Slavic philology and includes dictionaries and grammars for all the Slavic languages, historical and descriptive studies in Slavic linguistics, and histories of the various Slavic literatures.

In May 1974 the Library began issuing an acquisitions list, *Recent Acquisitions in Russian and East European Studies. No. 1, January 1973-December 1973* (compl. Stephen A. Maczko).

Nada Botkin, formerly of the
University of Pittsburgh

Polish Institute of Arts and Sciences in America

The Polish Institute of Arts and Sciences in America was founded in 1942 in New York by a group of outstanding Polish scholars and members of the Polish Academy of Sciences who hoped that after the liberation of Poland the Institute would become the American station of the Polish Academy of Sciences. Owing to the political events of 1945 this hope was frustrated and the Polish Institute of Arts and Sciences in America became an independent Polish-American scholarly organization.

The purpose of the Institute is to maintain, develop, and promote Polish-American cultural relations; to spread knowledge of Poland and her culture in the United States and of the United States in Poland; and to establish areas of cooperation between American and Polish scholars. To this end it organizes and supports research work pertaining to Poland in this country by offering facilities to scholars, including a private library and archives. It cooperates with research institutions in Poland by sending them American books and scholarly material.

The Library

The Library of the Polish Institute of Arts and Sciences in America is situated in the Institute's quarters at 59 East 66th Street, New York, N. Y. 10021. The Library is open Monday through Friday from 10:15 a.m. to 4:45 p.m. Prior to visiting the Library clients are requested to make an appointment by telephone with the Librarian (telephone 861-8694) or with the Secretary of the Institute (988-4338). The Library has a catalog arranged alphabetically by author and a subject catalog classified by the Dewey Decimal system. The catalog record cards can be accessed only in the presence of and with the guidance of the Librarian. The only special catalog maintained by the Institute is its file of belles lettres record cards.

In 1960 the Institute began to assemble its collections of books, periodicals, and brochures in its present headquarters. The Library's book collection has grown from ca. 2,500 books in 1960-61 to over 13,000 volumes, with an average annual intake of 500 volumes. This increment is based mainly on exchange with university libraries, museums, and various institutions of higher learning in Poland. Local donations by persons liquidating or reorganizing their private collections also comprise a very important source of books. Some of the books thus obtained are rare items, dating back to the 18th and 19th centuries.

The book library, located on the third floor of the Institute, contains a large collection of valuable, richly illustrated albums and volumes too heavy to be shelved, mainly relating to Fine Arts, and illustrated descriptions of cities and regions in Poland. Some of these were printed before World War I and during the interwar period. In addition, it holds books donated by the Consul General of West Germany in Chicago; this collection consists of books by prominent Polish prose writers translated into German by distinguished German authors.

The very large collection of periodicals, brochures, and other nonbook material is temporarily closed to the public owing to building remodeling, following which the collection will be reorganized. The most noteworthy items in this collection are: 22 folio volumes (1949-71) of *Wiadomości,* published in London; 38 bound volumes (1948-71) of *Kultura,* published in Paris; 21 volumes (1962-72) of *Zeszyty Historyczne,* published in Paris; a nearly complete collection

(1945-71) of *Twórczość,* published in Poland; and the *Polish Review,* an American scholarly journal published quarterly for the past 16 years by the Polish Institute of Arts and Sciences in America.

The Library's reference aids relating to Poland include volumes 1-16 of *Polski Słownik Biograficzny* (Kraków, 1936-39, and Warsaw, 1946-70) and a complete set of *Wielka encyklopedia powszechna,* 13 v. (Warsaw, 1962-70). The most valuable source in the collection is *Bibliografia Polska XIX Stulecia* (1881-90) by Karol Estreicher. Other noteworthy bibliographic sources are *Nowy Korbut,* a bibliography of Polish literature published by the Instytut Badań Literackich (9 v. to date); *Słownik współczesnych pisarzy polskich,* 4 v. (Warsaw, 1964); and the catalog of the Library of Kórnik, Poland, *Old Prints, Polonica XVI Century,* published by the Ossolineum in Wrocław. Among current reference aids mention should be made of yearbook *Informator nauki Polski* (1958-71), containing an alphabetical index of scholars. The Institute also has the most important recent dictionaries of the Polish language, including the two-volume set by Jan Stanisławski, *The Great English-Polish Dictionary* (Warsaw, 1968) and *The Great Polish-English Dictionary* (Warsaw, 1970).

The areas of strength of the Library are outlined in what follows.

History of Poland

The works on the predynastic period include those of Witold Hensel, Józef Kostrzewski, Gerard Labuda, Tadeusz Sulimirski, et al. On the Piast dynasty (963-1370) the Library holds a work by the contemporary writer Jan Długosz (Ioannis Dlugossii), *Annales seu cronicae incliti Regni Poloniae,* v. I and II, a milestone between the Middle Ages and the Renaissance. Sources on the Jagellonian dynasty (1386-1572) were published by the Library of Kórnik, *Lites ac res gestae inter Polonos ordinemque cruciferorum,* v. I, II (1890-92), v. III, 2d. ed. (1905). The Library holds writings of outstanding historians who have written on this period, among them Oskar Halecki and Tadeusz Korzon. The Library possesses many publications and albums about the Battle of Grünwald (1410). Among the holdings on the Electoral dynasty (1572-1795), special attention is called to the love letters of King Jan III Sobieski to his Queen, Maria Kazimierza, written during the campaign of Vienna (1683); and to the memoirs of Jędrzej Kitowicz, *Opis obyczajów i zwyczajów za panowania Augusta III* (Poznań-Warsaw, 1885). The Library has a selection of works by and about prominent contemporary historians Hugo Kołłątaj and Andrzej Frycz-Modrzewski. With respect to the partition period (1795-1918), extensive sources are held on the insurrections of November, 1831, and January, 1863; particular attention is called to *Dyaryusz Sejmu z r. 1830-1831,* compiled by Michał Rostworowski and published by the Polish Academy of Sciences in six volumes (Kraków, 1907-12).

The Institute's collection of sources on Polish history from World War I through World War II includes works by statesmen, politicians, and high-ranking military men, both contemporary accounts and works written in exile. Among those represented are Marian Seyda, Gen. Władysław Sikorski, Michał Sokolnicki, Gen. Władysław Anders, Marshal Józef Piłsudski, Kazimierz Iranek-Osmecki, Alfons Klafkowski, Col. Witold Urbanowicz, Gen. Tadeusz Bor-Komorowski, Jan Ciechanowski, Jan Karski, Józef Lipski, Stanisław Mikołajczyk, and Tytus Komarnicki. Sources on the mass deportations, forced-labor camps, and the Katyn massacre are also well represented.

Literature; Fine Arts; Theater; Film; Music; Folklore

The Library has a representative collection of Polish literature beginning with the 16th century, but with emphasis on the era of romanticism, for which the Library has nearly complete holdings of the works of the more famous authors as well as works about them. An item of special interest in the collection is a copy of Adam Mickiewicz's masterpiece *Pan Tadeusz* (Paris, A. Pinard, 1932-34), which belonged to the late poet Jan Lechoń.

The Institute's sources relating to Polish music are limited to Chopin's *Complete Works,* ed. I. J. Paderewski, et al. (Warsaw); Br. Edward Sydow's bibliography of Chopin; and the four-volume *Chopin-Życie i twórczość* by Ferdynand Hoesick, based on the prewar issue. An extensive two-volume edition of *Korespondencja Frederyka Chopina* by Br. Edward Sydow (Warsaw, State Institute of Publications, 1955) is available for study. The Library receives literature regarding the Chopin festivals which have been held periodically in Warsaw since 1927. With regard to modern composers and performers, the Library possesses literature about Ignacy Paderewski, his memoirs written jointly with Mary Lawton, and some works by persons of his entourage. Further, there is B. M. Maciejewski's *Karol Szymanowski: His Life and Music* (London, 1967) and the subject catalog of compositions and bibliography published by the Polskie Wydawnictwo Muzyczne (Kraków, 1967).

Painting; Drawing; and Polish Design

This field is represented by albums richly illustrated with biographical texts of famous artists: Alexander Michałowski, Alexander Orłowski, Jan Matejko, Stanisław Wyspiański, and for the interwar period, the prominent painter Stanisław Nowakowski. The art student will find the collections ample for research. The folklore collection comprises 34 volumes of regional songs and music by Oskar Kolberg, as well as his *Lud, jego zwyczaje, sposób życia, mowa, podania, przysłowia, obrzędy, gusła, zabawy, pieśni, muzyka i tańce* (Kraków, 1890).

Anna M. Lipski
Polish Institute of Arts and Sciences in America

Princeton University

The collection is integrated with the general holdings of Firestone Library for the purposes of catalog record, shelving, circulation, reference, interlibrary loan, and photoduplication. Book selection and specialized reference functions are performed primarily by the Slavic Bibliographer, Firestone Library B-6-M-1, tel. 609-452-3248. In 1971/72 the collection reached 31,325 cataloged volumes (including both monographs and bound periodicals) with an average annual intake over the last five years (1967/68-1971/72) of approximately 2,600 volumes.

The bulk of the collection is of rather recent origin. Prior to World War II only Hungarian and modern Greek publications received a fairly wide subject coverage. Acquisition of materials from other, especially Slavic, countries was limited largely to art, statistics, and public finance. After World War II new trends in teaching and research provided an impetus for the growth of the collection, especially with respect to the Slavic countries. A major milestone was the establishment of the Department of Slavic Languages and Literatures in 1961 in which Serbo-Croatian, Polish, and Czech were taught at various times. Graduate research was carried on in the history of Bulgaria, Poland, and Yugoslavia and eventually formal graduate courses were instituted in the history of East Central Europe (Czechoslovakia, Hungary, and Poland). In the late 1960s the interests of the Economics Department broadened to encompass Eastern Europe, particularly Hungary and Poland. A similar expansion of interests, especially with respect to Yugoslavia and Czechoslovakia, occurred in political science in conjunction with the growth of comparative communist studies.

In response to these trends the Library developed a selective program of acquiring publications in the languages of Bulgaria, Czechoslovakia, Poland, and Yugoslavia. A more limited program, and one restricted largely to history and social sciences, has been carried on in Hungarian and, to a lesser extent, Romanian literature. A limited acquisition program in modern Greek economics, linguistics, literature, education, and history was resumed in 1969 under the Cooperative Library Project of the Modern Greek Studies Association. Publications in Albanian are obtained only in exceptional cases, though scholarly works on Albania in Western languages and Russian are normally acquired.

Because of its relatively recent origin the principal strength of the collection lies in post-1945 imprints. Nevertheless, important older monographs and serial sets have also been obtained largely through retrospective acquisition. Thus the collection includes the journals of national banks and finance ministries of all East European countries, except Albania, for the period between the First and Second World War. It also contains impressive runs of series published by distinguished academic institutions and societies in Bulgaria (University of Sofia, Bulgarska akademiia na naukite), Czechoslovakia (Česká akademie věd a umění, Česká společnost nauk, Matice moravská, Národní museum) and Yugoslavia (Jugoslovenska akademija znanosti i umjetnosti, Matica srpska). Of perhaps unique value is a recently acquired collection of some two dozen Czech political and cultural reviews, a large proportion of which do not appear in the standard catalogs and lists of holdings of American libraries.

While no sections of the collection are as yet truly excellent, there are pockets of strength which may be classified as "good" or "very good" and are adequate to support advanced research.

There are other segments which may be classified as "fair" and are suitable at least for undergraduate research. The relative strengths and weaknesses of the collection in terms of size by individual countries and subjects are outlined in Appendix A.

As a reflection of the established acquisition trends the collection is markedly strong in publications concerning the four Slavic countries of the area, particularly Poland and Czechoslovakia. The Polish collection is very good in language and literature and history, good in economics, and fair in politics and law. The Czechoslovak collection is also very good in history, language, and literature, and fair in economics, politics and law, and art. The collections for the other two Slavic countries are somewhat weaker. The Yugoslav one is good in language and literature, and history; fair in economics, art, and politics and law. The Bulgarian one is good in language and literature, and fair in history. Of the four non-Slavic countries only two show minor strengths. The Hungarian collection, reflecting current research interests, is fair in history and economics. The Greek collection exhibits minor strength in history, and language and literature (see Appendix B). No aspect of the Albanian or Romanian collection appears to be significant. The current acquisition trends should lead to a relative improvement of the Hungarian, and probably also the Romanian, collection especially in history and the social sciences. There should also be a general improvement in the size and quality of the modern Greek collection.

From the subject point of view language and literature, and history show special strengths. In language and literature the collection is very good for Poland and Czechoslovakia, good for Yugoslavia and Bulgaria, and fair for Greece. In history it is very good for Poland and Czechoslovakia, good for Yugoslavia, and fair for Hungary, Greece, and Bulgaria. Economics, and politics and law are next in importance. The economics collection is good for Poland and fair for Czechoslovakia, Hungary, and Yugoslavia. The collection in politics and law is fair for Czechoslovakia, Poland, and Yugoslavia. Of the other subjects the art collection shows a minor strength for Czechoslovakia and Yugoslavia (see Appendix C). There are no areas of strength in ethnography, musicology, or philosophy. Though the number of specifically sociological volumes is low, the strength of the related subjects of history, economics, and politics and law can provide limited support for research in the sociology of Poland, Czechoslovakia, and Yugoslavia. In view of the current acquisition trends, the relative strength in the coverage of economics, politics and law, sociology, and possibly philosophy should increase.

Zdeněk V. David, formerly of
Princeton University

Appendix A

Number of Cataloged Volumes (Monographs and Bound Periodicals) by Subject and Country Held in August 1972

	Art	Economics	Ethnography	History	Language & Literature	Music	Philosophy	Politics & Law	Sociology	General Periodicals***	Bibliography	TOTAL
ALBANIA	5	13	2	118	68	1	0	5	0	0	4	216
BULGARIA	51	176	25	566	1,164	6	33	79	11	194	82	2,387
CZECHOSLOVAKIA	271	432	27	2,528	3,602*	91	97	330	38	1,152	357	8,925
GREECE (MODERN)	34	182	21	750	549	0	12	11	0	57	66	1,682
HUNGARY	227	341	9	887	364	126	7	73	3	75	151	2,263
POLAND	216	812	107	2,906	3,915	72	93	302	125	423	357	9,328
ROMANIA	152	224	18	475	220	0	3	19	2	28	77	1,218
YUGOSLAVIA	252	332	21	1,593	1,602**	7	18	228	14	997	242	5,306
TOTAL	1,208	2,512	230	9,823	11,484	303	263	1,047	193	2,926	1,336	31,325

*Czech 2,709
Slovak 893

**Macedonian 142
Serbo-Croat 1,220
Slovene 240

***Those periodicals which are not classified by subject. Volumes of other periodicals are included together with monographic volumes in the figures for the individual subjects.

Appendix B

Relative Strengths of the Collection by Countries*

	Fair	Good	Very Good
BULGARIA	History	Language & Literature	
CZECHOSLOVAKIA	Art Economics Politics & Law Sociology		Language & Literature History
GREECE	History Language & Literature		
HUNGARY	Economics History		
POLAND	Politics & Law Sociology	Economics	History Language & Literature
YUGOSLAVIA	Art Economics Language & Literature Politics & Law Sociology	History Language & Literature	

*No appreciable strengths for Albania and Romania.

Appendix C

Relative Strengths of the Collection by Subject*

	Fair	Good	Very Good
ART	Czechoslovakia Yugoslavia		
ECONOMICS	Czechoslovakia Hungary Yugoslavia	Poland	
HISTORY	Bulgaria Greece Hungary	Yugoslavia	Czechoslovakia Poland
LANGUAGE & LITERATURE	Greece	Bulgaria Yugoslavia	Czechoslovakia Poland
POLITICS & LAW	Czechoslovakia Poland Yugoslavia		
SOCIOLOGY	Czechoslovakia Poland Yugoslavia		

*No significant strengths in ethnography, musicology, or philosophy.

Stanford University

The Stanford University Main Library collection on East Central and Southeast Europe is quite young, systematic acquisition of Slavic materials having begun only in 1959. Considerable progress has been made since that time, however, particularly as a result of the Library's Resources Development Program, initiated in the academic year 1964-65, under which priority in the purchase of Slavic materials has been given to works relating to Russia and the Soviet Union (some 70 percent of the total appropriation). Secondary emphasis has been placed on materials from Poland, Czechoslovakia, and Bulgaria, in that order. The remaining East Central and Southeast European countries have received only marginal attention. The historical collection is designed to support the University's teaching and research program and to complement the Slavic collection of the Hoover Institution on War, Revolution, and Peace. The basic demarcation line between the Stanford and Hoover collections is the beginning of the 20th century, the latter collection stressing the more recent period. Subjects emphasized in the Stanford collection are linguistics, literature, and history.

The collection also benefited through participation, beginning in 1967, in the Public Law 480 Program, under which Stanford received from Yugoslavia scholarly monographs, serials, and reference materials in the fields of linguistics, literature, literary history and criticism, history, archeology, paleography, folklore, and art. An important recent acquisition was that of Vasil Mikov's collection of about 4,000 titles on Bulgaria as well as titles on Hungary, Yugoslavia, Romania, and Albania. This collection is strongest in the fields of Balkan affairs, ethnographic and demographic problems, and linguistics.

As of the end of 1971, the East European collections (excluding East Germany, for which no figures are available) contained about 12,000 books and over 1,300 serial titles. The current annual intake is ca. 2,500 titles.

The collection is incorporated into the general Library collections and may be used on the same terms. It is under the supervision of the Curator for Russian and East European Materials.

The collection is supported by a variety of reference works, including long runs of national bibliographies and numerous subject and author bibliographies. General information may also be obtained from various guides, handbooks, and encyclopedias such as *Kratka Bŭlgarska entsiklopediia, Enciklopedija Jugoslavije, Ottův slovník naučný, Révai nagy lexikona,* and *Wielka encyklopedia powszechna,* as well as from a number of prewar Polish encyclopedias and some others.

Although Stanford does not collect rare Slavic materials, special attention is given to catalogs of manuscripts and incunabula. Among the more prominent are the Polish union catalog of manuscripts and the listings of the National Library in Sofia; the National Museum in Prague; the University of Bratislava; numerous Polish scientific institutions, the public libraries in Croatia, Dubrovnik, and Hungary; and the Yugoslav Academy of Sciences. Similarly, general publications and guides provide information on various archives, e.g., the archives of the Bulgarian and Polish Academies of Sciences, the Czechoslovak National Archives, the archives of various universities, and the Sorbische Kulturarchiv in Bautzen, Germany. Holdings of the bulletins of the State Archives of Croatia date back to 1899, and those of Bosnia and Herzegovina to 1894.

The endeavors of the major learned institutions and societies of the East European countries are set forth in publications by and about them, including yearbooks and statistical compendia. This applies to all the academies of sciences, the national museums, and various universities. Among learned societies, publications by and about the following are especially well covered: Bŭlgarsko istorichesko druzhestvo; Arkheologichesko druzhestvo; Bŭlgarska Misŭl; Česká Společnost Nauk; Společnost Jaroslava Vrchlického; Pražský Lingvistický Kroužek; Slovanský Ústav; Matica Slovenská; Zakład Narodowy imienia Ossolińskich; learned societies of Warsaw, Łódź, Poznań, Toruń, and Wrocław; and almost all Yugoslav societies pursuing research in the social sciences and the humanities. Some of these are represented by serials beginning with the end of the 19th century.

The program for current acquisitions is quite well organized. Procurement of out-of-print materials is limited by lack of funds and faculty priorities. This has resulted in a basic research collection in the areas of language, literature, and history that has no strong specialty profile.

The noteworthy collection on the Church Slavonic language includes several grammars and works on phonetics, etymology, lexicology, lexicography, syntax, and history.

The modern Bulgarian language collection is satisfactory for research purposes in linguistics, including dialectology. Literature is represented by the output of numerous authors, many of them in first editions. Literary history and criticism are fairly well represented. Folklore, with the emphasis on folk songs, is an additional strong point of the Bulgarian collection. The most serious deficiency is in the field of 20th-century literature.

Materials on history are well balanced. There are numerous monographs for each period of Bulgarian history and about such personalities as V. Levski, Kh. Botev, and D. Petrov. The collection is generally oriented toward Balkan affairs.

The Czechoslovak collection is perhaps the best coordinated of all. The Library has current subscriptions to all important serials in Stanford's areas of interest, and it holds complete sets of such serials as *Časopis pro moderní filologii, Listy filologické, Český časopis historický,* the *Časopis* of the National Museum of Prague, and the *Časopis* of the Společnost Přátel starožitností československých. There are also well-selected collected works of Czech and Slovak writers, published mostly before 1939. Unfortunately, literary history and criticism are not satisfactorily represented; however, the works of the more prominent 20th-century critics may be found. The collection on linguistics includes the works of a number of authorities. Stanford also has a sizable collection of dictionaries of the Czech language.

The principal subjects covered in Czechoslovak history include: the foreign relations of Bohemia; the Hussite movement; and histories of Prague, Brno, Bratislava, and Olomouc. The following source materials are held: *Archiv český, Fontes rerum bohemicarum, Regesta diplomatica nec non epistolaria Bohemiae et Moraviae, Glossarium illustrans bohemico-moraviae historiae fontes, Dokumenty k protifeudálnym bojom slovenského ľudu,* and *Glossarium bohemoslavicum.* There are also critical editions of the first Czech historians, Cosmas of Prague and Dalimil. The collection in history provides good general information but offers limited research possibilities.

The largest of the East European collections is that on Poland. The following afford a basis for solid research: Monographs in all fields of linguistics beginning with the works of Jan Baudouin de Courtenay; specialized serials published by the Academy of Sciences and by leading universities and learned societies; dictionaries; histories of the Polish language; comprehensive grammars; dictionaries of Old Polish, of 16th-century Polish, and of the language of Jan Ch. Pasek and Adam Mickiewicz; a dictionary of dialects; and atlases of dialects. The collection is also strong in treatises on dialects in contemporary Poland, covering larger areas such as Masovia, Silesia, Pomerania, and Kashubia, as well as many small territories such as counties or even villages. The source materials in Old Polish may be found in critical editions of *Bogurodzica, Kazania gnieźnieńskie, Biblia królowej Zofii tzw. Szaroszpatacka, Wierszowane legendy średniowieczne* edited by Vrtel-Wierczyński, and some anthologies of Old Polish texts.

In 16th- and 17th-century Polish literature, Stanford has many collected works of the established authors, published in the series *Biblioteka pisarzów polskich* (holdings for the publication period 1889-1950 are extensive but not complete), in *Biblioteka Narodowa,* and in other editions. Old Polish drama, speeches, and poetry are critically discussed in a large selection of research works.

In sharp contrast to this positive picture stands the coverage of literature and literary criticism of the 19th and 20th centuries. Most authors of this period are not represented at all, and collected works of others are, for the most part, Polish publications of the 1950s. *Zbiór poetów polskich XIX w.* covers in part the Polish poets of this period. The fortuitous exception is that Stanford has numerous works of literary criticism on A. Mickiewicz.

Highlighting the Polish literary collection are numerous bibliographies and histories of literature, both comprehensive and specific. Among literary critics represented are: St. Adamczewski, K. Badecki, W. Borowy, J. Bartoszewicz, K. Chłędowski, B. Chlebowski, P. Chmielowski, W. Feldman, J. Kleiner, G. Korbut, J. Krzyżanowski, H. Kuraszkiewicz, J. Lorentowicz, J. Pigoń, St. Tarnowski, J. Tretiak, and K. Zawodziński.

The growing Polish scholarly interest in archeology is clearly reflected in the leading archeological serials as well as in several monographs. There are also works of competent scholars in folklore (Ł. Górnicki, J. J. Kraszewski, A. Brueckner, and O. Kolberg), numismatics (M. Gumowski), and ethnography.

Numerous monographs and ca. 80 serials provide a broad view of Polish history and exemplify various schools and trends in Polish historical scholarship. Here we may note Stanford's holdings of works by J. U. Niemcewicz (edition of 1822 in six volumes), A. Naruszewicz (edition of 1833-37 in 10 volumes), J. Lelewel, K. Szajnocha, and W. Sobieski; and by a number of modern historians.

Postwar Polish works predominate, with rather comprehensive holdings of scholarly publications appearing after 1965.

Among the more important source materials are critical editions of chronicles by Martinus Gallus, Wincenty Kadłubek, and Jan Długosz, together with *Lites ac res gestae inter Polonos ordinemque Cruciferorum; Monumenta medii aevi historica res gestas Poloniae illustrantia ab anno 1507 usque ad annum 1795* (19 v.); *Monumenta Poloniae Vaticana;* the archives of General J. Wybicki; the *acta* of Synods in Poznań, Kalisz, and Kraków (XVI-XVII c.); the diaries of the National Councils of 1555-57 and 1701-02; *Volumina legum,* 10 v. (1859-1952); the *acta* of the Insurrection of 1830-31; *Pomniki prawa Rzeczpospolitej Krakowskiej; Acta Silesiaca;* and others.

Despite its volume, the Polish history collection contains no subject specializations.

As indicated, the collection on Yugoslavia in the Stanford fields of interest is quite comprehensive beginning with items published after 1967. Up to that time the field of linguistics and literature was focused on Croatia. This resulted in a general collection on all facets of linguistics and a number of editions of the collected works of prominent Croatian authors. At present it is particularly strong in Serbian language and literature; however, literary criticism is still poorly represented (with the exception of materials on Vuk Karadžić).

In history, attention has been directed toward Balkan affairs in general rather than to any particular areas of interest. Most of the monographs are in English. However, a valuable source collection includes complete editions of *Monumenta spectantia historiam Slavorum Orientalium, Monumenta spectantia historiam Slavorum meridionalium, Codex diplomaticus regni Croatiae, Dalmatiae et Slavoniae, Monumenta historica civitatis Zagrebiae* (complete), the *Vjesnik* of the

Archeological Museum of Zagreb, and other materials. Among specific subjects, the period of Alexander I, King of Serbia (1876-1903), is relatively well covered.

This survey of the Slavic collection may be concluded by indicating Stanford's activity in collecting Sorbian-Lusatian materials. There are several bibliographies; some dictionaries; works by J. Młyńk, P. Nedo, Wjela, E. K. Mucke, G. Schwela, J. Bart, H. Zejler, and V. Zmeskal; and *Volkslieder der Serben in der Ober- und Nieder-Lausitz* edited by L. Haupt (Berlin, Akademie, 1953). Current publications are being acquired, especially those published by the Akademie der Wissenschaften, Berlin, and Bautzen.

A statistical survey of Stanford's East Central and Southeast Europe Collection indicates that significantly less attention has been given to the non-Slavic than to the Slavic countries. There is a lack of general reference sources; language teaching materials are suitable only to support the beginner's level; the literature is mainly in English translation and in limited perspective; and the history is discussed by English-speaking authors. Thus it is fair to say that the Stanford University Library does not offer a research collection on the non-Slavic countries. However, some characteristics of the materials on non-Slavic countries merit mention.

For Albania, Stanford subscribes to two serial publications by the University of Tirana—one in linguistics, one in history.

While there is an extremely good collection in the humanities and social sciences on Ancient Greece (thousands of volumes), coverage of subsequent historical periods and cultural events is poor. Among literary figures, only N. Kazantzakis is treated somewhat comprehensively. In history, attention is given to the Byzantine Empire, covered in a few valuable serial publications and in general historical works rather than by monographs (except for the War of Independence, 1821-29). Considerable stress is placed on histories and other general information on various Greek cities, as well as on descriptive works and folklore.

Stanford discontinued development of its Hungarian collection after the fall of the Austro-Hungarian Monarchy and the subsequent Hungarian liberation. The previous period is represented by long runs of serials such as *Acta Historica Academiae Scientiarum Hungariae, Studia Historica Academiae Scientiarum Hungariae, Biblioteca humanitatis historica, Monumenta Hungariae Historica, Monumenta Hungariae Archeologica,* and some other source materials, chiefly from the time of Rákóczy. Stanford also subscribes to some serial publications already well established in the collection, and is acquiring some basic reference sources as well as some literary works of the most prominent Hungarian writers.

With respect to Romania, in recent years Stanford has collected basic linguistic works dealing with the Romanian language. There has also been strong interest in collecting 20th-century literature. As a consequence, there are many literary histories and critical monographs, as well as the collected works of T. Arghezi, L. Blaga, G. Călinescu, C. Petrescu, L. Rebreanu, M. Sadoveanu, I. Teodereanu, and V. Voiculescu (original editions), and selected works of other writers. Representative of the 19th century are the collected works of G. Coşbuc, I. Creangă, O. Goga, S. Iosif, and A. Macedonski.

Stanford does not have an East German collection as such. The limited acquisitions of basic reference sources, linguistics, literary works, folklore, and archeology from East Germany are incorporated in the general German collection. Social science materials are collected by the Hoover Institution on War, Revolution, and Peace.

The Stanford University Library collection on East Europe and Southeast Europe exhibits the weaknesses of a collection in its early stages. However, it is developing steadily. The PL 480 Program for Poland will contribute to the future maturation of the collection. The values are the long runs of the various serial publications and a reasonable strength in linguistics, especially comparative linguistics, and dialectology. In history, there are only minimal possibilities fo.

research in very specialized subjects, but broad areas of interest are well covered. Despite its priority for Russian and Soviet materials, Stanford makes every reasonable effort to secure the important current scholarly publications in linguistics, literary criticism, and history, with some attention to related fields of knowledge.

Wojciech Zalewski
Stanford University

University of Texas at Austin

General Information

A small East European Studies fund was established at the University in 1954. Beginning in 1970, increased Library funding allowed the establishment of blanket-order programs for current scholarly materials published in many countries of the world. These programs have resulted in greatly improved coverage for titles relating to Eastern Europe published in North America, Western Europe, and the Soviet Union. The Library has recently initiated partial blanket-orders for the two East European countries that have received most attention at the University, Czechoslovakia (Czech imprints only) and Yugoslavia (Serbian and Croatian imprints).

Most of the Library's holdings relating to Eastern Europe are to be found in the Main Library, which for undergraduates is a closed-stack library, but which faculty, graduate students, and visiting scholars who obtain a stack pass are free to enter from 8 a.m. to midnight Monday through Friday, from 9 a.m. to midnight Saturday, and from 1 p.m. to midnight Sunday. Periodicals may not be checked out, but nonreserve books circulate for two-week periods. Visitors who wish to check out Main Library materials may do so, subject to the normal regulations, after paying a refundable "Non-Student Deposit" of $15.

Records of all holdings of the Main Library and of its branches are in the Public Catalog in the lobby of the Main Library; holdings of the library of the Population Research Center, the Documents Collection, and some holdings of the Humanities Research Library are, however, not at present listed in the Public Catalog, and inquiries on these collections should be addressed to their respective librarians.

There are no special East European or Slavic Reading Rooms, but both the Humanities and the Social Science Readings Rooms in the Main Library (hours are from 8 a.m. to 10 p.m. Monday through Friday and from 8 a.m. to 5 p.m. Saturday) contain relevant periodical and reference materials, which may not be checked out. These holdings include the printed catalog of the New York Public Library's Slavonic Collection, specialized bibliographies on the countries of Eastern Europe, current American and foreign periodicals, recent publications of the U.S. Foreign Broadcast Information Service and of Radio Free Europe, the Joint Translation Service's *Summary of the Yugoslav Press,* etc. Photocopying facilities are available both in the Main Library and in the other units discussed, but they are not numerous. Further information on the East European collections of the University may be obtained from the East European Studies Bibliographer, in the Main Library.

Humanities Research Library

The Humanities Research Library, which occupies several floors in the new Humanities Research Center on the University campus, houses the rare book collections acquired by the University through gift or purchase. It is open to University faculty and students (and to visiting scholars who have secured a reader's card) from 9 a.m. to 5 p.m. Monday through Friday and from 9 a.m. until noon on Saturday.

Though most of these collections are of no direct relevance to the student of Eastern Europe, there are both scattered early Western publications relating to the area, such as Jean Choisnyn's *Discovrs av vray, de tovt ce qvi s'est faict & passé pour l'entiere negociation de l'election dv roy de Pologne* (Paris, 1574) and Robert Townson's *Travels in Hungary, with a Short Account of Vienna in the Year 1793* (London, 1797), and, more importantly, special collections pertaining to Byron's activities in Greece and the Greek Revolution and to Czechoslovakia. Most noteworthy among the latter is the Charles Parish Bohemica Collection, which includes about a hundred volumes published from the 15th through the 18th centuries in Czech, Latin, and German. One example of this interesting collection is *Kalendář hystorycký* by Daniel Adam z Veleslavína published in Prague in 1590. Students of Czech history will also be interested in the Maresh Collection, which contains several hundred books and periodicals devoted to that subject.

Inquiries concerning these collections should be addressed to the Librarian in the Humanities Research Library.

Population Research Center

In addition to the population studies to be found in the Main Library, scholars will be particularly interested in the holdings of the library of the Population Research Center on the University campus. The Center, founded in the early 1960s, has one of the nation's outstanding collections of foreign census reports, including materials on all of the countries within the scope of this report. User facilities are still quite limited, but future expansion is projected. Inquiries regarding this collection should be addressed to the Librarian.

Documents Collection

The Documents Collection, located in the same building as the Main Library, is open from 9 a.m. to 5 p.m. Monday through Friday and from 9 a.m. until noon on Saturday. It is the University's main repository for documents issued by the U.S. Government, by the U.N. and its affiliated agencies, and by other international organizations. Included in its holdings are various series of translations of foreign (including East European) technical literature. Holdings of the Documents Collection are not listed in the Main Library's Public Catalog, and inquiries about the collection should be addressed to the Documents Librarian.

Law Library

The University Law Library's holdings concerning the countries of Eastern Europe are extremely limited, with less than a hundred volumes (nearly all in English) pertaining to the entire area. Inquiries should be directed to the Library's Director.

The Collections

ALBANIA.   The Library's hundred or so volumes, about a third of which are in Albanian, are divided among history, government, linguistics, and statistics.

BULGARIA.   Bulgarian holdings of the Library are by no means extensive (some 400 volumes, about half of which are in Bulgarian), but there are useful materials in the fields of geography, history, literature, and linguistics. Particular strengths include a virtually complete run, from its beginnings in 1933 to the present, of the *Izvestiia* of the Bulgarian Geographical Society, all published volumes of the *Izvestiia* of the Academy of Sciences' Geographical Institute, all volumes since 1959 of the *Statisticheski godishnik* of the Central Statistical Office, and reports on the censuses of 1920, 1926, and 1956 (the earlier two on microfilm). The Bulgarian literature collection, approximately 125 volumes, includes the works of Ivan Vazov, Elin Pelin, and others. About 150 studies on the Bulgarian language and on Old Church Slavonic are available.

CZECHOSLOVAKIA. Given the prominence and cultural vitality of the Czech population of Texas, it will come as no surprise that, with the relevant holdings numbering near 3,000 volumes, Library collections on Czechoslovakia are appreciably stronger than for the other East European countries. Czech has been taught at the University continuously since 1915 (decades before the establishment of the Slavic Language Department), and this is reflected in the fact that over half of the total number of volumes relating to Czechoslovakia deal with literary and linguistic subjects. In these fields, Czech holdings outnumber Slovak by a ratio of six to one. The Library possesses a relatively large number of the works of the major Czech writers and many of the basic studies on the Czech language. Numerous standing orders are maintained for current periodicals. Holdings of earlier journals are scattered. Linguists will be interested in the holdings of such Texas Czech publications as the journal *Bratrské listy* from Temple, Texas. Aside from language and literature, the collection has most strength in the fields of government (including some legal materials), 20th-century history, economics, and geography, though in all these fields the monographic coverage is substantially stronger for Western-language analyses than for publications in the local languages.

EAST GERMANY. While much of the older and current Library resources relating to the study of Germany as a whole is of obvious relevance to East Germany, holdings of the Library pertaining specifically to the GDR are quite limited. An adequate collection is available in geography, an area for which the Library has subscriptions to *Geographische Berichte,* the *Wissenschaftliche Veröffentlichungen* of the Deutsches Institut für Länderkunde, and *Petermanns geographische Mitteilungen.* For the last of these publications, a nearly complete backfile since 1855 is available. The collection in literature includes appreciable, though by no means exhaustive, collections of the writings of such figures as Arnold Zweig, Anna Seghers, Johannes R. Becher, Johannes Bobrowski, and Willi Bredel. Materials in government, economics, and statistics are somewhat less extensive, and those dealing with Sorbian history, culture, and language are not numerous.

MODERN GREECE. Acquisition by the Library of Modern Greek books did not begin until 1955, and such materials have not had a high priority in the subsequent years. The small collection is divided among history, modern Greek literature, and, to a lesser extent, geography. Most of these materials are in the Main Library, but a limited number are located in the Classics Library. The Humanities Research Library has a rich collection on Byron's activities in Greece and the Greek Revolution. Scholars visiting Austin will also be interested in the library of the Center for Neo-Hellenic Studies, located near the University campus.

HUNGARY. Hungary has not been an area of general interest at the University, and the small Hungarian holdings (about 500 volumes, of which perhaps a third are in Hungarian) are concentrated in linguistics, geography, and statistical publications. Holdings for the period from the late 1950s to the present are nearly complete for various Hungarian and English publications of the Hungarian Statistical Office, for geographical publications such as *Földrajzi Értesítő, Studies in Geography in Hungary,* and *Földrajzi Közlemények,* and for such linguistic publications as *Nyelvtudományi Közlemények* and *Nyelvtudományi Értekezések.* The Library also has fairly complete holdings of the Western-language writings and translations of Georg Lukács.

POLAND. University holdings relating to Poland amount to approximately a thousand volumes, about half of which are in Polish. Neither Polish literature nor the Polish language are at present taught at the University and the corresponding collections are small. Works of some major Polish authors are, however, present, and the Library has standing orders for several linguistic series. The strongest of the other fields are perhaps economics and history. While there is relatively little monographic material in geography, the Library has had standing orders since the 1950s for some of the major geographical journals and has a complete collection of the *Prace Geograficzne* of the Academy's Geographical Institute. The *Rocznik Statystyki* series is complete since 1956.

ROMANIA.   The Romanian collection—about 400 volumes, of which perhaps a quarter are in Romanian—is strongest in history, linguistics, and geography. Standing orders have existed for a few periodicals in these fields since the late 1950s and for a broader range since the mid-1960s. There are also reports on the 1930, 1941, and 1956 censuses.

YUGOSLAVIA.   Library holdings relating to Yugoslavia number approximately 2,000 volumes, about 80 percent of which are in the local languages. Most of these volumes are located in the Main Library, but since 1970 the Classics Library has begun acquiring archeological materials, largely serial publications such as *Archaeologica Iugoslavica* and the *Arheološki pregled* of the Arheološko društvo Jugoslavije (both with complete backfiles); this collection is being developed in connection with a University archeological excavation in Macedonia. Inquiries on these materials should be addressed to the Classics Librarian.

Within the Main Library, geography, statistical and census reports, economics, literature, linguistics, ethnography, and history are relatively strong. The collection of geographic and statistical periodicals is doubtless the outstanding single area: the Library has standing orders and, in most cases, complete backfiles for such publications as *Geografski glasnik, Geografski pregled, Geografski vestnik, Geografski zbornik,* the *Glasnik* of the Srpsko geografsko društvo, the *Zbornik radova* and *Posebna izdanje* of the Jovan Cvijić Geographical Institute in Belgrade, the *Posebna izdanje* of the Serbian Academy's Geographical Institute, and the *Geografski razgledi* of the Macedonian Geographical Society. Statistical and economic periodicals include the *Statisticki bilten* of the Narodna Bank and that of the Yugoslav Statistical Office, the *Statisticki godišnjak SFRJ, Statistička revija,* the *Journal of the Yugoslav Foreign Trade,* the *Statistika spoljne trgovine FNR Jugoslavije,* and others. Of the approximately 600 volumes in literature, nearly two-thirds pertain to Serbian literature and about a quarter to Croatian; this includes works of the major writers, nearly complete holdings of such series as *Srpska književnost v sto knjiga* and *Pet stoljeca hrvatske književnosti,* as well as current periodicals and critical studies. About 200 studies on the languages of Yugoslavia are also available.

Kirk Augustine, formerly of the
University of Texas, Austin

University of Toronto

General Information

The new University of Toronto Humanities and Social Sciences Research Library—the John P. Robarts Library—is located on St. George Street. It is open for service almost 100 hours per week.

There are two central card catalogs: the new catalog records all materials cataloged or recataloged in the Library of Congress classification system since 1959; the old catalog records the remainder of the material cataloged in the old scheme before 1959. Both catalogs have separate author-title and subject files.

Several information leaflets on the Library and its services have been printed. These deal with such topics as microfilms, Reference Department, Rare Books Department, and special services for faculty and graduate students.

There is a general reference room with a collection of over 28,000 volumes. The Reference Department provides, among its many services, group Library orientation tours, individual guidance, and interlibrary loan services. The Humanities and Social Sciences Periodicals Reading Room houses the current year's issues of approximately 5,000 of the more important periodicals. A Government Publications Section contains all publications of government agencies acquired since 1967. Materials purchased before that date are located in the general stack area of the Library. A Microfilm Reading Room and photocopy facilities are available for student and faculty use.

History and Development of Collection

The Slavic and East European collection at the University of Toronto totals more than 120,000 volumes, approximately 34,000 of which cover East Central and Southeast Europe. Included in the latter figure are about 2,000 volumes of microreproductions, 875 reference works, 450 government publications, and some 900 periodical titles. In 1971 alone, over 4,000 titles were added to the East Central and Southeast European collection. Most of the works are purchased from Library funds, but there are also many gifts each year and a small number of East European exchanges. In addition, special trust funds have greatly aided in the purchase of materials to strengthen the East European holdings.

Albania

The Albanian collection comprises about 300 titles, with emphasis on the language. Of special significance are several rare old Albanian grammars by Italian scholars, for example, the first edition of Vincenzo Librandi's *Grammatica albanese* (Milan, 1897).

The Library has only a few fundamental monograph series and multivolume sets such as *Albanische Forschungen,* 8 v. (Wiesbaden, 1964-68), *Albania,* 5 v. (Paris, 1925-35), and *Studi Albanesi,* 6 v. (Rome, 1931-36). A work on Albanian archeology by Luigi M. Ugolini, entitled *Albania antica,* 3 v. (Rome, 1927-42), is housed in the Rare Books Department.

Bulgaria

Some 2,000 volumes in the Library are devoted to Bulgaria, including about 1,000 in language and literature and slightly over 500 dealing with history. In addition, the Library subscribes to 29 periodicals published in Bulgaria and receives 14 others as gifts or exchanges.

The Library has several standard bibliographies, dictionaries, and encyclopedias. There are complete files of *Bŭlgarska dialektologiia, Bŭlgarski ezik, Bŭlgarski ezik i literatura,* and the *Izvestiia* of the Seminar of Slavonic Philology of the University of Sofia, incomplete files of the *Izvestiia* of the Institute of Bulgarian Literature of the Bulgarian Academy of Sciences, *Plamŭk,* and *Septemvri,* and a complete set of *Bŭlgarski starini,* 13 v. (1906-36). Some general histories and several anthologies of Bulgarian literature are available but few works of literary criticism. The collected works of such leading writers as K. Botev, I. Iovkov, D. Ivanov, P. Slaveikov, K. Smirnenski, A. Strashimirov, O. Vasilev, and I. Vazov are available. Bulgarian folklore is represented by the collection *Bŭlgarsko narodno tvorchestvo,* 12 v. (Sofia, 1961-63). The Bulgarian history collection was developed only after 1960, and shows very large gaps.

Czechoslovakia

Current holdings in the Czech collection total approximately 9,000 volumes. The Library receives 169 periodicals published in or dealing with Czechoslovakia. Strong emphasis has been placed on the acquisition of reference materials. Most of the general and some specialized bibliographies, both current and retrospective, are in the Library, as is an almost complete collection of the important Czech and Slovak encyclopedias, including six different encyclopedic dictionaries and the encyclopedic geographic and historical work *Čechy,* edited by F. A. Šubert, 14 v. in 15 (1883-1908).

In the field of Czechoslovak history the Library's objective has been to collect works on the 19th and 20th centuries. Czechoslovak history since World War II is well covered, and the collection dealing with the events of 1968 is expanding rapidly. Moreover, the Rare Books Department has a small but interesting collection of broadsides, handbills, political cartoons, manuscripts, and issues of newspapers such as *Rudé právo, Pravda, Práce, Lidová demokracie,* and *Mladá fronta* dealing with the August 1968 intervention. The collection is especially strong in Czech and Slovak historical periodicals and includes complete or nearly complete files of the following: *Časopis Matice moravské* (1869-1963), *Časopis Společnosti přátel starožitností českých* (1895-1959), *Český časopis historický, Československý časopis historický* (since 1953), *Historica* (since 1959), *Historický archiv* (since 1893), *Historický časopis* (since 1953), *Historické štúdie* (since 1955), *Sborník historický* (since 1953), and *Slovenský národopis* (since 1954). Also available are such comparatively rare publications as *Codex diplomaticus et epistolaris Moraviae,* v. 1-15 (1836-1903), F. Pubička's *Chronologische Geschichte Böhmens,* 6 v. in 10 (1770-1801), and *Series chronologica rerum Slavo-Bohemicarum* (1768). The collection contains many general histories of the Czech lands but is notably weak in more specialized studies of the medieval and early modern period.

In the field of political science, law, and government, the Library has some of the most important primary sources, including a file of *Sbírka zákonů* for 1918-64. The official newspaper of the Communist Party, *Rudé právo,* is available on microfilm from 1953, but most of the scholarly journals in these disciplines are lacking and monographic holdings are far from adequate. In the area of foreign relations, the collection includes a file of *Zahraniční politika* from 1922 to 1939. In economics, the Library has subscriptions to and fairly complete files of *Czechoslovak Economic Papers* (since 1959); *Kontrola, Lidová kontrola, Plánované hospodářství* (since 1965), and *Politická ekonomie* (since 1966). Holdings of government documents include some statistical material such as *Statistická ročenka* (from 1957). On the whole, there is a scarcity of research material for the period before World War II.

The Library's Czech language and literature collection numbers about 4,000 volumes. This includes more than 1,000 titles on Czech literary history and criticism recently purchased as a collection. Among the authors best represented are: V. Beneš-Třebízský, K. Čapek, K. M. Čapek-Chod, S. Čech, V. Dyk, E. B. Frida, A. Heyduk, A. Jirásek, J. S. Machar, J. Mužaková, B. Němcová, J. Neruda, K. V. Rais, F. X. Šalda, J. K. Tyl, Z. Winter, and J. Zeyer. The strongest areas in the Czech literature collection are the prose of the second half of the 19th century and the poetry of the 1920s. The weakest are probably Old Czech literature and that of the period after 1948. The Library has a number of important anthologies, a small collection of histories of Czech literature, and the comprehensive series of monographs *Sbírka pramenů k poznání literárního života československého,* 29 v. (1926-48). An invaluable asset to the study of Czech language and literature and to Czech studies in general is a complete set of the oldest and most important Czech scholarly journal, the *Časopis* of the National Museum in Prague. Other literary and general periodicals include *Česká literatura* (since 1957), *Česká revue, Cesta,* 12 v. (1918-30), *Literární noviny* (1952-68), *Lumír* (1873-1933), *Maj* (1903-14), *Naše doba* (1894-1949), *Slovanský přehled* (1899-1945), *Tvorba* (1926-62), and *Zvon* (1901-41).

As far as Czech and Slavic linguistics and philology are concerned, the Library's main strength is in periodical literature. Complete or nearly complete files of *Časopis pro moderní filologii* (since 1911), *České museum filologické* (1894-1904), *Český časopis filologický* (1942-44), *Listy filologické* (since 1874), *Naše řeč* (since 1917), *Slavia* (since 1922), and *Slovo a slovesnost* are available, as are the important Czech dictionaries. Holdings of linguistic monographs leave much to be desired, however, with the exception of a representative selection of studies by J. Dobrovský, J. Gebauer, K. Horálek, V. Machek, and F. Trávníček.

The collection in the field of Slovak language and literature amounts to some 750 volumes. Periodical holdings include *Bratislava* (1927-37), *Jazykovedné štúdie* (since 1956), *Slovenská literatúra* (since 1954), *Slovenská reč* (since 1932), *Kultúrny život* (since 1946), and *Slovenské pohľady* (since 1922). Holdings of Slovak literature are rather fragmentary, although the most important writers are well represented by collected editions of their works (J. Gregor-Tajovský, J. Holly, Hviezdoslav, S. Hurban Vajanský, M. Kukučín). Literary criticism is almost entirely absent.

The Library has more than 100 volumes devoted to the Hussite movement and the Reformation in Bohemia, including collections of documents as well as studies by V. Kybal, V. Novotný, J. Sedlak, and others. There are also various editions of the works of Jan Amos Komenský.

One of the notable features of the collection is a partial set of the publications of the Czech Academy of Sciences and Arts, covering most fully the period between 1891 and 1948.

East Germany

All the basic East German bibliographies are available. Reference aids are somewhat less complete, lacking up-to-date biographical handbooks and complete yearbook sets.

The Library subscribes to about 24 GDR serials, mostly political. The organ of the SED, *Einheit,* is available from 1963 to the present, and the Library has all of the *Beiträge zur Geschichte der Arbeiterbewegung* as well as almost all the monographs in the series *Bonner Bericht aus Mittel- und Ostdeutschland.* Also in the collection is a rare cultural and political journal, *Ost und West,* 3 v. (Berlin, 1947-49).

In the early 1960s subscriptions were placed for two major literary periodicals: *Neue Deutsche Literatur* and *Beiträge zur Literaturkunde,* a reference publication of the Zentral Institut für Bibliothekswesen. The Library has a full set of *Sinn und Form,* 22 v. (Berlin, 1949-) and all but the first two volumes of the literary journal *Weimarer Beiträge,* 14 v. (Berlin, 1955-).

East German foreign policy and relations are well covered. The Library has many monographs and receives *German Foreign Policy, Dokumente zur Aussenpolitik der DDR,* and the bulletins on foreign relations of the DDR Auswärtiges Amt.

The collection includes the fundamental writings of such authorities on East Germany as G. Castellan, J. Childs, E. W. Gniffke, F. Kopp, S. Mampel, J. P. Nettl, and C. Stern. Some 26 works by Walter Ulbricht are available, including a first edition of his *Legende vom "deutschen Sozialismus"* (Berlin, 1945).

The following bodies are represented by a large number of research publications: Institut für Marxismus-Leninismus, Berlin; Institut für Gesellschaftswissenschaften, Berlin; Partei Hochschule "Karl Marx," Berlin; Institut für Deutsche Militärgeschichte, Berlin; Deutsche Akademie der Wissenschaften, Berlin; Institut für Politik, Ausländisches Öffentliches Recht und Völkerrecht, Leipzig; and Bundesministerium für Gesamtdeutsche Fragen, Bonn. Among the important economic publications of the Deutsches Institut für Wirtschaftsforschung in Berlin is *Deutsche Industrie im Kriege, 1939-1945* (Berlin, 1954). The principal works on the Sozialistische Einheitspartei Deutschlands are available, as well as its *Dokumente.* The indispensable periodical index on Marx-Engels literature, *Internationale Bibliographie der marxistischen Zeitschriftenliteratur,* 10 v. (Berlin, 1950-59), is held in full.

There is an extensive collection on East German museums, art galleries, libraries, and archives including the valuable 94 volumes of *Prussia. Archiv-verwaltung. Publikationen aus den Preussischen Staatsarchiven* (Leipzig, 1878-1938).

In the field of literature, Bertolt Brecht is best covered, with over 100 critical works on his writing. The following authors are represented by the number of works shown: J. Bobrowski (13), W. Bredel (10), S. Heym (7), D. Noll (1), A. Seghers (16), E. Strittmatter (4), C. Wolf (4), and A. Zweig (25).

Sorbian

The collection on the Sorbs of Lusatia is one of North America's best, chiefly owing to the generous gifts of Rev. J. C. E. Riotte, a Sorbian priest who has special contacts with Domowina in Bautzen (Budyšin). Since 1967 he has been supplying the Library with almost all of Domowina's publications which are of research value. A great many works published before 1967 have been acquired through a retrospective buying program by the Library's Book Selection Department.

The Library has all the major bibliographies, including Jakub Wjacsławk's *Serbska bibliografija* (Berlin, 1952), Jurij Młyńk's two works covering the years 1945-65, and Heinz Schuster-Šewc's *Bibliographie der Sorbischen Sprachwissenschaft* (Bautzen, 1966).

The *Časopis Maćicy Serbskeje,* which appeared regularly from 1848 to 1937, is in the collection from 1862 to 1937 with only a few issues lacking.

Sets of the following journals, among others, are available from 1966 onwards: *Katolski posoł, Serbska šula, Serbska protyka.* The Library has a complete set of the cultural and literary monthly *Rozhlad.*

The *Spisy* as well as the *Lětopis* of the Instituta za Serbski ludospyt, with its three separate series on language and literature, history, and folklore, are all in the Library.

The collection contains over 70 titles on the Wendic language alone, including numerous grammars and dictionaries, as well as the important multivolume sets of *Sorbische Dialekttexte* and the *Sorbischer Sprachatlas.*

Literature is well covered, with most of the major writers represented, including 19 works of the important novelist Jurij Brězan. There are good critical editions of writers such as Jurij

Młyńk, Paweł Nowotny, Josef Páta, and Jerzy Śliziński. Among the rarer items is the early work of A. N. Pypin, in German translation, *Das serbischwendische Schriftthum in der Ober- und Niederlausitz* (Leipzig, 1884).

Greece

The University's Modern Greek holdings (covering the period since 1821) are limited in comparison with the fine classical collection. There is an excellent range of Byzantine periodicals, series, and collections (47 titles). The materials on the Eastern Orthodox Church are extensive (over 500 titles in various languages), with numerous directories, encyclopedias, histories, and liturgical works.

Periodical holdings until recently have concentrated on archeology; there are full or nearly full sets of *Archaiologikē Ephēmeris, Archaiologikē Hetaireia. Bibliothēkē, Archaiologikē Hetaireia. Praktika, Archaiologikon Deltion,* and *Polemōn.* The Library has recently increased its holdings of historical periodicals, which now include *Akadēmia Athēnōn.Mnēmeia tēs hellēnikēs historias, Byzantinisch-neugriechische Jahrbücher,* and *Thēsaurismata.* A subscription was recently entered for the literary journal *Nea Hestia,* but as yet the back file is limited to 72 special issues *(Aphieromata)* dealing with particular authors or subjects. In the field of folklore, the *Epetēris* of the *Kentron Ereunēs tēs Hellēnikēs Laographias,* 19 v. (Athens, 1939-) has recently been acquired. The Library now has about 50 volumes of the literary series *Neoellēnikē Logotechnia* and a complete set of 48 volumes of *Basikē Bibliothēkē.* The collection includes a rare complete set of the general journal *Panathēnaia,* 28 v. (Athens, 1900-14).

In Modern Greek history, the War of Independence is covered in greatest detail; however, the works are mainly in languages other than Greek and there is scant source material. As yet the Library has not built up its collection of historical, political, and economic works on the period from 1830 up to the present.

The serious acquisition of Modern Greek language and literary texts was begun only two years ago, when courses in these disciplines were first offered. Best represented are the works of Nikos Kazantzakēs (37 titles and 6 critical studies). The Library has complete editions of the poets K. Karyotakēs, K. Palamas, A. Sikelianos, and D. Solōmos. The following authors are represented by the number of titles shown: K. Kabaphēs (13), A. Karkabitsas (6), E. Mellos (10), S. Myribēlēs (11), G. Sepheriadēs (19), G. Sphakianakēs (6), A. Terzakēs (8), and G. Theotokas (8). Through the generosity of many contemporary Greek authors who have presented the Library with their books, a number of works of prose and poetry have been acquired which may not be easily accessible elsewhere in North America.

Hungary

The Hungarian collection contains approximately 6,000 titles. The period of the 1848 revolution and its aftermath is very well covered, with many historical, political, and economic works by such writers as István Széchenyi and Lajos Kossuth. The strong point of the collection lies in its 19th-century historical works. Included are important source materials, for example, the diaries and memoirs of Széchenyi, Kossuth, and Generals Görgey and Klapka, as well as a five-volume set on the revolution by György Gracza: *Az 1848-49-iki magyar szabadságharcz története* (Budapest, 1894-98).

Hungarian bibliographical and reference works are well represented. Among them is the complete national bibliography *Magyar Könyvészet,* which covers publications from 1473 onwards. One of the general reference sets is the 22-volume handbook on the history, geography, and demography of Hungary, *Magyarország vármegyéi és városai* (Budapest, 1896-1911).

The periodical literature on Hungary spans many fields. The *Acta* of the Hungarian Academy of Sciences alone encompass literature, linguistics, history, archeology, anthropology, economics, ethnology, and the arts. In addition the Library has such important linguistic and literary journals as *Magyar Nyelv, Nyugat, Magvető,* and *Kortárs,* as well as an incomplete set from 1921 of the major philological publication *Ural-altäische Jahrbücher,* formerly known as *Ungarische Jahrbücher.* Besides a complete set of the official journal of the Hungarian Historical Society, *Századok,* and of the theoretical journal of the Hungarian Communist Party, *Társadalmi Szemle,* other historical periodicals of the 20th century such as *Huszadik Század* (37 v.) and *Magyar Szemle* (46 v.) have been obtained in their entirety. Another valuable publication, *Külügyi Szemle* (21 v.), the review of foreign affairs, is available and there is a good run from 1887 of one of the world's oldest geographical journals, *Földrajzi Közlemények.* Two periodicals dealing with the question of minorities not only in Hungary but in the whole of Eastern Europe form a special part of the Hungarian holdings: *Kisebbségvédelem,* 7 v. (Budapest, 1938-44) and *Kisebbségi Körlevél,* v. 3-8 (Pécs, 1939-44).

With regard to monographs, generally speaking the Hungarian collection is strongest on foreign relations, economics, politics, and government. Strong holdings are also evident in Transylvanian history. There is a good survey of 20th-century belles lettres and poetry of the post-1945 period. The following writers are very well represented: Ady, Jókai, Mikszáth, L. Németh, Babits, Móricz, Déry, and Gy. Illyés.

Poland

The Polish collection is the largest division of the Library's East European holdings. It now contains more than 14,000 volumes, and there are 270 periodical subscriptions. Special emphasis has been placed on reference materials, and the Library has acquired the important bibliographies, encyclopedias, and dictionaries.

The Polish linguistic collection contains, among others, the following periodicals: *Język Polski* (since 1914), *Prace Filologiczne* (1885-1937), *Rocznik Slawistyczny* (since 1908), and *Prace Językoznawcze* of the University of Kraków.

Polish literature is well covered, especially the classic works. The collection includes many of the best critical editions of the works of C. Norwid, K. Brodziński, Z. Krasiński, and W. Pol, as well as the most complete postwar editions of A. Fredro, J. Kochanowski, A. Mickiewicz, H. Sienkiewicz, J. Słowacki, S. Wyspiański, and S. Żeromski. Other prominent writers whose works are fully covered include: W. L. Anczyc, M. Bałucki, J. Bandrowski, H. Boguszewska, K. Brandys, M. Dąbrowska, W. Gombrowicz, J. Kasprowicz, J. Korzeniowski, I. Krasicki, J. I. Kraszewski, E. Orzeszkowa, T. Parnicki, B. Prus, L. Staff, J. Tuwim, B. Zaleski, and T. Żeleński (Boy). The Rare Books Department has the first edition of *Pan Tadeusz* by A. Mickiewicz (1834). Among Polish literary periodicals, complete files are available of *Chimera,* the unofficial organ of the Young Poland movement (10 v.; 1901-07), *Archiwum Literackie* (since 1955), *Dialog* (since 1956), *Miesięcznik Literacki* (since 1966), *Ruch Literacki* (since 1960), *Twórczość* (since 1945) and the two émigré publications *Kultura* and *Wiadomości.* The Library has partial sets, some on microfilm, of *Krytyka, Pamiętnik Literacki, Przegląd Współczesny, Tygodnik Ilustrowany,* and *Wiadomości Literackie.* Altogether the Polish language and literature collection amounts to nearly 7,500 volumes.

The Polish history holdings of more than 4,000 volumes are strongest in periodicals and collections of documents. The two leading scholarly journals, *Kwartalnik Historyczny* (since 1887) and *Przegląd Historyczny* (since 1905), are available, as well as *Niepodległość* (1929-30 and 1948-), *Polish Perspectives* (since 1958), *The Polish Review* (since 1956), *Polish Western Affairs* (since 1960), *La Pologne* (1920-34), *Przegląd Zachodni* (since 1945), *Roczniki Historyczne* (since 1947), *Teki Historyczne* (since 1947), and *Zeszyty Historyczne* (since 1962). Documentary collections of important historical source materials include *Acta historica res gestas Poloniae illustrantia* (incomplete), *Akta Grodzkie i Ziemskie,* 25 v. (1868-1935), *Akta powstania Kościuszki,* 3 v. (1918-55), *Monumenta medii aevi historica res gestas Poloniae illustrantia,* reprint, 19 v. (1874-1927), *Monumenta Poloniae historica,* reprint (6 v.), and *Vetera monumenta Poloniae et Lithuaniae,* reprint (4 v.). In addition to the writings of the most prominent Polish historians, the Library has a number of rare 17th- and 18th-century publications in Western European languages dealing with contemporary developments in Poland. Of interest also are two collections, one of more than 500 volumes devoted to the city and region of Gdańsk, and the other of about 200 Polish pamphlets and monographs published mostly in Great Britain during World War II. The Library has a strong collection on Polish heraldry and genealogy, but the holdings in archeology are limited. On the whole, the 19th and 20th centuries are best covered in the Library's Polish history collection, with special emphasis on political and, for the interwar period, diplomatic history.

The Library's holdings in political science reflect the development of Polish political thought from the 16th century to modern times and include the works of A. Frycz-Modrzewski, a reprint of the 1760 edition of S. Konarski's *O skutecznym rad sposobie,* and a selection of the works of Polish political thinkers of the 19th and 20th centuries. The history of Polish political parties and ideological movements is less adequately covered, although most of the important studies and collections of documents published in the last decade are available. An important primary source for the study of Poland's political system is a set of *Dziennik Ustaw Rzeczypospolitej Polskiej.* A fairly complete file of *Nowe Drogi,* the theoretical and political organ of the Central Committee of the Polish United Workers' Party (since 1947), is available.

Periodical literature in economics is extensive, monographic holdings covering most fully the economic development of Poland since 1945.

The Library also has several important periodicals in the field of philosophy. *Mediaevalia philosophica Polonorum* is available in the Pontifical Institute of Medieval Studies, which is affiliated with the University. Holdings on the history of the Church in Poland are rather fragmentary, although there are some surveys and collections of documents (especially dealing with the Eastern Church in the Polish-Lithuanian Commonwealth), as well as monographic studies (notably several works by S. Kot).

Romania

No planned or systematic effort has ever been made to build up the Romanian collection; as a result, books and bound periodicals dealing with Romania account for only about 1,500 volumes. In the field of Romanian bibliography the Library has *Bibliografia românească veche 1508-1830,* by I. Bianu (1968 reprint) and N. Gergescu-Tistu's *Bibliografia literară română* (1932). However, other basic bibliographical tools are lacking. Similarly, the most comprehensive reference work, *Enciclopedia României,* 4 v. (1936-41), is not in the Library, although the postwar *Dicţionar enciclopedic român,* 4 v. (1962-66) is available. There are considerable gaps in the holdings in Romanian language studies. The three-volume *Dicţionariul limbei române,* by A. T. Laurianu and J. C. Massimu (Bucharest, 1871), is in the collections, but the set of the *Dicţionarul limbii române,* published by the Romanian Academy of Sciences, is incomplete. The Library has *Atlasul lingvistic romîn,* new series (1956-) and some of the representative periodical publications in linguistics and Romanian philology such as *Cercetări de lingvistică* (since 1955). Very few specialized monographic studies dealing with the Romanian language are available. Romanian literature holdings consist of several general surveys, notably those by N. Iorga (including his *Istoria litera-turii române în secolul al XVIII-lea, 1688-1821*) and G. Ivaşcu, a small selection of critical studies and anthologies, and a somewhat larger collection of belles lettres. Best represented authors include G. Călinescu, B. Delavrancea, M. Eminescu, O. Goga, E. Lovinescu, A. Macedonski, Perpessicius, C. Petrescu, L. Rebreanu, I. M. Sadoveanu, I. Slavici, Z. Stancu, I. Teodoreanu, and G. Topîrceanu. Folklore is also represented, especially that of Transylvania.

The collection in the field of Romanian history comprises some 650 volumes and is strongest in documentary publications. Of the important collections of source materials, the Library has *Documente privitóre la istoria Românilor*, 43 v. (1872-1942), edited by E. de Hurmuzachi, *Documente privitoare la istoria Ardealului, Moldovei şi Ţării-Româneşti*, 8 v. (1929-35), and *Documente privind istoria României*, 37 v. (1951-55). The collection is weak in periodicals, with the exception of *Dacia* (1927-47 and new series), *Revue roumaine d'histoire*, and *Revue des études roumaines*. General histories include an incomplete set of Giurescu's *Istoria Românilor*, v. 1-2 (1935-37) and N. Iorga's *Histoire des Roumains et de la romanité orientale*, 4 v. in 5 (1937).

The Library has little general or specialized material dealing with political science, government and economics (in all, approximately 50 volumes), except for the period since 1966, for which the selection of contemporary publications is adequate. Government documents are represented mostly by statistical yearbooks and bulletins, such as *Anuarul statistic al R.S.R.* (since 1957) and *Statistical yearbook of the R.P.R.* (since 1958). The Library regularly receives 44 periodicals published in or dealing with Romania.

Yugoslavia

The Library has approximately 9,000 volumes in its Yugoslav collection and subscribes to about 136 periodicals published in or dealing with Yugoslavia. The Yugoslav reference collection is adequate. Encyclopedias include the prewar *Narodna enciklopedija srpsko-hrvatsko-slovenačka*, 4 v. (1925-29), the *Hrvatska enciklopedija*, v. 1-4 (1941-45), the encyclopedic survey *Jugoslawien*, edited by W. Markert (1954), and the postwar *Enciklopedija Jugoslavije*.

The collection in the field of Serbo-Croatian language and literature amounts to 3,500 volumes. A complete set is available of *Rječnik hrvatskoga ili srpskoga jezika* (since 1880) and *Rečnik srpsko hrvatskog književnog i narodnog jezika*, published since 1954 by the Institute of Serbo-Croatian Language of the Serbian Academy of Sciences. There is also a fairly good selection of English-Serbo-Croatian and Serbo-Croatian-English dictionaries. In the field of linguistics the Library has *Jezik* (since 1952), *Južnoslovenski filolog* (since 1913), *Makedonski jazik* (since 1950), *Naš jezik* (1933-35 and 1949-62), and *Zbornik za filologiju i lingvistiku* (since 1957). Monographic holdings are not strong, but the collection offers an adequate introduction to the study of the Serbo-Croatian, Slovenian, and Macedonian languages.

In the literary field, the Library has fairly complete sets of the valuable collections *Srpska Književna zadruga* (since 1893), *Stari pisci hrvatski* (since 1869), and *Srpski pisci*. A good selection of medieval Serbian literature and the literature of Dubrovnik is lacking. The Library has almost all outstanding literary works in the Serbo-Croatian language. The best represented authors are I. Andrić, D. Baranin, B. Ćopić, O. Davićo, V. Karadžić, M. Krleža, J. Matko, B. Nušić, P. Njegoš, I. Sekulić, A. Šenoa, and T. Ujević. The Library has most of the literary criticism published after World War II but lacks many critical works of the interwar period. Holdings of literary and general periodicals include *The Bridge, Delo, Forum, Hrvatska revija, Hrvatsko kolo, Književnost, Kolo, Republika, Savremenik,* and *Srpski književni glasnik* (1901-14 and 1920-41), as well as a partial file of *Letopis matice srpske* and a fairly complete set of *Zbornik za istoriju, jezik i književnost srpskoga naroda* (1905-39). The Slovenian collection numbers about 500 volumes, and Macedonian holdings total about 200 volumes.

Yugoslav history is represented by a good selection of the important periodicals in the field, including *Brastvo* (1887-1940), *Godišnjica Nikole Čupića* (1877-1941), *Glasnik* of the Historical Society in Novi Sad (1928-36), *Historijski zbornik* (since 1948), *Istoriski časopis* (1948-60), *Jugoslovenski istoriski časopis* (1935-38), *Narodna starina* (1927-35), *Otadžbina* (1875, 1880-83, 1887-92), and *Zgodovinski časopis* (since 1948). Also available are the *Sabrana djela* of Serbia's great historian S. Jovanović, 17 v. (1932-40) and some standard works of J. K. Jireček, F. P. Kanitz, M. Kos, and F. Šišić. The history of Serbia is better represented than that of the other constituent republics of Yugoslavia. However, there is a scarcity of specialized monographic studies and books on the medieval period of Balkan history.

There are large gaps in the holdings of contemporary Yugoslav history, politics, law, and government. The Library has practically all important descriptive and interpretative accounts of the Yugoslav variety of communism in English, but, with the exception of *Istorijski arhiv Komunističke partije Jugoslavije,* v. 1-7 (1949-51), it lacks most of the original source materials. Also, Tito's collected works and those of such leading party ideologists as E. Kardelj and M. Pijade are absent. Another deficiency is found in the field of economics, where the major part of the Library's collection on the industrial and agricultural development of Yugoslavia is in English. Few original publications are available in this field, other than statistical surveys (over 20 titles, representing also federal republics of Yugoslavia).

The major works in the Library's collection of Yugoslav folklore and ethnography are *Srpske narodne pjesme,* 9 v. (1891-1902), edited by V. S. Karadžić, and a partial set of *Zbornik za narodni život i običaje južnih Slavena* (since 1896).

East European Music

One of the distinctive features of the East European holdings at the University of Toronto is the collection of music scores and books located in the Music Library. This Library receives a major portion of all music scores published since 1966 in the U.S.S.R., Poland, Hungary, Czechoslovakia, and the German Democratic Republic. In addition, there is a good complement of music books from postwar Hungary and Poland.

Mary Stevens
University of Toronto

Foreign Demographic Analysis Division
U.S. Bureau of Economic Analysis

East European studies have been conducted in the Foreign Demographic Analysis Division (FDAD) of the U.S. Bureau of Economic Analysis (until January 1972, the Bureau of the Census) since the Division was formed in 1951. The main focus of the work within the Division has been on the population, manpower, and socioeconomic characteristics of the Soviet Union and the Communist countries of Eastern Europe and the Far East. One of the primary functions of the Division has been to prepare detailed age-sex projections of the population of these countries, and the results are published periodically. A list of these publications is available from the Division.

An extensive collection of research materials for work in these areas is maintained in the Division. Approximately 2,000 volumes (primarily in the original languages) have been collected for studies on Eastern Europe, and about 50 journals on demography, sociology, labor, planning, economics, and statistics are received regularly. This material is particularly strong and relatively complete in the postwar period. Older statistical and census materials are maintained in the Social and Economics Statistics Administration (SESA) library, Suitland, Maryland. In addition, Joint Publications Research Service (JPRS) translations are received, reviewed, and filed. No catalog is available for East European holdings. There is a limited Xerox facility. Since this is a research library, books and materials are generally not available for loan. A bibliography of FDAD publications is available upon request.

Responsible researchers are invited to make use of these materials in the Division. Inquiries should be addressed to the Chief, U.S.S.R./East Europe Branch, Foreign Demographic Analysis Division, 24M Annex, Dept. of Commerce, Washington, D.C. 20230 (telephone 202-634-7137). The office hours of the Division are Monday-Friday, 8:15 a.m.-4:45 p.m.

Murray Feshbach
U.S. Bureau of Economic Analysis

University of Washington

General Information

The University of Washington (UW) has one of the largest research libraries on the West Coast, a fact reflected by its size and the degree of its collecting activity. The research resources for East Central and Southeastern Europe at the University Library are very rich. Whereas only 16 years ago, the then Slavic Bibliographic Coordinator, Henry Drennan, described the materials in the languages of the East European countries, excluding Russian, as "sparse," today the Library holds more than 30,000 titles between Bulgaria, Czechoslovakia, Hungary, Poland, Romania, and Yugoslavia, not including publications in the "hard sciences." Slavic and East European studies became so important over the past decade throughout the academic community at UW that in 1967 a separate Slavic and East European Section was formed within the Catalog Division of the Library. Although the Section is located in the technical services area and is open only on Monday through Friday from 7:30 a.m. to 6 p.m., it does group together in one place all of the Library's Slavic specialists, with the purpose of acquiring, processing, and servicing Slavic and East European materials. Slavic students and faculty regularly come into the Section with order requests, and with bibliographic and reference questions, as do other patrons who are referred from the General Reference Desk. However, the Library does not maintain a separate Slavic collection, nor are there special reading rooms or special catalogs for Slavic studies. Rather, there is one main dictionary card catalog representing all books classified in both the Library of Congress and Dewey systems, by subject, and further divided among the main and 17 affiliated branch libraries, exclusive of the Law Library, which is autonomous. The librarians and specialists in the Slavic and East European Section are the connecting link between the Library and Slavic area researchers, giving special Library tours, preparing bibliographies based on the Library's holdings, and otherwise providing whatever assistance is needed when questions arise requiring in-depth knowledge of the area and the languages.

The Collections

In compiling the survey which follows, Paul Horecky's area-studies bibliographies *Southeastern Europe* and *East Central Europe* were used as the basic measuring stick, together with a few other standard bibliographic guides, such as Rudolf Sturm's *Czechoslovakia* and Marin Pundeff's *Bulgaria*.

Albania

Although Albania is not a country whose publications the University of Washington actively seeks, the Library does receive on exchange their national bibliography, Hoxha's speeches, and the current political pamphlets. It is a limited program, since the language is still a barrier and the exchange partners' efforts are, at best, erratic. Actually, the Albanian collection is richest in materials from the Albanian minority in Yugoslavia, especially for the period of the Library's participation in the Public Law 480 Program for Yugoslavia (1967-72). Otherwise, the University's collecting activity in this area is virtually nonexistent and the holdings weak. The collection totals fewer than 350 titles, 15 of which are serials, three in English.

Bulgaria

The Bulgarian collection is strongest in general bibliographies and reference works, history, geography, ethnology and demography, and language and literature, especially individual authors. The collection is weakest in the military, economics, and sociology. All told, there are approximately 4,000 titles, most of them in Bulgarian. In addition to titles specific to Bulgaria, there is a substantial collection of about 750 titles dealing with the Balkan Peninsula. The Library's holdings comprise about 35 percent of the items listed in Horecky and 50 percent of those in Pundeff.

There is also a great deal of material not listed in these references, since the volume and quality of scholarly publication in Bulgaria has expanded considerably in recent years, as has the Library's exchange activity with the Cyril and Methodius National Library, the University Library in Sofia, and the Library of the Bulgarian Academy of Sciences. Of distinction are the Library's nearly complete long runs of scholarly serial publications from Bulgaria, including all the publications of the Bulgarian Academy of Sciences.

Czechoslovakia

The Czech collection is distinguished by its numerous early and rare reprints, many of which are in Latin. The University's collecting activities in Bohemica began much before its interest developed in the Balkans. Resources for studying the Hussite period in Bohemia, 1380-1620, for example, are excellent, often unparalleled in this country. The holdings of *Archiv český,* v. 1-37 (Prague, 1840-1941); Prague. Národní museum. *Časopis* (1827-1946); and Matica moravská, Brünn. *Sborník* (1878-1954) are complete or nearly complete.

Generally, the collection is strongest in history, particularly religious history, linguistics, literature (especially literary history and criticism), and music (some 350 scores by Czech composers). The weaker areas include the military, economics, sociology, and the fine arts. The reference collection is inconsistent, lacking some basic bibliographies and dictionaries but including other rather specialized and rare items such as L'udovit V. Rizner, *Bibliografia písomníctva slovenského na spôsob slovníka od najstarích čias do konca r. 1900,* 6 v. (1929-34) and Vincenc Brandl, *Glossarium illustrans bohemico-moravicae historiae fontes* (Brünn, 1876). The Library also has *Ottův slovník naučný; illustrovaná encyklopaedie obecných vědomostí,* 28 v. (Prague, 1888-1909).

Though a good-sized collection (3,200 titles in the social sciences and humanities), when measured against Sturm and Horecky it yields only about 25 percent of the former and 40 percent of the latter. These figures are somewhat misleading, however, when checking on older titles insomuch as cataloging in years past was inadequate and it is extremely difficult to locate books through a subject approach; even title entries are sometimes lacking.

Hungary

The Hungarian collection at the University of Washington comprises about 4,000 titles divided among many fields, though not very evenly. No clear-cut policy has existed on what Hungarica to collect, and the resources have thus been developed to serve the needs of the few individual professors who could use the material. Since the University offers no Hungarian language or literature courses, emphasis has been on the development of historical resources. The collection reflects the fact that a variety of courses in Eastern European history is offered at the University of Washington, and to support these courses, the Library has developed a good collection for study and research. The Library also has an extensive collection of scores by Hungarian musicians, including more than 300 scores by Béla Bartók, Zoltán Kodály, and Franz Liszt.

In history and allied areas, the Library has some surprising rarities, as for instance, J. M. Korabinsky, *Atlas regni Hungariae* (Vienna, 1805); *Századok,* 1867- (complete set of over 100 volumes); György Fejér, *Codex Diplomaticus Hungariae,* 41 v. (1828-44; complete), a collection of Hungarian official documents from the beginnings of recorded history to 1440, in Latin; and *Corpus juris hungarici, 1896-1919* (42-volume set of all laws of Hungary from 1000 to 1916).

The greatest weaknesses of the collection are in the fields of geography and the cinema arts.

Poland

The University's Polish holdings comprise about 7,500 titles, among them roughly 50 percent of the items mentioned in Horecky. The reference materials, particularly encyclopedias, dictionaries, general surveys, and guidebooks are often much more comprehensive. Overall, the Polish collection is strongest in history, language, and literature. There is excellent coverage for both contemporary authors (Słowomir Mrożek, Adolf Rudnicki, Tadeusz Różewicz), where often both the Polish text and the English translation are available, as well as for the writers of the 19th century and the early part of the 20th century. The three romantic poets of Poland are very well represented: Adam Mickiewicz by 33 titles (55 v.) and 74 volumes about him, Juliusz Słowacki by 17 titles (35 v.) and 19 volumes about him, and Zygmunt Krasiński by nine titles (17 v.) and nine volumes about him. Furthermore, there is a considerable representation of Polish émigré literature (about 70 individual authors), as well as 45 volumes of Oskar Kolberg's complete works (still in progress), a milestone in folklore.

In history, the Library has almost all of the items listed in Horecky; although some of the prewar publications are lacking, there is much more material in other areas than is listed. The collection is weakest in economics, sociology, education, religion, geographic/cartographic materials, and the cinema. As a result of the Public Law 480 Program for Poland, however, the Library's current holdings in all major subject areas have greatly expanded.

Romania

The University's Romanian collection did not really develop until after 1957, when exchanges with the major libraries in Romania began to show promise. Since then, the University has acquired about 4,000 titles in the Romanian language, mostly through a strong exchange program, which includes some 250 ongoing serials. Overall, these titles represent about 30 percent of the items listed in Horecky's *Southeastern Europe* and reveal definite strengths in language, history, and literature.

The Library receives the most important current monographs in language, literature, history, economics, and political science on an exchange basis with Romania. In addition, since 1960 the Library has received most of the publications, serial and monographic, of the Romanian Academy of Sciences and its various institutes, and since 1960, all the *Analele* of the University of Bucharest.

The University's resources also include some rare and out-of-print books, such as Nicolae Iorga, *Histoire des Roumains et de la roumanité orientale,* 4 v. (Bucharest, 1937): George Bibescu, *România, de la Adrianopol la Balta-Liman 1829-1849,* 2 v. (Bucharest, Göbl, 1893-94); and Jean Louis Carra, *Histoire de la Moldavie et de la Valachie* (Neuchâtel, Société Typographique, 1781). In addition to the 4,000 titles in the Romanian language, there are about 750 monographs on the

Balkans, and approximately 1,000 additional volumes on Eastern Europe in general, in various languages.

The main weaknesses of the Romanian collection are the lack of manuscripts, the incomplete serial holdings (most of them beginning after 1960), the general shortage of Romanian material translated into English, and the lack of important pre-World War II encyclopedias and bibliographies.

Yugoslavia

As a participant in the Public Law 480 Program for Yugoslavia, the Library acquired nearly everything of current research value from the area between 1967 and 1972. Holdings prior to 1967 are inconsistent, except for the major scholarly series, where most holdings are now complete. The Library has developed extensive exchange agreements since the Public Law 480 Program expired at the end of 1972, so that at this time (1975) the Yugoslav collection totals more than 6,500 titles.

As a whole, the East European resources at the University of Washington Libraries have come into their own and rate a much longer look than they did a decade ago. Today these resources represent a significant research collection. Not only do acquisitions in this area continue to increase at a healthy rate, but processing and cataloging are being done more efficiently and rapidly than ever before.

Darlene J. Rácz
University of Washington,
Seattle

University of Wisconsin at Madison

General Information

THE MEMORIAL LIBRARY is open to all students and faculty of the University and to scholars from other institutions upon presentation of appropriate documentation. Hours of service, except for holidays, are from 8 a.m. to midnight during the academic year, from 8 a.m. to 5 p.m. when the University is not in session, and from 8 a.m. to 10 p.m. during the summer session. With very few exceptions materials may be borrowed on interlibrary loan utilizing usual procedures. Photocopying but not microfilming facilities are available in the Library.

All East German holdings are listed in the general Library card catalog. In addition, the Bibliographer for Western Europe maintains a card file on books and periodicals in the East German collection. No publications describing the East German collection are now available, but a list of political ephemera and of East German periodicals in the collection is planned.

East Germany

FEW SPECIFIC DETAILS about the development of the East German collection are available; expansion through accretion, rather than specific *en bloc* purchases, has been characteristic. However, the strength of the collection in the immediate post-1945 to mid-1955 period can be identified with the activities of two librarians, Louis Kaplan and Maurice Leon, who were concerned with European political parties, and the large-scale purchases by Erwin K. Welsch of long runs of periodicals in 1969 and of political ephemera in 1971.

The collection on the whole is adequate to support research on most aspects of the German Democratic Republic (GDR), comprising abundant primary and secondary sources and some holdings of distinction in the fields of history, political science, economics, and literature; satisfactory supporting materials for the study of society, education, and intellectual life; and lesser strength in such fields as military and naval science, mass media, and popular culture. Periodical holdings are notably strong and marked by long runs dating from the immediate post-World War II period to the present.

For the period to about 1949, holdings are strong and in many instances unique, ranging from rare pamphlets and periodicals published by political parties to some of the first literary works produced by the new publishing houses in the Soviet sector of Berlin. From the fall of 1949 to approximately the mid-1950s, in-depth collection continued and solid documentation from the East was acquired. For the next 10 years, to the mid-1960s, although all serial subscriptions were maintained, fewer new titles were ordered, and acquisition of East German monographs also declined. After the mid-1960s, purchases for the collection increased substantially. Secondary works on the GDR published elsewhere were acquired with almost uniform regularity: periodicals, serial publications, and monographs about the GDR are abundant, and approximately 80 percent of research monographs and serials recommended in bibliographies about the GDR published in western languages outside the GDR can be found in the Wisconsin collection.

The Library relies on the Center for Research Libraries in Chicago for newspaper titles such as *Neues Deutschland,* the *Leipziger Volkszeitung,* and the *Neue Berliner Illustrierte.*

Individuals

The Library acquires books and pamphlets written by prominent individuals from all spheres of activity, intellectual as well as governmental. Walter Ulbricht is most extensively represented, with more than 100 items, including pamphlets and collected speeches and writings in English as well as German, with comparable holdings for Wilhelm Pieck (29 items), Otto Grotewohl (33), and other members of the government such as Willi Stoph (five), Kurt Hager (seven), and Albert Norden (23). Other government officials are represented. Those who differed with the regime and those who were implicated in the 1953 opposition to Ulbricht are also represented. Works by Wolfgang Harich, editor of the *Deutsche Zeitschrift für Philosophie;* Joachim Streisand, a revisionist historian who supported Harich; and Ernst Bloch document intellectual opposition. There are numerous works by prominent intellectuals in other fields: historians Leo Stern and Jürgen Kuczynski; economists Gerhard Richter and Osmar Spitzner; and the literary critic Günter Albrecht.

Scholarship and Learned Societies

The Library has an outstanding collection of the publications of the Academies of Sciences in Berlin and Leipzig, university periodicals and publications, and the publications of various scholarly research institutions. Holdings of the Academies' publications are quite complete and are not restricted by subject, including yearbooks, annuals, and other publications such as *Sitzungsberichte*. East German universities issue scholarly periodicals (Wissenschaftliche Zeitschriften), which are usually divided into natural science and humanities sections, are not usually issued through the book trade, and are somewhat difficult to obtain. However, the Library has complete sets of these periodicals, usually in both sections, from the universities at Berlin (1951/52 to date), Greifswald (1951 to date), Halle (1951 to date), Jena (1951/52 to date), Leipzig (1957/58 to date) and Rostock (1951 to date). The Library also collects other university serial publications such as lecture series (e.g., *Jenaer Reden und Schriften*), publications of research institutions and libraries (e.g., the *Schriftenreihe* of the Institute for German History at the University of Leipzig), and specialized series (e.g., the *Fichte-Schriften* of Berlin University). The Library collects only one periodical published by a technical school, the School of Pedagogy in Potsdam. Access to the contents of these periodicals is provided through the *Gesamtinhaltsverzeichnis der wissenschaftlichen Zeitschriften der Universitäten und Hochschulen der Deutschen Demokratischen Republik* (1951/52 to date).

Holdings of research institutions would, for example, include more than 60 publications of the Institut für Marximus-Leninismus, more than 35 of the Institut für Gesellschaftswissenschaften, and more than 20 of the Deutsches Institut für Zeitgeschichte.

An outstanding area of East German scholarship is historical research, where the University has made a conscientious effort to collect in all fields of history. Collecting areas include the publications of the joint commissions of historians of the GDR and the Soviet Union, Czechoslovakia, and Poland; and the basic periodicals such as complete runs of the *Zeitschrift für Geschichtswissenschaft,* of regional periodicals such as the *Jahrbuch für Regionalgeschichte,* of periodicals in special fields of history such as the *Jahrbuch für Wirtschaftsgeschichte* or the *Militärgeschichte,* and, of course, basic reference works and monographs.

Bibliography and Reference

Wisconsin collects a wide range of basic bibliographical publications from the GDR. Holdings include sections of the *Deutsche Nationalbibliographie* and publications of the Deutsche Bücherei, including its *Jahrbuch* (1965 to date), as well as bibliographies on specific topics, e.g., *Bibliographie fremdsprachiger Werke über Deutschland* (1963 to date), and related materials on libraries, information services, and archives in the GDR. Only the first volume is lacking in the Library's set of the invaluable *Jahrbuch der Bibliotheken, Archive, und Informationsstellen der DDR*. The run of the distinguished *Zentralblatt für Bibliothekswesen* is complete and includes the monographic series of *Beihefte*. Other relevant holdings include a complete set by *ZIID—Zeitschrift, Probleme der Information und Dokumentation in Wirtschaft und Wissenschaft*, a *Benutzungsführer* of the Deutsche Staatsbibliothek, the *Veröffentlichungen* of the Rostock University Library, and the three-volume *Bestandskatalog der Zentralbibliothek der Gewerkschaften*.

Archive-related publications, although not complete, are strong. Difficult-to-obtain sets of publications of the Main State Archives (Landeshauptarchive) include archival registers such as the *Schriftenreihe* of the German Central Archives, as well as treatises on using archives. The leading archival periodical *Archivmitteilungen* is available only for recent years and the Library does not have copies of those archival descriptions and inventories issued only for limited distribution.

The Library has reference works published in the GDR and issued outside the area regardless of language. The *Handbuch der Deutschen Demokratischen Republik* published in 1964 summarizes the developments and provides charts and maps. Of those reference works published in West Germany perhaps the most useful are the 11 individual distinct editions of *A bis Z* (formerly *SBZ von A bis Z*). From 1950 through 1959 the Institute for Marxism and Leninism in East Berlin issued the *Internationale Bibliographie der marxistischen Zeitschriftenliteratur*, which the Library has complete. Since 1967, *Bibliographie Philosophie* has provided broad coverage of European literature with emphasis on Marxist philosophy. Unusual bibliographic sources include the series "Spezialbibliographien zu den Fragen des Staates" published by the Deutsche Akademie für Staats-und Rechtswissenschaft Walter Ulbricht. These surveys of the literature of specific areas are detailed—a good example is the 1969 publication *Stellung und Aufgaben der Staatsanwaltschaft bei der Kriminalitätsforschung- und Bekämpfung*.

Government Publications

The Library has an extensive collection of documentary materials for the period 1945-49 from all four zones of military occupation. For the Soviet zone, the collection includes the complete *Zentralverordnungsblatt* of the Deutsche Justizverwaltung, issued from 1947 through October 1949, the two Sammelhefte, *Befehle des Obersten Chefs der Sowjetischen Militärverwaltung in Deutschland,* and volumes of collected ordinances on specific topics such as *Sozialrecht in der sowjetischen Besatzungszone Deutschlands* (Berlin, 1949).

Basic volumes and three supplements of the *Liste der auszusondernden Literatur* issued by the Deutsche Verwaltung für Volksbildung between 1946 and 1953 and the two volumes of the *Volks- und Berufszählung vom 29. Oktober 1946 in der sowjetischen Besatzungszone Deutschlands* (Berlin, 1948) are in the Library. Serial sets of official government agencies include such items as the 1947/48 *Jahrbuch, Arbeit und Sozialfürsorge* on labor and welfare, *Das deutsche Gesundheitswesen* on health conditions, *Deutsche Landwirtschaft* on agriculture (issued from 1947 through 1950), and the periodical of the Deutsche Wirtschaftskommission, *Deutsche Finanzwirtschaft*.

For the period after 1949 the Library is strongest in those areas relating to political, economic, and government affairs, with less depth in the areas of education or social policy.

STATISTICS. Statistical publication holdings include the *Statistisches Jahrbuch* from 1956 to date, the *Vierteljahreshefte zur Statistik der Deutschen Demokratischen Republik* issued from 1957 to 1959, as well as the *Ergebnisse der Volks- und Berufszählung am 31. Dezember 1964* (Berlin, 1967), and a set dating from 1950 of the periodical containing monthly statistics and notes on statistical activities, *Statistische Praxis*. A representative title of the numerous individual volumes containing statistical information is *Bilanz unserer Erfolge; 20 Jahre DDR in Zahlen und Fakten* (Berlin, 1969).

LAWS AND STATUTES.   The Library has a complete set of the *Gesetzblatt der Deutschen Demokratischen Republik* from 1949 to date, as well as various collections with commentaries on topics such as labor law and legislation, cultural law, and social welfare law. The leading journal of jurisprudence, *Neue Justiz,* is complete from 1949 to the present, and the journal *Staat und Recht* has also been received since its inception in 1952.

Many editions of the 1949 and 1968 GDR Constitutions are held, including annotated editions and translations into various languages. Three editions prepared by Siegfried Mampel and the two-volume work on the 1968 Constitution complete with documents and commentary edited by Klaus Sorgenicht in East Germany are also in the Wisconsin collection.

LEGISLATIVE SYSTEM.   Complete sets of the stenographic transcripts of the Volkskammer and its *Drucksachen* from its beginnings on October 11, 1949, to the present, are available, as are such volumes as the *Handbuch 3. Wahlperiode* and a rare two-volume publication by the Informationsbüro West, *Handbuch der Sowjetzonenvolkskammer 2. Legislaturperiode* (1954-58). The series "Aus der Tätigkeit der Volkskammer und ihrer Ausschüsse" is almost complete from the fifth legislative term (that of 1967).

Holdings of the publications of the Staatsrat (Council of State), in particular its "Schriftenreihe," are incomplete before 1967. Several documentary publications relating to the State Council are available, such as the 900-page *Der Staatsrat der Deutschen Demokratischen Republik 1960-1970* (1970) containing SED and Volkskammer records relating to the political and legal basis of the State Council.

OTHER OFFICIAL PUBLICATIONS.   Approximately 400 items published by other government agencies range from three issued by the Deutsches Institut für Berufsbildung and a dozen publications of the Deutsches Pädagogisches Zentralinstitut concerning educational problems to those of the Ministry of Finance on planning. Perhaps most strongly represented are the publications of the GDR that present its views of the Federal Republic and of international affairs. The Library has systematically attempted to collect representative titles from the various agencies concerned with propaganda activities. From the Amt für Information, which was active in the early 1950s there is a set of its *Dokumente* (1949-52), *Schriftenreihe* (1950-53), and its English-language periodical, *German Democratic Republic in Construction* (1952-56). From the Ausschuss für Deutsche Einheit there are about 20 items published in the 1950s. The Ministerium für Auswärtige Angelegenheiten has published similar items on foreign affairs. English translations of primary sources such as speeches by political leaders are found in a series of "Documents on the National Policy of the GDR."

Political Parties

The Library has impressive holdings on East German parties, including major secondary works in German and other Western and non-Western languages and primary sources such as party periodicals, documents, and collected works by party leaders.

The collection on the Sozialistische Einheitspartei Deutschlands (SED) is both the largest and most noteworthy, represented by approximately 300 entries in the card catalog. Of the protocols of the "Parteitage" only the first is lacking. Many related publications from both Germanies are available: *Der VI. Parteitag der SED, vom 15. bis 21 Januar 1963. Kommentar, Materialien und Dokumente* (1963) published in Bonn by the Bundesministerium für Gesamtdeutsche Fragen or the *Berichte des ZK an den 8. Parteitag der SED. Berichterstatter: Erich Honecker* (1971). The series *SED Dokumente; Beschlüsse und Erklärungen des ZK sowie seines Politbüros und seines Sekretariats* is complete, including the first three rare volumes. The protocols of the party conferences include those for 1949, 1952, and 1956. The Library also has volumes of "Reports and Resolutions" from the 2d and 3d party conferences. Numerous publications of the central committee include a number of volumes relating to each of its conventions.

The SED has also sponsored documentary volumes on various topics, e.g. *Arbeitereinheit, 1946-1966;* its relationship with the FDGB has produced various volumes for party functionaries and for party workers, which are very well represented. The Library holds a complete set of *Neuer Weg,* dating from Jan./Feb. 1946, dealing with practical aspects of party work. There is also a partial set of *Wille und Weg; Funktionärorgan der SED-Landesverband Gross Berlin (1946-1948).* Other serials include the SED's loose-leaf *Referenten-Material* published in 1946, the 15 published issues of the *Schriftenreihe für den Parteiarbeiter* (1949-55), and the complete *Der Parteiarbeiter* (1959 to the present).

In addition, there is a complete run of *Einheit,* the major theoretical journal of the central committee, from its first issue in 1946. Sets of *Sozialistische Einheit,* issued in both a Weimar and an East Berlin edition for a few months in early 1946, are also available and unusual.

Holdings of primary documents of minor political parties of East Germany are significant. Library acquisitions include about 20 publications of the East German Christlich-Demokratische Union, including its *Politisches Jahrbuch,* the report of the 12th *Parteitag,* and numbers from the series *Hefte aus Burgscheidungen,* which contains statements on party policy and programs, and, since 1969, the *Union Pressedienst.* There are also the *Reden und Aufsätze,* in two volumes, by former party chairman Otto Nuschke, and works of other party officials. The Liberal-Demokratische Partei Deutschlands is represented chiefly by the *Schriften der LDPD, 9 v., (1965-68)* and its *Zwanzig Jahre Liberal-Demokratische Partei Deutschlands* (1965). For the National-Demokratische Partei there is the 11-volume set, *Demokratie der erprobten Leistungen,* which focuses on the party's activities in the Volkskammer and contains numerous documents, a complete set of the *Stenographische Niederschrift* of each Parteitag from the first in June 1949 through the ninth in 1967, the *Dokumente der Partei* (1950-54), and an incomplete run of the *National-demokratische Schriftenreihe* (1948-57), as well as collected speeches and other books by party leaders.

Wisconsin's holdings of pamphlets and other political ephemera from the period 1945-49 should be of particular interest to students of the origins of Germany's postwar division and to those concerned with political propaganda. Virtually all parties are represented, many by the publications of local subdivisions.

Economics and Commerce

There has been a concerted and largely successful effort to obtain reference and monographic works on GDR economic policies. Included among the reference sources are both editions of the comprehensive *Ökonomisches Lexikon* (Berlin, 1967 and 1970), the volumes published to date of the *Lexikon der Wirtschaft* (Berlin, 1968-), and such compendia as Hellmuth Kalus' *Wirtschaftszahlen aus der SBZ,* 4th ed. (Bonn, 1964). The monograph collection includes works by East German economists as well as critical studies by West German economists. Periodical holdings are not substantial. The leading journal on political economy—the yearbook of the Institut für Wirtschaftswissenschaft—is complete (1957 to date). The commerce journals *Sozialistische Aussenwirtschaft* (formerly *Aussenhandel*) and *Sozialistische Finanzwirtschaft* (formerly *Deutsche Finanzwirtschaft*) are complete, as is the monographic series *Schriftenreihe Wirtschaftspraxis,* 31 parts (1955-56) dealing with practical problems of national economy, including planning. But other journals such as *Wirtschaftswissenschaft* and *Die Wirtschaft* are available only for recent years. Other monographic series such as *Plannung und Leitung der Volkwirtschaft* are incomplete. Relatively few works deal with individual industries or branches of trade; one can find information on the general question of land transportation but very little on specific means of transportation, e.g., railroads. The economics collection will support some research, but is not distinctive.

Freier deutscher Gewerkschaftsbund (FDGB) and the Workers' Movement

By tradition Wisconsin has a strong interest in the collection of publications of German trade unions, including those of the FDGB. The approximately 60 publications with an FDGB entry in the card catalog include several early publications rarely held by American libraries, long runs of key periodicals, and monographs. The protocol of the first congress in 1946 and the *Geschäftsbericht* for the same year are unusual. The Library's set of the FDGB's propaganda and instructional bulletin, *Schulungs- und Referentenmaterial,* although incomplete, is represented in neither the NUC nor the ULS, and the run of its *Referate und Dokumente aus der Gewerkschaftsbewegung,* nos. 1-35 (1951-53) is apparently the most complete set available in this country. Other publications include congress protocols, manuals on industrial safety methods, and even guidebooks to tours organized by the FDGB.

Runs of basic periodicals include *Die Arbeit,* theoretical journal of the FDGB, complete from February 1947 to December 1956; *Das Gewerkschaftsaktiv,* the journal dealing with labor union work, is complete from 1952 to 1956. *Die Arbeit* incorporated the latter in 1957 and included a supplement containing decisions of the FDGB governing body. *Blick vorwärts,* the periodical for workers in the cooperative movement, is complete from 1952 until its cessation in 1962. *Sozialistische Arbeitswissenschaften,* which began publication in 1957 as *Arbeitsökonomik und Arbeitsschutz,* is concerned with labor productivity and is available in a complete set. The periodical focusing on labor law and legislation, *Arbeit und Arbeitsrecht* (originally *Arbeit und Sozialfürsorge*), is complete from 1950 together with a broken but rare run of its *Schriftenreihe* published in the mid-1950s.

There has also been a conscientious attempt to collect monographs and serials related to the history of the German workingmen's movement as expressed in East German historiography. The basic series, *Archivalische Forschungen zur Geschichte der deutschen Arbeiterbewegung* and *Beiträge zur Geschichte der deutschen Arbeiterbewegung* (with its *Sonderhefte*) form the basis of a collection which includes numerous monographic studies of the movement on a local or national level, biographies of labor leaders or other prominent personalities, and works by the Institute for Marxism and Leninism in Berlin, such as the *Geschichte der deutschen Arbeiterbewegung* and its *Schriftenreihe: Beiträge zur Geschichte und Theorie der Arbeiterbewegung,* 22 v. (1954-60).

Other Organizations

The Library does not have substantial holdings of the publications of other organizations. For example, it has only 13 publications of the Freie Deutsche Jugend (FDJ), including the first two volumes of *Neues Leben; Zeitschrift der freien deutschen Jugend* (1945-46), the volume resulting from its 1955 'Kulturtagung,' and the first two volumes of its *Dokumente* (1960-61). Essentially the collection consists of monographs dealing with questions of youth in a socialist society. There are only a few monographs for other organizations such as the Demokratischer Frauenbund Deutschlands or the Nationalkomitee für ein Freies Deutschland.

Literature

Evaluation of the literature collection from East Germany is difficult, the basic question being which authors qualify for consideration. Rather than entering further into this question, this survey has chosen to include those authors commonly found in literary histories of East Germany.

The literary history of the GDR can be categorized according to domination of various ideological or artistic theories, but the collection can more realistically be judged by comparing the holdings of those authors who established reputations before 1945 with those whose fame came primarily after that date.

The Library's collection of the older generation of major authors with international reputations is quite substantial. For the outstanding dramatist, Bertolt Brecht, there are more than 100 entries and the same for the leading exponent of East German literature, Johannes R. Becher. There are 80 for Arnold Zweig, 55 for Friedrich Wolf, and 50 for Anna Seghers, a leading exponent of socialist realism in fiction.

Holdings of what may be considered the second rank of older authors are also substantial. Willi Bredel is a good example. The Library has 43 of his works, virtually all those he published. Although his earliest works are lacking in first editions, most are available. Some of his works published while in exile, e.g., *Die Prüfung* (Moscow-Leningrad, 1935), are available in those rare editions, and the corpus of his work published after 1945 is almost complete. Other examples include 24 works by Alfred Kurella and a similar number for Ludwig Renn, 17 works by Stefan Heym, who spent his youth in the United States and writes in English, and 21 works of Bodo Uhse, a former Hitler Youth turned Communist.

Library holdings of Franz Fühmann's works are indicative of its holdings of the works of younger writers, who achieved prominence after 1945. Fühmann has written approximately 25 books since his debut in 1953 with *Die Nelke Nikos, Gedichte*. He has written serious poetry, has adapted classic fables and stories for children, and has authored some original works for children. Of his works, the Library owns 12.

The Library has all but one of the works cited in John Flores' *Poetry in East Germany*. No attempt has been made to collect all works, even for prominent authors; only serious works have been collected. Consequently, numerical holdings of books by younger authors are not high—eight works of Christa Wolf who acquired fame with publication in 1961 of *Moskauer Novelle*, 11 by Rosemarie Schuder and 10 by Uwe Berger—but the quality of works selected is excellent. Over 80 percent of the overall serious output of GDR authors can be found in the collection.

From this examination it is possible to generalize further that, although there are some representatives of "popular" literature—a few of Fühmann's works might be placed in that category—there has been no attempt to collect systematically what one critic has defined as "the slew of sentimental, trashy stories and prose anecdotes by 'talented' workers" and the superficial, totally unreadable 'industry novels' (Betriebsromane) by recognized writers."

The collection of basic literary history and criticism is truly superior, including all reference materials necessary to support research and complete runs of most of the basic journals of literary criticism or those with literary content. From East Germany there are long runs of the major journals: *Aufbau* (1945-58), edited by the Kulturbund zur demokratischen Erneuerung Deutschlands; *Heute und Morgen* (1947-54), a literary monthly edited by Willi Bredel; *Sinn und Form* (1949 to date), edited by the German Academy of the Arts in Berlin; *Weimarer Beiträge, Zeitschrift für Literaturgeschichte* (1952 to date); *Neue Deutsche Literatur* (1953 to date), edited by the Deutsche Schriftstellerverband; and *Neue Texte, Almanach für deutsche Literatur* (1962-68). In addition to these lengthy runs there are incomplete holdings of numerous journals, some of which only existed briefly: *Beiträge zur Gegenwartsliteratur,* nos. 1-28 (1955-63) and a volume of *Dramatiker und Komponisten auf den Bühnen der Deutschen Demokratischen Republik* (1968-69) are examples of the diversity of titles available. The Wisconsin collection consists primarily of major journals containing contributions by serious authors; the Library has not made any concentrated effort to purchase journals intended for a mass audience.

The Library also holds basic sources not published in East Germany, such as the complete set of the *Deutschland Archiv* (until 1968 the *SBZ-Archiv*), and the more than 50 publications of the Bundesministerium für Gesamtdeutsche Fragen; in fields such as education, the Library has virtually complete runs of the five major East German education journals and numerous supporting serials and monographs; and in other fields such as cultural affairs the collection includes recent runs of the most important journals of music and art, the *Deutsche Zeitschrift für Philosophie*, and numerous journals of general cultural affairs ranging from a set of the FDGB's *Kulturelles Leben* (1954 to date) to the recent issues of the East German equivalent of *Playboy, Das Magazin*.

Finally, the Library can claim real strength in the field of East German-West German relations. Basic publications issued in the East, such as the *Dokumente zur Aussenpolitik der Regierung der Deutschen Demokratischen Republik* (1954 to date) and the *Dokumentation der Zeit* (1955 to date) issued by the Deutsches Institut für Zeitgeschichte, as well as all the comparable publications from the West, are being collected. The Library has a current commitment to continued development of the collection which ensures that the basic materials will be available at Wisconsin to support this research as well as other topics related to the GDR.

Erwin K. Welsch
University of Wisconsin

Other Countries

THIS SURVEY COVERS Albania, Bulgaria, Czechoslovakia, Greece, Hungary, Poland, Romania, and Yugoslavia. The German Democratic Republic is treated in a separate survey.

It is extremely difficult to establish the exact number of holdings in the University of Wisconsin Library on the countries of Eastern and Southeastern Europe. However, it is clear that the aggregate total, unevenly distributed among particular countries, is substantial. Numerically speaking, the greatest strength is in the field of language and literature, where some 2,500 titles pertain to Poland, 2,500 to Yugoslavia, and 1,100 to Czechoslovakia. As will be noted more fully below, historical holdings are also substantial. There are well over 3,000 titles pertaining to various aspects of the history of the East European countries exclusive of the Balkan countries, for which no aggregate tally exists. Poland is especially well covered, at least for certain periods of her modern history. Czechoslovakia and Hungary follow, with augmented strength to be expected in the near future for the Balkans, especially for Bulgaria. A 1972 Wisconsin Library in-house survey shows over 1,300 historical titles on Greece; most of this collection, however, pertains to classical antiquity.

Quantitatively and qualitatively, one may divide the total collection for the countries surveyed here into four categories in descending order of strength: I. Poland, II. Yugoslavia and Czechoslovakia, III. Hungary, Romania, Bulgaria, and Greece, IV. Albania.

The Wisconsin collection on *Poland* enjoys a national reputation as outstanding, but this evaluation, while basically justified, deserves qualification in two respects. First, although Polish holdings are relatively large in number, they probably rank only seventh or eighth in the United States as a whole. Secondly, with certain important exceptions, the Polish collection does not contain any particularly rare, much less unique, items. The basic strengths of the Polish collection still owe much to the early efforts of a distinguished Polish exchange scholar, Professor Witold Doroszewski, who was brought to Madison by a special appropriation of the Wisconsin Legislature in 1935 to establish a Department of Polish, the direct predecessor of our present Department of Slavic Languages, established in 1944. Through the zeal of Professor Doroszewski and other resident Slavicists, the Library acquired much of its present strength not only in Polish language and literature but also in Polish history. With respect to the latter, the interwar period is particularly well covered and the University of Wisconsin Library also possesses a substantial collection of books and other materials produced by émigré authors on a range of political and historical subjects. Various Polish treatments of the immediate background of World War II are especially noteworthy. Unfortunately, coverage of post-World War II Poland pales by comparison. Acquisitions for the first two decades of the postwar period were few and far between, but the situation has improved considerably in recent years. Thanks to PL 480, an annual intake of over 600 serial titles and approximately 1,300 monographs is expected.

As concerns *Yugoslavia,* the regular inflow of PL 480 materials, over 900 serials (including engineering, science, etc.) and 2,000 monographs, greatly strengthened the existing collection. As present Yugoslav publishing policy includes reprints of out-of-print and formerly taboo historical works, memoirs, biographies, diaries, and the like, gaps in our holdings are being filled. Given the active scholarly interest in Yugoslavia on the part of a distinguished senior faculty member, Professor Michael Petrovich of the History Department, the outlook for both a quantitative and a qualitative growth in strength of our present, already quite substantial Yugoslav collection is extremely favorable.

As is the case with Poland, Wisconsin's holdings on *Czechoslovakia* are particularly strong, indeed, in one respect actually outstanding, on the history of the interwar period, but considerably less impressive for the post-World War II period, especially for the two decades following the Communist takeover in 1948. Thus, one will find items such as the basic *Dokumenty z historie československé politiky, 1939-1943* and the invaluable periodical *Naše doba* (with a run from the 1890s to 1947) but few comparable primary sources for the Communist period. The single most noteworthy aspect of our Czechoslovak holdings is the collection of books, monographs, and other materials by and concerning Edvard Beneš. The Beneš materials held by the University of Wisconsin Library are purported to compare favorably with the collection at the British Museum. The collection is also strong on materials relating to the Munich agreement of 1938 and to the Sudeten problem, both before and after World War II, from both the Czech and the German point of view.

For *Hungary,* where historical holdings far exceed those in the humanities, the pre-World War II coverage is once again quite respectable, with good coverage of many primary as well as most secondary sources. Once again, however, the Communist period is far weaker, with the notable exception of the literature generated by the 1956 Hungarian Revolution which is adequately represented. Some thought has been given to acquiring material relating to Hungary's recent economic reforms and the literature pertaining to the New Economic Mechanism but, as of the date of this survey, not much has been accomplished in this regard.

The same basic pattern of relative strength in the pre-World War II period and major gaps and overall weakness for the Communist period applies also to *Romania* and is true of all fields, i.e., humanities, history, economics, politics, and society. At present the Library is seeking to work up exchange relations with Romanian institutions. If these efforts are successful, this should greatly augment recent and current material. For the moment, however, Wisconsin's holdings on Romania must be regarded as rather unimpressive.

Unimpressive would also seem to be the proper adjective to apply to Wisconsin's holdings on *Bulgaria,* except for recent developments which promise to change the picture significantly and may soon serve to elevate Bulgaria from Category III to Category II of our holdings. On the University of Wisconsin (Madison) campus several scholars from different disciplines joined forces a few years ago to foster their common intellectual interest in Bulgarian affairs. Their endeavors in Madison led directly to the establishment of the new Bulgarian Studies Group, an international, interdisciplinary association, and also resulted in the allocation at Wisconsin of funds earmarked for building the Library's Bulgarian collection. A major effort is under way to acquire out-of-print material, including out-of-print serial titles. Turkish cooperation has been obtained for the acquisition of materials pertaining to the Ottoman period in the Balkans.

The Library's holdings on *Albania* are quite weak, with little or no immediate prospect for a strengthening of the collection.

For further information concerning University of Wisconsin Library holdings on the countries covered in this survey, consult Alexander Rolich, Slavic Bibliographer, 320-C Memorial Library, University of Wisconsin, Madison, Wisconsin. For specific aspects of the collection pertaining to the Balkans, and to Yugoslavia and Bulgaria in particular, contact Professor Michael B. Petrovich, Department of History, University of Wisconsin, Madison.

Melvin Croan
University of Wisconsin

Yale University

General Information

The Slavic and East European Collections are located in the Sterling Memorial Library. The Slavic Reading Room and the Office of Collections are situated in Room 406. A non-Yale reader must obtain a special card for admittance to the stacks at the side of the Circulation Desk, near the entrance to the elevators.

The Slavic Librarians are on duty Monday through Friday from 8:30 a.m. until 5 p.m. The Slavic Reading Room is open during these same hours and also on Monday through Thursday from 7 p.m. to 10 p.m., on Saturday from 1 p.m. to 5 p.m., and on Sunday from 6 p.m. to 10 p.m. Requests for information on specific aspects of the collections should be addressed to the Curator or Assistant Curator.

The catalog cards for materials relating to East Central and Southeastern Europe are to be found in the public card catalog located on the main floor of Sterling Memorial Library. The catalog in the Slavic Reading Room (SRR) indicates the books contained in the room itself. In addition, microfilms, microfiches, and pamphlets which are not listed in the public card catalog are to be found in the SRR catalog, and are kept on the SRR's premises. There is also a working Slavic and East European serials catalog which may eventually appear in printed form.

The Slavic and East European Collections at Yale are an integral part of the Yale Library; thus, materials are scattered according to subject. The collections must be used in the stacks in conformity with the subject location. All catalog cards for Slavic materials are interfiled in the Public Card Catalog; the materials themselves are located in the 16 floors of stacks in the Library's tower, and in the Cross Campus annex. Excluded are materials on medicine, the technical sciences, and certain special fields, such as art, law, music, and theater, which are kept in the appropriate departmental libraries. The SRR is the Library's center for Slavic and East European Studies. The materials in this room consist of reference tools, some basic monographic studies, and collections of the works of some well-known authors. The SRR provides space for 20 readers. A microfiche reader is available. All materials are to be used only in the SRR. Overnight loans may be arranged for certain titles.

Books from the stacks must be charged out at the Circulation Desk. Yale undergraduates and nonmembers of the University with library cards may borrow eight books at a time for outside use; Yale graduate students may borrow 16 books and Yale faculty, an unlimited number. The borrowing period for stack books is one month, subject to recall after two weeks. Books from out-of-town libraries may be requested through the interlibrary loan service. The Library has its own Photographic Services Department.

The Collections

The estimated size of the collections and the annual intake are as follows:

Country	Approximate size of collection in 1973 (volumes)	Average annual intake (volumes)
Albania	1,500	20
Bulgaria	7,000	350

Country	Approximate size of collection (volumes)	Average annual intake (volumes)
Czechoslovakia	23,000	1,000
Hungary	7,000	300
Poland	25,000	1,500
Romania	6,000	300
Yugoslavia	22,000	2,500

Viewing the area collection as a whole, approximately 65 percent of all the books are in the social sciences and 35 percent in the humanities. Consultation of standard bibliographies of the area indicates that only about 25 percent of the titles shown are not in the Yale Library (the gaps vary from field to field). The most serious deficiency in Yale's holdings is the frequency of broken sets of serials and periodicals. Another weak spot is in the area of regional and local materials.

In the East European area (not including Greece or East Germany), Yale subscribes to 321 periodicals and 84 newspapers.

Of the national collections mentioned, the Polish and Czech are especially appreciated by the scholars. For example, Yale has a splendid collection of Conradiana. It is rich in first editions of great Polish writers, Kochanowski, for example, and contains a copy of Copernicus' *De revolutionibus* as well as other rare books. A rare collection of Polish historical maps is kept in the Library's Map Collection Division. The Manuscripts and Archives Division has manuscripts of Paderewski, Miłosz, and others. In the Diplomatic Archives, directly relevant to Poland are the papers of Arthur Bliss Lane, the first U.S. Ambassador to Poland after the Second World War. Yale has financed the microfilming of the deteriorating Belweder Archive, which belongs to the Pilsudski Institute in New York and comprises some 40,000 documents from Pilsudski's Adjutant General's Office for the years 1918-22. Yale is thus far the only library in the world to possess on microfilm this archive, a basic source for study in recent Polish history.

In the areas of Czech and Slovak studies, the Yale Library has recently acquired the 15,000-volume Harrison Thomson Collection, which is strong in both rare medieval and modern materials, predominantly in history. In addition to a fine Czech working collection in the social sciences and humanities, Yale is rich in first editions of Czech scholars and writers, supplemented by some magnificent illuminated manuscripts, as well as incunabula and rare old maps of Bohemia and Moravia.

The Serbo-Croatian, Slovenian, and Macedonian collections are uneven in respect to older materials, with the exception of academy publications, encyclopedias, bibliographies, and studies in linguistics (special emphasis has been given to collecting historical grammars). Modern publications on the social sciences and the humanities are abundant. From the archival materials, the papers of Ante Trumbich and the Yugoslav delegation to the Paris Peace Conference of 1919 are of special value.

Hungarian is not taught at Yale, and the collections at present reflect primarily an interest in Hungarian social studies. Hungarian belles lettres are represented only by the most outstanding works of authors; modern publications on linguistics and other social sciences are well covered, but the gaps in the 18th and 19th centuries are considerable. The strongest area is history, which is covered mainly in Western languages. There is a large collection of Hungarian historical maps in the Library's Map Collection Division, and a small collection of first editions and rare Bibles in the Beinecke Rare Book and Manuscript Library. In addition, the Manuscripts and Archives Division has numerous papers of Edward M. House, Ambassador John F. Montgomery, and Henry L. Stimson dealing with 20th-century Hungarian history.

The Romanian collection is comparatively strong in modern economics, history, and philology in general, especially in the fields of philosophy and criticism. The literature on minorities is well represented.

The Bulgarian collection is comparatively strong in government documents and other government publications, such as those concerning statistics, diplomatic relations, and minorities; it is also strong in history and linguistics. The Albanian collection is small and uneven, although some rare lexicographic works are present.

Aleksis Rannit
Yale University

Greece

The Modern Greek collection at the Yale University Library, although not as well rounded or large as a few other major collections in this field, is of interest to the scholar of Modern Greek studies for some of its rare and unusual holdings. Yale was the first American university to include Modern Greek in its curriculum, albeit for only a brief period. Evangelinos Apostolides Sophocles started his teaching career at Yale as "Instructor in Modern Greek," and his name is listed in the *Catalogue of the Officers and Students in Yale College* for the years 1837/1838 to 1839/1840. While at Yale Sophocles published anonymously his first work, a syllabus for the use of his students entitled *Koinai phraseis kai idiōmata tēs neōteras hellēnikēs dialektou* (New Haven, 1837). A good many of Sophocles' subsequent publications in Ancient, Medieval, and Modern Greek are included in the Library's holdings. Besides the publications concerned with ancient Greek, one can find his *A Romaic Grammar, Accompanied by a Chrestomathy with a Vocabulary* (Hartford, 1842), together with a second edition published under the title *Romaic or Modern Greek Grammar* (Boston, 1857), as well as his *Glossary of Later Byzantine Greek* (Boston, 1860) and several editions of his *Greek Lexicon of the Roman and Byzantine Periods . . .* (Boston, 1870, and later editions).

Yale has in its collection a number of early grammars and lexicons in Romaic or Modern Greek which include, among others, the works of J. van Meurs, *Glossarium Graecobarbarum* (Leiden, 1610 and 1614); Alexis de Sommevoire, *Tesoro . . .* (Paris, 1709); two editions of V. D. Skarlatos, *Lexikon tēs kath' hēmas hellēnikēs dialektou* (Athens, 1833 and 1874); St. A. Koumanoudēs, *Synagōgē neōn lexeōn . . .* (Athens, 1900 2 v.); and works by E. Legrand, H. Pernot, M. Triantaphyllidēs, and G. Psycharēs. To these must be added A. Koraēs, *Atakta,* 6 v. (Paris, 1828-35), and the work of his arch enemy, P. Kodrikas, *Meletē tēs koinēs hellēnikēs dialektou* (Paris, 1818); N. Vamvas, *Grammatikē tēs archaias kai tēs sēmerinēs hellēnikēs glōssēs* (Hermoupolis, 1835 and 1836); G. Chrysovergēs, *Grammatikē tēs kath' hēmas hellēnikēs glōssēs* (Athens, 1839); J. Franz, *Grammatica lingua Graecae* (Rome, 1837), and others.

One item that deserves special mention here is a little-known work of the Patriarch of Alexandria, Metrophanēs Kritopoulos, *Emendationes et animadversiones in Ioannis Meursii Glossarium Graecobarbarum* (Stendaliae, 1787, edited posthumously by J. Franz). Kritopoulos was one of the first Greeks to study at Balliol College at Oxford, between 1617 and 1622. After leaving England to return to Constantinople, Kritopoulos visited Germany and other Protestant countries. It was during his stay at Strassburg in 1627 that he came across van Meurs' work and wrote his *Emendationes*. The manuscript was left with friends there and was printed after his death. Yale also has another work of Kritopoulos, written in Helmstadt in 1625 and published posthumously. This is a confession of faith of the Orthodox Church, written to acquaint the reformed theologians with the tenets of the Orthodox Church. This work was finally printed under the editorship of J. Horneius as *Confessio Catholicae et Apostolicae in Oriente Ecclesiae* (Helmstadt, 1661); title page also in Greek). The Library has two rare editions of the controversial confession of faith of Kyrillos Loukarēs, *The confession of Faith . . . to those who desire to understand the religion of the Easterne Church* (London, 1629); this is an English translation with Latin text; the other edition is his *Confessio christianae fidei* (Amsterdam, 1645). The collection includes one of the editions of the confession of faith of Petr Mogila, Metropolitan of Kiev, *Orthodoxa confessio* (Moscow, 1781); this is a polyglot edition in Russian, Greek, Latin, and German. Also available is a confession of faith by Eugenios Voulgarēs, *Orthodoxos homologia . . .* (Aigina, 1828).

On the whole, the holdings on the Orthodox Church are adequate, with a good representation of histories of the Orthodox Church in several languages and some editions of the liturgical books; there is an early, rare edition of the *Hōrologion* (Venice, 1535). The Library also has a title unrecorded in either E. Legrand's *Bibliographie hellénique . . . au dix-huitième siècle* (Paris, 1918-1928) or in G. Ladas and A. Chatzēdēmos' *Hellēnikē vivliographia; symvole sto dekato ogdoo aiōna* (Athens, 1964), and therefore worthy of note: *Synopsis hiera diēremenē eis B'mere: To prōton periechei tinas akolouthias hekastou christianou . . .* (Venice, 1762); the second part of this item contains the "Hevdomadeucharion" of Athanasios of Crete, also known as Athanasios Varouchas. Other books that deserve mention are D. Rysios, *Latinōn thrēskeias elenchoi 36 . . .* (Amsterdam, 1748); *Akolouthia heterophthalmou kai Antichristou Christodoulou tou ex Akarnanias* (Leipzig? 1793); *Christianikē apologia syntetheisa . . .* (Constantinople, 1798); Athanasios Parios, *Epitomē eitē Syllogē tōn theiōn tēs pisteōs dogmatōn* (Leipzig, 1806); Athanasios Varouchas, *Logoi psychopheleis eis to sōtērion pathos* (Venice, 1819); A. Sturdza, *Encheiridion tou Orthodoxou Christianou* (St. Petersburg, 1828) and *Peri klērou kai thrēskeias* (Athens? 1832).

The Library also possesses (from the J. J. Robertson collection, which is described later in this survey) some of the pamphlets on the polemics between Neophytos Vamvas and Kōnstantinos Oikonomos concerning the translation into Modern Greek of the Holy Scriptures by Protestant missionaries: K. Oikonomos, *Epikrisis eis tēn peri Neoellēnikēs Ekklēsias syntomon apantēsin tou . . . Vamva* (Athens, 1839); N. Vamvas, *Peri tēs Neoellenikēs Ekklēsias . . . Oikonomos . . . symperainei ek tēs metaphraseōs tōn Hierōn Graphōn syntomos apantēsis* (Athens, 1838); and his *Antepikrisis eis tēn hypo . . . Oikonomou . . . epikrisin* (Athens, 1839). It is not surprising to find quite a few of the works of Neophytos Vamvas in the Robertson collection, since Vamvas came into early contact with American and British missionaries. He taught Greek to the first American missionaries when he was principal of the school at Chios (as early as 1820). He later came into contact with Robertson himself at Hermoupolis and perhaps elsewhere. Robertson printed the first edition of Vamvas' *Grammatikē* cited earlier in this report. Some of the works were presented to Robertson by Vamvas himself, as shown by the dedications written in the volumes, such as Vamvas' *Stoicheia tēs philosophikēs ēthikēs* (Venice, 1818) or his *Peri psychikēs ōphelias* (Kerkyra, 1829) and his *Logos tēs Megalēs Paraskeuēs* (Kerkyra, 1828) and others.

The collection includes two editions of the work of another Greek cleric, Christophoros Angelos, who left his native Peloponnesus in order to avoid Turkish persecution, studied at Balliol College, Oxford, in 1610, and later became tutor in Greek there. Angelos' books in the Yale collection are his *Encheirion peri tēs katastaseōs tōn sēmeron heuriskomenōn Hellēnōn* (Cambridge, 1619) and a later edition, in both Greek and Latin, entitled *Peri tēs katastaseōs . . . De statu hodiernorum Graecorum Enchiridion* (Franequerae, 1678).

In the field of Greek history, Yale's collection has most of the histories of Modern Greece, especially those written in foreign languages. The 6th edition of Paparrēgopoulos' *Historia tou Hellēnikou Ethnous,* 8 v. (Athens, 1938) and the major works of A. Vakalopoulos are available. The main strength of the collection in this area lies in its various books and pamphlets on the Greek War of Independence. This section comprises some 150 items on the Greek Revolution, mostly dating back to contemporary accounts of the event by foreign observers, Philhellenes, etc., but including the memoirs of Ph. Chrysanthopoulos or Phōtakos, *Apomnēmoneumata* (Athens,

1855) and the work of A. Phrantzēs, *Epitomē tēs historias tēs Anagennētheisēs Hellados,* 4 v. (Athens, 1839-41). The Library also has the basic works written since then, especially those of foreign scholars.

Yale has some interesting pamphlets pertaining to the Philhellenic movement in England and, especially, in the United States, with such items as appeals, sermons, speeches in Congress, etc., for the Greek cause. It has a collection of five pamphlets which deal with the history of the granting of a commission to build, in New York, two Greek frigates (*Hope* and *Hellas*) for the revolutionary forces and the disputes which ensued between the building company and the Greek Government. These pamphlets were all printed in New York in 1826.

The Library's holdings of government documents is negligible and of recent date, the only item of note being the two-volume collection entitled *Archeia tēs Hellēnikēs Palingenesias mechri tēs Enkatastaseōs tēs Vasileias* (Athens, 1856-62), which contain the early acts of the various provisional governments and other government documents up to the advent of King Otho in 1832.

Surprisingly, Yale has several books on the history of Greek education, such as G. Chassiotis, *L' instruction publique chez les Grecs* (Paris, 1881); K. Dendrinou Antonakaki, *Greek Education* (New York, 1955); G. M. Wilcox, *Education in Modern Greece* (Tiffin, 1933); S. M. Bourlotos, *Die Entwicklung des griechischen Erziehungs-Schulwesens seit der Einnahme Konstantinopels* (Weida, 1916); M. Papamavros, *Vorschläge zur einer Reform der griechischen Schulverfassung* (Jena, 1916); Th. Haralambidis, *Die Schulpolitik Griechenlands . . . 1821-1935* (Berlin, 1935).

Yale also has two little-known pamphlets which are reports of the New Haven Ladies' Greek Association, *First annual report . . .* (New Haven, 1831) and *Report of the proceedings of the New-Haven . . . August 19, 1833* (New Haven, 1833). Both the reports deal with the efforts of the above Association to promote the education of women in Greece by sending the Reverend Josiah Brewer and Miss Mary Raynolds to that country in 1829 to establish and support one or more schools in Greece or Asia Minor. Another rare pamphlet in the collection is a 12-page item containing the oration delivered in Athens, May 3, 1837, by Misaēl Apostolidēs on the occasion of the inauguration of the University of Athens, *Logidrion ekphonēthen eis tēn hēmeran tēs enkathidryseōs tou Panepistēmiou Othōnos* (Athens, 1837).

Yale has some of the early collections of folk songs and of other folk literature such as Cl. Fauriel, *Chants populaires . . .,* 2 v. (Paris, 1824-25); Ch. B. Sheridan, *The songs of Modern Greece* (London, 1825); D. Sanders, *Das Volksleben der Neugriechen . . .* (Mannheim, 1844); A. Passow, *Carmina popularia . . .* (Leipzig, 1860); G. Chasiotēs, *Syllogē tōn kata tēn Ēpeiron dēmotikōn asmatōn* (Athens, 1866); M. Lelekos, *Dēmotikē anthologia* (Athens, 1868); J. M. Firmenich-Richartz, *Neugriechische Volksgesänge* (Berlin, 1867); A. Iatridēs, *Syllogē dēmotikōn asmatōn* (Athens, 1859); B. Klein, *Neugriechische Volkslieder* (Berlin, 1826); I. Varettas, *Syllogē paroimiōn tōn neōterōn Hellēnōn . . .* (En Lamia, 1860) and other such older collections to which are added works of a more recent vintage.

In the area of Medieval and Modern Greek literature the Library has the Legrand sets such as his *Bibliothèque grecque vulgaire* (Paris, 1880-1913); W. Wagner, *Das ABC der Liebe* (Leipzig, 1879); his *Carmina graeca medii aevi* (Leipzig, 1874); his *Medieval Greek Texts* (London, 1870); and his *Trois poèmes du moyen-âge* (Berlin, 1881); it also has Sp. Lampros, *Collection de romans grecs en langue vulgaire* (Paris, 1880); A. Ellissen, *Analekten der mittel- und neugriechischen Litteratur,* 5 v. (Leipzig, 1855-62); K. Sathas, *Hellēnika anekdota* (Athens, 1867, 2 v.); and his *Mesaiōnikē vivliothēkē,* 7 v. (Venice, 1872-94).

Among histories of Modern Greek literature the Library has E. Voutieridēs, *Historia tēs neoēllenikēs logotechnias* (Athens, 1924; v. 1 only); K. Dieterich, *Geschichte der byzantinischen und neugriechischen Litteratur* (Leipzig, 1902); Ch. Gidel, *Nouvelles études sur la littérature grecque moderne* (Paris, 1873); D. C. Hesseling, *Histoire de littérature grecque moderne* (Paris, 1924) and its Dutch original published in Haarlem in 1921; it also has the more recent histories

of K. Dēmaras, B. Knös, A. Mirambel, R. Nicolai, H. Pernot, as well as the earlier works of
I. Rizos Neroulos, *Cours de littérature grecque moderne* (Genève, 1828) and the various editions
of the works on this subject by A. Rizos Rankavēs, *Geschichte der neugriechischen Litteratur*
(Leipzig, 1886); his *Histoire littéraire de la Grèce moderne* (Paris, 1877); his *Perilēpsis historias
tēs neoellēnikēs philologias* (Athens, 1855) and his *Précis d' une histoire de la littérature néo-
hellénique,* 2 v. (Berlin, 1877). The Library receives all important material on medieval and
modern Greek literature on a current basis. These include histories, anthologies, complete works
of single authors, etc. It has also recently made an effort to buy retrospectively.

The most interesting holdings in Yale's Modern Greek collection are from the collection of
John Jacob Robertson, which probably came to Yale in 1881. Robertson was the first American
Episcopal minister to go to Greece (in 1829). He later settled in Hermoupolis, on the island of
Syros, and established a printing press there which published missionary tracts and school books.
His collection includes a good number of the publications of his press at Syros, along with some
rare early tracts from the Greek presses of Malta and Smyrna which were operated by the American
Board of Commissioners for Foreign Missions. Of particular interest are some of the imprints
from presses established on Greek soil after the outbreak of the Greek Revolution, as well as
those described earlier from the presses of Venice, Vienna, Amsterdam, Bucharest, St. Petersburg,
Halle, Hydra, Nauplia, Aigina, etc. Some of these are known from only one or two copies. One
such imprint from the prerevolutionary Greek press of Kydōniai (Ayvalik, Turkey) is a Modern
Greek translation by Euanthia N. Kaïrē of Jean Nicolas Bouilly's *Conseils à ma fille,* under the
title *Symvoulai pros tēn thygatera mou* (Kydoniai, 1820).

Other interesting items are first editions of the works of Alexandros Soutsos, Panagiotēs
Soutsos, and I. Rizos Neroulos, and a rare pamphlet by Rizos Neroulos containing the memorial
oration for the death of the revolutionary hero Karaïskakēs and those who died during the siege
of Athens, *Logos epitaphios eis ton aoidimon G. Karaïskakē* . . . (Athens, 1835). Another oration
commemorating the dead of the siege of Athens is that of D. Sourmelēs, *Tous hyper patridos
apothanontas en tē poliorkia tōn Athēnōn* . . . (Aigina, 1828). The Library also has S. Valetas,
Hepta plēgai tēs Hellados (Nauplia, 1827), printed by the revolutionary press of Nauplia.

From the same collection come two works of Prince Nikolaos Mavrokordatos, *Peri kathē-
kontōn vivlos* . . . (Leipzig, 1722) and his posthumous novel, *Philotheou parerga* (Vienna, 1800);
the poem of D. Gouzelēs of Zante, *Hē krisis tou Paridos* (Trieste, 1817); the work of Ath. Christopoulos, *Politika parallēla* (Paris, 1833); and two works by Andreas Laskaratos, *To Lēxouri eis
to 1836* (Athens, 1845) and his *Apokrisē eis tōn aphorēsmon tou klērou tēs Kephalōnias tōn 1856*
(Kephallenia, 1867). First editions of A. Valaoritēs *Mnēmosyna* (Athens, 1861) and D. Sōlomos'
Ta heuriskomena (Kerkyra, 1859) are also available. The Library has numerous works edited or
written by Adamantios Koraēs.

Yale currently receives some 50 journals in the fields of Byzantine studies, Modern Greek
literature, history, folklore, etc. Three earlier journals in the Library's collection (from the
Robertson collection) are *Philistōr* (Athens, 1861-63), edited by S. Koumanoudēs and others,
and two very rare items, *Aiginaia* (Aigina, 1831), edited by G. Apostolidēs Kosmētēs, and *Melissa*
(Paris, 1819-20), edited by S. Kondos.

Recently Yale has been purchasing all important current Greek materials and is trying to fill
the many gaps in the collection. At present the Library purchases about 350 monographs annually
on a current basis.

Evro Layton
Modern Greek Studies Association
Cooperative Library Project
Setauket, N.Y.

YIVO Institute for Jewish Research

The Library and the Archives of the YIVO Institute for Jewish Research, located at 1048 Fifth Avenue, New York, N. Y. 10028, are open to the public from 9:30 a.m. to 5:30 p.m., Monday through Friday, except for Jewish and civil holidays. The professional staff of the two departments is composed of the Librarian and two Assistant Librarians, the Archivist and two Assistant Archivists. Collections are available for legitimate research to qualified users except in cases of donor-imposed restrictions.

Library

The Library holdings consist of printed matter—books and periodicals; the Archives are repositories of manuscripts, pictorial materials, and other nonbook records. The card catalog to the Library collections consists of an alphabetical main entry file and of a classified catalog with an index of subjects and geographic divisions. Stacks are closed and access to the collections is possible only through the examination of the card catalog. An open shelf reference collection is available in the reading room. Interlibrary loans and photocopying facilities are among the services the Library offers. An index to the publications of the Institute is available for the years 1925-50. The catastrophe period 1939-45 is covered by a series of guides and bibliographies compiled in cooperation with Yad Vashem in Jerusalem.

The collections of the Institute were started in Vilno in 1925, the year of its founding. The main purpose of the Institute was to centralize and stimulate research on the history and life of East European Jewry. In 1941, with the German invasion, the collections were looted, partially destroyed, and partially shipped to Germany, where they were recovered after the end of the war and returned to the Institute, reestablished in 1940 in New York.

There are no exact figures available on the number of holdings by geographic areas. An estimate of 12,000 volumes of books and 1,700 periodical titles for East Central Europe does not include the special Rabbinics collection, the collection of Yiddish belles lettres and miscellaneous publications originating in the area under survey, or the special collection of Nazi books. On the eve of World War II the Jewish population of the region consisted of approximately six million people. The internal life of this community and its mutual relations with the non-Jewish population are the subject of primary concern to the YIVO Library and Archives.

The Rabbinics and Rare Book Collection of the Library contains about 100 titles of books published in the printing presses of Eastern Europe prior to the 19th century. These are books of religious and moralistic content, as well as responsa published in Prague, Kraków, and Lublin, and later in Korzec, Żółkiew, Ostróg, Lwów, and elsewhere. Among the rarest items of this period is a Bible translated into excellent contemporary Yiddish, including commentaries, published in Prague in 1602.

The end of the 18th and first half of the 19th centuries was the period of the Jewish Enlightenment or Haskalah. This period is represented in the YIVO library by both its Western founders and its Eastern European followers and adherents. The East European Haskalah is very well covered in the YIVO collections. Besides the important Vilno Group, the Galician or Southern Polish "Maskilim" are represented by the works of Isaac Erter, Judah Loeb Mieses, and Joseph Perl, to mention just a few leading figures. Especially rare are the first edition of Joseph Perl's

Megale Tmirin (Vienna, 1819), a sharp satirical attack on the Hassidic traditional way of life and thinking; the curriculum of the first reformed schools for Jewish children in Eastern Europe, *Kurze Uebersicht in der Tarnopoler Israelitischen Freyschule eingeführten Lehrplans* . . . (Tarnopol, 1815); the translation into spoken Yiddish of "Proverbs"—*Mishley Shloyme* (Tarnopol, 1814), by Mendl Lefin, a proponent of reforms for Jews in Poland; and *Tsofnas Paneakh,* by Haykl Halevi Hurwitz, (Berdichev, 1817), one of the first works of Enlightenment in Russia. Besides using modern square type (instead of the traditional "meshkit"), *Tsofnas Paneakh* has the distinction of being the earliest Yiddish "Americana," since its subject is the discovery of America by Columbus. The work is so rare that no copy is known to exist in the country of its origin. To the list of rare books of this period should be added *Dos Shterntikhl,* published in Leipzig, 1862, by Yisroel Aksenfeld, a follower of Joseph Perl who, like his predecessor, made the Hassidic group a primary target of his satirical attacks. The Hassidic community, however, represented a very considerable portion of the Jewish population and created its own folk culture which is very essential to Jewish values. The YIVO Library has a large collection of materials which the historian of Hasidism, Simon Dubnow, characterized as "Hasidic legends" and "Hasidic teachings." Besides tales and sayings, there are histories of Hasidic dynasties, biographical dictionaries, and encyclopedias of ethical precepts, together with early scholarship on the subject.

Modern Yiddish and Hebrew literature, which originated in Eastern Europe in the second half of the 19th century, is most exhaustively covered in the YIVO collections. These collections may be one of the richest sources in this field and cover both the masters, and the minor figures, poetry and prose, books, pamphlets and periodicals, recognized works, as well as popular folk literature. The YIVO resources also include material on the sociolinguistic problem of coexistence of two Jewish languages—Hebrew and Yiddish—among the Jews, and extensive scholarship in the field of the Yiddish language, literature, and folklore.

As far as individual political units are concerned, Poland represents the area of the greatest concentration of resources. Bibliographies created by modern scholarship are available, as well as some older and less accessible sources. Among the more important primary source materials included in the collections are: *Akty o evreiakh,* by the Vilenskaia Komissiia dlia Rabora Drevnikh Aktov (Vilno, 1901); S. A. Bershadskii, *Russko-evreiskii arkhiv* (St. Peterburg, 1882-1903); and Mathias Bersohn, *Dyplomataryusz dotyczący Żydów w dawnej Polsce* (Warsaw, 1910). The Library also owns complete or partial sets of other standard collections of Polish State laws and statutes, as well as geographic and ethnographic dictionaries, publications of the Komisja Historji Sztuki (Kraków, 1934-35), and several important series of the government census of 1921. Research on Jewish life in Poland is represented by works of several generations of historians, starting with the pioneers: H. J. Gurland, E. N. Frenk, Mathias Bersohn, Al. Kraushar, Hilary Nussbaum. Included also are the monumental contributions of the second generation of historians, the monographs of Moses Schorr, Meir Bałaban, and Itskhok Schipper, as well as the works of the host of younger, academically trained scholars of the interbellum period. The present-day historical research conducted in Poland and, even more intensively, abroad, particularly in Israel and the United States, is covered as well.

An important part of the accumulated scholarship is formed by numerous publications of the Yiddish Scientific Institute, founded in Vilno in 1925 (now YIVO Institute for Jewish Research in New York) with its *Yivo Bleter, Historishe Shriftn,* and many others, and the postwar publications of the Jewish Historical Institute in Warsaw (Żydowski Instytut Historyczny) with its *Bleter far Geshikhte* and *Biuletyn ZIH.* Research on Jewish topics originating from the Polish Academy of Sciences in Kraków is also available, especially its series "Pomniki Dziejowe Polski" dealing with the earliest Jewish sources in Slavic countries and with Jewish customs and traditions in those areas, as the famous studies of Regina Lilientalowa *Święta żydowskie w przeszłości i teraź-*

niejszości (Kraków, 1919), and *Dziecko żydowskie* (Kraków, 1927). A rare and important study in the same area is Fr. Rawita-Gawroński's *Żydzi w historii i literaturze ludowej na Rusi* (Warsaw, n. d.). There are also studies of Jews in Polish literature and culture, among others *Powieści i nowele żydowskie Elizy Orzeszkowej,* by Irena Butkiewiczówna (Lublin, 1937), *Żydzi w kulturze polskiej,* by Dr. Alexander Hertz, (Paris, 1961), and an unpublished paper by Prof. Khone Shmeruk "Yiddish and Polish Literature: their Mutual Relations," (Jerusalem, 1972). The Library makes an effort to acquire current Polish scholarship bearing on Jews: general histories of Poland, annuals dedicated to cities with significant prewar concentrations of the Jewish population (Warsaw, Białystok, Łódź), studies of industrial and economic development of the country in which Jews played an important role are being acquired, as well as such current periodicals as *Kultura* (Paris), *Zeszyty Historyczne* (Paris), and *Kwartalnik Historyczny* (Warsaw). A special aspect of Jewish life in Poland was the struggle against anti-Semitism. The YIVO Library possesses a wide variety of pamphlets dealing with this problem, ranging from the writings of the famous Polish novelist Eliza Orzeszkowa *O Żydach i kwestji żydowskiej* (Vilno, 1882) to the hostile attacks of Ignacy Grabowski *W sprawie żydowskiej: niewdzięczni goście* (Warsaw, 1912) and Bogusław Miedziński *Uwagi o sprawie żydowskiej, wraz z uchwalami Rady Naczelnej OZN* (Warsaw, 1938). The need to defend the rights and interests of the Jewish population against the rising tide of anti-Semitism largely determined the activities of Jewish communal and political leaders. The YIVO Library has such important documents of the period as *Inwazja bolszewicka a Żydzi,* zbiór dokumentów (Warsaw, 1921) and *Materiały w sprawie żydowskiej w Polsce,* by I. Grünbaum (Warsaw, 1922), speeches of Jewish representatives in the Polish parliament collected and published in book form by their authors, and the bulletin published by the Jewish National Council, an organization formed by Jewish representatives in the parliament. Part of this defense action was carried on abroad by the Comité des Délégations Juives which was active in the years 1919-36. The YIVO Library contains all of its memoranda and the reports it submitted to the League of Nations and to other international bodies. The struggle for the right of the Jews to exist on Polish soil also produced a literature designed to prove the successful integration of Jews into Polish life and their contributions to its welfare. As an example we cite Janusz Konrad Urbach's *The Participation of Jews in the Struggle for Polish Independence* (Warsaw, 1938), and Mateusz Mieses' *Christian Poles of Jewish Origin* (Warsaw, 1938). The anti-Jewish camp pursued similar research but with a different purpose in mind; as witness Ludwik Korwin's *The Mosaic Nobility* (Kraków, 1938), a biographical dictionary in which the author isolated Polish nobility of "impure" origin.

The rich social and cultural life of Polish Jewry was reflected in activities of numerous Jewish organizations which sprang up to deal with the needs and problems of this hard-pressed community. The YIVO Library possesses records of Jewish cooperatives organized for economic self-help, and other organizations such as Centos Association of Societies for Child Protection and Care of Orphans; TOZ, a society to protect the health of Jews; Wuzet, an organization to develop vocational education among Jews; and Tor, a society to settle Jews on the soil. There were networks of Jewish schools of disparate affiliations, from secularist to religious, from Yiddishist to Hebraist and assimilationist, which recorded their activities and achievements in reports and periodicals. There were, finally, labor and union groups with their own periodicals and with other occasionally published literature.

The radical and labor movements in Poland are represented by numerous contemporary publications, as well as later studies, among them the important collection *Z pola walki* (London, 1904), and subsequent publications under the same title (Moscow-Leningrad, 1926-34), (Warsaw, 1956-59). The antiradical publications, which were at the same time violently anti-Jewish, include such items as *Nasze stronnictwa skrajne* by Skriptor (Kraków, 1903), and W. Sedecki's *Socjal-Litwactwo w Polsce* (Kraków, n.d.).

The Jewish press in Poland deserves special attention. It includes such rare items as *Varshoyer Yudishe Tsaytung* (1867-68), first Yiddish language paper in Poland, which was followed by the Hebrew language *Hatsefira* (1869-1918) and the Polish language *Jutrzenka* (1861-63), and *Izraelita* (1866-1905), all published in Warsaw. Very rare is a complete set of the first Zionist paper in Galicia, *Przyszłość* (1892-99), published in Lwów. A host of other papers is represented.

The great Yiddish and Hebrew dailies in Eastern Europe were started at the beginning of this century. The first of them, *Der Fraynd* (Petersburg-Warsaw, 1903-13) is available as a complete set with all its supplements. Others are partially represented. Very well covered are the nondaily periodicals of the interbellum period, among them such important organs as *Literarishe Bleter* (Warsaw, 1924-39), central organ of Yiddish writers in Poland; *Yidisher Landvirt* (Lwów, 1933-39), organ of the Jewish Agricultural Society in Poland; and *Sotsiale Meditsin* (Warsaw, 1927-39), organ of the Society for the Protection of the Health of the Jewish People in Poland. Of the postwar Jewish press, almost everything published is available, including complete sets of the main organ of the Central Committee of Jews in Poland, *Dos Naye Lebn* (Łódź-Warsaw, 1945-50), and *Folks-Shtime* (Warsaw, 1946 to date), organ of the Polish Communist Party.

Romania

The resources on Romania consist of 19th- and 20th-century books in various European languages describing the country. The majority of non-Yiddish literature, however, deals with the Jewish question in that country and it was produced by various Jewish bodies and ad hoc committees alarmed by the situation of the Jewish minority. Among the organizations actively interceding on behalf of the Jews and issuing various reports and memoranda were the Board of Deputies of British Jews, the World Zionist Organization, the Comité des Délégations Juives, the Alliance Israelite Universelle, and many others. Hebrew and Yiddish literature in Romania is represented in the Library by the writings of Jacob Psantir, the earliest historian of Romania Jewry, and by the works of many prominent Yiddish writers who were natives of Romania, as Itsik Manger, Shloyme Bikl, and Yankev Botoshanski. Many memoirs of immigrants, originating from Romania, include recollections of life in their native country. The works of the historians Itskhok Korn, Jacob Lestshinsky, Joseph Kisman, and several important collective publications issued by organizations of Romanian Jews, as well as by scholarly societies in Israel, are available, among them the monumental publication *Rumania,* issued by Yad Vashem in Jerusalem, as the first volume in its series on the "History of Jewish Communities." The Jewish press in Romania is represented by an almost complete set of the daily *Egalitatea* (Bucharest, 1890-1940) edited by the prominent communal leader Dr. M. Schwarzfeld; *Fraternitatea* (Iasi, 1882-83); and the Hebrew language *Hayoetz Lebaith Yisroel Berumania,* later *Der Vahre Hayoetz* (Bucharest, 1874-1904); the Library set is not complete. The Yiddish press developed in the interbellum period and is represented by periodicals published in Bucharest, Cernauţi, Kishinev, and Sighet (Máramarossziget).

Hungary

Many important contributions to the research on the Jewish community in Hungary are currently being published in Israel and the United States and are being acquired by the Library. The 19th- and early 20th-century Jewish historians and writers dealing with internal problems, education, customs, and the Jewish way of life in Hungary are represented by the works of F. Chorin, M. Ehrentheil, Yekuthiel Judah Gruenwald, T. Fritsch, A. Fürst, and A. Jellinek. Individual Jewish communities are dealt with in the works of Sándor Büchler (Budapest), M. S. Herzog (Stomfa), and Bernhard Wachstein (Eisenstadt). Statutes adapted by the Delegates of the Jewish communities of Hungary and Siebenbürgen (Transylvania) at the Great Congress which took place in Budapest on December 14, 1869, and subsequently published approvals of the statutes by Rabbinic authorities at home and abroad are available. The reports of the Landes-Rabbinerschule in Budapest covering the years 1877-1916 constitute an important and extensive series. The Library has also documentary sources related to the famous blood-accusation and trial of Tisza-Eszlár.

The interbellum period was characterized by the rise of anti-Semitism spurred by the emergence of Hitlerism in Germany. Publications reflecting the reaction of Jewish organizations to these events, and some literature on the "Numerus Clausus" introduced by Hungarian universities to limit the access of Jews, are also available. To the anti-Jewish literature belongs also the three-volume compilation by Béla Empelen, listing Jewish families and families of Jewish origin in Hungary (Budapest, 1937-39). The Jewish defense issued a reply entitled *Itéljetek* (Budapest, 1939), describing the Jewish contribution to Hungarian history and culture. The Jewish press of Hungary is represented in the Library by some news organs, literary and professional publications, and scholarly journals, some of them quite rare and valuable, as *Ben Chananja* (Szegedin, 1857-67).

Czechoslovakia

Research on Jewish history and communal life in Czechoslovakia was spurred by the establishment of the "Gesellschaft für Geschichte der Juden in der Czechoslovakischen Republik." The Library has its *Quellen zur Geschichte der Juden in Mähren* . . . (Prague, 1935), and *Jahrbuch* (Prague, 1929-36). It has also the *Zeitschrift für Geschichte der Juden in Tschechoslovakei* (Prague-Brno, 1930-34). Of older studies, the monumental two-volume publication *Zur Geschichte der Juden in Böhmen, Mähren u. Schlesien* . . . edited by Gottlieb Bondy in 1906, and studies by Heinrich Leo Weber, Samuel Kraus, Theodor Haas, L. Kompert, and M.H. Friedlander are available.

Contemporary scholarship in Israel and the diaspora is also covered. The Library has a number of monographs on individual Jewish communities and regions. The richest is the literature on Prague, which includes, among others, legends and folklore on the Great Rabbi Loew of Prague and his famous creation the "Golem." An important contribution is a volume in Hebrew, entitled *Karpatorus* (Jerusalem, 1959), dealing with the little-explored region adjacent to the Carpathian Mountains. Some periodical holdings deserve mention. Here belong *Die Wahrheit* (Prague, 1872), *Kalendář česko-židovský* (Prague, 1911-32), *Selbstwehr* and *Jüdischer Almanach* (Prague, 1934-38), and *Ozar Ha-Chaim,* edited by Rabbi Ch. J. Ehrenreich (Humenné, 1925-35). Of contemporary publications the Library receives regularly *Informations Bulletin,* published by the Rat der Jüdischen Gemeinden in Böhmen und Mähren zu Prag (1962 to date); *Věstník židovské obce nabožensté v Praze* (1945 to date); and *Židovská ročenka* (Prague, 1954-55-1963-64).

The Catastrophe Years

An area of extensive concentration in the YIVO Library, which cuts across geographic boundaries of individual countries, is the period 1933-45, the years of the Jewish Catastrophe in Europe. Here belong some of the very rare publications of Jewish underground organizations, as well as official organs of Jewish representative bodies, published with permission of the German occupation authorities: *Gazeta Żydowska* (Kraków, 1940-41), *Jüdisches Nachrichtenblatt* (Vienna and Berlin, 1938-43), *Informations Juives* (Paris, 1941-44). All the published series on the Nuremberg trials, the books and bulletins issued by Government Commissions to investigate German Crimes in Russia and Poland, the proceedings of international conferences on resistance movements in Europe, accounts of trials of German war criminals, scholarly periodicals devoted to the history of World War II, publications of the organizations of former inmates of concentration camps, scholarly series published by Jewish research organizations in Warsaw, Paris, London, New York, and Jerusalem—all these materials are located in the YIVO Library. Perhaps even more characteristic of the YIVO collection is the vast literature of eyewitness accounts which sprang up spontaneously after the war, the literature by and on the inmates of the D.P. camps between 1945 and 1952, and the ever increasing flow of memorial volumes (''yizkor-bikher'') published by organizations scattered on several continents which commemorate their destroyed native communities. Separate mention should be made of the collection of Nazi publications—books, periodicals, and official documents—issued in Germany between the years 1933 and 1945. It consists of 2,354 titles of books and periodicals amounting to approximately 4,500 volumes. A separate card catalog of this collection is available. [For the description of this collection see Bruno Blau, ''Das Yiddish Scientific Institute YIVO in New York,'' *Vierteljahrhefte für Zeitgeschichte,* v. 2 (Stuttgart, July 1954), p. 326-328.]

Archives

The YIVO Archives consist of at least 10,000,000 items (more than 5,000 linear feet of records) relating to many phases of modern Jewish history and culture throughout the world. Heavy emphasis is on records of all phases of life of Eastern European Jewry residing in Eastern European countries and on all other countries in which Eastern European Jews now reside.

MAJOR FIELDS OF SPECIALIZATION

A. History and culture of Eastern European Jewry.

B. Jewish mass immigrations and settlements, especially in the Western Hemisphere.

C. Jewish labor movements, 1870s to 1960.

D. Yiddish culture, with particular emphasis on language, literature, theater, press, education, and folklore.

E. The holocaust and its aftermath.

F. Jewish personalities.

The records are primarily in Yiddish, Hebrew, and English; other languages are represented. Researchers are encouraged to contact the YIVO Archives authorities in advance to determine the languages in which their desired records may be written.

In addition to paper records, the YIVO Archives include sizable collections of microfilm, photographs, recordings, portraits, and other audiovisual documentary materials.

MAJOR COLLECTIONS BY MAJOR FIELD OF SPECIALIZATION

A. History and culture of Eastern European Jewry. (Records are included in this section that do not fall specifically within the subsequent sections.)

1. Records of the YIVO-Vilno Archives moved from Europe to New York after World War II. Selected record series include:

a. Records on political, economic, cultural, social welfare, and other aspects of Jewish life and institutions in Lithuania, Poland, Romania, and other European countries.

b. Records of Jewish organizations between the two World Wars, including the Organization for Rehabilitation and Training (ORT) and the Organization for the Protection of the Health of Jews in Poland (TOZ).

c. Autobiographies (some 500) written in Yiddish or Polish for YIVO in Vilno during the 1930s by Jews age 16-22.

2. Records of numerous European *Kehilloth* and other communal organizations.

a. About 100 Jewish communities in Lithuania during the autonomy period 1919-63. The records contain minutes of meetings of communal councils and other organizations pertaining to vital statistics, finances, health, religion, and other aspects of Jewish life. Also records of the Jewish Ethnographic Society in Lithuania and other materials up to 1940.

b. Various Jewish communities in Poland and Russia, among them the Vilno Jewish community (The records form a part of the YIVO-Vilno Archives.) and the communities in Ostrów (Poznań area), Wąbrzeźo (Gdańsk area), Minsk, Kiev, and many others.

3. Papers of Elias Tcherikower including records on the pogroms in the Ukraine and Byelorussia during and after World War I, national autonomous movements in the Ukraine, and the Jewish labor movement. Also his collection of the papers of Simon Dubnow, Baron Horace Ginsburg, Sholem Schwartzbard and Maxim Vinaver; papers of Mark B. Ratner and Harash Sejmists and of the Zionist-Socialist movements (1906-18), and records of the Union of Jewish Students (1910-14).

4. Papers of David Moschowitch containing records of the Conjoint Foreign Committee of the British Board of Deputies and the Anglo-Jewish Association and relating to political and economic conditions of Jews in various countries, and papers of Lucien Wolf (1869-1956).

5. Records of the Educational Alliance (1890s-1960s), the National Conference of Jewish Social Service (1920s-1950s), the National Desertion Bureau (1920s-1960s), the Detroit Jewish Family and Children's Service (1930s-1960s), and the Jewish Occupational Council, 1940s. There are also microfilmed minutes of the meetings of the Boards of Directors of the Young Men's Hebrew Association (YMHA) and the Young Women's Hebrew Association (YWHA) of New York, 1874-1943.

6. Papers of Horace Kallen pertaining to his activities in the fields of education and social work in political movements.

7. Records of Polish, Russian, Romanian, and other *landsmanshaftn* in the United States.

8. Records of the American Joint Reconstruction Foundation (AJRF), European Office, 1922-1937.

B. Jewish migrations, settlements, and colonization, especially in the Western Hemisphere.

1. Leah Eisenberg and Julius Borenstein collection, pertaining to Jewish migration and settlement in various countries, 1869-1920s.

2. Autobiographies by Russian, Polish, and Romanian Jewish immigrants (ca. 300), 1882-1955. Subjects covered relate to life in the Eastern European *shtetl* (towns) at the end of the 19th and early 20th centuries, factory conditions, trade unions, and educational opportunities in the United States.

3. Records of the Jewish Colonization Association (JCA), 1891-1913, including materials relating to Argentina and other areas of interest to JCA.

4. Records of the United Hebrew Immigrant Aid Society (HIAS) and HICEM (HIAS, JCA-EMIGDIRECT), 1907-1950s.

5. Papers of Mayer Berman relating to Jews and Jewish refugees in Harbin, Shanghai, and other Far-Eastern localities, 1918-1940s.

6. Papers of Lazar Ran concerning Jews in Cuba, 1920s-1940s.

7. Papers of Joseph Rosen, Agro-Joint leader in the USSR, which contain records of the Agro-Joint concerning its activities to settle Soviet Jews on the land, 1925-38. Included are reports of engineers establishing Jewish colonies in the Ukraine and Crimea, periodic reports of supervisors, charts, maps, surveys, and circulars; and correspondence with Soviet government officials and other persons.

8. Records of the National Coordinating Committee for Aid to Refugees (NCC), 1930s.

9. Papers of Joseph Chamberlain relating to refugee work, 1930s-1940s.

10. Records of the German-Jewish Children's Aid (renamed European Jewish Children's Aid), 1930s-1950s.

11. Records of the Union for the Protection of the Health of Jews (OSE), 1930s-1960s. Relates also to the immigration of children to America.

12. Records of the National Refugee Service (NRS), 1939-1940s.

13. Records of the Lisbon offices of the American Jewish Distribution Committee and HICEM, and of the AJDC Transmigration Bureau in New York during World War II.

14. Records of the United Service for New Americans, 1947-1950s.

15. Records of the Committee for the Study of Recent Immigration from Europe, 1940-47.

16. Records of the United States HIAS Service.

C. Jewish Labor Movements, 1870s-1960s.

1. Records of Jewish Labor Bund, of the Poale-Zion, and other political parties in Tsarist Russia and in Poland before and after World War I.

2. Records of Workmen's Circle's Central Office and departments and local branches, 1893-1960s. Includes correspondence, minutes of meetings, reports, journals, and other papers concerning administration of the Workmen's Circle and its cemetery, education, insurance, medical, recreational, and other programs.

3. Records of the Hebrew-American Typographical Union, 1890s-1960s, including correspondence and minutes of meetings.

4. Papers of personalities active in Jewish labor movements, including Nathan Chanin, William Edlin, Isaac A. Hourwich, Aaron Liberman, Kalman Marmor, David Pinski, Maxim Kovensky, Morris Seskind.

5. Records of the Labor Zionist Movement in the United States 1907-1960s. A partial microfilm copy may be obtained from the American Jewish Archives.

D. Yiddish culture with particular emphasis on its language, literature, press, education, theater, music, and folklore. Included in this section are materials that may not be in the Yiddish language but which are essentially Yiddish-related in origin and content.

1. Yiddish literature, including an almost complete manuscript of Sholom Aleichem's *Funem yarid,* a number of smaller stories in manuscript, more than 100 letters, numerous bibliographical notations and clippings, and personal documents, photographs, and other memorabilia, 1901-16. Manuscripts of a number of Sholom Asch's novels, plays, and essays, over 200 Asch letters, numerous bibliographical notations and critical reviews, notes and photographs, 1918-1950s.

2. Manuscripts and other papers of Yiddish writers in America in the 1880s and 1890s, including Morris Rosenfeld, poet; Morris Winchevsky, poet, editor, socialist leader; and David Edelstadt, poet and anarchist.

3. Manuscripts and correspondence and other papers of Yiddish writers in Europe and America, primarily in the 20th century, including Kalman Marmor, publicist, editor, and historian of American Yiddish literature, 1870-1952; Chaim Zhitlovsky, philosopher, critic, socialist theoretician, and lecturer, 1880s-1943; Samuel Charney-Niger, literary critic, 1907-55; H. Leivick, poet and playwright, 1908-58; Abraham Liessin, poet and editor of the monthly *Di Tsukunft,* 1913-38; Joseph Opatoshu, novelist, 1920-1940s; Moyshe Leyb Halpern, poet, 1920s-1930; Borukh Rivkin, critic and editor, 1920s-1945; and Aaron Glantz-Leyeles, poet, publicist, essayist, and editor of *In Zikh,* 1920s-1965. Among the papers of Abraham Liessin there are manuscripts of many American and European Yiddish writers, and among the papers of Mendel Osherowitch there are scores of letters of Ab. Cahan, editor of the *Forverts.*

4. Records of the central offices of the dailies: *Der Tog, Tog-Morgn Zhurnal,* and *Forverts.* [Over a thousand sets of Jewish periodicals in Yiddish and in other languages are available in the YIVO Library. They were issued in various countries throughout the world, generally in the 19th and 20th centuries.]

5. Records relating to the education of Jews in Eastern Europe and in the United States in the 19th and 20th centuries. Include records of the Rabbinical Seminary and Teachers Seminary of Vilno, 1850s-1914; correspondence, reports, lists, and other records of the Central Office of the *yeshivot* in Poland, 1919-39, dealing with *yeshivot* in numerous Jewish communities and pertaining to administrative and educational matters; records relating to Jewish secular and religious schools in Poland and the Baltic states up to 1939; records relating to ORT and other Jewish vocational schools in Poland, the Baltic states, and other countries; records of the Workmen's Circle and Sholom Aleichem Yiddish Schools in New York City and other cities; and papers of Aaron Bromberg, A. Friedman, Liebush Lehrer, Yudl Mark, Anna Novick, and other Jewish educators.

6. Handwritten and printed plays, programs, posters, announcements, advertisements, and photographs relating to the Yiddish theater throughout the world. Include papers and other material of Mendl Elkin, Morris Schwartz, and Mark Schweid; and records of the Union of Jewish Actors in Poland between the two world wars.

7. Records of the Jewish Ethnographical Society of Vilno; collection of rabbinic *kvitlekh* (supplicatory notes), of Rosh Hashanah cards, wedding and Bar Mitzvah cards and other items relating to various religious ceremonies; papers of A. Litwin and Judah Leib Cahan pertaining to Jewish folklore.

E. The holocaust and its aftermath.

1. Papers of Joseph Tanenbaum relating also to the anti-Nazi boycott.

2. Papers of Nachman Zonabend on the Łódź ghetto, including the ghetto newspaper, department reports of the Jewish ghetto administration, the ghetto industry, reports on the daily life in the ghetto, the daily chronicle, photographs (over 400), and other materials.

3. Papers of A. Sutzkewer-Sh. Kaczerginski, on the Vilno ghetto, including diaries, chronicles, and reports relating to administration, police, the ghetto court, educational and cultural activities, forced labor, food supply, and other matters.

4. Records relating to the Warsaw ghetto, including contemporary eyewitness accounts on conditions in the ghetto, forced labor, social welfare, sanitary conditions, the Jewish council and the ghetto police; notes by Emanuel Ringelbaum; contemporary reports about Nazi brutality and the extermination of Jews in other parts of Poland; and some issues of the Jewish and Polish underground press.

5. Records of the Union Générale des Israélites de France (UGIF), the French *Judenrat.*

6. Records of Colonie Secolaire (''Rue Amélot''), a committee to save Jewish children during the Nazi occupation of France.

7. Papers of Rabbi Hirshler relating to the work of the Jewish Chaplaincy in camps in France during World War II.

8. Records of *Kehilas Ha-haredim* (the Orthodox Jewish Community in France) during World War II.

9. The Berlin Collection, about 40,000 pages of Nazi documents pertaining to Jews, especially those of the *Reichskommissariat Ostland* and the Government General, including documents from the Propaganda Ministry, the Ministry of Interior, the *Einsatzstab Rosenberg,* and Goering's Office and Ministry; and some 1350 dossiers of the *Hauptamt Wissenschaft* pertaining to German academicians.

10. Records of *Der Stürmer,* of the *Institut zur Erforschung der Judenfrage* and other agencies in Germany.

11. Records relating to the Nazi persecution of Jews in the Netherlands, Romania, and in the Theresienstadt Camp.

12. Some 2,000 eyewitness accounts and other reports by victims of Nazi persecution in occupied Europe.

13. Records of Jewish displaced person camps and transitory settlements in Germany, Austria, and Italy, 1946-50s.

 F. Jewish Personalities.

The YIVO Archives has hundreds of collections of papers of Jewish personalities on a great variety of subjects. A preliminary listing is available at the YIVO Archives as well as additional descriptive information and guides to the archival holdings.

Dina Abramowicz and Isaiah Trunk
YIVO Institute for Jewish Research

Area and Subject Guide

THIS HANDBOOK IS intended as a broad area and subject guide to significant library and archival collections in the United States and Canada, that is, a series of collection profiles rather than exhaustive listings of holdings. Consequently, an author and title index would be of limited value and is not included here. Categories of materials such as maps, newspapers, prints, photographs, and films are listed under country entries. The guide provides access to countries and main subjects. Also included are entries for special collections, geographic names, categories, and names of contributors.

P. H.
D. K.

Area and Subject Guide

About the Editors

Paul L. Horecky is a noted USSR and East European library specialist and bibliographer, and editor or author of other reference works related to Eastern Europe. The associate editor, David H. Kraus, is a seasoned bibliographer with expertise and experience in this geographic area.

]467[

East Central and Southeast Europe: A Handbook of Library and Archival Resources in North America was compiled and edited under the editorship of Paul L. Horecky and David H. Kraus. The text was designed by Shelly Lowenkopf. Composition: Chapman's Phototypesetting, Fullerton, California. Proofing: John R. "Jack" Raup. Offset and bound by Banta West, Inc., Reno, Nevada, using a 50# Glatfelter RRR in A-69 long grain white sheet. The cover, which was designed and executed by Raymond Glass, prints on Kivar 6 Cambric finish, which is applied over .080 boards.